3×5   formula card

8-10
12-3   office hours

30% Ratios

p. 52

50 questions
10 T-F
40 Mult.

⑦①⓪ **BOOK STORE**
Top CASH For BOOKS Anytime

"YOURS—FOR LOWER COSTS
OF HIGHER EDUCATION"

FUNDAMENTALS OF FINANCIAL MANAGEMENT

THIRD EDITION

JAMES C. VAN HORNE

Stanford University

PRENTICE-HALL, INC., *Englewood Cliffs, N.J. 07632*

Library of Congress Cataloging in Publication Data

Van Horne, James C.
  Fundamentals of financial management.

  Includes bibliographies.
  1. Corporations—Finance. I. Title.
HG4011.V36 1977   658.1'5   76-16093
ISBN 0-13-339341-0

FUNDAMENTALS OF FINANCIAL MANAGEMENT, *Third Edition*

by James C. Van Horne

10 9 8 7 6 5 4 3 2 1

PRENTICE-HALL INTERNATIONAL, INC., London
PRENTICE-HALL OF AUSTRALIA, PTY. LTD., Sydney
PRENTICE-HALL OF CANADA, LTD., Toronto
PRENTICE-HALL OF INDIA PRIVATE LIMITED, New Delhi
PRENTICE-HALL OF JAPAN, INC., Tokyo
PRENTICE-HALL OF SOUTHEAST ASIA PTE. LTD., Singapore
WHITEHALL BOOKS LIMITED, Wellington, New Zealand

Preface

The purpose of *Fundamentals of Financial Management* is to equip the reader with a basic understanding of the allocation of funds within a business enterprise and the raising of funds. The book is designed for use in an introductory course in financial management. Its stress is not only on understanding what business finance is, but also on applying certain theoretical concepts to financial problems. Most of these concepts are expressed in verbal terms; but in certain cases, elementary mathematics provide a more rigorous and clearer understanding. The mathematics employed involve no more than elementary algebra; moreover, every effort is made to provide full and extensive explanations of the terms used.

The primary emphasis in this revision has been on the capital investment decision and on relating this decision to the valuation of the firm through an appropriate acceptance criterion. In this regard, Chapter 12, "Mathematics of Finance," Chapter 15, "The Valuation Process," and Chapter 16, "Required Returns on Capital Investments," are new. A major revision also was undertaken in Chapter 14, "Risk and Capital Budgeting"; and improvements were made in Chapter 13 "Capital Budgeting," including an appendix on the effect of inflation. Hopefully, these changes will permit a deeper and more thorough understanding of this important area.

Other changes include an important revision of Chapter 11, "Intermediate-Term Financing"; moving up the part on short- and intermediate-term financing so that it follows the part on current-asset management; an expansion of Chapter 26, "Growth through Multi-national Operations"; the extension of Chapter 27 "Failure and Re-organization," to consider the likely reform of the Bankrupty Act; and moderate, though nonetheless significant improvements in a number of other chapters, including Chapter 10, "Short-Term Loans," Chapter 19, "Dividend Policy and Retained Earnings," Chapter 22, "Long-Term Debt," and Chapter 24, "Convertible Securities and Warrants." Pertinent improvements and updating were made in the remaining chapters. Questions, problems, and references have been revised.

I am grateful to a number of professors who have used the book and have offered helpful comments and criticism. In particular, I wish to thank Professors Moustafa H. Abdelsamad, Virginia Commonwealth University; George Catsiapis, University of Illinois; Glenn V. Henderson, Jr., Arizona State University; Hildegard Hendrickson, Seattle University; J. Ronald Hoffmeister, University of Missouri-St. Louis; John D. Martin, Virginia Polytechnic Institute; Robert M. Niendorf, University of Wisconsin; Michael Rice, University of North Carolina; Michael S. Rozeff, University of Iowa; Donald L. Stevens, University of Tennessee; Roger Stover, University of Minneapolis; Charles E. Wade, Texas Technological University. Finally, I am grateful to Ann Marie Ventura, who typed this revision.

Palo Alto, California   JAMES C. VAN HORNE

Contents

To my father, Ralph Van Horne

Introduction I

1 *The Role of Financial Management*

At any moment in time, a business firm can be viewed as a pool of funds. These funds come from a variety of sources: investors in the company's stock, creditors who lend it money, and past earnings retained in the business. Funds provided from these sources are committed to a number of uses: fixed assets used in production of a good or service, inventories used to facilitate production and sales, accounts receivable owed by customers, and cash and marketable securities used for transactions and liquidity purposes. At a given moment, the pool of funds of the firm is static. Over time, however, the pool changes; and these changes are known as funds flows. In an ongoing business, funds flow continually throughout the enterprise. The term *financial management* connotes that these flows are directed according to some plan; it is with managing the flow of funds within the firm that this book deals.

The financial manager is concerned with the following responsibilities:[1]

1. The proper amount of funds to employ in the firm, i.e., how large it will be and how fast it will grow
2. The efficient allocation of funds to specific assets
3. Raising funds on as favorable terms as possible, i.e., determining the composition of liabilities

[1]See Ezra Solomon, *The Theory of Financial Management* (New York: Columbia University Press, 1963), Chapter 1.

In years gone by, the financial manager was concerned with only the last of these functions. Gradually, however, his role has expanded to where it now involves the totality of the enterprise. Put another way, the financial manager now is involved in general management, while before his concern was primarily with raising funds and managing the firm's cash position. In recent years, the combination of increased competition among firms, persistent inflation, an explosion in technological improvements that has required considerable capital, increased national concern with environmental and social issues, heightened government regulation of firms, and the growing importance of international operations have had an enormous influence in pushing the financial manager into a general management role. Moreover, these factors have required considerable flexibility in order to cope with ever-present change. The "old way of doing things" simply is not good enough in a world in which old ways quickly become obsolete. Competition requires continual adaption to changing conditions.

How well the financial manager adapts to change and how efficient he is in planning the proper amount of funds to employ in the firm, in overseeing the allocation of these funds, and in raising funds affects not only the success of the firm in which he is employed but the overall economy as well. To the extent that funds are misallocated, the growth of the economy will be slowed. In an era of unfilled economic wants and scarcity, this may well work to the detriment of society. Efficient allocation of resources in an economy is vital to optimal growth in that economy; it also is vital in assuring that individuals obtain the highest level of want satisfaction possible. Through effectively allocating funds, the financial manager contributes to the fortunes of his firm and to the vitality and growth of the economy as a whole.

THE GOAL OF THE FIRM

Efficient management of the flow of funds within the firm implies the existence of an objective or goal, because judgment as to whether or not a financial decision is efficient must be made in the light of some standard. Although various objectives are possible, we assume in this book that the goal of the firm is to maximize the wealth of its present owners.

Ownership in a corporation is evidenced by shares of common stock. Each share indicates that its holder owns $1/n$th of the company involved, where n is the total number of shares outstanding.[2] For our purposes, shareholder wealth is represented by the market price per

---

[2]For a discussion of the characteristics of common stock, see Chapter 23.

share of the firm's stock. While the market price may not be a perfect measure of wealth for all stockholders, it is the best measure available. When a public market does not exist for the stock, an opportunity price must be used. By analyzing similar companies whose stock is traded publicly, one can approximate the market value of the company involved.[3]

Profit maximization versus wealth maximization

Frequently, maximization of profits is regarded as the proper objective of the firm, but it is not as inclusive a goal as that of maximizing shareholder wealth. For one thing, total profits are not as important as earnings per share. Even maximization of earnings per share, however, is not a fully appropriate objective, partly because it does not specify the timing or duration of expected returns. Is the investment project that will produce a $100,000 return five years from now more valuable than the project that will produce annual returns of $15,000 in each of the next five years? An answer to this question depends upon the time value of money to the firm and to investors at the margin. Few existing stockholders would think favorably of a project that promised its first return in one hundred years, no matter how large this return. We must take into account the time pattern of returns in our analysis.

Another shortcoming of the objective of maximizing earnings per share is that it does not consider the risk of the prospective earnings stream. Some investment projects are far more risky than others. As a result, the prospective stream of earnings per share would be more risky if these projects were undertaken. In addition, a company will be more or less risky depending upon the amount of debt in relation to equity in its capital structure. This risk is known as financial risk; and it, too, contributes to the overall risk to the investor. Two companies may have the same expected earnings per share, but if the earnings stream of one is subject to considerably more risk than the earnings stream of the other, the market price per share of its stock may be less.

Finally, this objective does not allow for the effect of dividend policy on the market price of the stock. If the objective were only to maximize earnings per share, the firm would never pay a dividend. At the very least, it could always improve earnings per share by retaining earnings and investing them in Treasury bills. To the extent that the

---

[3]For a landmark earlier article on the subject, see L. R. Johnson, Eli Shapiro, and Joseph O'Meara, Jr., "Valuation of Closely Held Stock for Tax Purposes: Approaches to an Objective Method," *University of Pennsylvania Law Review,* 100 (November 1951), 166–95.

payment of dividends can affect the value of the stock, the maximization of earnings per share will not be a satisfactory objective by itself.

For the reasons given above, an objective of maximizing earnings per share may not be the same as maximizing market price per share. The market price of a firm's stock represents the focal judgment of all market participants as to what the value is of the particular firm. It takes into account present and prospective future earnings per share, the timing and risk of these earnings, the dividend policy of the firm, and any other factors that bear upon the market price of the stock. The market price serves as a performance index or report card of the firm's progress; it indicates how well management is doing in behalf of its stockholders. Management is under continuous review. If a stockholder is dissatisfied with management's performance, he may sell his stock and invest in another company. This action, if taken by other dissatisfied stockholders, will put downward pressure on market price per share. In this case, the market price of the stock would be an index of stockholder discontent.

Management versus stockholders

In certain situations, the objectives of management may differ from those of the firm's stockholders. In a large corporation whose stock is widely held, stockholders exert very little control or influence over the operations of the company. When the control of a company is separate from its ownership, management may not always act in the best interests of the stockholders.[4] Managements sometimes are said to be "satisficers" rather than "maximizers";[5] they may be content to "play it safe" and seek an acceptable level of growth, being more concerned with perpetuating their own existence than with maximizing the value of the firm to its shareholders. The most important goal to a management of this sort may be its own survival. As a result, it may be unwilling to take reasonable risks for fear of making a mistake and thereby being conspicuous to outside suppliers of capital. In turn, these suppliers may pose a threat to management's survival. It is true that in order to survive over the long run, management may have to behave in a manner that is reasonably consistent with maximizing shareholder wealth. Nevertheless, the goals of the two parties do not necessarily have to be the same.

[4]For a discussion of this question, see Gordon Donaldson, "Financial Goals: Management vs. Stockholders," *Harvard Business Review,* 41 (May–June 1963), 116–29; and J. W. Elliott, "Control, Size, Growth, and Financial Performance in the Firm," *Journal of Financial and Quantitative Analysis,* 7 (January 1972), 1309–20.

[5]Herbert A. Simon, "Theories of Decision Making in Economics and Behavioral Science," *American Economic Review,* 49 (June 1959), 253–83. See also J. Fred Weston, *The Scope and Methodology of Finance* (Englewood Cliffs, N.J.: Prentice-Hall, 1966), Chapter 2.

A normative goal

Maximization of shareholder wealth is an appropriate guide for how a firm *should* act in a normative or ideal sense, but not necessarily how it does act. The purpose of capital markets is to efficiently allocate savings in an economy from ultimate savers to ultimate users of funds who invest in real assets. If savings are to be channeled to the most promising investment opportunities, a rational economic criterion must exist that governs their flow. By and large, the allocation of savings in an economy occurs on the basis of expected return and risk. The market value of a firm's stock embodies both of these factors. It therefore reflects the market's tradeoff between risk and return. If decisions are made in keeping with the likely effect upon the market value of its stock, a firm will attract capital only when its investment opportunities justify the use of that capital in the overall economy.

Put another way, the equilibration process by which savings are allocated in an economy occurs on the basis of expected return and risk. Holding risk constant, those economic units (business firms, households, financial institutions, or governments) willing to pay the highest yield are the ones entitled to the use of funds. If rationality prevails, the economic units bidding the highest yields will be the ones with the most promising investment opportunities. As a result, savings will tend to be allocated to the most efficient uses. Maximization of shareholder wealth then embodies the risk-return tradeoff of the market and is the focal point by which funds should be allocated within and among business firms. Any other objective is likely to result in the suboptimal allocation of funds and therefore lead to less than optimal capital formation and growth in the economy as well as a less than optimal level of economic want satisfaction.

This is not to say that management should ignore the question of social responsibility. As related to business firms, social responsibility concerns such things as protecting the consumer, paying fair wages to employees, maintaining fair hiring practices, supporting education, and becoming actively involved in environmental issues like clean air and water. Many people feel that a firm has no choice but to act in socially responsible ways; they argue that shareholder wealth and, perhaps, the corporation's very existence depend upon its being socially responsible. However, the criteria for social responsibility are not clearly defined, making formulation of a consistent objective function difficult.

Moreover, social responsibility creates certain problems for the firm. One is that it falls unevenly on different corporations. Another is that it sometimes conflicts with the objective of wealth maximization. Certain social actions, from a long-range point of view, unmistakably are in the best interests of stockholders, and there is little question that they should be undertaken. Other actions are less clear, and to engage in them may result in a decline in profits and in shareholder wealth in the long run. From the standpoint of society, this decline may produce a conflict. What is gained in having a socially desirable goal achieved may be offset in whole or part by an accompanying less-efficient allocation of resources in society. The latter will result in a less than optimal growth of the economy and a lower total level of economic want satisfaction. In an era of unfilled wants and scarcity, the allocation process is extremely important.

Many people feel that management should not be called upon to resolve the conflict posed above. Rather, society, with its broad general perspective, should make the decisions necessary in this area. Only society, acting through Congress and other representative governmental bodies, can judge the relative tradeoff between the achievement of a social goal and the sacrifice in the efficiency of apportioning resources that may accompany realization of the goal. With these decisions made, corporations can engage in wealth maximization and thereby efficiently allocate resources, subject, of course, to certain governmental constraints. Under such a system, corporations can be viewed as producing both private and social goods, and the maximization of shareholder wealth remains a viable corporate objective.

FUNCTION OF THE FINANCIAL MANAGER

As suggested earlier, the financial manager is concerned with (1) the efficient allocation of funds within the enterprise and (2) the raising of funds on as favorable terms as possible. These functions are pursued with the objective of maximizing shareholder wealth. By and large, this book is organized according to the two functions mentioned above. Embodied in the first is consideration of the total amount of funds to employ in the enterprise.

Before proceeding to examine the allocation and raising of funds, we take up certain background material and tools of analysis. In the next chapter, we examine the legal setting for financial management as it relates in particular to organizational form and taxes. In allocating and raising funds, the financial manager uses certain tools of analysis, planning, and control. Financial analysis is a necessary condition, or prerequisite, for making sound financial decisions. In order to raise funds efficiently and allocate them, the financial manager must plan carefully. For one thing, he must project future cash flows and then assess the likely effect of these flows on the financial condition of the firm. On the basis of these projections, he plans for adequate liquidity to pay bills and other obligations as they come due. These obligations may make it necessary to raise additional funds. In order to control performance, the financial manager needs to establish certain norms. These norms are then used to compare actual performance with planned performance. Because financial analysis, planning, and control underlie a good deal of the discussion in this book, we examine these topics in Chapters 3 and 4.

Allocation of funds

The financial manager oversees the allocation of funds among alternative uses. This allocation must be made in accordance with the underlying objective of the firm, to maximize shareholder wealth. In Part II, we examine cash, marketable securities, accounts receivable, and inventories. Our concern is with ways of efficiently managing these current assets in order to maximize profitability relative to the amount of funds tied up in the assets. Determining a proper level of liquidity for the firm is very much a part of this management. The optimal level of a current asset depends on the profitability and flexibility associated with that level in relation to the cost involved in maintaining it. In the past, the management of working capital dominated the role of the financial manager. Though this traditional function continues to be vital, his role has expanded to involve longer-term assets and liabilities.

The allocation of funds among fixed assets is considered in Part IV, under capital investment. Capital budgeting involves allocating capital to investment proposals whose benefits will be realized in the future. When a proposal embodies a current-asset component, the latter is treated as part of the capital-budgeting decision and not as a separate working-capital decision. Because the expected future benefits from an investment proposal are uncertain, risk necessarily is involved. Changes in the business-risk complexion of the firm can have a significant influence on its value in the marketplace. Because of this important effect, attention is devoted to the problem of measuring risk for a capital investment project. Capital is apportioned according to an acceptance criterion. It is important that the return required of the project be in accord with the objective of maximizing shareholder wealth. Accordingly, we spend a good deal of time exploring certain concepts in valuation. These concepts are then used in determining a required rate of return for the investment project.

In Part VII, we consider mergers and acquisitions from the standpoint of the firm's allocation of funds. Many of the concepts applicable to capital budgeting are applicable here. Growth of a company can be internal, external, or both. Moreover, it can be essentially domestic or international in flavor. In Part VII, then, we consider growth through international operations. In recent years, the multinational firm has become increasingly important, so its consideration is particularly germane. Finally, in this part, we take up failures and reorganizations, which involve a decision to liquidate a company or to rehabilitate it, often by changing its capital structure. This decision should be based on the same economic considerations that govern the allocation of capital.

In summary, the allocation of funds within the firm determines the total amount of assets of the firm, the composition of these assets, and the business-risk complexion of the firm. All of these factors have an important influence upon its value.

The raising of funds

The second facet of financial management is the acquisition of funds. A wide variety of sources is available. Each has certain characteristics as to cost, maturity, availability, the encumbrance of assets, and other terms imposed by the supplier of capital. On the basis of these factors, the financial manager must determine the best mix of financing for the firm. Its implications upon shareholder wealth must be considered when this decision is made.

In Part V, the question of the appropriate capital structure of a firm is considered. The concept of leverage is explored from a number of different angles in an effort to obtain a better understanding of financial risk and how this risk is interrelated with operating risk. In addition, retained earnings are analyzed as a source of funds. Because this source represents dividends foregone by stockholders, dividend policy very much impinges on financing policy and vice versa. In Part III, we examine the various sources of short- and intermediate-term financing; and in Part VI, the sources of long-term financing. In both parts, the features, concepts, and problems associated with alternative methods of financing are explored.

Financial management, then, involves the allocation of funds within the firm and the acquisition of funds. The two are interrelated in that a decision to invest in a particular asset necessitates the financing of that asset, whereas the cost of financing affects the decision to invest. The focus of this book is upon the allocation and acquisition of funds; together, these activities determine the value of the firm to its shareholders. Mastering the concepts involved is the key to understanding the role of financial management.

QUESTIONS

1. The maximization of wealth objectives suggests that management attempt to minimize dollar cost of production at a given level of output. Some costs of production are not paid for by the company (i.e., pollution). Is the objective of maximizing wealth functional from society's point of view? If the answer is no, which objective would you substitute in its place?

2. Contrast the objective of maximizing earnings and that of maximizing wealth.

3. Maximizing wealth implies maximizing the price of the stock of the firm. Scandals involving stock manipulations such as Equity Funding, Inc., suggest that stock prices are not an infallible yardstick of performance. Discuss conditions created by management which maximize stock prices but which do not necessarily mean efficiency in financial decision making.

4. Is the goal of zero profits for some finite period (3 to 5 years, for example) consistent with the maximization of wealth objective? Explain.

5. Explain why the existence of a goal is necessary to judge the efficiency of any financial decision.

SELECTED REFERENCES

ANDERSON, LESLIE P., VERGIL V. MILLER, and DONALD L. THOMPSON, *The Finance Function,* Scranton, Pa.: Intext, 1971.

ANTHONY, ROBERT N., "The Trouble with Profit Maximization," *Harvard Business Review,* 38 (November–December 1960), 126–34.

BRANCH, BEN, "Corporate Objectives and Market Performance," *Financial Management,* 2 (Summer 1973), 24–29.

DE ALESSI, LOUIS, "Private Property and Dispersion of Ownership in Large Corporations," *Journal of Finance,* 28 (September 1973), 839–51.

DONALDSON, GORDON, "Financial Goals: Management vs. Stockholders," *Harvard Business Review,* 41 (May–June 1963), 116–29.

FINDLAY, M. CHAPMAN, III, and G. A. WHITMORE, "Beyond Shareholder Wealth Maximization," *Financial Management,* 3 (Winter 1974), 25–35.

"The Issues in Social Responsibility," *Financial Analysts Journal,* 27 (September–October 1971), 26–34.

LEWELLEN, WILBUR G., "Management and Ownership in the Large Firm," *Journal of Finance,* 24 (May 1969), 299–322.

SCANLON, JOHN J., "Bell System Financial Policies," *Financial Management,* 1 (Summer 1972), 16–26.

SIMKOWITZ, MICHAEL A., and CHARLES P. JONES, "A Note on the Simultaneous Nature of Finance Methodology," *Journal of Finance,* 27 (March 1972), 103–8.

SOLOMON, EZRA, *The Theory of Financial Management,* Chapters 1 and 2. New York: Columbia University Press, 1963.

WESTON, J. FRED, "New Themes in Finance," *Journal of Finance,* 29 (March 1974), 237–43.

————, *The Scope and Methodology of Finance.* Englewood Cliffs, N.J.: Prentice-Hall, 1966.

Organizational Form and Taxes 2

To understand the role of a financial manager, one must be familiar with the legal setting in which he operates. In this chapter, we examine two aspects of this setting—the basic form of the business organization, and its tax environment. In connection with the first, we look into the advantages and disadvantages of the various forms of business organization. With respect to tax environment, our purpose is not to become experts on the subject. Indeed, such expertise would require many volumes. However, we do hope to gain a basic understanding of the tax implications of various financial decisions to be considered in this book.

FORM OF ORGANIZATION

In the United States, there are three basic forms of business organization: the sole proprietorship, the partnership, and the corporation. The sole proprietorship is the largest form of organization with respect to numbers, but the corporation is the most important with respect to the total amount of sales, assets, profits, and contribution to national income. There are several important advantages to the corporate form, which will be investigated as this section unfolds.

The sole proprietorship

The sole proprietorship is the oldest form of business organization. As the title suggests, a single person owns the business, holding title to all its assets, as well as being personally responsible for all of its liabilities. Because of its simplicity, a sole proprietorship can be established with few complications. This simplicity is its greatest virtue. Its principal shortcoming is that the proprietor is legally responsible for all obligations the organization incurs. If the organization is sued, he as an individual is sued. As a result, the proprietor has unlimited liability, which means that his personal property as well as the assets of the business may be seized to settle claims. Obviously, this liability places the individual in a risk-prone position.

Another problem with a sole proprietorship is the difficulty in raising capital. In general, this form of organization is not as attractive to creditors as are other forms of organizations. Moreover, the proprietorship has certain tax disadvantages. Fringe benefits, such as medical coverage and group insurance, are not regarded by the Internal Revenue Service as expenses of the firm and therefore are not deductible for tax purposes. In the case of a corporation, these benefits often are deductible. The proprietor, however, must pay for them from income he has left over after paying taxes. In addition to these drawbacks, the proprietorship form makes the transfer of ownership more difficult than does the corporate form. In estate planning, no portion of the enterprise can be transferred to members of the family during the proprietor's lifetime. For these reasons, this form of organization does not afford the flexibility other forms do.

The partnership

A partnership is similar to a proprietorship in all aspects except that there is more than one owner. In a *general partnership,* all partners have unlimited liability; they are jointly liable for the liabilities of the partnership. Because an individual partner can bind the partnership with obligations, it is important that general partners be selected with care. In most cases, there is a formal arrangement, or partnership agreement; this sets forth the powers of an individual partner, the distribution of profits, the amounts of capital to be invested by the partners, procedures for admitting new partners, and procedures for reconstituting the partnership in case of the death or withdrawal of a partner. Legally, the partnership is terminated if one of the partners dies or withdraws. In such cases, settlements invariably are "sticky," and reconstitution of the partnership is a difficult matter. For these reasons, many people view the partnership as an unattractive form of business organization.

The decision-making process of a partnership is often cumbersome. Unless the agreement specifies otherwise, important decisions must be made by majority vote. In most cases, group decisions are difficult, to say the least. On less important matters, individual partners may transact business for the firm but must be careful to keep the other partners informed. The powers of an individual partner will vary according to the formal or informal agreement among partners. Some partnerships specify a hierarchy of two or more layers of partners. This hierarchy determines the magnitude of decision an individual partner can make and the degree to which he can commit the firm.

In a number of states, *limited partnerships* are permitted. A limited partner contributes capital, and his liability is confined to that amount of capital. There must, however, be at least one general partner in the partnership; his liability is unlimited. Limited partners do not participate in the operation of the business; this is left to the general partner(s). The limited partners are strictly investors, and they share in the profits or losses of the partnership according to the terms of the partnership agreement. This type of arrangement is frequently used in financing real estate ventures.

The corporation

Because of the importance of the corporate form in the United States, the focus of this book is upon corporations. A corporation is an "impersonal" entity created by law which can own assets and incur liabilities. In the famous *Dartmouth College* decision in 1819, Justice Marshall concluded that

a corporation is an artificial being, invisible, intangible, and existing only in contemplation of the law. Being a mere creature of law, it possesses only those properties which the charter of its creation confers upon it, either expressly or as incidental to its very existence.[1]

The principal feature of this form is that the corporation exists separately and apart from its owners. An owner's liability is limited to his investment. Limited liability represents an important advantage over the proprietorship and the general partnership. Capital can be raised in the corporation's name without exposing the owners to unlimited liability. Therefore, personal assets cannot be seized in the settlement of claims. Ownership itself is evidenced by shares of stock, with each stockholder owning that proportion of the enterprise represented by his shares in relation to the total number of shares outstanding.[2] These shares are transferable, representing another important advan-

[1] *The Trustees of Dartmouth College* v. *Woodward,* 4 Wheaton 636 (1819).
[2] See Chapter 23 for a detailed discussion of common stock.

tage of the corporate form. Moreover, the corporation can continue even though individual owners may die or wish to sell their stock.

A corporation is incorporated in a specific state. To establish a corporation, the owners must file an application with the secretary of state or some other state official. This application includes the location of the company, the purpose of the business, the names of the owners and directors, the names of the management, the number of shares of stock authorized, the paid-in capital, and the length of the corporation's life, which in most cases is perpetual. Upon approval by the appropriate state official, a *charter* is issued that establishes the corporation as a legal entity and spells out the conditions under which it can exist.

Because of the advantages associated with limited liability, transferability of ownership, and the ability of the corporation to raise capital apart from its owners, the corporate form of business organization has grown enormously in importance during the last century. With the large demands for capital that accompany an advanced economy, the proprietorship and partnership have proven unsatisfactory, and the corporation has emerged as the most important organizational form. A possible disadvantage of the corporation is the tax treatment, which we take up shortly. Even here, the disadvantage exists only under certain circumstances. Minor disadvantages include the length of time required to incorporate and the red tape involved, as well as the incorporation fee that must be paid to the state. Thus, a corporation is more difficult to establish than either a proprietorship or a partnership. For a moderate-sized organization, however, this is not a serious problem.

CORPORATE INCOME TAXES

Few business decisions are not affected either directly or indirectly by taxes. Through their taxing power, federal, state, and local governments have a profound influence upon the behavior of business organizations and that of their owners. What might be an optimal business decision in the absence of taxes may prove to be a very inferior one with taxes. In this section, we trace through some of the essentials of taxation. This basic understanding is used in later chapters when we consider specific financial decisions. We begin with the corporate income tax and then go on to consider personal income taxes.

A corporation's taxable income is found by deducting from income all expenses, including depreciation and interest. Since 1975, the first $25,000 in taxable income is taxed at a rate of 20 percent, the second $25,000 at a rate of 22 percent, while all income over $50,000 is taxed at a rate of 48 percent. This scaling gives preferential treatment to small and moderate-sized corporations.

Corporations of any reasonable size are required to make quarterly tax payments on essentially a current basis. More specifically, they are required to pay 25 percent of their estimated taxes in any given year on April 15, June 15, September 15, and December 15 of that year. When actual income differs from that which has been estimated, adjustments are made. Assuming the company is on a calendar-year basis of accounting, it must make final settlement by April 15 of the subsequent year.

Depreciation

Because depreciation charges are deductible as an expense, they affect the amount of tax to be paid. The greater these charges, the lower the tax, all other things remaining constant. There are three methods for depreciating a capital asset: straight-line, double-declining-balance, and sum-of-the-years'-digits methods. The last two are forms of *accelerated* depreciation. Whatever method is used, it is necessary to start with the depreciable life of the asset. The IRS has established depreciable value and depreciable life guidelines for most types of assets. In general, one simply consults these guidelines to determine the depreciable life of an asset. If an asset costing $15,000 has a depreciable life of five years, annual depreciation charges using straight-line depreciation would be $15,000/5, or $3,000.

With the double-declining-balance method, depreciation charges in any year are

$$2(BV/n) \qquad (2\text{-}1)$$

where BV is the undepreciated book value of the asset at the start of the year, and n is the depreciable life of the asset. For a $15,000 asset, depreciation charges in the first year would be

$$2(\$15{,}000/5) = \$6{,}000$$

Depreciation charges in the second year are based upon an undepreciated book value of $9,000; we arrive at the $9,000 by subtracting the first year's depreciation charges, $6,000, from the asset's original book value. Depreciation charges in the second year would therefore be

$$2(\$9{,}000/5) = \$3{,}600$$

In the third year, they would be

$$2(\$5,400/5) = \$2,160$$

In the fourth year

$$2(\$3,240/5) = \$1,296$$

and in the fifth

$$2(\$1,944/5) = \$777$$

By using the double-declining-balance method of depreciation, the asset is never fully depreciated. For this reason, the IRS permits a firm to change from the double-declining-balance to the straight-line method at any time. If our hypothetical firm switches methods in the fifth year, depreciation charges in that year would simply be the undepreciated book value of the asset at the start of that year, or $1,944.

With the sum-of-the-years'-digits method, we must first compute the number of digits to be used. This can be determined by

$$\text{Digits} = n\left(\frac{n+1}{2}\right) \tag{2-2}$$

where n is again the depreciable life of the asset. For an asset with a depreciable life of five years,

$$\text{Digits} = 5\left(\frac{5+1}{2}\right) = 15$$

Depreciation charges for any year are found by dividing the remaining years of depreciable life by the digits and multiplying the result by the original depreciable value. For our example, depreciation charges in each year are

$$\text{Year } 1 = (5/15)(15,000) = \$5,000$$

$$\text{Year } 2 = (4/15)(15,000) = \$4,000$$

$$\text{Year } 3 = (3/15)(15,000) = \$3,000$$

$$\text{Year } 4 = (2/15)(15,000) = \$2,000$$

$$\text{Year } 5 = (1/15)(15,000) = \$1,000$$

The method of depreciation employed does not affect the total amount of depreciation charges, but it does affect the timing of those charges. With accelerated depreciation, depreciation charges are higher in the early years and lower in the later years than they would be if straight-line depreciation were used. As a result, taxes are lower in the early years and higher in the later years. Hence, only the timing is changed, and not the total amount of taxes. Because money has a time value, most companies choose to depreciate assets on an accelerated basis. The effect of this on the economic value of an asset is discussed in Chapter 12, when the time value of money is reviewed.

Interest expense

Interest charges on debt issued by a corporation are treated as an expense and are deductible for tax purposes. This treatment contrasts with that for common- and preferred-stock dividends, which are not deductible for tax purposes. If a company is profitable and pays taxes, the use of debt in its financing mix results in a significant tax advantage relative to the use of preferred or common stock. If the marginal tax rate is 48 percent, the firm would need to earn approximately $1.92 before taxes for every $1 paid out in dividends, ($1/(1 − tax rate)), versus only $1 for the payment of $1 of interest. Thus, we see the tax advantages associated with using debt.

Dividend income

A corporation may own stock in another company. If it receives dividends on this stock, 85 percent of these dividends is tax exempt. The remaining 15 percent is taxed at the corporate income tax rate. For example, suppose a firm receives $10,000 in dividend income from Alpha Duo Company. It would only pay taxes on $1,500 of this income. At a tax rate of 48 percent, taxes would amount to $720 as opposed to $4,800 if the entire dividend income were treated as taxable income.

Carry-back and carry-forward

If a corporation sustains a net operating loss, this loss may be carried back three years and forward five years to offset taxable income in those years. The loss must be applied first to the earliest preceding year. For example, if a firm sustained an operating loss of $200,000 in 1977, it would first carry this loss back to 1974. If the company had net profits of $200,000 in that year and paid taxes of $89,500, it would recompute its taxes for 1974 to show zero profit for tax purposes. Consequently, the company would be eligible for a tax refund of $89,500.

If the 1977 operating loss was greater than operating profits in 1974, the residual would be carried back to 1975 and taxes recomputed for that year. If part of the loss was not used in that year, it would be carried back to 1976. However, if the net operating loss was greater than net operating income in all three years, the residual would be carried forward to future profits in 1978, 1979, 1980, 1981, and 1982, in that sequence. Profits in each of these years would be reduced for tax purposes by the amount of the unused loss carry-forward. This feature of the tax law is designed to avoid penalizing the company with sharply fluctuating net operating income.

Capital gains and losses

When a capital asset is sold, a capital gain or loss is incurred. If the asset is held for less than six months, the gain or loss is defined as short-term; if held more than six months, it is long-term. Short-term capital losses are subtracted from short-term capital gains and any net gain is added to a corporation's ordinary income where it is subject to regular taxation. In contrast, long-term capital gains usually are subject to a more favorable tax treatment. The effective tax rate on the excess of net long-term capital gains (long-term gains less long-term losses) over net short-term capital losses (short-term losses less short-term gains) is 30 percent. If total income were below $50,000, however, the firm would elect to use the regular corporate rates of 20 percent and 22 percent, for it results in a lower tax.

To illustrate, suppose Boyle Manufacturing Company had ordinary taxable income of $40,000 and an excess of net long-term capital gain over short-term capital loss of $10,000. If it paid the regular tax rate of 20 percent on the first $25,000 and 22 percent on the next $25,000, its tax would be $10,500. If it used the capital-gains alternative, however, it would pay the following tax.

Regular income	$25,000 × 20 percent rate =	$5,000
Regular income	15,000 × 22 percent rate =	3,300
Capital gain	10,000 × 30 percent rate =	3,000
Total tax		$11,300

Obviously, it would not choose the capital-gains alternative. If the company's regular taxable income were $70,000, however, the alternative capital-gains tax would be worthwhile. Figuring the tax in the regular way on $80,000 of total income, we have:

First $25,000 regular income	$25,000 × 20 percent rate =	$5,000
Second $25,000 regular income	25,000 × 22 percent rate =	5,500
Amount over $50,000	30,000 × 48 percent rate =	14,400
Total tax		$24,900

Using the capital-gains tax alternative, we have:

First $25,000 regular income	$25,000 × 20 percent rate =	$5,000
Second $25,000 regular income	25,000 × 22 percent rate =	5,500
Amount over $50,000 reg. inc.	20,000 × 48 percent rate =	9,600
Capital gain	10,000 × 30 percent rate =	3,000
Total tax		$23,100

Here, the capital-gains alternative works to the advantage of the company, as it does in other situations where reasonable profits exist.

A *capital gain* is defined as the sales price of an asset less its original cost. If a capital asset is sold for a price in excess of its depreciated book value but for less than its original cost, the excess is subject to the regular tax rate. For example, suppose that a machine is purchased for $15,000 and, at the end of the third year, sold for $10,000, at which time its depreciated book value is $6,000. The $4,000 difference between sales price and depreciated book value is taxed at the regular corporate tax rate. In other words, this difference is classified as ordinary income. It represents a recapture of depreciation and not a capital gain. In contrast, if the asset were sold for $18,000, $3,000 of the gain would be subject to the more favorable capital-gains tax rate, while $9,000 ($15,000 − $6,000) would be treated as ordinary income for tax purposes. Thus, the sale of a capital asset is subject to the capital-gains tax only when the gain exceeds the total depreciation that has been taken.

If the depreciable property involved were a building or structural component, the recapture of depreciation treatment would be somewhat different. Here recapture of depreciation usually pertains to depreciation in excess of that which would have been taken under the straight-line method.

A capital loss cannot be deducted for tax purposes; it can be used only to offset capital gains. If, after deducting all capital gains from all capital losses, a company has a net capital loss for the year, this net loss may be carried back for three years and forward for five years to offset capital gains during that period. If the carry-over capital loss is not completely absorbed during this eight-year period, the amount left over is lost forever as a tax deduction.

Installment sales

If a company has installment sales, it is able to take advantage of a special tax provision. This provision allows the taxpayer to spread profits from installment sales over the years payments are received. For example, suppose Zakor Tool Company sells a $10,000 lathe, where $2,500 is required at the time of the sale and $2,500-installments in each of the next three years. Assuming the sale is profitable, Zakor can postpone reporting profitability until the installments are received. (If a loss is incurred, it is recognized at the time of the sale.) The advantage, of course, is that Zakor does not have to pay income taxes on profits arising from the sale until proceeds are actually received.

In our example, assume Zakor's marginal tax rate is 48 percent and its profit margin on the machine 40 percent. The reported profits and taxes paid on the sale of the lathe are as follows:

	Installment Receipt	Gross Profit	Taxes
Year of sale	$2,500	$1,000	$480
First year following sale	2,500	1,000	480
Second year following sale	2,500	1,000	480
Third year following sale	2,500	1,000	480

If the installment method of reporting sales were not used, Zakor would need to report the full $10,000 sale and $4,000 profit in the year of the sale, in which case it would pay $1,920 in taxes. Thus, the installment method allows a company, or individual, to defer the payment of taxes, but it does not reduce the total amount of taxes to be paid, assuming the tax rate stays unchanged.

Investment tax credit

The investment tax credit is available to corporations and individuals who invest in certain types of assets. This credit was conceived in 1962 to provide an incentive for investment in capital assets. The credit was later repealed, reinstated, and repealed in a countercyclical manner designed to dampen or stimulate modernization, depending on the phase of the economy. In 1971, it was restored; and in the Tax Reduction Act of 1975, the maximum credit was increased from 7 percent to 10 percent.

The maximum credit is available on qualified property with a useful life of seven or more years. (The useful life of an asset can be the same as that for computing depreciation.) The credit itself is available only at the time the property is placed into service. Suppose that Zakor Tool Company purchased plant equipment costing $100,000 which had a useful life of eight years. If the equipment were placed in service in 1977, Zakor would be able to claim an investment tax credit of $10,000 in that year. This credit reduces the amount of 1977 income taxes Zakor pays by $10,000. Moreover, the credit does not alter the basis for depreciation; it remains at $100,000.

The amount of qualified investment depends upon the useful life of the property. If the useful life were seven or more years, one could claim a 10 percent credit on the full investment. However, if the useful life were at least five but less than seven years, only two-thirds of the total investment would qualify. To illustrate, suppose Zakor invested in office machinery costing $9,000 with a useful life of six years. In this case, only two-thirds of the $9,000 investment, or $6,000, would be eligible for the 10 percent investment tax credit. If the useful life were at least three years but less than five years, only one-third of the investment would qualify. If Zakor invested in a truck costing $6,000 with a three-year useful life, only $2,000 would qualify for the 10 percent investment tax credit. Property with a useful life of less than three years is not eligible. Thus, we see that the emphasis is on stimulating investment in assets with relatively long economic lives.

PERSONAL INCOME TAXES

The subject of personal taxes is extremely comprehensive, but here our main concern is with the personal taxes of individuals owning stock in corporations. Any income reported by a sole proprietorship or a partnership becomes income of the owner(s), and it is taxed at the personal tax rate. This rate is graduated according to the amount of taxable income, going from a marginal tax rate of 14 percent all the way up to 70 percent for individuals having large taxable incomes.

For the individual, dividend income is taxed at the ordinary income tax rate. However, the first $100 of such income is tax exempt. If stock is jointly owned by husband and wife, the exemption is $200. As with the corporation, long-term capital gains for individuals are taxed more favorably than is ordinary income. Short-term capital gains, however, are treated as regular income and are taxed at the normal income tax rate. In order to establish a long-term capital gain, the asset must be held longer than six months. If the asset is a stock, the gain is simply the price for which the stock is sold, less the amount paid for it.

If the excess of net long-term capital gain over short-term capital loss for a year is less than $50,000, the individual may figure his tax in two ways and choose the one that results in the lower tax. Using the regular method, one-half the excess net long-term capital gain is added to taxable income and the tax figured accordingly. In other words, the individual pays taxes on only one-half the total excess net gain. The alternative way of computing taxes is to pay taxes equal to 25 percent of the excess net long-term gain. An individual in a marginal tax bracket of less than 50 percent will naturally choose the first method, while an individual in a tax bracket greater than 50 percent will choose the second. To illustrate the second situation, suppose that in 1975 Wayne Wheeler had a salary of $66,000 and an excess of net long-term capital gain over net short-term capital loss of $20,000. If he were married, had no children, and had $3,150 in itemized deductions, his taxes figured in the regular manner would be:

Salary		$66,000
Net long-term capital gain	$20,000	
Less 50 percent deduction	10,000	10,000
Adjusted gross income		$76,000
Less: Itemized deductions	3,150	
Deductions for exemptions ($750 each)	1,500	4,650
Taxable income		$71,350
Tax on this income		$28,463

If Mr. Wheeler chooses the alternate tax method, his taxes would be:

Salary		$66,000
Less: Itemized deductions	$3,150	
Deductions for exemptions	1,500	4,650
Taxable income		$61,350
Tax on this income		$23,016
Add: 25 percent of excess of net long-term gain over net short-term capital loss ($20,000)		5,000
Total taxes		$28,016

Thus, Mr. Wheeler would be better off choosing the alternative tax method for capital gains.

If the excess net long-term capital gain exceeds $50,000, the alternate tax treatment is modified. In essence, the portion of the total gain in excess of $50,000 is taxed at a higher rate than 25 percent. The rate used for this excess portion is one-half the marginal tax rate of the individual up to a maximum of 35 percent (one-half the maximum rate of 70 percent). The first $50,000 of the gain, however, still enjoys a tax rate of 25 percent, or $12,500 in taxes on this portion. It is only the amount in excess of $50,000 that is taxed at a higher rate.

If an individual has an excess of net short-term capital loss over net long-term capital gain, this excess loss may be deducted from ordinary income up to a maximum $1,000 in a taxable year. Any balance in excess of $1,000 may be carried forward as a short-term capital loss until it is used up. If an individual has an excess of net long-term capital loss over net short-term capital gain, however, only one-half of this excess may be deducted up to the maximum $1,000 in a taxable year. Any unused loss may be carried forward until it is used up. Thus, if an individual has a net long-term capital loss of $6,000 and no net short-term capital gains, he may deduct one-half of $2,000, or $1,000, from ordinary income in the year the loss is incurred. This leaves $4,000 to be carried forward as a long-term capital loss. If the individual had no capital gains or losses in the succeeding two years, he could deduct $1,000 in each of these years, after which the loss carry-forward would be used up.

The difference in tax treatment between ordinary income and capital gains has significant implications for dividend and other financial decisions. We shall see in subsequent chapters that this tax differential is particularly important when it comes to certain evaluation concepts.

Subchapter S

Subchapter S of the Internal Revenue Code allows the owners of small corporations—those having ten or fewer stockholders—to use the corporate organizational form but to be taxed as though the firm were a proprietorship or a partnership. Thus, the owners are able to avail themselves of the legal advantages extended to corporations, but they are able to avoid any tax disadvantage that might result. They simply declare any corporate profits as personal income and pay the appropriate tax on this income. This treatment eliminates the double taxation normally associated with dividend income—that is, the corporation paying dividends from after-tax income, and shareholders paying taxes on the dividend income they receive.

SUMMARY

In this chapter, the three basic forms of business organization were considered—the sole proprietorship, the partnership, and the corporation. Advantages and disadvantages of each were discussed, and it was concluded that, in a modern economy, the corporate form offers a number of advantages. As a result, we have seen a significant growth in the importance of the corporation in the last century.

The tax environment has a profound influence upon business decisions. We briefly examined certain basic features of the tax law as they apply to corporations and individuals. The impact of depreciation, interest charges, and installment sales on the amount of taxes paid was investigated. Moreover, we looked into the difference in taxes upon ordinary income and upon capital gains. This chapter serves only as an introduction to the issue; relevant taxes and the implication of these taxes will be discussed throughout the book when we consider specific financial decisions.

QUESTIONS

1. What is the principal advantage of the corporate form of business organization? Discuss the importance of this advantage to the owner of a small family restaurant. Discuss the importance of this advantage to a wealthy entrepreneur who owns several businesses.

2. What is the impact on earnings of the different methods of depreciation? Explain.

3. The method of depreciation does not alter the total amount of deductions from income during the life of an asset. What does it alter and why is that important?

4. Is there any theoretical justification for allowing the deduction of debt service charge from income for tax purposes, yet disallowing the deduction of dividends on preferred and common stock? Discuss.

5. Tax laws have become extremely complex. In addition, there is little theoretical or moral justification for a substantial number of tax incentives (loopholes). Why and how are these incentives created? In your opinion, is there any indication that these incentives will be eliminated?

6. The United States has a progressive federal tax on personal income. What impact will inflation have on the proportion of GNP going to the government? Discuss.

7. As a term project, evaluate the tax incentive known as the Domestic International Sales Corporation (DISC).

PROBLEMS

1. In 1972 the Kyle Company purchased, for $30,000, a special-purpose machine that had a depreciable life of five years and an expected salvage value of zero. (The company uses straight-line depreciation.) Three years later it sold the machine for $35,000.
   (a) If the company has a marginal tax rate of 48 percent on income and 30 percent on capital gains, how much in taxes would it pay on the sale of the machine?
   (b) If the machine were sold for $20,000, how much in taxes would be paid?

2. The Ross X-ray Company is going to purchase a new piece of equipment for $48,000 that has a depreciable life of three years and zero salvage value. Ross expects to earn $25,000 a year before depreciation and taxes from the use of the equipment in each of the three years. The company must decide whether to use straight-line depreciation or sum-of-the-years'-digits depreciation.

(a) Determine the taxable income arising from the use of the equipment in each of the three years under both methods of depreciation.

(b) What is the total taxable income under both methods of depreciation?

(c) Which method of depreciation is preferable?

3. The P. Breaux Construction Company was founded in 1969 and had the following taxable income through 1976:

1969	$ 0
1970	25,000
1971	40,000
1972	40,000
1973	− 125,000
1974	40,000
1975	60,000
1976	75,000

Compute the corporate income tax or tax refund in each year, assuming a rate of 22 percent on the first $25,000 earned and a rate of 48 percent on all income in excess of $25,000 through 1974. In 1975 and 1976, the rate was 20 percent on the first $25,000, 22 percent on the second $25,000, and 48 percent on all income in excess of $50,000.

4. R. F. O'Connell, who is married, owns a large sporting goods store, which is currently organized as a sole proprietorship. Annual income from the store averages $55,000 before taxes. O'Connell draws $30,000 a year and leaves $25,000 in the business to finance the increased inventory required in the face of competition, as well as for the store's other capital needs. With personal deductions, O'Connell's taxable income as an individual is $44,000. His taxes can be computed by using the following table. O'Connell is considering incorporating and wishes to determine whether total taxes, both personal and corporate, will be more or less under the corporate form than under the sole proprietorship. In this regard, he would draw a salary of $25,000 and pay $5,000 in dividends from the corporation to himself, leaving $25,000 in the business as before. Assume that O'Connell is able to claim $11,000 in personal deductions regardless of the organizational form of the business.

Personal Income Tax (Joint Return)

Taxable Income	Base Amount of Tax	Plus Marginal Tax Rate Times Balance Over Lower Amount in Range
$12,000–$16,000	$ 2,260	25%
16,000– 20,000	3,260	28
20,000– 24,000	4,380	32
24,000– 28,000	5,600	36
28,000– 32,000	7,100	39
32,000– 36,000	8,660	42
36,000– 40,000	10,340	45
40,000– 44,000	12,140	48

5. P. Pelley Corporation has a marginal tax rate of 48 percent. It sells forklift trucks at a price of $7,500 apiece with a gross profit margin of 33 ⅓ percent. It sells its trucks both on an installment basis and on a straight cash basis. For an installment sale, one-fifth of the purchase price is required as down payment at the time of the sale and one-fifth at the end of each of the next four years. With a cash sale, the full purchase price is due at the time of the sale.
   (a) Which type of sale results in the greater amount of taxes being paid?
   (b) Which type is more favorable with respect to taxes?
   (c) Should any other factors be considered?

6. As a term project, evaluate the impact of continued inflation on the tax burden borne by a corporation vis-à-vis that borne by individuals.

SELECTED REFERENCES

BITTKER, BORIS I., and JAMES S. EUSTICE, *Federal Income Taxation of Corporations and Shareholders.* Boston: Warren Gorham & Lamont, 1971.

DAVIES, ROBERT M., and MELVYN H. LAWRENCE, *Choosing a Form of Business Organization.* Durham, N.C.: Duke University Law School, 1963.

Federal Tax Course. Englewood Cliffs, N.J.: Prentice-Hall, 1976.

HOLZMAN, R. S., *Tax Basis for Managerial Decisions.* New York: Holt, Rinehart & Winston, 1965.

SMITH, DAN THROOP, *Tax Factors in Business Decisions.* Englewood Cliffs, N.J.: Prentice-Hall, 1968.

Financial Analysis 3

Financial analysis means different things to different people. A trade creditor, for example, is primarily interested in the liquidity of the firm being analyzed. His claim is short-term in nature, and the ability of the firm to pay this claim can best be judged by an analysis of its liquidity. The claim of a bondholder, on the other hand, is long-term. Accordingly, he is interested in the cash-flow ability of the firm to service debt over a long period of time. The bondholder may evaluate this ability by analyzing the capital structure of the firm, the major sources and uses of funds, the firm's profitability over time, and projections of future profitability. Finally, an investor in a company's common stock is concerned principally with present and expected future earnings as well as with the stability of these earnings about a trend. As a result, the investor usually concentrates his analysis on the profitability of the firm.

The point of view of the analyst may be either external or internal. In the cases described, it was external, involving suppliers of capital. From an internal standpoint, the firm needs to undertake financial analysis in order to effectively plan and control. To plan for the future, the financial manager must assess realistically the firm's present financial position and evaluate opportunities in relation to their effect on this position. With respect to internal control, the financial manager is particularly concerned with return on investment in the various assets of the company and in the efficiency of asset management. Finally, in order to bargain effectively for outside funds, the financial manager needs to be attuned to all aspects of financial analysis that outside suppliers of capital use in evaluating the firm. We see, then, that the type of financial analysis varies according to the particular interests of the analyst.

A POSSIBLE FRAMEWORK FOR ANALYSIS

There are a number of conceptual frameworks that might be used in analyzing a firm. Many analysts have a favorite procedure for coming to some generalizations about the firm being analyzed. At the risk of treading on some rather sacred ground, we present a conceptual framework which lends itself to situations in which external financing is contemplated. The factors to be considered are shown in Figure 3-1.

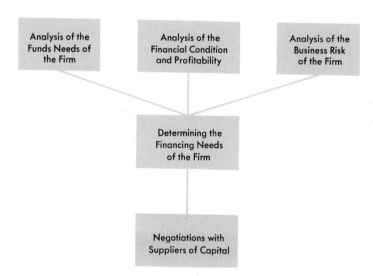

FIG. 3 · 1

Framework for
financial analysis

Taking them in order, our concern in the first case is with the trend and seasonal component of a firm's funds requirements. How much will be required in the future and what is the nature of these needs? Is there a seasonal component to the needs? Analytical tools used to answer these questions include source and use of funds statements and the cash budget, both of which are considered in Chapter 4. The tools used to assess the financial condition and performance of the firm are financial ratios, a topic taken up in this chapter. With these ratios, the skilled analyst dissects the company being analyzed from a number of different angles, in the hope of obtaining valuable insight into its financial condition and profitability. The last factor in the first row of Figure 3-1, business risk, relates to the risk inherent in the operations of the enterprise. Some companies are in highly volatile lines of endeavor, while others are in very stable lines. A machine tool company would fall in the former category, while an electric utility would be in the latter. The analyst needs to estimate the degree of business risk of the firm being analyzed.

All three of these factors should be used in determining the financing needs of the firm. Moreover, they should be considered jointly. The greater the funds requirements, of course, the greater the total financing that will be necessary. The nature of the funds needs influences the type of financing that should be used. If there is a seasonal component to the business, this component lends itself to short-term financing, and bank loans in particular. The basic business risk of the firm also has an important effect on the type of financing that should be used. The greater the business risk, the less desirable debt financing usually becomes relative to common-stock financing. In other words, equity financing is safer in that there is no contractual obligation to pay interest and principal as there is with debt. A firm with a high degree of business risk generally is ill advised to take on considerable financial risk as well. The financial condition and performance of the firm also influence the type of financing that should be used. The greater the liquidity, the stronger the overall financial condition, and the greater the profitability of the firm, the more risk that can be incurred with respect to type of financing. That is, debt financing becomes more attractive with improvements in liquidity, financial condition, and profitability.

The last box in Figure 3-1 gives recognition to the fact that it is not sufficient simply to determine the best financing plan from the standpoint of the firm and assume that it can be consummated. The plan needs to be sold to outside suppliers of capital. The firm may determine that it needs $1 million in short-term financing, but lenders may not go along with either the amount or the type of financing. In the end, the firm may have to compromise its plan to meet the realities of the marketplace. The interaction of the firm with these suppliers of capital determine the amount, terms, and price of financing. The fact that the firm must negotiate with outside suppliers of capital serves as a feedback mechanism to the other four factors in Figure 3-1. Analysis cannot be undertaken in isolation of the fact that ultimately an appeal will need to be made to suppliers of capital. Similarly, suppliers of capital must recognize that a company may approach the question of financing from a different point of view than their own and learn to appreciate the difference.

Thus, there are a number of facets to financial analysis. Presumably, analysis will be in relation to some structural framework similar to that presented above. Otherwise, it is likely to be loose and not really answer the questions for which it was intended. As we have seen, an integral part of financial analysis is the analysis of financial ratios; and that will occupy our attention in the remainder of this chapter.

Use of financial ratios

To evaluate the financial condition and performance of a firm, the financial analyst needs certain yardsticks. The yardstick frequently used is a ratio, or index, relating two pieces of financial data to each other. Analysis and interpretation of various ratios should give an experienced and skilled analyst a better understanding of the financial condition and performance of the firm than he would obtain from analysis of the financial data alone.[1]

The analysis of financial ratios involves two types of comparison. First, the analyst can compare a present ratio with past and expected future ratios for the same company. For example, the current ratio (the ratio of current assets to current liabilities) for the present year-end could be compared with the current ratio for the previous year-end. When financial ratios are arrayed on a spread sheet over a period of years, the analyst can study the composition of change and determine whether there has been an improvement or a deterioration in the financial condition and performance of the firm over time. Financial ratios also can be computed for projected, or *pro forma,* statements and compared with present and past ratios.

The second method of comparison involves comparing the ratios of one firm with those of similar firms or with industry averages at the same point in time. Such a comparison gives insight into the relative financial condition and performance of the firm. Financial ratios for various industries are published by Robert Morris Associates, Dun & Bradstreet, Leo Troy's *Almanac of Business and Industrial Financial Ratios,* and various other credit agencies and trade associations.[2] The analyst should avoid using "rules of thumb" indiscriminately for all industries. For example, the criterion that all companies should have

---

[1] For an excellent discussion of the history of ratio analysis, see James O. Horrigan, "A Short History of Financial Ratio Analysis," *Accounting Review,* 43 (April 1968), 284–94.

[2] Robert Morris Associates, an association of bank credit and loan officers, publishes industry averages based upon financial statements supplied to banks by borrowers. Eleven ratios are computed annually for 156 lines of business. In addition, each line of business is broken down according to four size categories. Dun & Bradstreet annually calculates fourteen important ratios for 125 lines of business. Troy, *Almanac of Business and Industrial Financial Ratios* (Englewood Cliffs, N.J.: Prentice-Hall, 1974), shows industry averages for some twenty-two financial ratios. Over 75 industries are reported, and some of the sublistings under each industry are quite extensive. Industry classifications include such things as farms and small retail stores as well as the more usual industries.

at least a 2-for-1 current ratio is inappropriate. The analysis must be in relation to the type of business in which the firm is engaged and to the firm itself. Many sound companies have current ratios of less than 2 to 1. Only by comparing the financial ratios of one firm with those of similar firms can one make a realistic judgment.

Because reported figures and the ratios computed from these figures are numerical, there is a tendency to regard them as precise portrayals of a firm's true financial status. For some firms, the accounting data may closely approximate economic reality. On many occasions, however, it is necessary to go beyond the reported figures in order to analyze properly the financial condition and performance of the firm. Such accounting data as depreciation, reserve for bad debts, and other reserves at best are estimates and may not reflect economic depreciation, bad debts, and other losses.

Moreover, accounting data from different companies should be standardized as much as possible. It is important to compare apples with apples and oranges with oranges. Even with standardized figures, however, the analyst should use caution in interpreting the comparisons.

Types of ratios

For our purposes, financial ratios can be divided into four types: liquidity, debt, profitability, and coverage ratios. The first two types are ratios computed from the balance sheet; the last two are ratios computed from the income statement and, sometimes, from both the income statement and the balance sheet. It is important to recognize from the outset that no one ratio gives us sufficient information by which to judge the financial condition and performance of the firm. Only when we analyze a group of ratios are we able to make reasonable judgments. In addition, it is important to take into account any seasonal character in a business. Underlying trends may be assessed only through a comparison of raw figures and ratios at the same time of year. For example, we would not compare a December 31 balance sheet with a May 31 balance sheet but would compare December 31 with December 31.

Although the number of financial ratios that might be computed increases geometrically with the amount of financial data, only the more important ratios are considered in this chapter. Actually, the ratios needed to assess the financial condition and performance of a company are relatively few in number. To compute unneeded ratios adds not only complexity to the problem but also confusion. In order to illustrate the ratios taken up in this chapter, we use the balance sheet and income statements of the Aldine Manufacturing Company shown in Tables 3-1 and 3-2.

TABLE 3 · 1

Aldine Manufacturing Company Balance Sheet

Assets	March 31, 1977	March 31, 1976
Cash and marketable securities	$ 177,689	$ 175,042
Accounts receivable	678,279	740,705
Inventories, at lower of cost (Fifo) or market	1,328,963	1,234,725
Prepaid expenses	20,756	17,197
Accumulated tax prepayments	35,203	29,165
Current assets	$2,240,890	$2,196,834
Fixed assets at cost	1,596,886	1,538,495
Less accumulated depreciation	856,829	791,205
Net fixed assets	$ 740,057	$ 747,290
Investment—Long-term	65,376	—
Goodwill	205,157	205,624
	$3,251,480	$3,149,748

Liabilities and Net Worth	March 31, 1977	March 31, 1976
Bank loans *and notes payable*	$ 448,508	$ 356,511
Accounts payable	148,427	136,793
Accrued taxes	36,203	127,455
Other accrued liabilities	190,938	164,285
Current liabilities	$ 824,076	$ 785,044
Long-term debt	630,783	626,460
Stockholders' equity		
Common stock, $1.00 par value	420,828	420,824
Capital surplus	361,158	361,059
Retained earnings	1,014,635	956,361
Total stockholders' equity	$1,796,621	$1,738,244
	$3,251,408	$3,149,748

TABLE 3·2

	Year Ended March 31, 1977	Year Ended March 31, 1976
Aldine Manufacturing Company Statement of Earnings		
Net sales	$3,992,758	$3,721,241
Cost of goods sold	2,680,298	2,499,965
Selling, general, and administrative expenses	801,395	726,959
Depreciation	111,509	113,989
Interest expense	85,274	69,764
Earnings before taxes	$ 314,282	$ 310,564
Income taxes (federal and state)	163,708	172,446
Earnings after taxes	$ 150,574	$ 138,118
Cash dividends	92,300	88,634
Increase in retained earnings	$ 58,274	$ 49,484

7,000

Current ratio

Liquidity ratios are used to judge a firm's ability to meet short-term obligations. From them, much insight can be obtained into the present cash solvency of the firm and its ability to remain solvent in the event of adversities. One of the most general and most frequently used of these ratios is the *current ratio:*

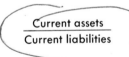

$$\frac{\text{Current assets}}{\text{Current liabilities}}$$

For Aldine, the ratio for the 1977 year-end is

$$\frac{\$2,240,890}{\$824,076} = 2.72$$

Aldine is engaged in making household electrical appliances. Its current ratio is somewhat above the median ratio for the industry of 2.1. (The median for the industry is taken from Robert Morris Associates, *Statement Studies.*) Though comparisons with industry averages do not always reveal financial strength or weakness, they are meaningful in identifying companies that are out of line. Where a significant deviation occurs, the analyst will want to determine the reasons for this occurrence. Perhaps the industry is overly liquid and the company being examined is basically sound despite a lower current ratio. In another situation, the company being analyzed may be too liquid, relative to the industry, with the result that it foregoes profitability. Whenever a "red flag" is raised, it is important for the analyst to search out the reasons behind it.

Supposedly, the higher the current ratio, the greater the ability of the firm to pay its bills. However, the ratio must be regarded as crude because it does not take into account the liquidity of the individual components of the current assets. A firm having current assets composed principally of cash and current receivables is generally regarded as more liquid than a firm whose current assets consist primarily of inventories.[3] Consequently, we must turn to "finer" tools of analysis if we are to evaluate critically the liquidity of the firm.

Acid-test ratio

A somewhat more accurate guide to liquidity is the *quick,* or *acid-test, ratio:*

$$\frac{\text{Current assets less Inventories}}{\text{Current liabilities}}$$

For Aldine, this ratio is

$$\frac{\$2,240,890 - \$1,328,963}{\$824,076} = 1.11$$

This ratio is the same as the current ratio except that it excludes inventories—presumably the least liquid portion of current assets—from the numerator. The ratio concentrates on cash, marketable securities, and receivables in relation to current obligations and thus provides a more penetrating measure of liquidity than does the current ratio. Aldine's acid-test ratio is slightly above the industry median of 1.1, indicating that it is in line with the industry.

---

[3]We have defined *liquidity* as the ability to realize value in money—the most liquid of assets. Liquidity has two dimensions: (1) the time required to convert the asset into money, and (2) the certainty of the realized price. To the extent that the price realized on receivables is as predictable as that realized on inventories, receivables would be a more liquid asset than inventories, owing to the shorter time required to convert the asset into money. If the price realized on receivables is more certain than that on inventories, receivables would be regarded as being even more liquid.

Liquidity of receivables

To the extent that there are suspected imbalances or problems in various components of the current assets, the financial analyst will want to examine these components separately in his assessment of liquidity. Receivables, for example, may be far from current. To regard all receivables as liquid, when in fact a sizable portion may be past due, overstates the liquidity of the firm being analyzed. Receivables are liquid assets only insofar as they can be collected in a reasonable amount of time. For our analysis of receivables, we have two basic ratios, the first of which is the *average collection period ratio*:

$$\frac{\text{Receivables} \times \text{Days in year}}{\text{Annual credit sales}}$$

For Aldine, this ratio is

$$\frac{\$678,279 \times 365}{\$3,992,758} = 62 \text{ days}$$

The average collection period tells us the average number of days receivables are outstanding.

The second ratio is the *receivable turnover ratio:*

$$\frac{\text{Annual credit sales}}{\text{Receivables}}$$

For Aldine, this ratio is

$$\frac{\$3,992,758}{\$678,279} = 5.89$$

Actually, these two ratios are inverses of each other. The number of days in the year, 365, divided by the average collection period, 62 days, gives the receivable turnover ratio, 5.89. The number of days in the year divided by the turnover ratio gives the average collection period. Thus, either of these two ratios can be employed.

When credit sales figures for a period are not available, we must resort to total sales figures. The receivable figure used in the calculation ordinarily represents year-end receivables. However, when sales are seasonal or have grown considerably over the year, using the year-end receivable balance may not be appropriate. With seasonality, an average of the monthly closing balances may be the most appropriate figure to use. With growth, the receivable balance at the end of the ·

year will be deceptively high in relation to sales. In this case, an average of receivables at the beginning and at the end of the year might be appropriate, if the growth in sales was steady throughout the year.

The median industry receivable turnover ratio is 8.1, which tells us that Aldine's receivables are considerably slower in turning over than is typical for the industry (62 days versus 45 days). This finding should cause the analyst concern. One thing he should check is the billing terms given on sales. For example, if the average collection period is 62 days and the terms given are 2/10, net 30,[4] he would know that a sizable proportion of the receivables are past due beyond the final due date of thirty days. On the other hand, if the terms are net 60, the typical receivable is being collected only two days after the final due date. Suppose that upon further investigation, the analyst finds Aldine's credit policy to be too liberal. As a result, many receivables are past due, with some uncollectible. Profits are less than those possible owing to bad-debt losses and the need to finance a large investment in receivables. In short, the investigation reveals that Aldine is considerably less liquid with respect to receivables than is suggested by a cursory glance at its current asset position.

Although too high an average collection period is usually bad, a very low average collection period may not necessarily be good. It may be that credit policy is excessively restrictive. The receivables on the book may be of prime quality and yet sales may be curtailed unduly—and profits less than they might be—because of this policy. In this situation, credit standards for an acceptable account might be relaxed somewhat.

Another means by which we can obtain insight into the liquidity of receivables is through an *aging of accounts*. With this method, we categorize the receivables at a moment in time according to the proportions billed in previous months. For example, we might have the following hypothetical aging of accounts receivable at December 31:

Proportion of Receivables Billed in

December	November	October	September	August and Before	Total
67%	19%	7%	2%	5%	100%

If the billing terms are 2/10, net 30, this aging tells us that 67 percent of the receivables at December 31 are current, 19 percent are up to one month past due, 7 percent are one to two months past due, and so on.

---

[4]The notation means that the supplier gives a 2 percent discount if the receivable invoice is paid within ten days and that payment is due within thirty days if the discount is not taken.

Depending upon the conclusions drawn from our analysis of the aging, we may want to examine more closely the credit and collection policies of the company. In the example above, we might be prompted to investigate the individual receivables that were billed in August and before, in order to determine if any should be charged off. The receivables shown on the books are only as good as the likelihood that they will be collected.

An aging of accounts receivable gives us considerably more information than the calculation of the average collection period, because it pinpoints the trouble spots more specifically. Of particular value is a comparison of different agings over time. With this comparison, we obtain an accurate picture of the investment of a firm in receivables and changes in the basic composition of this investment over time. Comparison of agings for different firms is difficult because most published reports do not include such information.

From a creditor's point of view, it is sometimes desirable to obtain an *aging of accounts payable*. This measure, combined with the less exact turnover of payables (annual purchases divided by payables), allows us to analyze payables in much the same manner as we do receivables. Also, one can compute the average age of a firm's accounts payable. The average age of payables is

$$\frac{\text{Accounts payable} \times 365}{\text{Purchase of raw materials}}$$

where accounts payable is the average balance outstanding for the year; and the denominator is the purchase of raw material during the year. This information is valuable in evaluating the probability that a credit applicant will pay on time. If the average age of payables is 48 days, and the terms in the industry are net 30, we know that a portion of the applicant's payables are not being paid on time. A credit check of other suppliers will give insight into the severity of the problem.

Liquidity of inventories

We may compute the *inventory turnover ratio* as an indicator of the liquidity of inventory:

$$\frac{\text{Cost of goods sold}}{\text{Average inventory}}$$

For Aldine, the ratio is

$$\frac{\$2,680,298}{\$1,281,844} = 2.09$$

The figure for cost of goods sold used in the numerator is for the period being studied—usually one year; the average inventory figure used in the denominator typically is an average of beginning and ending inventories for the period. As was true with receivables, however, it may be necessary to compute a more sophisticated average when there is a strong seasonal element. The inventory turnover ratio tells us the rapidity with which the inventory is turned over into receivables through sales. This ratio, like other ratios, must be judged in relation to past and expected future ratios of the firm and in relation to ratios of similar firms, the industry average, or both.

Generally, the higher the inventory turnover, the more efficient the inventory management of a firm. However, a relatively high inventory turnover ratio may be the result of too low a level of inventory and frequent stockouts. It might also be the result of too many small orders for inventory replacement. Either of these situations may be more costly to the firm than carrying a larger investment in inventory and having a lower turnover ratio. Again, caution is necessary in interpreting the ratio. When the inventory turnover ratio is relatively low, it indicates slow-moving inventory or obsolescence of some of the stock. Obsolesence may necessitate substantial write-downs, which, in turn, would negate the treatment of inventory as a liquid asset. Because the turnover ratio is a somewhat crude measure, we would want to investigate any perceived inefficiency in inventory management. In this regard, it is helpful to compute the turnover of the major categories of inventory to see if there are imbalances, which may indicate excessive investment in specific components of the inventory. Once we have a hint of a problem, we must investigate it more specifically to determine its cause.

Aldine's inventory turnover ratio of 2.09 compares with a median turnover for the industry of 3.3. This unfavorable comparison suggests the company is less efficient in inventory management than is the industry and that it holds excessive stock. A question also arises as to whether the inventory on the books is worth its stated value. If not, the liquidity of the firm is less than the current or quick ratio alone suggests. Once we have a hint of an inventory problem, we must investigate it along the lines of our previous discussion to determine its cause.

Summary of Aldine's liquidity

Although comparisons of Aldine's current and quick ratios with medians for the industry are favorable, a more detailed examination of receivables and inventory reveals some problems. The turnover ratios for both of these assets are significantly less than the median ratios for the industry. These findings suggest that the two assets are not entirely current, and this factor detracts from the favorable current and quick ratios. A sizable portion of receivables are slow and there appear to be inefficiencies in inventory management. On the basis of our analysis, we conclude that these assets are not particularly liquid in the sense of turning over into cash in a reasonable period of time.

DEBT RATIOS

Extending our analysis to the long-term liquidity of the firm (i.e., its ability to meet long-term obligations), several debt ratios may be used. The *debt-to-net-worth* ratio is computed by simply dividing the total debt of the firm (including current liabilities) by its net worth:

$$\frac{\text{Total debt}}{\text{Net worth}}$$

For Aldine, the ratio is

$$\frac{\$1,454,859}{\$1,796,621} = 0.81$$

The median debt-to-worth ratio for the electrical appliance industry is 0.8, so Aldine is right in line with the industry. Presumably it would not experience difficulty with creditors because of an excessive debt ratio.

When intangible assets are significant, they frequently are deducted from net worth to obtain the tangible net worth of the firm. Depending upon the purpose for which the ratio is used, preferred stock sometimes is included as debt rather than as net worth. Preferred stock represents a prior claim from the standpoint of the investor in common stock; consequently, he might include preferred stock as debt when analyzing a firm. The ratio of debt to equity will vary according to the nature of the business and volatility of cash flows. An electric utility, with very stable cash flows, usually will have a higher debt ratio than will a machine tool company, whose cash flows are far less stable. A comparison of the debt ratio for a given company with those of similar firms gives us a general indication of the credit-worthiness and financial risk of the firm.

In addition to the ratio of total debt to equity, we may wish to compute the following ratio, which deals with only the long-term capitalization of the firm:

$$\frac{\text{Long-term debt}}{\text{Total capitalization}}$$

where total capitalization represents all long-term debt and net worth. For Aldine, the ratio is

$$\frac{\$630,783}{\$2,427,404} = 0.26$$

This measure tells us the relative importance of long-term debt in the capital structure. Again this ratio is in line with the median ratio for the industry of 0.23. The debt ratios computed above have been based upon book value figures; it is sometimes useful to calculate these ratios using market values. The use of debt ratios is considered in Chapter 18, where we take up the problem of capital structure.

PROFITABILITY RATIOS

Profitability ratios are of two types: those showing profitability in relation to sales, and those showing profitability in relation to investment. Together, these ratios give us indication of the firm's efficiency of operation.

Profitability in relation to sales

The first ratio we consider is the *gross profit margin:*

$$\frac{\text{Sales less Cost of goods sold}}{\text{Sales}}$$

For Aldine, the gross profit margin is

$$\frac{\$1,312,460}{\$3,992,758} = 32.9 \text{ percent}$$

This ratio tells us the profit of the firm relative to sales after we deduct the cost of producing the goods sold. It indicates the efficiency of operations as well as how products are priced. Aldine's gross profit margin is significantly above the median for the industry of 23.8 percent, indicating that it is relatively more efficient in producing appliances.

A more specific ratio of profitability is the *net profit margin:*

$$\frac{\text{Net profits after taxes}}{\text{Sales}}$$

For Aldine, this ratio is

$$\frac{\$150,574}{\$3,992,758} = 3.77 \text{ percent}$$

The net profit margin tells us the relative efficiency of the firm after taking into account all expenses and income taxes, but not extraordinary charges. Aldine's net profit margin is above the median margin for the industry of 2.7 percent, which indicates it is more profitable on a relative basis than most other firms in the industry.

By considering both ratios jointly, we are able to gain considerable insight into the operations of the firm. For example, if the gross profit margin essentially is unchanged over a period of several years, but the net profit margin has declined over the same period, we know that the cause is either higher expenses relative to sales or a higher tax rate. Therefore, we would analyze these factors more specifically to determine the cause of the problem. On the other hand, if the gross profit margin falls, we know that the cost of producing the goods relative to sales has increased. This occurrence, in turn, may be due to lower prices or to lower operating efficiency in relation to volume. If expenses are constant in relation to sales, we would know that the lower net profit margin is due entirely to the higher cost of producing the goods relative to sales.

There are any number of combinations of changes possible in the gross and net profit margins. Indications of the sort illustrated above tell us where we should investigate further. In our analysis, it is useful to examine over time each of the individual expense items as a percentage of sales. By so doing, we can pick out specific areas of deterioration or improvement.

Profitability in relation to investment

The second group of profitability ratios relates profits to investments. One of these measures is the *rate of return on common stock equity:*

$$\frac{\text{Net profits after taxes less Preferred stock dividend}}{\text{Net worth less Par value of preferred stock}}$$

For Aldine, the rate of return is

$$\frac{\$150,574}{\$1,796,621} = 8.38 \text{ percent}$$

This ratio tells us the earning power on shareholders' book investment and is frequently used in comparing two or more firms in an industry. Aldine's rate of return is somewhat below the median return for the industry of 10.6 percent. Thus, while Aldine has a higher profit margin on its sales than the industry, it has a lower return on its net worth. This phenomenon suggests that Aldine needs relatively greater assets to produce sales than do most other firms in the industry.

To investigate the problem more directly, we turn to the *return on assets ratio:*

$$\frac{\text{Net profits after taxes}}{\text{Total tangible assets}}$$

For Aldine, the ratio is

$$\frac{\$150,574}{\$3,046,323} = 4.94 \text{ percent}$$

where goodwill is deducted from total assets to obtain total tangible assets. This ratio compares with a median for the industry of 5.2 percent. With higher profitability per dollar of sales but a slightly lower return on assets, we know that Aldine must employ more assets to generate a dollar of sales than does the industry on the average.

Turnover and earning power

The relationship of sales to total assets is known as the *turnover ratio:*

$$\frac{\text{Sales}}{\text{Total tangible assets} \leftarrow \text{Goodwill}}$$

Aldine's turnover for the 1977 fiscal year was

$$\frac{\$3,992,758}{\$3,046,323} = 1.31$$

The median turnover for the industry is 1.66, so it is clear that Aldine employs more assets per dollar of sales than does the industry on average. The turnover ratio tells us the relative efficiency with which a firm utilizes its resources to generate output. In the case of Aldine, it is less efficient than the industry in this regard. From our previous analysis of Aldine's liquidity, this occurrence could well be due to excessive investments in receivables and inventories.

When we multiply the asset turnover of the firm by the net profit margin, we obtain the return on assets ratio, or *earning power* on total tangible assets:

$$\text{Earning Power} = \frac{\text{Sales}}{\text{Total tangible assets}} \times \frac{\text{Net profits after taxes}}{\text{Sales}}$$

$$= \frac{\text{Net profits after taxes}}{\text{Total tangible assets}}$$

For Aldine, we have

$$\frac{\$3,992,758}{\$3,046,323} \times \frac{\$150,574}{\$3,992,758} = 4.94 \text{ percent}$$

Neither the net profit margin nor the turnover ratio by itself provides an adequate measure of operating efficiency. The net profit margin ignores the utilization of assets, whereas the turnover ratio ignores profitability on sales. The return on assets ratio, or earning power, resolves these shortcomings. An improvement in the earning power of the firm will result if there is an increase in turnover on existing assets, an increase in the net profit margin, or both. The interrelation of these ratios is shown in Figure 3-2. Two firms with different asset turnovers and net profit margins may have the same earning power. For example, Firm *A*, with an asset turnover of 4 to 1 and a net profit margin of 3 percent, has the same earning power—12 percent—as Firm *B*, with an asset turnover of 1½ to 1 and a net profit margin of 8 percent.

With all of the profitability ratios, comparisons of a company with similar companies are extremely valuable. Only by comparison are we able to judge whether the profitability of a particular company is good or bad, and why. Absolute figures provide some insight, but it is relative performance that is most important.

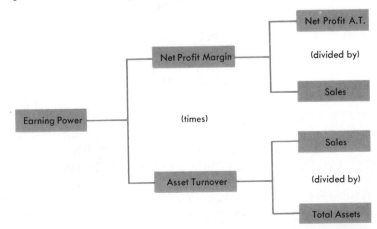

FIG. 3 · 2

Determination of earning power

Coverage ratios are designed to relate the financial charges of a firm to its ability to service them. Such bond rating services as Moody's Investors Service and Standard & Poor's make extensive use of these ratios. One of the most traditional of the coverage ratios is the *interest coverage ratio,* simply the ratio of earnings before interest and taxes for a particular reporting period to the amount of interest charges for the period. It is important to differentiate which interest charges should be used in the denominator. The *overall coverage method* stresses the importance of a company's meeting all fixed interest, regardless of the seniority of the claim. Suppose that we have the following financial data for a hypothetical company:

Average earnings	$2,000,000
Interest on senior 7% bonds	−400,000
	$1,600,000
Interest on junior 8% bonds	160,000

The overall interest coverage would be $2,000,000/$560,000, or 3.57. This method implies that the credit-worthiness of the senior bonds is only as good as the firm's ability to cover all interest charges.

Of the various coverage ratios, the most objectionable is the *prior deductions method.* Using this method, we deduct interest on the senior bonds from average earnings and then divide the residual by the interest on the junior bonds. We find that the coverage on the junior bonds in our example is ten times ($1,600,000/$160,000). Thus, the junior bonds give the illusion of being more secure than the senior obligations. Clearly, this method is inappropriate.

The *cumulative deduction method,* perhaps, is the most widely used method of computing interest coverage. Under this method, coverage for the senior bonds would be five times, as above. However, coverage for the junior bonds is determined by adding the interest charges on both bonds and relating the total to average earnings. Thus, the coverage for the junior bonds would be $2,000,000/$560,000 = 3.57 times.

One of the principal shortcomings of an interest coverage ratio is that a firm's ability to service debt is related to both interest and principal payments. Moreover, these payments are not met out of earnings per se, but out of cash. Hence, a more appropriate coverage ratio relates the cash flow of the firm (approximated by earnings before interest and taxes plus depreciation) to the sum of interest and principal payments. The *cash-flow coverage ratio* may be expressed as

$$\frac{\text{Annual cash flow before interest and taxes}}{\text{Interest} + \text{Principal payments} (1/1 - t))}$$

where t is the federal income tax rate. As principal payments are made after taxes, it is necessary to adjust this figure by $(1/(1 - t))$ so that it corresponds to interest payments, which are made before taxes.

A broader type of analysis would evaluate the ability of the firm to cover all charges of a fixed nature in relation to its cash flow. In addition to interest and principal payments on debt obligations, we would include preferred-stock dividends, lease payments, and possibly even certain essential capital expenditures. As we take up in Chapter 18, an analysis of this type is a far more realistic gauge than is a simple interest coverage ratio in determining whether a firm has the ability to meet its long-term obligations.

TREND OVER TIME

Up to now, our concern has been with presenting the various financial ratios, explaining their use in analysis, and comparing the ratios computed for our example company with industry averages. As we pointed out earlier, it also is valuable to compare the financial ratios for a given company over time. In this way, the analyst is able to detect any improvement or deterioration in its financial condition and performance.

To illustrate, Table 3-3 shows some of the financial ratios we have studied for Aldine Manufacturing Company over the 1968–77 period. As can be seen, the current and acid-test ratios tended to fluctuate through the late sixties and then increase through 1976, falling off somewhat in 1977. Paralleling this behavior were movements in the average receivable collection period and the inventory turnover ratio. The former increased steadily from 1972 through 1976, after which it declined somewhat while the latter decreased steadily throughout. The trends here tell us that there has been a relative buildup in receivables and inventory. The turnover of both has slowed, which raises questions as to the quality of these assets. When a trend analysis of receivables and inventory is coupled with a comparison with the median ratios for the industry, the only conclusion possible is that a problem exists. The analyst would want to investigate the credit policies of Aldine, the company's collection experience, and its bad-debt losses. Moreover, he should investigate inventory management, obsolescence of inventory, and any imbalances that might exist. Thus, despite the overall improvement in current and acid-test ratios in the seventies, the apparent deterioration in receivables and inventory is a matter of concern and needs to be investigated in depth.

TABLE 3·3

Financial Ratios of Aldine Manufacturing Company for Fiscal Years 1968–77										
	1968	1969	1970	1971	1972	1973	1974	1975	1976	1977
Current ratio	2.21	2.09	2.11	2.06	1.98	2.19	2.41	2.37	2.79	2.72
Acid-test ratio	0.94	0.86	0.92	0.90	0.88	0.95	1.01	1.02	1.22	1.11
Average receivable collection period (days)	38	37	45	41	39	46	48	55	72	62
Inventory turnover	3.61	3.34	3.28	3.55	3.40	3.19	2.94	2.68	2.17	2.09
Total debt/Net worth	0.95	0.92	0.98	0.97	0.93	0.90	0.87	0.86	0.81	0.81
Gross profit margin	35.8%	32.6%	28.4%	29.7%	30.9%	27.4%	28.9%	30.6%	32.8%	32.9%
Net profit margin	4.63%	4.02%	2.68%	3.07%	3.36%	2.04%	2.67%	3.02%	3.71%	3.77%
Return on assets	8.45%	7.53%	4.82%	5.92%	6.47%	4.23%	4.97%	5.21%	4.69%	4.94%
Turnover ratio	1.82	1.87	1.85	1.93	1.93	2.07	1.83	1.72	1.26	1.31

The debt-to-net-worth ratio has declined somewhat since 1970, indicating some improvement in overall condition from the standpoint of creditors, all other things the same. The gross profit margin and net profit margin have fluctuated over time. Since 1973, however, both ratios have shown steady improvement, which is encouraging. There is no particular disparity between the two series which would indicate less efficiency in controlling expenses vis-à-vis the cost of producing appliances or vice versa. The return on assets has fluctuated over the 1968–77 period. Abstracting from these fluctuations, however, it is disturbing that the return on assets did not increase in the 1976–77 period, a span during which the net profit margin showed steady improvement. With greater profitability in absolute terms, there must have been offsetting increases in total assets that caused the return on assets to remain relatively flat for the period. This reasoning is confirmed when we analyze the turnover ratio (Sales/Total assets). During the last four years it declined overall, indicating that more assets were needed to generate a dollar of sales. From our analysis of liquidity, we know that the primary cause was the large relative increase in receivables and inventory.

We see then that the analysis of the trend of financial ratios over time can give the analyst valuable insight into the changes that have occurred in a firm's financial condition and performance. When a trend analysis is combined with comparisons with like companies and the industry average, the depth of analysis possible is magnified considerably.

Financial analysis involves the analysis of the funds needs of the firm, its financial condition and performance, and its business risk. Upon analysis of these factors, one is able to determine the financing needs of the firm and negotiate with outside suppliers of capital. The framework proposed provides an interlocking means for structuring analysis. The analytical tools used to analyze financial condition and performance are financial ratios. These ratios can be divided into four types: liquidity, debt, profitability, and coverage. No one ratio is sufficient in itself to realistically assess the financial condition and performance of a firm. With a group of ratios, however, reasonable judgments can be made. The number of ratios needed for this purpose is not particularly large—about a dozen.

The ratios taken up in this chapter are extensively employed by outside creditors and investors. These ratios are also helpful for managerial control and for providing a better understanding of what outside suppliers of capital expect in the way of financial condition and performance. The usefulness of the ratios depends upon the ingenuity and experience of the financial analyst who employs them. By themselves, financial ratios are fairly meaningless; they must be analyzed on a comparative basis. A comparison of ratios of the same firm over time is important in evaluating changes and trends in the firm's financial condition and profitability. This comparison may be historical; it may also include an analysis of the future based upon projected financial statements. Ratios may also be judged in comparison with those of similar firms in the same line of business and when appropriate, with an industry average. Much can be gleaned from a thorough analysis of financial ratios about the financial condition and performance of the firm.

1. Why is the analysis of trends in financial ratios important?

2. Zakor Manufacturing Company has a current ratio of 4 to 1 but is unable to pay its bills. Why?

3. Can a firm generate a 25 percent return on assets and still be technically insolvent? Explain.

4. The traditional definitions of *collection period* and *investment turnover* are criticized because in both cases balance sheet figures that are a result of the last month of sales are related to annual sales. Why do these definitions present problems? Suggest a solution.

5. Compare the current and quick ratios with a *pro forma* cash budget and in this regard discuss their efficiency as measures of liquidity.

6. Explain why a long-term creditor should be interested in liquidity ratios.

7. Which financial ratios would you be most likely to consult if you were the following? Why?
   (a) A banker considering the financing of seasonal inventory
   (b) A wealthy equity investor
   (c) The manager of a pension fund considering the purchase of bonds
   (d) The president of a consumer products firm

8. Ratio analysis is valuable in assessing the financial position of a firm only when the ratios are compared with industry norms. In the current business environment, many corporations are conglomerates whose holdings cut across all industries. Suggest methods for analyzing conglomerates.

9. Why might it be possible for a company to make large operating profits, yet still be unable to meet debt payments when due? What financial ratios might be employed to detect such a condition?

10. Does increasing a firm's inventory turnover ratio increase its profitability? Why is this ratio computed using cost of goods sold (rather than sales, as is done by some compilers of financial statistics, such as Dun & Bradstreet)?

11. Which financial ratios are likely to be affected if the firm's accounting statements are reported on a cost basis rather than on a market basis?

12. Which firm is more profitable? Firm A with a turnover of 10.0 and a net profit margin of 2 percent, or Firm B with a turnover of 2.0 and a net profit margin of 10 percent? Provide examples of both types of firms.

13. Why do short-term creditors, such as banks, emphasize balance sheet analysis when considering loan requests? Should they also analyze projected income statements? Why?

1. The data for various companies in the same industry and of about the same size are as follows:

Company	A	B	C	D	E	F
Sales (in millions)	$10	$20	$ 8	$ 5	$12	$17
Total assets (in millions)	8	10	6	2.5	4	8
Net income (in millions)	0.7	2	0.8	0.5	1.5	1

(a) Determine the asset turnover, net profit margin, and earning power for each of the companies.
(b) Which firms appear to be out of line? What might their problems be? What additional data would you need to confirm your analysis?

2. Using the following information, complete the balance sheet below:

Long-term debt to net worth	.5 to 1
Total asset turnover	2.5 times
Average collection period*	18 days
Inventory turnover	9 times
Gross profit margin	10%
Acid-test ratio	1 to 1

*Assume a 360-day year, and all sales on credit.

Cash	$_____	Notes and payables	$100,000
Accounts receivable	_____	Long-term debt	_____
		Common stock	$100,000 } 200,000 N.W.
Inventory	_____	Retained earnings	100,000
Plant and equipment	_____	Total liabilities and worth	
Total assets	$_____		$_____

400,000

3.

U.S. REPUBLIC CORPORATION BALANCE SHEET, DECEMBER 31, 1976

Assets		Liabilities and Stockholders' Equity	
Cash	$ 1,000,000	Notes payable—Bank	$ 4,000,000
Accounts receivable	5,000,000	Accounts payable	2,000,000
Inventory	7,000,000	Accrued wages and	
Fixed assets, net	15,000,000	taxes	2,000,000
Excess over book		Long-term debt	12,000,000
value of assets		Preferred stock	4,000,000
acquired	2,000,000	Common stock	2,000,000
		Retained earnings	4,000,000
		Total liabilities and	
Total assets	$30,000,000	equity	$30,000,000

U.S. REPUBLIC CORPORATION STATEMENT OF INCOME AND RETAINED EARNINGS, YEAR ENDED DECEMBER 31, 1976

Net sales:		
Credit		$16,000,000
Cash		4,000,000
Total		$20,000,000
Costs and expenses		
Cost of goods sold	$12,000,000	
Selling, general, and administrative expenses	2,000,000	
Depreciation	1,400,000	
Interest on long-term debt	600,000	16,000,000
Net income before taxes		$ 4,000,000
Taxes on income		2,000,000
Net income after taxes		$ 2,000,000
Less: Dividends on preferred stock		240,000
Net income available to common		$ 1,760,000
Add: Retained earnings at 1/1/76		2,600,000
Subtotal		$ 4,360,000
Less: Dividends paid on common		− 360,000
Retained earnings at 12/31/76		$ 4,000,000

(a) Fill in the 1976 column.

U.S. REPUBLIC CORPORATION

Ratio	1974	1975	1976	Industry Norms
1. Current ratio	250%	200%		225%
2. Acid-test ratio	100%	90%		110%
3. Receivables turnover	5.0X	4.5X		6.0X
4. Inventory turnover	4.0X	3.0X		4.0X
5. Long-term debt/Total capitalization	35%	40%		33%
6. Gross profit margin	39%	41%		40%
7. Net profit margin	17%	15%		15%
8. Rate of return on equity	25%	30%		20%
9. Return on assets	15%	12%		10%
10. Tangible asset turnover	0.9X	0.8X		1.0X
11. Overall interest coverage	11X	9X		10X

(b) Evaluate the position of the company from the above table. Cite specific ratio levels and trends as evidence.

(c) Indicate which ratios would be of most interest to you and what your decision would be in each of the following situations:

(1) U.S. Republic wants to buy $500,000 worth of raw materials from you, with payment to be due in 90 days.

(2) U.S. Republic wants you, a large insurance company, to pay off its note at the bank and assume it on a ten-year maturity basis at the current coupon of 9 percent.

(3) There are 100,000 shares outstanding and the stock is selling for $80 a share. The company offers you an opportunity to buy 50,-000 additional shares at this price.

4. Selected financial ratios for RMN Incorporated are as follows:

	1974	1975	1976
Current ratio	4.2	2.6	1.8
Quick ratio	2.1	1.0	0.6
Debt to total assets	23	33	47
Inventory turnover	8.7X	5.4X	3.5X
Average collection period	33	36	49
Fixed assets turnover	11.6X	10.6X	12.3X
Total assets turnover	3.2X	2.6X	1.9X
Profit margin on sales	3.8	2.5	1.4
Return on total assets	12.1	6.5	2.8
Return on net worth	15.7	9.7	5.4

(a) Why did return assets decline?

(b) Was the increase in debt a result of greater current liabilities or of greater long-term debt? Explain.

5. **MOTORIZED HOMES, INC., BALANCE SHEET**
   MARCH 31, 1975 THROUGH MARCH 31, 1977
   (IN THOUSANDS)

	1975	1976	1977
ASSETS:			
~~Cash~~	$ 500	$ 1,550	$20,600
Accounts receivable	4,600	6,510	12,900
Inventories	18,700	12,800	27,000
Other	300	420	730
Current assets	$24,100	$21,280	$61,230
Property and equipment	8,300	11,400	18,300
Less accumulative depreciation	1,130	1,660	2,800
~~Net Fixed assets~~	$ 7,170	$9,740	$15,500
Investments in subsidiaries	558	1,570	4,100
Total assets	$31,828	$32,590	$80,830
LIABILITIES AND EQUITY:			
Notes	$ 7,000	$ 1,000	$ 0
Accounts payable	4,204	5,600	10,600
Accruals	300	1,000	2,200
Taxes payable	974	1,540	8,040
Current liabilities	$12,478	$ 9,140	$20,840
Stockholders' equity			
C.S. (12,100,000 shares in 1975 and 1976; 12,600,000 shares in 1977)	$ 6,050	$ 6,050	$ 6,300
Capital surplus	5,250	5,250	28,040
Retained earnings	8,050	12,150	25,650
Total liabilities and net worth	$31,828	$32,590	$80,830

MOTORIZED HOMES, INC., INCOME STATEMENT
(IN THOUSANDS)

	1975	1976	1977
Sales	$44,960	$70,860	$133,160
Cost of goods	36,100	56,500	101,000
Gross profit	$ 8,860	$14,360	$ 32,160
Selling expenses	1,070	1,460	3,500
Income from operations	$ 7,790	$12,900	$28,660
Interest and other income	91	300	660
Taxable income	$ 7,881	$13,200	$29,320
Taxes	3,783	6,336	14,074
Net income	$ 4,098	$ 6,864	$ 15,246
EPS (fully diluted)	.27	.38	1.22
Market price of common	$8	$15	$36

    (a)   Prepare a financial ratio analysis of Motorized Homes, Inc.

    (b)   Comment on the weakness and strengths of the corporation.

6.   A company has total annual sales (all credit) of $400,000, and a gross profit margin of 20 percent. Its current assets are $80,000; current liabilities, $60,000; inventories, $30,000; and cash, $10,000.

    (a)   How much average inventory should be carried if management wants the inventory turnover to be 4?

    (b)   How rapidly (in how many days) must accounts receivable be collected if management wants to have an average of $50,000 invested in receivables? (Assume a 360-day year.)

7.   The long-term debt section of the balance sheet of the Diters Corporation appears as follows:

7 ¼ % mortgage bonds of 1995	$2,500,000
7 ⅝ % second mortgage bonds of 1990	1,500,000
8 ⅜ % debentures of 1988	1,000,000
9 ⅛ % subordinated debentures of 1992	1,000,000
	$6,000,000

    (a)   If the average earnings before interest and taxes of the Diters Corporation are $1.5 million, what is the overall interest coverage?

    (b)   Using the cumulative deduction method, determine the coverage for each issue.

SELECTED REFERENCES

ALTMAN, EDWARD I., *Corporate Bankruptcy in America*, Lexington, Mass.: Heath Lexington Books, 1971.

————, "Financial Ratios, Discriminant Analysis and the Prediction of Corporate Bankruptcy," *Journal of Finance*, 23 (September 1968), 589–609.

————, "Railroad Bankruptcy Propensity," *Journal of Finance*, 26 (May 1971), 333–45.

BEAVER, WILLIAM H., "Financial Ratios as Predictors of Failure," *Empirical Research in Accounting: Selected Studies* in *Journal of Accounting Research* (1966), pp. 71–111.

BENISHAY, HASKELL, "Economic Information in Financial Ratio Analysis," *Accounting and Business Research*, 2 (Spring 1971), 174–79.

EDMISTER, ROBERT O., "An Empirical Test of Financial Ratio Analysis for Small Business Failure Prediction," *Journal of Financial and Quantitative Analysis*, 7 (March 1972), 1477–93.

GITMAN, LAWRENCE J., "Measuring Overall Corporate Liquidity: A New and Better Ratio," Paper presented at Financial Management Association Meetings, San Diego, October 24–26, 1974.

GORDON, MYRON J., "Towards a Theory of Financial Distress," *Journal of Finance*, 26 (May 1971), 347–56.

HELFERT, ERICH A., *Techniques of Financial Analysis,* 3rd ed., Chapter 2. Homewood, Ill.: Richard D. Irwin, 1972.

HORRIGAN, JAMES C., "The Determination of Long-Term Credit Standing with Financial Ratios," *Empirical Research in Accounting: Selected Studies in Journal of Accounting Research* (1966), pp. 44–62.

————, "A Short History of Financial Ratio Analysis," *Accounting Review,* 43 (April 1968), 284–94.

JAEDICKE, ROBERT K., and **ROBERT T. SPROUSE,** *Accounting Flows: Income, Funds, and Cash,* Chapter 7. Englewood Cliffs, N.J.: Prentice-Hall, 1965.

LEV, BARUCH, *Financial Statement Analysis: A New Approach.* Englewood Cliffs, N.J.: Prentice-Hall, 1974.

MURRAY, ROGER F., "The Penn Central Debacle: Lessons for Financial Analysis," *Journal of Finance,* 26 (May 1971), 327–32.

O'CONNOR, MELVIN C., "On the Usefulness of Financial Ratios to Investors in Common Stock," *Accounting Review,* 48 (April 1973), 339–52.

SORTER, GEORGE H., and **GEORGE BENSTON,** "Appraising the Defensive Position of a Firm: The Internal Measure," *Accounting Review,* 35 (October 1960), 633–40.

TROY, LEO, *Almanac of Business and Industrial Financial Ratios.* Englewood Cliffs, N.J.: Prentice-Hall, 1974.

Source and Use Statements and Financial Forecasting

4

The second portion of our examination of the tools of financial analysis and control deals with the analysis of fund flows and financial forecasting. A funds-flow statement is a valuable aid to a financial manager or a creditor in evaluating the uses of funds by a firm and in determining how those uses are financed. In addition to studying past flows, the analyst can evaluate future flows by means of a funds statement based upon forecasts. Such a statement provides an efficient method for the financial manager to assess the growth of the firm and its resulting financial needs, and to determine the best way to finance those needs. In particular, funds statements are very useful in planning intermediate- and long-term financing.

Closely related to a projected funds-flow statement are the cash budget and *pro forma* statements. The cash budget is indispensable to the financial manager in determining the short-term cash needs of the firm and, accordingly, in planning its short-term financing. When cash budgeting is extended to include a range of possible outcomes, the financial manager can evaluate the business risk and liquidity of the firm and plan a more realistic margin of safety. This margin of safety might come from adjusting the firm's liquidity cushion, rearranging the maturity structure of its dept, arranging a line of credit with a bank, or a combination of the three. Cash budgets prepared for a range of possible outcomes are valuable also in appraising the ability of the firm to adjust to unexpected changes in cash flows. The preparation of *pro forma* balance sheets and income statements enables the financial manager to analyze the effect of various policy decisions on the future financial condition and performance of the firm. We examine each of these three tools in turn.

FUNDS STATEMENTS

The flow of funds in a firm may be visualized as a continuous process. For every use of funds, there must be an offsetting source. In a broad sense, the assets of a firm represent the net uses of funds; its liabilities and net worth represent net sources. A funds-flow cycle for a typical manufacturing company is illustrated in Figure 4-1. For the going concern, there is really no starting or stopping point. A finished product is produced with a variety of inputs—namely, raw material, net fixed assets, and labor. These inputs ultimately are paid for in cash. The product then is sold either for cash or on credit. A credit sale involves a receivable, which, when collected, becomes cash. If the selling price of the product exceeds all costs (including depreciation on assets) for a period of time, there is a profit for the period; if not, there is a loss. The reservoir of cash, the focal point in the figure, fluctuates over time with the production schedule, sales, collection of receivables, capital expenditures, and financing. On the other hand, reservoirs of raw materials, work in process, finished goods inventory, accounts receivable, and trade payables fluctuate with sales, the production schedule, and policies with respect to managing receivables, inventories, and trade payables.

The funds statement is a method by which we study the net funds flow between two points in time. These points conform to beginning and ending financial statement dates for whatever period of examination is relevant—a quarter, a year, or five years. It is important to emphasize that the funds statement portrays net rather than gross changes between two comparable financial statements at different dates. For example, gross changes might be thought to include all changes that occur between the two statement dates rather than the sum of these changes—the net change as defined. Although an analysis of the gross funds flow of a firm over time would be much more revealing than an analysis of net funds flow, we are usually constrained by the financial information available—namely, balance sheets and income statements that span particular periods of time. Funds may be defined in several different ways, depending upon the purpose of the analysis. While they are often defined as cash, many analysts treat funds as working capital (current assets less current liabilities)—a

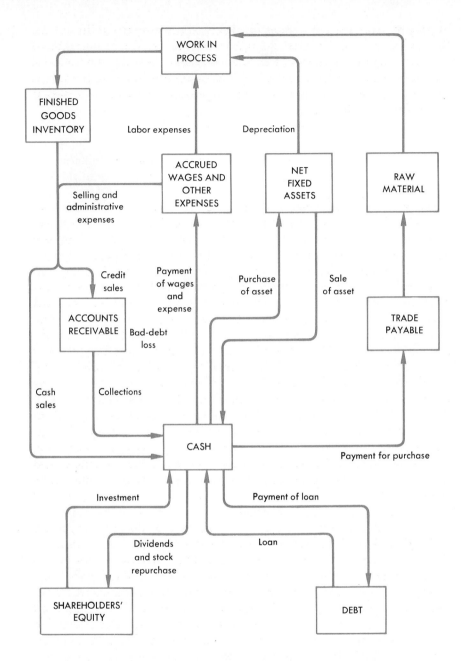

FIG. 4 · 1
Funds flow within the firm

somewhat broader definition. Other definitions are possible, although the two described are the most common by far. Depending upon the analyst's objective, the definition can be broadened or narrowed. Because a funds-flow analysis on a cash basis serves as a building block for analyses using broader definitions of funds, we begin by defining funds as cash.

Funds statement on a cash basis

Basically, one prepares a funds statement on a cash basis by (1) classifying net balance sheet changes that occur between two points in time into changes that increase cash and changes that decrease cash; (2) classifying, from the income statement and the surplus statement, the factors that increase cash and the factors that decrease cash; and (3) consolidating this information in a source and use of funds statement form. The first of these steps simply involves placing one balance sheet beside the other and computing the changes in the various accounts.

Sources of funds that increase cash are

1. A net decrease in any asset other than cash or fixed assets
2. A gross decrease in fixed assets
3. A net increase in any liability
4. Proceeds from the sale of preferred or common stock
5. Funds provided by operations

Funds provided by operations usually are not expressed directly on the income statement. To determine them, one must add back depreciation to net income after taxes. For Aldine Manufacturing Company, our example in the preceding chapter, we have:

Net income after taxes	$150,574
Add noncash expenses: Depreciation	111,509
Funds provided by operations	$262,083

Thus, the net income of Aldine understates funds provided by operations by $111,509. Depreciation is not a source of funds, for funds are generated only from operations.[1] If operating losses before depreciation are sustained, funds are not provided regardless of the magnitude of depreciation charges.

Uses of funds include

1. A net increase in any asset other than cash or fixed assets
2. A gross increase in fixed assets
3. A net decrease in any liability
4. A retirement or purchase of stock
5. Cash dividends

To avoid double counting, we compute gross additions to fixed assets by adding depreciation for the period to net fixed assets at the ending financial statement date, and subtract from this amount net fixed assets at the beginning financial statement date. The residual repre-

---

[1] For an extensive discussion of this concept, see Robert K. Jaedicke and Robert T. Sprouse, *Accounting Flows: Income, Funds, and Cash* (Englewood Cliffs, N.J.: Prentice-Hall, 1965), pp. 80–86.

sents the gross increase or decrease in fixed assets for the period. Once all sources and uses are computed, they may be arranged in statement form so that we can analyze them better. Table 4-1 shows a source and use of funds statement for the Aldine Manufacturing Company for the fiscal year ended March 31, 1977. The balance sheet and income statement for this corporation, on which the funds statement is based, are shown in Tables 3-1 and 3-2 of Chapter 3. When we subtract the total uses of funds in Table 4-1 from the total sources, the difference should equal the actual change in cash between the two statement dates. If it does not, then the analyst must search for the cause of the discrepancy. Frequently, discrepancies will be due to surplus adjustments; and the analyst should be alert to this possibility.[2]

TABLE 4 · 1

Aldine Manufacturing Company Sources and Uses of Funds March 31, 1976 to March 31, 1977 (in thousands)

Sources		Uses	
Funds provided by operations:			
Net profit	$150	Dividends	$ 92
Depreciation	112	Additions to fixed assets	104
		Increase—inventories	94
Decrease—accounts receivable	62	Increase—prepaid expenses	4
Increase—bank loans	92	Increase—tax prepayments	6
Increase—accounts payable	12	Increase—investments	65
Increase—other accruals	27	Decrease—accrued taxes	91
Increase—long-term debt	4		
		Increase—cash position	3
	$459		$459

In Table 4-1, we see that the principal uses of funds for the 1977 fiscal year were additions to fixed assets, increases in inventories and in investments, and a sizable decrease in taxes payable. These uses were financed primarily by funds provided by operations in excess of dividends; a decrease in accounts receivable; and by increases in bank loans, payables, and accruals. As sources exceeded slightly the uses of funds, the cash balance rose by $3,000. In a sources and uses of funds analysis it is useful to place cash dividends opposite net profits, and additions to fixed assets opposite depreciation. Doing this allows the analyst to evaluate easily both the amount of dividend payout and the net increase in fixed assets.

[2]For a more detailed description of the preparation of a funds-flow statement, see Myron J. Gordon and Gordon Shillinglaw, *Accounting: A Management Approach,* 4th ed. (Homewood, Ill.: Richard D. Irwin, 1969), pp. 497–512.

Funds as working capital

Financial analysts frequently prepare also a source and use of working capital statement. This statement is very similar to the source and use of funds statement, but takes into account working capital instead of cash. A source and use of working capital statement for Aldine Manufacturing Company for the year ended March 31, 1977, is shown in Table 4-2. We see that the only difference between this statement and a funds statement on a cash basis is the omission of changes in the various components of current assets and current liabilities. This statement is analyzed in much the same way as before. A source and use of working capital statement is used frequently by bankers, for they often require a borrower to maintain some sort of minimum working capital. It is used also by other lenders and by management for purposes of internal control.

TABLE 4 · 2

Aldine Manufacturing Company Sources and Uses of Working Capital March 31, 1976 to March 31, 1977 (in thousands)

Sources		Uses	
Funds provided by operations:			
Net profit	$150	Dividends	$ 92
Depreciation	112	Additions to fixed assets	104
Increase—long-term debt	4	Increase—investments	65
		Increase—working capital	5
	$266		$266

Implications

The analysis of cash and working capital funds statements gives us a rich insight into the financial operations of a firm—an insight that is especially valuable to the financial manager in analyzing past and future expansion plans of the firm and the impact of these plans on liquidity. He can detect imbalances in the uses of funds and undertake appropriate actions. For example, an analysis spanning the past several years might reveal a growth in inventories out of proportion with the growth of other assets and with sales. Upon analysis, he might find that the problem was due to inefficiencies in inventory management. Thus, a funds statement alerts the financial manager to problems that he can analyze in detail and take proper actions to correct. When a company has a number of divisions, individual funds statements may prove useful. These statements enable top management to appraise the performance of divisions in relation to the funds committed to them.

Another use of funds statements is in the evaluation of the firm's financing. An analysis of the major sources of funds in the past reveals what portion of the firm's growth was financed internally and what portion externally. In evaluating the firm's financing, the analyst will wish to evaluate the ratio of dividends to earnings relative to the firm's total need for funds. Funds statements are useful also in judging whether the firm has expanded at too fast a rate and whether financing is strained. For example, we can determine if trade credit has increased out of proportion to increases in current assets and to sales. If trade credit has increased at a significantly faster rate, we would wish to evaluate the consequences of increased slowness in trade payments on the credit standing of the firm and its ability to finance in the future. It is also revealing to analyze the mix of short- and long-term financing in relation to the funds needs of the firm. If these needs are primarily for fixed assets and permanent increases in working capital, we might be disturbed if a significant portion of total financing came from short-term sources.

An analysis of a funds statement for the future is extremely valuable to the financial manager in planning the intermediate- and long-term financing of the firm. It tells him the firm's total prospective need for funds, the expected timing of these needs, and their nature—that is, whether the increased investment is primarily for inventories, fixed assets, and so forth. Given this information, along with the expected changes in trade payables and the various accruals, he can arrange the firm's financing more effectively. In addition, he can determine the expected closing cash position of the firm simply by adjusting the beginning cash balance for the change in cash reflected on the projected source and use statement. In essence, the projected change in cash is a residual. Alternatively, the financial manager can forecast future cash positions of the firm through a cash budget, where direct estimates of future cash flows are made.

CASH BUDGETING

A cash budget involves a projection of future cash receipts and cash disbursements of the firm over various intervals of time. It reveals to the financial manager the timing and amount of expected cash inflows and outflows over the period studied. With this information, he is better able to determine the future cash needs of the firm, plan for the financing of these needs, and exercise control over the cash and liquidity of the firm.

Cash budgets may be for almost any period of time. For near-term forecasts, monthly periods probably are the ones used most frequently, because they take into account seasonal variations in cash flows. When cash flows are extremely volatile but predictable, budgets at more frequent intervals may be necessary for determining peak cash requirements. By the same token, when cash flows are relatively stable, budgeting at quarterly or even longer intervals may be justified. Generally, the further in the future the period for which one is trying to predict cash flows, the more uncertain the forecast. The expense of preparing monthly cash budgets usually is warranted only for predictions concerning the near future. As we shall see, the cash budget is only as useful as the accuracy of the forecasts that are used in its preparation.[3]

Preparation of the cash budget

Receipts. The key to the accuracy of most cash budgets is the forecast of sales. This forecast can be based upon an internal analysis, an external one, or both. With an internal approach, salesmen are asked to project sales for the forthcoming period. The product sales managers screen these estimates and consolidate them into sales estimates for product lines. The estimates for the various product lines then are combined into an overall sales estimate for the firm. The basic problem with an internal approach is that it can be too myopic. Often, important trends in the economy and in the industry are overlooked.

For this reason, many companies use an external analysis as well. With an external approach, economic analysts make forecasts of the economy and of industry sales for several years to come. In this regard, regression analysis may be used to estimate the association between industry sales and the economy in general. Given these basic predictions of business conditions and industry sales, the next step is to estimate market share by individual products, prices that are likely to prevail, and the expected reception of new products. Usually, these estimates are made in conjunction with marketing managers. However, the ultimate responsibility should lie with the economic forecasting

[3]For an excellent analysis of cost of inaccuracy versus the cost of the forecast itself, see John C. Chambers, Satinder K. Mullick, and Donald D. Smith, "How to Choose the Right Forecasting Technique," *Harvard Business Review,* 49 (July–August 1971), 45–74.

department. Given this information, an external forecast of sales can be prepared.

When the internal forecast of sales differs from the external one, as it is likely to do, a compromise must be reached. Past experience will show which of the two forecasts is more accurate. In general, the external forecast should serve as the foundation for the final sales forecast. However, it often will need to be modified by the internal forecast. For example, the firm might expect to receive several large orders from customers, and these orders might not show up in the external forecast. By basing the final sales forecast on both internal and external analyses, it usually is more accurate than is either an internal or an external forecast by itself. The final sales forecast should be based upon prospective demand and not be modified initially by internal constraints such as physical capacity. The decision to remove these constraints will depend upon the forecast. The importance of accurate sales forecasts cannot be overestimated, for most of the other forecasts, in some measure, are based upon expected sales.

Given the sales forecast, the next job is to determine the cash receipts from these sales. With cash sales, cash is received at the time of the sale; with credit sales, however, the receipts do not come until later. How much later will depend upon the billing terms given, the type of customer, and the credit and collection policies of the firm. Suppose, for purposes of illustration, that the terms offered by Continental Sheetmetal Company are net 30, meaning that payment is due within thirty days after the invoice date. Assume also that in the company's experience, 90 percent of receivables are collected, on the average, one month from the date of the sale, and that 10 percent are collected two months from the date of the sale, with no bad-debt losses. Moreover, on the average, 10 percent of total sales are cash sales.

If the sales forecasts are those shown in the first line of Table 4-3, we can compute a schedule of the expected sales receipts based upon the above assumptions. This schedule appears in Table 4-3. For January, we see that total sales are estimated to be $250,000, of which $25,000 are cash sales. Of the $225,000 in credit sales, 90 percent, or $202,500, is expected to be collected in February; and 10 percent, or $22,500, is expected to be collected in March. Similarly, sales in other months are broken down according to the same percentages. The firm should be alert to change its assumptions with respect to collections when there is an underlying shift in the payment habits of its customers. For example, if there is a slowdown in the economy, certain customers are likely to become slower in their trade payments. The firm must take account of this change if its cash budget is to be realistic.

From this example, it is easy to see the effect of a variation in sales upon the magnitude and timing of cash receipts, all other things held constant. For most firms, there is a degree of correlation between sales

TABLE 4 · 3

Schedule of Sales Receipts (in thousands)

	Nov.	Dec.	Jan.	Feb.	Mar.	Apr.	May	June
Total sales	$300.0	$350.0	$250.0	$200.0	$250.0	$300.0	$350.0	$380.0
Credit sales	270.0	315.0	225.0	180.0	225.0	270.0	315.0	342.0
Collections— one month		243.0	283.5	202.5	162.0	202.5	243.0	283.5
Collections— two months			27.0	31.5	22.5	18.0	22.5	27.0
Total collections			$310.5	$234.0	$184.5	$220.5	$265.5	$310.5
Cash sales			25.0	20.0	25.0	30.0	35.0	38.0
Total sales receipts			$335.5	$254.0	$209.5	$250.5	$300.5	$348.5

and collection experience. In times of recession and sales decline, the average collection period is likely to lengthen and bad-debt losses increase. Thus, the collection experience of a firm may reinforce a decline in sales, magnifying the downward impact upon total sales receipts.

Cash receipts may arise from the sale of assets, as well as from sales of the product. Suppose, for example, that the firm intends to sell $40,000 in fixed assets in February. Total cash receipts in February, then, would be $294,000. For the most part, the sale of assets is planned in advance and, therefore, is easily predicted for purposes of cash budgeting.

Disbursements. Next comes a forecast of cash disbursements. Given the sales forecast, a production schedule may be established. Management may choose either to gear production closely to sales or to produce at a relatively constant rate over time. With the former production strategy, inventory carrying costs generally are lower, but total production costs are higher than with the latter strategy. With steady production, the opposite usually occurs. If sales fluctuate, finished goods inventories build up during certain periods and require storage. Because storage is uneven throughout the year, inventory carrying costs are generally higher than they would be if production were geared to sales. On the other hand, production typically is more efficient. Which alternative is best will depend upon the added cost of carrying inventory when production is geared to sales relative to the savings available if production is steady. The final production schedule embodies decisions with respect to inventory management, a topic taken up in Chapter 8.

Once a production schedule has been established, estimates can be made of the materials that will need to be purchased, the labor that will be required, and any additional fixed assets the firm will need to acquire. As with receivables, there is a lag between the time a purchase is made and the time of actual cash payment. If the average billing terms given by suppliers are net 30, and the firm's policy is to pay its bills at the end of this period, there is approximately a one-month lag between a purchase and the payment. If the production program of Continental Sheetmetal calls for the manufacture of goods in the month preceding forecasted sales, we might have a schedule of expenses like that in Table 4-4. As we see, there is a one-month lag between the time of purchase and the payment for the purchase.

TABLE 4 · 4

Schedule of Expenses (in thousands)

	Dec.	Jan.	Feb.	Mar.	Apr.	May	June
Purchases	$100	$ 80	$100	$120	$140	$150	$150
Cash payment for purchases		100	80	100	120	140	150
Wages paid		80	80	90	90	95	100
Other expenses		50	50	50	50	50	50
Total cash expenses		$230	$210	$240	$260	$285	$300

Wages are assumed to increase with the amount of production. Generally, wages are more stable over time than are purchases. When production dips slightly, workers are usually not laid off. When production picks up, labor becomes more efficient with relatively little increase in total wages. Only after a certain point is overtime work required or do new workers have to be hired to meet the increased production schedule. Included in other expenses are: general, administrative, and selling expenses; property taxes; interest expenses; power, light, and heat expenses; maintenance expenses; and indirect labor and material expenses. These expenses tend to be reasonably predictable over the short run.

In addition to cash expenses, we must take into account capital expenditures, dividends, federal income taxes, and any other cash outflows. Because capital expenditures are planned in advance, they usually are predictable for the short-term cash budget. As the forecast becomes more distant, however, prediction of these expenditures becomes less certain. Dividend payments for most companies are stable and are paid on specific dates. Estimation of federal income taxes must be based upon projected profits for the period under review. Other cash outlays might consist of the repurchase of stock or payment of long-term debt. These outlays are combined with total cash expenses to obtain the schedule of total cash disbursements shown in Table 4-5.

TABLE 4 · 5

	Jan.	Feb.	Mar.	Apr.	May	June
Total cash expenses	$230	$210	$240	$260	$285	$300
Capital expenditures		150	50			
Dividend payments			20			20
Income taxes	30			30		
Total cash disbursements	$260	$360	$310	$290	$285	$320

Net cash flow and cash balance. Once we are satisfied that we have taken into account all foreseeable cash inflows and outflows, we combine the cash receipts and cash disbursements schedules to obtain the net cash inflow or outflow for each month. The net cash flow may then be added to beginning cash in January which is assumed to be $100,000, and the projected cash position computed month by month for the period under review. This final schedule is shown in Table 4-6.

TABLE 4 · 6

	Jan.	Feb.	Mar.	Apr.	May	June
Total cash receipts	$335.5	$294.0*	$209.5	$250.5	$300.5	$348.5
Total cash disbursements	260.0	360.0	310.0	290.0	285.0	320.0
Net cash flow	$ 75.5	$(66.0)	$(100.5)	$(39.5)	$ 15.5	$ 28.5
Beginning cash without financing	100.0	175.5	109.5	9.0	(30.5)	(15.0)
Ending cash without financing	175.5	109.5	9.0	(30.5)	(15.0)	13.5

*Includes sales receipts of $254,000 and cash sale of assets of $40,000.

The cash budget shown indicates that the firm is expected to have a cash deficit in April and May. This deficit is caused by a decline in collections through March, capital expenditures totaling $200,000 in February and March, and a cash dividend of $20,000 in March. With the increase in collections in May and June, the cash balance without financing rises to $13,500 in June. The cash budget indicates that peak cash requirements occur in April. If the firm has a policy of maintaining a minimum cash balance of $75,000 and of borrowing from its bank to maintain this minimum, it will need to borrow an additional $66,000 in March. Additional borrowings will peak at $105,500 in

April, after which they will decline to $61,500 in June, if all goes according to prediction.

Alternative means of meeting the cash deficit are available. The firm may be able to delay its capital expenditures or its payments for purchases. Indeed, one of the principal purposes of a cash budget is to determine the timing and magnitude of prospective financing needs so that the most appropriate method of financing can be arranged. A decision to obtain long-term financing should be based upon long-range funds requirements and upon considerations apart from a cash forecast. In addition to helping the financial manager plan for short-term financing, the cash budget is valuable to him in managing the firm's cash position. On the basis of a cash budget, he can plan to invest excess funds in marketable securities. The result is an efficient transfer of funds from cash to marketable securities and back.

Deviations from expected cash flows

Often, there is a tendency to place considerable faith in the cash budget simply because it is expressed in figures. It is important to stress again that a cash budget represents merely an *estimate* of future cash flows. Depending upon the care devoted to preparing the budget and the volatility of cash flows resulting from the nature of the business, actual cash flows will deviate more or less widely from those that were expected. In the face of uncertainty, we must provide information about the range of possible outcomes. To analyze cash flows only under one set of assumptions, as is the case with conventional cash budgeting, results in a faulty perspective of the future.

To take into account deviations from expected cash flows, it is desirable to work out additional cash budgets. For example, we might want to base one cash forecast upon the assumption of a maximum probable decline in business, and another upon the assumption of the maximum probable increase in business. By bringing possible events into the open for discussion, management is better able to plan for contingencies. Not only will such discussion sharpen its perspective on the probability of occurrence of a particular event, but it will give management a better understanding of the magnitude of its impact on the firm's cash flows.[4] Given the preparation of a cash budget based upon expected cash flows, it is often a simple matter to trace through a change in one or a series of figures in order to take into account a large number of possibilities. Examples of a change in assumptions include a decline in sales or an increase in the average collection period. For each set of assumptions and resulting cash budget, a probability of occurrence should be attached.

[4]See Gordon Donaldson, "Strategy for Financial Emergencies," *Harvard Business Review*, 47 (November–December 1969), 69.

The expected cash position plus the distribution of possible outcomes gives us a considerable amount of information. We can see the additional funds required or the funds released under various possible outcomes. This information enables us to determine more accurately the minimum cash balance, maturity structure of debt, and borrowing power necessary to give the firm a margin of safety.[5]

We also can analyze the ability of the firm to adjust to deviations from the expected outcomes. For example, if sales should fall off, how flexible are our expenses? What can be cut? By how much? How quickly? How much effort should be devoted to the collection of receivables? In the case of an unexpected increase in business, what additional purchases will be required, and when? Can labor be expanded? Can the present plant handle the additional demand? How much in funds will be needed to finance the buildup? Answers to these questions provide valuable insight into the efficiency and flexibility of the firm under a variety of conditions.[6]

From the standpoint of internal planning, it is far better to allow for a range of possible outcomes than to rely solely upon the expected outcome. This allowance is particularly important for firms whose business is relatively unstable in character. If the plans of the firm are based only upon expected cash flows, the firm is likely to be caught flat-footed in the case of a significant deviation from the expected outcome, and have difficulty making an adjustment. An unforeseen deficit in cash may be difficult to finance on short notice. Therefore, it is extremely important for the firm to be honest with itself and attempt to minimize the costs associated with deviations from expected outcomes by taking the steps necessary to assure accuracy and by preparing additional cash budgets so as to take into account the range of possible outcomes. When significant deviations from expected outcomes occur, the cash budget should be revised in keeping with new information.

FORECASTING FINANCIAL STATEMENTS

In addition to projecting the cash flow of a firm over time, it often is useful to prepare a projected, or *pro forma*, balance sheet and income statement for selected future dates. A cash budget gives us information

---

[5]For a detailed discussion of the appropriate margin of safety, see Chapter 5.

[6]Donaldson, "Strategy for Financial Emergencies," pp. 71–79, develops a framework for evaluating the resources available to meet adverse financial contingencies. These resources include surplus cash, unused lines of credit, negotiated bank loans, long-term debt, new equity, the reduction of planned outflows, and the liquidation of certain assets. Once these resources have been determined, together with the time necessary to put them to use, a strategy of response can be formulated. This strategy lays out the sequence in which resources will be brought into play to deal with an unanticipated event.

only as to the prospective future cash positions of the firm, whereas
pro forma statements embody forecasts of all assets and liabilities as
well as of income-statement items. Much of the information that goes
into the preparation of the cash budget, however, can be used to derive
a *pro forma* statement. As before, the key to accuracy is the sales
forecasts.

Pro forma balance sheet

To illustrate the preparation of a *pro forma* balance sheet, suppose
that we wish to prepare a *pro forma* statement for Continental Sheetmetal for June 30 and that the company has the following balance
sheet the previous December 31:

Assets (in thousands)		Liabilities (in thousands)	
Cash	$ 100	Bank borrowings	$ 50
Receivables	342	Accounts payable	200
Inventory	350	Accrued wages and expenses	250
		Accrued income taxes	70
Current assets	$ 792	Current liabilities	$ 570
Net fixed assets	800	Net worth	1,022
Total assets	$1,592	Total liabilities and net worth	$1,592

Receivables at June 30 can be estimated by adding to the receivable
balance at December 31 the total projected credit sales from January
through June, less total projected credit collections for the period. On
the basis of the information in the cash budget, receivables at June 30
would be $342,000 + $31,500, or $373,500.

If a cash budget is not available, the receivable balance may be estimated on the basis of a turnover ratio. This ratio, which depicts the
relationship between credit sales and receivables, should be based
upon past experience. To obtain the estimated level of receivables,
projected sales simply are divided by the turnover ratio. If the sales
forecast and turnover ratio are realistic, the method will produce a
reasonable approximation of the receivable balance. The estimated investment in inventories at June 30 may be based upon the production
schedule, which, in turn, is based upon the sales forecast. This schedule should show expected purchases, the expected use of inventory in
production, and the expected level of finished goods. On the basis of
this information, together with the beginning inventory level, a *pro
forma* estimate of inventory can be made. Rather than use the produc-

tion schedule, estimates of future inventory can be based upon a turn-over ratio of cost of goods sold to inventory. This ratio is applied in the same manner as for receivables. Suppose that on the basis of a turn-over ratio, we estimate inventory to be $420,000 on June 30, a figure that represents a moderate increase over the inventory level of December 31, in keeping with the buildup in sales.

Future net fixed assets are estimated by adding planned expenditures to existing net fixed assets and subtracting from this sum depreciation for the period, plus any sale of fixed assets at book value. From the cash budget, we note that capital expenditures are estimated at $200,000 over the period and that $40,000 in fixed assets will be sold at what we assume to be their depreciated book values. If depreciation for the period is expected to be $110,000, the expected net addition to fixed assets would be $50,000, ($200,000 − 40,000 − 110,000), and projected net fixed assets at June 30 would be $850,000. Because capital expenditures are planned in advance, fixed assets generally are fairly easy to forecast.

Turning now to the liabilities, accounts payable are estimated by adding total projected purchases for January through June, less total projected cash payments for purchases for the period, to the December 31 balance. Our estimate of accounts payable, therefore, is $200,000 + $50,000, or $250,000. The calculation of accrued wages and expenses is based upon the production schedule and the historical relationship between these accruals and production. We assume the estimate of accrued wages and expenses to be $240,000. Accrued income taxes are estimated by adding to the current balance taxes on forecasted income for the six-month period, less the actual payment of taxes. If income taxes for the period are forecast at $60,000, and the firm is scheduled to make $60,000 in actual payments, estimated accrued income taxes at June 30 would be $70,000.

Net worth at June 30 would be the net worth at December 31 plus profits after taxes for the period, less the amount of cash dividends paid. If profits after taxes are estimated at $65,000, net worth at June 30 would be $1,022,000 plus $65,000 minus dividends of $40,000, or $1,047,000. Two items remain: cash and bank loans. We see from the cash budget that estimated cash at June 30 would be $13,500 without additional financing. If the firm has the policy of maintaining a minimum cash balance of $75,000 and borrowing from its bank to maintain this balance, cash at June 30 would be $75,000, and bank borrowings would increase by $61,500 to $111,500. In general, cash and notes payable serve as balancing factors in the preparation of *pro forma* balance sheets, whereby assets and liabilities plus net worth are brought into balance.

Once we have estimated all the components of the *pro forma* balance sheet, they are combined into a balance sheet format. The *pro forma* balance sheet at June 30 is:

Assets (in thousands)		Liabilities (in thousands)	
Cash	$ 75.0	Bank borrowings	$ 111.5
Receivables	373.5	Accounts payable	250.0
Inventories	420.0	Accrued wages and expenses	240.0
		Accrued income taxes	70.0
Current assets	$ 868.5	Current liabilities	$ 671.5
Net fixed assets	850.0	Net worth	1,047.0
Total assets	$1,718.5	Total liabilities and net worth	$1,718.5

The cash-budget method is but one way to prepare a *pro forma* statement; one can also make direct estimates of all of the items on the balance sheet by projecting financial ratios into the future and then making estimates on the basis of these ratios. Receivables, inventories, accounts payable, and accrued wages and expenses frequently are based upon historical relationships to sales and production when a cash budget is not available.

Pro forma income statement

The *pro forma* income statement is a projection of income for a period of time in the future. As was true with our other projections, the sales forecast is the key input. Given this forecast, production schedules can be formulated and estimates made of production costs for the product or products. The analyst may wish to evaluate each component of the cost of goods sold. A detailed analysis of purchases, production wages, and overhead costs is likely to produce the most accurate forecasts. Often, however, costs of goods sold are estimated on the basis of past ratios of costs of goods sold to sales.

Selling and administrative expenses are estimated next. Because both of these expenses usually are budgeted in advance, estimates of them are fairly accurate. Typically, these expenses are not overly sensitive to changes in sales in the very short run, particularly to reductions in sales. Next, we estimate other income and expenses as well as interest expenses to obtain net income before taxes. Income taxes are then computed based upon the applicable tax rate and deducted, to arrive at estimated net income after taxes. All of these estimates are then combined into an income statement.

Pro forma statements allow us to study the composition of expected future balance sheets and income statements. Financial ratios may be computed for analysis of the statements; these ratios and the raw figures may be compared with those for present and past balance sheets. Using this information, the financial manager can analyze the direction of change in the financial condition and performance of the firm over the past, the present, and the future. If the firm is accustomed to making accurate estimates, the preparation of a cash budget, *pro forma* statements, or both literally forces it to plan ahead and to coordinate policy in the various areas of operation. Continual revision of these forecasts keeps the firm alert to changing conditions in its environment and in its internal operations. Again, it is useful to prepare more than one set of *pro forma* statements in order to take into account the range of possible outcomes.

SUMMARY

In this chapter, we continued our examination of the analytical tools of the financial manager; we looked at source and use of funds statements, the cash budget, and *pro forma* statements. The source and use of funds statement gives the financial analyst considerable insight into the uses of funds and how these uses are financed over a specific period of time. Funds-flow analysis is valuable in analyzing the commitment of funds to assets and in planning the firm's intermediate- and long-term financing. The flow of funds studied, however, represents net rather than gross transactions between two points in time.

A cash budget is a forecast of the future cash receipts and cash disbursements of a firm. This forecast is particularly useful to the financial manager in determining the probable cash balances of the firm over the near future and in planning for the financing of prospective cash needs. In addition to analyzing expected cash flows, the financial manager should take into account possible deviations from the expected outcome. An analysis of the range of possible outcomes enables management to better assess the efficiency and flexibility of the firm and to determine the appropriate margin of safety.

Finally, we considered the preparation of *pro forma* balance sheets and income statements. These statements give the financial manager insight into the prospective future financial condition and performance of the firm, giving him yet another tool for financial planning and control.

1. Contrast the *pro forma* source and use of funds statements with a *pro forma* cash budget as planning tools.

2. In constructing a *pro forma* cash budget, which variable is most important in order to arrive at accurate projections? Explain.

3. Discuss the benefits that can be derived by the firm from cash budgeting.

4. Explain why a decrease in cash constitutes a source of funds while an increase in cash is a use of funds.

5. Explain why selling inventory to credit customers is considered as a source of funds when in fact no funds were generated.

6. Why do most audited financial reports to the stockholders include a source and use of funds statement in addition to the balance sheet and income statement?

7. Is depreciation a source of funds? Under what conditions might the "source" dry up?

8. Why do bankers closely analyze the source and use of funds statement in considering credit applications?

9. Which of the following are sources of funds and which are uses of funds?
    (a) Sale of land
    (b) Quarterly dividend payment
    (c) Lease payment
    (d) Decrease in raw-materials inventory
    (e) Increase in depreciation charges
    (f) Sale of government bonds

10. What are the major points of difference between a cash budget and the source and use of funds statement?

11. On what items should the financial manager concentrate to improve the accuracy of the cash budget? Explain your reasoning.

12. Is the *pro forma* cash budget a better measure of liquidity than traditional measures such as the current ratio and quick ratio?

13. Why is the sales forecast so important in preparing the cash budget?

14. What is the purpose of the cash budget? Would a cash budget be advisable even with money in the bank? For a sole proprietor?

1. (a) Prepare a source and use of funds statement on a cash basis for Motorized Homes, Inc. (Problem 5, Chapter 3) for 1976 and 1977.
    (b) Prepare a source and use of working capital statement for Motorized Homes, Inc., for 1976 and 1977.
    (c) Do the source and use statements reveal additional information about the firm? Explain.

2. Financial statements for the Sennet Corporation follow.

Sennet Corporation Balance Sheet at December 31 (in millions)

	1975	1976		1975	1976
Cash	$ 4	$ 5	Accounts payable	$ 8	$10
Accounts receivable	7	10	Notes payable	5	5
Inventory	12	15	Accrued wages	2	3
Total current assets	$23	$30	Accrued taxes	3	2
Net plant	40	40	Total current liabilities	$18	$20
			Long-term debt	20	20
			Common stock	10	10
			Retained earnings	15	20
Total	$63	$70	Total	$63	$70

Sennet Corporation Income Statement 1976 (in millions)

Sales		$100
Cost of goods sold	$50	
Selling, general, and administrative expenses	15	
Depreciation	3	
Interest	2	70
Net income before taxes		$ 30
Taxes		15
Net income		$ 15

(a) Prepare a source and use of funds statement for Sennet.
(b) Prepare a source and use of working capital statement.

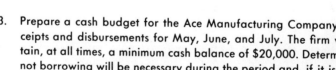

3. Prepare a cash budget for the Ace Manufacturing Company, indicating receipts and disbursements for May, June, and July. The firm wishes to maintain, at all times, a minimum cash balance of $20,000. Determine whether or not borrowing will be necessary during the period and, if it is, when and for how much. As of April 30, the firm had a balance of $20,000 in cash.

Actual Sales		Forecasted Sales	
January	$50,000	May	$ 70,000
February	50,000	June	80,000
March	60,000	July	100,000
April	60,000	August	100,000

Accounts Receivable: 50 percent of total sales are for cash. The remaining 50 percent will be collected equally during the following two months (the firm incurs a negligible bad-debt loss).

Cost of Goods Manufactured: 70 percent of sales. 90 percent of this cost is paid during the first month after incurrence; the remaining 10 percent is paid the following month.

Selling and Administrative Expenses: $10,000 per month plus 10 percent of sales. All of these expenses are paid during the month of incurrence.

Interest Payments: A semiannual interest payment on $300,000 of bonds outstanding (6 percent coupon) is paid during July. An annual $50,000 sinking-fund payment is also made.

Dividends: A $10,000 dividend payment will be declared and made in July.

Capital Expenditures: $40,000 will be invested in plant and equipment in June.

Taxes: Income tax payments of $1,000 will be made in July.

4. Given the information that follows, prepare a cash budget for the Central City Department Store for the first six months of 1977.
  (a) All prices and costs remain constant.
  (b) Sales are 75 percent for credit and 25 percent for cash.
  (c) With respect to credit sales, 60 percent are collected in the month after the sale, 30 percent in the second month, and 10 percent in the third. Bad-debt losses are insignificant.
  (d) Sales, actual and estimated, are:

October 1976	$300,000	March 1977	$200,000
November 1976	350,000	April 1977	300,000
December 1976	400,000	May 1977	250,000
January 1977	150,000	June 1977	200,000
February 1977	200,000	July 1977	300,000

  (e) Purchases of merchandise are 80 percent of sales, and the store pays for each month's anticipated sales in the preceding month.
  (f) Wages and salaries are:

January	$30,000	April	$50,000
February	40,000	May	40,000
March	50,000	June	35,000

  (g) Rent is $2,000 a month.
  (h) Interest on $500,000 of 6 percent bonds is due on the last day of the calendar quarter.
  (i) A tax prepayment on 1977 income of $50,000 is due in April.
  (j) A capital addition of $30,000 is planned in June, to be paid for then.
  (k) The company has a cash balance of $100,000 at December 31, 1976, which is the minimum desired level for cash. Funds can be borrowed in multiples of $5,000 on a monthly basis at 6 percent per annum. Interest is payable on the first of the month following the borrowing.

5. Use the cash budget worked out in Problem 4 and the following additional information to prepare a *pro forma* income statement for the first half of 1977 for the Central City Department Store.

(a) Inventory at 12/31/76 was $200,000.

(b) Depreciation is taken on a straight-line basis on $250,000 of assets with an average remaining life of ten years and no salvage value.

(c) The tax rate is 50 percent.

6. Given the following information and that contained in Problems 4 and 5, construct a *pro forma* balance sheet as of June 30, 1977, for the Central City Department Store.

Central City Department Store Balance Sheet at December 31, 1976

Assets		Liabilities and Equity	
Cash	$100,000	Accounts payable	$130,000
Accounts receivable	427,500	Notes	500,000
Inventory	200,000	Common stock and	
Fixed assets, net	250,000	retained earnings	347,500
	$977,500		$977,500

SELECTED REFERENCES

ANSOFF, H. IGOR, "Planning as a Practical Management Tool," *Financial Executive,* 32 (June 1964), 34–37.

CHAMBERS, JOHN C., SATINDER K. MULLICK, and **DONALD D. SMITH,** "How to Choose the Right Forecasting Technique," *Harvard Business Review,* 49 (July–August 1971), 45–74.

DONALDSON, GORDON, "Strategy for Financial Emergencies," *Harvard Business Review,* 47 (November–December 1969), 67–79.

GORDON, MYRON J., and **GORDON SHILLINGLAW,** *Accounting: A Management Approach,* 4th ed., Chapter 16. Homewood, Ill.: Richard D. Irwin, 1969.

HELFERT, ERICH A., *Techniques of Financial Analysis,* 3rd ed., Chapters 1 and 3. Homewood, Ill.: Richard D. Irwin, 1972.

JAEDICKE, ROBERT K., and **ROBERT T. SPROUSE,** *Accounting Flows: Income, Funds, and Cash,* Chapters 5 and 6. Englewood Cliffs, N.J.: Prentice-Hall, 1965.

LERNER, EUGENE M., "Simulating a Cash Budget," *California Management Review,* 11 (Winter 1968), 79–86.

PARKER, GEORGE G. C., and **EDILBERTO L. SEGURA,** "How to Get a Better Forecast," *Harvard Business Review,* 49 (March–April 1971), 99–109.

TRUMBULL, WENDELL P., "Developing the Funds Statement as the Third Major Financial Statement," *N.A.A. Bulletin,* 45 (April 1963), 21–31.

WESTON, J. FRED, "Forecasting Financial Requirements," *Accounting Review,* 33 (July 1958), 427–40.

Management of Current Assets II

5 *Working Capital Management*

Current assets, by accounting definition, are assets normally converted into cash within one year. Working capital management usually is considered to involve the administration of these assets—namely, cash and marketable securities, receivables, and inventories—and the administration of current liabilities. Administration of *fixed assets* (assets normally not converted into cash within the year), on the other hand, is usually considered to fall within the realm of capital budgeting, which we take up in Part IV. By and large, investment in current assets is more divisible than investment in fixed assets, a fact that has important implications for flexibility in financing. Differences in divisibility as well as in durability of economic life are the essential features that distinguish current from fixed assets.

Determining the appropriate levels of current assets and current liabilities, which determine the level of working capital, involves fundamental decisions with respect to the firm's liquidity and the maturity composition of its debt.[1] In turn, these decisions are influenced by a tradeoff between profitability and risk. In a broad sense, the appropriate decision variable to examine on the asset side of the balance sheet is the maturity composition, or liquidity, of the firm's assets—i.e., the

[1] Parts of this chapter are adapted from James C. Van Horne, "A Risk-Return Analysis of a Firm's Working-Capital Position," *Engineering Economist,* 14 (Winter 1969), 71–90.

78

turnover of these assets into cash. Decisions that affect the asset liquidity of the firm include the management of cash and marketable securities, credit policy and procedures, inventory management and control, and the administration of fixed assets. For purposes of illustration, we hold constant the last three factors; the efficiency in managing them is taken up elsewhere in the book.[2] We assume also that the cash and marketable securities held by the firm (hereafter called liquid assets) yield a return lower than the return on investment in other assets.

For current assets, then, the lower the proportion of liquid assets to total assets, the greater the firm's return on total investment. Profitability with respect to the level of current liabilities relates to differences in costs between various methods of financing and to the use of financing during periods when it is not needed. To the extent that the explicit costs of short-term financing are less than those of intermediate- and long-term financing, the greater the proportion of short-term debt to total debt, the higher the profitability of the firm. Although short-term rates occasionally exceed long-term rates, generally they are less, making short-term financing a less-expensive financing alternative. Moreover, the use of short-term debt as opposed to longer-term debt is likely to result in higher profits because debt will be paid off on a seasonal basis during periods when it is not needed.

The profitability assumptions above suggest a low proportion of current assets to total assets and a high proportion of current liabilities to total liabilities. This strategy, of course, will result in a low level of working capital, or, conceivably, even negative working capital. Offsetting the profitability of this strategy is the risk to the firm. For our purposes, risk is the probability of technical insolvency. In a legal sense, insolvency occurs whenever the assets of a firm are less than its liabilities—negative net worth. Technical insolvency, on the other hand, occurs whenever a firm is unable to meet its cash obligations.[3]

The evaluation of risk necessarily involves analysis of the liquidity of the firm. *Liquidity* may be defined as the ability to realize value in money, the most liquid of assets. Liquidity has two dimensions: (1) the time necessary to convert an asset into money, and (2) the certainty of the conversion ratio, or price, realized for the asset. An investment in real estate, for example, is generally a less-liquid investment than an investment in marketable securities. Not only does it usually take longer to sell real estate than to sell securities, but the price realized is more uncertain. The two dimensions are not independent. If an asset must be converted into money in a short time, the price is likely to be

---

[2]See Chapters 7 and 8 and Part IV.

[3]James E. Walter, "Determination of Technical Solvency," *Journal of Business,* 30 (January 1957), 30–43.

more uncertain than if the holder has a reasonable time in which to sell the asset.[4]

In this chapter, we study the extent to which possible adverse deviations from expected net cash flows (cash inflows less cash outflows) are protected by the liquid assets of the firm. The risk involved with various levels of current assets and current liabilities must be evaluated in relation to the profitability associated with those levels. The discussion that follows concerns the financing of current assets and the level of those assets that should be maintained from a broad theoretical standpoint.

FINANCING CURRENT ASSETS

The way in which current assets are financed involves a tradeoff between risk and profitability. For purposes of analysis, we assume that the company has an established policy with respect to payment for purchases, labor, taxes, and other expenses. Thus, the amounts of accounts payable and accruals included in current liabilities are not active decision variables.[5] These liabilities finance a portion of the current assets of the firm and tend to fluctuate with the production schedule and, in the case of taxes, with profits. As the underlying investment in current assets grows, accounts payable and accruals also tend to grow, in part financing the buildup in current assets. Our concern is with how current assets not supported by accounts payable and accruals are financed.[6]

Hedging approach

If the firm adopts a hedging approach to financing, each asset would be offset with a financing instrument of the same approximate maturity. With a hedging approach, short-term or seasonal variations in current assets would be financed with short-term debt; the permanent component of current assets would be financed with long-term debt or

---

[4]James C. Van Horne and David A. Bowers, "The Liquidity Impact of Debt Management," *Southern Economic Journal*, 34 (April 1968), 537.

[5]Delaying the payment of accounts payable can be a decision variable for financing purposes. However, there are limits to the extent to which a firm can "stretch" its payables. For simplicity, we assume in the above analysis that the firm has a definite policy with respect to paying its bills, such as taking advantage of all cash discounts and paying all other bills at the end of the credit period. See Chapter 9 for a discussion of trade credit as a means of financing.

[6]We assume the financing of fixed assets as given.

equity. This policy is illustrated in Figure 5-1. If total funds requirements behave in the manner shown, only the short-term fluctuations shown at the top of the figure would be financed with short-term debt. To finance short-term requirements with long-term debt would necessitate the payment of interest for the use of funds during times when they were not needed. This occurrence could be illustrated if we drew a straight line to represent the total amount of long-term debt and equity across the seasonal humps at the top of Figure 5-1. It is apparent that financing would be employed in periods of seasonal lull when it was not needed. With a hedging approach to financing, the borrowing and payment schedule for short-term financing would be arranged so as to correspond to the expected swings in current assets, less payables and accruals. Fixed assets and the permanent component of current assets would be financed with long-term debt, equity, and the permanent component of current liabilities.

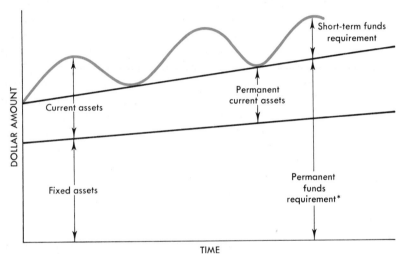

*Financed by long-term debt, equity, and the permanent component of current liabilities (accounts payable and accruals).

FIG. 5 · 1
Funds requirement

A hedging approach to financing suggests that apart from current installments on long-term debt, a firm would show no current borrowings at the seasonal troughs in Figure 5-1. Short-term borrowings would be paid off with surplus cash. As the firm moved into a period of seasonal funds needs, it would borrow on a short-term basis, again paying the borrowings off as surplus cash was generated. In this way, financing would be employed only when it was needed. Permanent funds requirements would be financed with long-term debt and equity. In a growth situation, permanent financing would be increased in keeping with increases in permanent funds requirements.

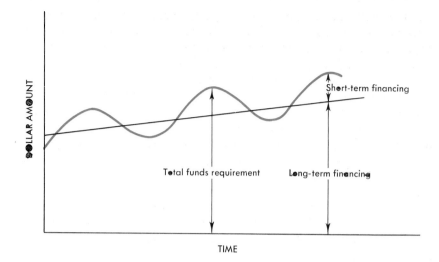

FIG. 5 · 2

Funds requirement

Maturity of debt. Although an exact synchronization of the schedule of expected future net cash flows and the payment schedule of debt is appropriate under conditions of certainty, it usually is not under uncertainty. Net cash flows will deviate from expected flows in keeping with the business risk of the firm. As a result, the schedule of maturities of the debt contracts is very important in the risk-profitability tradeoff. The question is what margin of safety should be built into the maturity schedule in order to allow for adverse fluctuations in cash flows. The shorter the maturity schedule of the debt, the greater the risk that the firm will be unable to meet principal and interest payments. The longer the maturity schedule, the less risky the financing of the firm, all other things held constant.

The composite maturity schedule of debt for a firm will depend upon management's risk preferences. Generally, the longer the maturity schedule of debt in relation to expected net cash flows, the less the risk of inability to meet principal and interest payments. However, the longer the maturity schedule, the more costly the financing is likely to be. For one thing, the explicit cost of long-term financing usually is more than that of short-term financing.[7] In addition to the generally higher costs of long-term borrowings, the firm may well pay interest on debt over periods of time when the funds are not needed. Thus, there usually is an inducement to finance funds requirements on a short-term basis.

Consequently, we have a tradeoff between risk and profitability. The margin of safety, or lag between expected net cash flows and payments

---

[7]We ignore at this time consideration of implicit costs that might be associated with short-term financing. These costs are analyzed in Chapter 18.

on debt, will depend upon the risk preferences of management. In turn, its decision as to the maturity breakdown of the firm's debt will determine the portion of current assets financed by current liabilities and the portion financed on a long-term basis.

To allow for a margin of safety, management might decide upon the proportions of short-term and long-term financing shown in Figure 5-2. Here, we see, the firm finances a portion of its expected seasonal funds requirement, less payables and accruals, on a long-term basis. If the expected net cash flows do occur, it will pay interest on debt during seasonal troughs when the funds are not needed. As we shall see in the subsequent section, however, the firm can also create a margin of safety by increasing the proportion of liquid assets. Thus, the firm can reduce the risk of cash insolvency either by increasing the maturity schedule of its debt or by decreasing the relative "maturity" of its assets. At the end of the chapter, we explore the interdependence of these two facets.

LEVEL OF CURRENT AND LIQUID ASSETS

In determining the appropriate level of current assets, management must again consider the tradeoff between profitability and risk.[8] To illustrate this tradeoff, we hold constant the amount of the firm's fixed assets and vary the amount of current assets. Moreover, we assume that the management of receivables and inventories is efficient and consistent throughout the range of output under consideration. In other words, at every level of output, the investment in receivables and inventories is predetermined.[9] As a result, we are concerned only with the cash and marketable securities portion of the current assets of the firm.[10]

Suppose that with existing fixed assets a firm can produce up to 100,000 units of output a year. Assume also that production is continuous throughout the period under consideration, given a particular level of output. For each level of output, the firm can have a number of different levels of current assets. We assume initially three current-asset alternatives. The relationship between output and current-asset

---

[8]The development of this section draws in part upon Ernest W. Walker, "Towards a Theory of Working Capital," *Engineering Economist,* 9 (January–February 1964), 21–35.

[9]The efficiency of management of receivables and inventory is examined in Chapters 7 and 8, respectively. The quality of these assets, as determined by the efficiency of their management, has a significant bearing upon the liquidity of the firm.

[10]The allocation of funds between cash and marketable securities, near cash, is taken up in Chapter 6.

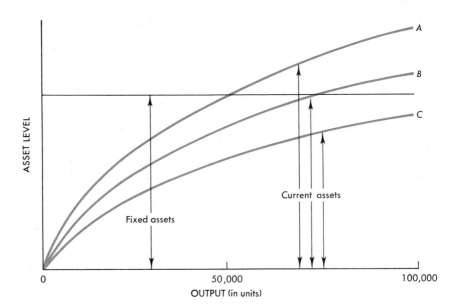

FIG. 5 · 3
Current to fixed assets

level for these alternatives is illustrated in Figure 5-3. We see from the figure that the greater the output, the greater the need for investment in current assets. However, the relationship is not linear; current assets increase at a decreasing rate with output. This relationship is based upon the notion that it takes a greater proportional investment in current assets when only a few units of output are produced than it does later on when the firm can use its current assets more efficiently. Fixed assets are assumed not to vary with output.

Of the three alternatives, alternative A is the most conservative level of current assets, for the ratio of current assets to fixed assets is greatest at every level of output. The greater the proportion of current to fixed assets, the greater the liquidity of the firm and the lower the risk of technical insolvency, all other things held constant. Alternative C is the most aggressive policy, because the ratio of current assets to fixed assets is lowest at all levels of output. The probability of technical insolvency is greatest under alternative C if net cash flows are less than expected.

Suppose that for the forthcoming year a firm expects sales of $2 million on 80,000 units of output and expects to realize a profit margin before interest and taxes of 10 percent, or $200,000 in total profits. We assume that this figure will not vary with the levels of current assets considered. Suppose also that fixed assets are $500,000 for the period under review and that management is considering current asset positions of $400,000, $500,000, or $600,000. Given this information, we are able to make the profitability calculations shown in Table 5-1. As evidenced in this table, the greater the proportion of current assets

TABLE 5 · 1

	A	B	C
			Profitability under Alternative Current-Asset Positions
Sales	$2,000,000	$2,000,000	$2,000,000
Earnings before interest and taxes	200,000	200,000	200,000
Current assets	600,000	500,000	400,000
Fixed assets	500,000	500,000	500,000
Total assets	1,100,000	1,000,000	900,000
Asset turnover (sales/total assets)	1.82:1	2:1	2.22:1
Rate of return (earnings/total assets)	18.2%	20%	22.2%

to fixed assets, the lower the rate of return. Alternative *A*, the most conservative plan, gives the firm the greatest liquidity cushion to meet unexpected needs for funds. However, it also provides the lowest rate of return of the three alternatives. Alternative *C*, on the other hand, provides the highest rate of return but has the lowest liquidity and, correspondingly, the greatest risk.

This is a very simple example of the tradeoff between risk and profitability. Our assumptions were such that changes in the level of current assets were comprised entirely of changes in liquid assets—cash and marketable securities. We should recognize that the generalizations possible become far more complicated when it comes to changes in accounts receivable and inventory. Although receivables do not provide the buffer against running out of cash that cash and marketable securities do, they provide more of a buffer than do inventories or fixed assets. By the same token, the profit foregone by holding receivables generally is less than that for holding cash or marketable securities, but greater than that for holding inventories and fixed assets. Though we may have some idea of relative ordering of receivables and inventories with respect to risk and profits foregone, the differences are extremely difficult to quantify. In subsequent chapters, we deal with the optimal level of each of these assets, taking into consideration both profitability and risk. However, for now, we continue to restrict our definition of liquid assets to cash and marketable securities.

INTERDEPENDENCE OF TWO FACETS

In the preceding sections, we examined two broad facets of working capital management—the decision as to how current assets are to be financed, and the decision as to the proportion of liquid assets to maintain. The two facets are interdependent. All other things held constant, a firm with a high proportion of liquid assets is better able to finance its current assets on a short-term basis than is a firm with a low proportion of liquid assets. On the other hand, a firm that finances its current assets entirely with equity will have less need for liquidity than it would if it financed these assets entirely with short-term borrowings. Because of their interdependence, these two facets of working capital management must be considered jointly.

If the firm knows its future cash flows with certainty, it will be able to arrange its maturity schedule of debt to correspond exactly with its schedule of future net cash flows. As a result, profits will be maximized, for there will be no need to hold low-yielding liquid assets nor to have more long-term financing than is absolutely necessary. When cash flows are subject to uncertainty, however, the situation is changed. As discussed in Chapter 4, cash forecasts can be prepared for a range of possible outcomes, with a probability attached to each. This information enables management to assess the possibility of technical insolvency and to plan accordingly for a margin of safety.[11] The greater the dispersion of the probability distribution of possible net cash flows, the greater the margin of safety that management will wish to provide. We assume initially that the firm cannot borrow on short notice to meet unexpected cash drains. As a result, it can provide a margin of safety only by (1) increasing the proportion of liquid assets, and (2) lengthening the maturity schedule of financing. Both these actions affect profitability. In the former case, funds are committed to low-yielding assets; in the latter, the firm may pay interest on borrowings over periods of time when the funds are not needed. In addition, long-term debt usually has a higher explicit cost than does short-term debt.

A decision as to the appropriate margin of safety will be governed by considerations of risk and profitability and by the utility preferences of management with respect to bearing risk. To the extent that the cost of running out of cash is measurable, the optimal margin of safety can be determined by comparing the expected costs of running out of cash with the profits foregone when a particular solution is used to avoid that possibility. The expected cost of a cash stockout is the cost associated with a particular stockout times its probability of occurrence. For example, suppose that associated with a particular solution there is a 10 percent probability for a cash stockout of $50,000, and a 5 percent probability that the stockout will be $100,000. If the costs of these stockouts are $10,000 and $25,000, respectively, the expected costs will be $0.10(\$10,000) = \$1,000$ and $0.05(\$25,000) =$

---

[11] In addition to the discussion in Chapter 4, see the section on cash-flow analysis of debt in Chapter 18.

$1,250, respectively. The total expected cost of cash stockout for that solution is $2,250. The optimal solution could be determined by comparing the reduction in the expected cost of cash stockout accompanying a particular solution with the opportunity cost of implementing that solution. The optimal solution would be where the marginal opportunity cost equaled the marginal decrease in the expected cost of cash stockout. The difficulty with this approach, however, is in estimating the cost of a cash stockout. Such costs as deterioration in a firm's credit standing and the inability to pay certain obligations are intangible and defy precise quantification.

Because of this difficulty, it may be easier for management to consider subjectively the costs associated with various cash stockouts and then simply specify a tolerable level of risk. Suppose, for example, we find that there is a 5 percent probability that the cash balance of the firm will be − $300,000 or less during the next several periods. If management is willing to tolerate a 5 percent probability of running out of cash, the firm should increase its liquid assets by $300,000. If it does so, there will be only a 5 percent probability that possible deviations from expected cash flows will result in the firm's running out of cash. However, the firm may be able to achieve the same results by lengthening its maturity schedule of financing. For example, by refinancing existing debt that matures within two years into intermediate-term debt maturing in five to seven years, the firm may be able to reduce the probability of technical insolvency to 5 percent. Likewise, various combinations of liquidity increase and debt lengthening may achieve this result.

Each solution (increasing liquidity, lengthening the maturity structure, or a combination of the two), will cost the firm something in profit-making ability. For a given risk tolerance, management may determine which solution is least costly and then implement that solution. On the other hand, management might determine the least costly solution for various levels of risk. Then management could formulate risk tolerances on the basis of the cost involved in providing a margin of safety. Hopefully, these tolerances would be in keeping with an objective of maximizing shareholder wealth. The approach, however, has been to provide an information framework specifying risk and profitability that management can use to make informed and rational decisions.

If the firm can borrow in times of emergency, the above analysis needs to be modified. The greater the ability of the firm to borrow, the less it needs to provide for a margin of safety by the means discussed previously. Certain companies can arrange for lines of credit or revolving credits that enable them to borrow on short notice.[12] When a company has access to such credit, it must compare the cost of these

---

[12]For a discussion of these methods, see Chapter 10.

arrangements (compensating balances, interest costs, and use of debt capacity) with the cost of other solutions. There are, of course, limits to how much a firm may borrow on short notice. Consequently, it must provide for some margin of safety on the basis of the considerations discussed above.

SUMMARY

Working capital management involves deciding upon the amount and composition of current assets and how to finance these assets. These decisions involve tradeoffs between risk and profitability. The greater the relative proportion of liquid assets, the less the risk of running out of cash, all other things being equal. However, profitability also will be less. The longer the composite maturity schedule of securities used to finance the firm, the less the risk of cash insolvency, all other things being equal. Again, however, the profits of the firm are likely to be less. Resolution of the tradeoff between risk and profitability with respect to these decisions depends upon the risk preferences of management.

In this chapter, we have been concerned with working capital management in a broad sense. We assumed, for example, the efficient management of the various components of current assets. The efficiency of credit and collection procedures and inventory control have a significant bearing upon the liquidity of the firm. Moreover, we did not differentiate between cash and marketable securities (near cash) or consider the optimal split between these two assets. In the three subsequent chapters, we analyze specifically the management of cash and marketable securities, the management of receivables, and the management of inventories. In Part III, we consider methods of short- and intermediate-term financing.

QUESTIONS

1. Evaluate the following statement: "Returns on current assets are insignificant; therefore, a business firm should minimize its investment in these assets."

2. The amount of current assets that a firm will maintain will be determined by the tradeoff between risk and profitability.
   (a) Is there a unique combination of risk and profitability for each level of current assets?
   (b) Discuss the factors that will affect the risk associated with holding current assets.

3. Utilities hold 10 percent of total assets in current assets while retail trade industries hold 60 percent of total assets in current assets. Explain how industry characteristics account for this difference.

4. Some firms finance their permanent working capital with short-term lia-bilities (commercial paper and short-term notes). Explain the impact of this decision on the profitability and risk parameters of these firms.

5. Suppose a firm finances its seasonal (temporary) current assets with long-term funds. What is the impact of this decision on the profitability and risk parameters of this firm?

6. Risk associated with the amount of current assets is assumed to decrease with increased levels of current assets. Is this assumption correct for all levels of current assets? Explain.

7. Compare the net working capital position with the *pro forma* cash budget as tools to measure the ability of a firm to meet maturing obligations.

8. At times long-term interest rates are lower than short-term rates, yet the discussion in the chapter suggests that long-term financing is more expen-sive. If long-term rates are lower, shouldn't the firm finance itself entirely with long-term debt?

9. How does shortening the maturity composition of the firm's outstanding debt increase the risk of the firm? Why does increasing the liquidity of the firm's assets reduce that risk?

10. Why do firms invest in any current assets at all if the returns on those as-sets are less than the returns from fixed assets?

11. What are the costs of maintaining too large a net working capital posi-tion? Too small a net working capital position?

12. What are the main disadvantages of the use of the net working capital position as an indication of a firm's financial solvency?

PROBLEMS

1. The Anderson Corporation has a sales level of $280,000 with a 10 percent net profit margin before interest and taxes. To generate this sales volume, the firm maintains a fixed asset investment of $100,000. Currently, the firm maintains $50,000 in current assets.
   (a) Determine the asset turnover for the firm and compute the rate of return on assets.
   (b) Compute the rate of return on assets at different levels of current as-sets starting with $10,000 and increasing in $15,000 increments to $100,000.
   (c) What implicit assumption is being made about sales in part (b)? Ap-praise the significance of this assumption along with the policy to choose the level of current assets that will maximize the return on in-vestments as computed in (b).

2. The Malkiel Corporation has made the three-year projection of its asset investment given in the following table. It has found that payables and ac-cruals tend to equal one-third of current assets. It currently has $50 million in equity and the remainder of its capitalization in long-term debt. The earn-ings retained quarterly amount to $1 million/quarter.

Date	Fixed Assets	Current Assets
3/31/77 (now)	$50 (*in millions*)	$21 (*in millions*)
6/30/77	51	30
9/30/77	52	25
12/31/77	53	21
3/31/78	54	22
6/30/78	55	31
9/30/78	56	26
12/31/78	57	22
3/31/79	58	23
6/30/79	59	32
9/30/79	60	27
12/31/79	61	23

(a) Graph the time path of total and fixed assets.

(b) Devise a financing plan, assuming your objective is to use a hedging approach.

(c) If short-term rates average 5 percent and long-term rates average 7 percent, how much would the firm save if its entire current assets were financed by short-term rates?

3. Barnstap Aviation Company, founded three years ago, sells fuel and certain parts to private plane users at El Teton Airport, a small municipal airport in the Central Valley of California. The company has been successful in filling an economic need and has experienced good profitability. Up to the present time, however, it has been unable to obtain term financing. As a result, it has had to finance itself by "stretching" its accounts payable and recently by borrowing from a local finance company. At the end of June, Barnstap had the following debt and net worth:

Accounts payable	$60,000
Short-term debt	40,000
Net worth	60,000
	$160,000

Willie Brown, the president of Barnstap, estimates that the effective cost of stretching payables is 30 percent per annum, comprised of cash discounts foregone and, in certain cases, by paying higher prices than would otherwise prevail. However, only $30,000 of the total payables is stretched; that is, the company would have had $30,000 in normal payables at the end of June. The rate of interest on the finance company loan is 24 percent. It would appear that both sources of financing will be available in the future at the same effective rates of interest.

The company has a seasonal element to its business, with peak requirements in June. In June just passed, it required $100,000 in payables and debt. By the end of December, its requirements usually decline by 30 percent. Mr. Brown estimates that the company's requirements for payables and debt will be the following next June under three possible states of the economy:

State	Requirements	Probability of State Occurring
Boom	$160,000	.20
Normal	120,000	.60
Recession	90,000	.20

Recently, the company has been exploring the use of a term loan. It has been approached by Monument Southern Life Insurance Company for a five-year term loan at 18 percent interest. The amount is $80,000, and the insurance company is neither willing to lend more nor willing to lend less.

Mr. Brown wishes to evaluate the interest costs of the term loan in relation to the present method of financing at four times: June 30 and December 31 of this year, and June 30 and December 31 of next year. For ease of calculation, one can assume that the amounts are outstanding six months, as increases and decreases in total financing requirements are steady. Moreover, one can assume that 30 percent of the total payables and debt requirements is comprised of normal payables, for which there is no effective interest cost. The company would then borrow up to $40,000 from the finance company at 24 percent, with anything over that amount obtained from stretching accounts payable at an effective rate of 30 percent.

Which financing alternative has the lower six-month interest costs for each of the four dates and under each of the three possible states of the economy? Why?

SELECTED REFERENCES

ARCHER, STEPHEN H., "A Model for the Determination of Firm Cash Balances," *Journal of Financial and Quantitative Analysis*, 1 (March 1966), 1–11.

BEAN, VIRGINIA L., and REYNOLDS GIFFITH, "Risk and Return in Working Capital Management," *Mississippi Valley Journal of Business and Economics*, 1 (Fall 1966), 28–48.

BUDIN, MORRIS, and ROBERT J. VAN HANDEL, "A Rule-of-Thumb Theory of Cash Holdings by Firm," *Journal of Financial and Quantitative Analysis*, 10 (March 1975), 85–108.

COSSABOOM, ROGER A., "Let's Reassess the Profitability-Liquidity Tradeoff," *Financial Executive*, 39 (May 1971), 46–51.

GLAUTIER, M.W.E., "Towards a Reformulation of the Theory of Working Capital," *Journal of Business Finance*, 3 (Spring 1971), 37–42.

MEHTA, DILEEP R., *Working Capital Management*. Englewood Cliffs, N.J.: Prentice-Hall, 1974.

SMITH, KEITH V., *Management of Working Capital*. New York: West Publishing, 1974.

VAN HORNE, JAMES C., "A Risk-Return Analysis of a Firm's Working-Capital Position," *Engineering Economist*, 14 (Winter 1969), 71–89.

WALKER, ERNEST W., "Towards a Theory of Working Capital," *Engineering Economist*, 9 (January–February 1964), 21–35.

WALTER, JAMES E., "Determination of Technical Solvency," *Journal of Business*, 30 (January 1959), 30–43.

6 Cash and Marketable Securities

Our concern in the preceding chapter was with the overall level of liquid and current assets of the firm. By examining the tradeoff between profitability and risk, we were able to determine in a general way the proper amount of liquid assets the firm should carry. Recall that *liquid assets* were defined as cash and marketable securities. Once the overall level of liquid assets is determined, the question becomes how much will be carried in cash and how much will be carried in marketable securities. The purpose of this chapter is to present ways for determining the appropriate amounts to carry in each of these assets, to examine methods for improving the efficiency of cash management, and to study the investment of excess funds in marketable securities.

TRANSACTIONS AND PRECAUTIONARY BALANCES

Keynes has identified three motives for holding cash: the transactions motive, precautionary motive, and the speculative motive. The trans-

---

[1]John Maynard Keynes, *The General Theory of Employment, Interest, and Money* (New York: Harcourt, Brace & Jovanovich, 1936), pp. 170–74.

actions motive is the need for cash to meet payments arising in the ordinary course of business. These payments include such things as purchases, labor, taxes, and dividends. The precautionary motive for holding cash has to do with maintaining a cushion or buffer to meet unexpected contingencies. The more predictable the cash flows of the business, the fewer precautionary balances that are needed. Ready borrowing power to meet emergency cash drains also reduces the need for this type of balance. It is important to point out that not all of the firm's transactions and precautionary balances need to be held in cash; indeed, a portion may be held in marketable securities—near-money assets.

The speculative motive relates to the holding of cash in order to take advantage of expected changes in security prices. When interest rates are expected to rise and security prices to fall, this motive would suggest that the firm should hold cash until the rise in interest rates ceases. When interest rates are expected to fall, cash may be invested in securities; the firm will benefit by any subsequent fall in interest rates and rise in security prices. For the most part, companies do not hold cash for the purpose of taking advantage of expected changes in interest rates. Consequently, we concentrate only upon the transactions and precautionary motives of the firm, with these balances held both in cash and in marketable securities.

Influences on the amount of transactions and precautionary balances held by the firm include

1. Expected net cash flows of the firm as determined by the cash budget. These cash forecasts should encompass both the short- and long-run cash needs of the firm.

2. Possible deviations from expected net cash flows. As we discussed in Chapter 4, probability concepts can be applied to the cash budget to determine the variation in cash flows under different circumstances. Every effort should be made to take into account the magnitude of possible dispersions.

3. Maturity structure of the firm's debt.

4. Firm's borrowing capacity to meet emergency needs beyond transactions and precautionary balances.

5. Utility preferences of management with respect to the risk of cash insolvency.

6. Efficiency of cash management.

Factors 1 through 5 were discussed in the preceding chapter in our study of working capital management. We assume that the first four of these factors have been evaluated by management in keeping with that discussion and that the appropriate transactions and precautionary balances, exclusive of the last factor, have been determined. The efficiency of cash management, however, remains to be considered. This factor, together with the previous five, will determine the appropriate level of total transactions and precautionary balances for the firm. Obviously, the more efficient the cash management of the firm, the fewer transactions and precautionary balances that will need to be maintained.

CASH MANAGEMENT

In this section, we analyze various collection and disbursement methods by which a firm can improve its cash management efficiency. These methods constitute two sides of the same coin; they exercise a joint impact on the overall efficiency of cash management. We consider first the acceleration of collections, or reducing the delay between the time a customer pays his bill and the time the check is collected and becomes usable funds for the firm. A number of methods have been employed in recent years to speed up this collection process and maximize available cash. These methods are designed to do one or all of the following: (1) speed the mailing time of payments from customers to the firm; (2) reduce the time during which payments received by the firm remain uncollected funds; and (3) speed the movement of funds to disbursement banks.

Concentration banking

Concentration banking is a means of accelerating the flow of funds of a firm by establishing strategic collection centers. Instead of a single collection center located at the company headquarters, multiple collection centers are established. The purpose is to shorten the period between the time a customer mails in his payment and the time when the company has the use of the funds. Customers in a particular geographic area are instructed to remit their payments to a collection center in that area. The selection of the collection centers usually is based upon the geographic areas served and the volume of billings in a given area. When payments are received, they are deposited in the collection center's local bank. Surplus funds are then transferred from these local bank accounts to a concentration bank or banks. A bank of concentration is one with which the company has a major account— usually a disbursement account. For example, a company headquartered in New York City might have but one concentration bank, a New York bank. Concentration banking is one way to reduce the size of the float, the difference between the amount of deposit and the amount of usable funds in a bank. A company usually cannot withdraw a deposit until the bank actually collects the checks. Until collected, the deposited checks represent float.[2]

An illustration.   To illustrate concentration banking and the transfer of funds, we examine the case of an actual large company with over twenty collection centers. At the time of the study, each collection center billed customers in its area and made daily deposits in its local bank of payments received from customers. On the average, the checks deposited in a bank were collected in one and one-fourth days. In other words, the company had use of the funds one and one-fourth days after deposit. In each of its local banks, the company maintained sufficient collected balances to compensate the bank for the costs of servicing the account.

A daily *wire transfer* arrangement was used to transfer collected balances in excess of compensating balances to one of several concentration banks. The managers of the collection centers initiated the transfer on the basis of a daily report of estimated collected balances from their local banks. Because the wire transfers were made through the Federal Reserve System, the funds transferred became available immediately at the concentration banks.

This method of transfer differs from a *depository transfer check* arrangement for the movement of funds, whereby a depository check is drawn on the local bank, payable to a concentration bank. Funds are not immediately available at the concentration bank, for the check must be collected through the usual channels. The check itself is not signed but bears the company's printed name as drawer. Given a resolution by the board of directors to the drawee bank, the printed name is sufficient authority for withdrawal. Whereas a transfer check costs only about $0.10 to process, it is not as fast as a wire transfer, which costs about $1.50. The delay must be analyzed in relation to the difference in cost. For small transfers, a wire transfer is too costly compared with a depository transfer check and should not be used. The

---

[2] Checks deposited with a bank usually are processed for collection by that bank either through the Federal Reserve System, through a correspondent bank, or through a clearing-house system of a group of banks in a particular city. A check becomes collected funds when it is presented to the drawee bank and actually paid by that bank. In order to streamline the availability of credit, however, the Federal Reserve has established a schedule specifying the availability of credit for all checks deposited with it for collection. This schedule is based upon the average time required for a check deposited with a specific Federal Reserve bank to be collected in a particular geographic area of the country. The maximum period for which credit is deferred is two business days. This means that a check deposited with a Federal Reserve bank for collection at a distant point would become available credit for the depositing bank two days later. Correspondent banks frequently set up deferment schedules based upon that of the Federal Reserve. From the standpoint of a company, the length of the float depends upon the time it takes the bank to obtain available credit on checks processed for collection. In turn, this time will depend upon where the drawee banks are located.

earnings possible on investing the released funds simply do not cover the differential in cost.[3]

The advantage of a system of decentralized billings and collections over a centralized system is twofold. (Recall that we compare a system of multiple collection centers with a single collection center located at company headquarters.)

1. The time required for mailing is reduced. Because the collection center bills customers in its area, these customers usually receive their bills earlier than if the bills were mailed from the head office. In turn, when customers pay their bills, the mailing time to the nearest collection center is shorter than the time required for the typical remittance to go to the head office. The company estimated that there was a saving of approximately one day in mailing time from the customer to the company.

2. The time required to collect checks is reduced, because remittances deposited in the collection center's local bank usually are drawn on banks in that general area. The company estimated that the average collection period would be two and one-fourth days if all remittances were deposited in the company's head office bank, compared with one and one-fourth days under the present system. At the margin, then, the company was able to speed up the collection of customer checks by one day.

Thus, the company was able to accelerate overall collections by two days; one day was gained by reducing the mailing time and one day by reducing the time during which deposited checks remained uncollected. At the time of the study, average daily remittances by customers were $2.1 million. By saving two days in the collection process, approximately $4.2 million in funds were released for investment elsewhere. With the recent high levels of interest rates, it is not difficult to see the opportunity cost of tying up funds. However, profits from the investment of the released funds must be compared with any additional costs of a decentralized system over a centralized one. Also, it is important to consider any differences between the two systems in total compensating balances. The greater the number of collection centers, the more local bank accounts that must be maintained.

Lock-box system

Another means of accelerating the flow of funds is a lock-box arrangement. With concentration banking, remittances are received by a collection center and deposited in the bank after processing. The purpose of a lock-box arrangement is to eliminate the time between the receipt of remittances by the company and their deposit in the bank. A lock-box arrangement usually is on a regional basis, with the com-

[3] See Frederick W. Searby, "Use Your Hidden Cash Resources," *Harvard Business Review*, 46 (March–April 1968), 74–75.

pany choosing regional banks according to its billing patterns. Before determining the regions to be used, a feasibility study is made of the availability of checks that would be deposited under alternative plans. If a company divided the country into five sections on the basis of a feasibility study, it might pick New York City for the Northeast, Atlanta for the Southeast, Chicago for the Midwest, Dallas for the Southwest, and San Francisco for the West Coast.

The company rents a local post-office box and authorizes its bank in each of these cities to pick up remittances in the box. Customers are billed with instructions to mail their remittance to the lock-box. The bank picks up the mail several times a day and deposits the checks in the company's account. The checks are microfilmed for record purposes and cleared for collection. The company receives a deposit slip and a list of payments, together with any material in the envelope. This procedure frees the company from handling and depositing the checks.

The main advantage of a lock-box system is that checks are deposited at banks sooner and become collected balances sooner than if they were processed by the company prior to deposit. In other words, the lag between the time checks are received by the company and the time they actually are deposited at the bank is eliminated. The principal disadvantage of a lock-box arrangement is the cost. The bank provides a number of services additional to the usual clearing of checks and requires compensation for them, usually preferring increased deposits. Because the cost is almost directly proportional to the number of checks deposited, lock-box arrangements usually are not profitable if the average remittance is small.

The appropriate rule for deciding whether or not to use a lock-box system, or, for that matter, concentration banking, is simply to compare the added cost of the more efficient system with the marginal income that can be generated from the released funds. If costs are less than income, the system is profitable; if not, the system is not a profitable undertaking. The degree of profitability depends primarily upon the geographical dispersion of customers, the size of the typical remittance, and the earnings rate on the released funds.

Other procedures

Frequently, firms give special attention to the handling of large remittances so that they may be deposited in a bank as quickly as possible. This special handling may involve personal pickup of these checks or the use of airmail or special delivery. When a small number of remittances account for a large proportion of total deposits, it may be very worthwhile to initiate controls to accelerate the deposit and collection of these large checks. The firm should exercise tight control over interbank transfers of cash and transfers between various units of the company, such as divisions or subsidiaries. Excessive funds may be tied up in various divisions of the firm.

Some companies maintain too many bank accounts, thereby creating unnecessary pockets of idle funds. A company that has an account in every city where it has either a sales office or a production facility might be able to reduce cash balances considerably if it were to eliminate some of these accounts. The banking activities of a sales office can often be handled from a larger account with little loss in service or availability of funds. Even though small accounts may create a degree of goodwill with bankers, they make little sense in the overall cash management of the firm. By closing such unnecessary accounts, a firm may be able to release funds that it then can put to profitable use.

Control of disbursements

In addition to accelerating collections, effective control of disbursements can result in a faster turnover of cash. Whereas the underlying objective of collections is maximum acceleration, the objective in disbursements is to slow them down as much as possible. The combination of fast collections and slow disbursements will result in maximum availability of funds.

For a company with multiple banks, it is important to be able to shift funds quickly to those banks from which disbursements are made, to prevent excessive balances from building up temporarily in a particular bank. Operating procedures for disbursements should be well established. If cash discounts are taken on accounts payable, procedures should aim toward eliminating or minimizing the loss of discounts due to clerical inefficiencies. The timing of payments is important. For maximum use of cash, payments should be made on the due dates, not before and not after.

A company can delay disbursements through the use of drafts. Unlike an ordinary check, the draft is not payable on demand. When it is presented to the issuer's bank for collection, the bank must present it to the issuer for acceptance. The funds then are deposited by the issuing firm to cover payment of the draft. The advantage of the draft arrangement is that it delays the time the firm actually has to have funds on deposit to cover the draft. Consequently, it allows the firm to maintain smaller deposits at its banks.

Another way of maximizing cash availability is "playing the float." In this case, float is the difference between the total dollar amount of checks drawn on a bank account and the amount shown on the bank's books. It is possible, of course, for a company to have a negative balance on its books and a positive bank balance, because checks outstanding have not been collected from the account on which they are drawn. If the size of float can be estimated accurately, bank balances can be reduced and the funds invested to earn a positive return.

As mentioned earlier, optimizing cash availability involves accelerating collections as much as possible and delaying payments as long as is realistically possible. Because delaying payments may damage the firm's credit standing, the resulting cost to the firm must be taken into account. In the future, we can expect to see further improvements in check collection. As we move toward a "checkless society," the time funds remain uncollected will become shorter. In a checkless society where transfers are made entirely through computers, payments would be immediate. There would be no uncollected funds, for one party's account would be debited the instant another's was credited. While the firm's deposits would be collected faster, so too would the checks it wrote. Whether it gains or loses would depend upon the typical float on checks deposited relative to the float for checks written.

Many companies maintain a separate account for payroll disbursements. In order to minimize the balance in this account, one must predict when the payroll checks issued will be presented for payment. If payday falls on a Friday, for example, not all of the checks will be cashed on that day. Consequently, the firm need not have funds on deposit to cover its entire payroll.[4] Even on Monday, some checks will not be presented because of delays in their deposit. Based upon its experience, the firm should be able to construct a distribution of when, on the average, checks are presented for collection. An example is shown in Figure 6-1. With this information, the firm can approximate

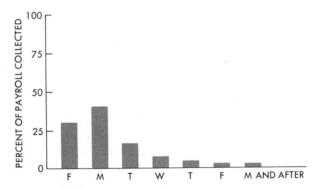

FIG. 6 · 1

Percentage of payroll checks collected

the funds it needs to have on deposit to cover payroll checks. Similar to the payroll account, many firms establish a separate account for dividends. Here too the idea is to predict when such checks will be presented for payment so as to minimize the cash balance in the account.

[4] See James McN. Stancill, *The Management of Working Capital* (Scranton, Pa.: Intext, 1971), pp. 19–22.

We assume that on the basis of the considerations in Chapter 5 and the efficient cash management principles taken up in the last section, the firm has determined a proper level of transactions and precautionary balances. This decision was made in keeping with expected net cash flows, possible deviations of cash flows from expectations, the maturity structure of the firm's debt, the availability of borrowing, the efficiency of cash management, and, finally, the risk preferences of management. Given the level of transactions and precautionary balances, which we identify as cash and marketable securities, we must determine an optimal split between the two assets. Our concentration will be on determining an optimal level of cash which, in turn, determines the optimal level of marketable securities under our assumption that the total level of liquid assets has been determined.

The cash balance maintained by the firm should be determined in keeping with one of two constraints. The first is the compensating balance requirement of the commercial bank(s) with which the firm maintains its account(s). The second constraint is self-imposed, and it depends upon expected cash flows, possible deviations in these flows, the interest rate on marketable securities, and the fixed cost associated with a security transaction. In the next section, we consider the first of these constraints, while in the following section we explore the self-imposed constraint. We will see that the optimal cash balance is the greater of the two constraints.

Compensating balances

Establishing a minimum level of cash balances depends in part upon the compensating balance requirements of banks. These requirements are set on the basis of the profitability of the accounts. A bank begins by calculating the average collected balances shown on the bank's books over a period of time. As brought out before, this balance often is higher than the cash balance shown on the company's books. From the average collected balance, the bank subtracts the percentage of deposits it is required to maintain at the Federal Reserve, around 17 percent. The residual constitutes the earnings base on which income is generated. Total income is determined by multiplying the base times the earnings rate of the bank. This rate fluctuates in keeping with money market conditions.

Once the income from an account is determined, the cost of the account must be computed. Most banks have a schedule of costs on a per

item basis for such transactions as transfers and processing checks. The account is analyzed for a typical month during which all transactions are multiplied by the per item cost and totaled. If the total cost is less than the total income from the account, the account is profitable; if more, it is unprofitable. The minimum average level of cash balances required is the point at which the account is just profitable. Because banks differ in the earnings rate they use as well as in their costs and method of account analysis, the determination of compensating balances varies. The firm, therefore, may be wise to shop around and determine the bank that requires the lowest compensating balances for a given level of activity. If a firm has a lending arrangement with a bank, the firm may well be required to maintain balances in excess of those required to compensate the bank for the activity in its account. Because we consider compensation for a lending arrangement in Chapter 10, no discussion of this form of compensation will be undertaken at this time.

In recent years, there has been a trend toward paying cash for services rendered by a bank instead of maintaining compensating balances. The advantage to the firm is that it may be able to earn more on funds used for compensating balances than the fee for the services. The higher the interest rate in the money markets, the greater the opportunity cost of compensating balances and the greater the advantage of service charges. It is an easy matter to determine if the firm would be better off with service charges as opposed to maintaining compensating balances. One simply compares the charges with the earnings on the funds released. Most banks resist placing normal services, such as clearing checks, on a fee basis. Nevertheless, an increasing number of bank services are being offered on such a basis.

The balances maintained at a bank and the services the bank performs should be analyzed carefully. If deposits are more than compensating, funds may be tied up unnecessarily. However, we must investigate the self-imposed constraint in the next section in order to determine if cash is truly excessive. It may well be that a firm should maintain a cash balance in excess of that required to compensate the bank.

Models for determining minimum cash

The purpose of this section is to provide a means for determining the minimum cash balance, ignoring for the moment compensating balance requirements imposed by a bank. One simple model for determining an optimal split between cash and marketable securities is the economic order quantity formula used in inventory management. (See Chapter 8.)

Inventory model

Under conditions of certainty, the economic order quantity formula may be used to determine the optimal average amount of transactions balances to maintain. This model provides a useful conceptual foundation for the cash management problem.[5] In the model, the carrying cost of holding cash—namely, the interest foregone on marketable securities—is balanced against the fixed cost of transferring marketable securities to cash, or vice versa. The model is illustrated by the sawtoothed lines in Figure 6-2.

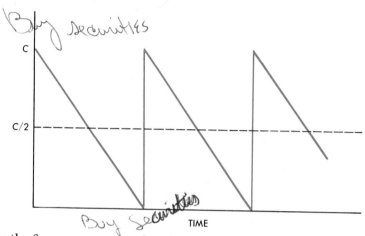

FIG. 6 · 2

Inventory model applied to cash management

In the figure, we assume that the firm has a steady demand for cash over some period of time, say one month. The firm obtains cash during this period by selling marketable securities. Suppose it starts out with C dollars in cash and when this amount is expended, it replenishes it by selling C dollars of marketable securities. Thus, the transfer of funds from securities to cash occurs whenever cash touches zero. If a cushion is desired or if lead times are necessary to effect a transaction, the threshold for initiating a transfer can be higher. The principle is the same regardless of whether or not a cushion is used.

The objective is to specify the value of C that minimizes total costs —that is, the sum of the fixed costs associated with transfers and the opportunity cost of earnings foregone by holding cash balances. These costs can be expressed as

$$b\left(\frac{T}{C}\right) + i\left(\frac{C}{2}\right) \qquad (6\text{-}1)$$

[5]The model was first applied to the problem of cash management by William J. Baumol, "The Transactions Demand for Cash: An Inventory Theoretic Approach," *Quarterly Journal of Economics,* 46 (November 1952), 545–56. It has been further refined and developed by a number of others.

where b is the fixed cost of a transaction that is assumed to be independent of the amount transferred, T is the total demand for cash over the period of time involved, and i is the interest rate on marketable securities for the period involved (assumed to be constant). T/C represents the number of transactions during the period, and when it is multiplied by the fixed cost per transaction, we obtain the total fixed cost for the period. $C/2$ represents the average cash balance, and when it is multiplied by the interest rate, we obtain the earnings foregone by virtue of holding cash. The larger the C, the larger the average cash balance, $C/2$, and the smaller the average investment in securities and earnings from these securities. Thus, there is a higher opportunity cost of interest income foregone. However, the larger the C, the fewer the transfers, T/C, that occur, and the lower the transfer costs. The object is to balance these two costs so that total costs are minimized.

The optimal level of C is found to be

$$C^* = \sqrt{\frac{2bT}{i}} \qquad (6\text{-}2)$$

Thus, cash will be demanded in relation to the square root of the dollar volume of cash payments. This phenomenon implies that as the level of cash payments increases, the amount of transaction cash the firm needs to hold increases by a lesser percentage. In other words, economies of scale are possible. The implication is that the firm should try to consolidate individual bank accounts into as few as possible in order to realize economies of scale in cash management. We see from Eq. (6-2) that C^* varies directly with order cost, b, and inversely with the interest rate on marketable securities, i.[6] However, the relationship is dampened by the square-root sign in both cases.

To illustrate the use of the economic order quantity (EOQ) formula, consider a firm with estimated cash payments of $6 million for a one-month period where these payments are expected to be steady over the period. The fixed cost per transaction is $100 and the interest rate on marketable securities is 6 percent per annum, or 0.5 percent for the one-month period. Therefore,

$$C = \sqrt{\frac{2bT}{i}} = \sqrt{\frac{2(100)(6,000,000)}{.005}} = \$489,898$$

[6] For a study involving the effect changing interest rates have on the relative level of cash held by the firm, see Morris Budin and Robert J. Van Handel, "A Rule-of-Thumb Theory of Cash Holdings by Firms," *Journal of Financial and Quantitative Analysis*, 10 (March 1975), 85–108.

Thus, the optimal transaction size is \$489,898 and the average cash balance \$489,898/2 = \$244,949. This means the firm should make \$6,000,000/\$489,898 = 12 plus transactions of marketable securities to cash during the month.

It is useful now to consider in more detail the two costs involved. The interest rate is fairly straightforward; it simply represents the rate of interest on securities that would be sold to replenish cash. In most cases, this is the rate on short-term money market instruments and not the average rate of return on all marketable securities. The fixed cost associated with a transaction is more difficult to measure because it consists of both explicit and implied costs. Included are the fixed component of transaction costs, the time it takes the treasurer or other official to place an order with an investment banker, the time he consumes in recording the transaction, the secretarial time needed to type the transaction and the purchase order, the time needed to record the transaction on the books, and the time needed to record the safekeeping notification. Given a number of transactions, the procedures for placing an order can be streamlined to reduce the average fixed cost per transaction. Nevertheless, these costs do exist and too often are either overlooked or underestimated.

One limitation to the use of the EOQ model is that cash payments are assumed to be steady over the period of time specified. Only if this assumption is a reasonable approximation of the situation is the model applicable. When cash payments become lumpy, it may be appropriate to reduce the period for which calculations are made so that expenditures during the period are relatively steady. The EOQ model can be applied also when receipts are continuous and there are discontinuous large payments. The decision to be made then would be the optimal purchase size of marketable securities.

Another limitation to the use of the model is that cash payments are seldom completely predictable. For modest degrees of uncertainty, one need only add a cushion so that a transfer from marketable securities to cash is triggered at some level of cash above zero. In general, the EOQ model gives the financial manager a benchmark for judging the optimal cash balance. It does not have to be used as a precise rule governing his behavior. The model merely suggests what would be the optimal balance under a set of assumptions. The actual balance may be more if the assumptions do not entirely hold.

Stochastic models

In those cases in which the uncertainty of cash payments is large, the EOQ model may not be applicable and other models should be used to determine optimal behavior. If cash balances fluctuate randomly, one can apply control theory to the problem. Assume that the demand for cash is stochastic and unknown in advance. We then can set control limits such that when cash reaches an upper limit a transfer of cash to marketable securities is consummated, and when it hits a lower limit a transfer from marketable securities to cash is triggered. As long as the cash balance stays between these limits, no transactions take place.

How the limits are set depends in part upon the fixed costs associated with a securities transaction and the opportunity cost of holding cash. As before, we assume these costs are known and that the fixed cost of selling a marketable security is the same as that for buying it. In essence, we want to satisfy the demand for cash at the lowest possible total cost. Although there are a number of applications of control theory to the problem, we take up a relatively simple one. The Miller-Orr model specifies two control limits—h dollars as an upper bound and zero dollars as a lower bound.[7] The model is illustrated in Figure 6-3. When the cash balance touches the upper bound, $h - z$ dollars of marketable securities are bought and the new balance becomes z dollars. When the cash balance touches zero, z dollars of marketable securities are sold and the new balance again becomes z. This is illustrated in Figure 6-3. The minimum bound can be set at some amount

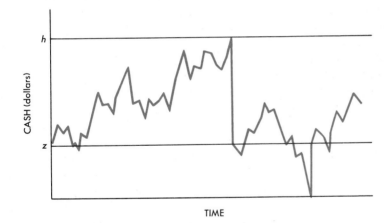

FIG. 6 · 3
Miller-Orr Model
using control limits

higher than zero and h and z would move up in the figure. However, we will use zero as the lower bound for purposes of illustration, recognizing that a firm can set the lower bound at some positive amount. This obviously would be necessary if there were delays in transfer.

The solution for the optimal values of h and z depends not only upon the fixed and opportunity costs but also upon the degree of likely

[7] See Merton H. Miller and Daniel Orr, "A Model of the Demand for Money by Firms," *Quarterly Journal of Economics*, 80 (August 1966), 413—35.

fluctuation in cash balances. The optimal value of z, the return-to-point for security transactions, is

$$z = \sqrt[3]{\frac{3b\sigma^2}{4i}} \tag{6-3}$$

where

b = fixed cost associated with a security transaction

σ^2 = variance of daily net cash flows (a measure of the dispersion of these flows)

i = interest rate per day on marketable securities

The optimal value of h is simply $3z$. With these control limits set, the model minimizes the total costs (fixed and opportunity) of cash management. Again, the critical assumption is that cash flows are random. The average cash balance cannot be determined exactly in advance, but it is approximately $(z + h)/3$. As experience unfolds, however, it can be easily calculated.

Optimal level of cash balances

We have presented two models for determining an optimal level of cash balances under the self-imposed constraint.[8] The EOQ model assumes that the demand for cash is predictable, while the control limit model assumes it is random. For most firms, the first model is more applicable than the second owing to near-term cash flows being relatively predictable. When there is only moderate uncertainty, the EOQ model can be modified to incorporate a cushion. The second model serves primarily as a benchmark for determining cash balances under a rather extreme assumption as to their predictability. The average cash balance generally will be much higher when this model is used as opposed to the EOQ one. Thus, when cash balances of a firm are higher than those dictated by a control-limit model and the demand for cash is relatively predictable, we know cash is too high.

The optimal average cash balance will be the higher of the compensating balance requirements of a bank and that suggested by a cash-marketable securities model. In most cases, the former will exceed the latter. However, when the fixed costs of a security transaction are high, the opportunity cost of holding cash is low, and/or cash flows are sub-

---

[8] For an analysis of the potential savings arising from the use of such models vis-à-vis simple heuristic cash management rules, see Hans G. Daellenbach, "Are Cash Management Optimization Models Worthwhile?" *Journal of Financial and Quantitative Analysis,* 9 (September 1974), 607–26. Only if fixed transaction costs are relatively large does Daellenbach find the use of optimization models to be worthwhile.

ject to great fluctuation, the average cash balance suggested by a model may be higher than that required by the bank. Therefore, average balances in excess of those considered compensating should be maintained.

INVESTMENT IN MARKETABLE SECURITIES

In the models presented in the preceding section, we assumed the yield on marketable securities was known with certainty and, accordingly, there was no risk of fluctuations in market price. In this section, we explore the types of marketable securities available to a company as near-money investments, allowing for varying yields and for fluctuations in market price. Regardless of whether the decision to invest excess funds in marketable securities is made according to some model or strictly by management judgment, someone must decide what type of investment to make. Where formerly corporations invested primarily in short-term government securities, they now seek a more varied portfolio in order to maximize investment income. In the remainder of this section, we describe certain important money-market instruments that serve the short-term investment needs of corporations.

Treasury securities

U.S. Treasury obligations constitute the largest segment of the money markets. The principal securities issued are bills, tax-anticipation bills, notes, and bonds. Treasury bills are auctioned weekly by the Treasury with maturities of 91 days and 182 days. In addition, one-year bills are sold periodically. Treasury bills carry no coupon but are sold on a discount basis. These securities are extremely popular with companies as short-term investments, in part because of the large amount outstanding. The market is very active, and the transaction costs involved in the sale of Treasury bills in the secondary market are small.

The original maturity on Treasury notes is one to ten years, whereas the original maturity on Treasury bonds is over ten years. With the passage of time, of course, a number of these securities have maturities of less than one year and serve the needs of short-term investors. Notes and bonds are coupon issues, and there is an active market for them. Overall, Treasury securities are the safest and most marketable investments. Therefore, they provide the lowest yield for a given maturity of the various instruments we consider.

Agency securities

Obligations of various agencies of the federal government are guaranteed by the agency issuing the security and not usually by the U.S. government as such. Principal agencies issuing securities are the Federal Housing Administration and the Government National Mortgage Association (Ginnie Mae). In addition, there are a number of government-sponsored, quasi-private agencies. The securities of these agencies are not guaranteed by the federal government, nor is there any stated "moral" obligation. In final analysis, however, there is an implied backing. It would be hard to imagine the federal government allowing them to fail. Major government-sponsored agencies include the Banks for Cooperatives, Federal Home Loan Banks, Federal Intermediate Credit Banks, Federal Land Banks, and Federal National Mortgage Association (Fannie Mae).

Although agency issues are being increasingly accepted by the investment community, they still provide a yield advantage over Treasury securities of the same maturity. These securities have a fairly high degree of marketability; they are sold in the secondary market through the same security dealers as are Treasury securities. With the sharp increase in agency financing in recent years, marketability has been enhanced considerably. Maturities range from a month up to approximately fifteen years. However, about one-half of the securities outstanding mature in less than a year.

Bankers' acceptances

Bankers' acceptances are drafts that are accepted by banks, and they are used in the financing of foreign and domestic trade. The credit-worthiness of bankers' acceptances is judged relative to the bank accepting the draft, not the drawer. Acceptances generally have maturities of less than 180 days and are of very high quality. They are traded in an over-the-counter market dominated by five principal dealers. The rates on bankers' acceptances tend to be slightly higher than rates on Treasury bills of like maturity; and both are sold on a discount basis.

Commercial paper

Commercial paper consists of short-term unsecured promissory notes issued by finance companies and certain industrial concerns. Commercial paper can be sold either directly or through dealers. A number of large sales finance companies have found it profitable, because of the volume, to sell their paper directly to investors, thus bypassing dealers. Among companies selling paper on this basis are the C.I.T. Financial Corporation, Ford Motor Credit Company, General Motors Acceptance Corporation (GMAC), and Sears Roebuck Acceptance Corporation.

Paper sold through dealers is issued by industrial companies and smaller finance companies. The dealer organization for commercial paper is dominated by three firms. Overall, the total volume of paper sold through dealers is considerably less than the total volume sold directly. Dealers screen potential issuers very carefully as to their credit-worthiness. In a sense, the dealer stands behind the paper he places with investors.

Rates on commercial paper are somewhat higher than rates on Treasury bills of the same maturity and about the same as the rates available on bankers' acceptances. Paper sold directly, however, generally commands a lower yield than paper sold through dealers. Usually, commercial paper is sold on a discount basis, and maturities generally range from 30 to 270 days. Most paper is held to maturity, for there is essentially no secondary market. However, direct sellers of commercial paper will often repurchase the paper on request. Arrangements may also be made through dealers for repurchase of paper sold through them. Commercial paper is sold only in fairly large denominations, usually of at least $25,000.

Repurchase agreements

In an effort to tap new sources of financing, government security dealers offer repurchase agreements to corporations. The repurchase agreement, or "repo" as it is called, is the sale of short-term securities by the dealer to the investor whereby the dealer agrees to repurchase the securities at a specified future time. The investor receives a given yield while he holds the security. The length of the holding period itself is tailored to the needs of the investor. Thus, repurchase agreements give the investor a great deal of flexibility with respect to maturity. Rates on repurchase agreements are related to the rates on Treasury bills, federal funds, and loans to government security dealers by commercial banks. There is little marketability to the instrument, but the usual maturity is only a few days. Because the instrument involved is a U.S. Treasury security, there is no default risk.

Negotiable certificates of deposit

Negotiable time certificates of deposit are a short-term investment that originated in 1961. The certificate (CD) is evidence of the deposit of funds at a commercial bank for a specified period of time and at a specified rate of interest. The most common denomination is $100,000, so its appeal is limited to large investors. Money-market banks quote rates on CDs; these rates are changed periodically in keeping with changes in other money-market rates. The maximum rate that banks are allowed to pay, however, is regulated by the Federal Reserve System under Regulation Q. Yields on CDs are greater than those on Treasury bills and repos and about the same as those on bankers' acceptances and commercial paper. Original maturities of CDs generally range from 30 to 360 days. A fair secondary market has developed for the CDs of the large money-market banks, so such CDs are marketable. Default risk is that of the bank failing, a possibility that is low in most cases.

Portfolio management

The decision to invest excess cash in marketable securities involves not only the amount to invest but also the type of security in which to invest. To some extent, the two decisions are interdependent. Both should be based upon an evaluation of expected net cash flows and the certainty of these cash flows. If future cash-flow patterns are known with reasonable certainty, the portfolio may be arranged so that securities will be maturing on approximately the dates when the funds will be needed. Such a cash-flow pattern gives the firm a great deal of flexibility in maximizing the average return on the entire portfolio, for it is unlikely that significant amounts of securities will have to be sold unexpectedly.

If future cash flows are fairly uncertain, the most important characteristics of a security become its marketability and risk with respect to fluctuations in market value. Treasury bills and short-term repos are perhaps best suited for the emergency liquidity needs of the firm. Higher yields can be achieved by investing in longer-term, less-marketable securities with greater default risk. Although the firm should always be concerned with marketability, some possibility of loss of principal is tolerable provided the expected return is high enough. Thus, the firm faces the familiar tradeoff between risk and return.

The larger the security portfolio, the more chance there is for specialization and economies of operation. A large enough security portfolio may justify a staff whose sole responsibility is managing the portfolio. Such a staff can undertake research, plan diversification, keep abreast of market conditions, and continually analyze and improve the firm's position. When investment is made a specialized function of the firm, the number of different securities considered for investment is likely to be diverse. Moreover, continual effort can be devoted to achieving the highest yield possible in keeping with the cash needs of the firm. Trading techniques in such a firm tend to be very sophisticated. For companies with smaller security positions, however, there may be no economic justification for a staff. Indeed, a single individual may handle investments on a part-time basis. For this type of company, the diversity of securities in the portfolio will probably be limited.

SUMMARY

In the management of cash, we should attempt to accelerate collections and handle disbursements so that a maximum of cash is available. Collections can be accelerated by means of concentration banking, a lock-box system, and certain other procedures. Disbursements should be handled so as to give maximum transfer flexibility and the optimum timing of payments.

Given the level of liquid assets, the determination of which was discussed in Chapter 5, it is necessary to determine on optimal split between cash and marketable securities. The optimal level of cash, which in turn determines the optimal level of marketable securities, is the greater of the compensating balance requirement of the bank and the level suggested by an appropriate model. The models examined were the inventory model applied to cash management and a control limit model. In both, the appropriate level of cash balances depends upon expected cash flows, the fixed cost of a securities transaction, and the interest foregone in holding cash.

There are a number of marketable securities in which the firm can invest. Specific securities considered included Treasury securities, government agency securities, bankers' acceptances, commercial paper, repurchase agreements, and certificates of deposit. As discussed, these securities differ somewhat in yield, maturity, marketability, and default risk.

QUESTIONS

1. Explain the concept of concentration banking.

2. Explain how the lock-box system can improve the efficiency of cash management.

3. Money-market instruments are used as an investment vehicle for idle cash. Discuss the primary criterion for asset selection in investing temporary idle cash.

4. The assumed objective of a business firm is to maximize the wealth of stockholders, which implies that priorities should be assigned to assets on the

basis of profitability. Reconcile this statement with the fact that corporations keep 5 to 10 percent of assets in idle cash.

5. Discuss the impact of lock-box banking on corporate cash balances.

6. Explain the application of the economic order quantity model to managing cash balances.

7. Contrast the Miller-Orr model for determining cash balances with the economic order quantity model.

8. Discuss the primary criterion for assigning priorities to assets that will serve as investment vehicles for a firm's temporary excess liquidity.

9. If the general level of interest rates is expected to fall, what maturity of securities should the firm invest in? If interest rates are expected to rise?

10. How can diversification reduce the risk of investment in marketable securities? What are the limits of such risk reduction?

PROBLEMS

1. The Zindler Company currently has a centralized billing system. Payments are made by all customers to the central billing location. It requires, on the average, four days for customers' mailed payments to reach the central location. Further, an additional one and one-half days are required to process payments before the deposit can be made. The firm has a daily average collection of $500,000.

   The company has recently considered the possibility of initiating a lock-box system. It has been estimated that such a system would reduce the time required for customers' mailed payments to reach the receipt location by two and one-half days. Further, the processing time could be reduced by an additional day, because each lock-box bank would pick up mailed deposits twice daily.

   (a) Determine the reduction in cash balances that can be achieved through the use of a lock-box system.

   (b) Determine the opportunity cost of the present system, assuming a 5 percent return on short-term instruments.

   (c) If the annual cost of the lock-box system were $75,000, should such a system be initiated?

2. The List Company, which can earn 7 percent on money-market instruments, currently has a lock-box arrangement with a New Orleans bank for its southern customers. The bank handles $3 million a day in return for a compensating balance of $2 million.

   (a) The List Company has discovered that it could divide the southern region into a southwestern region (with $1 million a day in collections, which could be handled by a Dallas bank for a $1 million compensating balance) and a southeastern region (with $2 million a day in collections, which could be handled by an Atlanta bank for a $2 million compensating balance). In each case, collections would be one-half day quicker than with the New Orleans arrangement. What would be the annual savings (or cost) of dividing the southern region?

(b) In an effort to retain the business, the New Orleans bank has offered to handle the collections strictly on a fee basis (no compensating balance). What would be the maximum fee the New Orleans bank could $105,000 charge and still retain List's business?

3. A broker suggests that your corporation move its temporary excess liquidity of $10 million from Treasury bills, which are yielding 6 percent, to AT&T preferred $4/yr. dividend stock selling for $60.

(a) Assuming the corporate tax rate is 48 percent and there is an 85 percent exclusion from taxes for dividends, compute the after-tax yield of each of the alternatives.

(b) Would you follow your broker's suggestion? Why or why not?

4. The Schriver Company expects to have $1 million in cash outlays for next year. The firm believes that it will face an opportunity interest rate of 5 percent and will incur a cost of $100 each time it borrows (or withdraws). Cash outlays are expected to be steady over the year. Using the inventory model:

(a) Determine the optimal borrowing or withdrawal lot size for the Schriver Company.

(b) What is the total cost for the use of cash needed for transactions 362.00 demand?

(c) What will be the cash cycle for the firm (velocity)? 63,246 23.1

(d) What will be the average cash balance for the firm? ½ of a

5. Assume that the Schriver Company (Problem 4) began the year with $1 million in cash.

(a) How much would initially be invested in securities?

(b) How much would be invested in securities after 231 days?

6. The Verloom Berloop Tulip Bulb Company has experienced a stochastic demand for its product, with the result that cash balances fluctuate randomly. The standard deviation of daily net cash flows, σ, is $1,000. The company wishes to make the transfer of funds from cash to marketable securities and vice versa as automatic as possible. It has heard that this can be done by imposing upper- and lower-bound control limits. The current interest rate on marketable securities is 6 percent. The fixed cost associated with each transfer is $100, and transfers are instantaneous.

(b) What are the optimal upper- and lower-bound control limits? (Assume a 360-day year.)

(b) What happens at these control limits?

7. Devise a profit-maximizing maturity schedule for investments in marketable securities if the XYZ Corporation expects the following monthly cash balances (net of transactions needs). The precautionary demand for cash is $100,000.

January	$300,000	July	$400,000
February	500,000	August	300,000
March	600,000	September	200,000
April	500,000	October	200,000
May	700,000	November	100,000
June	800,000	December	100,000

Why might such a schedule *not* be in the best interest of the shareholders?

An Analytical Record of Yields and Yield Spreads. New York: Salomon Brothers, 1976.

ARCHER, STEPHEN H., "A Model for the Determination of Firm Cash Balances," *Journal of Financial and Quantitative Analysis,* 1 (March 1966), 1–11.

BAUMOL, WILLIAM J., "The Transactions Demand for Cash: An Inventory Theoretic Approach," *Quarterly Journal of Economics,* 65 (November 1952), 545–56.

BUDIN, MORRIS, and **ROBERT J. VAN HANDEL,** "Rule-of-Thumb Theory of Cash Holdings by Firm," *Journal of Financial and Quantitative Analysis,* 10 (March 1975), 85–108.

DAELLENBACH, HANS G., "Are Cash Management Optimization Models Worthwhile?" *Journal of Financial and Quantitative Analysis,* 9 (September 1974), 607–26.

FROST, PETER A., "Banking Services, Minimum Cash Balances and the Firm's Demand for Money," *Journal of Finance,* 25 (December 1970), 1029–39.

MEHTA, DILEEP R., *Working Capital Management,* Chapters 6–8. Englewood Cliffs, N.J.: Prentice-Hall, 1974.

MILLER, MERTON H., and **DANIEL ORR,** "The Demand for Money by Firms: Extension of Analytic Results," *Journal of Finance,* 23 (December 1968), 735–59.

———, "A Model of the Demand for Money by Firms," *Quarterly Journal of Economics,* 80 (August 1966), 413–35.

ORGLER, YAIR E., *Cash Management.* Belmont, Calif.: Wadsworth, 1970.

REED, WARD L., JR., "Cash—The Hidden Asset," *Financial Executive,* 38 (November 1970), 54–63.

SEARBY, FREDERICK W., "Use Your Hidden Cash Resources," *Harvard Business Review,* 46 (March–April 1968), 74–75.

SMITH, KEITH V., *Management of Working Capital,* Section 2. New York: West Publishing, 1974.

STANCILL, JAMES McN., *The Management of Working Capital,* Chapters 2 and 3. Scranton, Pa.: Intext, 1971.

VAN HORNE, JAMES C., *The Function and Analysis of Capital Market Rates.* Englewood Cliffs, N. J.: Prentice-Hall, 1970.

———, "Interest-Rate Risk and the Term Structure of Interest Rates," *Journal of Political Economy,* 73 (August 1965), 344–51.

Accounts Receivable 7

As was discussed in Chapter 5, the investment of funds in accounts receivable involves a tradeoff between profitability and risk. The optimum investment is determined by comparing the benefits to be derived from a particular level of investment with the costs of maintaining that level. These costs involve not only the funds tied up in receivables but losses from accounts that do not pay. The latter arise from extending credit too leniently. The purpose of this chapter is to examine the key variables involved in managing receivables efficiently and to show how they can be varied to obtain the optimal investment. We consider first the credit and collection policies of the firm as a whole and then discuss credit and collection procedures for the individual account.

Actually, the two facets are closely related. For example, credit policy involves a tradeoff between the profits on sales that give rise to receivables on the one hand and the cost of carrying these receivables plus bad-debt losses on the other. Credit analysis is instrumental in determining the amount of credit risk to be accepted. In turn, the amount of risk accepted affects the slowness of receivables, and the resulting investment in receivables, as well as the amount of bad-debt losses. Collection procedures also affect these factors. Thus, the credit and collection procedures of the firm are essential to the firm's overall credit and collection policies. For expository purposes, however, it is useful to consider the two facets separately, keeping in mind their interrelationship.

Although the level of accounts receivable is affected importantly by the influence of economic conditions on credit sales, it is determined also by policy decisions. Economic conditions, of course, are largely beyond the control of the financial manager. As with other current assets, however, he can vary the level of receivables in keeping with the tradeoff between profitability and risk. By lowering quality standards and increasing the level of receivables, for example, the company hopes to stimulate demand which, in turn, should lead to higher profits. However, there is a cost to carrying the additional receivables as well as a greater risk of bad-debt losses. It is this tradeoff we wish to examine.

The policy variables we consider include the quality of the trade accounts accepted, the length of the credit period, the cash discount given, any special terms given, such as seasonal datings, and the collection program of the firm. Together, these elements largely determine the average collection period and the proportion of bad-debt losses. We analyze each element in turn, holding constant certain of the others as well as all exogenous variables that affect the average collection period and the percentage of bad-debt losses. In addition, we assume that the evaluation of risk is sufficiently standardized that degrees of risk for different accounts can be compared objectively.

Credit standards

Credit policy can have a significant influence upon sales. If competitors extend credit liberally and we do not, our policy may have a dampening effect upon the marketing effort. Trade credit is one of many factors that influence the demand for a firm's product. Consequently, the degree to which trade credit can promote demand depends upon what other factors are being employed. In theory, the firm should lower its quality standard for accounts accepted as long as the profitability of sales generated exceeds the added costs of the receivables. What are the costs of relaxing credit standards? One type of cost is the enlarged credit department and the clerical expenses involved in checking additional accounts and servicing the added volume of receivables. We assume that these costs are deducted from the profitability of additional sales to give a net profitability figure for computational purposes. Another cost comes from the increased probability of bad-debt losses. However, we postpone consideration of this cost to a subsequent section; we assume for now that there are no bad-debt losses.

Finally, there is the cost of the additional investment in receivables, resulting from (1) increased sales, and (2) a slower average collection period. If new customers are attracted by the relaxed credit standards, collecting from these customers is likely to be slower than collecting from existing customers. In addition, a more liberal extension of credit may cause certain existing customers to be less conscientious about paying their bills on time. Those who decide credit policy must consider this possibility.

To determine the profitability of a more liberal extension of credit, we must know the profitability of additional sales, the added demand for products arising from the relaxed credit standards, the increased slowness of the average collection period, and the required return on investment. Suppose a firm's product sells for $10 a unit, of which $7 represents variable costs before taxes, including credit department costs. Current annual sales are $2.4 million, represented entirely by credit sales, and the average total cost per unit at that volume is $9 before taxes. The firm is considering a more liberal extension of credit, which will result in a slowing in the average collection period from one to two months. However, existing customers are not expected to alter their payment habits. The relaxation in credit standards is expected to produce a 25 percent increase in sales, to $3 million annually.[1] The $600,000 increase represents 60,000 additional units if we assume that the price per unit stays the same. Finally, assume that the firm's required return on investment in receivables is 20 percent before taxes.

Given this information, our evaluation is reduced to a tradeoff between the added profitability on the additional sales and the required return on the additional investment in receivables; and we are able to make the calculations shown in Table 7-1. Inasmuch as the profitability on additional sales, $180,000, exceeds the required return on the additional investment, $42,000, the firm would be well advised to relax its credit standards. An optimal credit policy would involve extending trade credit more liberally until the marginal profitability on additional sales equals the required return on the additional investment in receivables necessary to generate those sales. However, as we take on poorer credit risks we also increase the risk of the firm, as depicted by the variance of the expected cash-flow stream. This increase in risk is largely reflected in additional bad-debt losses, a subject we deal with shortly.

Obviously, there are practical problems to consider. One assumption is that we have excess capacity and can produce 60,000 additional units at a variable cost of $7 per unit. After some point we no longer are able to meet additional demand with existing plant and would need to add plant. This occurrence would necessitate a change in anal-

---

[1]In estimating the effect of a change in credit policy on demand, it is important to take into account the reaction of competitors to this change. Their reaction will affect demand over the long run.

ysis, for we now would have a large block of incremental costs. One implication of all of this is that the firm should vary its credit quality standards in keeping with the level of production. As capacity is approached, the firm may wish to tighten credit standards. If the firm operates at a level below capacity, the lowering of credit quality standards becomes more attractive, all other things the same. Implied also in our analysis is that the conditions described will be permanent. That is, increased demand as a function of lowering credit quality standards as well as price and cost figures will remain unchanged. If the increase in sales that results from a change in credit policy were a one-shot as opposed to a continuing occurrence, we would need to modify our analysis accordingly.

TABLE 7 · 1

Profitability versus Required Return

Profitability of additional sales	= $3 × 60,000 units = $180,000
Present level of receivables	= (Annual sales/Receivable turnover) $2.4 million/12 = $200,000
Level of receivables after change in credit policy	= $3 million/6 = $500,000
Additional receivables	= $300,000
Additional investment in receivables	= Additional receivables × Variable costs as a percent of sales. $300,000 × 0.7 = $210,000
Required return on additional investment	= 0.20 × $210,000 = $42,000

Credit terms

Credit period.   Credit terms involve both the length of the credit period and the discount given. The terms "2/10, net 30" mean that a 2 percent discount is given if the bill is paid before the tenth day after the date of invoice; payment is due by the thirtieth day. The credit period, then, is thirty days. Although the customs of the industry frequently dictate the terms given, the credit period is another means by which a firm may be able to affect product demand—hoping to increase demand by extending the credit period. As before, the tradeoff is between the profitability of additional sales and the required return on the additional investment in receivables. Assume for the purpose of illustration that our example involves lengthening the credit period from thirty to sixty days instead of relaxing credit standards. Assume also that by lengthening the credit period, the firm expects sales to increase by 25 percent, and the average collection period to increase from one to two months. As the quality of account being accepted is the same, we assume that there is no change in bad-debt losses—in other words, that there are no losses. The analysis is the same as in Table 7-1. As seen, such a policy would be advantageous to the company because the profitability on additional sales—$180,000—exceeds the required return on the additional investment in receivables—$42,000.

Discount given and the discount period.   Varying the discount involves an attempt to speed up the payment of receivables. To be sure, the discount also may have an effect upon demand and upon bad-debt losses. However, we assume that the discount offered is not regarded as a means of cutting price and thereby affecting demand, and that the discount offered does not affect the amount of bad-debt losses. Holding constant these factors, we must determine whether a speedup in collections would more than offset the cost of an increase in the discount. If it would, the present discount policy should be changed.

Suppose, for example, that the firm has annual credit sales of $3 million and an average collection period of two months, and that the sales terms are net 45 days, with no discount given. Assume further that the annual turnover of receivables is six times. Consequently, the average receivable balance is $500,000. Now, suppose that by instigating terms of 2/10, net 45, the average collection period is reduced to one month and that 50 percent of the customers (in dollar volume) take advantage of the 2 percent discount. The opportunity cost of the discount to the firm is .02 × 0.5 × $3 million, or $30,000 annually. However, the turnover of receivables has improved to twelve times a year, so that average receivables are reduced from $500,000 to $250,000.

Thus, the firm realizes $250,000 from accelerated collections. The value of the funds released is their opportunity cost. If we assume a 20 percent rate of return, the opportunity saving is $50,000. In this case the opportunity saving arising from a speedup in collections is greater than the cost of the discount. Consequently, the firm should adopt a 2 percent discount. If the speedup in collections had not resulted in sufficient opportunity savings to offset the cost of discount, the discount policy would not be changed. It is possible, of course, that discounts other than 2 percent may result in an even greater difference between the opportunity saving and the cost of the discount.

In addition to the size of the discount offered, the length of the discount period also may affect the average collection period. Here, the effect is not as clear as before. When a firm lengthens the discount period, two forces influence the average collection period. If the credit period is held constant, certain customers will be tempted to take the discount where previously they did not do so. This practice will tend to shorten the average collection period. On the other hand, customers who have been taking the discount and paying at the end of the discount period now will postpone payment until the end of the new discount period, thereby lengthening the average collection period. Whether the first force dominates the second will depend upon the mix of payment habits of the firm's customers. Given estimates of the likely effect of a change in the discount period on the average collection period, the firm can balance this effect with the increased dollar cost associated with more customers taking the discount. For all practical purposes, the discount period is variable within only a narrow range. The minimum period for mailing invoices and receipt of checks is about ten days. To increase it significantly beyond ten days defeats its purpose. In reality, then, the discount period is not an important decision variable.

Default risk

In the above examples, we assumed no bad-debt losses. Our concern in this section is not only with the slowness of collection but also with the portion of the receivables defaulting. Different credit policies will involve both of these factors. Suppose that we are considering the present credit policy (sales of $2,400,000) together with two new ones and that these policies are expected to produce the following results:

	Present Policy	Policy A	Policy B
Additional demand (percentage)	0	25	35
Average collection period	1 month	2 months	3 months
Percentage of default losses	1	3	6

We assume that after six months an account is turned over to a collection agency and that, on the average, 1 percent of the total receivable volume under the present credit policy is never received by the firm, 3 percent is never received under policy A, and 6 percent is never received under policy B.

If we go through the same type of calculations as in the earlier example, we obtain the results shown in Table 7-2 for policies A and B. The profitability of the two credit policies in relation to the required return on investment can be summarized as follows:

	Policy A	Policy B
Profitability of additional sales less additional bad-debt losses, present policy to policy A	$114,000	
Profitability of additional sales less additional bad-debt losses, policy A to policy B		$(32,400)
Required return on additional investment	42,000	43,400
	$72,000	$(75,800)

Consequently, we would want to adopt policy *A* but would not want to go so far in relaxing our credit standards as policy *B*. As we see, the marginal benefit is positive in moving from the present policy to policy *A* but negative in going from policy *A* to policy *B*. It is possible, of course, that a relaxation of credit standards that fell on one side or the other of policy *A* would provide an even greater marginal benefit; the optimal policy is the one that provides the greatest marginal benefit.

TABLE 7 · 2

Profitability versus Required Return and Bad-Debt Losses

	Policy A	Policy B
Annual sales	$3,000,000	$3,240,000
Turnover of receivables	6	4
Level of receivables after change in credit policy	$500,000	$810,000
Additional receivables	$300,000	$310,000
Additional investment in receivables above present investment*	$210,000	
Additional investment in receivables above policy A investment*		$217,000
Required return on additional investment (20%)	$42,000	$43,400
Additional sales above present sales (units)	60,000	
Additional sales above policy A sales (units)		24,000
Profitability of additional sales	$180,000	$72,000
Bad-debt losses (percent of annual sales)	$90,000	$194,400
Additional bad-debt losses above present losses ($24,000)	$66,000	
Additional bad-debt losses above policy A losses ($90,000)		$104,400
Profitability of additional sales less additional bad-debt losses	$114,000	($32,400)

*(Additional receivables) (Variable cost per unit/Selling price per unit).

Collection policy

The overall collection policy of the firm is determined by the combination of collection procedures it undertakes. These procedures include such things as letters sent, phone calls, personal calls, and legal action, and they are described later in this chapter. One of the principal policy variables is the amount expended on collection procedures. Within a range, the greater the relative amount expended, the lower the proportion of bad-debt losses and the shorter the average collection period, all other things the same.

The relationships, however, are not linear. Initial collection expenditures are likely to cause little reduction in bad-debt losses. Additional expenditures begin to have a significant effect in reducing the amount of bad-debt losses. Beyond a point, however, additional expenditures tend to have little effect in further reducing these losses. The hypothesized relationship between expenditures and bad-debt losses is shown in Figure 7-1. Likewise, the relationship between the average collection period and the level of collection expenditure is likely to be similar to that shown in the figure.

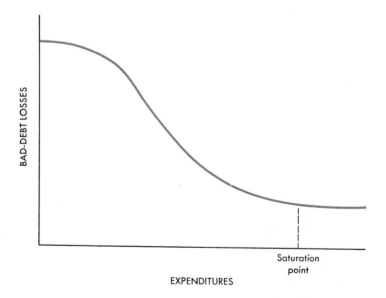

FIG. 7 · 1

Relationship between
amount of bad-debt losses
and collection
expenditures

If sales are independent of the collection effort, the appropriate level of collection expenditure again involves a tradeoff—this time between the level of expenditure on the one hand and the reduction in the cost of bad-debt losses and reduction in investment in receivables on the other. Suppose that we are considering the present collection program in relation to two new ones and that the programs were expected to produce these results:

	Present Program	Program A	Program B
Annual collection expenditures	$116,000	$148,000	$200,000
Average collection period	2 months	1 ½ months	1 month
Percentage of default	3	2	1

Assume that present sales are $2.4 million and that they are not expected to change with changes in the collection effort. If we go through the same type of reasoning as we did for the discount policy where receivables were reduced and for bad-debt losses, we obtain the results in Table 7-3. In the last three rows of the table, we see that the opportunity saving resulting from a speedup in collections plus the reduction in bad-debt losses exceeds the additional collection expenditures in going from the present program to program A, but not in going from program A to program B. As a result, the firm should adopt program A but not increase collection expenditures to the extent of program B.

TABLE 7 · 3

Evaluation of Collection Programs

	Present Program	Program A	Program B
Annual sales	$2,400,000	$2,400,000	$2,400,000
Turnover of receivables	6	8	12
Average receivables	$400,000	$300,000	$200,000
Reduction in receivables from present level		$100,000	
Reduction in receivables from program A level			$100,000
Return on reduction in receivables (20 percent)		$20,000	$20,000
Bad-debt losses (percent of annual sales)	$72,000	$48,000	$24,000
Reduction in bad-debt losses from present losses		$24,000	
Reduction in bad-debt losses from program A losses			$24,000
Opportunity saving on reduced receivables plus reduction in bad-debt losses		$44,000	$44,000
Additional collection expenditures from present expenditures		$32,000	
Additional collection expenditures from program A expenditures			$52,000

In the example above, we have assumed that demand is independent of the collection effort. In most cases, however, sales are likely to be affected adversely if the collection efforts of the firm become too intense, and customers become increasingly irritated. If they do, we must take into account the relationship between the collection effort and demand. Reduction in demand can be incorporated into the marginal analysis of collection expenditures in the same manner as was the increase in demand accompanying a relaxation in credit standards. In addition, if the collection effort has an effect on the percentage of total sales taking a cash discount, this factor must be considered. With increased collection efforts, for example, more customers might take the cash discount.

Credit and collection policies—summary

We see that the credit and collection policies of a firm involve several decisions as to (1) the quality of account accepted, (2) the credit period, (3) the cash discount given, and (4) the level of collection expenditures. In each case, the decision should involve a comparison of what is to be gained by a change in policy with the cost of the change. Optimal credit and collection policies would be those that resulted in the marginal gains equaling the marginal costs.

To maximize profits arising from credit and collection policies, the firm should vary these policies jointly until an optimal solution is achieved. That solution will determine the best combination of credit standards, credit period, cash discount policy, special terms, and level of collection expenditures. For most policy variables, profits increase at a decreasing rate up to a point and then decrease as the policy is varied from no effort to an extreme effort. This relationship is depicted in Figure 7-2 for the quality of account rejected. When there are no credit standards, that is, when all applicants are accepted, sales are maximized. However, the maximization of sales is offset by large bad-debt losses as well as by the opportunity cost of carrying a very large receivable position. As credit standards are initiated and applicants rejected, revenue from sales declines, but so do the average collection period and bad-debt losses. Because the latter two decline initially at a faster rate than do sales, profits increase. As credit standards are tightened increasingly, however, sales revenue declines at an increasing rate. At the same time, the average collection period and bad-debt losses decrease at a decreasing rate. Fewer and fewer bad credit risks are eliminated. Because of the combination of these influences, total profits of the firm increase at a diminishing rate with stricter credit standards up to a point, after which they decline. The optimal policy with respect to credit standards is represented by point X in the figure. In turn, this policy determines the level of accounts receivable held by the firm.

The analysis in the last several sections has purposely been rather general, to provide insight into the important concepts of credit and collection policies. Obviously, a policy decision should be based upon a far more specific evaluation than that contained in the examples above. Estimating the increased demand and increased slowness of collections that might accompany a relaxation of credit standards is extremely difficult. Nevertheless, management must make estimates of these relationships if it is to appraise realistically its existing policies.

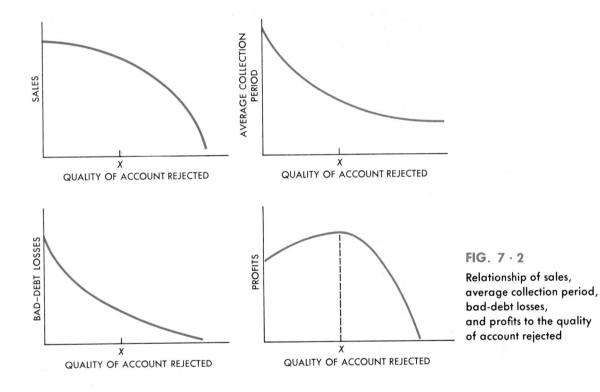

FIG. 7 · 2

Relationship of sales, average collection period, bad-debt losses, and profits to the quality of account rejected

ANALYZING THE CREDIT APPLICANT

Having established the terms of sale to be offered, the firm must evaluate individual credit applicants and consider the possibilities of a bad debt or slow payment. The credit evaluation procedure involves three related steps: obtaining information on the applicant, analyzing this information to determine the applicant's credit-worthiness, and making the credit decision. The credit decision, in turn, establishes whether credit should be extended and what the maximum amount of credit should be.

Sources of information

Though there are a number of sources of credit information, there necessarily are expenses incurred in collecting it. For some accounts, especially small ones, the cost of collecting comprehensive credit information may outweigh the potential profitability of the account. The firm extending credit may have to be satisfied with a limited amount of information on which to base a decision. In addition to cost, the firm must consider the time it takes to investigate a credit applicant. A shipment to a prospective customer cannot be delayed unnecessarily pending an elaborate credit investigation. Thus, the amount of information collected needs to be considered in relation to the time and expense required. Depending upon these considerations, the credit analyst may use one or more of the following sources of information.[2]

Financial statement. One of the most desirable sources of information for credit analysis is a financial statement that the seller may request from his customer at the time of the prospective sale. Some companies are perfectly willing to provide statements to suppliers, whereas others may refuse to do so. There is frequently a correlation between a company's refusal to provide a statement and weaknesses in its financial position. When possible, it is helpful to obtain interim statements, particularly for companies having seasonal patterns of sales. Needless to say, audited statements are far better than unaudited figures.

Credit ratings and reports. In addition to financial statements, credit ratings are available from various mercantile agencies. Dun & Bradstreet is perhaps the best known and most comprehensive of these agencies. It provides credit ratings to subscribers for a vast number of business firms throughout the nation. A key to its individual ratings is shown in Figure 7-3. As we see in the figure, D & B ratings give the credit analyst an indication of the estimated size of net worth and a credit appraisal for companies of a particular size, ranging from "high" to "limited." D & B also indicates when the information available is insufficient to provide a rating for a given business.

In addition to its rating service, D & B provides credit reports on business firms. These reports contain a brief history of the company and its principal officers, the nature of the business, certain financial information, and a trade check of suppliers as to the length of their experience with the company and as to whether payments are discount, prompt, or past due. The quality of the D & B reports varies

---

[2]For a good practical discussion of the ways a company should go about a credit investigation, see Robert S. Morrison, *Handbook for Manufacturing Entrepreneurs,* 2nd ed. (Cleveland: Western Reserve Press, 1974), Chapter 50.

New Key to Ratings
(Effective May 1, 1971)

ESTIMATED FINANCIAL STRENGTH		COMPOSITE CREDIT APPRAISAL			
		HIGH	GOOD	FAIR	LIMITED
5A	Over $50,000,000	1	2	3	4
4A	$10,000,000 to 50,000,000	1	2	3	4
3A	1,000,000 to 10,000,000	1	2	3	4
2A	750,000 to 1,000,000	1	2	3	4
1A	500,000 to 750,000	1	2	3	4
BA	300,000 to 500,000	1	2	3	4
BB	200,000 to 300,000	1	2	3	4
CB	125,000 to 200,000	1	2	3	4
CC	75,000 to 125,000	1	2	3	4
DC	50,000 to 75,000	1	2	3	4
DD	35,000 to 50,000	1	2	3	4
EE	20,000 to 35,000	1	2	3	4
FF	10,000 to 20,000	1	2	3	4
GG	5,000 to 10,000	1	2	3	4
HH	Up to 5,000	1	2	3	4

CLASSIFICATION FOR BOTH
ESTIMATED FINANCIAL STRENGTH AND CREDIT APPRAISAL

FINANCIAL STRENGTH BRACKET	EXPLANATION
1 $125,000 and Over	When only the numeral (1 or 2) appears, it is an indication that the estimated financial strength, while not definitely classified, is presumed to be within the range of the ($) figures in the corresponding bracket and that a condition is believed to exist which warrants credit in keeping with that assumption.
2 20,000 to 125,000	

NOT CLASSIFIED OR ABSENCE OF RATING

The absence of a rating, expressed by two hyphens (--), is not to be construed as unfavorable but signifies circumstances difficult to classify within condensed rating symbols. It suggests the advisability of obtaining a report for additional information.

FIG. 7 · 3
Dun & Bradstreet
key to ratings

with the information available externally and the willingness of the company being checked to cooperate with the D & B reporter. In addition to Dun & Bradstreet, there are a number of credit agencies that specialize in a particular line of business or in geographic areas, such as New York or Chicago.

Bank checking. Another source of information for the firm is a credit check through a bank. Many banks have large credit departments that undertake, as a service, credit checks for their customers. By calling or writing the bank(s) of account of the company being checked, a firm's bank is able to obtain information as to the average cash balance carried, loan accommodations, experience, and sometimes financial information. Because banks generally are more willing to share information with other banks than with a direct inquirer, it usually is best for the firm to initiate the credit check through its own bank rather than to inquire directly.

Exchange of information. Credit information frequently is exchanged among companies selling to the same customer. Through various credit organizations, credit men in a particular area become a closely knit group. A company is able to check other suppliers as to their experience with an account. Useful information includes the length of time they have had the account, the maximum credit extended, the amount of the line of credit, and whether payments are prompt or slow. In addition, there are various clearing houses of credit information. The largest of these is the National Association of Credit Management; credit information is provided by this agency in the form of a report.

The company's own experience. In addition to these sources, a company's own experience with an account is extremely important. A study of the promptness of past payments, including any seasonal patterns for example, is very useful. Frequently, the credit department will make written assessments of the quality of the management of a company to whom credit may be extended. These assessments are very important, for they pertain to the first of the famous "three C's" of credit: *character, collateral,* and *capacity.* For a prospective customer, frequently the salesman is able to supply useful information, based on his impressions of management and operations. Caution is necessary in interpreting this information, however, because a salesman has a natural bias toward granting credit and making the sale.

Credit analysis

Having collected credit information, the firm must undertake a credit analysis of the applicant. In practice, the collection of information and its analysis are closely related. If, on the basis of initial credit information, a large account appears to be relatively risky, the credit analyst will want to obtain further information. Presumably, the expected value of the additional information will exceed the cost of acquiring it.[3] Given the financial statements of an applicant, the credit analyst should undertake a ratio analysis, as described in Chapter 3. The analyst will be particularly interested in the applicant's liquidity and ability to pay bills on time.

In addition to analyzing financial statements, the credit analyst will consider the financial strength of the firm, the character of the company and its management, and various other matters. He then attempts to determine the ability of the applicant to service trade credit. In this regard, he assesses the probability of an applicant's not paying on time and of a bad-debt loss. The amount of information collected

[3] For a discussion of the value of additional information using probability concepts, see Harold Bierman, Jr., *et al., Quantitative Analysis for Business Decisions* (Homewood, Ill.: Richard D. Irwin, 1969).

should be determined in relation to the expected profit from an order and the cost of investigation. More sophisticated analysis should be undertaken only when there is a chance that a credit decision based upon the previous stage of investigation will be changed. If, for example, an analysis of a Dun & Bradstreet report resulted in an extremely unfavorable picture of the applicant, an investigation of the applicant's bank and its trade suppliers might have little prospect of changing the reject decision. Therefore, the added cost associated with this stage of investigation would not be worthwhile. With incremental stages of investigation each having a cost, they can be justified only if the information obtained has value in changing a prior decision.[4] Rather than perform all stages of investigation regardless of the profitability of the order, the firm should undertake investigation in stages and go to a new stage only when the expected net benefits of the additional information exceed the cost of acquiring it.

Although quantitative approaches have been developed to measure ability to service trade credit, the final decision for most companies extending trade credit rests upon the credit analyst's judgment in evaluating available information. Numerical evaluations have been used with success in consumer credit, where various characteristics of an individual are quantitatively rated and a credit decision is made on a total score.[5] Numerical ratings systems also are being used by companies extending trade credit. With the overall growth of trade credit, a number of companies are finding it worthwhile to use numerical credit-scoring systems to screen out clear accept and reject applicants. Credit analysts, then, can devote their energies to evaluating marginal applicants.

Credit decision

Once the credit analyst has marshaled the necessary evidence and has analyzed it, a decision must be reached as to the disposition of the account. In the case of an initial sale, the first decision to be made is whether or not to ship the goods and extend credit. If repeat sales are likely, the company will probably want to establish procedures so that it does not have to evaluate the extension of credit each time an order is received. One means for streamlining the procedure is to establish a

[4] For such an analysis, see Dileep Mehta, "The Formulation of Credit Policy Models," *Management Science*, 15 (October 1968), 30–50.

[5] See James H. Myers and Edward W. Forgy, "The Development of Numerical Credit Evaluation Systems," *Journal of the American Statistical Association*, 58 (September 1963), 799–806; William P. Poggess, "Screen-Test Your Credit Risks," in Keith V. Smith, ed., *Working Capital Management* (New York: West Publishing, 1974), pp. 109–20; and Robert O. Edmister and Gary G. Schlarbaum, "Credit Policy in Lending Institutions," *Journal of Financial and Quantitative Analysis*, 9 (June 1974), 335–56.

line of credit for an account. A line of credit is a maximum limit on the amount the firm will permit to be owing at any one time. In essence, it represents the maximum risk exposure that the firm will allow itself to undergo for an account. The establishment of a credit line streamlines the procedure for shipping goods, but the line must be reevaluated periodically in order to keep abreast of developments in the account. What was a satisfactory risk exposure today may be more or less than satisfactory a year from today. Despite comprehensive credit procedures, there will always be special cases that must be dealt with individually. Here, too, however, the firm can streamline the operation by defining responsibilities clearly.

ADDITIONAL CONSIDERATIONS

Collection procedures

In addition to credit procedures for the individual account, the firm must establish clear-cut collection procedures for past-due or delinquent accounts. The initial question to be answered is, How past due should an account be allowed to go before collection procedures are initiated? Because a receivable is only as good as the likelihood that it will be paid, a firm cannot afford to wait too long before initiating collection procedures. On the other hand, if it initiates procedures too soon, it may anger reasonably good customers who, for some reason, fail to make payments by the due date. Procedures, whatever they are, should be firmly established. Initially, a letter is usually sent, followed, perhaps, by additional letters that become ever more serious in tone. Next may come a telephone call from the credit manager and then, perhaps, one from the company's attorney. Some companies have collection men who make personal calls on the account.

If all else fails, the account may be turned over to a collection agency. The agency's fees are quite substantial—frequently, one-half the amount of the receivable—but such a procedure may be the only feasible alternative, particularly for a small account. Direct legal action is costly, sometimes serves no real purpose, and may only force the account into bankruptcy. When payment cannot be collected, compromise settlements may provide a higher percentage of collection.[6]

Similar to our analysis of the amount of collection expenditures in the aggregate, the amount spent on an individual account must be evaluated in relation to the likely benefits. In short, the firm should not spend $25 to collect a $15 account. The expected benefits should exceed the collection costs. Suppose that Z-REX Corporation was

[6] For an extended discussion of these settlements, see Chapter 27.

owed $1,000 from a delinquent customer. With a $60 collection expenditure, Z-REX expects the following:

Collection	Probability	Expected Outcome
$ 0	0.5	$ 0
100	0.2	20
200	0.1	20
300	0.1	30
400	0.1	40
		$110

Because the expected value of benefits, $110, exceeds the amount expended, $60, the collection effort provides an expected value of net benefits of $50. Of course, other collection efforts may result in even higher net benefits and they should be explored. Past experience may tell a firm what the optimal collection procedure is relative to profitability.

Credit insurance

To protect against unusual bad-debt losses in extending trade credit, a firm may take out credit insurance. Although the firm cannot insure against losses incurred normally in the industry (known as primary losses), it can insure against above-normal losses. Insurance companies usually restrict coverage to certain acceptable risks, as determined by Dun & Bradstreet ratings. In addition, these companies usually insist upon *coinsurance,* the participation of the collecting firm in a portion of the bad-debt loss—usually 10 to 20 percent. The insistence upon coinsurance safeguards the insurance company from the firm's becoming excessively liberal in the granting of credit. The cost of credit insurance varies directly with the risk of the accounts accepted and is calculated as a percentage of sales. The decision to use credit insurance depends upon the probability of extreme credit losses and the ability of the firm to bear these losses, as well as the amount of premiums.

Use of electronic data processing equipment

Computers have been used a great deal in credit management. Their use provides certain essential up-to-date information needed for analysis. All of the information previously placed on receivable ledgers can be placed on punched cards or tapes. As a result, the credit department has very quick access to this information. At frequent intervals, it can obtain a trial balance that gives a summary of all billings, payments, discounts taken, and amounts still owed. Also, it can obtain an aging of accounts showing the total amounts owed the firm, the portion that is current, the portion that is up to thirty days past due, that which is thirty to sixty days past due, and so forth.

In addition, the computer can be programmed to provide complete reports on all delinquent accounts; and delinquency letters can be sent out mechanically at regular intervals. Frequent reports on past-due accounts, which were not possible before the computer, alert the credit manager to problems as they develop. As a result, he is able to stay on top of them and take corrective action. Formerly, the situation might have deteriorated during the information lag. Management also may want to be informed when an account approaches the line of credit established for it, and computers can provide this information easily.

The computer helps the credit manager by providing timely and accurate information on the status of accounts. The payment history of a customer can be drawn from storage and printed out in seconds. Included in this history is information such as the date the account was opened, the amount owing currently, the customer's credit line, any numerical credit ratings, and the promptness of past payments. Special reports can be prepared that involve categorization or comparisons. For example, if several companies in the same industry are slow in their payments at a particular time of the year, management might want to know the firm's experience with all other companies in that particular industry. Such information enables the credit manager to analyze and deal with the problem more effectively. In another situation, management might wish to compare incoming orders from a particular customer with his payment history. This information also can be provided quickly.

Indeed, the computer can provide a vast array of detailed information, previously impractical to obtain, that may be useful not only to the credit manager but to other management as well. In addition to processing data, the computer can be programmed to make certain routine credit decisions.[7] In particular, small orders from good accounts can be approved by the computer without the order ever going to a credit analyst. All in all, electronic data processing can make a significant contribution to the credit department. As their volume of receivables grows, many firms find computer processing to be the only feasible means by which to handle receivables.

[7] For a discussion of credit decision making by simulation, see Roger L. Sisson and Norman L. Statland, "The Future of Computers in Credit Management," *Credit and Financial Management,* 65 (November 1963), 40, 44.

Credit and collection policies encompass the quality of accounts accepted, the credit period extended, the cash discount given, and the level of collection expenditures. In each case, the credit decision involves a tradeoff between the additional profitability and the cost resulting from a change in any of these elements. For example, by liberalizing the quality requirements for accounts, the firm might hope to make more on the additional sales than the cost of carrying the additional receivables plus the additional bad-debt losses. To maximize profits arising from credit and collection policies, the firm should vary these policies jointly until an optimal solution is obtained. The firm's credit and collection policies, together with its credit and collection procedures, determine the magnitude and quality of its receivable position.

In evaluating a credit applicant, the credit analyst is concerned with obtaining financial and other information about the applicant, analyzing this information, and reaching a credit decision. If the account is new, the firm must decide whether or not to accept the order. With repeat orders, the firm must usually decide upon the maximum credit to extend. This maximum, known as a line of credit, is based upon the credit-worthiness of the applicant. Collection procedures should be firmly established and applied consistently. The length of time an account may be delinquent before collection procedures are initiated will depend upon the billing terms and the nature of the account. To protect against unusual credit losses, a firm may take out credit insurance. We reviewed briefly some of the applications of electronic data processing to credit management. The uses of the computer are many and are likely to increase in importance.

1. Is it always good policy to reduce the firm's bad-debt losses by "getting rid of the deadbeats"?

2. What are the probable effects on sales and profits of each of the following credit policies:
   (a) A high percentage of bad-debt loss, but normal receivable turnover and rejection rate
   (b) A high percentage of past-due accounts and a low credit rejection rate
   (c) A low percentage of past-due accounts, but high receivable rejection and turnover rates
   (d) A low percentage of past-due accounts and a low rejection rate, but a high turnover rate

3. During the early 1960s, O. M. Scott, Inc., suffered severe financial problems resulting from the financing of dealer inventories through trust receipts. The trust receipt financing contributed to a substantial overstocking of inventory by the dealers.
   (a) What happens to Scott's sales as dealers work off excess inventory?
   (b) Should Scott recognize as sales its shipments to dealers on a trust receipt agreement or the sales of dealers to final consumers?

4. Many retailers have liberalized their credit policy to the extent that credit is offered to all customers, regardless of risk class, on a 1½ percent per month rate.
   (a) What is the effective annual cost of borrowing for customers utilizing these terms?
   (b) For a corporation with an average 40 percent markup, what is the return on the investment in receivables resulting from incremental sales? Assume a default rate of 35 percent on incremental sales.
   (c) Discuss the implications of (a) for individuals with a high credit rating.

5. Is an increase in the collection period necessarily bad? Explain.

6. Explain the difference between a bad-debt expense, the provision for bad debt, and a writeoff against the provision for bad debt.

7. Credit customers can be classified into risk classes where *risk* is defined as the expected default rate by customers in the risk class.
   (a) Construct a model for predicting the default rate of individual credit customers. (Hint: Select the variables, such as income, age, education, you would evaluate, and determine a weighting system.)
   (b) Construct a model for predicting the default rate of business firms.

8. Term Project: Test the predictive ability of your model in Question 7.

PROBLEMS

1. The Fletcher Corporation is a retail clothier whose variable costs have consistently been 85 percent of sales and fixed costs are $100,000 on sales of $1 million. The management is considering a change of credit policy to allow higher-risk customers to buy on 30-day credit terms. (These customers are expected to pay on the thirtieth day.)

Risk Class	Required Return before Tax	Percentage Default Rate	Total Sales
D	20%	5%	$1,100,000
E	25	7	1,175,000
F	30	10	1,225,000
G	35	14	1,250,000

On the basis of the risk characteristics of the incremental investment in receivables, management has established the required return for the investment, the expected sales level, and the expected default rate for each risk class.

(a) Determine which policy Fletcher should adopt.

(b) Discuss the qualitative factors one would have to consider in making a final decision.

2. The J. A. Richardson Company, a manufacturer of athletic equipment, is currently selling $2.5 million annually to dealers on 30-day credit terms. Management believes that sales could be substantially increased if dealers carried more inventory; however, dealers are unable to finance their inventory. As a result, management is considering changing credit policy. The following information is available. (The average collection period is now 30 days.)

Costs: Variable cost 80 percent
Fixed cost $300,000

Required (Pretax) Return on Investment: 20 percent

Credit Policy	Average Collection Period	Annual Sales
A	45 days	$2.80 million
B	60 days	3.00 million
C	75 days	3.10 million
D	90 days	3.15 million

(a) Determine which policy Richardson should adopt.

(b) Discuss the implicit assumptions made by the incremental profit/incremental investment approach to decision making.

3. The Chickee Corporation has a 12 percent opportunity cost of funds and currently sells on terms of n/10, EOM. The firm has sales of $10 million a year, which are 80 percent on credit and spread evenly over the year. The average collection period is currently 60 days. If Chickee offered terms of 2/10, net 30, 60 percent of its customers would take the discount, and the collection period would be reduced to 40 days. Should Chickee change its terms from net/10, EOM to 2/10, net 30?

4. The Pottsville Manufacturing Corporation is considering extending trade credit to the San Jose Company. Examination of the records of San Jose has produced the following financial statements.

SAN JOSE COMPANY BALANCE SHEET (in millions)

	19__1	19__2	19__3
Assets			
Current assets:			
Cash	$ 1.5	$ 1.6	$ 1.6
Receivables	1.3	1.8	2.5
Inventories (at lower of cost or market)	1.3	2.6	4.0
Other	.4	.5	.4
Total current assets	$ 4.5	$ 6.5	$ 8.5
Fixed assets:			
Buildings (net)	2.0	1.9	1.8
Machinery and equipment (net)	7.0	6.5	6.0
Total fixed assets	$ 9.0	$ 8.4	$ 7.8
Other assets	1.0	.8	.6
Total assets	$14.5	$15.7	$16.9
Liabilities:			
Current liabilities:			
Notes payable (8 ½ %)	$ 2.1	$ 3.1	$ 3.8
Trade payables	.2	.4	.9
Other payables	.2	.2	.2
Total	$ 2.5	$ 3.7	$ 4.9
Term loan (8 ½ %)	4.0	3.0	2.0
Total	$ 6.5	$ 6.7	$ 6.9
Net worth			
Common stock	$ 5.0	$ 5.0	$ 5.0
Preferred stock (6 ½ %)	1.0	1.0	1.0
Retained earnings	2.0	3.0	4.0
Total liabilities and equities	$14.5	$15.7	$16.9

SAN JOSE COMPANY INCOME STATEMENT (in millions)

	19__1	19__2	19__3
Net credit sales	$15.0	$15.8	$16.2
Cost of goods sold	11.3	12.1	13.0
Gross profit	$ 3.7	$ 3.7	$ 3.2
Operating expenses	1.1	1.2	1.2
Net profit before taxes	$ 2.6	$ 2.5	$ 2.0
Tax	1.3	1.2	1.0
Profit after taxes	$ 1.3	$ 1.3	$ 1.0
Dividends	.3	.3	.0
	$ 1.0	$ 1.0	$ 1.0

The San Jose Company has a Dun & Bradstreet rating of 4A-2. A bank check indicates that the firm generally carries balances in the low seven figures. A trade credit check of five suppliers to the San Jose Company reveals that the firm takes its discounts from the three creditors offering 2/10, net 30 terms, though it is about fifteen days slow in paying the two firms offering terms net 30.

Analyze the San Jose Company's application for credit.

5. The credit manager of C. E. Brown, Inc., feels that the credit policy of the firm needs to be tightened. In support of his argument to the president, the credit manager contrasts the 90-day terms of C. E. Brown with the 30-day terms of the industry. C. E. Brown is selling $1.6 million a year, and costs are 85 percent variable and $100,000 fixed. On the basis of a survey of Brown's customers, the credit manager expects the following relationship between terms and sales:

Policy	Terms	Annual Sales
A	90	$1,600,000
B	75	1,575,000
C	60	1,550,000
D	45	1,500,000
E	30	1,425,000
F	15	1,300,000

(a) If the opportunity cost of capital is 15 percent, which policy should be adopted? (Assume that the average collection period corresponds to the terms given.)

(b) Discuss the qualitative factors that should be considered before making a final decision.

6. Philbrick Castings Company currently (in April) is experiencing a lull in sales and has excess capacity. It has received an order for $5,000 in castings from a potential customer, with another $15,000 in orders likely to come before September. This potential customer has asked for a $10,000 line of credit, with payment due sixty days after delivery. Given the present situation, Philbrick can fill an order within a month of its receipt. Variable costs are 75 percent of sales, and because Philbrick has excess cash, it does not require a return on any additional investment in receivables. Management perceives a real need to attract orders and is willing to forego such return until business picks up and cash has a greater opportunity cost.

When investigating the potential customer, Philbrick finds that it is an extremely risky business. There appears to be only a 60 percent chance that this potential customer will be solvent by year-end and pay its bills. If the company becomes insolvent, unsecured creditors are likely to receive nothing. Given this information, should the account be accepted?

BERANEK, WILLIAM, *Analysis for Financial Decisions,* Chapter 10. Homewood, Ill.: Richard D. Irwin, 1963.

BROSKY, JOHN J., *The Implicit Cost of Trade Credit and Theory of Optimal Terms of Sale.* New York: Credit Research Foundation, 1969.

FRIEDLAND, SEYMOUR, *The Economics of Corporate Finance,* Chapter 4. Englewood Cliffs, N.J.: Prentice-Hall, 1966.

GREER, CARL C., "The Optimal Credit Acceptance Policy," *Journal of Financial and Quantitative Analysis,* 2 (December 1967), 399–415.

HERBST, ANTHONY F., "Some Empirical Evidence on the Determinants of Trade Credit at the Industry Level of Aggregation," *Journal of Financial and Quantitative Analysis,* 9 (June 1974), 377–94.

LANE, SYLVIA, "Submarginal Credit Risk Classification," *Journal of Financial and Quantitative Analysis,* 7 (January 1972), 1379–85.

MAO, JAMES C. T., "Controlling Risk in Accounts Receivable Management," *Journal of Business Finance & Accounting,* 1 (Autumn 1974), 395–403.

MARRAH, GEORGE L., "Managing Receivables," *Financial Executive,* 38 (July 1970), 40–44.

MEHTA, DILEEP, "The Formulation of Credit Policy Models," *Management Science,* 15 (October 1968), 30–50.

———, *Working Capital Management,* Chapters 1–3. Englewood Cliffs, N.J.: Prentice-Hall, 1974

MORRISON, ROBERT S., *Handbook for Manufacturing Entrepreneurs,* 2nd ed., Chapter 50. Cleveland: Western Reserve Press, 1974.

PATTERSON, HARLAN R., "New Life in the Management of Corporate Receivables," *Credit and Financial Management,* 72 (February 1970), 15–18.

SCHIFF, MICHAEL, "Credit and Inventory Management," *Financial Executive,* 40 (November 1972), 28–33.

SCHWARTZ, ROBERT A., "An Economic Model of Trade Credit," *Journal of Financial and Quantitative Analysis,* 9 (September 1974), 643–58.

SISSON, ROGER L., and **NORMAN L. STATLAND,** "The Future of Computers in Credit Management," *Credit and Financial Management,* 67 (May 1965), 13–15, 40, 44.

SMITH, KEITH V., *Management of Working Capital,* Section 3. New York: West Publishing, 1974.

SOLDOFSKY, ROBERT M., "A Model for Accounts Receivable Management," *N.A.A. Bulletin,* January 1966, pp. 55–58.

WELSHANS, MERLE T., "Using Credit for Profit Making," *Harvard Business Review,* 45 (January–February 1967), 141–56.

WRIGHTSMAN, DWAYNE, "Optimal Credit Terms for Accounts Receivable," *Quarterly Review of Economics and Business,* 9 (Summer 1969), 59–66.

Inventory Management and *Control* 8

prob.# 1 excluding D (A, B, C) & #4

Because inventories represent so important a segment of the total assets of most business firms, it is extremely important that they be managed efficiently. With the development of the computer, there have been considerable advances in the management of inventories during the last 25 years. As information on sales and inventory levels has become more reliable and more quickly obtainable, the need for inventory to buffer information lags has been greatly reduced. Moreover, there have been major improvements in inventory control, transportation, and warehousing. All of these developments have made possible a greater turnover of inventories. Our purpose in this chapter is to investigate techniques for efficiently managing inventory and to relate these methods to the financial manager's concern with controlling investment.

Inventories provide a very important link in the production and sale of a product. For a company engaged in manufacturing, a certain amount of inventory is absolutely necessary in the actual production of the product; this inventory is known as "goods in process." Although other types of inventory—namely, in-transit, raw-materials, and finished-goods inventory—are not absolutely necessary in the strictest sense, they are extremely important if the firm is to be at all flexible. For example, inventory in transit, that is, inventory between various stages of production or storage, permits efficient production scheduling and utilization of resources. Without this type of inventory, each stage of production would be dependent upon the preceding stage's finishing its operation on a unit of production. As a result, there would probably be delays and considerable idle time in certain stages of production. Thus, there is an incentive for the production area of the firm to maintain large in-transit inventory.

Raw-materials inventory gives the firm flexibility in its purchasing. Without it, the firm must exist on a hand-to-mouth basis, buying raw material strictly in keeping with its production schedule. Moreover, the purchasing department often is able to take advantage of quantity discounts. By so doing, raw-materials inventory may be bloated temporarily. Finished-goods inventory allows the firm flexibility in its production scheduling and in its marketing effort.[1] Production does not need to be geared directly to sales. Given the desire of the marketing department to fill orders promptly, large inventories allow efficient servicing of customer demands. If a certain product is temporarily out of stock, present as well as future sales to the customer may be lost. Thus, there is an incentive to maintain large stocks of all three types of inventory.

The advantages of increased inventories, then, are several. The firm can effect economies of production and purchasing and can fill customer orders more quickly. In short, the firm is more flexible. The obvious disadvantages are the total cost of holding the inventory, including storage and handling costs, and the required return on capital tied up in the investment in inventory. Inventories, like accounts receivable, should be increased as long as the resulting savings exceed the total cost of holding the added inventory. The balance finally reached depends upon the estimates of actual savings, the cost of carrying additional inventory, and the efficiency of inventory control. Obviously, this balance requires coordination of the production, marketing, and finance areas of the firm in keeping with an overall objective.

INVENTORY CONTROL

For a given level of inventory, the efficiency of inventory control affects the flexibility of the firm. Two essentially identical firms with the same amount of inventory may have significantly different degrees of flexibility in operations due to differences in inventory control. Inefficient procedures may result in an unbalanced inventory—the firm may frequently be out of certain types of inventory, and overstock other types, necessitating excessive investment. These ineffi-

---

[1]See John F. Magee, "Guides to Inventory Policy: Functions and Lot Sizes," *Harvard Business Review*, 34 (January–February 1956).

ciencies ultimately have an adverse effect upon profits. Turning the situation around, differences in the efficiency of inventory control for a given level of flexibility affect the level of investment required in inventories. The less efficient the inventory control, the greater the investment required. Similarly, excessive investment in inventories affects profits adversely. Thus, the effects of inventory control on flexibility and on the level of investment required in inventories represent two sides of the same coin. Our purpose in the subsequent sections is to examine various principles of inventory control.

Economic order quantity

The economic order quantity (EOQ) is an important concept in the purchase of raw materials and in the storage of finished-goods and in-transit inventories. In our analysis, we wish to determine the optimal order quantity for a particular item of inventory, given its forecasted usage, ordering cost, and carrying cost. Ordering can mean either the purchase of the item or its production. Assume for the moment that the usage of a particular item of inventory is known with certainty. Moreover, assume that this usage is stationary or steady throughout the period of time being analyzed. In other words, if usage is 2,600 items for a six-month period, 100 items would be used each week. Moreover, usage is assumed to be independent of the level of inventory.

We assume that ordering costs, O, are constant regardless of the size of the order. In the purchase of raw materials or other items, these costs represent the clerical costs involved in placing an order as well as certain costs of receiving and checking the goods once they arrive. For finished-goods inventories, ordering costs involve scheduling a production run. When start-up costs are large, as they are in a machined piece of metal for example, ordering costs can be quite significant. For in-transit inventories, ordering costs are likely to involve nothing more than record keeping. The total ordering cost for a period is simply the number of orders for that period, times the cost per order.

Carrying costs per period, C, represent the cost of inventory storage, handling, and insurance, together with the required rate of return on the investment in inventory. These costs are assumed to be constant per unit of inventory, per unit of time. Thus, the total carrying cost for a period is the average number of units of inventory for the period, times the carrying cost per unit. In addition, we assume for now that inventory orders are filled without delay. Because out-of-stock items can be replaced immediately, there is no need to maintain a buffer or safety stock. Although the assumptions made up to now may seem overly restrictive, they are necessary for an initial understanding of the conceptual framework that follows. Subsequently, we will relax some of them.

If the usage of an inventory item is perfectly steady over a period of time and there is no safety stock, average inventory (in units) can be expressed as

$$\text{Average inventory} = \frac{Q}{2} \tag{8-1}$$

where Q is the quantity (in units) ordered and is assumed to be constant for the period. The above problem is illustrated in Figure 8-1. Although the quantity demanded is a step function, we assume for analytical purposes that it can be approximated by a straight line. We see that zero inventory always indicates that further inventory must be ordered.

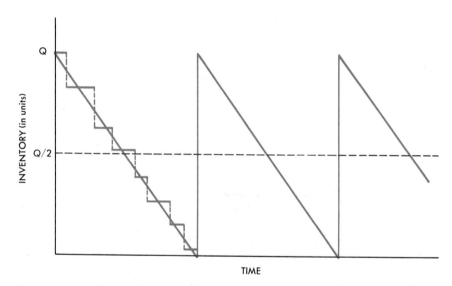

FIG. 8 · 1

Order quantity example

The carrying cost of inventory is the carrying cost per unit, times the average number of units of inventory, or $CQ/2$. The total number of orders for a period of time is simply the total usage (in units) of an item of inventory for that period, S, divided by Q. Consequently, total ordering costs are represented by the ordering cost per order, times the number of orders, or SO/Q. Total inventory costs, then, are the carrying costs plus ordering costs, or

$$TC = \frac{CQ}{2} + \frac{SO}{Q} \tag{8-2}$$

We see from Eq. (8-2) that the higher the order quantity, Q, the higher the carrying costs but the lower the total ordering costs. The lower the order quantity, the lower the carrying costs but the higher the total ordering costs. We are concerned with the tradeoff between the economies of increased order size and the added cost of carrying additional inventory.

From Eq. (8-2), we can obtain the optimal order quantity, Q^*:

$$Q^* = \sqrt{\frac{2SO}{C}} \qquad (8\text{-}3)$$

This equation is known as the economic lot-size formula. To illustrate its use, suppose that usage of an inventory item is 2,000 units during a 100-day period, ordering costs are $100 an order, and carrying costs are $10 per unit per 100 days. The most economic order quantity, then, is

$$Q^* = \sqrt{\frac{2(2,000)(100)}{10}} = 200 \text{ units}$$

With an order quantity of 200 units, the firm would order (2,000/200), or ten times, during the period under consideration or, in other words, every ten days. We see from Eq. (8-3) that Q^* varies directly with total usage, S, and order cost, O, and inversely with the carrying cost, C. However, the relationship is dampened by the square-root sign in both cases. As usage increases, then, the optimal order size and the average level of inventory increases by a lesser percentage. In other words, economies of scale are possible.

In our example, we have assumed that inventory can be ordered with no delay. However, there usually is a time lapse in procurement between the time a purchase order is placed and the time the inventory is actually received, or in the time it takes to manufacture an item after an order is placed. This lead time must be considered. If it is constant and known with certainty, however, the optimal order quantity is not affected. In the above example, the firm would still order 200 units at a time and place ten orders during the specified time period, or every ten days. If the lead time for delivery were three days, the firm simply would place its order seven days after delivery of the previous order.

The EOQ function is shown in Figure 8-2, p. 144. In the figure, we plot ordering costs, carrying costs, and total costs—the sum of the first two costs. We see that whereas carrying costs vary directly with the size of the order, ordering costs vary inversely with the size of the order. The total cost line declines at first as the fixed costs of ordering are spread over more units. The total cost line begins to rise, however, when the decrease in average ordering cost is more than offset by the additional carrying costs. Point X, then, represents the economic order quantity, which minimizes the total cost of inventory.

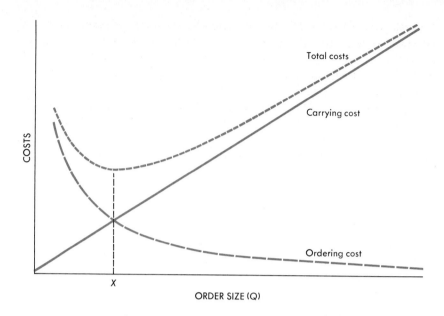

FIG. 8 · 2

Economic order
quantity relationship

When the total cost line around the EOQ point is not particularly sensitive to the number of units ordered, it may be appropriate to use an EOQ range instead of a point. To determine this sensitivity, we might compute the percentage change in total costs for, say, a 10 percent change in number of units ordered. If the sensitivity is not great, we may find that an EOQ range affords us greater flexibility in ordering without less economy.[2] The EOQ formula taken up in this section is a very useful tool for inventory control. In purchasing raw materials or other items of inventory, it tells us the amount to order and the best timing of our orders. For finished-goods inventory, it enables us to exercise better control over the timing and size of production runs. In general, the EOQ model gives us a rule for deciding when to replenish inventories and the amount to replenish. All inventory models, no matter how complex, address themselves to this problem of the timing and magnitude of replenishment.[3]

Quantity discounts

Frequently, the firm is able to take advantage of quantity discounts in ordering. Because these discounts affect the price per unit, they also influence the economic order quantity. However, the basic EOQ framework should still be used as a point of departure for analyzing the

[2]See Arthur Snyder, "Principles of Inventory Management," *Financial Executive,* 32 (April 1964), 16–19.

[3]See Harvey M. Wagner, *Principles of Operation Research* (Englewood Cliffs, N.J.: Prentice-Hall, 1969), pp. 786–89.

problem. In our example, we assumed 2,000 units of usage during a 100-day period, order costs of $100 an order, and carrying costs of $10 per unit per 100 days, resulting in an economic order quantity of 200 units. Suppose now that a quantity discount of $0.10 a unit in price is available if the firm increases its order size to 250 units, whereas currently it enjoys no discount. To determine whether or not the discount is worthwhile, we must analyze the benefits in relation to the costs involved.

The savings available to the firm in lower purchase price are

$$\text{Savings} = \text{Discount per unit} \times \text{Usage}$$

$$= \$0.10 \times 2,000 = \$200$$

The cost is the additional carrying cost less savings in ordering costs which result from fewer orders being placed. The additional carrying cost, where Q' is the new order size required, is

$$\frac{(Q' - Q^*)C}{2} = \frac{(250 - 200)10}{2} = \$250$$

The saving in ordering costs is

$$\frac{SO}{Q^*} - \frac{SO}{Q'} = \frac{(2000)(100)}{200} - \frac{(2000)(100)}{250} = \$200$$

Therefore, the net increase in costs is $250 − $200, or $50, for going from an order quantity of 200 units to 250 units. Because the net cost is less than the benefits to be derived, the firm should use an order quantity of 250 units. Similarly, other problems involving quantity discounts can be analyzed in this manner. The economic order quantity formula serves as a point of departure for balancing the benefits against the costs of a change in order size.

MARGINAL ANALYSIS OF INVENTORY POLICY

Another way to approach the question of optimal inventory level is through the use of marginal analysis similar to that used to analyze credit policy in the preceding chapter. The essence of the approach is to compare incremental benefits with incremental costs in going from one level of average inventory to another. If marginal benefits exceed marginal costs, the new level is better than the old. Let us begin our discussion by exploring the benefits associated with having more inventory.

Benefits of increased inventory

Recall that in the economic order quantity formula, the benefits derived from increasing the amount of inventory held were due to the reduction in number of orders. It is an easy matter to determine the reduction in total ordering costs over, say, one year's period of time which result from an increase in the average level of inventory. To illustrate, suppose that total one-year demand for finished goods inventory at AFD Tool Company is 400,000 units. If the order quantity is 10,000 units, inventory will be ordered 40 times during the year. Assume that the company maintains a safety stock of 2,000 units. Then the average inventory level is 2,000 + (10,000/2) = 7,000 units. If ordering costs are $3,000 per order, total ordering costs for the year would be 40 × $3,000 = $120,000. The cost of an order is due to the start-up costs of scheduling a new production run. Though we have treated these costs as linearly related to the number of orders per year, we also could handle nonlinear situations.

Suppose now that the company is considering increasing its average inventory level through an increase in its order quantity from 10,000 to 20,000 units. With a safety stock of 2,000 units, the average inventory level becomes 2,000 + (20,000/2) = 12,000 units. The total number of orders for the year becomes 400,000/20,000 = 20 orders, and total ordering costs for the year would be 20 × $3,000 = $60,000 as contrasted with $120,000 before. Thus, there is a savings of $60,000 in total ordering costs by going from an average inventory level of 7,000 units to 12,000 units.

Costs of increased inventory

Total benefits must be balanced against the cost of carrying the additional inventory. Carrying costs are comprised of increased warehousing costs, insurance, and handling costs, together with the required return on the additional investment. Suppose the increased warehousing, insurance, and handling costs in going from an average inventory level of 7,000 units to 12,000 units are estimated to be $10,000 per year. Moreover, suppose that the average investment per unit of inventory is $40. Thus, the incremental investment necessary to carry the additional inventory is 5,000 units × $40 = $200,000. If the required return on investment is 20 percent before taxes, the required return on the additional investment is $40,000. The total annual incremental cost of going from an average inventory level of 7,000 to 12,000 units is $10,000 in warehousing, insurance, and handling costs plus $40,000 in required return on additional investment, or $50,000 in total.

Balancing incremental benefits with costs

147
Chapter 8
Inventory
Management
and Control

The *net* annual incremental advantage in going from the present average level of inventory to the new level is:

Benefits to be realized	$60,000
Costs to be incurred	50,000
	$10,000

As incremental benefits exceed incremental costs, the firm would want to increase its average inventory level from 7,000 to 12,000 units.

Suppose now that AFD Tool Company is considering increasing its average level of inventory even further, to 14,500 units. As 2,000 units represent safety stock, this level implies an order quantity of 25,000 units. That is (14,500 − 2,000) times two. With total annual demand for inventory of 400,000 units, there would be 400,000/25,000 = 16 orders a year. With ordering costs of $3,000 per order, total ordering costs become $48,000. The incremental annual savings in ordering costs in going from an average level of inventory of 12,000 units to 14,500 units is $60,000 − $48,000 = $12,000.

On the cost side, suppose increased warehousing, insurance, and handling costs in going from 12,000 to 14,500 units of average inventory are estimated to be $7,000. Note that these costs may not bear a linear relationship with level of inventory; our example assumes the relationship is an increasing one. If investment per unit continues to be $40, the additional investment is 2,500 × $40 = $100,000. With a required rate of return of 20 percent, the required return on the additional investment is $20,000. Thus, total annual incremental costs are $7,000 plus $20,000 = $27,000.

The *net* annual incremental advantage in going from 12,000 units to 14,500 units of average inventory is:

Benefits to be realized	$12,000
Costs to be incurred	27,000
	−$15,000

As incremental benefits are less than incremental costs, AFD Tool Company would not want to increase its average inventory level from 12,000 units to 14,500 units. It would, however, want to go from the present level of 7,000 units to 12,000 units. It is possible, of course, that average inventory levels on one side or the other of 12,000 units would provide an even larger net advantage. This could be determined by undertaking analyses for other levels of average inventory.

The use of marginal analysis provides a useful alternative to the economic order quantity formula in arriving at an appropriate level of inventory. It allows us to take account of any nonlinear costs and benefits, which the EOQ formula does not. In the absence of nonlinear relationships, the two approaches should provide approximately the same answer. The EOQ formula is more exact in the sense that it produces a specific optimal level, while the marginal-analysis approach tells us whether one level of inventory is superior to another. If we consider enough possible levels, we can certainly come very close to the true optimum. The real advantage to the approach, however, is when benefits and/or costs bear a nonlinear relationship to levels of inventory. Our presentation also illustrates that the basic concepts behind inventory and receivable management are the same.

MODIFICATION FOR SAFETY STOCKS

In practice, the demand or usage of inventory generally is not known with certainty; usually it fluctuates during a given period of time. Typically, the demand for finished-goods inventory is subject to the greatest uncertainty. In general, the usage of raw-materials inventory and in-transit inventory, both of which depend upon the production scheduling, is more predictable. In addition to demand or usage, the lead time required to receive delivery of inventory once an order is placed is usually subject to some variation. Owing to these fluctuations, it is not feasible in most cases to allow expected inventory to fall to zero before a new order is expected to be received, as could be done when usage and lead time were known with certainty. A safety stock is necessary.

Order point and safety stock

Before discussing safety stocks in detail, it is necessary to consider at what point inventory will be ordered. Suppose that demand for inventory is known with certainty but that it takes five days before an order is received. In our previous illustration of the economic order quantity formula, we found that the EOQ for our example firm was 200 units, resulting in an order being placed every ten days. If usage is steady, the firm now would need to order five days before it ran out of stock, or at 100 units of stock on hand. Thus, the order point is 100 units. When the new order is received five days later, the firm will just have exhausted its existing stock. This example of an order point is illustrated in Figure 8-3.

When we allow for uncertainty in demand for inventory as well as in lead time, a safety stock becomes advisable. The concept here is illustrated in Figure 8-4. In the upper panel of the figure, we show what would happen if the firm had a safety stock of 100 units and if expected demand of 200 units every ten days and lead time of five days were to occur. Note that with a safety stock of 100 units, the order

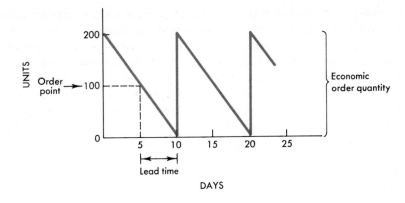

FIG. 8 · 3

Order point when
lead time is certain

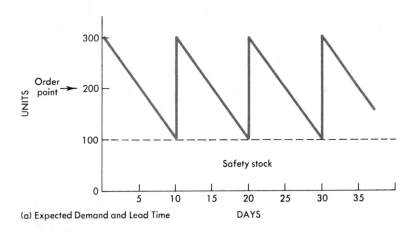

(a) Expected Demand and Lead Time

FIG. 8 · 4

Safety stock
when demand and
lead time are uncertain

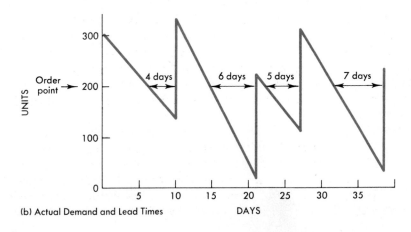

(b) Actual Demand and Lead Times

point must be set at 200 units of inventory on hand as opposed to the previous 100 units. In other words, the order point determines the amount of safety stock held.

In the bottom panel of the figure, the actual experience for our hypothetical firm is shown. In the first segment of demand, we see that actual usage is somewhat less than that which was expected. (The slope of the line is less than the expected demand line in the upper panel.) At the order point of 200 units of inventory held, an order is placed for 200 units of additional inventory. Instead of taking the expected five days for the inventory to be replenished, however, we see that it takes only four days. The second segment of usage is much greater than expected and, as a result, inventory is rapidly used up. At 200 units of remaining inventory, a 200-unit order again is placed, but here it takes six days for the inventory to be received. As a result of both of these factors, heavy inroads are made into the safety stock. In the third segment of demand, usage is about the same as expected; that is, the slopes of expected and actual usage lines are about the same. Because inventory was so low at the end of the previous segment of usage, an order is placed almost immediately. The lead time turns out to be five days. In the last segment of demand, usage is slightly greater than expected. The lead time necessary to receive the order is seven days, much longer than expected. The combination of these two factors again causes the firm to go into its safety stock. The example illustrates the importance of safety stock in absorbing random fluctuations in usage and in lead times. Without such stock, the firm would have run out of inventory on two occasions.

The amount of safety stock

The proper amount of safety stock to maintain depends upon several things. The greater the uncertainty associated with forecasted demand for inventory, the greater the safety stock the firm will wish to carry, all other things the same. Put another way, the risk of running out of stock is greater the larger the unforeseen fluctuations in usage. Similarly, the greater the uncertainty of lead time to replenish stock, the greater the risk of running out of stock, and the greater the safety stock the firm will wish to maintain, all other things being equal. Another factor influencing the safety-stock decision is the cost of running out of inventory. In the case of raw-materials and in-transit inventories, the cost of being out of stock is the delay in production. How much does it cost when production closes down temporarily? Where fixed costs are large, this cost will be quite high, as can be imagined in the case of an aluminum extrusion plant. The cost of running out of finished goods is customer dissatisfaction. Not only will the immediate sale be lost, but future sales will be endangered if the customer takes his business elsewhere. Although this opportunity cost is difficult to measure, it must be recognized by management and incorporated into the safety-stock decision. The greater the costs of running out of stock, of course, the greater the safety stock management will wish to maintain, all other things the same.

The final factor to consider is the cost of carrying additional inventory. If it were not for this cost, a firm could maintain whatever safety stock was necessary to avoid all possibility of running out of inventory. The greater the cost of carrying inventory, the more costly it is to maintain a safety stock, all other things being equal. Determination of the proper amount of safety stock involves balancing the probability and cost of a stockout against the cost of carrying enough safety stock to avoid this possibility. Ultimately, the question reduces to the probability of inventory stockout that management is willing to tolerate. In a typical situation, this probability is reduced at a decreasing rate as more safety stock is added. For example, a firm might be able to reduce the probability of inventory stockout by 20 percent if it adds 100 units of safety stock, but only by an additional 10 percent if it adds another 100 units. There comes a point when it becomes very expensive to reduce further the probability of stockout. Management will not wish to add safety stock beyond the point at which incremental carrying costs exceed the incremental benefits to be derived from avoiding a stockout.

RELATION TO FINANCIAL MANAGEMENT

The inventory control methods described in the last several sections give us a means for determining an optimal level of inventory, as well as how much should be ordered and when. These tools are necessary for managing inventory efficiently and balancing the advantages of additional inventory against the cost of carrying this inventory. With the use of computers, great improvements in inventory control have been made and are continuing to be made. Unfortunately, a review of the many applications of operations research to inventory management is beyond the scope of this book.[4]

Although inventory management usually is not the direct operating responsibility of the financial manager, the investment of funds in inventory is a very important aspect of financial management. Consequently, the financial manager must be familiar with ways to control inventories effectively so that capital may be allocated efficiently. The greater the opportunity cost of funds invested in inventory, the lower the optimal level of average inventory and the lower the optimal

[4] For such a review, see Arthur F. Veinott, Jr., "The Status of Mathematical Inventory Control," *Management Science*, 12 (July 1966), 745–77.

order quantity, all other things held constant. This statement can be verified by increasing the carrying costs, C, in Eq. (8-3). The EOQ model also can be used by the financial manager in planning for inventory financing.

When demand or usage of inventory is uncertain, the financial manager may try to effect policies that will reduce the average lead time required to receive inventory once an order is placed. The lower the average lead time, the lower the safety stock needed and the lower the total investment in inventory, all other things held constant. The greater the opportunity cost of funds invested in inventory, the greater the incentive to reduce this lead time. In the case of purchases, the purchasing department may try to find new vendors that promise quicker delivery or place pressure on existing vendors for faster delivery. In the case of finished goods, the production department may be able to schedule production runs for faster delivery by producing a smaller run. In either case, there is a tradeoff between the added cost involved in reducing the lead time and the opportunity cost of funds tied up in inventory. This discussion serves to point out the importance of inventory management to the financial manager. The greater the efficiency with which the firm manages its inventory, the lower the required investment in inventory, all other things held constant.

SUMMARY

The optimal level of inventories should be judged in relation to the flexibility inventories afford. If we hold constant the efficiency of inventory management, the lower the level of inventories, the less the flexibility of the firm. The higher the amount of inventories, the greater the flexibility of the firm. In evaluating the level of inventories, management must balance the benefits of economies of production, purchasing, and increased product demand against the cost of carrying the additional inventory. Of particular concern to the financial manager is the cost of funds invested in inventory.

The efficiency of inventory control very much affects the flexibility of the firm, given a level of inventory. Conversely, given a degree of flexibility, efficiency affects the level of inventory investment. In this chapter, we have examined several tools of inventory control. One is the economic order quantity (EOQ), whereby we determine the optimal size of order to place, on the basis of the demand or usage of the inventory, the ordering costs, and the carrying costs. Under conditions of uncertainty, the firm must usually provide for a safety stock, owing to fluctuations in demand for inventory and in lead times. By varying the point at which orders are placed, one varies the safety stock that is held.

Another way to determine the optimal level of inventory is through a marginal analysis of the benefits to be realized from additional inventory versus the costs of carrying it. Benefits derive from lower total ordering costs, satisfying more customer orders, and increased production efficiency. Carrying costs are comprised of increased warehousing and insurance and handling costs, together with the required return on the additional investment in inventory.

1. The analysis of inventory policy is analogous to the analysis of credit policy. Propose a measure to analyze inventory policy which is analogous to aging of accounts receivable policy.

2. What are the principal implications to the financial manager of ordering costs, storage costs, and cost of capital as they relate to inventory?

3. Contrast the EOQ model with the incremental profit/incremental investment approach to inventory management. What implicit assumption is made by the EOQ with respect to the relationship between inventory level and sales?

4. Some inventories, such as distilled spirits, must be kept for long periods (5 to 12 years) before being available to customers. Discuss the impact of this type of inventory on liquidity measures. How should one finance this type of inventory?

5. Explain how efficient inventory management affects the liquidity and profitability of the firm.

6. Explain methods by which a firm can reduce its investment in inventory and, at the same time, leave the risk characteristics unchanged.

7. The EOQ model does not provide any information about the safety stock that should be carried by a firm. Develop a conceptual model that will aid management in determining the correct amount of safety stock.

8. How can the firm reduce its investment in inventories? What costs might the firm incur from a policy of very low inventory investment?

9. Explain how a large seasonal demand complicates inventory management and production scheduling.

1. A college bookstore is attempting to determine the optimal order quantity for a popular book on financial management. The store sells 5,000 copies of this book a year at a retail price of $12.50, although the publisher allows the store a 20 percent discount from this price. The store figures that it costs $1 per year to carry a book in inventory and $100 to prepare an order for new books.

(a) Determine the total costs associated with ordering one, two, five, ten, and twenty times a year.

(b) Determine the economic order quantity.

(c) What implicit assumptions are being made about the annual sales rate?

(d) Develop the algebraic expression for determining total cost of ordering and holding inventory. (Hint: Let X be the EOQ and let Y be total cost.)

2. A firm that sells 5,000 gidgets per month is trying to determine how many gidgets to keep in inventory. The financial manager has determined that it costs $200 to place an order. The cost of holding inventory is 4¢/month per average gidget in inventory. A five-day lead time is required for delivery of goods ordered. (This lead time is known with certainty.)

(a) Develop the algebraic expression for determining the total cost of holding and ordering inventory.

(b) Plot the holding cost and the ordering cost on a graph where the abscissa represents size of order and the ordinate represents cost.

(c) Determine the EOQ from the graph.

(d) (Optional) Take the first differential of the total cost equation with respect to the size of order, set it equal to zero, and solve for the size of order.

(e) Compare the answer to (d) with the answer to (c).

(f) Determine the reorder point.

3. The Tahnya Athletic House is analyzing its inventory policy. Of particular concern is the deviation of inventory turnover from the industry average. Tahnya has an inventory turnover (cost of goods/inventory) of 12, while the industry average is 4. Sales average $350,000 per year on fixed costs of $20,000 and variable costs of 80 percent of sales. On the basis of stockout reports, the following estimates have been made:

Inventory Policy	Turnover	Sales
A	12	$350,000
B	6	400,000
C	4	425,000
D	3	440,000

(a) If the required pretax return on investment is 20 percent, which policy should be adopted?

(b) Discuss the implicit assumptions made in making your decision.

4. Favorite Foods Inc. buys 50,000 boxes of ice-cream cones every two months. Order costs are $100 per order and carrying costs are $0.40 per box.

(a) Determine the optimal order quantity.

(b) The vendor now offers Favorite Foods a quantity discount of $0.02 per box if it buys cones in order sizes of 10,000 boxes. Should Favorite Foods avail itself of the quantity discount?

AMMER, DEAN S., "Materials Management as a Profit Center," *Harvard Business Review,* 47 (January–February 1969), 72–89.

BERANEK, WILLIAM, "Financial Implications of Lot-Size Inventory Models," *Management Science,* 13 (April 1967), 401–8.

BIERMAN, HAROLD, JR., CHARLES P. BONINI, and WARREN H. HAUSMAN, *Quantitative Analysis for Business Decisions,* Chapters 10–12. Homewood, Ill.: Richard D. Irwin, 1969.

BROWN, ROBERT G., *Decision Rules for Inventory Management.* New York: Holt, Rinehart & Winston, 1967.

BUFFA, ELWOOD S., *Production-Inventory Systems: Planning and Control.* Homewood, Ill.: Richard D. Irwin, 1968.

HILLIER, FREDERICK S., and GERALD J. LIEBERMAN, *Introduction to Operations Research,* Chapter 12. San Francisco: Holden-Day, 1967.

MAGEE, JOHN F., "Guides to Inventory Policy," I–III, *Harvard Business Review,* 34 (January–February 1956), 49–60; (March–April 1956), 103–16 and (May–June 1956), 57–70.

MEHTA, DILEEP R., *Working Capital Management,* Chapters 4–5. Englewood Cliffs, N.J.: Prentice-Hall, 1974.

SMITH, KEITH V., *Management of Working Capital,* Section 4. New York: West Publishing, 1974.

SNYDER, ARTHUR, "Principles of Inventory Management," *Financial Executive,* 32 (April 1964), 16–19.

STANCILL, JAMES McN., *The Management of Working Capital,* Chapter 5. Scranton, Pa.: Intext, 1971.

STARR, MARTIN K., and DAVID W. MILLER, *Inventory Control—Theory and Practice.* Englewood Cliffs, N.J.: Prentice-Hall, 1962.

VIENOTT, ARTHUR F., JR., "The Status of Mathematical Inventory Theory," *Management Science,* 12 (July 1966), 745–77.

WAGNER, HARVEY M., *Principles of Operations Research—with Applications to Managerial Decisions,* Chapters 9, 19, and Appendix II. Englewood Cliffs, N.J.: Prentice-Hall, 1969.

Short- and Intermediate-Term Financing

II

Trade *Credit* and Commercial *Paper* 9

The three major sources of short-term financing that we examine are trade credit, commercial paper, and short-term loans. In this chapter, we consider the first two methods of financing; the last is examined in Chapter 10. From our analysis of working capital management in Chapter 5, we assume that the firm has decided on a proper proportion of short-term financing in relation to other types of financing; that is, the maturity composition of its debt. The decisions to be made here, then, are what types of short-term financing should be employed and what their composition should be. In this chapter and the next, we analyze alternative sources of short-term financing to see how they may be used to finance seasonal and temporary fluctuations in funds requirements, as well as the more permanent needs of the firm.

TRADE CREDIT AS A SOURCE OF FINANCING

Trade credit is a form of short-term financing common to almost all businesses. In fact, it is the largest source of short-term funds for business firms collectively. In an advanced economy, most buyers are not required to pay for goods upon delivery but are allowed a short deferment period before payment is due. During this period, the seller of the goods extends credit to the buyer. Because suppliers generally are more liberal in the extension of credit than are financial institutions, trade credit is an important source of funds for small companies in particular.

There are three types of trade credit: open account, notes payable, and trade acceptances. By far the most common type is the open-account arrangement. With this arrangement, the seller ships goods to the buyer along with an invoice that specifies the goods shipped, the price, the total amount due, and the terms of the sale. Open-account credit derives its name from the fact that the buyer does not sign a formal debt instrument evidencing the amount that he owes the seller. The seller extends credit based upon his credit investigation of the buyer (see Chapter 7).

In some situations, promissory notes are employed instead of open-account credit. In this case, the buyer is asked to sign a note that evidences his debt to the seller. The note itself calls for the payment of the obligation at some specified future date. Promissory notes have been used in such lines of business as furs and jewelry. This arrangement is employed when the seller wants the buyer to recognize his debt formally. For example, a seller might request a promissory note from a buyer if the latter's open account became past due.

A trade acceptance is another arrangement by which the indebtedness of the buyer is formally recognized. Under this arrangement, the seller draws a draft on the buyer ordering him to pay the draft at some date in the future. The seller will not release the goods until the buyer accepts the time draft.[1] When the buyer accepts the draft, he designates a bank at which the draft will be paid when it comes due. At that time, the draft becomes a trade acceptance, and depending upon the credit-worthiness of the buyer, it may possess some degree of marketability. If the trade acceptance is marketable, the seller of the goods can sell it at a discount and receive immediate payment for the goods. At final maturity, the holder of the acceptance presents it to the designated bank for collection.

Terms of sale

Because the use of promissory notes and trade acceptances is rather limited, the subsequent discussion will be confined to open-account trade credit. With this type of credit, the terms of the sale are an important consideration. These terms, which are specified in the invoice, may be placed in several broad categories according to the net period within which payment is expected and according to the terms of the cash discount.

COD and CBD—no extension of credit. COD terms mean cash on delivery of the goods. The only risk that the seller undertakes in this type of arrangement is that the buyer may refuse the shipment.

[1] If the instrument is a sight draft, the buyer is ordered to pay the draft upon presentation. Under this arrangement, trade credit is not extended.

Under such circumstances, the seller will be stuck with the shipping costs. Occasionally a seller might ask for cash before delivery (CBD) to avoid all risk. Under either COD or CBD terms, the seller does not extend credit. CBD terms must be distinguished from progress payments, which are very common in certain industries. With progress payments, the buyer pays the manufacturer at various stages of production prior to the actual delivery of the finished product. Because large sums of money are tied up in work in progress, aircraft manufacturers request progress payments from airlines in advance of the actual delivery of aircraft.

Net period—no cash discount.   When credit is extended, the seller specifies the period of time allowed for payment. For example, the terms "net 30" indicate that the invoice or bill must be paid within thirty days. If the seller bills on a monthly basis, it might require such terms as "net 15 EOM," which means that all goods shipped before the end of the month must be paid for by the fifteenth of the following month.

Net period with cash discount.   In addition to extending credit, the seller may offer a cash discount if the bill is paid during the early part of the net period. The terms "2/10, net 30" indicate that the buyer is offered a 2 percent discount if the bill is paid within ten days; if he does not pay within ten days, he must pay the full amount of the bill within thirty days. A cash discount differs from a trade discount and from a quantity discount. With a trade discount, one type of customer (a wholesaler for example) is given a lower price on goods purchased than is another type of customer, say a retailer. With a quantity discount, a customer is given a discount if the shipment is above a certain amount. Under most circumstances, a cash discount is offered as an incentive to the buyer to pay early. In Chapter 7, we considered the question of the optimal cash discount to be offered by a seller.

Datings.   Datings are used frequently in a seasonal business, where the seller wishes to encourage customers to place their orders before a heavy selling period. For example, a manufacturer of lawn mowers may give seasonal datings specifying that any shipment to a dealer in the winter or spring does not have to be paid for until summer. The arrangement is beneficial to the seller because, with earlier orders, he can gauge his demand more realistically and schedule production more efficiently. Also, the seller does not have to store certain finished goods inventory. The advantage of datings to the buyer is that he does not have to pay for the goods until he is able to sell them. Under this arrangement, credit is extended for a longer than normal period of time.

Trade credit as a means of financing

We have seen that trade credit is a source of funds, because the buyer does not have to pay for goods until after they are delivered. If the firm automatically pays its bills a certain number of days after the date of invoice, trade credit becomes a built-in source of financing that varies with the production cycle. As the firm increases its production and corresponding purchases, accounts payable increase and provide part of the funds needed to finance the increase in production. As production decreases, accounts payable tend to decrease. Although the variation of accounts payable with production may not be directly proportional, on account of shortages or gluts in inventory on hand, there is a strong degree of correspondence.

If a firm adheres strictly to the practice of paying its bills at a given time after invoice, trade credit is not a discretionary source of financing. It is entirely dependent upon the purchasing plans of the firm, which, in turn, are dependent upon its production cycle. In examining trade credit as a discretionary form of financing, we want to specifically consider situations in which (1) a firm does not take a cash discount but pays on the last day of the net period, and (2) a firm pays its bills beyond the net period.

Payment on the final due date

In this section, we assume that the firm foregoes a cash discount but does pay its bill on the final due date of the net period. If no cash discount is offered, there is no cost for the use of credit during the net period. By the same token, if a firm takes the discount, there is no cost for the use of trade credit during the discount period. However, if a cash discount is offered and it is not taken, there is a definite opportunity cost. For example, if the terms of sale are 2/10, net 30, the firm has the use of funds for an additional twenty days if it does not take the cash discount but pays on the final day of the net period. In the case of a $100 invoice, it would have the use of $98 for twenty days. The annual interest cost is[2]

$$\frac{2}{98} \times \frac{360}{20} = 36.7 \text{ percent}$$

Thus, we see that trade credit can be a very expensive form of short-term financing when a cash discount is offered.

[2] For ease of calculation, 360 rather than 365 is used as the number of days in the year.

The cost of trade credit declines the longer the net period is in relation to the discount period. For example, had the terms in the above example been 2/10, net 60, the annual interest cost would have been

$$\frac{2}{98} \times \frac{360}{50} = 14.7 \text{ percent}$$

The relationship between the annual interest cost of trade credit and the number of days between the end of the discount period and the end of the net period is shown in Figure 9-1. In the figure, we assume 2/10 discount terms. We see that the cost of trade credit decreases at a decreasing rate as the net period increases. The point is that if a firm does not take a cash discount, its cost of trade credit declines the longer it is able to postpone payment.

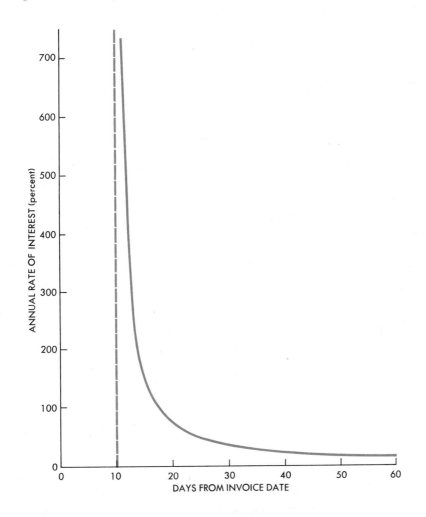

FIG. 9 · 1

Annual rate of interest
on accounts payable
with terms of 2/10, net 30

The following terms have been used by tufters in the carpet and floor-covering industry:[3]

$$5/10, \ 4/70, \ \text{net } 71$$

These terms mean that if a firm pays within ten days after invoicing, it is entitled to a 5 percent cash discount; whereas if it pays between day 10 and day 70, it is entitled to a 4 percent discount. The final due date is seventy-one days after invoicing. If a purchaser pays on day 70, it foregoes a 1 percent higher discount for the use of funds from day 10 to day 70. If the invoice is for $100, the annual interest cost is

$$\frac{1}{95} \times \frac{360}{60} = 6.3 \text{ percent}$$

Thus, the cost of foregoing the 5 percent discount in favor of the 4 percent one is relatively low in this case, and trade credit is an attractive means of financing. With these terms, the seller creates a powerful incentive to pay on the seventieth day. No one should pay on the final due date, for the cost of credit for the day is astronomical, as can be easily determined.

Stretching accounts payable

In the preceding section, we assumed that payment was made at the end of the due period. However, a firm may postpone payment beyond this period; we shall call this postponement "stretching" accounts payable or "leaning on the trade." The cost of stretching accounts payable is twofold: the cost of the cash discount foregone and the possible deterioration in credit rating. In Chapter 7, we discussed the rating system of such credit agencies as Dun & Bradstreet. If a firm stretches its payables excessively so that trade payables are significantly delinquent, its credit rating will suffer. Suppliers will view the firm with apprehension and may insist upon rather strict terms of sale if, indeed, they sell at all. Also, banks and other lenders do not regard excessive slowness in the trade very favorably in assessing a company. Although it is difficult to measure, there is certainly an opportunity cost to a deterioration in a firm's credit reputation.

Notwithstanding the possibility of a deteriorating credit rating, it may be possible to postpone certain payables beyond the net period without severe consequences. Suppliers are in business to sell goods, and trade credit may be a very important sales tool. A supplier may

---

[3]This example is drawn from John J. Brosky, *The Implicit Cost of Trade Credit and Theory of Optimal Terms of Sale* (New York: Credit Research Foundation, 1969), p. 3.

well be willing to go along with a certain stretching of his payables, particularly if the risk of bad-debt loss is negligible. If the funds requirement of the firm is seasonal, suppliers may not view the stretching of payables in an unfavorable light during periods of peak requirements, provided that the firm is current in the trade during the rest of the year. However, there may be an indirect charge for this extension of credit in the form of higher prices. The firm should be particularly careful to consider this possibility in evaluating the cost of stretching accounts payable.

Periodic and reasonable stretching of payables is not necessarily bad per se. It should be evaluated objectively in relation to its cost and in relation to alternative sources of short-term credit. When a firm does stretch its payables, effort should be made to keep suppliers fully informed of its situation. A large number of suppliers will allow a firm to stretch payables if the firm is honest with the supplier and consistent in its payments. Sometimes a firm with seasonal funds requirements is able to obtain a dating from a supplier. When a firm obtains a dating, it does not stretch its payables; as long as it pays the bill by the final date, no deterioration in its credit rating is likely.

Advantages of trade credit

The firm must balance the advantages of trade credit as a discretionary source of financing against the cost of foregoing a cash discount and the opportunity cost associated with a possible deterioration in credit reputation if it stretches its payables. There are several advantages of trade credit as a form of short-term financing. Probably the major advantage is its ready availability. The accounts payable of most firms represent a continuous form of credit. There is no need to arrange financing formally; it is already there. If the firm is now taking cash discounts, additional credit is readily available by not paying existing accounts payable until the end of the net period. There is no need to negotiate with the supplier; the decision is entirely up to the firm. In the case of stretching accounts payable, it will become necessary, after a certain degree of postponement, to negotiate with the supplier.

In other types of short-term financing, it is necessary to negotiate formally with the lender over the terms of the loan. The lender may impose restrictions on the firm and seek a secured position. Restrictions are possible with trade credit, but they are not nearly as likely. With other sources of short-term financing, there may be a lead time between the time the need for funds is recognized and the time the firm is actually able to borrow them. Trade credit is a more flexible means of financing. The firm does not have to sign a note, pledge collateral, or adhere to a strict payment schedule on the note. A supplier views an occasional delinquent payment with a far less critical eye than does a banker or other lender.

Trade credit is advantageous to small firms that have difficulty obtaining credit elsewhere, or cannot obtain it at all. Typically, a higher percentage of the total liabilities of a small firm is comprised of trade credit than is true of a large firm. In periods of tight money, it has been contended that large firms obtain credit more easily than do small firms. However, small firms still have access to trade credit as a means of financing; often this credit comes from large suppliers who, in turn, avail themselves of other sources of financing. On balance, it appears that trade credit in the economy flows from firms with easy access to the capital markets, or with idle money balances, to firms with little access to the capital markets. To the extent that the former category consists predominantly of large, well-established firms while the latter consists of smaller, newer firms, trade credit serves as an escape valve for the small firm in times of tight money.[4]

The advantages of using trade credit must be weighed against the cost. As we have seen, the cost may be very high when all factors are considered. Many firms utilize other sources of short-term financing in order to be able to take advantage of cash discounts. The savings in cost over other forms of short-term financing, however, must offset the flexibility and convenience of trade credit. For certain firms, moreover, there simply are no alternative sources of short-term credit.

Who bears the cost?

It is important to recognize that trade credit involves a cost for the use of funds over time. In the previous sections, it was implied that there is no explicit cost to trade credit if the buyer pays the invoice during the discount period or during the net period, if no cash discount is given. Although this supposition is valid from the standpoint of marginal analysis, it overlooks the fact that somebody must bear the cost of trade credit, for the use of funds over time is not free. The burden may fall on the supplier, the buyer, or both parties. The supplier may be able to pass the cost on to the buyer in the form of higher prices.

---

[4] For an excellent analysis of this question, see Robert A. Schwartz, "An Economic Analysis of Trade Credit," *Journal of Financial and Quantitative Analysis*, 9 (September 1974), 643–57. See also Arthur B. Laffer, "Trade Credit and the Money Market," *Journal of Political Economy*, 78 (March–April 1970); Allan H. Meltzer, "Monetary Policy and the Trade Credit Practices of Business Firms," in Commission on Money and Credit, *Stabilization Policies* (Englewood Cliffs, N.J.: Prentice-Hall, 1963), p. 494; Meltzer, "Mercantile Credit, Monetary Policy and the Size of Firms," *Review of Economics and Statistics*, 42 (November 1960), 429–37; and Thomas Mayer, "Trade Credit and the Discriminatory Effects of Monetary Policy," *National Banking Review* (June 1966), pp. 543–45.

In the case of a product for which demand is elastic, however, the supplier may be reluctant to increase prices and may end up absorbing most of the cost of trade credit. Under other circumstances, the supplier is able to pass the cost on to the buyer. The buyer should determine who is bearing the cost of trade credit; if he finds that he is bearing the cost, he may want to consider other suppliers to see if he can do better elsewhere. In addition, the buyer should recognize that the cost of trade credit changes over time. In periods of rising interest rates and tight money, suppliers may raise the price of their products to take account of the rising cost of carrying receivables. This rise in price should not be confused with other rises caused by changing supply and demand conditions in the product markets.

THE USE OF COMMERCIAL PAPER

Large, well-established companies sometimes borrow on a short-term basis through commercial paper. Commercial paper consists of unsecured short-term negotiable promissory notes sold in the money market. Because these notes are unsecured and are a money-market instrument, only the most credit-worthy companies are able to use commercial paper as a source of short-term financing. The development of the commercial paper market in this country began in the colonial period. Its explosive growth in the sixties and seventies (see Table 9-1, p. 166) was closely associated with growth of the whole economy and the growth of installment financing of durable goods. In addition, the growth in commercial paper financing in the late sixties and in 1973–74 was attributable in part to the fact that banks curtailed credit in general and credit to finance companies in particular. Borrowers then turned to the commercial paper market as an alternative source of financing.

Market for commercial paper

The commercial paper market is composed of two parts: the dealer market and the direct placement market.[5] Industrial firms, utilities, and medium-sized finance companies sell commercial paper through dealers. The dealer organization is composed of a half-dozen major dealers, who purchase commercial paper from the issuer and, in turn, sell it to investors. The typical commission a dealer earns is one-eighth percent, and maturities on dealer-placed paper generally range from one to six months. The market is a highly organized and sophisticated

[5] For a discussion of commercial paper from the standpoint of a short-term investor, see Chapter 6.

one; paper is sold in denominations ranging from $25,000 to several million dollars. Though the dealer market has been characterized in the past by a significant number of issuers who borrowed on a seasonal basis, the trend definitely is toward financing on a revolving or more permanent basis.

TABLE 9 · 1

Commercial Paper Rates and Amounts Outstanding, 1960–75

	Commercial Paper Outstanding at December 31 (in millions)			Commercial Paper Average Interest Rate for Year		
	Total	Dealer-placed	Directly Placed	Dealer-Placed 4–6 Mos.	Directly Placed 3–6 Mos.	Prime Rate on Bank Loans at June 30
1960	$ 4,497	$ 1,358	$ 3,139	3.85%	3.54%	5.00%
1965	9,058	1,903	7,155	4.38	4.27	4.50
1967	16,535	4,901	11,634	5.10	4.89	5.50
1969	31,624	11,817	19,807	7.83	7.16	8.50
1970	33,071	10,650	22,421	7.72	7.23	8.00
1971	32,126	10,095	22,031	5.11	4.91	5.50
1972	34,721	11,212	23,509	4.69	4.52	5.25
1973	41,073	10,926	30,147	8.15	7.40	7.50
1974	49,144	10,787	38,357	9.87	8.62	11.75
1975(0)	50,437	10,929	39,508	6.33	6.16	7.00

Source: *Federal Reserve Bulletins.*

Table 9-1 shows the surge in commercial paper placed through dealers during the 1965 through 1969 period. This growth resulted in part from industrial firms and utilities discovering commercial paper as an appropriate alternative source of funds in periods of tight money. During these periods, commercial banks are not able to accommodate their demand for loans; therefore, the utilities and industrial firms are forced to seek other sources of short-term financing.

Since the 1920s, a number of large sales finance companies, such as General Motors Acceptance Corporation, have bypassed the dealer organization in favor of selling their paper directly to investors. These issuers tailor both the maturity and the amount of the note to the needs of investors, most of which are large corporations with excess cash. Maturities on directly placed paper can range from as little as a few days up to nine months. Unlike many industrial issuers, finance companies use the commercial paper market as a permanent source of funds. With the development of the direct-placement market, pockets of idle investment funds have been tapped for short-term financing purposes. As shown in Table 9-1, directly placed paper has recently accounted for 60 to 80 percent of the total commercial paper outstanding. The growth in direct paper was caused by the increased demand for consumer credit, along with the substitution of commercial paper for bank credit by large finance companies.

Advantages to borrower

The principal advantage of commercial paper as a source of short-term financing is that it is generally cheaper than a short-term business loan from a commercial bank. Usually, the rate on prime commercial paper is 0.25 percent to 2 percent lower than the prime rate for bank loans to the highest-quality borrower. The differential tends to increase in periods of easy money and to decrease in periods of tight money. It is important to recognize that, unlike the prime rate on bank loans, commercial paper rates fluctuate considerably in keeping with money-market conditions. Table 9-1 shows the average rates for dealer-placed and directly placed commercial paper as well as the prime rate on business loans since 1960. In assessing commercial paper as a means of financing, the firm should weigh relative cost and availability in comparison with alternative sources of funds. In this comparison, the cost of bank credit should be adjusted upward for compensating-balance requirements (see the next chapter).

Many companies consider commercial paper a desirable supplement to bank credit. Ideally, a company would borrow heavily through commercial paper when the interest-rate differential was wide and borrow more from banks when the differential narrowed. This strategy would result in the lowest average interest cost and the maximum flexibility. However, commercial banks do not look favorably on credit requests only in periods of tight money. Switching from commercial paper to bank borrowings is possible, but a company must be careful not to impair relations with its bank. The commercial paper market is highly impersonal. If a firm cannot borrow from a commercial bank, it is at the mercy of the market. Therefore, it is important to maintain lines of credit at commercial banks in order to backstop adverse money-market conditions.

In addition to cost advantages, another reason commercial paper is used is that the legal limitations on the size of a loan that a commercial bank can extend precludes satisfying the requirements of the large finance companies. For example, the maximum loan a national bank can make to a single borrower is 10 percent of its capital and surplus. The total borrowing requirements of the three largest sales finance companies exceed the legal lending limits of the fifty largest banks in this country. Consequently, these companies must turn to other sources of short-term financing—namely, direct investors.

SUMMARY

Trade credit can be an important source of short-term financing for the firm. However, it is a discretionary source of financing only if a firm does not have a strict policy with respect to the number of days after invoice a bill is paid. When a cash discount is offered but not taken, the cost of trade credit is the cash discount foregone. However, the longer the period between the end of the discount period and the time the bill is paid, the less the opportunity cost. "Stretching" accounts payable involves postponement of payment beyond the due period. The opportunity cost of stretching payables is the possible deterioration in the firm's credit rating. The firm must balance the costs of trade credit against its advantages and the costs of other short-term credit. The major advantage of trade credit is the flexibility it gives the firm.

Commercial paper is used only by well-established, high-quality companies. The evidence of debt is an unsecured short-term promissory note that is sold in the money market. Commercial paper is sold either through dealers or directly to investors. The latter method is used by large sales finance companies, and about three-quarters of commercial paper is placed in this manner. The principal advantage of commercial paper is that its yield is less than the rate of interest a company would have to pay on a bank loan. When used properly, it therefore is a very desirable source of short-term funds.

QUESTIONS

1. Explain why trade credit is a "spontaneous source of funds."

2. Trade credit is a very costly source of funds when discounts are lost. Explain why many firms rely on this source of funds to finance their temporary working capital.

3. Stretching payables provides "free" funds to the customers for a short period. The supplier, however, can face serious financial problems if all of its customers stretch their accounts. Discuss the nature of the problems the supplier may face and suggest different approaches to cope with stretching.

4. What may be the impact of large-scale stretching on social welfare? Explain.

5. Why is the rate on commercial paper usually less than the prime rate charged by bankers and more than the Treasury bill rate?

6. Why would a firm borrow bank funds at higher rates instead of issuing commercial paper?

7. Why would a firm invest its temporary excess liquidity in Treasury bills instead of buying higher-yielding commercial paper?

8. Suppose a firm elected to tighten its trade credit policy from 2/10, net 90 to 2/10, net 30. What effect could the firm expect this change to have on its liquidity?

9. Why do small firms in particular rely heavily on trade credit as a source of funds? Why will suppliers advance credit to firms when banks will not?

1. Determine the effective annual cost of capital for the following terms, assuming discounts are lost:
   (a) 1/10, n/30
   (b) 2/10, n/30
   (c) 3/10, n/30
   (d) 10/30, n/60
   (e) 3/10, n/60
   (f) 2/10, n/90
   (g) 3/10, n/90
   (h) 5/10, n/100

2. The Dud Company purchases raw materials on terms of 2/10, net 30. A review of the company's records by the owner, Mr. Dud, revealed that payments are usually made fifteen days after purchases are received. When asked why the firm did not take advantage of its discounts, the bookkeeper, Mr. Grind, replied that it cost only 2 percent for these funds, whereas a bank loan would cost the firm 6 percent.
   (a) What mistake is Grind making?
   (b) What is the real cost of not taking advantage of the discount?
   (c) If the firm could not borrow from the bank and was forced to resort to the use of trade credit funds, what suggestion might be made to Grind which would reduce the annual interest cost?

3. The Sphinx Supply Company needs to increase its working capital by $100,000. It has decided that the following three alternatives of financing are available:
   (a) Forego cash discounts, granted on a basis of 3/10, net 30.
   (b) Borrow from the bank at 8 percent. This alternative would necessitate maintaining a 25 percent compensating balance.
   (c) Issue commercial paper at 7½ percent. The cost of placing the issue would be $500 each six months.
   Assuming the firm would prefer the flexibility of bank financing, provided the additional cost of this flexibility was no more than 1 percent, which alternative should be selected?

4. The manager of Wilstat Corporation is considering the benefits of switching from cash purchase of merchandise to credit purchase on net 60-day terms.

The manager feels that the increased liquidity of purchasing $5,000/month on 60-day terms will be reflected in the liquidity ratios. The working capital accounts of the corporation are as follows:

Cash	$15,000	Notes payable	$10,000
Receivables	25,000	Taxes payable	6,000
Inventories	40,000	Other accruals	4,000
	$80,000		$20,000

(a) What effect would the purchase of $10,000 of merchandise on 60-day terms have on (1) the current ratio and (2) the quick ratio?

(b) Do the ratios indicate increased liquidity? Explain.

5. Determine the annual percentage interest cost for each of the following terms of sale, assuming the firm does not take the cash discount but pays on the final day of the net period (assume a 360-day year):

(a) 1/20, net 30 ($500 invoice)

(b) 2/30, net 60 ($1,000 invoice)

(c) 2/5, net 10 ($100 invoice)

(d) 3/10, net 30 ($250 invoice)

6. Does the dollar size of the invoice affect the annual interest cost of not taking discounts? Illustrate with an example.

7. Recompute Problem 5, assuming a 10-day stretching of the payment date.

SELECTED REFERENCES

BAXTER, NEVINS D., *The Commercial Paper Market*. Princeton, N.J.: Princeton University Press, 1964.

BROSKY, JOHN J., *The Implicit Cost of Trade Credit and Theory of Optimal Terms of Sale*. New York: Credit Research Foundation, 1969.

LAFFER, ARTHUR B., "Trade Credit and the Money Market," *Journal of Political Economy*, 78 (March–April 1970).

ROBICHEK, A. A., D. TEICHROEW, and J. M. JONES, "Optimal Short Term Financing Decision," *Management Science*, 12 (September 1965), 1–36.

SCHADRACK, FREDERICK C., and FREDERICK S. BREIMYER, "Recent Developments in the Commercial Paper Market," *Monthly Review of the Federal Reserve Bank of New York*, 52 (December 1970), 280–91.

SCHWARTZ, ROBERT A., "An Economic Model of Trade Credit," *Journal of Financial and Quantitative Analysis*, 9 (September 1974), 643–58.

SEIDEN, MARTIN H., *The Quality of Trade Credit*, Occasional Paper No. 87. New York: National Bureau of Economic Research, 1964.

SELDEN, RICHARD T., *Trends and Cycles in the Commercial Paper Market*. New York: National Bureau of Economic Research, 1963.

SMITH, KEITH V., *Management of Working Capital*, Section 5. New York: West Publishing, 1974.

Short-Term Loans 10

In the preceding chapter, we considered two important sources of short-term financing for the firm—namely, trade credit and commercial paper. In this chapter, we examine short-term loans, the principal sources of which are commercial banks and finance companies. For expository purposes, it is convenient to separate business loans into two categories: unsecured loans and secured loans. Almost without exception, finance companies do not offer unsecured loans, simply because a borrower who deserves unsecured credit can borrow at a lower cost from a commercial bank. Consequently, our discussion of unsecured loans will involve only commercial banks.

UNSECURED BANK CREDIT

Short-term, unsecured bank loans typically are regarded as "self-liquidating" in that the assets purchased with the proceeds generate sufficient cash flows to pay the loan in less than a year. At one time, banks confined their lending almost exclusively to this type of loan. Fortunately, banks now provide a wide variety of business loans, tailored to the specific needs of the borrower. Still, the short-term, self-liquidating loan is an important source of business financing. It is particularly popular in financing seasonal buildups in accounts receivable and inventories. Unsecured short-term loans may be extended under a line of credit, under a revolving-credit agreement, or on a transaction basis. The debt itself is evidenced formally by a promissory note signed by the borrower, showing the time and amount of payment and the interest to be paid.

Line of credit

A line of credit is an arrangement between a bank and its customer with respect to the maximum amount of unsecured credit the bank will permit the firm to owe at any one time. Usually, credit lines are established for a one-year period and are subject to one-year renewals. Frequently, lines of credit are set for renewal after the bank receives the audited annual report and has had a chance to review the progress of the borrower. For example, if the borrower's year-end statement date is December 31, a bank may set its line to expire sometime in March. At that time, the bank and the company would meet to discuss the credit needs of the firm for the coming year in light of its past year's performance. The amount of the line is based upon the bank's assessment of the credit-worthiness of the borrower and upon his credit needs. Depending upon changes in these conditions, a line of credit may be adjusted at the renewal date, or before, if conditions necessitate a change.

The cash budget, perhaps, gives the best insight into the borrower's short-term credit needs. For example, if maximum or peak borrowing needs over the forthcoming year are estimated at $800,000, a company might seek a line of credit of $1 million to give it a margin of safety. Whether the bank will go along with the request, of course, will depend upon its evaluation of the credit-worthiness of the firm. If the bank agrees, the firm then may borrow on a short-term basis—usually ninety days—up to the full $1 million line. As banks tend to regard borrowing under lines of credit as seasonal or temporary financing, they usually require that the borrower be out of bank debt at some time during the year. Frequently, the borrower will be required to "clean up" bank debt for at least thirty days during the year. The understanding between the bank and the borrower with respect to a "cleanup," of course, is subject to negotiation. The "cleanup" itself is evidence to the bank that the loan is truly seasonal in nature and not a portion of the permanent financing of the firm.

Despite its many advantages to the borrower, a line of credit does not constitute a legal commitment on the part of the bank to extend credit. The borrower is usually informed of the line by means of a letter indicating that the bank is willing to extend credit up to a certain amount. An example of such a letter is shown in Figure 10-1. This letter is not a legal obligation of the bank to extend credit. If the credit-worthiness of the borrower should deteriorate over the year, the

```
                    Second National Bank
                    Palo Alto, California




                                         March 23, 197-

        Mr. Joseph A. Ralberg
        Vice President & Treasurer
        Barker Manufacturing Corporation
        Palo Alto, California

        Dear Mr. Ralberg:

        Based upon our analysis of your year-end audited statements,
        we are pleased to renew your $1 million unsecured line of
        credit for the forthcoming year.  Borrowings under this
        line will be at a rate of one-half percent (½%) over the
        prime rate.

        This line is subject to only the understanding that your
        company will maintain its financial position and that it
        will be out of bank debt for at least 45 days during the
        fiscal year.


                              Yours very truly,


                                 John D. Myers
                                 Vice President
```

FIG. 10 · 1
Sample letter
extending line of credit

bank may not want to extend credit and would not be required to do so. Under most circumstances, however, a bank feels bound to honor a line of credit.

Revolving-credit agreement

A revolving-credit agreement represents a legal commitment on the part of the bank to extend credit up to a maximum amount. While the commitment is in force, the bank must extend credit to the borrower any time he wishes to borrow, provided total borrowings do not exceed the maximum amount specified. If the revolving credit is for $1 million, and $700,000 is already owing, the borrower can borrow an additional $300,000 at any time. For the privilege of having this formal commitment, the borrower usually is required to pay a commitment fee on the unused portion of the revolving credit. For example, if the revolving credit is for $1 million, and borrowing for the year averages $400,000, the borrower will be required to pay a commitment fee on the $600,000 unused portion. If the fee is 0.5 percent, the cost of this privilege will be $3,000 for the year. Revolving-credit agreements frequently extend beyond one year. Because lending arrangements of more than a year must be regarded as intermediate rather than short-term credit, we shall examine revolving credits more extensively in Chapter 11. The purpose of introducing them at this time is to illustrate the formal nature of the arrangement in contrast to the informality of a line of credit.

Transaction loans

Borrowing under a line of credit or under a revolving-credit arrangement is not appropriate when the firm needs short-term funds for only one purpose. For example, a contractor may borrow from a bank in order to complete a job. When the contractor receives payment for the job, he pays the loan. For this type of loan, a bank evaluates each request by the borrower as a separate transaction. In these evaluations, the cash-flow ability of the borrower to pay the loan is usually of paramount importance.

Compensating balances

In addition to charging interest on loans, commercial banks often require the borrower to maintain demand-deposit balances at the bank in direct proportion to either the amount of funds borrowed or the amount of the commitment. These minimum balances are known as compensating balances. The amount required in the compensating balance varies according to the particular bank and the borrower, but many banks require balances equal to 15 percent of a line of credit. If the line is $1 million, the borrower will be required to maintain average balances of at least $150,000 during the year. The effect of a compensating-balance requirement is to raise the effective cost of borrowing if the borrower is required to maintain balances above the amount the firm would maintain ordinarily.

Bankers will argue that balances compensating a lending accommodation should be "free" in the sense that they are not needed to compensate the bank for deposit activity in the firm's demand-deposit account. In fact, however, many banks overlook this differentiation of compensation when it comes to evaluating whether the requirement is being met. In other words, if a firm needed to maintain a balance of $150,000 simply to compensate for the deposit and withdrawal activity in its account, it also might be able to obtain a $1 million line of credit without increasing its balances. To the extent that a compensating-balance requirement does not require the borrower to maintain balances above those that it would maintain ordinarily, such a requirement does not raise the effective cost of borrowing. However, if balances above the ordinary must be maintained, the effective cost of borrowing is raised. For example, suppose we borrow $1 million at 8 percent and are required to maintain $100,000 more in balances than we would ordinarily. We would then have use of only $900,000 of the $1 million loan. The effective annual interest cost is $80,000/$900,000 = 8.88 percent, rather than 8 percent.

Compensating-balance requirements may increase the liquidity position of the borrower from the bank's point of view. As a last resort, the bank can exercise its legal right of offset and apply the balances on deposit to pay off the loan or a portion of the loan. The compensating balance required of a firm may vary somewhat in keeping with general credit availability. When money is tight and loan demand high, commercial banks are able to enforce higher compensating-balance requirements than they are when credit is readily available.

There is some indication that the notion of compensating balances for loans is lessening somewhat in importance. Increasingly, banks are becoming more profit- as opposed to deposit-oriented and, accordingly, are "fine-tuning" their profitability analyses of customer relationships. This movement has led a number of banks to prohibit the use of balances to support both account activity and lending arrangements. With the rapid and significant fluctuation in the cost of funds to banks in recent years, some banks are making loans without compensating-balance requirements. The interest rate charged is higher and more in line with the bank's incremental cost of obtaining funds. The movement toward more sophisticated profitability analysis is likely to reduce further, though certainly not eliminate, the imposition of compensating-balance requirements in connection with lending arrangements.[1]

Interest rates

Unlike interest rates on such impersonal money-market instruments as Treasury bills, bankers' acceptances, and commercial paper, most business loans are determined through personal negotiation between

---

[1]For further discussion of this issue, see Paul S. Nadler, "Compensating Balances and the Prime at Twilight," *Harvard Business Review*, 50 (January–February 1972), 112–20.

the borrower and the lender(s). In some measure, banks try to vary the interest rate charged according to the credit-worthiness of the borrower; the lower the credit-worthiness, the higher the interest rate. Interest rates charged also vary in keeping with money-market conditions. One measure that varies to some extent with underlying market conditions is the *prime* rate. The prime rate is the lowest rate typically charged on business loans to large, well-established, and financially sound companies. The rate itself is usually set by large money-market banks and is relatively uniform throughout the country. In the past, the rate changed only slowly over time in keeping with underlying changes in market conditions. This phenomenon is evident in Figure 10-2 up to the mid-sixties.

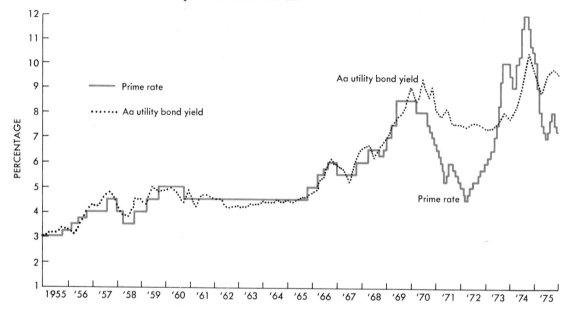

FIG. 10 · 2   Relationship between callable new issues of Aa utility bonds and the prime rate

After the mid-sixties, the prime rate changed much more rapidly. Several factors were responsible. For one thing, there was a greater volatility in overall market rates of interest. The early- to mid-sixties was a period of unprecedented stability in interest rates. This stability has not been witnessed since. Another factor was the cost of funds to banks. Over the years, time deposits and other liabilities on which interest is paid have increased significantly in relation to demand deposits. As a result, fluctuations in market rates of interest cause greater volatility in the cost of funds to banks than was true previously. Finally, certain banks have instigated "floating" prime rates. The floating prime is in keeping with changes in money-market rates. For example, the rate might be 0.5 percent above the commercial paper rate, with adjustments occurring on a weekly basis. The floating prime not only has resulted in those banks adjusting their prime rates more frequently than before but has brought pressure on "nonfloating" prime banks to change their rates more frequently than might otherwise be the case. All of these factors have caused frequent changes in the prime rate in recent years, as evidenced in Figure 10-2.

Given a prime rate for companies of the highest credit-worthiness, other borrowers are charged rates above the prime. For example, a bank might extend a line of credit to a company at a rate of 0.5 percent above prime. If the prime rate is 8.5 percent, the borrower will be charged an interest rate of 9 percent. If the prime rate changes to 8 percent, the borrower will pay 8.5 percent.

The interest-rate differential between the prime rate and the rate charged to a borrower will depend upon the relative bargaining power of the borrower and the bank. Supposedly, this differential should reflect only the borrower's credit-worthiness in relation to that of a "prime-risk" borrower. However, other factors influence the differential. The balances maintained and other business the borrower has with a bank (such as trust business) may be important considerations. A good customer who has maintained very attractive balances in the past may be able to obtain a more favorable interest rate than will a firm of equal credit-worthiness that has carried rather meager balances in the past. Although the prime rate reflects national credit conditions, many banks extend credit only in a specific geographic area. To the extent that credit conditions in that area differ from national conditions, the interest-rate differential from the prime rate will be affected. In addition, a bank that is aggressively seeking a relationship with a company may be willing to extend credit at a rate slightly lower than it might charge normally.

Thus, the interest rate charged on a short-term loan will depend upon the prevailing prime rate, the credit-worthiness of the borrower, his present and prospective relationship with the bank, and, sometimes, upon other considerations. Because of the fixed costs involved in credit investigation and in the processing of a loan, we would expect the interest rate on small loans to be higher than the rate on large loans.

Methods of computing interest rates. There are two ways in which interest on a loan may be paid: on a collect basis and on a discount basis. When paid on a collect basis, the interest is paid at the maturity of the note; when paid on a discount basis, interest is deducted from the initial loan. To illustrate, suppose we have a $10,000 loan at 7 percent interest for one year. The effective rate of interest on a collect note is

$$\frac{\$700}{\$10,000} = 7.00 \text{ percent}$$

On a discount basis, the effective rate of interest is not 7 percent but

$$\frac{\$700}{\$9,300} = 7.53 \text{ percent}$$

When we pay on a discount basis, we have the use of only $9,300 for the year but must pay back $10,000 at the end of that time. Thus, the effective rate of interest is higher on a discount note than on a collect note. We should point out that most bank business loans are on a collect note basis.

SECURED CREDIT

Many firms cannot obtain credit on an unsecured basis, either because they are new and unproven or because their ability to service debt is not regarded as adequate by bankers. In order to make a loan, lenders require security so as to reduce their risk of loss. With security, lenders have two sources of loan payment: the cash-flow ability of the firm to service the debt; and, if that source fails for some reason, the collateral value of the security. Most lenders will not make a loan unless the firm has sufficient expected cash flows to make proper servicing of debt probable. To reduce their risk further, however, they require security as well.

Collateral value

The excess of the market value of the security pledged over the amount of the loan determines the lender's margin of safety. If the borrower is unable to meet his obligation, the lender can sell the security to satisfy the claim. If the security is sold for an amount exceeding the amount of the loan and interest owed, the difference is remitted to the borrower. If the security is sold for less, the lender becomes a general, or unsecured, creditor for the amount of the difference. Because secured lenders do not wish to become general creditors, they usually seek security with a market value sufficiently above the amount of the loan to minimize the likelihood of their not being able to sell the security in full satisfaction of the loan. However, the degree of security protection a lender seeks varies with the creditworthiness of the borrower, the security the borrower has available, and the financial institution making the loan. Before taking up various short-term secured lending arrangements, we must examine briefly the means by which a lender protects himself under the Uniform Commercial Code.

Security devices

It is important to understand the implications of the Uniform Commercial Code for secured lending. Article 9 of the Code deals with security interests of lenders, the specific aspect with which we are concerned. Prior to the adoption of the Code, procedures by which a lender perfected a valid lien on collateral were complex and differed greatly among states. Article 9 consolidated rules governing security devices into one meaningful body of laws.[2] Because the lending arrangements discussed in subsequent sections involve security interests under the Uniform Commercial Code, we need to define certain terms in this section.

Whenever a lender requires collateral of a borrower, he obtains a *security interest* in the collateral. The collateral may be accounts receivable, inventory, equipment, or other assets of the borrower. The security interest in the collateral is created by a *security agreement*, also known as a *security device*. This agreement is signed by the borrower and lender and contains a description of the collateral. In order to "perfect" a security interest in the collateral, the lender must file a copy of the security agreement or a financing statement with a public office of the state in which the collateral is located. Frequently, this office is that of the secretary of state. The filing gives public notice to other parties that the lender has a security interest in the collateral described. Before accepting collateral as security for a loan, a lender will search the public notices to see if the collateral has been pledged previously in connection with another loan. Only the lender with a valid security interest in the collateral has a prior claim on the assets and can sell the collateral in settlement of his loan.

RECEIVABLE LOANS

Assignment of accounts receivable

Accounts receivable represent one of the most liquid assets of the firm, and, consequently, they make desirable security for a loan. From the standpoint of the lender, the major difficulties with this type of security are the cost of processing the collateral and the risk of fraud. To illustrate the nature of the arrangement, we trace through a typical assignment of accounts receivable loan. A company may seek a receivable loan from either a commercial bank or a finance company. As the interest rate charged by a bank usually is less than that charged by a finance company, the firm generally will try to borrow first from a bank.

[2]See Lester E. Denonn, "The Security Agreement," *Journal of Commercial Bank Lending,* 50 (February 1968), 32–40.

Quality and size of receivables. In evaluating the loan request, the lender will analyze the quality of the firm's receivables in order to determine the amount he is willing to lend against these receivables. The greater the quality of the accounts the firm maintains, the greater the percentage the lender is willing to advance against the face value of the receivables pledged. A lender does not have to accept all the borrower's accounts receivable; usually, he will reject accounts that have low credit ratings or that are unrated. Also, government and foreign accounts usually are ineligible unless special arrangements are made. Depending upon the quality of the receivables accepted, a lender typically advances between 50 percent and 85 percent of their face value.

The lender is concerned not only with the quality of receivables but also with their size. The lender must keep records on each account receivable that is pledged; the smaller the average size of the accounts, the more it costs per dollar of loan to process them. Consequently, a firm that sells low-priced items on open account will generally be unable to obtain a receivable loan regardless of the quality of the accounts. The cost of processing the loan is simply too high. Occasionally a "bulk" assignment of receivables will be used to circumvent the problem. With a "bulk" assignment, the lender does not keep track of the individual accounts but records only the total amounts in the accounts assigned and the payments received. Because preventing fraud is difficult with a "bulk" assignment, the percentage advance against the face value of receivables is likely to be low—perhaps 25 percent.

Procedure. Suppose a lender has decided to extend a loan to a firm on the basis of a 75 percent advance against the face value of accounts receivable assigned. The firm then sends in a schedule of accounts showing the name of the account, the date of billing(s), and the amounts owed. An example of an assignment schedule is shown in Figure 10-3. The lender will sometimes require evidence of shipment, such as an invoice. Having received the schedule of accounts, the lender has the borrower sign a promissory note and a security agreement. The firm then receives 75 percent of the face value of the receivables shown on the schedule of accounts.

A receivable loan can be on either a nonnotification or a notification basis. Under the former arrangement, the customer of the firm is not notified that his account has been pledged to the lender. When the firm receives payment on the account, it forwards this payment, together with other payments, to the lender. The lender checks the payments against its record of accounts outstanding, and reduces the amount the borrower owes by 75 percent of the total payments. The other 25 percent is credited to the borrower's regular checking account. With a nonnotification arrangement, the lender must take precautions

The undersigned hereby assigns to **WELLS FARGO BANK** the following accounts:

(LIST NAMES OR REFER TO ATTACHED)	GROSS AMOUNT	
Accounts receivable totalling_____		
evidenced by_____		
for (dates)_____		
Attached hereto and made a part hereof		
TOTAL		

The above accounts are assigned to **WELLS FARGO BANK** and a security interest is granted in accordance with the terms and conditions of the existing Continuing Security Agreement between undersigned and **WELLS FARGO BANK**, to which reference is made.

Date _____

Signed _____

By: _____

Schedule No. S _____

N503   —100/PAD—217—006

FIG. 10 · 3

Accounts-receivable assignment form

to make sure the borrower does not withhold a payment check, using the funds himself. With a notification arrangement, the account is notified of the assignment, and remittances are made directly to the lender. Under this arrangement, the borrower cannot withhold payments. Most firms naturally prefer to borrow on a nonnotification basis; however, the lender reserves the right to place the arrangement on a notification basis.

Means of financing. An accounts-receivable loan is a more or less continuous financing arrangement. As the firm generates new receivables that are acceptable to the lender, they are assigned, adding to the security base against which the firm is able to borrow. New receivables replace the old, and the security base and the amount of loan fluctuate accordingly. A receivable loan is a very flexible means of secured financing. As receivables build up, the firm is able to borrow additional funds to finance this buildup. Thus, it has access to "built-in" financing.

At a commercial bank, the interest cost of borrowing against accounts receivable usually is 2 to 5 percent higher than the prime rate. In addition, many banks have a service charge of an additional 1 to 2 percent for processing this type of loan. Costs at commercial finance companies are higher; the total interest cost of a receivable loan may range from 12 to 24 percent.

Factoring receivables

In the assignment of accounts receivable, the firm retains title to the receivables. When a firm *factors* its receivables, however, it actually sells them to a factor. The sale may be either with or without recourse, depending upon the type of arrangement negotiated. The factor maintains a credit department and makes credit checks on accounts. Based upon its credit investigation, the factor may refuse to buy certain accounts that it deems too risky. By factoring, a firm frequently relieves itself of the expense of maintaining a credit department and making collections. Any account that the factor is unwilling to buy is an unacceptable credit risk unless, of course, the firm wants to assume this risk on its own and ship the goods. Factoring arrangements are governed by a contract between the factor and the client. The contract frequently is for one year with an automatic provision for renewal and can be canceled only with prior notice of thirty to sixty days. Although it is customary in a factoring arrangement to notify the customer that his account has been sold and that payments on the account should be sent directly to the factor, in many instances notification is not made. The customer continues to remit payments to the firm, which, in turn, endorses them to the factor. These endorsements frequently are camouflaged to prevent the customer from learning that his account has been sold.

Factoring costs. For bearing risk and servicing the receivables, the factor receives a fee of around 1 to 3 percent of the face value of the receivables sold. This fee will vary according to the typical size of individual accounts, the volume of receivables sold, and the quality of the accounts. The typical fee is somewhat over 1 percent; it may go as low as 0.75 percent for the very best customer. We must recognize that the receivables sold to the factor will not be collected from the various accounts for a period of time. If the firm wishes to receive payment for the sale of its receivables before they are actually collected, it must pay interest on the advance. Advancing payment is a lending function of the factor in addition to his functions of risk bearing and of servicing the receivables. For this additional function, the factor requires compensation. For example, if the receivables sold total $10,000, and the factoring fee is 2 percent, the factor will credit the firm's account with $9,800. If the firm wants to draw on this account before the receivables are collected, however, it will have to pay an interest charge—say 1 percent a month—for the use of the funds. If it wishes a cash advance of the full $9,800, and the receivables are collected on the average, in one month, the interest cost will be approximately $0.01 \times 9,800$, or $98.[3] Thus, the total cost of factoring is composed of a

---

[3]The actual cash advance would be $9,800 less the interest cost, or $9,702.

factoring fee plus an interest charge if the firm draws upon its account before the receivables are collected. If the firm does not draw on its account until the receivables are collected, there is no interest charge. A third alternative is for the firm to leave its funds with the factor beyond the time when the receivables are collected and to receive interest on the account from the factor.

Flexibility. The typical factoring arrangement is continuous. As new receivables are acquired, they are sold to the factor, and the firm's account is credited. The firm then draws upon this account as it needs funds. Sometimes the factor will allow the firm to overdraw its account during periods of peak needs and thereby borrow on an unsecured basis. Under other arrangements, the factor may withhold a reserve from the firm's account as a protection against losses. There are about twenty old-line factors in the country, most of which are located in New York City. In recent years, commercial banks have entered the factoring business and, accordingly, are a source of such financing. As with the old-line factors, most banks that factor are located on the eastern seaboard.[4]

Factoring, like the assignment of accounts receivable, affords the firm flexibility in its financing. As sales increase and the firm needs funds, financing becomes available automatically. This eliminates the uncertainty associated with the collection cycle. Consequently, the cash flows of the firm are more predictable. Factoring is widely used in the textile and apparel industries and has found acceptance in the shoe and furniture industries as well. While some people attach a stigma to the company that factors, many others regard it as a perfectly acceptable method of financing. Its principal shortcoming is that it can be expensive. We must bear in mind, however, that the factor often relieves the firm of credit checkings, the cost of processing receivables, and collection expenses. For a small firm, the savings may be quite significant. All in all, factoring has found increasing acceptance as a means of financing, showing substantial growth in volume during the last fifteen years.

INVENTORY LOANS

Inventories also represent a reasonably liquid asset and are therefore suitable as security for a short-term loan. As with a receivable loan, the lender determines a percentage advance against the market value of the collateral. This percentage varies according to the quality of the

[4]For an analysis of the entry of commercial banks into factoring, see Robert P. Shay and Carl C. Greer, "Banks Move into High-Risk Commercial Financing," *Harvard Business Review,* 46 (November–December 1968), 149–53, 156–61.

inventory. Certain inventories, such as grains, are very marketable and resist physical deterioration over time. The margin of safety required by the lender on a loan of this sort is fairly small, and the advance may be as high as 90 percent. On the other hand, the market for a highly specialized piece of equipment may be so narrow that a lender is unwilling to make any advance against its reported market value. Thus, not every kind of inventory can be pledged as security for a loan. The best collateral is inventory that is relatively standard and for which a ready market exists apart from the marketing organization of the borrower.

Lenders determine the percentage that they are willing to advance by considering marketability, perishability, market-price stability, and the difficulty and expense of selling the inventory to satisfy the loan. The cost of selling some inventory may be very high indeed. The lender does not want to be in the business of liquidating collateral, but he does want to assure himself that the collateral has adequate value in case the borrower defaults in the payment of principal or interest. As is true with most secured loans, however, the actual decision to make the loan will depend upon the cash-flow ability of the borrower to service debt. There are a number of different ways a lender can obtain a secured interest in inventories, and we consider each in turn. In the case of the first methods (floating lien, chattel mortgage, and trust receipt), the inventory remains in the possession of the borrower. In the last two methods (terminal warehouse and field warehouse receipts), the inventory is in the possession of a third party.

Floating lien

Under the Uniform Commercial Code, the borrower may pledge his inventories "in general" without specifying the specific inventory involved. Under this arrangement, the lender obtains a floating lien on all inventory of the borrower. This lien is very general and difficult to police on the part of the lender. Frequently, a floating lien is requested only as additional protection and does not play a major role in determining whether or not the loan will be made. Even if the lender does regard the collateral as important, he usually is willing to make only a moderate advance because he cannot exercise tight control over the collateral. The floating lien can be made to cover both receivables and inventories, as well as the collection of receivables. This modification gives the lender a lien on a major portion of a firm's current assets. In addition, the lien can be made to encompass almost any length of time so that it includes future as well as present inventory as security.[5]

[5]For further discussion, see J. Carson Quarles, "The Floating Lien," *Journal of Commercial Bank Lending*, 53 (November 1970), 51–58.

Chattel mortgage

With a chattel mortgage, inventories are identified specifically either by serial number or by some other means. While the borrower holds title to the goods, the lender has a lien on inventory. This inventory cannot be sold unless the lender gives his consent. Because of the rigorous identification requirements, chattel mortgages are ill suited for inventory with rapid turnover and/or inventory that is not easily identified because of size or other reasons. They are well suited, however, for certain capital assets such as machine tools.

Trust receipt loans

Under a trust receipt financing arrangement, the borrower holds the inventory and proceeds from the sale of inventory in trust for the lender. This type of lending arrangement, known also as floor planning, has been used extensively by automobile dealers, equipment dealers, and consumer durable goods dealers. To illustrate trust receipt financing, suppose an automobile manufacturer ships cars to a dealer who, in turn, finances the payment for these cars through a finance company. The finance company pays the manufacturer for the cars shipped. The dealer signs a trust receipt security agreement, which specifies what can be done with the inventory. Figure 10-4 (p. 186) is a copy of the security device used under a trust receipt agreement. The car dealer is allowed to sell the cars but must turn the proceeds of the sale over to the lender in payment of the loan. Inventory in trust, unlike inventory under a floating lien, is specifically identified by serial number or by other means. In our example, the finance company periodically audits the cars the dealer has on hand. The serial numbers of these cars are checked against those shown in the security agreement. The purpose of the audit is to see if the dealer has sold cars without remitting the proceeds of the sale to the finance company.

As the dealer buys new cars from the automobile manufacturer, a new trust receipt security agreement is signed that takes account of the new inventory. The dealer then borrows against this new collateral, which he holds in trust. Although there is tighter control over collateral with a trust receipt agreement than with a floating lien, there is still the risk of inventory being sold without the proceeds being turned over to the lender. Consequently, the lender must exercise judgment in deciding to lend under this arrangement. A dishonest dealer can devise numerous ways to fool the lender.

Many durable goods manufacturers finance the inventories of their distributors or dealers. Their purpose is to encourage dealers or distributors to carry reasonable stocks of goods. It is reasoned that the greater the stock, the more likely the dealer or distributor is to make a

SECURITY AGREEMENT: FLOORING

DEALER'S REFERENCE

Pursuant to the California Uniform Commercial Code, the undersigned Borrower hereby grants to

_____
(Bank)

a security interest in the following described inventory, together with all replacements and substitutions thereof, all additions and accessions thereto, and all proceeds thereof.

YEAR	MAKE	ARTICLE	MODEL OR MOTOR NO.	SERIAL NO.	INVOICE NO.	COST	RELEASE PRICE	DATE RELEASED
								1.
								2.
								3.
								4.
								5.
								6.
								7.
								8.

1. BORROWER'S OBLIGATIONS: The security interest created hereby is given as security for the payment of $ _____ , together with interest thereon payable _____ from date hereof at the rate of _____ percent per annum, provided that said rate of interest may be changed upon not less than _____ days notice to Borrower. Borrower hereby agrees to pay said sum to Secured Party at its office as follows:

_____ % of the cost of each unit of collateral on or before _____ , 19 _____ ;
_____ % of the cost of each unit of collateral on or before _____ , 19 _____ ;
and the balance of principal and interest on or before _____ , 19 _____ ,
unless the maturity is extended by Secured Party. This Agreement also secures all other Indebtedness of Borrower to Bank, including all debts, obligations, or liabilities now or hereafter existing, absolute or contingent, and future advances.

2. LOCATION OF COLLATERAL: _____

3. USE OF COLLATERAL: The inventory Collateral of this agreement is to be held for ☐ Sale ☐ Lease

4. INCORPORATION OF PROVISIONS ON REVERSE: All provisions on the reverse side are incorporated herein as if set forth fully at this point.

Dated _____ , 19 _____

IF
CORPORATION
AFFIX
SEAL

By _____

BORROWER(S) - PRINT

_____
SIGNATURE OF BORROWER(S) - TITLE

_____
CHIEF PLACE OF BUSINESS OR RESIDENCE (INDIVIDUALS)

CBA-SA-3 (4-66)

ORIGINAL — TO BANK

FIG. 10·4   A trust receipt security agreement

sale. Because the manufacturer is interested in selling his product, financing terms often are more attractive than they are with an "outside" lender.

Terminal warehouse receipt loans

A borrower secures a terminal warehouse receipt loan by storing inventory with a public, or terminal, warehousing company.[6] The warehouse company issues a warehouse receipt, which evidences title to specified goods that are located in the warehouse. An example of a warehouse receipt is shown in Figure 10-5. The warehouse receipt

FIG. 10 · 5
Warehouse receipt

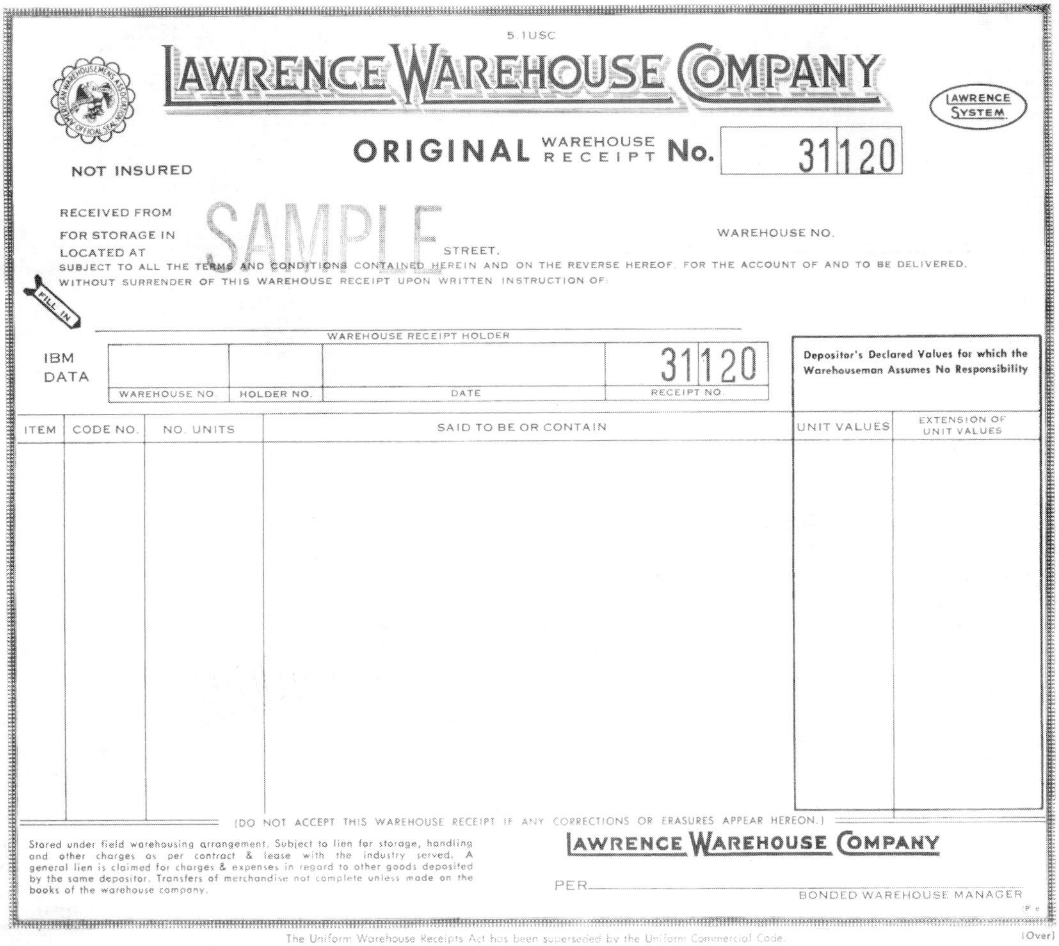
5.1USC

LAWRENCE WAREHOUSE COMPANY

LAWRENCE SYSTEM

NOT INSURED

ORIGINAL WAREHOUSE RECEIPT No. 31120

RECEIVED FROM

FOR STORAGE IN — WAREHOUSE NO.

LOCATED AT — STREET.

SAMPLE

SUBJECT TO ALL THE TERMS AND CONDITIONS CONTAINED HEREIN AND ON THE REVERSE HEREOF, FOR THE ACCOUNT OF AND TO BE DELIVERED, WITHOUT SURRENDER OF THIS WAREHOUSE RECEIPT UPON WRITTEN INSTRUCTION OF:

FILL IN

WAREHOUSE RECEIPT HOLDER

IBM DATA

WAREHOUSE NO.	HOLDER NO.	DATE	RECEIPT NO.
			31120

Depositor's Declared Values for which the Warehouseman Assumes No Responsibility

ITEM	CODE NO.	NO. UNITS	SAID TO BE OR CONTAIN	UNIT VALUES	EXTENSION OF UNIT VALUES

(DO NOT ACCEPT THIS WAREHOUSE RECEIPT IF ANY CORRECTIONS OR ERASURES APPEAR HEREON.)

Stored under field warehousing arrangement. Subject to lien for storage, handling and other charges as per contract & lease with the industry served. A general lien is claimed for charges & expenses in regard to other goods deposited by the same depositor. Transfers of merchandise not complete unless made on the books of the warehouse company.

LAWRENCE WAREHOUSE COMPANY

PER ________ BONDED WAREHOUSE MANAGER

The Uniform Warehouse Receipts Act has been superseded by the Uniform Commercial Code. (Over)

[6]For an excellent discussion of warehouse receipts, see Robert W. Rogers, "Warehouse Receipts and Their Use in Financing," *Bulletin of the Robert Morris Associates,* 46 (April 1964), 317–27.

gives the lender a security interest in the goods, against which he makes a loan to the borrower. Under such an arrangement, the warehouseman can release the collateral to the borrower only when authorized to do so by the lender. Consequently, the lender is able to maintain strict control over the collateral and will release collateral only when the borrower pays a portion of the loan. For his own protection, the lender usually requires the borrower to take out an insurance policy with a loss-payable clause in favor of the lender.

Warehouse receipts may be either nonnegotiable or negotiable. A nonnegotiable warehouse receipt is issued in favor of a specific party— in this case, the lender—who is given title to the goods and has sole authority to release them. A negotiable warehouse receipt can be transferred by endorsement. Before goods can be released, however, the negotiable receipt must be presented to the warehouseman. A negotiable receipt is useful when title to the goods is transferred from one party to another while the goods are in storage. With a nonnegotiable receipt, the release of goods can be authorized only in writing. Most lending arrangements are based upon nonnegotiable receipts.

Field warehouse receipt loans

In a terminal warehouse receipt loan, the goods are located in a public warehouse. Another arrangement, known as field warehousing, permits loans to be made against inventory that is located on the borrower's premises. Under this arrangement, a field warehousing company sets off a designated storage area on the borrower's premises for the inventory pledged as collateral. The field warehousing company has sole access to this area and is supposed to maintain strict control over it. (The goods that serve as collateral are segregated from the borrower's other inventory.) The field warehousing company issues a warehouse receipt as described in the preceding section, and the lender extends a loan based upon the collateral value of the inventory. The field warehouse arrangement is a useful means of financing when it is not desirable, either because of the expense or because of the inconvenience, to place the inventory in a public warehouse. Field warehouse receipt lending is particularly appropriate when a borrower must make frequent use of inventory. Because of the need to pay the field warehousing company's expenses, the cost of this method of financing can be relatively high.

It is important to recognize that the warehouse receipt, as evidence of collateral, is only as good as the issuing warehousing company. When administered properly, a warehouse receipt loan affords the lender a high degree of control over the collateral. However, there have been sufficient examples of fraud to show that the warehouse receipt does not always evidence actual value. The warehouseman must exercise strict control. A grain elevator that is alleged to be full may, in fact, be empty. Upon close examination, we may find that barrels reported to contain chemical concentrate actually contain water.

OTHER COLLATERAL FOR SHORT-TERM LOANS

Collateral other than the kinds we have discussed may be used in securing short-term loans. The owners of a corporation may have outside assets that they are willing to pledge to secure a loan. For example, stocks or bonds might be assigned to a lender as security for a loan. If the company defaults on the loan, the lender can sell the securities in settlement of its loan. For bonds and listed stocks, lenders usually are willing to advance a fairly high percentage of the market value. For bonds, the percentage may be as high as 90 percent. In addition to pledging securities, the owners of a company may pledge the cash surrender value of life insurance policies, a savings account passbook, or a building or house owned separately from the corporation itself.

Although not collateral in a strict sense, an outside party—either an individual or another company—may guarantee the loan of the borrower. A lender may not care to extend credit based upon the strength of the company but may be willing to do so if the loan is guaranteed by another party. If the borrower defaults in payment under this arrangement, the guarantor is liable for the payment of the loan. Before making the loan, the lender will analyze carefully the liquidity and net worth of the prospective guarantor. Unless the guarantor is a party of financial substance, the guarantee is meaningless as protection for a loan. An arrangement whereby the owners of a corporation guarantee a loan to the company insures that the owners will take a real interest in the fortunes of the firm. Other possible guarantors of a loan might be relatives of the owners, or a principal supplier.

COMPOSITION OF SHORT-TERM FINANCING

In this and the preceding chapter, we considered various sources of short-term financing. Because the total amount of short-term financing was assumed to have been determined according to the framework presented in Chapter 5, only determination of the best combination need be considered in this chapter. The appropriate mix, or the weighting, of alternative sources will depend upon considerations of cost, availability, timing, flexibility, and the degree to which the assets of the firm are encumbered. Central to any meaningful analysis of alternative sources of funds is a comparison of their costs, and inextricably related to the question of cost is the problem of timing. Differentials in cost between various alternatives are not necessarily constant over time. Indeed, they fluctuate in keeping with changing financial market conditions. Whereas the differential between the prime rate and the commercial paper rate was around 0.5 percent in the early seventies, it was slightly negative in 1973. Thus, timing bears heavily on the question of the most appropriate mix of short-term financing.

Naturally, the availability of financing is important. If a firm cannot borrow through commercial paper or through a bank because of its low credit standing, it must turn to alternative sources. The lower the credit standing of the firm, of course, the fewer the sources of short-term financing available to it. Flexibility with respect to short-term financing pertains to the ability of the firm to pay off a loan as well as to its ability to renew it or increase it. With factoring and also with a bank loan, the firm can pay off the loan when it has surplus funds. As a result, interest costs are reduced relative to the case, such as commercial paper, where the firm must wait until final maturity before paying off the loan. Flexibility relates also to how easily the firm can increase its loan on short notice. With a line of credit or revolving credit at a commercial bank, it is an easy matter to increase borrowings, assuming the maximum has not been reached. With other forms of short-term financing, the firm is less flexible. Finally, the degree to which assets are encumbered bears on the decision. With secured loans, lenders obtain a lien on the assets of the firm. This secured position constrains the firm in future financing. Whereas receivables are actually sold under a factoring arrangement, the principle is the same. In this case, the firm sells one of its most liquid assets, thus reducing its credit-worthiness in the minds of creditors.

All of these factors influence the firm in deciding upon the most appropriate mix of short-term financing. Because cost is perhaps the key factor, differences in other factors should be compared with differences in cost. What is the cheapest source of financing from the standpoint of explicit costs may not be the cheapest source when flexibility, timing, and the degree to which assets are encumbered are considered. Although it would be desirable to express sources of short-term financing in terms of both explicit and implicit costs, the latter are hard to quantify. A more practical approach is to list available sources according to their explicit costs and then consider the other factors to see if they change the ranking as it relates to total desirability. Because the financing needs of the firm change over time, multiple sources of short-term financing should be explored on a continuous basis.

Short-term loans can be divided into two types—unsecured loans and secured loans. Unsecured credit usually is confined to bank loans under a line of credit, under a revolving-credit agreement, or on a transaction basis. Typically, banks require balances to compensate for a lending arrangement. If the borrower is required to maintain balances above those that it would maintain ordinarily, the effective cost of borrowing is increased. Interest rates on business loans are a function of the existing prime rate, the credit-worthiness of the borrower, and the profitability of the relationship for the bank.

Many firms are unable to obtain unsecured credit and are required by the lender to pledge security. In giving a secured loan, the lender looks first to the cash-flow ability of the company to service debt and, if this source of loan repayment might fail, to the collateral value of the security. To provide a margin of safety, a lender usually will advance somewhat less than the market value of the collateral. The percentage advance varies according to the quality of the collateral pledged and the control the lender has over this collateral. Accounts receivable and inventory are the principal assets used to secure short-term business loans. Receivables may either be pledged to secure a loan or sold to a factor. Inventory loans can be under a general lien, under a trust receipt, or under terminal warehouse or field warehouse receipt arrangements. Certain collateral owned outside a corporation may be used to secure a loan for a corporation. The most appropriate mix of short-term financing will depend upon considerations of relative cost, availability, flexibility, timing, and the degree to which the assets of the firm are encumbered.

1. The Truth in Lending bill requires that lenders state the *true* annual interest rate to borrowers. What impact does this legislation have on the cost of borrowing for corporations?

2. Does the Truth in Lending legislation have any impact on the cost of borrowing for individuals? Explain.

3. A loan service offers to lend you $3,500 to be paid in twenty-four easy monthly installments of $201.
   (a) Compute the monthly cost of capital for this loan.
   (b) Is the "true" annual rate equal to twelve times the monthly rate? Explain.

4. Why might a company prefer an unsecured source of funds such as a line of credit or a revolving-credit agreement to some form of secured financing such as a receivable loan or chattel mortgage, even if the latter source is less expensive?

5. List assets that you would accept as collateral on a loan in your order of preference. Justify your priorities.

6. Inventory and accounts receivable are the most liquid assets a firm owns. Does this liquidity make them the safest security available to the lender? Explain.

7. The settlements in the cases of Billie Sol Estes (the fertilizer scandal), Anthony DeAngelis (the salad oil scandal), and many other less-notorious bankruptcies suggest that secured lenders are not really secure. Suggest methods of protecting the lender in short-term financing.

8. Which of the methods of short-term financing considered in this chapter would be most likely to be used by the following? Explain your reasoning.
   (a) A raw-material processor such as a mining or lumber company
   (b) A retail sales concern such as an appliance retailer or high fidelity equipment dealer
   (c) An international company
   (d) A consumer durable dealer such as an automobile sales agency

9. What reaction might a firm expect from trade creditors when it pledges its receivables to secure a bank loan?

10. As the firm's financial manager, what factors would you consider in choosing a primary bank?

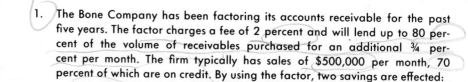

1. The Bone Company has been factoring its accounts receivable for the past five years. The factor charges a fee of 2 percent and will lend up to 80 percent of the volume of receivables purchased for an additional ¾ percent per month. The firm typically has sales of $500,000 per month, 70 percent of which are on credit. By using the factor, two savings are effected:

(a) $2,000 per month that would be required to support a credit department, and

(b) A bad-debt expense of 1 percent on credit sales.

The firm's bank has recently offered to lend the firm up to 80 percent of the face value of the receivables shown on the schedule of accounts. The bank would charge 8 percent per annum interest plus a 2 percent processing charge per dollar of receivables lending. The firm extends terms of net 30, and all customers who pay their bills do so by the thirtieth of the month. Should the firm discontinue its factoring arrangement in favor of the bank's offer if the firm borrows, on the average, $100,000 per month on its receivables?

2. The Sharpless Corporation is in financial difficulty. In order to continue operations, the firm must raise $100,000 in working capital. The firm is unable to secure bank credit, though a commercial sales company has agreed to lend the company up to $100,000 secured by a warehouse receipt. The loan will carry an annual interest charge of 20 percent. The additional cost of maintaining a field warehouse arrangement to issue negotiable receipts is $2,000 per year.

   A second alternative open to the firm is stretching its trade credit. The firm purchases on terms of 2/10, net 30. Stretching beyond the due date will result in a 3 percent per month penalty charge, though it is believed that stretching beyond the due date by over sixty days may impair the firm's ability to get trade credit.

   (a) If the firm purchases $80,000 of raw materials every thirty days, how much will discount losses and stretching penalties cost the firm each month after the required $100,000 is raised?

   (b) Which form of financing is cheaper?

3. The American Bank is offering the C. J. Hyde Corp. a line of credit of $1 million, renewable annually for a fee of ¼ percent on the unused portion of the line plus 8 percent on the amount of the line of credit that is outstanding. Currently, the Hyde Corp. is financing its seasonal working capital needs with trade credit, on which discounts of 3/10, n/90 are lost. The accounts payable balance averages $600,000 on purchases of $2,400,000.

   (a) How much alternative financing is needed to take advantage of the discounts?

   (b) What is the effective cost of capital of trade credit?

   (c) What is the effective cost of capital on the line of credit?

4. ABC Corporation borrows $100,000 for one year at 8 percent interest from a bank.

   (a) What is the effective interest cost if the loan is on a discount basis?

   (b) What is the effective interest cost if the bank requires compensating balances of 20 percent but the loan is on a collect basis?

5. The Barnes Corporation has just acquired a large account. As a result, it needs an additional $75,000 in working capital immediately. It has been determined that there are three feasible sources of funds:

   (a) Trade credit: the company buys about $50,000 of materials per month on terms of 2/30, net 90. Discounts are taken.

   (b) Bank loan: the firm's bank will loan $100,000 at 9 percent. A 20 percent compensating balance will be required.

(c) A factor will buy the company's receivables ($100,000 per month) which have a collection period of sixty days. The factor will advance up to 75 percent of the face value of the receivables for an annual charge of 8 percent. The factor will also charge a 2 percent fee on all receivables purchased. It has been estimated that the factor's services will save the company a credit department expense and bad-debts expense of $1,500 per month.

Which alternative should be selected?

6. The Coral Machine Tool Company had the following balance sheet at the close of its fiscal year last month:

Cash	$ 14,000	Accounts payable	$240,000
Receivables	196,000	Bank loan	170,000
Inventories	170,000	Current liabilities	$410,000
Current assets	$380,000	Mortgage loan	240,000
Fixed assets	473,000	Common stock	50,000
		Retained earnings	153,000
	$853,000		$853,000

The company had the following income statement for the year:

Sales		$2,000,000
Cost of goods sold:		
Purchases	$960,000	
Wages	600,000	
Depreciation	60,000	1,620,000
Gross profit		$ 380,000
Expenses		310,000
Profit before taxes		$ 70,000
Taxes		33,000
Profit after taxes		$ 37,000

The company has approached the bank to increase its loan so that the company can become more current in the trade and avail itself of certain cash discounts. Suppliers are becoming very difficult. Between higher prices being paid on purchases and cash discounts being foregone, Coral estimates that it is foregoing $40,000 per year over what would be the case if its average payable were thirty days in length.

(a) How much additional financing is necessary to bring the average payable collection period to thirty days?

(b) What are some of the problems from the standpoint of the bank? Is it likely to extend the additional credit on an unsecured basis?

ABRAHAM, ALFRED B., "Factoring—The New Frontier for Commercial Banks," *Journal of Commercial Bank Lending,* 53 (April 1971), 32–43.

BAXTER, NEVINS D., and **HAROLD T. SHAPIRO**, "Compensating Balance Requirements: The Results of a Survey," *Journal of Finance,* 19 (September 1964), 483–96.

CRANE, DWIGHT B., and **WILLIAM L. WHITE**, "Who Benefits from a Floating Prime Rate," *Harvard Business Review,* 50 (January–February 1972), 121–29.

Credit and Financial Management, 75 (December 1973). A special issue devoted to factoring.

DENONN, LESTER E., "The Security Agreement," *Journal of Commercial Bank Lending,* 50 (February 1968), 32–40.

HAYES, DOUGLAS A., *Bank Lending Policies: Domestic and International.* Ann Arbor, Mich.: University of Michigan, 1971.

NADLER, PAUL S., "Compensating Balances and the Prime at Twilight," *Harvard Business Review,* 50 (January–February 1972), 112–20.

QUARLES, J. CARSON, "The Floating Lien," *Journal of Commercial Bank Lending,* 53 (November 1970), 51–58.

ROBICHEK, ALEXANDER A., and **STEWART C. MYERS**, *Optimal Financing Decisions,* Chapter 5. Englewood Cliffs, N.J.: Prentice-Hall, 1965.

ROGERS, ROBERT W., "Warehouse Receipts and Their Use in Financing," *Bulletin of the Robert Morris Associates,* 46 (April 1964), 317–27.

SHAY, ROBERT P., and **CARL C. GREER**, "Banks Move into High-Risk Commercial Financing," *Harvard Business Review,* 46 (November–December 1968), 149–53, 156–61.

SMITH, KEITH V., *Management of Working Capital,* Section 5. New York: West Publishing, 1974.

STONE, BERNELL K., "Allocating Credit Lines, Planned Borrowing, and Tangible Services over a Company's Banking System," *Financial Management,* 4 (Summer 1975), 65–78.

11 Intermediate-Term Financing

The principal characteristic of short-term loans is that they are self-liquidating over a period of time of less than a year. Frequently, they are employed to finance seasonal and temporary funds requirements. Intermediate-term financing, on the other hand, is employed to finance more permanent funds requirements, such as fixed assets and underlying buildups in receivables and inventories. The means for payment of the loan usually come from the generation of cash flows over a period of years. As a result, most of these loans are paid in regular, periodic installments. We regard intermediate-term financing as involving final maturities of one to ten years. These boundaries are arbitrary, although the one-year boundary is rather commonly accepted. In this chapter, we examine various types of intermediate-term debt as well as lease financing.

TERM LOANS

Commercial banks have become increasingly involved in providing intermediate-term financing to industry. There are two features of a bank term loan that distinguish it from other types of business loans. First, it has a final maturity of more than one year, and second, it most often represents credit extended under a formal loan agreement. Both ordinary term loans and revolving credits are classified under the broad heading of bank term loans.

Ordinary term loans

An ordinary term loan is a business loan with an original, or final, maturity of more than one year, repayable according to a specified schedule. For the most part, these loans are repayable in periodic installments, for example, quarterly, semiannually, or annually. The payment schedule of the loan usually is geared to the borrower's cash-flow ability to service the debt. Typically, this schedule calls for equal periodic installments, but it may be irregular with respect to amounts or may simply call for repayment in a lump sum at final maturity. Sometimes the loan is amortized in equal periodic installments except for the final payment, known as a "balloon" payment, which is larger than any of the others.

Maturity. Most bank term loans are written with original maturities in the one- to six-year range. Some banks are willing to make longer term loans, but only rarely will a bank make a term loan with a final maturity of more than ten years. In recent years, however, banks have been making longer term loans. Whereas a four- to six-year loan once was considered dangerous to a bank's liquidity, term loans in this maturity range now are commoon.

Interest costs. Generally, the interest rate on a term loan is higher than the rate on a short-term loan to the same borrower. For example, if a firm could borrow at the prime rate on a short-term basis, it might pay 0.25 percent to 0.50 percent more on a term loan. The interest rate on a term loan can be set in one of two ways: (1) a fixed rate which is effective over the life of the loan may be established at the outset, or (2) a variable rate may be set that is adjusted in keeping with changes in the prime rate. In addition to interest costs, the borrower is required to pay the legal expenses that the bank incurs in drawing up the loan agreement. Also, a commitment fee may be charged for the time during the commitment period when the loan is not taken down. For an ordinary term loan, these additional costs usually are rather small in relation to the amount of the loan. An indirect cost to the borrower is the need to maintain compensating balances, which we discussed in Chapter 10.

Advantages. The principal advantage of an ordinary bank term loan is flexibility. The borrower deals directly with the lender, and the loan can be tailored to the borrower's needs through direct negotiation. The bank usually has had previous experience with the borrower, so it is familiar with the company's situation. Should the firm's requirements change, the terms and conditions of the loan may be revised. It is considerably more convenient to negotiate with a single lender or a reasonably small group of lenders than with a large number of public security holders, as there are with a bond issue. In addition, the borrower can deal confidentially with a bank, or, for that matter, with any private lending institution, and does not have to reveal certain financial information to the public.

In many instances, bank term loans are made to small businesses that do not have access to the capital markets and cannot readily float a public issue. Large companies also may find it quicker and more convenient to seek a bank term loan than to float a public issue. A term loan can be arranged in several weeks, whereas a public issue takes a good deal longer.

Limitations.　One of the limitations on the use of a bank term loan is the maturity. Banks seldom will make a term loan for more than ten years and usually want a shorter maturity. Another limitation is the restrictive provisions imposed in the loan agreement, which we will discuss in detail later in this chapter. Although the borrower is restricted by these provisions, he probably would encounter them with an insurance company term-loan agreement or a bond indenture. A possible disadvantage of a bank term loan is the legal restriction on the maximum amount a bank can lend to a single borrower. However, many term loans are extended by a group of banks rather than a single bank. Except for the very largest of loans, the legal lending limit on banks is not a barrier.

When making loans in periods of inflation, some banks ask for equity kickers in order to get a "piece of the action." These kickers usually take the form of stock purchase warrants, which enable the bank to purchase a number of shares of stock at a specified price. A percentage of net profit is another form of kicker, as is a percentage of the gross sales of a retail organization. These kickers, of course, work to the disadvantage of the borrower; they raise the effective cost of borrowing. If the firm is doing well, the effective cost can be very high indeed. A firm regarded as risky, however, may have little choice other than to provide a kicker. This may spell the difference between obtaining a loan or being refused term credit. Moreover, the kicker usually operates in only one direction. If the firm is doing poorly, the kicker it provides has negligible value and, accordingly, costs the firm very little. If, however, the firm is doing well, the kicker will have value; the firm also will be in a better position to incur the added cost.

Revolving credits

As we said in Chapter 10, a revolving credit is a formal commitment by a bank to lend up to a certain amount of money to a company over a specified period of time. The actual notes evidencing debt are short-term, usually ninety days; but the company may renew them or borrow additionally, up to the specified maximum, throughout the duration of the commitment. Many revolving-credit commitments are for three years, although it is possible for a firm to obtain a shorter commitment. As with an ordinary term loan, the interest rate is usually 0.25 to 0.50 percent higher than the rate at which the firm could borrow on a short-term basis under a line of credit. When a bank makes a revolving-credit commitment, it is legally bound under the loan agreement to have funds available whenever the company wants to borrow. The borrower usually must pay for this availability in the form of a commitment fee, perhaps 0.50 percent per annum, on the difference between the amount borrowed and the specified maximum.

Because most revolving-credit agreements are for more than one year, they are regarded as intermediate-term financing. This borrowing arrangement is particularly useful at times when the firm is uncertain about its funds requirements. A revolving-credit agreement has the features of both a short-term borrowing arrangement and a term loan, for the firm can borrow a fixed amount for the entire duration of the commitment. Thus, the borrower has flexible access to funds over a period of uncertainty and can make more definite credit arrangements when the uncertainty is resolved. Revolving-credit agreements can be set up so that at the maturity of the commitment, borrowings then owing can be converted into a term loan at the option of the borrower. To illustrate, suppose that a company introduces a new product and is faced with a period of uncertainty over the next several years. To provide maximum financial flexibility, the company might arrange a three-year revolving credit that is convertible into a five-year term loan at the expiration of the revolving-credit commitment. At the end of three years, the company, hopefully, would know its funds requirements better. If these requirements are permanent, or nearly so, the firm might wish to exercise its option and take down the term loan.

Loan agreements (Protective covenants)

When a bank makes a term loan or revolving-credit commitment, it provides the borrower with available funds for an extended period of time. Much can happen to the financial condition of the borrower during that period. In order to safeguard itself, the lender requires the borrower to maintain its financial condition and, in particular, its current position at a level at least as favorable as when the commitment was made. The provisions for protection contained in a loan agreement are known as protective covenants.

The loan agreement itself simply gives the bank legal authority to step in should the borrower default under any of the provisions. Otherwise, the bank would be locked into a commitment and would have to wait until maturity before being able to effect corrective measures. If the borrower should suffer losses or other adverse developments, he will default under a well-written loan agreement; the bank then will be able to act. The action usually takes the form of working with the company to straighten out its problems. Seldom will a bank demand immediate payment, although it has the legal right to do so in cases of default.

Formulation of provisions. The formulation of the different restrictive provisions should be tailored to the specific loan situation. These provisions are the tools by which the banker fashions the overall protection of his loan. No one provision is able by itself to provide the necessary safeguards, but together with the other provisions, it is designed to assure overall liquidity and ability to pay a loan. The important protective covenants of a loan agreement may be classified as follows: (1) general provisions used in most loan agreements, which are variable to fit the situation; (2) routine provisions used in most agreements, which usually are not variable; and (3) specific provisions that are used according to the situation. Although we focus on a bank loan agreement, the protective covenants used and the philosophy underlying their use are the same for an insurance company loan agreement or the indenture for a bond issue.

General provisions. The *working capital requirement* probably is the most commonly used and most comprehensive provision in a loan agreement. Its purpose is to preserve the company's current position and ability to pay the loan. Frequently, a straight dollar amount, such as $2 million, is set as the minimum working capital the company must maintain during the duration of the commitment. When the bank feels that it is desirable for a specific company to build working capital, it may increase the minimum working capital requirement throughout the duration of the loan. The establishment of a working capital minimum normally is based upon the amounts of present working capital and projected working capital, allowing for seasonal fluctuations. The requirement should not restrict the company unduly in the ordinary generation of profit. However, should the borrower incur sharp losses or spend too much for fixed assets, purchase of stock, dividends, redemption of long-term debt, and so forth, it would probably breach the working capital requirement.

The *cash dividend and repurchase-of-stock restriction* is another important restriction in this category. Its purpose is to limit cash going outside the business, thus preserving the liquidity of the company. Most often, cash dividends and repurchase of stock are limited to a percentage of net profits on a cumulative basis after a certain base date, frequently the last fiscal year-end prior to the date of the term-loan agreement. A less flexible method is to restrict dividends and repurchase of stock to an absolute dollar amount each year. In most cases, the prospective borrower must be willing to undergo a cash dividend and repurchase-of-stock restriction. If tied to earnings, this restriction still will allow adequate dividends as long as the company is able to generate satisfactory profits.

The *capital-expenditures limitation* is third in the category of general provisions. Capital expenditures may be limited to a fixed dollar amount each year. However, it probably is more common to limit annual capital expenditures either to depreciation or to a percentage thereof. The capital-expenditures limitation is another tool used by the banker to assure the maintenance of the borrower's current position. By limiting capital expenditures directly, the bank can be more sure that it will not have to look to liquidation of fixed assets for payment of its loan. Again, however, the provision should not be so restrictive as to prevent the adequate maintenance and improvement of facilities.

A *limitation on other indebtedness* is the last general provision. This limitation may take a number of forms, depending upon the circumstances. Frequently, a loan agreement will prohibit a company from incurring any other long-term debt. This provision protects the bank, inasmuch as it prevents future lenders from obtaining a prior claim on the borrower's assets. Usually a company is permitted to borrow within reasonable limits for seasonal and other short-term purposes arising in the ordinary course of business.

Routine provisions. The second category of restrictions includes routine, usually invariable, provisions found in most loan agreements. Ordinarily, the loan agreement requires the borrower to furnish the bank with financial statements and to maintain adequate insurance. Additionally, the borrower normally is required not to sell a substantial portion of its assets and is required to pay, when due, all taxes and other liabilities, except those contested in good faith. A provision forbidding the pledging or mortgaging of any of the borrower's assets is almost always included in a loan agreement; this important provision is known as a negative pledge clause.

Ordinarily, the company is required not to discount or sell its receivables. Moreover, the borrower generally is prohibited from entering into any leasing arrangement of property, except up to a certain dollar amount of annual rental. The purpose of this provision is to prevent the borrower from taking on a substantial lease liability, which might endanger its ability to pay the loan. A lease restriction also prevents the firm from leasing property instead of purchasing it and thereby getting around the limitations on capital expenditures and debt. Usually, too, there is a restriction on other contingent liabilities. The provisions in this category appear as a matter of routine in most bank loan agreements. Although somewhat mechanical, they are important because they close many loopholes and provide a tight, comprehensive loan agreement.

Special provisions. Special provisions are used in specific loan agreements by the banker in order to achieve a desired total protection of his loan. For instance, a loan agreement may contain a definite understanding regarding the use of the loan proceeds, so that there will be no diversion of funds to purposes other than those contemplated when the loan was negotiated. A provision for limiting loans and advances often is found in a bank term-loan agreement. Closely allied to this restriction is a limitation on investments, which is used to safeguard liquidity by preventing certain nonliquid investments.

If one or more executives are essential to a firm's effective operation, a bank may insist that the company carry life insurance on their lives. Proceeds of the insurance may be payable to the company or directly to the bank, to be applied to the loan. An agreement may also contain a management clause, under which certain key individuals must remain actively employed in the company during the time the loan is owing. Aggregate executive salaries and bonuses sometimes are limited in the loan agreement, to prevent excessive compensation of executives, which might reduce profits. This provision closes another loophole; it prevents large stockholders who are officers of the company from increasing their own salaries in lieu of paying higher dividends, which are limited under the agreement.

Negotiation of restrictions. The provisions described above represent the most frequently used protective covenants in a loan agreement. From the standpoint of the lender, the aggregate impact of these provisions should be to safeguard the financial position of the borrower and its ability to pay the loan. Under a well-written agreement, the borrower cannot get into serious financial difficulty without defaulting under the agreement, thereby giving the bank legal authority to take action. Although the lender is instrumental in establishing the restrictions, the restrictiveness of the protective covenants is subject to negotiation between the borrower and the lender. The final result will depend upon the relative bargaining power of each of the parties involved.[1]

Insurance company term loans

In addition to banks, life insurance companies lend money on a term basis. However, there are important differences in the maturity of the loan extended and in the interest rate charged. In general, life insurance companies are interested in term loans with final maturities

---

[1] For a linear-programming approach for evaluating the opportunity costs of the protective-covenant restrictions, see James Van Horne, "A Linear-Programming Approach to Evaluating Restrictions under a Bond Indenture or Loan Agreement," *Journal of Financial and Quantitative Analysis,* 1 (June 1966), 68–83.

in excess of ten years. Because these companies do not have the benefit of compensating balances or other business from the borrower, and because their loans usually have a longer maturity than bank term loans, typically, the rate of interest is higher. To the insurance company, the term loan represents an investment and must yield a return commensurate with the costs involved in making the loan, the risk, the maturity, and prevailing yields on alternative investments. Because an insurance company is interested in keeping its funds employed without interruption, it normally has a prepayment penalty, whereas usually the bank does not. One of the simpler prepayment formulas calls for a premium of 0.25 percent for each year remaining to maturity.

Insurance company term loans generally are not competitive with bank term loans. Indeed, they are complementary, for they serve different maturity ranges. Sometimes a bank and an insurance company will participate in the same loan. The bank may take the early maturities, perhaps the first five years, with the insurance company taking the remaining maturities. Including an insurance company in the credit permits a longer maturity range than the bank can provide, and the bank can offer a lower interest rate on the early maturities. Usually, there will be only one loan agreement, drawn up jointly by the bank and the insurance company. A term loan of this sort may serve both the intermediate- and long-term funds requirements of the firm.

Small business administration loans

The Small Business Act of 1953 gave the Small Business Administration, an agency of the federal government, the authority to make loans to small businesses when they are unable to obtain funds elsewhere.[2] The definition of a small business depends upon its sales in relation to those of the industry, and upon the number of employees. Any manufacturing firm with less than 250 employees is eligible for an SBA loan. (In some cases, 1,000 employees is the limit.) The SBA seeks to make sound business loans to credit-worthy borrowers, as private lenders do. A company wishing to borrow files an application with the SBA; the application receives thorough analysis before the decision to make the loan is made.

When possible, the SBA prefers to participate with a private lending institution in extending credit. In fact, it can make direct loans only when borrowing from other sources is not available on reasonable terms. The participation by the SBA may be up to 90 percent of

[2] See *Organization and Operation of the Small Business Administration,* Select Committee on Small Business, House of Representative, 88th Cong., 2d sess. (Washington, D.C.: Government Printing Office, 1964).

the loan, with the balance being provided by the private lender. This participation does not necessarily have to consist of a loan from the SBA; the SBA may instead guarantee payment of up to 90 percent of a loan by a private investor. In recent years, participation loans have been stressed and accordingly have tended to dominate direct lending. The application process for a participating loan has been streamlined, with a considerable reduction in the length of time needed for a decision.

Some SBA loans are short-term, but the vast majority are term loans with an average maturity of about five years. Increasingly, longer-term loans are being made and ten-year loans, the maturity ceiling, are common. Although the maximum guarantee the SBA can extend is $350,000, a participating lending institution can extend credit beyond this limit if it so desires. However, most loans are small; the great majority made by the SBA are less than $25,000. Beginning in 1970, the SBA offered economic opportunity loans to socially or economically disadvantaged persons. The maximum loan here is $25,000 with a fifteen-year maturity limitation.

EQUIPMENT FINANCING

Equipment represents another asset of the firm that may be pledged to secure a loan. If the firm either has equipment that is marketable or is purchasing such equipment, it is usually able to obtain some sort of secured financing. Because such loans usually are for more than a year, we consider them in this chapter rather than under short-term secured loans. As with other secured loans, the lender is concerned with the marketability of the collateral. Depending upon the quality of the equipment, he will make a percentage advance against the equipment's market value. Frequently, the repayment schedule for the loan is set in keeping with the depreciation schedule of the equipment. For example, a trucking company usually will depreciate its tractors over four years and its trailers over six years. A lender might set a four-year installment payment schedule for a loan secured by tractors and a six-year schedule for a loan secured by trailers. In setting the repayment schedule, the lender wants to be sure that the market value of the tractor or trailer always exceeds the balance of the loan.

The excess of the expected market value of the equipment over the amount of the loan represents the margin of safety, which will vary according to the specific situation. In the case of the rolling stock of a trucking company, the collateral is movable and reasonably marketable. As a result, the advance may be as high as 80 percent. Less-marketable equipment, such as that with a limited use, will not command as high an advance. A certain type of lathe, for example, may have a thin market; and a lender might not be willing to advance more than 50 percent of its reported market value. Some equipment is of such a special-purpose nature that it has no value for collateral purposes. Frequently, the lender either will have its own appraiser or will hire an appraiser to estimate the approximate value of a piece of equipment if it should have to be sold. As with other collateral, the lender is interested not only in the estimated market price of the equipment but also in the cost of selling it.

Sources of equipment financing

Sources of equipment financing include commercial banks, finance companies, and the sellers of equipment. Because the interest charged by a finance company on an equipment loan usually is higher than that charged by a commercial bank, a firm will turn to a finance company only if it is unable to obtain the loan from a bank. The seller of the equipment may finance the purchase either by holding the secured note itself or by selling the note to its captive finance subsidiary. The interest charge will depend upon the extent to which the seller uses financing as a sales tool. If the seller uses financing extensively, it may charge only a moderate interest rate, and may make up for part of the cost of carrying the notes by charging higher prices for the equipment. The borrower must consider this possibility in judging the true cost of financing. Equipment loans may be secured either by a chattel mortgage or by a conditional sales contract arrangement.

Chattel mortgage

A chattel mortgage is a lien on property other than real property. The borrower signs a security agreement which gives the lender a lien on the equipment specified in the agreement. In order to perfect the lien, the lender files a copy of the security agreement or a financing statement with a public office of the state in which the equipment is located. Given a valid lien, the lender can sell the equipment if the borrower defaults in the payment of principal or interest on the loan.

Conditional sales contract

With a conditional sales contract arrangement, the seller of the equipment retains title to it until the purchaser has satisfied all the terms of the contract. The buyer signs a conditional sales contract security agreement under which he agrees to make periodic installment payments to the seller over a specified period of time. These payments usually are monthly or quarterly. Until the terms of the contract are satisfied completely, the seller retains title to the equipment. Thus, the seller receives a down payment and a promissory note for the balance of the purchase price upon the sale of the equipment. The note is secured by the contract, which gives the seller the authority to repossess the equipment if the buyer does not meet all the terms of the contract.

The seller may either hold the contract himself or sell it, simply by endorsing it, to a commercial bank or finance company. The bank or finance company then becomes the lender and assumes the security interest in the equipment. If the buyer should default under the terms of the contract, the bank or finance company could repossess the equipment and sell it in satisfaction of its loan. Often, the vendor will sell the contract to a bank or finance company with recourse. Under this arrangement, the lender has the additional protection of recourse to the seller in case the buyer defaults.

LEASE FINANCING

A *lease* is a means by which a firm can acquire the economic use of an asset for a stated period of time. This financing device has developed rapidly in the decades of the sixties and seventies with a wide variety of applications, as well as a substantial increase in the sheer volume of transactions. Although this type of financing can be long-term, most lease financing is for periods of less than ten years. Hence, we take it up under intermediate-term financing. Our concern is with financial leases rather than with operating leases. A *financial lease* is a noncancelable contractual commitment on the part of a lessee to make a series of payments to a lessor for the use of an asset. The lessee acquires most of the economic values associated with outright ownership of the asset, even though the lessor retains title to it. With a financial lease, the lease period generally corresponds to the economic life of the asset. In addition, the total payments the lessee agrees to make must exceed the purchase price of the asset.[3] The distinguishing feature between a financial and an operating lease is cancelability— an operating lease can be canceled by giving proper notice, whereas a financial lease cannot. An example of an operating lease is one for telephone service.

In lease financing, the nature of the obligations of the lessor and the lessee is specified in the lease contract. This contract contains

1.   The basic lease period during which the lease is noncancelable.

---

[3] See Richard F. Vancil, "Lease or Borrow: New Methods of Analysis," *Harvard Business Review,* 39 (September–October 1961), 22–36.

2. The timing and amounts of periodic rental payments during the basic lease period.

3. Any option to renew the lease or to purchase the asset at the end of the basic period.

4. Provision for the payment of the costs of maintenance and repairs, taxes, insurance, and other expenses. With a "net lease," the lessee pays all of these costs. Under a "maintenance lease," the lessor maintains the asset and pays the insurance.

Forms of lease financing

There are three main types of lease financing: a sale and leaseback arrangement, the direct acquisition of an asset under a lease, and leveraged leasing. Virtually all lease-financing arrangements fall into one of these three categories. In this section, we briefly describe these categories, and in subsequent sections, we present a framework for the analysis of lease financing and we discuss the basic valuation implications.

Sale and leaseback. Under a sale and leaseback arrangement, a firm sells an asset it owns to another party, and this party leases it back to the firm. Usually, the asset is sold at approximately its market value. The firm receives the sales price in cash and the economic use of the asset during the basic lease period. In turn, it contracts to make periodic lease payments and, of course, gives up title to the asset. As a result, the lessor realizes any residual value the asset might have at the end of the lease period, whereas before this would have been realized by the firm. Lessors engaged in sale and leaseback arrangements include insurance companies, other institutional investors, finance companies, and independent leasing companies.

Direct leasing. Under direct leasing, a company acquires the use of an asset it did not own previously. For example, a firm simply may lease an asset from the manufacturer: IBM leases computers; Kearney & Trecker Corporation leases machine tools. Indeed, a number of capital goods are available today on a lease-financed basis. There are a wide variety of direct leasing arrangements available to meet various needs of the firm. The major types of lessors are manufacturers, finance companies, banks, independent leasing companies, special-purpose leasing companies, and partnerships. For leasing arrangements involving all but the first, the vendor sells the asset to the lessor and he, in turn, leases it to the lessee. As in any lease arrangement, the lessee has use of the asset, along with a contractual obligation to make lease payments to the lessor.

Since 1963, commercial banks have been allowed to engage in direct leasing; their entry represents an important development in the leasing industry. Independent leasing companies, such as Boothe

Leasing and Nationwide Leasing, finance the purchase of a wide variety of equipment. In doing so, they frequently borrow from banks, securing the loan with the assignment of the lease payments. Special-purpose leasing companies confine their operations to certain types of assets; computer leasing companies, for example, mainly lease computer hardware and peripheral equipment. In recent years, individuals in high tax brackets have formed partnerships for the purpose of purchasing equipment and leasing it to companies. The tax shield afforded by accelerated depreciation charges and interest paid on borrowings is more valuable to them than to a corporation. As a result, both the lessor and the lessee may benefit.

Leveraged leasing. A special form of leasing has recently developed in conjunction with the financing of assets requiring large capital outlays. This device it is known as *leveraged leasing.* In contrast to the two parties involved in the forms of leasing previously described, there are three parties involved in leveraged leasing: (1) the lessee, (2) the lessor, or equity participant, and (3) the lender. We examine each in turn.[4]

From the standpoint of the lessee, there is no difference between a leveraged lease and any other type of lease. The lessee contracts to make periodic payments over the basic lease period and, in return, is entitled to the use of the asset over that period of time. The role of the lessor, however, is changed. The lessor acquires the asset in keeping with the terms of the lease arrangement. This acquisition is financed in part by an equity investment by the lessor of, say, 20 percent (hence the name *equity participant*). The remaining 80 percent is provided by a long-term lender or lenders. Usually, the loan is secured by a mortgage on the asset, as well as by the assignment of the lease and lease payments.[5] The lessor, however, is the borrower.

As owner of the asset, the lessor is entitled to deduct all depreciation charges associated with the asset, as well as utilize the entire investment tax credit. The cash-flow pattern for the lessor typically involves (1) a cash outflow at the time the asset is acquired, which represents its equity participation less the investment tax credit; (2) a period of cash inflows represented by lease payments and tax benefits, less payments of the debt (principal and interest); and (3) a period of net cash outflows where, because of declining tax benefits, the sum of lease payments and tax benefits falls below the debt payments due. If there is any residual value at the end of the lease period, this of course rep-

[4] For a discussion of leveraged leasing, see "FASB Discussion Memorandum: Accounting for Leases" (Stamford, Conn.: *Financial Accounting Standards Board,* July 2, 1974), Sec. VIII; Robert C. Wiar, "Economic Implications of Multiple Rates of Return in the Leveraged Lease Context," *Journal of Finance,* 28 (December 1973), 1275–86; and E. Richard Packham, "An Analysis of the Risks of Leveraged Leasing," *Journal of Commercial Bank Lending,* 57 (March 1975), 2–29.

[5] Sometimes in addition, the lessee guarantees the debt.

resents a cash inflow to the lessor. While the leveraged lease may seem the most complicated of the three forms of leasing we have described, it reduces to certain basic concepts. From the standpoint of the lessee, which is our concern, the leveraged lease can be analyzed in the same manner as any other lease. Therefore, we will not treat it separately in the rest of this chapter.

Accounting for leases

In recent years, the accounting treatment of leases has involved greater and greater disclosure. Where once leases did not have to be disclosed, rulings by the Accounting Principles Board and its successor, the Financial Accounting Standards Board, have resulted in enough disclosure that the financial statement user is able to judge the impact of this contractual obligation in the same way as he is the impact of debt payments. Therefore, the attraction of lease financing as an "off-balance-sheet" method of financing has diminished from the standpoint of the firm.

The omission of consideration of the lease obligation can of course have a favorable, and deceptive, effect upon the financial condition of a firm, as depicted by financial ratios, over what would be the case if the asset were purchased and financed with debt. For one thing, the company that leases would show a faster turnover of its assets and better earnings power than an identical company that engaged in debt financing. Moreover, it would appear to have less financial risk under the leasing alternative. The debt-to-equity ratio would be less, and the coverage ratio of times interest earned higher. Close analysis of the financial statement, however, would show that the better financial ratios of the lease-financed company were an illusion. The lease payments represent just as much a contractual obligation on the part of the company as does the payment of principal and interest on debt.

At the time of this writing, the accounting treatment of leases was undergoing change. At the very least, the lease obligation must be disclosed in a footnote to the audited financial statements. However, the Financial Accounting Standards Board has come out with a proposal that calls for capitalization on the balance sheet of certain types of leases. By *capitalization*, it is meant that annual lease payments are capitalized at an appropriate discount rate and the capitalized liability is shown on the balance sheet, together with the amortized value of the asset. **The proposal** is complex, but in principle it classifies certain types of leases as capital leases which must be shown on the balance sheet.[6]

[6]*Accounting for Leases Exposure Draft* (Stamford, Conn.: Financial Accounting Standards Board, August 26, 1975).

A lease is regarded as a capital lease if it satisfies any one of the following conditions:

1. The lease transfers title to the asset to the lessee by the end of the lease period.

2. The lease contains an option to purchase the asset at a bargain price.

3. The lease period is equal to or greater than 75 percent of the estimated economic life of the asset.

4. The estimated fair value of the asset at the end of the lease period is less than 25 percent of what it was at the beginning.

5. The asset is of special purpose for the lessee and would not be readily marketable to others.

If a lease meets one or more of these conditions, it would need to be capitalized on the asset side of the balance sheet. The amount reflected would be the present value of minimum lease payments over the lease period, using the lessee's incremental borrowing rate as the discount rate. The associated lease obligation would be shown on the liability side of the balance sheet, with the present value of payments due within one year being reflected as current liabilities and the present value of payments due after one year being shown as noncurrent liabilities.

In addition, the firm would need to show captions on the balance sheet for operating leases. An operating lease is any lease that does not meet one of the five criteria listed above for a capital lease. The same present-value information would need to be shown for operating leases, with the exception that it would be reflected under a caption as opposed to under the asset or liability columns. With a combination of capital and operating leases, the balance sheet might look like the following:

Assets		Liabilities	
Leased Property:		Current:	
Capital leases less		Obligations under	
accumulated depreciation	$1,000	capital leases	$150
Operating leases ($2,250)		Long-term:	
		Obligations under	
		capital leases	850
		Commitments under	
		operating leases	
		($2,250)	

For both capital and operating leases, more detailed information would be required in footnotes. Relevant information here would include the gross amounts of leases by major property categories, a schedule by years of future minimum lease payments required, the range and weighted average of discount rates used to reduce these payments to present value, and a general description of the leasing arrangements. The last-named would include a discussion of the terms of renewal or purchase option, any restrictions on the company, the basis on which any contingent rental payments were determined, and the relative importance of the lease arrangements to the company.

If this proposal ultimately is made a final ruling by the Financial Accounting Standards Board, it will cause the reflection of many leased assets and their associated contractual obligations on the balance sheet. The board is the accounting profession's rule-making body. Accountants must conform to its rulings if they are to give unqualified opinions on the financial statements of the companies they audit. If leases are capitalized on the balance sheet, it will permit an easier analysis of the contractual nature of the obligation by creditors and investors. The obligation is less likely to be overlooked, as can sometimes now occur when it is "buried" in a footnote. As a result, one of the purported advantages of leasing as opposed to borrowing will cease to exist. (Whether or not it ever was an advantage with respect to the valuation of the firm is problematical.)

Tax considerations

A lease payment is deductible as an expense for federal income tax purposes. If the asset is purchased, it must be capitalized; and the annual depreciation charge then is deducted as an expense. Prior to the 1954 tax code, lease financing permitted a faster tax writeoff over the basic lease period than was generally possible with a purchased asset subject to depreciation. With the passage of the 1954 tax code, which permitted accelerated depreciation, this tax advantage was largely eliminated. However, if a company is not sufficiently profitable to realize completely the tax benefits associated with accelerated depreciation, leasing as opposed to buying an asset may result in a tax advantage.

With leasing, the cost of any land is amortized in the lease payments. By deducting the lease payments as an expense for federal income tax purposes, in essence, the lessee is able to write off the original cost of the land. If the land is purchased, the firm cannot depreciate it for tax purposes. When the value of land represents a significant portion of the asset acquired, lease financing can offer a tax advantage to the firm. Offsetting this tax advantage, however, is the likely residual value of land at the end of the basic lease period. The firm also may gain certain tax advantages in a sale and leaseback arrangement when the assets are sold for less than their depreciated value.

An important tax consideration is the investment tax credit, which is available to corporations and individuals who invest in certain types of assets. This credit was described in Chapter 2, and we know that it is available at the time the asset is placed in service. The credit itself can be taken by the lessor or the lessee, depending upon the leasing arrangement. When the lessor retains the tax credit, lease payments generally are lower than what they would be in the absence of the credit. This reduction is occasioned by the forces of competition among lessors. However, the exact amount by which lease payments are lowered depends upon negotiations between the lessor and the lessee.

When the lessee is unable to utilize the full tax credit because of an insufficient tax liability, but the lessor is able to use it, both parties tend to gain. The lessee realizes part of the tax credit through lease payments that are lower than they would otherwise be. In turn, the lessor is able to use the full tax credit. Perhaps the most important illustration of this arrangement is the lease financing of jet airplanes by airlines. Often the profits of airline companies are not sufficient to utilize the full tax credit available on a significant purchase of aircraft. However, through a lease arrangement, the airline is able to avail itself of a greater portion of the benefits than it could with a straight purchase.

LEASING VERSUS BORROWING[7]

Whether lease financing or borrowing is favored will depend upon the patterns of cash outflows for each financing method and upon the opportunity cost of funds. To illustrate a method of analysis, we compare lease financing with debt financing, using a hypothetical example. We assume that the firm has decided to invest in a project on the basis of considerations that will be discussed in Part IV. In other words, the investment-worthiness of the project is evaluated separately from the specific method of financing to be employed.[8] We assume also that the firm has determined an appropriate capital structure and has decided to finance the project with a fixed-income type of instrument—either debt or lease financing. We turn now to examining the two alternatives.

[7] The development of this section assumes that the reader is familiar with present-value calculations. If not, Chapter 12 should be read in advance.

[8] For an analysis in which the leasing contract is viewed as an investment rather than a financing decision, see Robert W. Johnson and Wilbur G. Lewellen, "Analysis of the Lease-or-Buy Decision," *Journal of Finance,* 27 (September 1972), 815–23. They hold that the lease is a long-term acquisition of services and that the relevant comparison is lease versus buy, not lease versus borrow. For a comparison of various methods for analyzing lease versus borrowing, see Richard S. Bower, "Issues in Lease Financing," *Financial Management,* 2 (Winter 1973), 25–34.

No Resp.

Suppose a firm has decided to acquire an asset costing $200,000 and having an expected economic life of ten years, after which the asset is not expected to have any residual value. Once the investment decision is made, the question becomes, Is it better to finance the asset by leasing or by borrowing? If leasing is used, the lessor requires that the cost of the asset be completely amortized over the ten-year period and that it yield a 9 percent return. As is customary, lease payments are to be made in advance—that is, at the end of the year prior to each of the ten years. The amount of annual lease payment may be calculated by solving the following equation for x:

$$\$200,000 = \sum_{t=0}^{9} \frac{x}{(1.09)^t}$$

$$\$200,000 = x + 5.9852x$$

$$x = \frac{\$200,000}{6.9852}$$

$$x = \$28,600$$

(11-1)

Because lease payments are made in advance, we solve for the annual lease payment which equates the cost of the asset, $200,000, with the present value of one lease payment at time 0, plus the present value of nine lease payments at the end of each of the next nine years. Because the discount rate is 9 percent, we find in Table A-2 at the end of the book that the present-value discount factor for an even stream of cash flows for nine years, discounted at 9 percent, is 5.9852. Therefore, the annual lease payment necessary to amortize the cost of the asset completely and to return the lessor 9 percent is $28,600.

From our previous discussion, we know that the firm will make annual lease payments of $28,600 if the asset is leased. Because these payments are an expense, they are deductible for tax purposes. However, they are deductible only in the year for which the payment applies. For example, the $28,600 payment at the end of year 0 represents a prepaid expense and is not deductible for tax purposes until year 1. Similarly, the other nine payments are not deductible until the following year. If we assume a federal income tax rate of 50 percent, cash outflows after taxes each year would be those on page 214 in column 3 of Table 11-1. Suppose that the appropriate opportunity cost of funds on an essentially risk-free investment is 5 percent after taxes. The reason for using this rate as our discount rate is that the difference in cash flows between lease financing and debt financing involves little or no risk. Therefore, it is not appropriate to use the cost of capital, which embodies a risk premium for the firm as a whole, as the discount rate.

Given the information in the paragraph above, we are able to compute the present value of cash outflows. The computations are shown in the last column of Table 11-1. We see that the present value of the total cash outflows under the leasing alternative is $121,463. This figure, then, must be compared with the present value of cash outflows under the borrowing alternative.

TABLE 11 · 1

Schedule of Cash Outflows: Leasing Alternative

End of Year	(1) Lease Payment	(2) Tax Shield	(3) Cash Outflow after Taxes (1) − (2)	(4) Present Value of Cash Outflows (5%)
0	$28,600	—	$28,600	$ 28,600
1–9	28,600	$14,300	14,300	101,642
10	—	14,300	− 14,300	− 8,779
				$121,463

Borrowing

If the asset is purchased, the firm is assumed to finance it entirely with a 10 percent unsecured term loan. For tax purposes, the firm is able to deduct depreciation charges as well as avail itself of the investment tax credit. If straight-line depreciation is used, annual depreciation charges are $20,000. The investment tax credit is available at the time the asset is placed in service. We assume this is at time 0 and that the applicable credit is 10 percent. This deduction effectively lowers the purchase price by $20,000 to $180,000 if the asset is purchased. A loan of this amount is assumed to be taken out at time 0 and is payable over ten years in equal annual payments of $29,294.[9] The proportion of interest in each payment depends upon the unpaid balance of the principal amount owing during the year. For example, the principal amount owing during year 1 is $180,000; therefore, the annual interest for that year is $18,000. Table 11-2 shows the schedule of debt payments.

Given annual interest and depreciation, we are able to compute the cash outflows after taxes for the borrowing alternative; these outflows are shown in Table 11-3. Because both depreciation and interest are deductible for tax purposes, they provide a tax shield equal to their sum times the tax rate. When this shield is deducted from the total

[9]This amount is computed in the same manner as in Eq. (11-1) with the exception that time goes from $t = 1$ through 10 instead of $t = 0$ through 9. Because of rounding to the nearest dollar, the payment in year 10 is slightly higher.

TABLE 11·2

End of Year	Interest plus Principal Payments	Principal Amount Owing at End of Year	Annual Interest
0	$ —	$180,000	$ —
1	29,294	168,706	18,000
2	29,294	156,283	16,871
3	29,294	142,617	15,628
4	29,294	127,585	14,262
5	29,294	111,049	12,758
6	29,294	92,860	11,105
7	29,294	72,852	9,286
8	29,294	50,843	7,285
9	29,294	26,633	5,084
10	29,296		2,663

payment of $29,294, we obtain the cash outflow after taxes at the end of each year. Finally, we compute the present value of these outflows; and they are found to total $102,785. According to this analysis, the firm should acquire the asset through debt financing, because the present value of cash outflows with borrowing is less than that with leasing.

TABLE 11·3

Schedule of Cash Outflows: Borrowing Alternative

End of Year	(1) Loan Payment	(2) Interest	(3) Depreciation	(4) Tax Shield [(2) + (3)] 0.5	(5) Cash Outflow after Taxes (1)-(4)	(6) Present Value of Cash Outflows (5%)
1	$29,294	$18,000	$20,000	$19,000	$10,294	$9,804
2	29,294	16,871	20,000	18,435	10,859	9,849
3	29,294	15,628	20,000	17,814	11,480	9,917
4	29,294	14,262	20,000	17,131	12,163	10,007
5	29,294	12,758	20,000	16,379	12,915	10,119
6	29,294	11,105	20,000	15,552	13,742	10,255
7	29,294	9,286	20,000	14,643	14,651	10,412
8	29,294	7,285	20,000	13,642	15,652	10,594
9	29,294	5,084	20,000	12,542	16,752	10,799
10	29,296	2,663	20,000	11,331	17,965	11,029
						$102,785

This conclusion arises despite the fact that the implied interest rate embodied in the lease payments, 9 percent, is less than the explicit interest rate on the debt, 10 percent. The major relative advantage of purchasing the asset and financing it with debt is the realization of the investment tax credit at the outset. This credit effectively reduces the purchase price and the amount of debt to be incurred. In the case of the lease, the lessor is entitled to the investment tax credit. This advantage may be passed off in part to the lessee in the form of lease payments lower than would otherwise be the case. While the lower interest rate embodied in the lease payments in our example reflects this occurrence, it is not sufficient to cause the lease alternative to be more attractive. Another factor that favors the debt alternative is the deductibility of interest payments for tax purposes. Because the amount of interest embodied in a "mortgage-type" debt payment is high at first and declines with successive payments, the tax benefits associated with these payments follow the same pattern over time. From a present-value standpoint, this pattern benefits the firm relative to the pattern of lease payments, which typically are constant over time.

Other considerations

The decision to borrow rests upon the relative timing and magnitude of cash flows under the two financing alternatives as well as upon the discount rate employed. If the asset is expected to have a residual value, the results of our calculations will be changed. Suppose that the asset is expected to have a market value of $40,000 at the end of the tenth year. If we assume a capital gains tax of 30 percent, the net cash flow after taxes is $28,000 at the end of the tenth year.[10] The present value of $28,000 at the end of year 10, discounted at 5 percent, is $17,190. When this value is subtracted from the present value of cash outflows after taxes, the total present value under the borrowing alternative becomes $85,595. Thus, if an asset is expected to have a significant residual value, borrowing becomes relatively more attractive.

In our example above, we assumed straight-line depreciation. If the company uses accelerated depreciation, it obtains a greater tax shield in the early years and a lower one in later years. As a result, cash outflows after taxes in the early years are reduced relative to cash outflows

---

[10] For simplicity, we assume that the depreciation schedule is the same as before. If the depreciable life is longer than before, total tax payments during the ten years will be greater, and net cash flows after taxes smaller.

in later years, and the present value under the borrowing alternative is increased. Thus, accelerated depreciation makes borrowing more attractive than it is with straight-line depreciation.

As we can see, deciding between leasing and borrowing involves some rather extensive calculations. Each situation requires a separate analysis. The analysis is complicated if the two alternatives involve different amounts of financing. If we finance less than the total cost of the asset by borrowing, but finance 100 percent of the cost by leasing, we must consider the difference in the amount of financing both from the standpoint of explicit as well as implicit costs. These considerations and the others mentioned throughout this chapter make the evaluation of lease financing a complex matter.

SUMMARY

Intermediate-term financing generally is thought to include maturities of one to ten years. There are a number of sources of intermediate-term financing. Commercial banks, insurance companies, and other institutional investors make term loans to business firms. Banks also provide financing under a revolving-credit arrangement, which represents a formal commitment on the part of the bank to lend up to a certain amount of money over a specified period of time. Lenders who offer unsecured credit usually impose restrictions on the borrower. These restrictions are called protective covenants and are contained in a loan agreement. If the borrower defaults under any of the provisions of the loan agreement, the lender may initiate immediate corrective measures. On a secured basis firms can obtain intermediate-term financing by pledging equipment that they own or are purchasing. Banks, finance companies, and sellers of the equipment are active in providing this type of secured financing. Finally, the Small Business Administration (SBA) extends intermediate-term credit.

Typically, intermediate-term debt financing is self-liquidating. For this reason, it resembles short-term financing. However, intermediate-term debt also can satisfy more permanent funds requirements and, in addition, can serve as an interim substitute for long-term financing. If a firm wishes to float long-term debt or issue common stock but conditions are unfavorable in the market, it may seek intermediate-term debt to bridge the gap until long-term financing can be undertaken on favorable terms. Thus, intermediate-term debt may give a firm flexibility in the timing of long-term financing. It can also provide flexibility when the firm is uncertain as to the size and nature of its future funds requirements. As uncertainty is resolved, intermediate -term financing can be replaced by a more appropriate means of financing. (A bank revolving credit is well suited for providing this type of flexibility.) The most important use of inter-mediate-term financing, however, is to provide credit when the expected cash flows of the firm are such that the debt can be retired steadily over a period of several years. Even though it sometimes is linked to a particular asset, such as a piece of equipment, intermediate-term debt must be considered in relation to the firm's total funds requirements. It can play a major role in the overall financing decisions of the firm.

Lease financing involves the acquisition of the economic use of an asset through a contractual commitment to make periodic lease payments to a lessor who owns the asset. Because of this contractual obligation, leasing is regarded as a method of financing similar to borrowing. Leasing can involve the direct acquisition of an asset under a lease, a sale and lease-back arrangement, or a leveraged lease. The accounting treatment of leases and the tax implications were discussed. One of the principal economic reasons for leasing is the inability of a firm to utilize all the tax benefits associated with ownership of an asset (depreciation and the investment tax credit). This can arise not only because of unprofitable operations but because earnings are not of sufficient size to effectively utilize all of the possible tax benefits. One means for analyzing lease financing in relation to debt financing is to discount to present value the net cash outflows after taxes under each alternative, using the risk-free rate as the discount rate. The preferred alternative is the one that provides the lower present value.

QUESTIONS

1. What reasons can you cite for the firm's use of intermediate-term debt? Why isn't long-term debt substituted in its place? Short-term debt?

2. Why don't insurance companies compete more actively with banks for short- and intermediate-term financing?

3. What is the purpose of protective covenants in a term-loan agreement?

4. Chapter 1 suggests that the decision-making processes of investing funds (buying assets) and of raising funds (financing assets) are two separate and distinct functions of the financial manager. This chapter suggests that, at least in the case of leasing, the decision-making processes cannot be separated. Discuss the problems raised by this sort of situation and prepare your analytical method for making decisions in this situation.

5. Explain the concept of sale and leaseback. Compare this arrangement with a mortgage loan on the leased asset.

6. Discuss the probable impact that a sale and leaseback arrangement will have on
   (a) Liquidity ratios *Curr.* ↑
   (b) Return on investment ↑
   (c) Return on equity ↑
   (d) The risk class of the corporation's stock ↑
   (e) The price of the stock ↓

7. Some businessmen consider that the risk of obsolescence and inflexibility is being transferred from the lessee to the lessor. How is the lessor induced to accept higher risk and greater inflexibility?

8. Leasing is often called off-balance-sheet financing. It is argued that this method of financing allows a firm to use greater financial leverage without changing stockholders' perception of the risk class of the stock. Please evaluate.

9. In your opinion, would the following factors tend to favor borrowing or leasing as a financing alternative? Why?
   (a) Increased corporate tax rate
   (b) Accelerated depreciation
   (c) Rising price level
   (d) Increased residual value of the leased asset
   (e) An increase in the risk-free interest rate

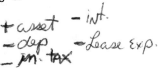

+ asset   − int.
− dep   − Lease Exp.
− in. tax

Lssee → Lessee

PROBLEMS

1. Equilease Company offers to buy any equipment you select and lease it on a noncancelable, twenty-four month, financial lease at the following rates:

Plans	A	B	C
Monthly payment per $100 of purchase price	$4.90	$4.80	$4.70

PLAN A Advance rental (payment due at the start of the month) and abandon equipment to lessee at expiration of lease.

PLAN B. Advance rental and sell equipment to lessee for 10% of original purchase price.

PLAN C. Two-month advance rental and sell equipment to lessee for 10% of original purchase price.

Determine the cost of capital for each of the three plans.

2. The Simone Corporation, which has a 40 percent tax rate, wishes to acquire a $100,000 stamping machine, which would be depreciated on a straight-line basis with an eight-year life and no salvage value. It would be possible to lease the machine for $20,000 per year, payable in advance. It would

also be possible to borrow the $100,000 at 10 percent; this would require annual payments of $18,745.

(a) Which is the superior method of financing if the risk-free rate is 4 percent?

(b) Rework the problem, assuming a 60 percent tax rate.

3.

THE MESTAYER CORPORATION BALANCE SHEET (IN MILLIONS)

Current assets	$10
Fixed assets (30 years, straight-line depreciation)	30
Total assets	$40
Current liabilities	$ 5
Long-term debt (6%)	15
Total debt	$20
Net worth	20
Total liabilities and net worth	$40

INCOME STATEMENT

Sales	$100,000,000
Operating income	7,900,000
Depreciation	1,000,000
Interest	900,000
Net income before taxes	$ 6,000,000
Taxes (50%)	3,000,000
Net income	$ 3,000,000

The Mestayer Corporation is contemplating the sale and twenty-five year leaseback of $10 million of fixed assets. The proceeds would be used to retire long-term debt. Annual lease payments for the twenty-five years will be $1 million and the property will be abandoned to the lessee at the end of the lease.

(a) Reformulate the financial statements under the assumption that this transaction took place.

(b) Show the effects of this sale upon the following ratios:
   (1) Asset turnover
   (2) Return on assets
   (3) Debt to net worth
   (4) Times interest earned

(c) What is the real impact of this transaction? Has the corporation's fundamental position improved?

4. The McDonald Company wishes to buy a $1.2 million piece of equipment over a two-year period. The bank has offered to loan the required money on the basis of a two-year note with a $300,000 amortization payment every six months. The loan would require a compensating balance equal to

15 percent of the outstanding balance and would bear 10 percent interest on the unpaid balance. The seller of the equipment has offered McDonald a conditional sales contract with four equal semiannual payments. How large could the payments be before McDonald would find the bank loan more attractive?

5. The Buda Company is contemplating investing in a project that will generate the following net cash flows (after taxes):

Year	Net Flows (end of year)
0	− $9,000,000
1	+5,000,000
2	+5,000,000
3	+5,000,000

The firm has decided to finance the project through using intermediate-term debt; for this there appear to be two alternatives:

(1) Utilize an additional $9 million of the firm's three-year revolving bank credit. Currently $3 million of the $15 million commitment is used. The bank charges 1 percent over prime on the balance and 0.5 percent on the unused portion. Prime is expected to average 7 percent in year 1, 8 percent in year 2, and 7 percent in year 3. Treasury bills can always be bought to yield 1.5 percent less than the prevailing prime rate.

(2) Privately place a $9 million, unsecured three-year note with Atonement Mutual. The note would bear 7.5 percent interest and involve a 0.5 percent placement fee. The note agreement would also require the firm to maintain $1 million more in working capital than would otherwise be held.

(a) Which alternative is to be preferred? What other factors might be considered?

(b) Suppose that the Atonement note provided for an equal amortization of principal, and Buda had no other investment opportunities (except Treasury bills) over the three-year period. Would this affect your answer?

SELECTED REFERENCES

Accounting for Leases Exposure Draft. Stamford, Conn.: Financial Accounting Standards Board, August 26, 1975.

AXELSON, KENNETH S., "Needed: A Generally Accepted Method for Measuring Lease Commitments," *Financial Executive,* 39 (July 1971), 40–52.

BEECHY, THOMAS H., "The Cost of Leasing: Comment and Correction," *Accounting Review,* 45 (October 1970), 769–73.

———, "Quasi-Debt Analysis of Financial Leases," *Accounting Review,* 44 (April 1969), 375–81.

BOWER, RICHARD S., "Issues in Lease Financing," *Financial Management,* 2 (Winter 1973), 25–34.

BOWER, RICHARD S., FRANK C. HERRINGER, and J. PETER WILLIAMSON, "Lease Evaluation," *Accounting Review,* 41 (April 1966), 257–65.

COOPER, KERRY, and ROBERT H. STRAWSER, "Evaluation of Capital Investment Projects Involving Asset Leases," *Financial Management,* 4 (Spring 1975), 44–49.

DOENGES, R. CONRAD, "The Cost of Leasing," *Engineering Economist,* 17 (Fall 1971), 31–44.

FERRARA, WILLIAM L., and JOSEPH F. WOJDAK, "Valuation of Long-Term Leases," *Financial Analysts Journal,* 25 (November–December 1969), 29–32.

FINDLAY, M. CHAPMAN, III, "A Sensitivity Analysis of IRR Leasing Models," *Engineering Economist,* 20 (Summer 1975), 231–42.

GORDON, MYRON J., "A General Solution to the Buy or Lease Decision: A Pedagogical Note," *Journal of Finance,* 29 (March 1974).

GRITTA, RICHARD D., "The Impact of the Capitalization of Leases on Financial Analysis," *Financial Analysts Journal,* 30 (March–April 1974), 1–6.

HAYES, DOUGLAS A., *Bank Lending Policies: Domestic and International.* Ann Arbor, Mich.: Bureau of Business Research, University of Michigan, 1971.

JOHNSON, ROBERT W., and WILBUR G. LEWELLEN, "Analysis of the Lease-or-Buy Decision," *Journal of Finance,* 27 (September 1972), 815–23.

KELLER, THOMAS F., and RUSSELL J. PETERSON, "Optimal Financial Structure, Cost of Capital, and the Lease-or-Buy Decision," *Journal of Business Finance & Accounting,* 1 (Autumn 1974), 405–14.

MIDDLETON, J. WILLIAM, "Term Lending—Practical and Profitable," *Journal of Commercial Bank Lending,* 50 (August 1968), 31–43.

MOYER, R. CHARLES, "Lease Financing and the Investment Tax Credit: A Framework for Analysis," *Financial Management,* 4 (Summer 1975), 39–44.

PACKHAM, E. RICHARD, "An Analysis of the Risks of Leveraged Leasing," *Journal of Commercial Bank Lending,* 57 (March 1975), 2–29.

ROENFELDT, RODNEY L., and JEROME S. OSTERYOUNG, "Analysis of Financial Leases," *Financial Management,* 2 (Spring 1973), 74–87.

ROGERS, DEAN E., "An Approach to Analyzing Cash Flow for Term Loan Purposes," *Bulletin of the Robert Morris Associates,* 48 (October 1965), 79–85.

SCHALL, LAWRENCE D., "The Lease-or-Buy and Asset Acquisition Decisions," *Journal of Finance,* 29 (September 1974), 1203–14.

VANCIL, RICHARD F., "Lease or Borrow: New Method of Analysis," *Harvard Business Review,* 39 (September–October 1961), 122–36.

VAN HORNE, JAMES, "A Linear-Programming Approach to Evaluating Restrictions under a Bond Indenture or Loan Agreement," *Journal of Financial and Quantitative Analysis,* 1 (June 1966), 68–83.

WIAR, ROBERT C., "Economic Implications of Multiple Rates of Return in the Leverage Lease Context," *Journal of Finance,* 28 (December 1973), 1275–86.

WYMAN, HAROLD E., "Financial Lease Evaluation under Conditions of Uncertainty," *Accounting Review,* 48 (July 1973), 489–93.

Capital Investments and Valuation

IV

12 Mathematics of Finance

Compound int rates
12-5 formula
compound uniform
f.v.
p.v.

Because finance is concerned with decisions involving monetary variables, and because the price of money is the interest rate, most financial decisions involve interest-rate considerations. This chapter deals with the mathematics of compound interest and present value. While this material is introductory in nature, we have placed it here because of the important role it plays in the ensuing development of the book. In capital budgeting, valuation, and cost of capital, which we take up in the remaining chapters of this part, it is particularly relevant. However, we also draw on this material when we consider such things as capital structure, dividend policy, refunding a bond issue, convertible securities, and mergers. Therefore, a mastery of the material contained within this chapter is important for the subsequent comprehension of the book. Although obviously mathematical in orientation, we focus only on a handful of formulas in order that the essentials can be easily understood. The examples frequently involve numbers that must be raised to the nth power. Although difficult to work by hand, we assume that most readers have access to a calculator where these examples can be easily verified.

COMPOUND INTEREST

The notion of compound interest is central to understanding the mathematics of finance. The term itself merely implies that interest paid on a loan or an investment is added to the principal; as a result, interest is earned on interest. In this section, we examine a class of problems that can be solved using the same concept; these problems will be illustrated with a number of examples. To begin our discussion, consider a person who has $100 in a savings account. If the interest rate is 5 percent compounded annually, how much will he have at the end of a year? The formula for solving this problem is simply

$$TV_1 = X_0(1 + r) \qquad (12\text{-}1)$$

where TV_1 = terminal value at the end of one period
        X_0 = amount of savings at beginning
        r = interest rate

Therefore, the individual's savings account will have in it at the end of the year:

$$TV_1 = \$100(1 + .05) = \$105$$

At the end of two years, the terminal value of an initial balance of X_0 is

$$TV_2 = X_0(1 + r)^2 \qquad (12\text{-}2)$$

For our example problem, the terminal value would be $100 times (1.05) squared, or times 1.1025. Thus,

$$TV_2 = \$100 (1 + .05)^2 = \$110.25$$

For the two-year case, $100 in savings will become $105 at the end of the first year at 5 percent interest. Going to the end of the second year, $105 becomes $110.25, as $5 is earned on the initial $100 and $0.25 is earned on the $5 in interest paid at the end of the first year.

At the end of three years, the individual would have

$$TV_3 = X_0(1 + r)^3 \qquad (12\text{-}3)$$

which for our example problem is

$$TV_3 = \$100(1 + .05)^3 = \$115.76$$

Similarly, at the end of n years, the terminal value of a deposit is

$$TV_n = X_0(1 + r)^n \qquad (12\text{-}4)$$

TABLE 12 · 1

**Illustration of Compound Interest with $100
Initial Deposit and 5 Percent Interest**

Period	Beginning Value	Interest Earned during Period (5 percent of beginning value)	Terminal Value
1	$100.00	$5.00	$105.00
2	105.00	5.25	110.25
3	110.25	5.51	115.76
4	115.76	5.79	121.55
5	121.55	6.08	127.63
6	127.63	6.38	134.01
7	134.01	6.70	140.71
8	140.71	7.04	147.75
9	147.75	7.38	155.13
10	155.13	7.76	162.89

In Table 12-1, we show the terminal values for our example problem at the end of years 1 through 10. This table illustrates the concept of interest being earned on interest.

Equation (12-4) is our fundamental formula for calculating terminal values. As can be visualized, the greater the interest rate r, and the greater the number of periods n, the greater the terminal value. In Figure 12-1, we graph the growth in terminal value for a $100 initial deposit with interest rates of 5, 10, and 15 percent. As can be seen, the greater the rate, the steeper the growth curve by which terminal value increases.

While our concern has been with interest rates, the concept involved applies to compound growth of any sort. For example, we might wish to determine the future earnings of a firm if they were expected to grow at a 10 percent compound rate. If earnings were $100,000 now, they would be the following at the end of years 1 through 5:

Year	Growth Factor	Expected Earnings
1	(1.10)	$110,000
2	$(1.10)^2$	121,000
3	$(1.10)^3$	133,100
4	$(1.10)^4$	146,410
5	$(1.10)^5$	161,051

Similarly, we can determine the level at the end of so many years for other problems involving compound growth. The principle is particu-

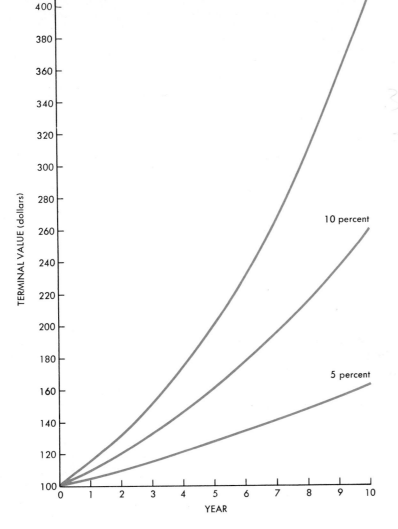

FIG. 12 · 1

Compound values with $100 initial deposit and 5, 10, and 15 percent interest rates

larly important when we consider certain valuation models for common stock later in Part IV.

Compound value with uniform payments or receipts

Consider now a situation where an individual makes an initial deposit but adds to it a given amount at the end of each period. Continuing with our previous example, suppose the initial deposit is $100 and the compound annual interest rate 5 percent, but the individual adds to it $50 per year. At the end of one year, the terminal value would be

$$TV_1 = \$100(1.05) + \$50 = \$155$$

At the end of two years, it would be

$$TV_2 = \$155(1.05) + \$50 = \$212.75$$

While we could calculate the terminal value at the end of any period in this step-by-step manner, a more general formula is available for solution of the problem. It is

$$TV_n = \left(X_o + \frac{x}{r}\right)(1 + r)^n - \frac{x}{r} \qquad (12\text{-}5)$$

For the above example, the terminal value at the end of two years would be

$$TV_2 = \left(\$100 + \frac{\$50}{.05}\right)(1.05)^2 - \frac{\$50}{.05}$$

$$= (\$100 + \$1,000)(1.1025) - \$1,000$$

$$= \$212.75$$

which, of course, is the same as calculated before. The terminal value at the end of five years would be

$$TV_5 = (\$100 + \$1,000)(1.05)^5 - \$1,000$$

$$= \$403.91$$

Consider now a situation where there are payments of $200 at the end of each of four years, where the interest rate is 8 percent, but where there is no initial deposit. The terminal value at the end of four years for this problem would be

$$TV_4 = \frac{\$200}{.08}(1.08)^4 - \frac{\$200}{.08}$$

$$= \$901.22$$

Annuities. An *annuity* can be defined as a series of uniform receipts for a specified number of years which result from an initial deposit. Suppose you inherit $10,000 and wish to have a steady income over the next ten years. A life insurance company sells annuities that will pay you, or your beneficiary if you should die, a fixed dollar amount annually for ten years. The insurance company calculates the amount of distribution on the basis of a 5 percent return. What is the annual amount it will pay? Referring to Eq. (12-5), the terminal value at the end of ten years would be zero, as everything would be paid out. We know also that X_o is \$10,000, r is .05, and n is 10. Therefore, we must solve for x, which we know will be negative as it is a withdrawal. Setting the problem up in this manner, we have

$$0 = \left(\$10,000 - \frac{x}{.05}\right)(1.05)^{10} + \frac{x}{.05}$$

$$= (\$10,000 - 20x)(1.628894) + 20x$$

$$32.57788x - 20x = 16,288.94$$

$$12.57788x = 16,288.94$$

$$x = \$1,295.05$$

Thus, the individual is able to obtain \$1,295.05 per year for ten years with an annuity.

Reversing the previous problem, we also are able to determine the amount of initial deposit or balance that is necessary to afford a person a withdrawal of a certain amount over so many years. To illustrate, suppose a person wanted to be able to withdraw \$5,000 per year over the next ten years and a savings institution pays 5 percent per annum. How much will the individual need to deposit for this to happen? In this case, x in Eq. (12-5) is $-\$5,000$. At the end of ten years, there will be no terminal value, so $TV_n = 0$. With an interest rate of 5 percent, we have

$$0 = \left(X_o - \frac{\$5,000}{.05}\right)(1.05)^{10} + \frac{\$5,000}{.05}$$

where we wish to solve for X_o. We have

$$0 = (X_o - \$100,000)(1.62889) + \$100,000$$

$$1.62889 X_o = \$62,889$$

$$X_o = \$38,609$$

Therefore, \$38,609 must be deposited initially in order for the annuity to pay \$5,000 at the end of each of the next ten years.

Compounding more than once a year

Up to now, we have assumed that interest was paid annually. While it is easiest to work with this assumption, we consider now the relationship between terminal value and interest rates for different periods of compounding. To begin, suppose that interest is paid semiannually. If one then deposited \$100 in a savings account at 5 percent, the terminal value at the end of six months would be

$$TV_{1/2} = \$100\left(1 + \frac{.05}{2}\right) = \$102.50$$

and at the end of a year it would be

$$TV_1 = \$100\left(1 + \frac{.05}{2}\right)^2 = \$105.0625$$

This amount compares with \$105.00 if interest were paid only once a year. The \$0.0625 difference is attributable to the fact that during the second six months, interest is earned on the \$2.50 in interest paid at the end of the first six months. The more times during a year that interest is paid, the greater the terminal value at the end of a given year.

The general formula for solving for the terminal value at the end of year n is

$$TV_n = X_o\left(1 + \frac{r}{m}\right)^{mn} \qquad (12\text{-}6)$$

To illustrate, suppose that in our previous example interest were paid quarterly and that we wished again to know the terminal value at the end of one year. It would be

$$TV_1 = \$100\left(1 + \frac{.05}{4}\right)^4 = \$105.09$$

which, of course, is higher than that which occurs either with semi-annual or with annual compounding.

The terminal value at the end of three years for the above example with quarterly interest payments is

$$TV_3 = \$100\left(1 + \frac{.05}{4}\right)^{12} = \$116.0754$$

This compares with a terminal value with semiannual compounding of

$$TV_3 = \$100\left(1 + \frac{.05}{2}\right)^6 = \$115.9693$$

and with annual compounding of

$$TV_3 = \$100\left(1 + \frac{.05}{1}\right)^3 = \$115.7625$$

The greater the number of years, the greater the difference in terminal values that occur between two different methods of compounding.

If interest were compounded daily on the basis of a 365-day year, the terminal value of an X_o initial deposit at the end of n years would be

$$TV_n = X_o\left(1 + \frac{r}{365}\right)^{365n} \qquad (12\text{-}7)$$

As m approaches infinity, the term $(1 + r/m)^{mn}$ approaches e^{rn}, where e is approximately 2.71828 and is defined as

$$e = \lim_{m \to \infty} \left(1 + \frac{1}{m}\right)^m \qquad (12\text{-}8)$$

where ∞ is the sign for infinity. To see that e approaches 2.71828 as m increases, simply increase m in the above expression from, say, 5 to 10 to 20 and solve for e. The terminal value at the end of n years of an initial deposit of X_o where interest is compounded continuously at a rate of r is

$$TV_n = X_o e^{rn} \qquad (12\text{-}9)$$

For our example problem, the terminal value at the end of twenty years would be

$$TV_{20} = \$100(2.71828)^{(.05)(20)} = \$271.828$$

This compares with a terminal value with annual compounding of

$$TV_{20} = \$100(1.05)^{20} = \$265.330$$

and with semiannual compounding of

$$TV_{20} = \$100\left(1 + \frac{.05}{2}\right)^{40} = \$268.506$$

Continuous compounding results in the maximum possible terminal value at the end of n periods for a given rate of interest. As m is increased in Eq. (12-6), the terminal value increases at a decreasing rate until ultimately it approaches that achieved with continuous compounding.

Having considered compound interest, we now are ready to take up present values. In any economy in which capital has value, a dollar today is worth more than a dollar to be received one year, two years, or three years from now. Therefore, we need a means for standardizing differences in timing of cash flows so that the time value of money is properly recognized. Calculating the present value of future cash flows allows us to isolate differences in the timing of these cash flows.

To illustrate the method, suppose that you were given the opportunity to receive $1,000 at the end of each of the next two years with complete certainty. If the opportunity cost of funds is 8 percent per annum, what is this proposal worth to you today? We might begin by asking, What amount today would grow to be $1,000 at the end of one year at 8 percent interest? In calculating the terminal value in the preceding section, we multiplied the initial deposit by $(1 + r)$, where r is the rate of interest, to obtain the terminal value. In this case, we are given the terminal value as well as the required interest rate and must solve for the appropriate beginning value. Consequently, we divide the terminal value by the required rate of interest, and this operation is known as discounting. For our example, the present value of $1,000 to be received at the end of one year is

$$PV = \frac{\$1,000}{(1.08)} = \$925.93$$

Similarly, the present value of $1,000 to be received at the end of two years is

$$PV = \frac{\$1,000}{(1.08)^2} = \$857.34$$

Thus, the opportunity is worth $925.93 + $857.34 = $1,783.27 today.

The general formula for finding the present value of x_n to be received at the end of year n where k is the required rate of discount is

$$PV = \frac{x_n}{(1 + k)^n} \qquad (12\text{-}10)$$

This formula tells us that the present worth of a given dollar amount decreases the further in the future it is to be received. Note that Eq. (12-10) for discounting is simply the reciprocal of the formula for finding the terminal value, Eq. (12-4), of x dollars so many years hence.

Figure 12-2 illustrates the present value of $100 received from one through ten years in the future with discount rates of 5, 10, and 15

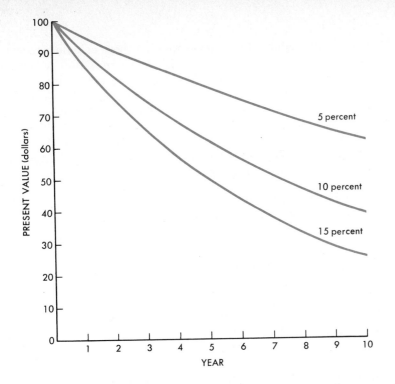

FIG. 12 · 2

Present values with $100
cash flow and 5, 10,
and 15 percent
discount rates

percent. This graph shows that the present value of $100 decreases by a decreasing rate the further in the future it is to be received. The greater the interest rate, of course, the lower the present value but also the more pronounced the curve. At a 15 percent discount rate, $100 to be received ten years hence is worth only $24.72 today.

Construction of present-value tables

Fortunately, one does not have to calculate present values by hand using Eq. (12-10). Present-value tables exist which allow us to easily determine the present value of $1 received so many years from now at such and such a rate. To illustrate the construction of such a table, we make a few calculations using a discount rate of 10 percent. Suppose we wish to know the present value of $1 to be received one year from today. The formula is

$$PV = \frac{1}{(1 + 0.10)} = 0.90909 \qquad (12\text{-}11)$$

Similarly, if we wish to know the present value of $1 received two years from today, the formula is

$$PV = \frac{1}{(1 + 0.10)^2} = \frac{1}{1.21} = 0.82645 \qquad (12\text{-}12)$$

A present-value table relieves us of making these calculations every time we have a problem to solve; it is shown in Table A-1 in the Appendix at the end of the book. We see in the table that for a 10 percent discount rate, the discount factors for one and two years in the future are 0.90909 and 0.82645, respectively—just as we calculated by hand.

If we had an uneven series of cash flows—$1 one year hence, $3 two years hence, and $2 three years from now—the present value of this series, using a 10 percent discount rate, would be:

PV of $1 to be received at the end of one year $1(0.90909) = $0.90909
PV of $3 to be received at the end of two years $3(0.82645) = 2.47935
PV of $2 to be received at the end of three years $2(0.75131) = 1.50262
Present value of series $4.89106

Given a present-value table, we are able to calculate the present value for any series of future cash flows in the above manner.

However, the procedure can be simplified for a series if the cash flows in each future period are the same, that is, for an annuity. Suppose that in a series of future cash flows, $1 was to be received at the end of each of the next three years. The calculation of the present value of this stream, using the above procedure, would be:

PV of $1 to be received in one year   = $0.90909
PV of $1 to be received in two years   = 0.82645
PV of $1 to be received in three years = 0.75131
Present value of series $2.48685

With an even series of future cash flows, it is unnecessary to go through these calculations. The discount factor, 2.48685, can be applied directly. We would simply multiply $1 by 2.48685 to obtain $2.48685. Present-value tables for even series of cash flows have been developed that allow us to look up the appropriate compound discount factor. An example is shown in Table A-2 in the Appendix at the end of the book. We note that the discount factor for an even series of cash flows for three years, using a 10 percent discount rate, is 2.4868—as we calculated. Thus, for an even series of cash flows, we simply multiply the appropriate discount factor times the cash flow. If we wish to know the present value, using an 8 percent discount rate, of a future stream of $5 cash flows to be received at the end of each year over a four-year period, the calculation would be

$$\$5(3.3121) = \$16.56 \qquad (12\text{-}13)$$

Using the present-value tables shown in Tables A-1 and A-2 at the end of the book, we are able to calculate the present value of various future streams of cash flows.

As a final illustration of the use of these tables, suppose that we wished to determine the present value of $500 to be received at the end of one year, $400 to be received at the end of two years, $300 to be received at the end of three years, and $200 to be received at the end of years four through ten, all at a discount rate of 12 percent. Here we have an uneven series for the first three years and an even series, or annuity, for years four through ten. Consequently, we use Table A-1 for the first series and Table A-2 for the second. For the first series, the present value is

PV of $500 at the end of one year — $500(.89286)   = $446.43
PV of $400 at the end of two years — $400(.79719)   =   313.88
PV of $300 at the end of three years—$300 (.71178) =   213.53
$$\overline{\$978.84}$$

For the second series, the annuity begins not at time 0 but at the beginning of the fourth year. Referring to Table A-2, we calculate the present value of an annuity of ten years and subtract from it the present value of an annuity of three years to obtain the present value of an annuity from years four through ten:

PV of $200 for 10 years — $200(5.6502) = $1,130.04
PV of $200 for 3 years — $200(2.4018) =   480.36
$$\overline{\$649.68}$$

Thus, the present value of the whole series is

PV of uneven series $978.84
PV of annuity   649.68
$$\overline{\$1,628.53}$$

A wide variety of present-value problems could be illustrated. The reader is encouraged to do the problems at the end of this chapter.

Present value when interest is compounded more than once a year

When interest is compounded more than once a year, the formula for calculating present values must be revised along the same lines as for the calculation of terminal value. Instead of dividing the future cash flow by $(1 + k)^n$ as we do when annual compounding is involved, the present value is determined by

$$PV = \frac{x_n}{\left(1 + \dfrac{k}{m}\right)^{mn}} \qquad (12\text{-}14)$$

where, as before, x_n is the cash flow at the end of year n, m is the number of times a year interest is compounded, and k is the discount rate.

The present value of $100 to be received at the end of year 3, where the discount rate is 10 percent compounded quarterly, is

$$PV = \frac{\$100}{\left(1 + \dfrac{.10}{4}\right)^{(4)(3)}} = \$74.36$$

The present value of $100 at the end of one year with a discount rate of 100 percent compounded monthly is

$$PV = \frac{\$100}{\left(1 + \dfrac{1}{12}\right)^{12}} = \$38.27$$

When interest is compounded continuously, the present value of a cash flow at the end of year n is

$$PV = \frac{x_n}{e^{rn}} \qquad\qquad (12\text{-}15)$$

where e is approximately 2.71828. The present value of $1,000 to be received at the end of ten years with a discount rate of 20 percent compounded continuously is

$$PV = \frac{\$1,000}{2.71828^{(.20)(10)}} = \$135.34$$

While it is important to understand discounting where interest is compounded more than once a year, all of the present-value calculations in this book will involve annual compounding. However, the reader should be able to adjust any of the discount calculations undertaken for compounding more than once a year.

Solving for the number of periods

In the preceding section, we solved for the present value, given the interest rate, number of periods, and cash flows. In this section, we wish to solve for the number of periods given the other three variables. To illustrate such a problem, suppose that for $10,000 one can acquire an asset that will generate cash inflows of $2,000 at the end of each year until it becomes obsolete, after which no more cash flows are generated and the asset has no salvage value. If the opportunity cost of funds is 9 percent, how long must the asset last to be a worthwhile investment? In this case, we have an annuity producing $2,000 a year.

Setting up the problem, we have

$$\$10,000 = \frac{\$2,000}{(1.09)} + \frac{\$2,000}{(1.09)^2} + \cdots + \frac{\$2,000}{(1.09)^n}$$

We must determine that value of n where the cumulative sum on the right-hand side of the equation equals $10,000. To do so, we first divide the amount of the investment, $10,000, by the annual cash flow, $2,000, and obtain 5.0. When we go to Table A-2 at the back of the book, we find that for 9 percent, the discount factor is 5.0329 for seven years, whereas it is 4.4859 for six years. Therefore, the asset must last nearly seven years if it is to be a worthwhile investment.

SUMMARY

Mastering the concept of compound interest and growth is fundamental to understanding much of what goes on in financial management. In an economy where capital has value, interest rates are positive and these rates must be embodied in any analysis where payments or receipts occur in the future. In this chapter, we considered the determination of terminal, or compound, values as well as the determination of present values.

The terminal value at the end of year n for an initial deposit of X_o that grows at a compound annual rate of r is

$$TV = X_o(1 + r)^n$$

This basic formula may be modified to take account of interest being paid more than once a year by

$$TV = X_o\left(1 + \frac{r}{m}\right)^{mn}$$

where m is the number of times during the year interest is paid. Also in this chapter, we considered how to determine the terminal value where there were uniform payments or receipts over n years. Where receipts are involved, the situation is known as an *annuity*.

The second major concept we considered was the determination of the present value of a future cash flow. It can be expressed as

$$PV = \frac{x_n}{(1 + k)^n}$$

where x_n is a cash flow at the end of year n, and k is the discount rate or interest rate required. As in the previous case, this formula may be modified for compounding more than once a year. We proceeded to show how present-value tables are constructed and used. Finally, we considered how to solve for *n*, given the other three variables in the present-value equation.

QUESTIONS

1. What is compound interest? Why is it important?

2. What kinds of personal financial decisions have you made which involve compound interest?

3. In calculating the terminal value, we multiply by one plus the interest rate to the *n*th power, whereas to calculate the present value we divide by this amount. If the initial deposit and cash flow were $100, would the present value be the reciprocal of the terminal value?

4. What is an annuity? Is it worth more or less than a lump sum equal to the sum of the annuity payments?

5. If you had a savings account, what type of compounding would you prefer? Why?

6. Contrast the calculation of terminal value with the calculation of present value. What is the difference?

7. What is the advantage of present-value tables over hand calculations?

8. If you were to receive a sum of money five years hence but wished to sell your contract for its present value, which type of compounding would you prefer? Why?

9. In order to solve for the number of periods in a present-value situation, what do you need to know?

PROBLEMS

1. Do the following exercises on terminal values:
    (a) $100 initial deposit is worth how much at the end of three years?
        (1) Assuming an annual interest rate of 10 percent
        (2) Assuming an annual interest rate of 100 percent
        (3) Assuming an annual interest rate of 0 percent
    (b) $500 initial deposit plus annual payments of $100 is worth how much at the end of five years?
        (1) Assuming an annual interest rate of 10 percent
        (2) Assuming an annual interest rate of 5 percent
        (3) Assuming an annual interest rate of 0 percent
    (c) $100 initial deposit is worth how much at the end of three years?
        (1) Assuming an interest rate of 10 percent compounded quarterly
        (2) Assuming an interest rate of 100 percent compounded quarterly
    (d) Why does your answer to (c) differ from that to (a)?

(e) $100 initial deposit is worth how much at the end of ten years?
- (1) Assuming an interest rate of 10 percent compounded annually
- (2) Assuming an interest rate of 10 percent compounded semi-annually
- (3) Assuming an interest rate of 10 percent compounded quarterly
- (4) Assuming an interest rate of 10 percent compounded continuously $= X_0 e^{rn}$

Do the following exercises on present values:

(a) $100 at the end of three years is worth how much today?
- (1) Assuming a discount rate of 10 percent
- (2) Assuming a discount rate of 100 percent
- (3) Assuming a discount rate of 0 percent.

(b) What is the aggregate present value of $500 received at the end of each of the next three years?
- (1) Assuming a discount rate of 4 percent
- (2) Assuming a discount rate of 25 percent

(c) $100 is received at the end of one year, $500 at the end of two years, and $1,000 at the end of three years. What is the aggregate present value of these receipts?
- (1) Assuming a discount rate of 4 percent
- (2) Assuming a discount rate of 25 percent

(d) $1,000 is to be received at the end of one year, $500 at the end of two years, and $100 at the end of three years. What is the aggregate present value of these receipts?
- (1) Assuming a discount rate of 4 percent
- (2) Assuming a discount rate of 25 percent

(e) Compare your solutions in (2c) with those in (2d) and explain the reason for the differences.

3. At an annual growth rate of 7 percent, how long does it take $1 to double in value? At a 10 percent rate, how long does it take?

4. Joe Hernandez has inherited $25,000 and wishes to purchase an annuity that will provide him with a steady income over the next twelve years. He has heard that the local savings and loan association is currently paying 6 percent on an annual basis. If he were to deposit his funds here, how much would he be able to withdraw annually?

5. You need to have $50,000 at the end of ten years. To accumulate this sum, you have decided to save a certain amount at the end of each of the next ten years and deposit it in the bank. The bank pays 5 percent interest. How much will you have to save each year?

6. Mr. Joel Dunway wishes to borrow $10,000 for three years. A group of individuals agree to lend him this amount if he contracts to pay them $18,000 at the end of the three years. What is the implicit annual interest rate to the nearest percentage?

7. You have been offered a note with four years to maturity which will pay $3,000 at the end of each of the four years. The price of the note to you is $10,200. What is the implicit interest rate you will receive?

8. The H. L. Cramer Company sales were $500,000, and they are expected to grow at a compound rate of 20 percent for the next six years. What will the sales be at the end of each of the next six years?

9. The H & L Bark Company is considering the purchase of a scraping machine that is expected to provide cash flows as follows:

Year	1	2	3	4	5	6	7	8	9	10
Cash flow	$1,200	$2,000	$2,400	$1,900	$1,600	$1,400	$1,400	$1,400	$1,400	$1,400

If the appropriate discount rate is 14 percent, what is the present value of this cash-flow stream?

SELECTED REFERENCES

DRAPER, JEAN E., and JANE S. KLINGMAN, *Mathematical Analysis*. New York: Harper & Row, 1967.

HOWELL, JAMES E., and DANIEL TEICHROEW, *Mathematical Analysis for Business Decisions,* Chapter 10. Homewood, Ill.: Richard D. Irwin, 1963.

KEMENY, JOHN G., ARTHUR SCHLEIFER, JR., J. LAURIE SNELL, and GERALD L. THOMPSON, *Finite Mathematics,* 2nd ed., Chapter 7. Englewood Cliffs, N.J.: Prentice-Hall, 1972.

Capital Budgeting 13

[handwritten marginal notes: "ave. rate of r / payback / IRR / adv. dis of each / Prob: 2,3,5,9"]

Having covered the mathematics of present values in the preceding chapter, we now are ready to consider capital investments. Generally, the financial manager is not involved in managing the ongoing operations of the firm. This is the responsibility of the production manager or, in the case of a service company, the operations manager. However, the financial manager is instrumental in the initial allocation of funds to fixed assets. The process by which funds are allocated is known as capital budgeting. A capital expenditure is made with the expectation of future benefits being realized. Usually, these benefits are expected beyond one year in the future. Examples include investment in such assets as equipment, buildings, and land, as well as the introduction of a new product, a new distribution system, or a new program for research and development. Thus, the future success and profitability of the firm depends upon investment decisions made currently.

An investment proposal should be judged in relation to whether it provides a return equal to or greater than that required by investors. To simplify our investigation of the methods of capital budgeting in this chapter, we assume the required rate of return is given and is the same for all investment projects. This assumption implies that the selection of any investment project does not alter the business-risk complexion of the firm as perceived by suppliers of capital. In Chapters 15 and 16, we investigate how to measure the required rate of return, and, in Chapter 14, we allow for the fact that different investment projects have different degrees of business risk. As a result, the selection of an investment project may affect the business-risk complexion of the firm, which, in turn, may affect the rate of return required by investors. In Chapter 14, then, we take up methods by which the firm can take risk into account in reaching capital-budgeting decisions. For purposes of introducing capital budgeting in this chapter, however, we hold risk constant.

INFORMATION REQUIRED

Capital budgeting involves the generation of investment proposals, the estimate of cash flows for the proposals, the evaluation of cash flows, the selection of projects based upon an acceptance criterion, and, finally, the continual reevaluation of investment projects after their acceptance.

Depending upon the firm involved, investment proposals can emanate from a variety of sources. For purposes of analysis, projects may be classified into one of five categories:

1. New products or expansion of existing products
2. Replacement of equipment or buildings
3. Research and development
4. Exploration
5. Others

The last category comprises miscellaneous items such as the expenditure of funds to comply with certain health standards or the acquisition of a pollution-control device. In the case of a new product, the proposal usually originates in the marketing department. On the other hand, a proposal to replace a piece of equipment with a more sophisticated model usually emanates from the production area of the firm. In each case, it is important to have efficient administrative procedures for channeling investment requests.

Most firms screen proposals at multiple levels of authority. For a proposal originating in the production area, the hierarchy of authority might run from section chiefs to (1) plant managers to (2) the vice-president for operations to (3) a capital-expenditures committee under the financial manager to (4) the president to (5) the board of directors.

How high a proposal must go before it is finally approved usually depends upon its size. The greater the capital outlay, the greater the number of screens usually required. Plant managers, for example, may be able to approve moderate-sized projects on their own; but final approval for larger projects is received only at higher levels of authority. Because the administrative procedures for screening investment proposals vary greatly from firm to firm, it is not possible to generalize. The best procedure will depend upon the circumstances. Where projects are approved at multiple levels, it is important that the same acceptance criterion be applied objectively and consistently throughout the organization.[1] Otherwise, capital is likely to be misallocated in the sense that one division might accept a project that another would reject.

Estimating cash flows

One of the most important tasks in capital budgeting is estimating future cash flows for a project. The final results we obtain are really only as good as the accuracy of our estimates. The reason we express the benefits expected to be derived from a project in terms of cash flows rather than in terms of income is that cash is what is central to all decisions of the firm. The firm invests cash now in the hope of receiving cash returns in a greater amount in the future. Only cash receipts can be reinvested in the firm or paid to stockholders in the form of dividends.[2] Thus, cash, not income, is what is important in capital budgeting.

For each investment proposal, we need to provide information on expected future cash flows on an after-tax basis. In addition, the information must be provided on an incremental basis so that we analyze only the difference between the cash flows of the firm with and without the project. For example, if a firm contemplates a new product that is likely to compete with existing products, it is not appropriate to ex-

---

[1] For surveys of the administrative practices of companies with respect to capital budgeting as well as of the evaluation techniques being used, see J. William Petty, David F. Scott, Jr., and Monroe M. Bird, "The Capital Expenditure Decision-Making Process of Large Corporations," *Engineering Economist,* 20 (Spring 1975), 159–72; and Thomas Klammer, "Empirical Evidence of the Adoption of Sophisticated Capital Budgeting Techniques," *Journal of Business,* 45 (July 1972), 387–97. See also James B. Weaver, "Organizing and Maintaining a Capital Expenditure Program," *Engineering Economist,* 20 (Fall 1974), 1–36, for a discussion of administrative procedures. Finally, for a discussion of the importance of a postcompletion audit as well as of its form, see James S. Schnell and Roy S. Nicolosi, "Capital Expenditure Feedback: Project Reappraisal," *Engineering Economist,* 19 (Summer 1974), 253–61.

[2] See D. E. Peterson, *A Quantitative Framework for Financial Management* (Homewood, Ill.: Richard D. Irwin, 1969), p. 335.

press cash flows in terms of the estimated sales of the new product. We must take into account that probably "cannibalization" of existing products will come about and make our cash-flow estimates on the basis of incremental sales.

To illustrate the information needed for a capital-budgeting decision, consider the following situation. Suppose a firm is considering the introduction of a new product. To launch the product, it will need to spend $150,000 for special equipment and the initial advertising campaign. The marketing department envisions the product life to be six years and expects incremental sales revenue to be:

Year 1	Year 2	Year 3	Year 4	Year 5	Year 6
$60,000	$120,000	$160,000	$180,000	$110,000	$50,000

Cash outflows include labor and maintenance costs, material costs, and various other expenses associated with the product. As with sales, these costs must be estimated on an incremental basis. In addition to these outflows, the firm will need to pay higher taxes if the new product generates higher profits; and this incremental outlay must be included. Suppose that on the basis of these considerations the firm estimates total incremental cash outflows to be:

Year 1	Year 2	Year 3	Year 4	Year 5	Year 6
$40,000	$70,000	$100,000	$100,000	$70,000	$40,000

Because depreciation is a noncash expense, it is not included in these outflows. The expected net cash flows from the project are:

	Initial Cost	Year 1	Year 2	Year 3	Year 4	Year 5	Year 6
Cash inflows		$60,000	$120,000	$160,000	$180,000	$110,000	$50,000
Cash outflows	$150,000	40,000	70,000	100,000	100,000	70,000	40,000
Net cash flows	−$150,000	$20,000	$50,000	$60,000	$80,000	$40,000	$10,000

Thus, for an initial cash outflow of $150,000, the firm expects to generate net cash flows of $20,000, $50,000, $60,000, $80,000, $40,000, and $10,000 over the next six years. These cash flows represent the relevant information we need in order to judge the attractiveness of the project.

To go to a somewhat more complicated replacement-decision example, suppose that we are considering the purchase of a turret lathe to replace an old lathe and that we need to obtain cash-flow information in order to evaluate the attractiveness of this project. The purchase price of the new machine is $18,500; and it will require an additional $1,500 to install, bringing the total cost to $20,000. The old machine can be sold for its depreciated book value of $2,000. The initial net cash outflow for the investment project, therefore, is $18,000. The new machine is expected to cut labor and maintenance costs and effect other cash savings totaling $7,600 a year before taxes for the next five years, after which it is not expected to provide any savings, nor is it expected to have a salvage value. These savings represent the net savings to the firm if it replaces the old machine with the new. In other words, we are concerned with the difference between the cash flows resulting from the two alternatives—continuing with the old machine or replacing it with a new one.

Because machines of this sort have useful lives in excess of one year, their cost cannot be charged against income for tax purposes but must be depreciated over the depreciable life of the asset. Depreciation then is deducted from income in order to compute taxable income. If the firm employs straight-line depreciation, the annual depreciation charge is 20 percent of the total depreciable cost of $20,000, or $4,000 a year. Assume additionally that the corporate federal income tax rate is 50 percent. Moreover, assume that the old machine has a remaining depreciable life of five years, that there is no expected salvage value at the end of this time, and that the machine also is subject to straight-line depreciation. Thus, the annual depreciation charge on the old machine is 20 percent of its depreciated book value of $2,000, or $400 a year. Because we are interested in the incremental impact of the project, we must subtract depreciation charges on the old machine from depreciation charges on the new one to obtain the incremental depreciation charges associated with the project. Given the information cited, we now are able to calculate the expected net cash flow (after taxes) resulting from the acceptance of the project.

	Book Account	Cash-Flow Account
Annual cash savings	$7,600	$7,600
Depreciation on new machine	4,000	
Less depreciation on old machine	400	
Additional depreciation charge	$3,600	
Additional income before taxes	4,000	
Income tax (50%)	2,000	2,000
Additional income after taxes	$2,000	
Annual net cash flow		$5,600

In figuring the net cash flow, we simply deduct the additional cash outlay for federal income taxes from the annual cash savings. The expected annual net cash inflow for this replacement proposal is $5,600 for each of the next five years; this figure compares with additional income after taxes of $2,000 a year. The cash-flow and net-profit figures differ by the amount of additional depreciation. Because our concern is not with income, as such, but with cash flows, we are interested in the right-hand column. For an initial cash outlay of $18,000, then, we are able to replace an older lathe with a new one that is expected to result in net cash savings of $5,600 a year over the next five years. As in the previous example, the relevant cash-flow information for capital-budgeting purposes is expressed on an incremental, after-tax basis.

METHODS FOR EVALUATING PROJECTS

Once we have collected the necessary information, we are able to evaluate the attractiveness of the various investment proposals under consideration. The investment decision will be either to accept or to reject the proposal. In this section, we evaluate four approaches to capital budgeting: the average-rate-of-return method; the payback method; the internal-rate-of-return method; and the net-present-value method. The first two represent approximate methods for assessing the economic worth of a project. For simplicity, we assume throughout that the expected cash flows are realized at the end of each year.

Average rate of return

doesn't take in to consideration time-value

The average rate of return is an accounting method and represents the ratio of the average annual profits after taxes to the average investment in the project. In our first example, the average annual book earnings for the five-year period are $2,000; and the average net investment in the project, assuming straight-line depreciation, is $18,000/2, or $9,000. Therefore,

$$\text{Average rate of return} = \frac{\$2,000}{\$9,000} = 22.22 \text{ percent} \qquad (13\text{-}1)$$

The average-rate-of-return method is sometimes based upon the original investment rather than upon the average investment. In the above example, the average rate of return would be $2,000/$18,000 = 11.11 percent under this version of the average-rate-of-return method.

The principal virtue of the average rate of return method is its simplicity; it makes use of readily available accounting information. Once the average rate of return for a proposal has been calculated, it may be compared with a required, or cutoff, rate of return to determine if a particular proposal should be accepted or rejected. The principal shortcomings of the method are that it is based upon accounting income rather than upon cash flows and that it fails to take account of the timing of cash inflows and outflows. The time value of money is ignored; benefits in the last year are valued the same as benefits in the first year.

Suppose that we have three investment proposals, each costing $9,000 and each having an economic and depreciable life of three years. Assume that these proposals are expected to provide the following book profits and cash flows over the next three years:

| | Project A | | Project B | | Project C | |
Period	Book Profit	Net Cash Flow	Book Profit	Net Cash Flow	Book Profit	Net Cash Flow
1	$3,000	$6,000	$2,000	$5,000	$1,000	$4,000
2	2,000	5,000	2,000	5,000	2,000	5,000
3	1,000	4,000	2,000	5,000	3,000	6,000

If straight-line depreciation is employed, each proposal will have the same average rate of return–$2,000/$4,500, or 44 percent. However, few, if any, firms would be equally favorable to all three projects. Most would prefer project *A*, which provides a large portion of total cash benefits in the first year. For this reason, the average rate of return leaves much to be desired as a method for project selection.

Payback method *60% of co.*
use this #1 of years to recover invest.

The payback period of an investment project tells us the number of years required to recover our initial cash investment. It is the ratio of the initial fixed investment over the annual cash inflows for the recovery period. For our example,

$$\text{Payback period} = \frac{\$18,000}{\$5,600} = 3.2 \text{ years} \qquad (13\text{-}2)$$

If the annual cash inflows are not equal, the job of calculation is somewhat more difficult. Suppose that annual cash inflows are $4,000 in the first year, $6,000 in the second and third years, and $4,000 in the fourth and fifth years. In the first three years, $16,000 of the original investment will be recovered, followed by $4,000 in the fourth year.

With an initial cash investment of $18,000, the payback period is 3 years + ($2,000/$4,000), or 3½ years.

If the payback period calculated is less than some maximum acceptable payback period, the proposal is accepted; if not, it is rejected. For example, if the required payback period is four years, the project in our example would be accepted. The major shortcoming of the payback method is that it fails to consider cash flows after the payback period; consequently, it cannot be regarded as a measure of profitability. Two proposals costing $10,000 each would have the same payback period if they both had annual net cash inflows of $5,000 in the first two years. However, one project might be expected to provide no cash flows after two years, while the other might be expected to provide cash flows of $5,000 in each of the next three years. Thus, the payback method can be very deceptive as a yardstick of profitability. In addition to this shortcoming, the method does not take account of the magnitude or timing of cash flows during the payback period; it considers only the recovery period as a whole.

Internal-rate-of-return method

Because of the various shortcomings in the average-rate-of-return and payback methods described above, it generally is felt that discounted cash-flow methods provide a more objective basis for evaluating and selecting investment projects. These methods take account of both the magnitude and the timing of expected cash flows in each period of a project's life. In any economy in which capital has value, the time value of money is an important concept. For example, stockholders place a higher value on an investment project that promises returns over the next five years than on a project that promises identical returns for years six through ten. Consequently, the timing of expected future cash flows is extremely important in the investment decision.

Discounted cash-flow methods enable us to isolate differences in the timing of cash flows for various projects by discounting these cash flows to their present values, a topic considered in the preceding chapter. The present values can then be analyzed to determine the desirability of the projects. The two discounted cash-flow methods are the internal-rate-of-return method and the present-value method, and we consider each in turn.

The internal rate of return for an investment proposal is the discount rate that equates the present value of the expected cash outflows with the present value of the expected inflows. If the initial cash outlay or cost occurs at time 0, it is represented by that rate, r, such that

$$A_0 = \frac{A_1}{(1 + r)} + \frac{A_2}{(1 + r)^2} + \cdots + \frac{A_n}{(1 + r)^n} \qquad (13\text{-}3)$$

Thus, r is the rate that discounts the stream of future cash flows—A_1 through A_n—to equal in present value the initial outlay at time 0—A_0. For our example, the problem can be expressed as

$$18,000 = \frac{5,600}{(1 + r)} + \frac{5,600}{(1 + r)^2} + \frac{5,600}{(1 + r)^3} + \frac{5,600}{(1 + r)^4} + \frac{5,600}{(1 + r)^5} \qquad (13\text{-}4)$$

Solving for the internal rate of return, r, sometimes involves a trial-and-error procedure using present-value tables. Fortunately, there are computer programs for solving for the internal rate of return; and these programs eliminate the arduous computations involved in the trial-and-error procedure. To illustrate the latter method, however, consider again our example. The cash-flow stream is represented by an even series of cash flows of $5,600, to be received at the end of each of the next five years. We want to determine the discount factor that, when multiplied by $5,600, equals the cash outlay of $18,000 at time 0. Suppose that we start with the discount rates—14 percent, 16 percent, and 18 percent—and calculate the present value of the cash-flow stream. For the different discount rates, we find, using Table A-2 in the Appendix at the end of the book:

Discount Rate	Discount Factor	Cash Flow Each Year	Present Value of Stream
18%	3.1272	$5,600	$17,512.32
16	3.2743	5,600	18,336.08
14	3.4331	5,600	19,225.36

When we compare the present value of the stream with the initial outlay of $18,000, we see that the internal rate of return necessary to discount the stream of $18,000 falls between 16 and 18 percent, being closer to 16 than to 18 percent. To approximate the actual rate, we interpolate between 16 and 17 percent as follows:

	Discount Rate	Present Value
	16%	$18,336.08
	17	17,916.08
Difference	1%	$ 420.00

$$\frac{336.08}{420.00} = 0.80 \qquad 16\% + 0.80\% = 16.8\%$$

Thus, the internal rate of return necessary to equate the present value of the cash inflows with the present value of the outflows is approximately 16.8 percent. It should be noted that interpolation gives only an approximation of the exact percentage; the relationship between the two discount rates is not linear with respect to present value.

When, as above, the cash-flow stream is an even series, and the initial outlay occurs at time 0, there really is no need for trial and error. We simply divide the initial outlay by the cash flow and search for the nearest discount factor. Using our example, we divide $18,000 by $5,600, obtaining 3.214. The nearest discount factor on the five-year row in Table A-2 at the end of the book is 3.2743, and this figure corresponds to a discount rate of 16 percent. Inasmuch as 3.214 is less than 3.2743, we know that the actual rate lies between 16 and 17 percent and we interpolate accordingly. When the cash-flow stream is an uneven series, the task is more difficult; and here we must resort to trial and error. However, given practice, a person can come surprisingly close in selecting discount rates from which to start.

When solving for r, it is important to recognize the possibility that there may be more than one internal rate of return that equates the present value of the cash inflows with the present value of cash outflows. Although the existence of multiple internal rates of return is unusual, we do examine the problem in Appendix A to this chapter.

Acceptance criterion.   The acceptance criterion generally employed with the internal-rate-of-return method is to compare the internal rate of return with a required rate of return, known also as the cutoff, or hurdle, rate. If the internal rate of return exceeds the required rate, the project is accepted; if not, it is rejected. For example, if the required rate of return were 10 percent and this criterion is used, the investment proposal considered above would be accepted. If the required rate of return is the return investors expect the firm to earn on the project, accepting a project with an internal rate of return in excess of the required rate of return should result in an increase in the market price of the stock, because the firm accepts a project with a return greater than that required to maintain the present market price per share. Much more will be said in Chapter 16 about relating the investment decision to the objective of the firm. We assume for now that the required rate of return is given.

Present-value method

Like the internal-rate-of-return method, the present-value method is a discounted cash-flow approach to capital budgeting. With the present-value method, all cash flows are discounted to present value using the required rate of return. The net-present value of an investment proposal is

$$NPV = A_0 + \frac{A_1}{(1 + k)} + \frac{A_2}{(1 + k)^2} + \cdots + \frac{A_n}{(1 + k)^n} \qquad (13\text{-}5)$$

where k is the required rate of return. If the sum of these discounted cash flows is equal to, or greater than, 0, the proposal is accepted; if not, it is rejected. Another way to express the acceptance criterion is to say that the project will be accepted if the present value of cash inflows exceeds the present value of cash outflows. The rationale behind the acceptance criterion is the same as that behind the internal-rate-of-return method. If the required rate of return is the return investors expect the firm to earn on the investment proposal, and the firm accepts a proposal with a net-present value greater than 0, the market price of the stock should rise. Again, the firm is taking on a project with a return greater than that necessary to leave the market price of the stock unchanged.

If we assume a required rate of return of 10 percent after taxes, the net-present value of our example problem is

$$NPV = -18{,}000 + \frac{5{,}600}{(1.10)} + \frac{5{,}600}{(1.10)^2} + \frac{5{,}600}{(1.10)^3} + \frac{5{,}600}{(1.10)^4} + \frac{5{,}600}{(1.10)^5}$$

$$= -18{,}000 + 21{,}228.48 = \$3{,}228.48 \qquad (13\text{-}6)$$

An easier way to solve this problem, of course, is by direct reference to Table A-2 in the Appendix at the end of the book, where we find the appropriate discount factor—3.7908—and multiply $5,600 by it to obtain $21,228.48. Subtracting the initial outlay of $18,000, we obtain $3,228.48. Inasmuch as the net-present value of this proposal is greater than 0, the proposal should be accepted, using the present-value method.

With the internal-rate-of-return method, we are given the cash flows and solve for the rate of discount that equates the present value of the cash inflows with the present value of outflows. The internal rate of return is then compared with the required rate of return to determine whether the proposal should be accepted. With the present-value method, we are given the cash flows and the required rate of return and solve for the net-present value. The acceptability of the proposal is determined by whether the net-present value is equal to, or greater than, zero.

It is obvious that different net-present values will be given for different required rates of return. With a 10 percent required rate, the following cash-flow streams have equivalent net-present values—namely, $3,228:

	Proposal		
Year	1	2	3
0	−$18,000	−$18,797	−$16,446
1	5,600	4,000	7,000
2	5,600	5,000	6,000
3	5,600	6,000	5,000
4	5,600	7,000	4,000
5	5,600	8,000	3,000

However, with different required rates of return, the net-present values of the proposals are:

	Proposal Net-Present Value		
Discount Rate	1	2	3
0%	$10,000	$11,203	$8,554
4	6,930	7,565	6,162
8	4,359	4,546	4,131
10	3,228	3,228	3,228
12	2,187	2,019	2,390
16	336	−114	888
20	−1,253	−1,928	−418

We see that the relative desirability of the proposals changes with changes in the discount rate. The higher the discount rate, the more valued is the proposal with early cash inflows, proposal 3. The lower the discount rate, the less important the timing of the cash flows and the more valued is the proposal with the greatest absolute amount of cash inflows, proposal 2. The example serves to illustrate the importance of the discount rate used in the calculations. Different answers will be given, depending upon the discount rate employed.

Mutual exclusion and dependency

In evaluating a group of investment proposals, it is important to determine whether the proposals are independent of each other. A proposal is said to be mutually exclusive if the acceptance of it precludes the acceptance of one or more other proposals. For example, if the firm is considering investment in one of two temperature-control systems, acceptance of one system will rule out acceptance of the other. Two mutually exclusive proposals cannot both be accepted.

A *contingent* or *dependent* proposal is one whose acceptance depends upon the acceptance of one or more other proposals. An example of a contingent proposal might be an investment in a large machine, which depends upon the construction of an addition to a plant. A combination of investment proposals containing a contingent proposal must contain the proposal(s) upon which it is dependent. When an investment proposal is not independent of all other proposals, this occurrence must be recognized and investment decisions made accordingly.

Profitability index

The profitability index, or benefit-cost ratio, of a project is the present value of future net cash flows over the initial cash outlay. It can be expressed as

$$PI = \frac{\sum_{t=1}^{n} \frac{A_t}{(1 + k)^t}}{A_0}, \qquad (13\text{-}7)$$

where the Greek sigma means the sum of discounted cash flows from period 1 through period n. For our example,

$$PI = \frac{\$21,228.48}{\$18,000.00} = 1.18 \qquad (13\text{-}8)$$

As long as the profitability index is equal to or greater than 1.00, the investment proposal is acceptable. For any given project, the net-present-value method and the profitability index give the same accept-reject signals. If we must choose between mutually exclusive projects, however, the net-present-value measure is preferred because it expresses in absolute terms the expected economic contribution of the project. In contrast, the profitability index expresses only the relative profitability. To illustrate, consider the following mutually exclusive projects:

	Project A	Project B
Present value of net cash flows	$20,000	$8,000
Initial cash outlay	15,000	5,000
Net present value	$ 5,000	$3,000
Profitability index	1.33	1.60

According to the net-present-value method, project A would be preferred, whereas according to the profitability indexes, project B would be preferred. Because the net-present value represents the expected economic contribution of a project, we should prefer A to B. Thus, the net-present-value method is the better of the two methods when we must choose between mutually exclusive projects that involve different initial cash outlays.[3]

COMPARISON OF PRESENT-VALUE AND INTERNAL-RATE-OF-RETURN METHODS

In general, the present-value and internal-rate-of-return methods lead to the same acceptance or rejection decision. In Figure 13-1, we illustrate graphically the two methods applied to a typical investment project. The figure shows the relationship between the net-present value of a project and the discount rate employed. When the discount rate is 0, net-present value is simply the total cash inflows less the total cash outflows of the project. Assuming that total inflows exceed total outflows and that outflows are followed by inflows, the typical project will have the highest net-present value when the discount rate is 0. As the discount rate increases, the present value of future cash inflows decreases relative to the present value of cash outflows. At the intercept, the net-present value of the project is 0. The discount rate at that point represents the internal rate of return that equates the present value of cash inflows with the present value of cash outflows. For discount rates greater than the internal rate of return, the net-present value of the project is negative.[4]

If the required rate of return is less than the internal rate of return, we would accept the project using either method. Suppose that the required rate were 10 percent. As seen in Figure 13-1, the net-present value of the project then would be Y. Inasmuch as Y is greater than 0, we would accept the project using the present-value method. Similarly, we would accept the project using the internal-rate-of-return method because the internal rate exceeds the required rate. For required rates greater than the internal rate of return, we would reject the project under either method. Thus, we see that the internal-rate-of-return and present-value methods give us identical answers with respect to the acceptance or rejection of an investment project.

[3]See Bernhard Schwab and Peter Lusztig, "A Comparative Analysis of the Net-Present Value and the Benefit-Cost Ratio as Measures of the Economic Desirability of Investments," *Journal of Finance*, 24 (June 1969), 507–16.

[4]Again, we must recognize the possibility of multiple internal rates of return. See Appendix A to this chapter.

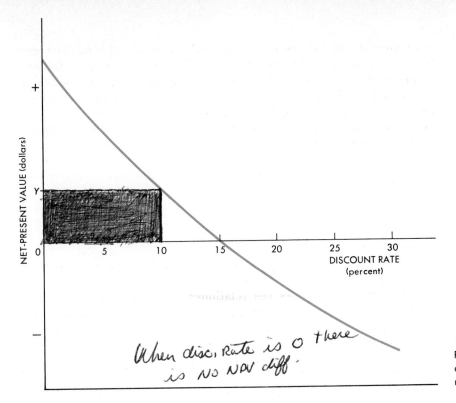

When disc, Rate is 0 there is NO NPV diff.

FIG. 13 · 1

Relation between discount rate and net-present value

Differences between methods

However, important differences exist between the methods and they must be recognized. When two investment proposals are mutually exclusive, so that we can select only one, the two methods may give contradictory results. To illustrate the nature of the problem, suppose a firm had two mutually exclusive investment proposals that were expected to generate the following cash flows:

	Cash Flows	
Year	Proposal A	Proposal B
0	−$23,616	−$23,616
1	10,000	0
2	10,000	5,000
3	10,000	10,000
4	10,000	32,675

Internal rates of return for proposals *A* and *B* are 25 percent and 22 percent, respectively. If the required rate of return is 10 percent, however, and we use this figure as our discount rate, the net-present values of proposals A and B are \$8,083 and \$10,347, respectively. Thus, proposal A is preferred if we use the internal-rate-of-return method, whereas proposal B is preferred if we use the present-value method. If we can choose but one of these proposals, we obviously have a conflict.

Reinvestment rate. The conflict between these two methods is due to different assumptions with respect to the reinvestment rate on funds released from the proposals. The internal-rate-of-return method implies that funds are reinvested at the internal rate of return over the remaining life of the proposal. For proposal A, the assumption is that cash flows of \$10,000 at the end of years 1, 2, and 3 can be reinvested to earn a return of 25 percent, compounded annually. The present-value method implies reinvestment at a rate equivalent to the required rate of return used as the discount rate. Because of these differing assumptions, the two methods can give different rankings of investment proposals as we have seen.

To illustrate further the nature of the problem, consider two additional mutually exclusive proposals with the following cash flows:

	Cash Flows	
Time	Proposal C	Proposal D
0	−\$155.22	−\$155.22
1	100.00	0
2	0	0
3	100.00	221.00

The net-present value of each of these proposals is \$10.82 if we assume a required rate of return of 10 percent. However, we would be indifferent between the two proposals only if the firm had opportunities for reinvestment at a rate of 10 percent. This concept is illustrated in Figure 13-2, where the functional relationship between net-present value and the discount rate is graphed for the two proposals. The intercepts on the 0 horizontal line represent the internal rates of return of the two proposals that equate their net-present values with 0. For proposal C, the internal rate of return is 14 percent; for proposal D, it is 12.5 percent. The intercepts on the vertical axis represent total cash inflows less total cash outflows for the two proposals, because the discount rate is 0. We see that proposal D ranks higher than proposal C if the reinvestment rate is below 10 percent and lower if it is above 10 percent. At the point of intersection, 10 percent, the proposals have identical net-present values. Given a reinvestment rate of 10 percent,

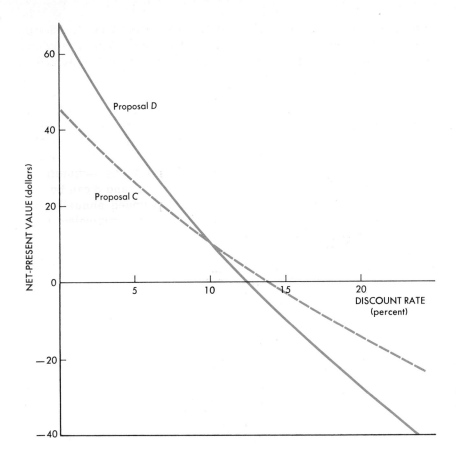

FIG. 13 · 2

Relation between
discount rate and
net-present values,
proposals C and D

then, the two proposals would have equal ranking. For reinvestment
rates other than this percentage, we would prefer one proposal to the
other. In a similar manner, other mutually exclusive investment proposals can be evaluated according to the intersections.

Which method provides the better results?

The question to be answered is which method—the internal-rate-
of-return method or the present-value method—is better for purposes
of evaluating investment proposals. Actually, the question hinges
upon what is the appropriate rate of reinvestment for the intermediate
cash flows. We have demonstrated that the internal-rate-of-return
method implies a reinvestment rate equal to the internal rate of return, whereas the present-value method implies a reinvestment rate
equal to the required rate of return used as the discount factor. Per-

haps the ideal solution would be to take the expected rate of reinvestment for each period and calculate a terminal value. However, this procedure involves additional computational steps that many do not feel to be worthwhile.

If a choice must be made, the present-value method generally is considered to be superior theoretically. With the internal-rate-of-return method, the implied reinvestment rate will differ depending upon the cash-flow stream for each investment proposal under consideration. For proposals with a high internal rate of return, a high reinvestment rate is assumed; for proposals with a low internal rate of return, a low reinvestment rate is assumed. Only rarely will the internal rate of return calculated represent the relevant rate for reinvestment of intermediate cash flows. With the present-value method, however, the implied reinvestment rate—namely, the required rate of return—is the same for each proposal. To the extent that we can regard the required rate as an approximate measure of the opportunity rate for reinvestment, the present-value method is preferred over the internal-rate-of-return method.

However, many financial managers feel that, in practice, the internal rate of return is easier to visualize and to interpret than is the net-present-value measure. In addition, one does not have to specify a required rate of return in the calculations. To the extent that the required rate of return is but a rough estimate, the use of the internal-rate-of-return method may permit a more realistic comparison of projects. The principal shortcoming of the method is the possibility of multiple internal rates of return, a subject that we take up in Appendix A to this chapter.

DEPRECIATION AND SALVAGE VALUE

In our replacement example, we assumed straight-line depreciation and no salvage value. For continuity, we then investigated the various methods for evaluating investment proposals, using this example as our illustration throughout. We need now to digress for awhile in order to examine the effects of accelerated depreciation and of salvage value upon the cash flows. Recall that the replacement of the old machine with a new one was expected to result in annual cash savings of $7,600 a year over the next five years. Straight-line depreciation charges on the new machine were $4,000 a year; and when we subtracted $400 annual depreciation charges on the old machine, we obtained incremental depreciation charges of $3,600 a year. Thus, the additional income before taxes was $4,000, resulting in additional taxes of $2,000 a year, assuming a 50 percent tax rate. When this $2,000 outlay was subtracted from the $7,600 cash savings, the net cash inflow became

$5,600 a year. Consider now the modification of the example occasioned by accelerated depreciation and salvage value.

Accelerated depreciation

As we know from Chapter 2, accelerated depreciation can be either the double-declining-balance method or the sum-of-the-years'-digits method. In the case of a five-year depreciable life, the annual depreciation charge would be 2(1/5), or 40 percent of the depreciated book value balance at the beginning of the year for the double-declining-balance method. If the depreciable value were $10,000 initially, depreciation charges would be $4,000 in the first year, $2,400 in the second (40 percent of ($10,000 − 4,000)), and so on. For the sum-of-the-years'-digits method, the first-year depreciation charge on an asset having a five-year depreciable life would be 5/15, followed by 4/15, 3/15, 2/15, and 1/15 for the remaining years. Given a depreciable value of $20,000 in our example and a five-year depreciable life, the annual depreciation charges for these accelerated methods are:

Year	Double-Declining Balance (40%)	Sum-of-the-Years' Digits
1	$ 8,000.00	$ 6,666.67
2	4,800.00	5,333.33
3	2,880.00	4,000.00
4	1,728.00	2,666.67
5	2,592.00	1,333.33
	$20,000.00	$20,000.00

If the old machine were still depreciated on a straight-line basis of $400 a year, the incremental depreciation charge and annual net cash flow for these two methods over the five-year period would be:

Year	Double-Declining Balance (40%)		Sum-of-the-Years' Digits	
	Incremental Depreciation	Net Cash Flow	Incremental Depreciation	Net Cash Flow
1	$7,600.00	$7,600.00	$6,266.67	$6,933.33
2	4,400.00	6,000.00	4,933.33	6,266.67
3	2,480.00	5,040.00	3,600.00	5,600.00
4	1,328.00	4,464.00	2,266.67	4,933.33
5	2,192.00	4,896.00	933.33	4,266.67

We see that the use of accelerated depreciation increases the depreciation charge in the early years of the project's life over what it would be if straight-line depreciation were used, resulting in lower taxes and higher cash flows in these years. The use of accelerated depreciation changes the timing of cash flows from what they would be if straight-line depreciation were used. If money does have a time value, accelerated depreciation is advantageous to the firm. For example, the internal rate of return using the double-declining-balance method is 18.7 percent, compared with 16.8 percent when the straight-line method of depreciation is employed. The net-present value, assuming a required rate of return of 10 percent, is $3,743.33 under the double-declining-balance method, compared with $3,228.48 under the straight-line method. For the sum-of-the-years' digits method, the internal rate of return is 18.5 percent and the net-present value, $3,708.30. Thus, the method of depreciation affects the timing of cash flows and the resulting attractiveness of the investment project. The total amount of taxes is not reduced with accelerated depreciation; taxes simply are paid at a date later than would be the case with straight-line depreciation.

Salvage value and taxes

The cash-flow pattern also will differ from that shown in the example if the new machine is expected to have a salvage, or scrap, value at the end of the five-year period. When there is a salvage value, it may affect depreciation charges as well as the cash flow in the last year. Assume that the salvage value of the new machine is expected to be $2,000 at the end of the fifth year. The total depreciable value becomes $18,000 instead of $20,000; and, assuming straight-line depreciation, annual depreciation charges for the new machine become $3,600 instead of $4,000. If we follow through with the previous calculations, we find that the annual net cash flow for years 1 through 4 is $5,400 instead of $5,600. The net cash flow in the fifth year is $5,400, plus the salvage value of $2,000, or $7,400.

In addition to the salvage value, there are other tax considerations. If the machine can be sold for more than its depreciated book value, the difference is subject to income taxes if the sales price is less than the machine's original cost. For example, if the machine could be sold for $4,000 instead of $2,000, there would be a gain of $2,000. If the corporate tax rate were 50 percent, the total cash proceeds realized from the sale would be $3,000. As long as the gain is less than the total depreciation claimed, it is reported as fully taxable income. In our example, the machine cost $20,000 and $18,000 in depreciation is claimed through year 5. As the $2,000 gain is less than the total depreciation claimed, it is taxed at the ordinary corporate tax rate of 50 percent. If the machine could be sold for $23,000, however, $18,000 of the total gain of $21,000 would be reported as fully taxable income, while $3,000 would be subject to the capital-gains tax treatment, which usually is more favorable.[5] There are many other variations that we could illustrate, but these examples are enough to show that tax considerations are important in calculating the cash flow.

CAPITAL RATIONING

Capital rationing occurs anytime there is a budget ceiling, or constraint, on the amount of funds that can be invested during a specific period of time, such as a year. Such constraints are prevalent in a number of firms, particularly in those that have a policy of financing all capital expenditures internally. Another example of capital rationing is when a division of a large company is allowed to make capital expenditures only up to a specified budget ceiling, over which the division usually has no control. With a capital-rationing constraint, the firm attempts to select the combination of investment proposals that will provide the greatest profitability.

To illustrate, suppose a firm had the following investment opportunities, ranked in descending order of profitability indexes (the ratio of the present value of future net cash flows over the initial cash outlay):

Proposal	Profitability Index	Initial Outlay
4	1.25	$400,000
7	1.19	100,000
2	1.16	175,000
3	1.14	125,000
6	1.09	200,000
5	1.05	100,000
1	0.97	150,000

If the budget ceiling for initial outlays during the present period were $1 million, and the proposals were independent of each other, we would select proposals in descending order of profitability until the

[5] See *Federal Tax Course* (Englewood Cliffs, N.J.: Prentice-Hall, 1975), Chapters 6 and 22.

budget was exhausted. With capital rationing, we would accept the first five proposals, totaling $1 million in initial outlays. In other words, we do not necessarily invest in all proposals that increase the net-present value of the firm; we invest in an acceptable proposal only if the budget constraint allows such an investment. In the above example, we do not invest in proposal 5, even though the profitability index in excess of 1 would suggest its acceptance. The critical aspect of the capital-rationing constraint illustrated is that capital expenditures during a period are strictly limited by the budget ceiling, regardless of the number of attractive investment opportunities.

Opportunity costs and objections to capital rationing

The cost to the firm of a budget ceiling might be regarded as the opportunity foregone on the next most profitable investment after the cutoff. In our example, the opportunity foregone by the $1 million budget ceiling is proposal 5, which has a profitability index of 1.05. Although all cash flows are discounted at the required rate of return, we do not necessarily accept proposals that provide positive net-present values. Acceptance is determined by the budget constraint, which tells us which proposals can be accepted before the budget is exhausted. To be sure, the required rate of return sets a lower limit; we would not accept proposals yielding less than this required rate even if the budget were not exhausted.[6] However, we may reject projects that provide positive net-present values, as was shown with proposal 5. Under capital rationing, the required rate of return is not the acceptance criterion. Should it then be used as the discount rate in present-value calculations, or should the opportunity cost be used? The implied discount rate in any budget period is the yield foregone on the most profitable investment opportunity rejected, or the required rate of return, whichever is the higher. This implied discount rate can vary significantly from period to period, depending upon variations in the total amount of investment projects from period to period and in the budget constraints.

Capital rationing usually results in an investment policy that is less than optimal. In some periods, the firm accepts projects down to its required rate of return; in others, it may reject projects that would provide returns substantially in excess of the required rate. If the firm actually can raise capital at that approximate real cost, should it not invest in all projects yielding more than the required rate of return? If it rations capital and does not invest in all projects yielding more than the required rate, is it not foregoing opportunities that would enhance the market price of its stock?

---

[6]The exception is contingent projects, as illustrated earlier.

From a theoretical standpoint, a firm should accept all projects yielding more than the required rate of return.[7] By so doing, it should increase the market price per share because projects are accepted that will provide a return higher than that necessary to maintain the present market price per share. This proposition assumes that the firm actually can raise capital, within reasonable limits, at the required rate of return. Certainly, unlimited amounts of capital are not available at any one cost. However, most firms are involved in a more or less continual process of making decisions to undertake capital expenditures and to finance these expenditures. Given the assumptions above, the firm should accept all proposals yielding more than the required rate of return and raise capital to finance these proposals at that approximate real cost. Certainly, there are circumstances that complicate the use of this rule. However, in general, this policy should tend to maximize the market price of the stock over the long run. If capital is rationed, and projects are rejected that would yield more than the required rate of return, its investment policy, by definition, is less than optimal. Management could increase the value of the firm to the shareholders by accepting these projects.

In this chapter, we have examined various methods of capital budgeting, concentrating in particular on the internal-rate-of-return and present-value methods. An important topic taken up initially was the collection of the cash-flow information essential for the evaluation of investment proposals. Capital-budgeting methods, including the average-rate-of-return and payback methods, were evaluated under the assumption that the acceptance of any investment proposal does not change the total business-risk complexion of the firm. It was shown that the two discounted cash-flow methods—internal rate of return and net-present value—were the only appropriate means by which to judge the economic contribution of an investment proposal.

The important distinction between the internal-rate-of-return method and the present-value method is the implied reinvestment rate. Depending upon the situation, contrary answers can be given with respect to the acceptance of mutually exclusive investment proposals. On theoretical grounds, a case can be made for the superiority of the present-value method. The problem of capital rationing was examined, and we concluded that such a policy is likely to result in investment decisions that are less than optimal.

[7]We shall examine the rationale for this criterion in Chapter 16.

Multiple internal rates of return

In a well-known article, Lorie and Savage pointed out that certain streams of cash flows may have more than one internal rate of return.[8] To illustrate the problem, suppose that we had the following stream of cash flows corresponding to the "pump" proposal of Lorie and Savage:

Year	0	1	2
Cash flow	−$1,600	$10,000	−$10,000

In this example, a new, more effective pump is substituted for an existing pump. On an incremental basis, there is an initial outlay followed by net cash inflows resulting from the increased efficiency of the new pump. If the quantity of oil, for example, is fixed, the new pump will exhaust this supply more quickly than the old pump would. Beyond this point of exhaustion, the new pump alternative would result in an incremental outflow, because the old pump would still be productive.

When we solve for the internal rate of return for the above cash-flow stream, we find that it is not one rate, but two: 25 percent and 400 percent. This unusual situation is illustrated in Figure 13-3, where the discount rate is plotted along the horizontal axis and net-present value along the vertical axis. At a 0 rate of discount, the net-present value of the project, −$1,600, is negative, owing to the fact that total nondiscounted cash outflows exceed total nondiscounted inflows. As the discount rate increases, the present value of the second-year outflow diminishes with respect to the first-year inflow, and the present value of the proposal becomes positive when the discount rate exceeds 25 percent. As the discount rate increases beyond 100 percent, the present value of all future cash flows (years 1 and 2) diminishes relative to the initial outflow of −$1,600. At 400 percent, the present value of all cash flows again becomes 0.

This type of proposal differs from the usual case, shown in Figure 13-1 in this chapter, in which net-present value is a decreasing function of the discount rate, and in which there is but one internal rate of return that equates the present value of all inflows with the present value of all outflows. An investment proposal may have any number of

[8]See James H. Lorie and Leonard J. Savage, "Three Problems in Rationing Capital," *Journal of Business,* 28 (October 1955), 229–39.

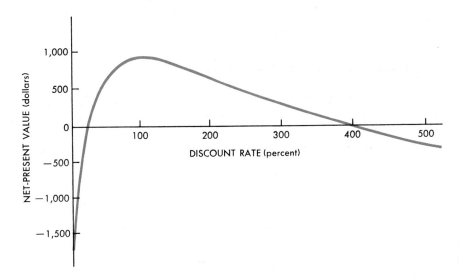

FIG. 13 · 3
Dual rates of return

internal rates of return, depending upon the cash-flow pattern. Consider the following series of cash flows:

Year	0	1	2	3
Cash flow	−$1,000	$6,000	−$11,000	$6,000

In this example, discount rates of 0, 100 percent, and 200 percent result in the net-present value of all cash flows equaling 0.

The number of internal rates of return is limited to the number of reversals of sign in the cash-flow stream. In the above example, we have three reversals and three internal rates of return. Although a multiple reversal in signs is a necessary condition for multiple internal rates of return, it is not sufficient for such an occurrence. The occurrence of multiple internal rates of return also depends upon the magnitude of cash flows. For the following series of cash flows, there is but one internal rate of return (32.5 percent), despite two reversals of sign:

Year	0	1	2
Cash flow	−$1,000	$1,400	−$100

When confronted with a proposal having multiple rates of return, how does one decide which is the correct rate? In our dual-rate example, is the correct rate 25 percent or 400 percent? Actually, neither rate is correct, because neither is a measure of investment worth.[9] In essence, the firm has "borrowed" $10,000 from the project at the end of the year 1 and will pay it back at the end of year 2. The relevant question is, What is it worth to the firm to have the use of $10,000 for one year? This question, in turn, depends upon the rate of return on investment opportunities available to the firm for that period of time. If the firm could earn 20 percent on the use of these funds and realize these earnings at the end of the period, the value of this opportunity would be $2,000, to be received at the end of year 2. The internal rate of return that equates the present value of this amount to the present value of the initial outlay of $1,600 is 11.8 percent. Similarly, other proposals can be evaluated to find one meaningful rate of return.[10]

Inflation and cash-flow estimates

In estimating cash flows, it is important that anticipated inflation be taken into account. Often there is a tendency to assume that price levels remain unchanged throughout the life of the project. Frequently, this assumption is imposed unknowingly; future cash flows simply are estimated on the basis of existing prices. However, a bias arises in the selection process in that the required rate of return for the project usually is based on current capital costs, which in turn embody a premium for anticipated inflation. The purpose of this appendix is to illustrate this bias.[11]

Assume a situation where the hurdle rate for a project is its required rate of return as perceived by investors and creditors. (The ways by which it is measured are taken up in Chapter 16.) There is general agreement that security prices depend on anticipated changes in prices. In fact, over eighty years ago Irving Fisher expressed the nominal rate of interest on a financial instrument as the sum of the real rate and the rate of price change expected over the life of the instrument.[12] This observed phenomenon has come to be known as the *Fisher effect.* Implied is that the required rate of return for a project is

[9]Ezra Solomon, "The Arithmetic of Capital-Budgeting Decisions," *Journal of Business,* 29 (April 1956), 424–29.

[10]For a rigorous analysis of the problem of multiple rates of return, see Daniel Teichroew, Alexander A. Robichek, and Michael Montalbano, "An Analysis of Criteria for Investment and Financing Decisions under Certainty," *Management Science,* 12 (November 1965), 151–79.

[11]Appendix B is based on James C. Van Horne, "A Note on Biases in Capital Budgeting Introduced by Inflation," *Journal of Financial and Quantitative Analysis,* 6 (January 1971), 653–58.

[12]*Appreciation and Interest* (New York: Macmillan, 1896).

$$R_j = R_j^* + \rho \qquad (13B-1)$$

where R_j is the required rate of return in nominal terms, R_j^* is the required rate in real terms, and ρ is the weighted-average anticipated rate of inflation over the life of the project.

If anticipated inflation is embodied in the acceptance criterion, it is important that it be reflected in the estimated cash flows for the project as well. The expected cash flows of a project are affected by anticipated inflation in several ways. If cash inflows ultimately arise from the sale of a product, these inflows are affected by expected future prices. As for cash outflows, inflation affects both expected future wages and material costs. Note that future inflation does not affect depreciation charges on existing assets. Once the asset is acquired, these charges are known with certainty. The effect of anticipated inflation on cash inflows and cash outflows will vary with the nature of the project. In some cases, cash inflows, through price increases, will rise faster than cash outflows; in other cases, the opposite will hold. No matter what the relationship, it is important that it be embodied in the cash-flow estimates. Otherwise, a bias of the type described before arises.

To illustrate this bias, assume that a project that cost $100,000 at time 0 was under consideration and was expected to provide cash-flow benefits over the next five years. Assume further straight-line depreciation of $20,000 a year and a corporate tax rate of 50 percent. Suppose that cash flows were estimated on the basis of price levels at time 0, with no consideration to the effect of future inflation upon them, and that these estimates were:

	Period				
	1	2	3	4	5
Expected cash inflow, I_t	$30,000	$40,000	$50,000	$50,000	$30,000
Expected cash outflow, O_t	10,000	10,000	10,000	10,000	10,000
	$20,000	$30,000	$40,000	$40,000	$20,000
Times $(1 - \text{tax rate})$	.50	.50	.50	.50	.50
	$10,000	$15,000	$20,000	$20,000	$10,000
Depreciation $\times$ Tax rate	10,000	10,000	10,000	10,000	10,000
Net cash flow	$20,000	$25,000	$30,000	$30,000	$20,000

If the project's required rate of return were 12 percent, the net-present value of the project would be $-\$3,192$. As this figure is negative, the project would be rejected.

However, the results are biased in the sense that the discount rate embodies an element attributable to anticipated future inflation, whereas the cash-flow estimates do not. Suppose that the existing rate of inflation, as measured by changes in the price-level index, were 5 percent, and that this rate was expected to prevail over the next five years. If both cash inflows and cash outflows were expected to increase at this rate, the net-present value of the project would be

$$NPV_0 = \sum_{t=1}^{5} \frac{[I_t(1.05)^t - O_t(1.05)^t][.5] + 20,000,[.5]}{(1.12)^t} - 100,000 \qquad (13B\text{-}2)$$

$$= \$5,450$$

where I_t is the cash inflow in year t, O_t is the cash outflow in year t, and \$20,000 is the annual depreciation in year t which is multiplied by the tax rate to give the tax-shield cash savings. Because the net-present value is positive, the project would now be acceptable, whereas before it was not. To reject it under the previous method of estimating cash flows would result in an opportunity loss to stockholders, for the project provides a return in excess of that required by investors.

This example serves to illustrate the importance of taking anticipated inflation into account explicitly when estimating future cash flows. Too often, there is a tendency not to consider its effect in these estimates. Because anticipated inflation is embodied in the required rate of return, not to take account of it in the cash-flow estimates will result in a biased appraisal of the project and, in turn, the possibility of a less than optimal allocation of capital.

QUESTIONS

1. Explain what is meant by the time value of money. Why is a bird in the hand worth two (or so) in the bush? Which capital-budgeting approaches ignore this concept? Are they optimal?

2. In evaluating the return from investments, why is depreciation included in the cash flows from a project and not deducted as are other expenses such as wages or taxes?

3. In capital budgeting for a new machine, should the following items be added or subtracted from the new machine's purchase price?
   (a) The market value of the old machine is $500.
   (b) An investment in inventory of $2,000 is required.
   (c) The book value of the old machine is $1,000.
   (d) $200 is required to ship the new machine to the plant site.
   (e) A concrete foundation for the new machine will cost $250.
   (f) Training of the machine operator will cost $300.
   (g) The investment tax credit on the new machine.

4. Why does the payback period bias the process of asset selection toward short-lived assets?

5. Contrast the internal rate of return with the net-present value. Why might these two time-value approaches to asset selection give conflicting decision rules?

6. Why is the rate of return of future periods important in selecting a measure with which to assign priorities to projects in the current period?

7. The payback period, although it is conceptually unsound, is very popular in business as a criterion for assigning priorities to investment projects. Why is it unsound and why is it popular?

8. Why are capital-budgeting procedures not applied to working capital decisions?

9. Discuss the adjustments in the capital-budgeting decision one should make to compensate for expected inflation.

10. Discuss the relationship between the payback period of an annuity and its internal rate of return.

11. Is the economic efficiency of a country enhanced by the use of modern capital-budgeting techniques? Why?

PROBLEMS

1. Do the following exercises on internal rates of return:
   (a) An investment of $1,000 today will return $2,000 at the end of ten years. What is its IRR?
   (b) An investment of $1,000 today will return $500 at the end of each of the next three years. What is its IRR?
   (c) An investment of $1,000 today will return $1,000 at the end of one year, $500 at the end of two years, and $100 at the end of three years. What is its IRR?
   (d) An investment of $1,000 will return $60 per year forever. What is its IRR?

2. Two mutually exclusive projects have projected cash flows as follows:

Period	0	1	2	3	4
A	−$2,000	$1,000	$1,000	$1,000	$1,000
B	−$2,000	0	0	0	$6,000

   (a) Determine the internal rate of return for each project.
   (b) Determine the present value for each project at different discount rates, varying from 0 to 35 percent.
   (c) Plot a graph of the present value of each project at the different discount rates.
   (d) Which project would you select? Why? What assumptions are inherent in your decision?

MARY ALLEN IS A DOPE

3. The Homes Corporation is faced with two mutually exclusive investment proposals. One would cost $100,000 and provide *net cash flows* of $30,000 per year for five years. The other would cost $50,000 and provide *net cash flows* of $16,000 for five years. Homes has a 10 percent after-tax opportunity cost of funds. Compute the net-present value and profitability index of each project. Which should be accepted?

4. Rework Problem 3, assuming a 17 percent opportunity cost of funds. How would this change your answer?

5. The L. C. Scott Company is considering the purchase of a machine tool to replace an existing tool that has a book value of $3,000 and can be sold for $1,500. The salvage value of the old machine in four years is zero, and it is depreciated on a straight-line basis. The proposed machine will perform the same function the old machine is performing; however, improvements in technology will enable the firm to reap cash benefits (before depreciation and taxes) of $7,000 *per year* in materials, labor, and overhead. The new machine has a four-year life, costs $14,000, and can be sold for an expected $2,000 at the end of the fourth year. Assuming straight-line depreciation, a 40 percent tax rate, and a required rate of return of 16 percent, find the payback period, NPV, and IRR.

6. An existing machine whose original cost was $4,500 has a book value of $2,100; it can be operated for seven years during which it will be depreciated to zero terminal value. Alternatively, a new machine that has an expected life of seven years can be purchased to replace the existing machine for $12,500. The new machine is expected to have a salvage value of $2,000 and is expected to provide cash savings (before depreciation and taxes) of $3,300 per year. The tax rate is 40 percent, the required rate of return is 16 percent, and straight-line depreciation is used. The existing machine can be sold for $2,600.
   (a) Compute the payback period.
   (b) Compute the internal rate of return.
   (c) Compute the net-present value and the profitability index.
   (d) Would you replace the machine?
   (e) Answer (a)–(d) above assuming the old machine could not be sold.

7. An insurance company agrees to pay you $3,300 at the end of twenty years if you contribute $100 per year at the beginning of each year for the twenty years.
   (a) Find the net-present value of this alternative if your required rate of return is 5 percent.
   (b) Find the internal rate of return.

8. The P. Breaux Company agrees to lend you $10,000 payable in twenty-four monthly installments of $500. (Ignore taxes.)
   (a) Compute the internal rate of return (IRR) to P. Breaux (expressed as a monthly rate).
   (b) Is the annual rate equal to twelve times the monthly rate? Explain.
   (c) If P. Breaux's required rate of return is $\frac{1}{2}$ of 1 percent per month, find the net-present value of making the loan.

9. The N. Marks Company is using a machine whose original cost was $45,000. The machine is five years old and is expected to last an additional ten years. It is being depreciated on a straight-line basis over its fifteen-year life to an expected zero salvage. It can be sold currently for $10,000. A replacement is being contemplated. The new machine costs $40,000 and will have zero salvage at the end of ten years. The machine will produce savings (before interest and depreciation) of $6,000/yr. The tax rate is 40 percent and the required rate of return is 10 percent.
   (a) Compute the internal rate of return.
   (b) Compute the net-present value and profitability index.
   (c) Compute the payback period.

SELECTED REFERENCES

ABDELSAMAD, MOUSTAFA, *A Guide to Capital Expenditure Analysis*. New York: American Management Association, 1973.

BERNHARD, RICHARD H., "Mathematical Programming Models for Capital Budgeting— A Survey, Generalization, and Critique," *Journal of Financial and Quantitative Analysis,* 4 (June 1969), 111–58.

BIERMAN, HAROLD, JR., and SEYMOUR SMIDT, *The Capital Budgeting Decision*. New York: Macmillan, 1971.

DUDLEY, CARLTON L., JR., "A Note on Reinvestment Assumptions in Choosing between Net Present Value and Internal Rate of Return," *Journal of Finance,* 27 (September 1972), 907–15.

FOGLER, H. RUSSELL, "Ranking Techniques and Capital Rationing," *Accounting Review,* 47 (January 1972), 134–43.

HASTIE, K. LARRY, "One Businessman's View of Capital Budgeting," *Financial Management,* 3 (Winter 1974), 36–44.

JOHNSON, ROBERT W., *Capital Budgeting*. Belmont, Calif.: Wadsworth, 1970.

LORIE, JAMES H., and LEONARD J. SAVAGE, "Three Problems in Rationing Capital," *Journal of Business,* 28 (October 1955), 229–39.

MAO, JAMES C. T., "The Internal Rate of Return as a Ranking Criterion," *Engineering Economist,* 11 (Winter 1966), 1–13.

MURDICK, ROBERT G., and DONALD D. DEMING, *The Management of Corporate Expenditures*. New York: McGraw-Hill, 1968.

OAKFORD, ROBERT V., *Capital Budgeting*. New York: Ronald Press, 1970.

PETTY, J. WILLIAM, DAVID F. SCOTT, JR., and MONROE M. BIRD, "The Capital Expenditure Decision-Making Process of Large Corporations," *Engineering Economist,* 20 (Spring 1975), 159–72.

ROBICHEK, ALEXANDER A., and STEWART C. MYERS, "Conceptual Problems in the Use of Risk-Adjusted Discount Rates," *Journal of Finance,* 21 (December 1966), 727–30.

SCHNELL, JAMES S., and ROY S. NICOLOSI, "Capital Expenditure Feedback: Project Reappraisal," *Engineering Economist,* 19 (Summer 1974), 253–61.

SCHWAB, BERNHARD, and PETER LUSZTIG, "A Comparative Analysis of the Net-Present Value and the Benefit-Cost Ratios as Measures of the Economic Desirability of Investments," *Journal of Finance,* 24 (June 1969), 507–16.

SOLOMON, EZRA, "The Arithmetic of Capital-Budgeting Decisions," *Journal of Business,* 29 (April 1956), 124–29.

————, *The Management of Corporate Capital*. New York: Free Press, 1959.

————, *The Theory of Financial Management*. New York: Columbia University Press, 1963.

SWALM, RALPH O., "Utility Theory—Insights into Risk Taking," *Harvard Business Review*, 44 (November–December 1966), 123–36.

TEICHROEW, DANIEL, ALEXANDER A. ROBICHEK, and MICHAEL MONTALBANO, "An Analysis of Criteria for Investment and Financing Decisions under Certainty," *Management Science*, 12 (November 1965), 151–79.

————, "Mathematical Analysis of Rates of Return under Certainty," *Management Science*, 11 (January 1965), 395–403.

VAN HORNE, JAMES C., "A Note of Biases in Capital Budgeting Introduced by Inflation," *Journal of Financial and Quantitative Analysis*, 6 (January 1971), 653–58.

WEAVER, JAMES B., "Organizing and Maintaining a Capital Expenditure Program," *Engineering Economist*, 20 (Fall 1974), 1–36.

WEINGARTNER, H. MARTIN, *Mathematical Programming and the Analysis of Capital Budgeting Problems*. Copyright © H. Martin Weingartner, 1963.

————, "Some New Views on the Payback Period and Capital Budgeting Decisions," *Management Science*, 15 (August 1969), 594–607.

Risk and Capital Budgeting 14

In the preceding chapter, we assumed that the acceptance of any investment proposal under consideration did not change the business-risk complexion of the firm as perceived by suppliers of capital. This assumption allowed us to hold risk constant and base our analysis of an investment project on its expected future cash flows. When we relax this assumption, we must allow for the possibility of investment projects having different degrees of risk. Because suppliers of capital to the firm (investors and creditors) tend to be risk-averse, the acceptance of a project that changes the risk complexion of the firm may cause them to change their required rates of return for investing or extending credit.

When we allow for changes in risk, then, we must take into account possible changes in the firm's value. The project that is expected to provide a high return may be so risky as to cause a significant increase in the perceived risk of the firm. In turn, this may cause a decrease in the firm's value despite the project's considerable profitability potential.

In this chapter, we consider various ways by which management can assess the risk of a project or a group of projects. Our ultimate objective is to come to an understanding of how risk affects value. First, however, we must measure project risk under a variety of circumstances, and that is the purpose of this chapter. We will cover the

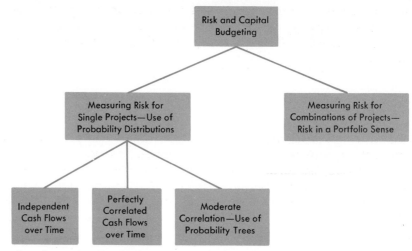

FIG. 14 · 1

Development of the chapter

topics shown in Figure 14-1. As the figure indicates, we are concerned with measuring risk for single investment proposals and for combinations, or portfolios, of investment proposals. In this regard, certain elementary probability concepts will be employed in the treatment of risk. Because cash flows arising from an investment proposal occur over time, it is necessary to consider the relationship between cash flows from period to period. That is the reason for the boxes reflecting independent and dependent assumptions as to the correlation of cash flows over time. As we shall see, the assumption made has a significant effect on measured risk.

Given information about the expected risk of an investment proposal or proposals, together with information about the expected return, management must then evaluate this information and reach a decision. As the decision to accept or reject an investment proposal depends on the valuation of the firm, we defer consideration of the evaluation of risky investments until we have convered certain valuation concepts in the next chapter. In this chapter, then, we develop the information necessary to evaluate risky investments. In Chapter 16, we examine the use of this information in reaching capital-budgeting decisions consistent with an objective of maximizing shareholder wealth. We begin this chapter with a general introduction to project risk and then move on to consider the topics shown in Figure 14-1.

THE PROBLEM OF PROJECT RISK

We define the riskiness of an investment project as the variability of its cash flows from those that are expected. The greater the variability, the riskier the project is said to be. For each project under consideration, we can make estimates of the future cash flows. Rather than estimate only the most likely cash-flow outcome for each year in the future as we did in Chapter 13, we estimate a number of possible out-comes. In this way, we are able to consider the range of possible cash flows for a particular future period rather than just the most likely cash flow.

An illustration

To illustrate the formulation of multiple cash-flow forecasts for a future period, suppose we had two investment proposals under con-sideration. Suppose further that we were interested in making fore-casts for the following states of the economy: normal, deep reces-sion, mild recession, major boom, and minor boom. After assessing the future under each of these possible states, we estimate the following cash flows for next year:

	Annual Cash Flows	
State	Proposal A	Proposal B
Deep recession	$3,000	$2,000
Mild recession	3,500	3,000
Normal	4,000	4,000
Minor boom	4,500	5,000
Major boom	5,000	6,000

We see that the dispersion of possible cash flows for proposal B is greater than that for proposal A, and, therefore, we could say that it was riskier. In order to quantify our analysis of risk, however, we need additional information. More specifically, we need to know the likeli-hood of the various states of the economy occurring. Suppose our esti-mate of the odds for a deep recession is 10 percent, of a mild recession 20 percent, of a normal economy 40 percent, of a minor economic boom 20 percent, and of a major economic boom 10 percent. Given this information, we now are able to formulate a probability distribution of possible cash flows for posposals A and B:

Proposal A		Proposal B	
Probability	Cash Flow	Probability	Cash Flow
0.10	$3,000	0.10	$2,000
0.20	3,500	0.20	3,000
0.40	4,000	0.40	4,000
0.20	4,500	0.20	5,000
0.10	5,000	0.10	6,000

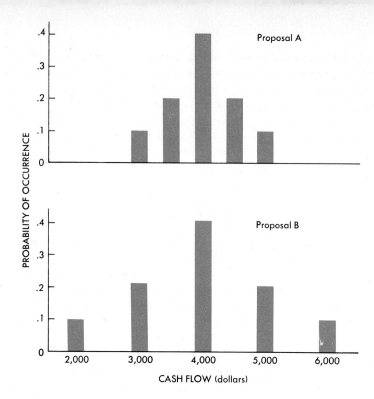

FIG. 14 · 2

Comparison of two proposals

We can graph these probability distributions, and the results are shown in Figure 14-2. As we see, the dispersion of cash flows is greater for proposal B than it is for proposal A, despite the fact that the most likely outcome is the same for both investment proposals, $4,000. According to the discussion in Chapter 13, the firm would rank the proposals equally. The critical question is whether dispersion should be considered. If risk is associated with the probability distribution of possible cash flows such that the greater the dispersion the greater the risk, proposal B would be the riskier investment. If management, stockholders, and creditors are averse to risk, proposal A then would be preferred to proposal B.

Measurement of dispersion

Rather than always having to resort to graph paper, we need a measure of the dispersion of a probability distribution. The tighter the distribution, the lower this measure should be, while the wider the distribution, the greater it should be. The conventional measure of dispersion is the *standard deviation,* which will be presented first mathematically and then illustrated with the previous example. The *standard deviation* can be expressed mathematically as

$$\sigma = \sqrt{\sum_{x=1}^{n} (A_x - \bar{A})^2 P_x} \qquad (14\text{-}1)$$

where A_x is the cash flow for the xth possibility, P_x is the probability of occurrence of that cash flow, and $\bar{A}$ is the *expected value* of cash flows, to be defined in Eq. (14-2). The Greek sigma, Σ, means the sum of the bracketed amounts from possibility #1 through possibility #n. In other words, n is the total number of possibilities—five in our example. The square-root sign, $\sqrt{}$, indicates that we take the square root of the calculated amount. The *expected value* of a probability distribution can be defined as

$$\bar{A} = \sum_{x=1}^{n} A_x P_x \qquad (14\text{-}2)$$

It is simply a weighted average of the possible cash flows, with the weights being the probabilities of occurrence.

The standard deviation is simply a measure of the tightness of a probability distribution. For a normal, bell-shaped distribution, such as that shown in Figure 14-3, approximately 68 percent of the total area of the distribution falls within one standard deviation on either side of the expected value. This means that there is only a 32 percent chance that the actual outcome will be more than one standard deviation from the mean. The probability that the actual outcome will fall within two standard deviations of the expected value of the distribution is approximately 95 percent, and the probability that it will fall within three standard deviations is over 99 percent. A table showing the area of a normal distribution that is so many standard deviations to the right or left of the expected value is given in Appendix B to this chapter. As we shall see later in the chapter, the standard deviation is used to assess the likelihood of an event occurring.

An illustration. To illustrate the derivation of the expected value and standard deviation of a probability distribution of possible cash flows, consider again our previous example. The expected value of the distribution for proposal A is

$$\bar{A}_a = 0.10(3{,}000) + 0.20(3{,}500) + 0.40(4{,}000)$$
$$+ 0.20(4{,}500) + 0.10(5{,}000) = 4{,}000$$

which is the same as that for proposal B:

$$\bar{A}_b = 0.10(2{,}000) + 0.20(3{,}000) + 0.40(4{,}000)$$
$$+ 0.20(5{,}000) + 0.10(6{,}000) = 4{,}000$$

However, the standard deviation for proposal A is

$$\sigma_a = [0.10(3{,}000 - 4{,}000)^2 + 0.20(3{,}500 - 4{,}000)^2$$
$$+ 0.40(4{,}000 - 4{,}000)^2 + 0.20(4{,}500 - 4{,}000)^2$$
$$+ 0.10(5{,}000 - 4{,}000)^2]^{1/2} = [300{,}000]^{1/2} = 548$$

where $[\ ]^{1/2}$ is simply the square root, the same as $\sqrt{\ }$. Note also that when we square a minus number, such as $(3,000 - 4,000)^2$, it becomes positive. The standard deviation for proposal B is

$$\sigma_b = [0.10(2,000 - 4,000)^2 + 0.20(3,000 - 4,000)^2$$
$$+ 0.40(4,000 - 4,000)^2 + 0.20(5,000 - 4,000)^2$$
$$+ 0.10(6,000 - 4,000)^2]^{1/2} = [1,200,000]^{1/2} = 1,095$$

Thus, proposal B has a higher standard deviation, indicating a greater dispersion of possible outcomes. Therefore, we would say that it had greater risk.

Coefficient of variation. A measure of relative dispersion is the coefficient of variation, which simply is the standard deviation of a probability distribution over its expected value. For proposal A, the coefficient of variation is

$$CV_a = 548/4,000 = 0.14$$

while that for proposal B is

$$CV_b = 1,095/4,000 = 0.27$$

Because the coefficient of variation for proposal B exceeds that for proposal A, we would say that it had a greater degree of risk. One might question the use of the coefficient of variation when in our example it was obvious that proposal B had greater risk owing to its larger standard deviation. In our example, however, the expected values of the probability distributions of possible cash flows for the two proposals were the same. What if they were different? Here we need a measure of relative dispersion, and the coefficient of variation is such a measure. Frequent reference to the expected value, standard deviation, and coefficient of variation will be made in the remainder of this chapter.[1]

Definition of business risk

Given these statistical measures, we now can give a more precise definition to business risk. We use the term to mean the risk associated

---

[1] We assume that risk can be judged solely in relation to the expected value and standard deviation of a probability distribution. Implied is that the shape of the distribution is unimportant. This holds when the distribution is relatively symmetric or "bell-shaped." However, if it is significantly skewed to the right or left, management may wish to take account of this fact as well. Although it is possible to incorporate a skewness measure into our analysis of risk, it is difficult mathematically to do so. For simplicity, we shall deal with only the expected value and standard deviation of a probability distribution.

with the operations of the firm. Business risk exists apart from the risk inherent in the way the firm is financed. The latter is known as financial risk, which we consider in Chapter 17. We define *business risk* as the relative dispersion of the net cash flows of the firm as a whole, as measured by the coefficient of variation.

For example, suppose that the expected net cash flows over the next five years for Firms C and D could be expressed in terms of probability distributions. Suppose further that the expected values of the distribution were $500,000 and $2 million, respectively; and that the standard deviations were $200,000 and $600,000, respectively. For Firm C, the relative dispersion of the probability distribution, as measured by the coefficient of variation, is

$$CV_c = \frac{\$200,000}{\$500,000} = 0.40$$

while for Firm D, it is

$$CV_d = \frac{\$600,000}{\$2,000,000} = 0.30$$

As the coefficient of variation for Firm C is greater than that for Firm D, we would say that it had the greater degree of business risk.

MEASURING RISK FOR INDIVIDUAL INVESTMENT PROJECTS

If investors and creditors are risk-averse, and all available evidence suggests that they are, it is important that management incorporate the risk of an investment proposal into its analysis of the proposal's worth. Otherwise, capital-budgeting decisions are unlikely to be in accord with an objective of maximizing share price. Having established the importance of taking risk into account, we proceed to measure it for individual investment proposals. Our concern will be with measuring risk under varying assumptions as to the dependence of cash flows from period to period. We begin with the situation where cash flows are independent over time and then move on to consider various degrees of dependency.

Independence of cash flows over time

Suppose that we are evaluating an investment proposal in which the probability distributions of cash flows for various future periods are independent of one another. In other words, the outcome in period t does not depend upon what happened in period $t - 1$. The expected value of the probability distribution of net-present value for the proposal is

$$NPV = \sum_{t=0}^{n} \frac{\bar{A}_t}{(1 + i)^t} \qquad (14\text{-}3)$$

where $\bar{A}_t$ is the expected value of net-cash flow in period t, and i is the risk-free rate. The risk-free rate is used as the discount rate in this analysis because we attempt to isolate the time value of money. To include a premium for risk in the discount rate would result in double counting with respect to our evaluation.[2] Given the assumption of mutual independence of cash flows for various future periods, the standard deviation of the probability distribution of net-present values is[3]

$$\sigma = \sqrt{\sum_{t=0}^{\infty} \frac{\sigma_t^2}{(1 + i)^{2t}}} \qquad (14\text{-}4)$$

where σ_t is the standard deviation of the probability distribution of possible net cash flows in period t.

To illustrate the calculations involved in Eq. (14-3) and Eq. (14-4), suppose that we had an investment proposal costing \$10,000 at time 0 that was expected to generate cash flows during the first three periods with the probabilities shown in Table 14-1. The expected values of net cash flows for periods 1, 2, and 3 are \$5,000, \$4,000, and \$3,000, respectively. The standard deviation of possible cash flows for period t, σ_t, is computed by

$$\sigma_t = \sqrt{\sum_{x=1}^{5} (A_{xt} - \bar{A}_t)^2 P_{xt}} \qquad (14\text{-}5)$$

where A_{xt} is the xth net cash flow, $\bar{A}_t$ is the expected value of net cash flow for period t, and P_{xt} is the probability of occurrence of A_{xt}. In the

[2] The cost of capital, for example, embodies a premium for business risk. If this rate is used as the discount rate, we would be adjusting for risk in the discounting process itself. That is, we would adjust the cash-flow benefits of a proposal for the risk associated with the enterprise as a whole. (From Eq. (14-4), it is clear that as the discount rate embodies in it greater and greater risk premiums, σ becomes smaller.) We then would use the probability distribution of net-present values to judge the risk of the proposal. In essence, we would be adjusting for risk a second time in our evaluation of the relative dispersion of the probability distribution of possible net-present values.

[3] The derivation of this formula is relatively complicated and beyond the scope of this book. For additional discussion, see Frederick S. Hillier, "The Derivation of Probabilistic Information for Evaluation of Risky Investments," *Management Science,* 9 (April 1963), 443–57.

above example, the standard deviation of possible net cash flows for period 1 is

$$\sigma_1 = [0.10(3,000 - 5,000)^2 + 0.25(4,000 - 5,000)^2$$
$$+ 0.30(5,000 - 5,000)^2 + 0.25(6,000 - 5,000)^2$$
$$+ 0.10(7,000 - 5,000)^2]^{\frac{1}{2}} = \$1,140 \qquad (14\text{-}6)$$

Because the probability distributions for periods 2 and 3 have the same dispersion about their expected values as that for period 1, σ_2 and σ_3 are \$1,140 also. Given this information, we are able to calculate the expected value of net-present value for the proposal as well as the standard deviation about this expected value. If we assume a risk-free rate of 4 percent, the expected value of net-present value for the proposal is

$$NPV = -10,000 + \frac{5,000}{(1.04)} + \frac{4,000}{(1.04)^2} + \frac{3,000}{(1.04)^3} = \$1,173 \qquad (14\text{-}7)$$

Using Eq. (14-4), under the assumption of mutual independence of cash flows over time, the standard deviation about the expected value is

$$\sigma = \sqrt{\frac{1,140^2}{(1.04)^2} + \frac{1,140^2}{(1.04)^4} + \frac{1,140^2}{(1.04)^6}} = \$1,827 \qquad (14\text{-}8)$$

TABLE 14 · 1

Cash Flows for Example Problem

Period 1		Period 2		Period 3	
Probability	Net Cash Flow	Probability	Net Cash Flow	Probability	Net Cash Flow
0.10	$3,000	0.10	$2,000	0.10	$1,000
0.25	4,000	0.25	3,000	0.25	2,000
0.30	5,000	0.30	4,000	0.30	3,000
0.25	6,000	0.25	5,000	0.25	4,000
0.10	7,000	0.10	6,000	0.10	5,000

Standardizing the dispersion

The expected value and the standard deviation of the probability distribution of possible net-present values give us a considerable amount of information by which to evaluate the risk of the investment proposal. If the probability distribution is approximately normal, we are able to calculate the probability of the proposal's providing a net-present value of less or more than a specified amount. For example, suppose that we wish to determine the probability that the net-present value of the project will be 0 or less. To determine this probability, we first calculate the difference between 0 and the expected value of net-present value for the project.

In our example, this difference is − $1,173. We then standardize this difference by dividing it by the standard deviation of possible net-present values. The formula is

$$S = \frac{X - \overline{NPV}}{\sigma} \qquad (14\text{-}9)$$

where X is the outcome in which we are interested, $\overline{NPV}$ is the expected value of net-present value, and σ the standard deviation of the probability distribution. In our case,

$$S = \frac{0 - 1,173}{1,827} = -0.642$$

This figure tells us that a net-present value of 0 lies .642 standard deviations to the left of the expected value of the probability distribution of possible net-present values.

To determine the probability that the net-present value of the project will be 0 or less, we consult a normal probability distribution table found in most statistics texts or in Appendix B at the end of this chapter. We find that for the normal distribution, there is a 0.26 probability that an observation will be less than − .642 standard deviations from the expected value of that distribution. Thus, there is a 0.26 probability that the net-present value of the proposal will be zero or less. If we assume a continuous distribution, the probability density function of our example problem can be shown in Figure 14-3.

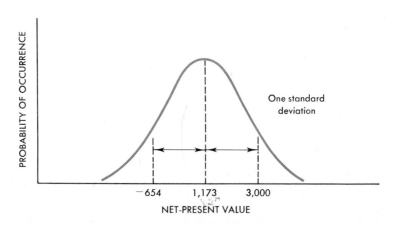

FIG. 14 · 3

Probability density
function for
example problem

The mean of the probability distribution of possible net-present values is $1,173. One standard deviation on either side of the mean gives us net-present values of −$654 and $3,000. With a normal distribution, 0.683 of the distribution or area under the curve falls within one standard deviation on either side of the mean or expected value. We know then that there is approximately a two-thirds probability that the net-present value of the proposal examined will be between −$654 and $3,000. We know also that there is a 0.26 probability that the net-present value will be less than 0 and a 0.74 probability that it will be greater than 0. By expressing differences from the expected value in terms of standard deviations, we are able to determine the probability that the net-present value for an investment proposal will be greater or less than a particular amount.[4]

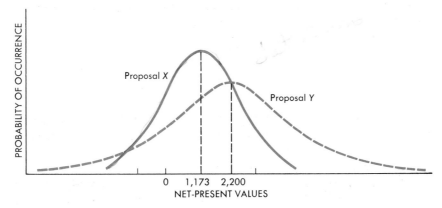

FIG. 14 · 4

Probability distribution of net-present value for proposals X and Y

Knowledge of these probabilities is fundamental for a realistic assessment of risk. For example, suppose that the firm is considering another investment project, proposal Y. The probability density function for this proposal is shown in Figure 14-4, as is that for our example problem, which we shall call proposal X. We see that the expected value of net-present value for proposal Y, $2,200, is higher than that for proposal X, $1,173; but there is also greater dispersion of the probability distribution about the expected value. If risk is directly related to dispersion, proposal Y has both a higher expected profitability and a greater risk than does proposal X. Which proposal is preferable depends on the risk tolerances of management. We address ourselves to this question in Chapter 16. For now, our concern is only with measuring risk.

---

[4] In the above examples, we have assumed normal probability distributions. Although this property is very desirable for purposes of calculation, it is not necessary for use of the above approach. Even when the distribution is not normal, we usually are able to make relatively strong probability statements by using Chebyshev's inequality.

Perfect correlation of cash flows over time

In the preceding section, we assumed mutual independence of cash flows from one future period to another. For most investment proposals, however, the cash flow in one future period depends in part upon the cash flows in previous periods. If an investment proposal turns bad in the early years, the probability is high that cash flows in later years also will be lower than originally expected. To assume that an extremely unfavorable or favorable outcome in the early life of an investment proposal does not affect the later outcome is unrealistic in most investment situations. What are the consequences of our assumption that cash flows are dependent? The expected value of the probability distribution of possible net-present values for a proposal is the same as before; it is determined by Eq. (14-3). However, when cash flows are correlated over time, the standard deviation of the probability distribution about the expected value will be larger than it would be if we assumed independence. The greater the degree of correlation, the greater the dispersion.

Cash flows are perfectly correlated over time if the deviation of an actual cash flow for a period from the mean of the probability distribution of expected cash flows for that period implies that cash flows in all other periods deviate in exactly the same manner. In other words, the cash flow in period t depends entirely upon what happened in previous periods. If the actual cash flow in period t is X standard deviations to the right of the expected value of the probability distribution of expected cash flows for that period, actual cash flows in all other periods will be X standard deviations to the right of the expected values of their respective probability distributions. The formula for the standard deviation of a perfectly correlated stream of cash flows over time is[5]

$$\sigma = \sum_{t=0}^{\infty} \frac{\sigma_t}{(1 + i)^t} \qquad (14\text{-}10)$$

To illustrate its use, consider the same example as before. The standard deviation about the expected value of net-present value for the proposal, using Eq. (14-10), is

$$\sigma = \frac{1,140}{(1.04)} + \frac{1,140}{(1.04)^2} + \frac{1,140}{(1.04)^3} = \$3,164$$

[5] Again, the derivation of this formula is beyond the scope of this book.

This compares with a standard deviation of $1,827 when we used Eq. (14-4) under the assumption of mutual independence over time. Thus, the standard deviation, and risk, for a perfectly correlated stream of cash flows is significantly higher than the standard deviation for the same stream under the assumption of mutual independence. The reason is that an extreme outcome in one period implies an extreme outcome in all other periods. In the case of independence over time, an extreme outcome in one period is not likely to be followed by an extreme outcome in the next. In other words, there is an averaging process over time which tends to "tighten" the probability distribution of possible net-present values relative to the case of perfect correlation of cash flows over time.

The assessment of project risk with a perfectly correlated stream of cash flows over time is the same as that illustrated previously for a project with an uncorrelated stream. We standardize the dispersion and determine the probability that the actual net-present value of the project will be more or less than certain amounts.

The use of probability trees with moderate correlation

From our discussion of the implications of independent and perfectly correlated cash-flow streams over time, it should be clear that the standard deviation for a less than perfectly correlated stream will be somewhere between the two values calculated previously. The greater the degree of dependence, the closer the standard deviation will be to that calculated with Eq. (14-10). The difficulty with correlation between the two extremes of independence and perfect positive correlation is that the problem does not lend itself to mathematical solution. There exist, however, methods for dealing with it. One means is with a probability tree. To illustrate, suppose that the investment in a project costing $250 at time 0 were expected to generate the possible net cash flows shown in Table 14-2.

Given a cash flow of −$100 in period 1, the probability is 0.40 that this negative flow will become −$400 in period 2, 0.40 that it will remain at −$100, and 0.20 that it will be $200. The joint probability that a −$100 cash flow in period 1 will be followed by a −$400 cash flow in period 2 is simply the product of the initial probability and the conditional probability, or 0.25 × 0.40 = 0.10. Similarly, the joint probability that a cash flow of −$100 in period 1 will be followed by a cash flow of −$100 in period 2 is 0.25 × 0.40 = 0.10, and the probability that a −$100 cash flow in period 1 will be followed by a $200 cash flow in period 2 is 0.25 × 0.20 = 0.05. If the cash flow in period 1 turns out to be $200, there is a 0.20 probability it will become −$100 in period 2, 0.60 it will remain at $200 in period 2, and 0.20 it will become $500. In the same manner as before, we can calculate the joint probabilities for this branch, and they are found to be 0.10, 0.30, and 0.10, respectively. Similarly, the joint probabilities for the last branch, where a $500 net cash flow in period 1 occurs, can be determined.

TABLE 14 · 2

Illustration of a Probability Tree

Period 1		Period 2		
Initial Probability P(1)	Net Cash Flow	Conditional Probability (2 | 1)	Net Cash Flow	Joint Probability P(1, 2)
0.25	− $100	0.40	− $400	0.10
		0.40	− 100	0.10
		0.20	200	0.05
0.50	200	0.20	− 100	0.10
		0.60	200	0.30
		0.20	500	0.10
0.25	500	0.20	200	0.05
		0.40	500	0.10
		0.40	800	0.10

Initial Investment at time o = $250.

The expected value of the probability distribution of possible net-present values is

$$\overline{NPV} = \sum_{x=1}^{z} NPV_x P_x \qquad (14\text{-}11)$$

where NPV_x is the net-present value for series X of net cash flows, covering all periods, P_x is the probability of occurrence of that series, and z is the total number of cash-flow series. For our example, there are nine possible series of net cash flows, so $z = 9$. The first series is represented by a cash flow of −$100 in period 1, followed by a −$400 cash flow in period 2. The probability of occurrence of that cash flow is .10. Assuming a risk-free discount rate of 4 percent, the net-present value of this series is

$$NPV_1 = -250 - \frac{100}{(1.04)} - \frac{400}{(1.04)^2} = -\$715.98$$

The second cash-flow series is represented by a cash flow of $-\$100$ in period 1, followed by a $-\$100$ cash flow in period 2. The net-present value of this series is

$$NPV_2 = -250 - \frac{100}{(1.04)} - \frac{100}{(1.04)^2} = -\$438.61$$

In the same manner, the net-present values for the seven other cash-flow series can be determined. When these values are multiplied by their respective probabilities of occurrence (the last column in Table 14-2) and summed, we obtain the expected value of net-present value of the probability distribution of possible net-present values. The calculations are shown in Table 14-3 and we see that the expected value of net-present value is $127.22.

TABLE 14 · 3

Calculation of Expected Value of Net-Present Value for Example Problem

(1) Cash-Flow Series	(2) Net-Present Value	(3) Probability of Occurrence	(4) (2) × (3)
1	− $715.98	0.10	− $71.60
2	− 438.61	0.10	− 43.86
3	− 161.24	0.05	− 8.06
4	− 150.15	0.10	− 15.02
5	127.22	0.30	38.17
6	404.59	0.10	40.46
7	415.68	0.05	20.78
8	693.05	0.10	69.31
9	970.41	0.10	97.04
Weighted average			$127.22

The standard deviation of the probability distribution of possible net-present values can be determined by

$$\sigma = \sqrt{\sum_{x=1}^{z} (NPV_x - \overline{NPV})^2 P_x} \qquad (14\text{-}12)$$

where the symbols are the same as for Eq. (14-11). The standard deviation for our example problem is

$$\sigma = [0.10(-715.98 - 127.22)^2 + 0.10(-438.61 - 127.22)^2$$
$$+ 0.05(-161.24 - 127.22)^2 + 0.10(-150.15 - 127.22)^2$$
$$+ 0.30(127.22 - 127.22)^2 + 0.10(404.59 - 127.22)^2$$
$$+ 0.05(415.68 - 127.22)^2 + 0.10(693.05 - 127.22)^2$$
$$+ 0.10(970.41 - 127.22)^2]^{1/2} = [229,937]^{1/2} = \$480$$

With information about the expected value and standard deviation of the probability distribution of possible net-present values, we are able to analyze the project in the same manner as before. The purpose of this section was to show the calculations involved in determining the expected value and standard deviation for a probability tree. Although the mathematical calculation of the standard deviation is feasible for simple cases, it is not for complex situations. Here, one should resort to simulation to approximate the standard deviation. This technique is explained in Appendix A to this chapter when we examine the Hertz model for evaluating risky investments.

Correlation of cash flows over time—summary. We have seen that the standard deviation of a probability distribution of possible net-present values varies according to the assumptions made about the correlation of cash flows over time. The least risky situation is when cash flows are independent over time. However, we should not invoke this assumption unless it fits the case. The important thing is to use that method for calculating the standard deviation—Eq. (14-4), Eq. (14-10), or a probability-tree approach—which best describes the cash-flow pattern of the project being considered. An improper assumption as to correlation of cash flows over time will result in a biased assessment of risk and the possibility of a suboptimal capital-budgeting decision.

RISK IN A PORTFOLIO SENSE

Heretofore our concern has been with measuring risk for a single investment proposal. When multiple investment projects are involved and one is concerned with their combined risk, the measurement procedure differs from that for a single project. The approach we take corresponds to a portfolio approach in security analysis.[6] The circum-

---

[6]See, for example, William F. Sharpe, *Portfolio Analysis and Capital Markets* (New York: McGraw-Hill, 1970); and Jack Clark Francis, *Investments: Analysis and Management* (New York: McGraw-Hill, 1972), Part 4.

stances under which the approach is feasible are taken up in Chapter 16 when we examine acceptance criteria for risky investments. Our purpose here is only to show how to measure risk for combinations of risky investments, assuming that such a measure is desired.

If a firm adds a project whose future cash flows are likely to be highly correlated with those of existing assets, the total risk of the firm will increase more than if it adds a project that has a low degree of correlation with existing assets. The idea is that projects can be combined in such a way as to reduce relative risk.

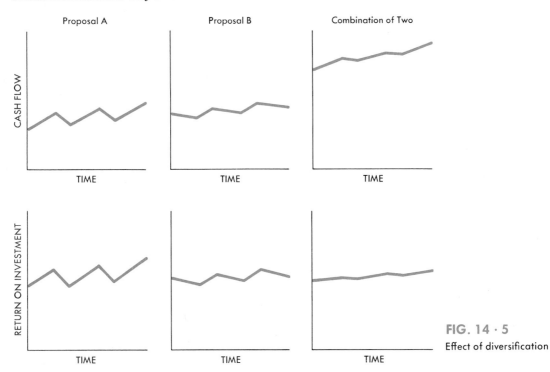

FIG. 14 · 5
Effect of diversification

To illustrate, Figure 14-5 shows the expected cash-flow patterns for two projects over time. Proposal A is cyclical, while proposal B is mildly countercyclical. By combining the two projects, we see that total cash-flow dispersion is reduced and the dispersion of the return on investment is reduced even more. The combination of projects in such a way as to reduce risk is known as diversification, and the principle is the same as diversification in securities. One attempts to reduce deviations in return from the expected value of return.

Measurement of portfolio risk

The standard deviation of the probability distribution of possible net-present values for a portfolio is more difficult to calculate than before. It is not the summation of the standard deviations of the individual projects making up the portfolio, but

$$\sigma = \sqrt{\sum_{j=1}^{m} \sum_{k=1}^{m} \sigma_{jk}} \qquad (14\text{-}13)$$

where j refers to project j, k to project k, m is the total number of projects in the portfolio, σ_{jk} is the variance about the expected value of net-present value when $j = k$[7] and the covariance between possible net-present values for projects j and k when j does not equal k.

The two capital Greek sigmas mean that we consider the covariances for all possible pairwise combinations of projects in the portfolio. For example, suppose that m were four. The matrix of possible pairwise combinations would be:

$$
\begin{array}{cccc}
\sigma_{1,1} & \sigma_{1,2} & \sigma_{1,3} & \sigma_{1,4} \\
\sigma_{2,1} & \sigma_{2,2} & \sigma_{2,3} & \sigma_{2,4} \\
\sigma_{3,1} & \sigma_{3,2} & \sigma_{3,3} & \sigma_{3,4} \\
\sigma_{4,1} & \sigma_{4,2} & \sigma_{4,3} & \sigma_{4,4}
\end{array}
$$

The combination in the upper left-hand corner is 1,1, which means that $j = k$ and that our concern is with the variance of project #1. That is, $\sigma_1 \sigma_1 = \sigma_1^2$ in Eq. (14-13), or the standard deviation squared. As we trace down the diagonal, there are four situations in all where $j = k$, and we would be concerned with the variances in all four. The second combination in row 1 is $\sigma_{1,2}$, which signifies the covariance between possible net-present values for projects #1 and #2. Note, however, that the first combination in row 2 is $\sigma_{2,1}$, which signifies the covariance between projects #2 and #1. In other words, we count the covariance between projects #1 and #2 twice. Similarly, we count the covariances between all other combinations not on the diagonal twice. The double summation signs in Eq. (14-13) mean that we sum all variances and covariances in the matrix of possible pairwise combinations. In our matrix above, it is sixteen, represented by four variances and six covariances counted twice.

The covariance term in Eq. (14-13) is

$$\sigma_{jk} = r_{jk}\sigma_j\sigma_k \qquad (14\text{-}14)$$

where r_{jk} is the expected correlation between possible net-present values for projects j and k, σ_j is the standard deviation for project j,

[7] That is, the standard deviation squared of the probability distribution of possible net-present values for investment project j.

and σ_k is the standard deviation for project k. The standard deviations of the probability distributions of possible net-present values for projects j and k are determined by the methods taken up in the previous section under the appropriate assumption as to correlation of cash flows over time. When $j = k$ in Eq. (14-14), the correlation coefficient is 1.0, and $\sigma_j \sigma_k$ becomes σ_j^2. That is, we are concerned only with the variance of projects along the diagonal of the matrix.

Correlation between projects

YES

Estimating the correlation between possible net-present values for two projects in Eq. (14-14) is the key ingredient in analyzing risk in a portfolio context. When two projects are similar to projects with which the company has had experience, it may be feasible to compute the correlation coefficients using historical data. For other investments, however, estimates of the correlation coefficients must be based solely upon an assessment of the future.

Management might have reason to expect only slight correlation between investment projects involving research and development for an electronic transistor and a new consumer product. On the other hand, it might expect high positive correlation between investments in a milling machine and a turret lathe if both machines were used in the production of industrial lift trucks. The profit from a machine to be used in a production line will be highly, if not completely, correlated with the profit for the production line itself.

The correlation between expected net-present values of various investments may be positive, negative, or 0, depending upon the nature of the association. A correlation coefficient of 1.00 indicates that the net-present values of two investment proposals vary directly in exactly the same proportional manner; a correlation coefficient of -1.00 indicates that they vary inversely in exactly the same proportional manner; and a 0 correlation coefficient indicates that they are independent or unrelated. For most pairs of investments, the correlation coefficient lies between 0 and 1.00. The reason for the lack of negatively correlated investment projects is that most investments are correlated positively with the economy.

Estimates of the correlation coefficients must be as objective as possible if the total standard deviation figure obtained in Eq. (14-13) is to be realistic. However, it is not unreasonable to suppose that management is able to make fairly accurate estimates of these coefficients. To the extent that actual correlation differs from expected correlation, future correlation estimates on existing projects should be revised in keeping with the learning process. The learning process applies also to future estimates of correlation between investments that are similar to existing investments.

An illustration

To illustrate these concepts, suppose that a firm has a single existing investment project, 1, and that it is considering investing in an additional project, 2. Assume further that the projects have the following expected values of net-present value, standard deviations, and correlation coefficients:

	Expected Value of Net-Present Value	Standard Deviation	Correlation Coefficient
Project 1	$12,000	$14,000	1.00
Project 2	8,000	6,000	1.00
Projects 1 and 2			0.40

The expected value of the net-present value of the combination of projects is simply the sum of the two separate net-present values.

$$NPV = \$12{,}000 + \$8{,}000 = \$20{,}000 \qquad (14\text{-}15)$$

The standard deviation for the combination, using Eqs. (14-13) and (14-14), is

$$\sigma = \sqrt{r_{11}\sigma_1^2 + 2r_{12}\sigma_1\sigma_2 + r_{22}\sigma_2^2}$$
$$= \sqrt{(1.00)(14{,}000)^2 + (2)(0.40)(14{,}000)(6{,}000) + (1.00)(6{,}000)^2}$$
$$= \$17{,}297 \qquad (14\text{-}16)$$

Thus, the expected value of net-present value of the firm increases from $12,000 to $20,000 and the standard deviation of possible net-present values from $14,000 to $17,297 with the acceptance of project 2. The coefficient of variation (standard deviation over expected value of net-present value) is $14{,}000/12{,}000 = 1.17$ without project 2 and $17{,}297/20{,}000 = 0.86$ with the project. If we employ the coefficient of variation as a measure of relative business risk, we would conclude that acceptance of project 2 would lower the business risk of the firm.

By accepting projects with relatively low degrees of correlation with existing projects, a firm diversifies and in so doing may be able to lower its overall business risk. We note that in Eq. (14-16) the lower the degree of positive correlation, r_{12}, or the higher the degree of negative correlation, the lower the standard deviation of possible net-present values, all other things being equal. Whether the coefficient of variation declines when an investment project is added, however, depends also upon the expected value of net-present value for the project.

Combinations of risky investments

N O

We now have a procedure for determining the total expected value and the standard deviation of a probability distribution of possible net-present values for a combination of investments. For our purposes, we define a *combination* as including all existing investment projects and one or more proposals under consideration. We assume, then, that the firm has existing investment projects and that these projects are expected to generate future cash flows. Thus, existing projects constitute a subset that is included in all combinations. We denote this portfolio of projects by the letter E.

Suppose now that the firm has under consideration four investment proposals which are independent of one another, that is, they are not contingent or mutually exclusive. If these proposals are labeled #1, #2, #3, and #4, we have the following possible combinations of risky investments:

E	$E,1$	$E,1,2$	$E,1,2,3$	$E,1,2,3,4$
	$E,2$	$E,1,3$	$E,1,2,4$	
	$E,3$	$E,1,4$	$E,1,3,4$	
	$E,4$	$E,2,3$	$E,2,3,4$	
		$E,2,4$		
		$E,3,4$		

Thus, sixteen combinations of projects are possible, with one possibility being the rejection of all of the proposals under consideration so the firm is left with only its existing projects, E. The expected value of net-present value and standard deviation for each of these combinations can be computed in the manner described previously. The results can then be graphed.

Figure 14-6 depicts a scatter diagram of the sixteen possible combinations. Here the expected value of net-present value is along the horizontal axis, and the standard deviation is on the vertical axis. Each dot represents a combination. Collectively, these dots constitute

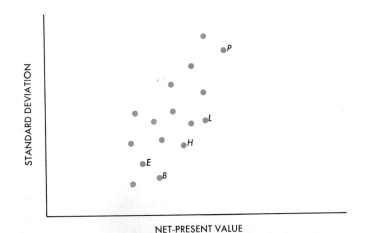

FIG. 14 · 6

Opportunity set of combinations of projects

NET-PRESENT VALUE

the total set of feasible combinations of investment opportunities available to the firm.

We see that certain dots dominate others in the sense that they represent a higher expected value of net-present value and the same standard deviation, a lower standard deviation and the same expected value of net-present value, or both a higher expected value and a lower standard deviation. The dominating dots are those that are farthest to the right in the figure. Four of them have been identified specifically—combinations B, H, L, and P. (The dot E represents all existing investment projects.)

Although the selection process itself is deferred until Chapter 16, it is important to realize that the combination ultimately chosen determines the new investment proposal or proposals that will be accepted. For example, if combination H were selected and it consisted of E, #1, and #4, investment proposals #1 and #4 would be accepted. Those investment proposals not in the combination finally selected would be rejected. In our case, they would be proposals #2 and #3. If the combination finally selected consists only of existing investment projects, E, all investment proposals under consideration would be rejected. However, the selection of any other combination implies the acceptance of one or more of the investment proposals under consideration.

The incremental expected value of net-present value and standard deviation can be determined by measuring on the horizontal and vertical axes the distance from dot E to the dot representing the combination finally selected. These distances can be thought of as the incremental contribution of expected value of net-present value and standard deviation to the firm as a whole. In Chapter 16, we explore how the actual selection can be made and under what circumstances this approach is appropriate. Our purpose here has been to measure risk for combinations of risky investments in order to provide management with such information.

SUMMARY

The risk of an investment project can be defined as the deviation in actual cash flows from those that were expected. Expressing the future in terms of probability distributions of possible cash flows, risk can be expressed quantitatively as the standard deviation of the distribution. The coefficient of variation is simply the standard deviation of a probability distribution over its expected value, and it serves as a relative measure of risk. Business risk is the risk associated with the operations of the firm, and it can be expressed in terms of the coefficient of variation.

One approach to the evaluation of risky investments is the direct analysis of the probability distribution of possible net-present values of a project. Given the expected value and standard deviation of the distribution, management can determine the probability that the actual net-present value will be lower than such and such an amount. This type of information is extremely valuable in judging the risk of a project.

When analyzing investment projects, it is important to make the proper assumption as to the likely correlation of cash flows over time. An independence assumption implies that a cash flow in one period is unrelated to cash flows in other periods, whereas an assumption of perfect correlation implies that cash flows in every period deviate in exactly the same manner. The standard deviation, or risk, under the latter assumption is considerably larger than the standard deviation under the former assumption. For cases of moderate correlation, a probability-tree series of conditional probabilities approach may be used.

Investment projects also can be judged with respect to their portfolio risk. Here we are concerned with the marginal risk of a project to the firm as a whole. By diversifying into projects not having high degrees of correlation with existing assets, a firm is able to reduce the standard deviation of its probability distribution of possible net-present values relative to the expected value of the distribution. The likely degree of correlation between projects is the key to measuring portfolio risk, and we examined this issue.

Our purpose in this chapter has been to explore the means by which risk can be quantified for investment proposals and combinations of proposals. With this information, together with information about the expected profitability of the investment(s), one is able to reach much more informed and, we would hope, better decisions. In Chapter 16, we consider how this information can be employed in the decision process. The acceptance criterion should be rooted in valuation, a topic we turn to in the next chapter.

APPENDIX A

Hertz simulation approach to risky investments

In an important contribution to evaluating risky investments, David B. Hertz proposed the use of a simulation model to obtain the expected return and dispersion about this expected return for an investment proposal.[8] Hertz considers the following factors in evaluating an investment proposal:

Market Analysis
1. Market size
2. Selling price
3. Market growth rate
4. Share of market (which results in physical sales volume)

[8] David B. Hertz, "Risk Analysis in Capital Investment," *Harvard Business Review*, 42 (January–February 1964), 95–106.

Investment Cost Analysis

5. Investment required
6. Residual value of investment

Operating and Fixed Costs

7. Operating costs
8. Fixed costs
9. Useful life of facilities

Probability distributions are assigned to each of these factors, based upon management's assessment of the probable outcomes. Thus, the possible outcomes are charted for each factor according to their probability of occurrence; examples of these probability distributions are shown in Figure 14-7.

FIG. 14 · 7   Probability distributions of nine key factors

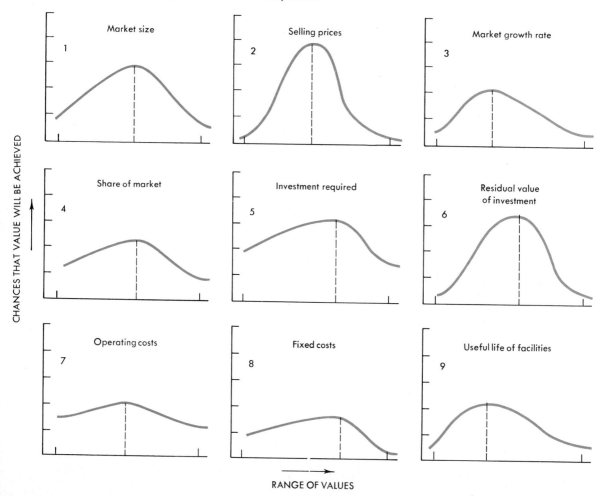

SOURCE: Hertz, "Risk Analysis in Capital Investment," p. 102.

Once the probability distributions are determined, the next step is to determine the average rate of return that will result from a random combination of the nine factors listed above. To illustrate the simulation process, assume that the market-size factor had the following probability distribution:

Market size (in thousand units)	450	500	550	600	650	700	750
Probability	.05	.10	.20	.30	.20	.10	.05

Now suppose that we have a roulette wheel with 100 numbers, on which numbers 1 to 5 represent a market size of 450,000 units, 6 to 15 represent a market size of 500,000, 16 to 35 a market size of 550,000 units, and so on through 100. As in roulette, we spin the wheel, and the ball falls in one of the 100 slots—number 26. For this trial, then, we simulate a market size of 550,000 units. Fortunately, we do not have to have a roulette wheel to undertake a simulation; the same type of operation can be carried out on a computer in a much more efficient manner.

Simulation trials are undertaken for each of the other eight factors. The first four factors (market analysis) give us the annual sales per year, while factors 7 and 8 give us the operating costs and fixed costs per year. Together, these six factors enable us to calculate the annual earnings per year. When trial values for these six factors are combined with trial values for the required investment, the useful life, and the residual value of the project, we have sufficient information to calculate the return on investment for that trial run. Thus, the computer simulates trial values for each of the nine factors and then calculates the return on investment based upon the values simulated. The process is repeated a number of times: each time we obtain a combination of values for the nine factors and the return on investment for that combination. When the trial is repeated often enough, the rates of return obtained can be plotted in a frequency distribution like that shown in Figure 14-8.

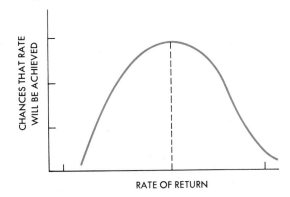

FIG. 14 · 8

Probability distribution for rate of return

SOURCE: Hertz, "Risk Analysis in Capital Investment," p. 102.

From this frequency distribution, we are able to evaluate the expected return and the dispersion about this expected return, or risk, in the same manner as before—in other words, we can determine the probability that an investment will provide a return greater or less than a certain amount. By comparing the probability distribution of rates of return for one proposal with the probability distribution of rates of return for another, management is able to evaluate the respective merits of different risky investments.

Two points should be mentioned with respect to Hertz's simulation method. Although the simulation model computes the average rate of return on investment, the method could easily be modified to calculate the internal rate of return, the net-present value, or the profitability index. In addition, although Hertz allows for dependency among the nine factors, the model presented treats the factors as though they were independent. To the extent that dependency exists among factors, it must be taken into account in determining the probability distributions. For example, there is likely to be significant correlation between the market size and the selling price. These interrelationships add considerable complexity to the estimating procedure. Notwithstanding the added complexity of estimating and specifying in the model the relationships between factors, it must be done if the model is to provide realistic results. These estimates may be based upon empirical testing when such testing is feasible. Once the relationships are incorporated in the model, those factors that are correlated would then be simulated jointly. Rates of return for the simulated trials would be calculated and a frequency distribution of simulated trials formed in the same manner as before.

APPENDIX B

Normal probability distribution table

Table 14-4 shows the area of the normal distribution that is X standard deviations to the left or to the right of the mean. The test is "one-tail" in the sense that we are concerned with one side of the distribution or the other. For example, if we wished to know the area of the curve, or probability, that was 1.5 standard deviations or more from the arithmetic mean on the right, it would be depicted by the tinted area in Figure 14-9. In Table 14-4, we see that this corresponds to 6.68 percent of the total area of the normal distribution. Thus, we would say that there was a 6.68 percent probability that the actual outcome would exceed the mean by 1.5 standard deviations. In a similar manner, the table can be used to determine the probability associated with other distances from the mean.

TABLE 14 · 4

Area of Normal Distribution That Is X Standard Deviations to the Left or Right of the Mean

Number of Standard Deviations from Mean (X)	Area to the Left or Right (One tail)	Number of Standard Deviations from Mean (X)	Area to the Left or Right (One tail)
0.00	.5000	1.55	.0606
0.05	.4801	1.60	.0548
0.10	.4602	1.65	.0495
0.15	.4404	1.70	.0446
0.20	.4207	1.75	.0401
0.25	.4013	1.80	.0359
0.30	.3821	1.85	.0322
0.35	.3632	1.90	.0287
0.40	.3446	1.95	.0256
0.45	.3264	2.00	.0228
0.50	.3085	2.05	.0202
0.55	.2912	2.10	.0179
0.60	.2743	2.15	.0158
0.65	.2578	2.20	.0139
0.70	.2420	2.25	.0122
0.75	.2264	2.30	.0107
0.80	.2119	2.35	.0094
0.85	.1977	2.40	.0082
0.90	.1841	2.45	.0071
.095	.1711	2.50	.0062
1.00	.1577	2.55	.0054
1.05	.1469	2.60	.0047
1.10	.1357	2.65	.0040
1.15	.1251	2.70	.0035
1.20	.1151	2.75	.0030
1.25	.1056	2.80	.0026
1.30	.0968	2.85	.0022
1.35	.0885	2.90	.0019
1.40	.0808	2.95	.0016
1.45	.0735	3.00	.0013
1.50	.0668		

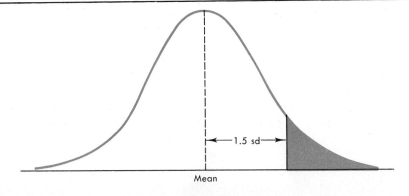

FIG. 14 · 9
Normal distribution

← 1.5 sd →

Mean

1. The literature on finance assumes that the risk associated with an investment is a measurable phenomenon equivalent to the variability of returns of an investment. In your opinion, is this definition of risk adequate for asset selection by average investors? Explain.

2. In Chapter 13, the importance of the assumed reinvestment rate was discussed. Discuss the biases introduced in capital budgeting if an adjusted discount rate is used to assign priorities to capital expenditures.

3. Discuss the importance of correlation among the expected returns of different projects.

4. Contrast conditions of uncertainty with conditions of risk.

5. Risk in capital budgeting can be judged by analyzing the probability distribution of possible returns. What shape distribution would you expect to find for a safe project whose returns were absolutely certain? For a very risky project?

6. If project A has an expected value of net-present value of $200 and a standard deviation of $400, is it more risky than project B whose expected value is $140 and standard deviation $300?

1. R. A. Rice, Inc., can invest in one of two mutually exclusive projects. The two proposals have the following discrete probability distributions of net cash flows for period p:

A		B	
Probability	Cash Flow	Probability	Cash Flow
.20	$2,000	.10	$2,000
.30	4,000	.40	4,000
.30	6,000	.40	6,000
.20	8,000	.10	8,000

(a) Without calculating a mean and a coefficient of variation, can you select the better proposal, assuming a risk-averse management?
(b) Verify your intuitive determination.

2. Dewitt Corporation has determined the following discrete probability distributions for net cash flows generated by a contemplated project:

	Period 1		Period 2		Period 3
Prob.	Cash Flow	Prob.	Cash Flow	Prob.	Cash Flow
.10	$1,000	.20	$1,000	.30	$1,000
.20	2,000	.30	2,000	.40	2,000
.30	3,000	.40	3,000	.20	3,000
.40	4,000	.10	4,000	.10	4,000

(a) Assume the probability distributions of cash flows for future periods are independent. Also, assume that the after-tax, risk-free rate is 4 percent. If the proposal will require an initial outlay of $5,000, determine the expected value of the net-present value.

(b) Determine the standard deviation about the expected value.

3. The Hume Corporation is faced with several possible investment projects. For each, the total cash outflow required will occur in the initial period. The cash outflows, expected net-present values, and standard deviations are given in the following table. All projects have been discounted at the risk-free rate of 4 percent, and it is assumed that the distributions of their possible net-present values are normal.

Project	Cost	Net-present Value	σ
A	$100,000	$10,000	$20,000
B	50,000	10,000	30,000
C	200,000	25,000	10,000
D	10,000	5,000	10,000
E	500,000	75,000	75,000

(a) Construct a risk profile for each of these projects in terms of the profitability index.

(b) Ignoring size problems, are there some projects that are clearly dominated by others?

(c) May size problems be ignored?

(d) What is the probability that each of the projects will have a net-present value ≥ 0?

4. The probability distribution of possible net-present values for project X has an expected value of $20,000 and a standard deviation of $10,000. Assuming a normal distribution, calculate the probability that the net-present value will be zero or less; that it will be greater than $30,000; and that it will be less than $5,000.

5. The Windrop Company is considering investment in two of three possible proposals, the cash flows of which are normally distributed. The expected net-present value (discounted at the risk-free rate of 4 percent) and the standard deviation for each proposal are given as follows:

	1	2	3
Expected net-present value	$10,000	$8,000	$6,000
Standard deviation	4,000	3,000	4,000

Assuming the following correlation coefficients for each possible combination, which combination dominates the others?

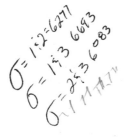

Proposals	Correlation Coefficients
1	1.00
2	1.00
3	1.00
1 and 2	.60
1 and 3	.40
2 and 3	.50

6. The Plaza Corporation is confronted with several combinations of risky investments.

Combinations	Net-present Value	σ
A	$100,000	$200,000
B	20,000	80,000
C	75,000	100,000
D	60,000	150,000
E	50,000	20,000
F	40,000	60,000
G	120,000	170,000
H	90,000	70,000
I	50,000	100,000
J	75,000	30,000

(a) Plot the above portfolios.
(b) Which combinations dominate the others?

BRIGHAM, EUGENE F., and **RICHARD H. PETTWAY,** "Capital Budgeting by Utilities," *Financial Management,* 2 (Autumn 1973), 11–22.

CARTER, E. EUGENE, *Portfolio Aspects of Corporate Capital Budgeting.* Lexington, Mass.; D. C. Heath, 1974.

GRAYSON, C. JACKSON, JR., *Decisions under Uncertainty: Drilling Decisions by Oil and Gas Operators.* Boston: Division of Research, Harvard Business School, 1960.

GREER, WILLIS R., JR., "Capital Budgeting Analysis with the Timing of Events Uncertain," *Accounting Review,* 45 (January 1970), 103–14.

———, "Theory versus Practice in Risk Analysis: An Empirical Study," *Accounting Review,* 49 (July 1974), 496–505.

HAYES, ROBERT H., "Incorporating Risk Aversion into Risk Analysis," *Engineering Economist,* 20 (Winter 1975), 99–121.

HERTZ, DAVID B., "Investment Policies That Pay Off," *Harvard Business Review,* 46 (January–February 1968) 96–108.

———, "Risk Analysis in Capital Investment," *Harvard Business Review,* 42 (January–February 1964), 95–106.

HESPOS, RICHARD F., and **PAUL A. STRASSMANN,** "Stochastic Decision Trees for the Analysis of Investment Decisions," *Management Science,* 11 (August 1965), 244–59.

HILLIER, FREDERICK S., "A Basic Model for Capital Budgeting of Risky Interrelated Projects," *Engineering Economist,* 17 (Fall 1971), 1–30.

———, "The Derivation of Probabilistic Information for the Evaluation of Risky Investments," *Management Science,* 9 (April 1963), 443–57.

JARRETT, JEFFREY E., "An Abandonment Decision Model," *Engineering Economist,* 19 (Fall 1973), 35–46.

KEELEY, ROBERT, and **RANDOLPH WESTERFIELD,** "A Problem in Probability Distribution Techniques for Capital Budgeting," *Journal of Finance,* 27 (June 1972), 703–9.

LESSARD, DONALD R., and **RICHARD S. BOWER,** "Risk-Screening in Capital Budgeting," *Journal of Finance,* 28 (May 1973).

LEVY, HAIM, and **MARSHALL SARNAT,** "The Portfolio Analysis of Multiperiod Capital Investment under Conditions of Risk," *Engineering Economist,* 16 (Fall 1970), 1–19.

LEWELLEN, WILBER G., and **MICHAEL S. LONG,** "Simulation versus Single-Value Estimates in Capital Expenditure Analysis," *Decision Sciences* 3 (1972), 19–33.

MAGEE, J. F., "How to Use Decision Trees in Capital Investment," *Harvard Business Review,* 42 (September–October 1964), 79–96.

PETTY, J. WILLIAM, DAVID F. SCOTT, JR., and **MONROE M. BIRD,** "The Capital Expenditure Decision-Making Process of Large Corporations," *Engineering Economist,* 20 (Spring 1975), 159–72.

ROBICHEK, ALEXANDER A., "Interpreting the Results of Risk Analysis," *Journal of Finance,* 30 (December 1975), 1384–86.

ROBICHEK, ALEXANDER A., and **JAMES VAN HORNE,** "Abandonment Value and Capital Budgeting," *Journal of Finance,* 22 (December 1967), 577–89; Edward A. Dyl and Hugh W. Long, "Comment," *Journal of Finance,* 24 (March 1969), 88–95; and Robichek and Van Horne, "Reply," ibid., 96–97.

SALAZAR, RUDOLFO C., and **SUBRATA K. SEN,** "A Simulation Model of Capital Budgeting under Uncertainty," *Management Science,* 15 (December 1968), 161–79.

VAN HORNE, JAMES C., "The Analysis of Uncertainty Resolution in Capital Budgeting for New Products," *Management Science*, 15 (April 1969), 376–86.

———, "Capital-Budgeting Decisions Involving Combinations of Risky Investments," *Management Science*, 13 (October 1966), 84–92.

———, "Capital Budgeting under Conditions of Uncertainty as to Project Life," *Engineering Economist*, 17 (Spring 1972), 189–99.

———, "Variation of Project Life as a Means for Adjusting for Risk," *Engineering Economist*, 21 (Summer 1976).

WESTON, J. FRED, "Investment Decisions Involving the Capital Asset Pricing Model," *Financial Management*, 2 (Spring 1973), 25–33.

The *Valuation Process* 15

Def of bond val.
Cost of debt cap.

In this chapter, we investigate the valuation of securities. By *valuation,* we mean the process by which the market price of a security is determined. In particular, we will be concerned with the valuation of bonds, preferred stock, and common stock, though the principles discussed apply to other financial instruments as well. As much of what we take up builds upon the concept of compound interest, we assume that the reader has covered Chapter 12. In the preceding chapter on capital budgeting, we saw that the discount rate is the vehicle by which a firm should judge the attractiveness of an investment opportunity. Before we can analyze the required rate of return, however, we first must explore the valuation of market instruments. In a sense, this chapter and the next, where we take up the required rate of return, form the foundation on which we build our discussion of the theory of finance.

VALUATION IN GENERAL

A key factor in the valuation of any financial instrument is an implied positive relationship between risk and expected return. It has been shown that investors overall dislike risk. As a result, they must be offered additional expected return the greater the expected risk of the security involved. Assume for purposes of illustration that investors concentrate upon some common holding period—say one year. Assume further that they are concerned with what we shall call *unavoidable risk*. This is simply the risk that cannot be avoided by diversification of the securities they hold. Implied is that some of the risk associated with an individual security can be avoided by efficient diversification. Much more will be said about this later in the chapter; for now, our purpose is to illustrate a simple but fundamental concept.

If financial markets are highly efficient, and we believe they are, there exists a market-determined relationship between expected return and unavoidable risk similar to that depicted in Figure 15-1. The relationship presented is known as the *security market line;* it depicts the tradeoff between unavoidable risk and expected return. The expected one-year return is shown on the vertical axis, and unavoidable risk is on the horizontal. At zero risk, the security market line has an intercept on the vertical axis at a positive expected rate of return. As no risk is involved, this rate is known as the *risk-free rate.* As risk in-

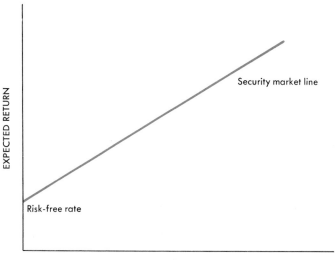

FIG. 15 · 1

The security market line

creases, the required rate of return increases in the manner depicted. Thus, there is a positive relationship between risk and expected return, which, as we shall see, governs the valuation of marketable securities.[1]

It is important to recognize that the security market line depicts the tradeoff between expected return and unavoidable risk at a moment in time. This line can change over time with changes in interest rates and investor psychology. If interest rates in general were to rise, for example, it would shift upward. This shift might be depicted by the

---

[1]The concepts underlying the security market line will be explored in more depth in the latter part of this chapter when we take up the valuation of common stocks.

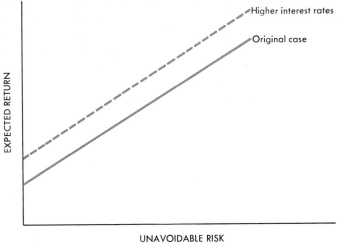

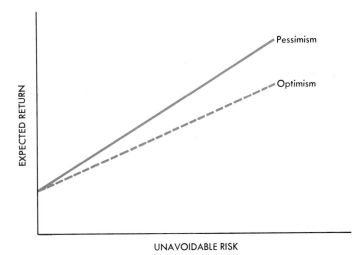

FIG. 15 - 2

Security market line
with changes
in interest rates
and investor psychology

graph in the upper panel of Figure 15-2. Note that the line shifts up-ward by a given amount throughout. In the lower panel of the figure, we show a hypothetical change in investor psychology from pessimism regarding the economy to optimism. Note here that the slope of the security market line decreases as opposed to a shift throughout. The same expected return is required for a risk-free security as before. However, lower returns are required for all risky securities; the greater the unavoidable risk, the lower the return required relative to before. Thus, we must allow for the fact that the relationship between risk and expected return is not necessarily stable over time. With this general valuation concept in mind, we are able to explore in more de-tail the valuation of specific types of securities.

Bond valuation

A bond is a fixed-income security in the sense that the interest and principal payments are specified at the time of the issue and are invariant over the duration of the obligation. The valuation equation for a bond where interest is paid at the end of the year and whose face value is $1,000 is

$$P = \frac{I}{(1 + k)} + \frac{I}{(1 + k)^2} + \cdots + \frac{I}{(1 + k)^n} + \frac{\$1,000}{(1 + k)^n} \qquad (15\text{-}1)$$

where P is the present value of the payment stream, I is the annual interest payment as given by the coupon rate, n is the number of years to final maturity, and k is the required rate of return, given its risk. The latter also is known as the *yield to maturity*.

To illustrate, suppose we wish to determine the market price necessary for a bond with an 8 percent coupon and ten years to maturity to provide a return of 7 percent. This coupon rate corresponds to interest payments of $80 a year. Therefore,

$$P = \frac{\$80}{(1.07)} + \frac{\$80}{(1.07)^2} + \cdots + \frac{\$80}{(1.07)^{10}} + \frac{\$1,000}{(1.07)^{10}}$$

Referring to Table A-2 at the back of the book, we find that the present value of $80 per year for ten years, discounted at 7 percent, is $561.89, and from Table A-1 that the present value of $1,000 received at the end of the tenth year is $508.35. The market price, P, is simply the sum of these two present values, or $1,070.24.

If interest is paid more than once a year, Eq. (15-1) needs to be modified along the lines of our discussion in Chapter 12 when we dealt with compound interest. If interest is paid semiannually, we have

$$P = \frac{I/2}{\left(1 + \frac{r}{2}\right)} + \frac{I/2}{\left(1 + \frac{r}{2}\right)^2} + \frac{I/2}{\left(1 + \frac{r}{2}\right)^3} + \cdots + \frac{I/2}{\left(1 + \frac{r}{2}\right)^{2n}} + \frac{\$1,000}{\left(1 + \frac{r}{2}\right)^{2n}}$$

$$(15\text{-}2)$$

In the example above,

$$P = \frac{\$40}{(1.035)} + \frac{\$40}{(1.035)^2} + \frac{\$40}{(1.035)^3} + \cdots + \frac{\$40}{(1.035)^{20}} + \frac{\$1,000}{(1.035)^{20}}$$

$$= \$1,071.06$$

Thus, an 8 percent bond with semiannual interest payments and a 7 percent required return assumption gives a slightly higher present value or market price than it does with annual interest payments.[2] Most bonds issued today involve semiannual interest payments. If interest is paid m times a year, however, the valuation equation is

$$P = \frac{I/m}{\left(1 + \frac{r}{m}\right)} + \frac{I/m}{\left(1 + \frac{r}{m}\right)^2} + \frac{I/m}{\left(1 + \frac{r}{m}\right)^3} + \cdots + \frac{I/m}{\left(1 + \frac{r}{m}\right)^{mn}} + \frac{\$1{,}000}{\left(1 + \frac{r}{m}\right)^{mn}}$$

$$(15\text{-}3)$$

All of this follows of course from our discussion of compound interest in Chapter 12, so we need not dwell further on the equation.

It is possible to have a bond that is a perpetuity. A case in point is the British Consul, a bond issued in the early nineteenth century with no maturity date; it carries the obligation of the British government to pay a fixed coupon perpetually. If an investment promises a fixed annual payment of I forever, its present value is[3]

$$P = \frac{I}{k} \qquad\qquad (15\text{-}4)$$

[2] If the required rate of return were greater than the coupon rate, semiannual payments would result in a lower present value than that which occurs with annual payments.

[3] The valuation equation for annual fixed payments through year n would be

$$P = \frac{I}{(1 + k)} + \frac{I}{(1 + k)^2} + \cdots + \frac{I}{(1 + k)^n}$$

When we multiply both sides of this equation by $(1 + k)$, we obtain

$$P(1 + k) = I + \frac{I}{(1 + k)} + \cdots + \frac{I}{(1 + k)^{n-1}}$$

Subtracting the first equation from the second, we have

$$P(1 + k) - P = I - \frac{I}{(1 + k)^n}$$

As n approaches infinity, $I/(1 + k)^n$ approaches zero. Thus

$$Pk = I$$

and

$$P = I/k$$

Here k is the yield required on a perpetual investment. To illustrate, suppose we had the opportunity to buy a security that paid $50 a year forever. If the appropriate yield, k, is 8 percent, the market value of the security would be

$$P = \frac{\$50}{.08} = \$625$$

If the appropriate yield were to change from 8 percent to 6 percent, the market value would be

$$P = \frac{\$50}{.06} = \$833$$

Market price changes. For a given change in yield, the market price of a security generally will change by a greater amount the longer its maturity.[4] To illustrate, consider a five-year bond with annual interest payments of $50 and a yield to maturity of 8 percent. Its valuation is

$$P = \frac{\$50}{(1.08)} + \frac{\$50}{(1.08)^2} + \frac{\$50}{(1.08)^3} + \frac{\$50}{(1.08)^4} + \frac{\$50}{(1.08)^5} + \frac{\$1,000}{(1.08)^5}$$

$$= \$885$$

If the yield were to decrease to 6 percent, we would have

$$P = \frac{\$50}{(1.06)} + \frac{\$50}{(1.06)^2} + \frac{\$50}{(1.06)^3} + \frac{\$50}{(1.06)^4} + \frac{\$50}{(1.06)^5} + \frac{\$1,000}{(1.06)^5}$$

$$= \$959$$

Thus, the perpetuity used in our example increases in value by $833 − 625 = $208, while the five-year bond increases by only $959 − $885 = $74. Similarly, one is able to take other maturities and demonstrate that, in general, the longer the maturity, the greater the price fluctuation associated with a given change in yield. One can think of the face value of $1,000 serving as an anchor. The closer it is to being realized, the less important are interest payments in determining the market price, and the less important is a change in yield to maturity on the market price of the security.

---

[4] For bonds selling at a discount with very long maturities, it is possible for prices to change by a lesser amount the longer the maturity. This occurrence is unusual, so we will not discuss it further. The interested reader is referred to Michael H. Hopewell and George G. Kaufman, "Bond Price Volatility and Term to Maturity," *American Economic Review*, 63 (September 1973), 749–53.

Preferred-stock valuation

Preferred stock is a fixed-income security in the sense that it specifies a fixed dividend to be paid at regular intervals. The features of this financial instrument are discussed in Chapter 23. While virtually all preferred-stock issues have a call feature and many are eventually retired, they have no maturity as such. Therefore, they can be treated as perpetuities when it comes to valuation. Thus, we have

$$P = \frac{D}{k} \qquad (15\text{-}5)$$

where P as before is the market price, D is the stated dividend per share, and k is the appropriate discount rate. If Hi-Lo Corporation had a 7 percent, $100 par value preferred-stock issue outstanding where the appropriate yield was 11 percent, its value per share would be

$$P = \frac{\$7}{.11} = \$63.64$$

Appropriate return for a fixed-income security

SKIP

As illustrated in several instances above, the valuation of a fixed-income security simply involves capitalizing interest payments or preferred-stock dividends, using an appropriate discount rate. This rate can be thought to be comprised of the risk-free rate plus a premium for risk. Thus,

$$k = i + \theta \qquad (15\text{-}6)$$

where i = risk-free rate
      θ = risk premium

If the security involved were a Treasury bill, there would be no risk of default and we would expect θ to approximate zero.[5] Fixed-income securities of corporations obviously possess greater default risk than do Treasury bills. Therefore, there must exist a risk premium. The risk involved varies according to the company. Moreover, the financial instruments of an individual company possess more or less risk depending upon their maturity, whether they are secured, and so forth.

---

[5] Even with Treasury bills, there are fluctuations in market price caused by changes in interest rates. Moreover, there is uncertainty as to the return available upon reinvestment at maturity if one's holding period is longer than the maturity of the instrument. Nonetheless, Treasury bills are thought to represent a good proxy for the risk-free rate.

While we would expect differences in risk to be greater *among* firms, there still will be differences in risk between different instruments of the same firm.

If we assume that investors overall are concerned with unavoidable risk, as described in the opening section of this chapter, the appropriate discount rate can be approximated by use of the security market line. Given the degree of risk, one traces up to the security market line in Figure 15-1, and then over to the vertical axis to obtain the appropriate required rate of return. Similar securities, such as thirty-year bonds issued by electric utilities and rated Aa by one of the major rating services, will cluster at approximately the same degree of risk and, accordingly, require about the same rate of return. However, the risk associated with five-year bonds of General Electric Company will be considerably less than that associated with, say, the preferred stock of a new company in the electronics industry.

While our discussion of risk has been general, it is possible to measure unavoidable risk and, as a result, approximate the required rate of return. As the work in this regard has been concerned primarily with the valuation of common stocks, we have deferred its illustration to the subsequent section. In closing, however, it is important to stress that the same concepts that apply to the valuation of fixed-income securities also apply to the valuation of common stocks.

VALUATION OF COMMON STOCKS

The theory surrounding the valuation of common stocks has undergone profound change over the last fifteen years. It is a subject of considerable controversy, and no one method for valuation is universally accepted. Still, in recent years there has emerged growing acceptance of the notion that individual common stocks should be analyzed as a part of a total portfolio of common stocks the investor might hold. While the development of portfolio selection has been mathematical in nature, the key concept itself is relatively simple and we shall explore it in the latter part of this section. First, however, we need to take up what is meant by the return to the common-stock investor.

Dividends and capital gains

If an investor's holding period were one year, most of us would agree that the return on investment in a common stock would be the sum of cash dividends received plus any capital gain or loss, all over the purchase price, minus one. To illustrate, suppose that an individual were to purchase a share of DSS Corporation for $50 a share. Furthermore, the company was expected to pay a $2 dividend at the end of the year, and its market price after the payment of the dividend was expected to be $53 a share. The expected return would be

$$k = \frac{\$2.00 + \$53.00}{\$50.00} - 1 = 10 \text{ percent} \qquad (15\text{-}7)$$

Another way to solve for k of course is

$$\$50.00 = \frac{\$2.00}{(1 + k)} + \frac{\$53.00}{(1 + k)} \qquad (15\text{-}8)$$

Now suppose that instead of holding the security one year, the individual intends to hold it two years and sell it at the end of that time. Moreover, suppose he expects the company to pay a $2.20 dividend at the end of year 2 and the market price of the stock to be $56.10 after the dividend is paid. His expected return can be found by solving the following equation for k:

$$\$50 = \frac{\$2.00}{(1 + k)} + \frac{\$2.20}{(1 + k)^2} + \frac{\$56.10}{(1 + k)^2} \qquad (15\text{-}9)$$

When we solve for k by the method described earlier, we find it to be 10 percent also. For general purposes, the formula can be expressed as

$$P_0 = \sum_{t=1}^{2} \frac{D_t}{(1 + k)^t} + \frac{P_2}{(1 + k)^2} \qquad (15\text{-}10)$$

where P_0 is the market price at time 0, D_t is the expected dividend at the end of period t, the capital Greek sigma denotes the sum of discounted dividends at the end of periods 1 and 2, and P_2 is the expected terminal value at the end of period 2.

If an investor's holding period were ten years, the expected rate of return would be determined by solving the following equation for k:

$$P_0 = \sum_{t=1}^{10} \frac{D_t}{(1 + k)^t} + \frac{P_{10}}{(1 + k)^{10}} \qquad (15\text{-}11)$$

Now, suppose that the investor were a perpetual trust fund and that the trustee expected to hold the stock forever. In this case, the expected return would consist entirely of cash dividends and perhaps a liquidating dividend. Thus, the expected rate of return would be determined by solving the following equation for k:

$$P_0 = \sum_{t=1}^{\infty} \frac{D_t}{(1 + k)^t} \qquad (15\text{-}12)$$

where ∞ is the sign for infinity.

It is clear that the intended holding period of different investors will vary greatly. Some will hold a stock only a few days, while others might expect to hold it forever. Investors with holding periods shorter than infinity expect to be able to sell the stock in the future at a price higher than they paid for it. This assumes, of course, that at that time there will be investors willing to buy it. In turn, these investors will base their judgments as to what the stock is worth on expectations of future dividends and future terminal value beyond that point. That terminal value, however, will depend upon other investors at that time being willing to buy the stock. The price they are willing to pay will depend upon their expectations of dividends and terminal value. And so the process goes through successive investors. Note that the total cash return to all successive investors in a stock is the sum of the dividends paid, including any liquidating dividend. Thus, cash dividends are all that stockholders as a whole receive from their investment; they are all the company pays out. Consequently, the foundation for the valuation of common stocks must be dividends.

The logical question to be raised at this time is, Why do the stocks of companies that pay no dividends have positive, and often quite high, values? The obvious answer is that investors expect to sell the stock in the future at a price higher than they paid for it. Instead of a dividend income plus terminal value, they rely only upon the terminal value. In turn, terminal value will depend upon the expectations of the market place at the end of the horizon period. The ultimate expectation is that the firm eventually will pay dividends, either regular or liquidating ones, and that future investors will receive a cash return on their investment. In the interim, however, investors are content with the expectation that they will be able to sell the stock at a subsequent time because there will be a market for it. In the meantime, the company is reinvesting earnings and, hopefully, enhancing its future earning power and ultimate dividends.

Growth models

We saw that the return on investment is the rate of discount that equates the present value of the stream of expected future dividends with the current market price of the stock. If dividends of a company are expected to grow at a constant rate, g, in keeping, say, with a growth in earnings, Eq. (15-12) becomes

$$P_0 = \frac{D_0(1 + g)}{(1 + k)} + \frac{D_0(1 + g)^2}{(1 + k)^2} + \cdots + \frac{D_0(1 + g)^\infty}{(1 + k)^\infty} \qquad (15\text{-}13)$$

where D_0 is the dividend per share at time 0. Thus, the dividend expected in period n is equal to the most recent dividend times the compound growth factor, $(1 + g)^n$.

Assuming k is greater than g, Eq. (15-13) can be expressed as[6]

$$P_0 = \frac{D_1}{k - g} \qquad (15\text{-}14)$$

Rearranging, the expected return becomes

$$k = \frac{D_1}{P_0} + g \qquad (15\text{-}15)$$

The critical assumption in this valuation model is that dividends per share are expected to grow perpetually at a compound rate of g. For many companies, this assumption may be a fair approximation of reality. To illustrate the use of Eq. (15-15), suppose that A & G Company's dividend per share at $t = 1$ was expected to be \$3, that it was expected to grow at a 4 percent rate forever, and that the appropriate discount rate was 9 percent. The market price would be

$$P_\bullet = \frac{\$3}{.09 - .04} = \$60 \qquad (15\text{-}16)$$

[6]If we multiply both sides of Eq. (15-13) by $(1 + k)/(1 + g)$ and subtract Eq. (15-13) from the product, we obtain

$$\frac{P_0(1 + k)}{(1 + g)} - P_0 = D_0 - \frac{D_0(1 + g)^\infty}{(1 + k)^\infty}$$

Because k is greater than g, the second term on the right side will be zero. Consequently,

$$P_0\left[\frac{1 + k}{1 + g} - 1\right] = D_0$$

$$P_0\left[\frac{(1 + k) - (1 + g)}{1 + g}\right] = D_0$$

$$P_0[k - g] = D_0(1 + g)$$

$$P_0 = \frac{D_1}{k - g}$$

When the pattern of expected growth is such that a perpetual growth model is not appropriate, modifications of Eq. (15-13) can be used. A number of valuation models are based upon the premise that the growth rate will taper off eventually.[7] For example, the transition might be from a present above-normal growth rate to one that is considered normal. If dividends per share were expected to grow at an 8 percent compound rate for five years and thereafter at a 4 percent rate, Eq. (15-13) would become

$$P_0 = \sum_{t=1}^{5} \frac{D_0(1.08)^t}{(1+k)^t} + \sum_{t=6}^{\infty} \frac{D_5(1.04)^{t-5}}{(1+k)^t} \qquad (15\text{-}17)$$

If the current dividend, D_0, were $2.00 per share and the required rate of return, k, were 10 percent, we would solve for P_0 in the following manner:

End of Year	Dividend			Present Value of Dividend at 10 Percent	
1	$2.00(1.08) =	$2.16	×	.90909 =	$1.96
2	2.00(1.08)^2 =	2.33	×	.82645 =	1.93
3	2.00(1.08)^3 =	2.52	×	.75131 =	1.89
4	2.00(1.08)^4 =	2.72	×	.68301 =	1.86
5	2.00(1.08)^5 =	2.94	×	.62092 =	1.83
			Present value of dividends: first five years =		$9.47

Dividend at the end of year 6 $= \$2.94(1.04) = \$3.06$

Market value at the end of year 5 $= \dfrac{D_6}{k-g} = \dfrac{\$3.06}{.10-.04} = \$51.00$

Present value of $51.00 at the end of year 5 $= 51.00 \times .62092 = \$31.67$

$P_0 = \$9.47 + \$31.67 = \$41.14$

The transition from an above-normal to a normal rate of growth could be specified as more gradual than the rate above. For example, we might expect dividends to grow at an 8 percent rate for three years,

[7]See W. Scott Bauman, "Investment Returns and Present Values," *Financial Analysts Journal*, 25 (November–December 1969), 107–18; Burton G. Malkiel, "Equity Yields, Growth, and the Structure of Share Prices," *American Economic Review*, 52 (December 1963), 1004–31; Charles C. Holt, "The Influence of Growth Duration on Share Prices," *Journal of Finance*, 17 (September 1962), 465–75; Eugene F. Brigham and James L. Pappas, "Duration of Growth, Changes in Growth Rates, and Corporate Share Prices," *Financial Analysts Journal*, 22 (May–June 1966), 157–62; Paul F. Wendt, "Current Growth Stock Valuation Methods," *Financial Analysts Journal*, 21 (March–April 1965), 3–15; and James M. Warren, "A Note on the Algebraic Equivalence of the Holt and Malkiel Models of Share Valuation," *Journal of Finance*, 29 (June 1974), 1007–10.

followed by a 6 percent rate for the next three years, and a 4 percent growth rate thereafter. The more growth segments that are added, the more closely the growth in dividends will approach a curvilinear function. It seems clear that a company will not grow at an above-normal rate forever. Typically, companies tend to grow at a very high rate initially, after which their growth opportunities slow down to a rate that is normal for companies in general. If maturity is reached, the growth rate may stop altogether. For any growth model, Eq. (15-13) can be modified so that it portrays the expected stream of future dividends.

It is important to point out that a dividend-valuation model encompasses both dividends and market-price changes. In the valuation of a stock, the investor may view the current market price as a combination of the present value of expected future dividends and the market price at the end of his holding period. Thus,

$$P_0 = \sum_{t=1}^{n} \frac{D_t}{(1 + k)^t} + \frac{P_n}{(1 + k)^n} \qquad (15\text{-}18)$$

The first term on the right represents the present value of expected future dividends during the holding period, while the last term is the market price at which the investor expects to be able to sell the stock at the end of period n. However, the expected price at the end of period n will depend on expected future dividends beyond that point. More specifically, it is the present value of expected future dividends from year $n + 1$ to infinity:

$$P_n = \sum_{t=n+1}^{\infty} \frac{D_t}{(1 + k)^{t-n}} \qquad (15\text{-}19)$$

Substituting Eq. (15-19) into Eq. (15-18), we obtain

$$P_n = \sum_{t=1}^{\infty} \frac{D_t}{(1 + k)^t} \qquad (15\text{-}20)$$

Thus, we see that a dividend-valuation model embodies the concept of expected market-price changes.

Required rate of return on a stock

The expected return on a stock is the rate of discount that equates the present value of the stream of expected future dividends with the market price of the stock. Conversely, the market price of a stock might be thought to be the stream of expected future dividends discounted to their present value using the required rate of return. Frequently, the terms *required* and *expected* are used interchangeably. While the two rates of return are the same in market equilibrium, they are not the same when disequilibrium prevails. To appreciate the distinction and to better understand the equilibrating process, we explore in more detail the required rate of return for a stock.

The capital-asset pricing model

Picking up on our previous discussion of the security market line, we now want to consider how this line is derived and how the required rate of return is determined for a common stock. We do this in the context of Sharpe's capital-asset pricing model, which was developed in the 1960s. Like any model, this one is a simplification of reality. However, it allows us to draw certain implications about the required rate of return for a stock, assuming the market for stocks overall is in equilibrium. As we shall see, the value of an individual security depends upon its risk in relation to the risk of other securities available for investment. Because a complete and mathematically rigorous presentation of the model is beyond the scope of an introductory book, we will concentrate on the general aspects of the model and its important implications.[8] Certain corners have been cut in the interest of simplicity.

As with any model, there are assumptions to be made. First, we assume that capital markets are highly efficient in that investors are well informed, transaction costs are low, there are negligible restrictions on investment, and no investor is large enough to affect the market price of the stock. We assume also that investors are in general agreement about the likely performance of individual securities and that their expectations are based on a common holding period, say one year. There are two types of investment opportunities with which we will be concerned.[9] The first is a risk-free security whose return over the holding period is known with certainty. Frequently, the rate on Treasury bills is used as surrogate for the risk-free rate. The second investment opportunity with which we are concerned is the market portfolio of common stocks. It is represented by all available stocks,

---

[8]See William F. Sharpe, *Portfolio Analysis and Capital Markets* (New York: McGraw-Hill, 1970); Eugene F. Fama and Merton H. Miller, *The Theory of Finance* (New York: Holt, Rinehart & Winston, 1972); and Jack Francis and Stephen Archer, *Portfolio Analysis* (Englewood Cliffs, N.J.: Prentice-Hall, 1971), for a more complete discussion of the model.

[9]The immediate subsequent development draws upon William F. Sharpe, "Efficient Capital Markets with Risk," Research Paper (Stanford Graduate School of Business, 1972).

weighted according to their market values outstanding. As the market portfolio is a somewhat unwieldy thing with which to work, most people use a surrogate such as Standard & Poor's 500-stock index or the Dow-Jones Industrials index.

Earlier we discussed the idea of *unavoidable risk;* it was defined as that risk that cannot be avoided by efficient diversification. Because one cannot hold a more diversified portfolio than the market portfolio, it represents the limit to attainable diversification. Thus, the risk associated with the market portfolio is unavoidable, or "systematic." Put another way, the only risk remaining after efficient diversification is systematic in the sense that it affects all securities. In essence, this is the risk of market swings caused by such things as changes in the economy or the political situation. It affects all stocks, no matter how efficiently one is diversified.

The characteristic line

We now are in a position to compare the expected return for an individual stock with the expected return for the market portfolio. In our comparison, it is useful to deal with returns in excess of the risk-free rate. The *excess return* is simply the expected return less the risk-free return. In Figure 15-3, an example of a comparison of expected excess returns for a specific stock with those for the market portfolio is shown. The colored line is known as the characteristic line; it depicts the expected relationship between excess returns for the stock and excess returns for the market portfolio. This expected rela-

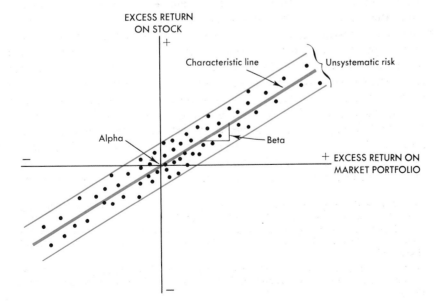

FIG. 15 · 3

Relationship between excess returns for stock and excess returns for market portfolio

tionship may be based upon past experience, in which case actual excess returns would be plotted on the graph and a line drawn which best characterized the historical relationship.

One notes in the graph that the greater the expected excess return for the market, the greater the expected excess return for the stock. Three measures are important.[10] The first is known as the *alpha,* and it is simply the intercept of the characteristic line on the vertical axis. If the excess return for the market portfolio were expected to be zero, the alpha would be the expected excess return for the stock. In theory, the alpha for an individual stock should be zero.[11] Using past data to approximate the characteristic line, however, alphas might be observed that differ from zero if the market were in disequilibrium or if there were market imperfections. We assume for now, however, that the alpha for a particular stock is zero.

The second measure with which we are concerned, and the most important, is the *beta.* The beta is simply the slope of the characteristic line. If the slope is one, it means that excess returns for the stock vary proportionally with excess returns for the market portfolio. In other words, the stock has the same unavoidable risk as the market as a whole. A slope steeper than one means that the stock's excess return varies more than proportionally with the excess return of the market portfolio. Put another way, it has more unavoidable risk than the market as a whole. This type of stock is often called an "aggressive" investment. A slope of less than one means that the stock has less unavoidable or systematic risk than the market as a whole. This type of stock is often called a "defensive" investment. Examples of the three types of relationships are shown in Figure 15-4.

The greater the slope of the characteristic line for a stock, as depicted by its beta, the greater its systematic risk. This means that for both upward and downward movements in market excess returns, movements in excess returns for the individual stock are greater or less depending on its beta. Thus, the beta is a measure of a stock's systematic or unavoidable risk.

The last of the three measures with which we are concerned is the unsystematic line for an individual stock. The greater the dispersion of the estimates involved in predicting a stock's characteristic line, the greater the unsystematic risk of the stock. By diversification, however, this risk can be reduced and even eliminated if diversification is efficient. While the extreme to completely efficient diversification is to hold the market portfolio, it has been shown that unsystematic risk is reduced at a decreasing rate toward zero as more stocks are added to

---

[10]Sharpe, "Efficient Capital Markets with Risk."

[11]The alpha for the market portfolio is simply a weighted average of the alphas for the individual stocks making up the portfolio. As efficient markets and the resulting arbitrage will assure that no alpha for an individual stock will be negative, every alpha must be zero for the weighted average to be zero. See ibid.

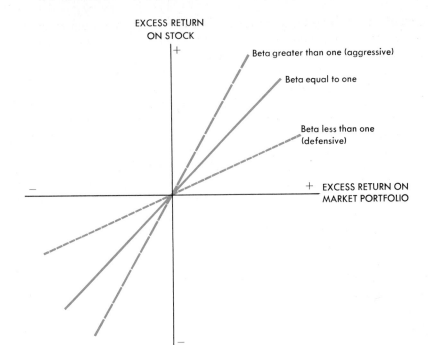

EXCESS RETURN
ON STOCK

+

Beta greater than one (aggressive)

Beta equal to one

Beta less than one
(defensive)

+ EXCESS RETURN ON
MARKET PORTFOLIO

−

FIG. 15 · 4

Examples of
characteristic lines
with different betas

the portfolio.[12] Thus, a substantial proportion of the unsystematic risk of a stock can be eliminated with a relatively moderate amount of diversification—say ten or fifteen stocks. For the well-diversified portfolio, then, unsystematic risk approaches zero. Therefore, the true risk of any stock in that portfolio is the responsiveness of its returns to the responsiveness of returns for the market portfolio. This risk is denoted by the slope of the characteristic line or beta.

Measuring the required rate of return

From the discussion above, we know that unsystematic risk is unique to the particular company involved, being independent of economic, political, and other factors that affect all securities in a systematic manner. If we assume that capital markets are efficient and that investors as a whole are efficiently diversified, unsystematic risk is of minor importance and the important risk associated with a stock becomes its unavoidable or systematic risk. The greater the beta of a stock, the greater the risk of that stock and the greater the return that

[12]See Jack Evans and Stephen H. Archer, "Diversification and the Reduction of Dispersion: An Empirical Analysis," *Journal of Finance,* 23 (December 1968), 761–67; and Bruce D. Fielitz, "Indirect versus Direct Diversification," *Financial Management,* 3 (Winter 1974), 54–62.

is required. If we assume that systematic risk is diversified away, the required rate of return for stock j is

$$\bar{R}_j = i + (\bar{R}_m - i)\beta_j \qquad (15\text{-}21)$$

where i is the risk-free rate, $\bar{R}_m$ is the expected return for the market portfolio, and β_j is the beta coefficient for stock j as defined earlier.

If the past is thought to be a good surrogate for the future, one can use past data on excess returns for the stock and for the market to calculate the beta. There are several services that provide betas on companies whose stocks are actively traded; these betas are based on historical monthly or quarterly returns for the past five or ten years. Services providing beta information include the Value Line Investment Survey and Merrill Lynch, Pierce, Fenner and Smith. The obvious advantage is that they allow one to obtain the historical beta for a stock without having to calculate it oneself.

From Eq. (15-21), we see that the greater the unavoidable risk of a stock, as denoted by its beta, the higher the return that is required.

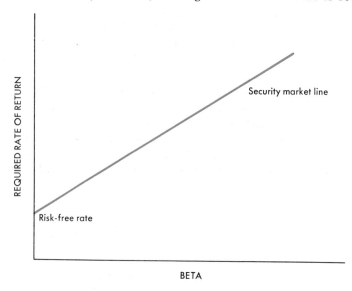

FIG. 15 · 5

The security market line

Given the assumptions of the model, there exists a linear and positive relationship between the beta of a particular stock and its required rate of return. This is shown in Figure 15-5, and, as before, the line is known as the security market line. This is exactly the same concept as that presented in Figure 15-1 when we were discussing fixed-income securities. However, in that case we implicitly assumed a market portfolio comprised of both fixed-income securities and common stocks. Given that definition of the market portfolio, the relevant measure of risk is the beta, and the required return on any fixed-income security or common stock can be determined by reference to the figure.

However, the work to date on devising return measures for combinations of fixed-income securities and common stocks leaves something to be desired. As a result, it is difficult in practice to derive satisfactory beta information for fixed-income securities and common stocks. In contrast, when the market portfolio is restricted to common stocks, beta information is well developed and readily available. For this reason, most of the practical work on the capital-asset pricing model has involved common stocks. However, the concept of the relationship between unavoidable risk and the required return is important for both fixed-income securities and common stocks. Given the fact that investors tend to be risk-averse, expected returns for individual securities should bear a positive relationship to their marginal contributions of risk to the market portfolio (i.e., unavoidable or systematic risk).

Returns in disequilibrium situations

We said earlier that in market equilibrium the required rate of return on a stock equals its expected return. What happens when this is not so? Suppose that in Figure 15-6, the security market line is drawn based on what investors as a whole know to be the appropriate relationship between the required rate of return and systematic or unavoidable risk. However, for some reason two stocks, call them X and Y, are improperly priced. Stock X is underpriced relative to the security market line, while stock Y is overpriced.

As a result, stock X provides a higher expected return than the security market line for the systematic risk involved, while stock Y provides a lower expected return. Investors seeing the opportunity for

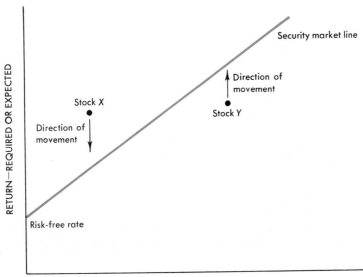

FIG. 15 · 6

Equilibrating process
in cases of
market disequilibrium

superior returns by investing in stock X should rush to buy it. This action would drive the price up and the expected return down. How long would this continue? It would continue until the market price was driven up and the expected return down to the point at which the expected return was on the security market line. In the case of stock Y, investors holding this stock would sell it, recognizing that they could obtain a higher return for the same amount of systematic risk with other stocks. This selling pressure would drive Y's market price down and its expected return up until the expected return was on the security market line.

When the expected returns for these two stocks were both on the security market line, market equilibrium would again prevail. As a result, the expected returns for the two stocks would equal their required returns. Available evidence suggests that disequilibrium situations in stock prices do not persist for long and that stock prices adjust rapidly to new information. Given the vast amount of evidence indicating market efficiency, the security market concept becomes a useful means for determining the expected and required rate of return for a stock. This rate then can be used as the discount rate in the valuation procedures described earlier.

This brings to a close our examination of valuation. Given the expected cash payments together with the appropriate required rate of return for a financial instrument, we are able to determine its present value and, accordingly, attach a proper valuation to the investment.

SUMMARY

The valuation of any financial instrument involves a capitalization of its expected income stream by a discount rate appropriate for the risk involved. The important risk to the investor is that which cannot be avoided by diversification. This risk, known as *unavoidable risk,* is systematic in the sense that it affects all securities, although in different degrees. If we assume that investors as a whole are efficiently diversified in the securities they hold, the important risk to the investor is the security's systematic risk.

The degree of systematic risk a security possesses can be determined by the drawing of a *characteristic line*. This line depicts the relationship between expected returns in excess of the risk-free rate for the specific security involved and for the market portfolio. The slope of this line is known as *beta,* and it is a measure of systematic risk. The greater the beta, the greater the unavoidable risk of the security involved. The relationship between the required rate of return for a security and its beta is known as the *security market line*. It is linear and reflects a positive relationship between the return investors require and systematic risk. Thus, the required return is the risk-free rate plus some premium for systematic risk.

With the security market line concept, one is able to approximate the appropriate discount rate for both fixed-income securities and common stocks. Bonds and preferred stocks represent fixed-income securities in the sense that the cash payment, whether it be interest or preferred dividend, is established at issuance and is invariant. We illustrated the calculation of the present value of a bond under various assumptions as to the number of times a year interest is paid as well as the valuation of a perpetuity.

We showed that expected future dividends are the foundation for the valuation of common stocks. The dividend-capitalization model embodies the notion of capital gains, so it is not inconsistent with much of the folk-lore regarding the importance of capital gains versus dividends. We went on to consider various growth models where dividends are expected to grow over time either at a constant rate or at different rates. In all cases, determination of value involves calculating the present value of the expected future stream of dividends. The key to valuation is determining the appropriate discount rate that properly takes account of risk. This is the reason for our stressing its measurement in this chapter. We continue our discussion of required rates of return in the next chapter when we investigate the cost of capital.

QUESTIONS

1. Define the *capitalization of income approach* to valuation.
2. Why do we treat bonds and preferred stock in the same way when it comes to valuation?
3. Why do bonds with long maturities fluctuate more in value than bonds with short maturities, given the same change in yield to maturity?
4. Why are dividends the basis for the valuation of common stock?
5. Suppose controlling stock of IBM Corporation were placed in a perpetual trust with an irrevocable clause that cash or liquidating dividends will never be paid. Earnings per share continue to grow. What is the value of the company?
6. Why is the growth rate in dividends of a company likely to taper off in the future? Couldn't the growth rate increase as well? If it did, what would be the effect?
7. Explain the importance of the assumption of efficient capital markets when it comes to deriving the security market line.
8. Define the *characteristic line* and its *alpha* and *beta*.
9. Why is beta a measure of systematic risk? What is its meaning?
10. What is the required rate of return of a stock? How can it be measured?
11. Is the security market line constant over time?

Bond pays 8% you went 10% value so bond less

1. Gonzalez Electric Company has outstanding a three-year, 8 percent bond issue with a face value of $1,000 per bond. Interest is payable annually. The bonds are privately held by Suresafe Fire Insurance Company. Suresafe wishes to sell the bonds and is negotiating with another party. It estimates that given current market conditions, the bonds should provide a return of 10 percent (yield to maturity). What price per bond should Suresafe be able to realize on their sale?

2. What would be the price per bond in Problem 1 if interest payments were semiannual?

3. Superior Cement Company has a 5 percent preferred-stock issue outstanding, with each share having a $100 face value. Currently, the return is 7 percent. What is the market price per share? If interest rates in general should rise so that the required return becomes 9 percent, what will happen to the market price per share?

4. The stock of the Health Corporation is currently selling for $20 and is expected to pay a $1 dividend at the end of the year. If an investor bought the stock now and sold it for $23 after receiving the dividend, what rate of return would he earn?

5. (a) The Pueblo Corporation paid a dividend of $1.50 per share last year; dividends of Pueblo are expected to grow at a rate of 10 percent indefinitely. The Pueblo stockholders are known to demand a 20 percent return. At what price should Pueblo stock sell? *16.50*

   (b) Suppose that Pueblo dividends were expected to grow at 10 percent for only five more years, after which they would grow at 6 percent forever. At what price should Pueblo stock now sell?

6. Delphi Products Corporation currently pays a dividend of $2 per share and this dividend is expected to grow at a 15 percent annual rate for three years, then at a 10 percent rate for the next three years, after which it is expected to grow at a 5 percent rate forever.

   (a) What value would you place on the stock if a 9 percent rate of return were required?

   (b) Would your valuation change if you expected to hold the stock only three years?

7. Suppose that you were given the following data for past excess quarterly returns for Karochi Corporation and for the market portfolio:

End of yr. Payment Disco 10%
80   90909
80   82645
1080   75131
1
2
3

Quarter	Excess Returns Karochi	Excess Returns Market Portfolio
1	.04	.05
2	.05	.10
3	−.04	−.06
4	−.05	−.10
5	.02	.02
6	.00	−.03
7	.02	.07
8	−.01	−.01
9	−.02	−.08
10	.04	.00
11	.07	.13
12	−.01	.04
13	.01	−.01
14	−.06	−.09
15	−.06	−.14
16	−.02	−.04
17	.07	.15
18	.02	.06
19	.04	.11
20	.03	.05
21	.01	.03
22	−.01	.01
23	−.01	−.03
24	.02	.04

On the basis of this information, graph the relationship between the two sets of excess returns and draw a characteristic line. What is the approximate alpha? The approximate beta? What can you say about the systematic risk of the stock, based upon past experience?

8. Assuming the capital-asset pricing model approach is appropriate, compute the required rate of return for each of the following stocks, given a risk-free rate of .05 and an expected return for the market portfolio of .10:

Stock	A	B	C	D	E
Beta	1.5	1.0	0.6	2.0	1.3

What implications can you draw?

SELECTED REFERENCES

BAUMAN, W. SCOTT, "Investment Returns and Present Values," *Financial Analysts Journal*, 25 (November–December 1969), 107–18.

BLUME, MARSHALL E., "On the Assessment of Risk," *Journal of Finance*, 26 (March 1971), 1–10.

BOWER, RICHARD S., and DOROTHY H. BOWER, "Risk and the Valuation of Common Stock," *Journal of Political Economy*, 77 (May–June 1969), 349–62.

BRIGHAM, EUGENE F., and JAMES L. PAPPAS, "Duration of Growth, Changes in Growth Rates, and Corporate Share Prices," *Financial Analysts Journal*, 22 (May–June 1966), 157–62.

ELTON, EDWIN J., and MARTIN J. GRUBER, "Earnings Estimates and the Accuracy of Expectational Data," *Management Science*, 18 (April 1972), 409–24.

EVANS, JACK, and STEPHEN H. ARCHER, "Diversification and the Reduction of Dispersion: An Empirical Analysis," *Journal of Finance*, 23 (December 1968), 761–67.

FAMA, EUGENE F., "Components of Investment Performance," *Journal of Finance*, 27 (June 1972), 551–67.

———, "Efficient Capital Markets: A Review of Theory and Empirical Work," *Journal of Finance*, 25 (May 1970), 383–417.

FAMA, EUGENE F., and MERTON H. MILLER, *The Theory of Finance*. New York: Holt, Rinehart & Winston, 1972.

FIELITZ, BRUCE D., "Indirect versus Direct Diversification," *Financial Management*, 3 (Winter 1974), 54–62.

HALEY, CHARLES W., and LAWRENCE D. SCHALL, *The Theory of Financial Decisions*, Chapters 5–7. New York: McGraw-Hill, 1973.

HOLT, CHARLES C., "The Influence of Growth Duration on Share Price," *Journal of Finance*, 17 (September 1962), 465–75.

LEV, BARUCH, *Financial Statement Analysis*. Englewood Cliffs, N.J.: Prentice-Hall, 1974.

LORIE, JAMES H., and MARY T. HAMILTON, *The Stock Market*. Homewood, Ill.: Richard D. Irwin, 1973.

MALKIEL, BURTON G., "Equity Yields, Growth, and the Structure of Share Prices," *American Economic Review*, 53 (December 1963), 467–94.

MAO, JAMES C. T., "The Valuation of Growth Stocks: The Investment Opportunities Approach," *Journal of Finance*, 21 (March 1966), 95–102.

MODIGLIANI, FRANCO, and GERALD A. POGUE, "An Introduction to Risk and Return," *Financial Analysts Journal*, 30 (March–April 1974), 68–80, and (May–June 1974), 69–86.

POGUE, GERALD A., and KISHORE LALL, "Corporate Finance: An Overview," *Sloan Management Review*, 15 (Spring 1974), 19–38.

ROBICHEK, ALEXANDER A., "Risk and the Value of Securities," *Journal of Financial and Quantitative Analysis*, 4 (December 1969), 513–38.

ROBICHEK, ALEXANDER A., and MARCUS C. BOGUE, "A Note on the Behavior of Expected Price/Earnings Ratios over Time," *Journal of Finance*, 26 (June 1971), 731–35.

SHARPE, WILLIAM F., "Capital Asset Prices: A Theory of Market Equilibrium under Conditions of Risk," *Journal of Finance*, 19 (September 1964), 425–42.

———, *Portfolio Analysis and Capital Markets*. New York: McGraw-Hill, 1970.

———, "A Simplified Model for Portfolio Analysis," *Management Science*, 10 (January 1963), 277–93.

VAN HORNE, JAMES C., *The Function and Analysis of Capital Market Rates*. Englewood Cliffs, N.J.: Prentice-Hall, 1970.

VAN HORNE, JAMES C., and **WILLIAM F. GLASSMIRE, JR.,** "The Impact of Unanticipated Changes in Inflation on the Value of Common Stocks," *Journal of Finance,* 27 (December 1972), 1081–92.

VAN HORNE, JAMES C., and **RAYMOND C. HELWIG,** *The Valuation of Small Bank Stocks.* East Lansing: Bureau of Business and Economic Research, Michigan State University, 1966.

WENDT, PAUL F., "Current Growth Stock Valuation Methods," *Financial Analysts Journal,* 33 (March–April 1965), 3–15.

16 *Required Returns on Capital Investments*

In the preceding chapter, we considered the valuation of debt and equity instruments. The concepts advanced there serve as a foundation for determining the required rate of return for the firm and for specific investment projects. The capital investment decision is directly related to the financing decision, because the acceptance of investment proposals depends upon how those proposals will be financed. In Chapter 13, we saw that the discount rate is the vehicle by which we judge the attractiveness of an investment opportunity. Our focus in this chapter is on determining an appropriate discount rate or required rate of return to employ. In so doing, we hope to come to an understanding of the link between the acceptance of investment proposals and the market price of the firm's stock.

The acceptance criterion for capital investments is perhaps the most difficult and controversial topic in finance. We know in theory that it should be the rate of return on a project that will leave unchanged the market price of the company's stock. The difficulty is in determining this rate in practice. Because predicting the effect of decisions on stock prices is an inexact science (some would call it an art form), estimating the appropriate required rate of return is inexact as well. Rather than skirt the issue, we address it head on and propose a general framework for measuring the required rate of return. We begin with the required rate of return for the company as a whole and then move on to consider the required rate of return for individual projects.

For a company as a whole, there is an aggregation of assets. As a result, the use of an overall cost of capital as the acceptance criterion for investment decisions is appropriate only under certain circumstances. These circumstances are that the assets of the firm are homogeneous with respect to risk and that investment proposals under consideration are of the same character. If investment proposals vary widely with respect to risk, the required rate of return for the company as a whole is not appropriate as an acceptance criterion. The advantage of using it is, of course, its simplicity. Once it is computed, projects can be evaluated using a single rate which does not change unless underlying conditions change. This avoids the problem of computing individual required rates of return for each investment proposal. However, it is important that if the firm's overall required rate of return is used as an acceptance criterion, projects correspond to the above conditions. Otherwise, one should determine an acceptance criterion for each project, a topic we take up in the latter part of this chapter.[1]

The overall cost of capital of a firm is comprised of the costs of the various components of financing. The most difficult of these costs to measure is the cost of equity capital, and this topic will occupy most of our attention. However, we consider also the costs of debt and preferred stock. Our concern throughout will be with the *marginal* cost of a specific source of financing. The use of marginal costs follows from the fact that we use the cost of capital to decide whether to invest in new projects. Past costs of financing have no bearing on this decision. All costs will be expressed on an after-tax basis, so as to conform to the expression of investment project cash flows on an after-tax basis. Once we have examined the explicit costs of various sources of financing, we shall combine these costs to obtain an overall cost of capital to the firm.

Cost of debt

The explicit cost of debt can be derived by solving for that discount rate, k, that equates the net proceeds of the debt issue with the present value of interest plus principal payments, and then adjusting the explicit cost obtained for the tax effect.[2] If we denote the after-tax cost of debt by k_i, it can be approximated by

$$k_i = k(1 - t) \qquad (16\text{-}1)$$

[1] See Wilbur G. Lewellen, "A Conceptual Reappraisal of Cost of Capital," *Financial Management*, 4 (Winter 1974), 63–70, for a discussion of the importance of required rates of return corresponding to the risk involved in the particular decision at hand.

[2] For the mathematics of interest, see Chapters 12 and 15.

where k is the internal rate of return or yield, and t is the marginal tax rate.[3] Because interest charges are tax-deductible, the after-tax cost of debt is substantially less than the before-tax cost. If a company were able to sell a new issue of twenty-year bonds with an 8 percent coupon rate and realize net proceeds (after underwriting expenses) of $1,000 for each $1,000 face value bond, k would be 8 percent. If the federal income tax rate were 50 percent,

$$k_i = 8.00(1 - 0.50) = 4.00 \text{ percent}$$

We note that the 4.00 percent after-tax cost in our example represents the marginal, or incremental, cost of additional debt. It does not represent the cost of debt already employed.

The explicit cost of debt is considerably cheaper than the cost of another source of financing having the same k but where the financial charges are not deductible for tax purposes. Implied in the calculation of an after-tax cost of debt is the fact that the firm is profitable. Otherwise, it does not gain the tax benefit associated with interest payments. The explicit cost of debt for an unprofitable firm is the before-tax cost, k.

Cost of preferred stock

The cost of preferred stock is a function of its stated dividend. As we discuss in Chapter 23, this dividend is not a contractual obligation on the part of the firm but is payable at the discretion of the board of directors. Consequently, unlike with debt, there is no risk of legal bankruptcy. However, from the standpoint of common stockholders, preferred stock represents a security senior to their interests. Because

---

[3]When the price paid for a bond differs from its face value, the premium or discount is amortized for federal income tax purposes. If the premium or discount is significant, the after-tax cost of debt should take it into account. The approximate cost of a bond sold at a discount or a premium is

$$k_i = \frac{(1 - t)\left[C_t + \dfrac{1}{n}(P - I_0)\right]}{\frac{1}{2}(P + I_0)}$$

where P is the face value of the bond (usually $1,000), I_0 is the price at which the bond is sold, n is the number of years to maturity, and C_t is the fixed interest cost in all periods. $(1/n)(P - I_0)$ represents the amortization of the discount or premium over the life of the bond, and the denominator represents the average amount outstanding. If sinking-fund payments are made, the formula must be revised. The formula above is but an approximation of the explicit cost because it does not take account of annual compounding. See G. David Quirin, *The Capital Expenditure Decision* (Homewood, Ill.: Richard D. Irwin, 1967), pp. 100–101. Because most bond issues are sold in the capital markets at close to their face values, we do not take account specifically of the tax effect of a premium or discount.

most corporations that issue preferred stock intend to pay the stated dividend, the dividend on the preferred stock represents a prior claim on income. As preferred stock has no maturity date, its cost may be represented as

$$k_p = \frac{D}{I_0} \qquad (16\text{-}2)$$

where D is the stated annual dividend and I_0 represents the net proceeds of the preferred-stock issue. If a company were able to sell a $7\frac{1}{2}$ percent preferred-stock issue ($100 par value) and realize net proceeds of $98\frac{1}{2}$ a share, the cost of the preferred stock would be $7\frac{1}{2}/98\frac{1}{2} = 7.61$ percent. Note that this cost is not adjusted for taxes, because the preferred-stock dividend is paid after taxes. Thus, the explicit cost of preferred stock is substantially greater than that for debt.

Cost of equity capital

The cost of equity capital is by far the most difficult cost to measure. In theory, it may be defined as the minimum rate of return that the company must earn on the equity-financed portion of an investment project in order to leave unchanged the market price of the stock. If the firm invests in projects where the expected return is less than this required return, the market price of the stock over the long run will suffer.

In the context of the dividend-capitalization model presented in the preceding chapter, the cost of equity capital can be thought of as the rate of discount that equates the present value of all expected future dividends per share, as perceived by investors at the margin, with the current market price per share. Recall from Chapter 15 that

$$P_0 = \frac{D_1}{(1 + k_e)} + \frac{D_2}{(1 + k_e)^2} + \cdots + \frac{D_\infty}{(1 + k_e)^\infty} \qquad (16\text{-}3)$$

$$P_0 = \sum_{t=1}^{\infty} \frac{D_t}{(1 + k_e)^t}$$

where P_0 is the value of a share of stock at time 0, D_t is the dividend per share expected to be paid in period t, k_e is the appropriate rate of discount, and the capital Greek sigma represents the sum of discounted expected future dividends from period 1 through infinity, where infinity is depicted by ∞.

Estimating future dividends. If we can successfully estimate the stream of future dividends that the market expects, it is an easy matter to solve for the rate of discount that equates this stream with the current market price of the stock. Because expected future dividends are not directly observable, they must be estimated. Herein lies the major difficulty in estimating the cost of equity capital. For reasonably stable patterns of past growth, one might project this trend into the future.[4] However, we must temper the projection to take account of current market sentiment. Insight into such sentiment can come from reviewing various analyses about the company in financial newspapers and magazines.

On the basis of the long-range plans of the company, the financial manager can make internal estimates of the expected future growth in earnings per share and in dividends per share. These estimates should take account of economic and other factors that bear on the firm's future operating performance. Because the financial manager has access to a great deal of relevant information, his estimates of future earnings may be the most accurate of all. However, it is important that investors also expect these earnings. There is an obvious bias if the financial manager uses his estimate of growth to solve for k_e and his estimate differs significantly from that of the market. The important question to ask is, What growth in dividends do investors at the margin expect that leads them to pay x dollars for a share of stock? Every effort should be made to get as accurate a handle as possible on this expected growth pattern. Thus, the financial manager must think as investors do when he estimates future dividends for his company.

Capital-asset pricing model approach to the cost of equity. Rather than estimating the future dividend stream of the firm and then solving for the cost of equity capital, one may approach the problem directly by estimating the required rate of return on the company's equity. From our discussion of the capital-asset pricing model in the preceding chapter, we know that it implies the following required rate of return for a stock:

$$R_j = i + (\bar{R}_m - i)\beta_j \qquad (16\text{-}4)$$

where i is the risk-free rate, $\bar{R}_m$ is the expected return for the market portfolio, and β_j is the beta coefficient for stock j.

Recall from Chapter 15 that beta is a measure of the responsiveness of the excess returns for security j (in excess of the risk-free rate) to those of the market, using some broad-based market index such as Standard & Poor's 500-stock index as a surrogate for the market port-

[4]For an analysis of the accuracy of earnings-per-share forecasts produced by various mechanical forecasting techniques using past data, see Edwin J. Elton and Martin J. Gruber, "Earnings Estimates and the Accuracy of Expectational Data," *Management Science,* 18 (April 1972), 409–24. The article also serves as a presentation of these techniques. For yet another method for estimating expected growth, see Aharon R. Ofer, "Investors' Expectations of Earnings Growth, Their Accuracy, and Effects on the Structure of Realized Rates of Return," *Journal of Finance,* 30 (May 1975), 509–23.

folio. If the historical relationship between security returns and those for the market portfolio is believed to be a reasonable proxy for the future, one can use past returns to compute the beta for a stock. This was illustrated in the preceding chapter where a characteristic line was fitted to the relationship between returns in excess of risk-free rate for the stock and those for the market index. *Beta* is defined as the slope of this line. Rather than calculate beta information directly, several services provide historical beta information on a large number of publicly traded stocks. These services allow one to obtain the beta for a stock with ease, thereby facilitating greatly the calculation of the cost of equity capital.

Again, if the past is thought to be a good proxy for the future, one can use Eq. (16-4) to compute the cost of equity capital for a company. To illustrate, suppose that the beta for the Silva-Chin Company were found to be 1.20, based on quarterly excess return data over the last five years. This coefficient tells us that the stock's excess return goes up or down by a somewhat greater percentage than does the excess return for the market. (A beta of 1.00 means that excess returns for the stock vary proportionally with excess returns for the market portfolio.) Thus, the stock of Silva-Chin Company has more unavoidable, or systematic, risk than does the market as a whole. Suppose that management believes that this past relationship is likely to hold in the future. Suppose further that the past rate of return of about 10 percent on stocks in general is expected to prevail in the future. Finally, suppose that a risk-free rate of 5 percent is expected in the future.

This is all the information we need to compute the required rate of return on equity for Silva-Chin Company. Using Eq. (16-4), the cost of equity capital would be

$$R_i = .05 + (.10 - .05) \, 1.20 = 11 \text{ percent}$$

Thus, the estimated required rate of return on equity for Silva-Chin Company is approximately 11 percent. In essence, we are saying that this is the rate of return that investors expect the company to earn on its equity.

If measurement were exact and certain assumptions held,[5] the cost

---

[5] As discussed in the preceding chapter, the capital-asset pricing model assumes the presence of perfect capital markets. When this assumption is relaxed to take account of real-world conditions, the residual risk of a stock may take on a degree of importance. Recall that the total risk of a security is comprised of its systematic as well as its residual risk. The assumption of the capital-asset pricing model is that the latter can be completely diversified away, which leaves only the former risk.

If imperfections exist in the capital markets, these may impede efficient diversification by investors. (One example of an imperfection is the presence of significant bankruptcy costs.) The greater the imperfections that are believed to exist, the greater the allowance that must be made for residual risk. As a result, it will be necessary to adjust upward the required rate of return. For amplification of this point, see James C. Van Horne, *Financial Management and Policy*, 4th ed. (Englewood Cliffs, N.J.: Prentice-Hall, 1977), Chapters 7–8.

of equity capital determined by this method would be the same as the required rate of return determined by solving for the rate of discount that equates the present value of the stream of expected future dividends with the current market price of the stock. By now it should be apparent that we can only hope to approximate the cost of equity capital. We believe that the methods suggested above enable such an approximation. However, we will be more or less accurate depending on the situation. Usually we are able to place far more confidence in estimates for a large company whose stock is actively traded on the New York Stock Exchange and whose systematic risk is close to that of the market as a whole than we are in estimates for a moderate-sized machine tool company whose stock is inactively traded in the over-the-counter market and whose systematic risk is very large. We must live with the inexactness involved in the measurement process and try to do as good a job as possible.

Flotation costs.   It is necessary to qualify our measured cost of equity capital for the flotation costs involved in the sale of common stock. If a company sells a new issue of common stock, the proceeds of the sale are usually less than the current market price per share. In general, a new issue must be priced below the current market price; in addition, there are out-of-pocket flotation costs.[6] As a result of these factors, the net proceeds from the sale of the stock are less than the current market price per share times the number of shares issued. Accordingly, the cost of equity capital calculations should be modified to take this into account.

For example, suppose the cost of equity capital for a company were found to be 12 percent. Suppose further that of the equity capital employed over time, one-fourth comes from the sale of new stock, with the balance coming from retained earnings. Finally, suppose that for a new issue, flotation costs and underpricing result in the company's receiving only 90 percent of the current market price of the stock. Making these adjustments, the cost of equity capital would be

$$\text{Adjusted } R_j = (.12/.90) .25 + (.12) .75 = .1233$$

Thus, for every $4 in equity capital, $1 must come from new issues of common stock. When one takes account of the flotation costs involved, it raises the cost of equity capital from 12 percent to 12.33 percent.

Flotation costs represent a capital market imperfection which make new issues of common stock a more "expensive" form of financing than retained earnings. While the type of adjustment illustrated above is approximate, it is necessary if the firm raises significant amounts of equity capital via the new-issue route. Our example assumes the issue

[6]See Chapter 21 for a discussion of these costs.

is sold to new investors. If the issue is a rights offering to existing shareholders, in theory the amount of underpricing does not matter. Therefore, the adjustment would involve only out-of-pocket flotation costs. As we will discuss the question of a rights offering versus a public offering in Chapter 21, a discussion of the differences at this time is not appropriate. This brings to a close our examination of the cost of equity capital.

Weighted-average cost of capital

Once the costs of the individual components of the capital structure have been computed,[7] these costs may be weighted according to some standard and a weighted-average cost of capital calculated. *As an illustration of only the mechanics* of the calculations, suppose that a firm had the following capital structure at the latest statement date:

	Amount	Proportion
Debt	$ 30 million	30%
Preferred stock	10 million	10
Common stock	20 million	20
Retained earnings	40 million	40
	$100 million	100%

Suppose further that the firm computed the following after-tax costs for these component methods of financing:

	Cost
Debt	4.0%
Preferred stock	8.0
Common stock	11.0
Retained earnings	10.0

[7]While equity, debt, and preferred stock are the major types of financing, there are other types. These include leasing, convertible securities, warrants, and other options. Because determining the costs of these methods of financing involves some special and rather complex valuation issues, we treat them in individual chapters where we are able to give such issues proper attention. For our purposes in this chapter, knowing the costs of equity, debt, and preferred-stock financing is sufficient for illustrating the overall cost of capital of a company. When costs are determined for other types of financing, they can be inserted in the weighting scheme to be discussed now.

The cost of common stock is based on the external sale of a new issue to the public, whereas the cost of retained earnings is taken to be the required rate of return on equity. The slight difference in these two costs is attributable to flotation costs and underpricing associated with the sale of a new issue. If the present weights are used, the weighted-average cost of capital for this example problem is:

(1) *Method of Financing*	*(2)* *Proportion*	*(3)* *Cost*	*(4)* *Weighted Cost (2 × 3)*
Debt	30%	4.0%	1.20%
Preferred stock	10	8.0	0.80
Common stock	20	11.0	2.20
Retained earnings	40	10.0	4.00
Weighted-average cost of capital			8.20%

Given the assumptions of this example, we find the measured weighted-average cost of capital to be 8.2 percent.

With the calculation of a weighted-average cost of capital, the critical question is whether the figure represents the firm's real cost of capital. The answer to this question depends upon how accurately we have measured the individual marginal costs, upon the weighting system, and upon certain other assumptions. Assume for now that we are able to measure accurately the marginal costs of the individual sources of financing, and let us examine the importance of the weighting system.

Weighting system. The critical assumption in any weighting system is that the firm will in fact raise capital in the proportions specified. Because the firm raises capital *marginally* to make a *marginal* investment in new projects, we need to work with the marginal cost of capital to the firm as a whole. This rate depends upon the package of funds employed to finance investment projects.[8] In other words, our concern is with new or incremental capital, not with capital raised in the past. In order for the weighted-average cost of capital to represent a marginal cost, the weights employed must be marginal; that is, the weights must correspond to the proportions of financing inputs the firm intends to employ. If they do not, capital is raised on a marginal basis in proportions other than those used to calculate this cost. As a result, the real weighted-average cost of capital will differ from that calculated and used for capital-investment decisions. An obvious bias

[8] See Wilbur G. Lewellen, *The Cost of Capital* (Belmont, Calif.: Wadsworth, 1969), p. 87.

results. If the real cost is greater than that which is measured, certain investment projects will be accepted that will leave investors worse off than before. On the other hand, if the real cost is less than the measured cost, projects will be rejected that could increase shareholder wealth. Therefore, the 8.2 percent weighted-average cost of capital computed in our example is realistic only if the firm intends to finance in the future in the same proportions as its existing capital structure.

It is recognized that the raising of capital is "lumpy," and strict proportions cannot be maintained. For example, a firm would have difficulty in financing each project undertaken with 35 percent debt, 10 percent preferred stock, and 55 percent retained earnings. In practice, it may finance with debt in one instance and with preferred stock or retained earnings in another. Over time, most firms are able to finance in roughly a proportional manner. It is in this sense that we try to measure the marginal cost of capital for the package of financing employed. Another problem is that retained earnings, an important source of funds for most firms, are constrained by the absolute amount of earnings. If a firm's investment opportunities warrant expansion at a rate faster than the growth in earnings, financing by means of retained earnings must diminish relative to other means. Where the expansion is expected to be continuous for a number of years, the financing mix of the firm is subject to a constraint with respect to the ability of the firm to retain earnings. This constraint must be recognized. Frequently, however, expansion is concentrated in a few years so that over the long run a firm is able to finance with a roughly constant proportion of retained earnings.

Rationale for weighted-average cost

The rationale behind the use of a weighted-average cost of capital is that by financing in the proportions specified and accepting projects yielding more than the weighted-average cost, the firm is able to increase the market price of its stock. This increase occurs because investment projects accepted are expected to yield more on their equity-financed portions than the cost of equity capital, k_e. Once these expectations are apparent to the marketplace, the market price of the stock should rise, all other things remaining the same, because expected future earnings per share (and dividends per share) are higher than those expected before the projects were accepted. The firm has accepted projects that are expected to provide a return greater than that required by investors at the margin, based on the risk involved.

We must return to the critical assumption that over time the firm finances in the proportions specified. If it does so, the financial risk of the company remains roughly unchanged. As we shall see in Chapter

18, the "implicit" costs of financing are embodied in the weighted-average cost of capital by virtue of the fact that a firm has to supplement nonequity financing with equity financing. It does not raise capital continually with supposedly cheaper debt funds without increasing its equity base. The firm's capital structure need not be optimal for the firm to employ the weighted-average cost of capital for capital-budgeting purposes. The important consideration is that the weights used be based upon the future financing plans of the company. If they are not, the weighted-average cost of capital calculated does not correspond to the actual cost of funds obtained; as a result, capital-budgeting decisions are likely to be suboptimal.

The use of a weighted-average cost of capital figure must be qualified also for the points raised earlier. It assumes that the investment proposals being considered do not differ in systematic, or unavoidable, risk from that of the firm and that the residual risk of the proposals does not provide any diversification benefits to the firm. Only under these circumstances is the cost of capital figure obtained appropriate as an acceptance criterion. These assumptions are extremely binding. They imply that the projects of a firm are completely homogeneous with respect to risk and that only projects of exactly the same risk will be considered.

In practice, of course, the issue is one of degree. If the conditions above are approximately met, then the company's weighted-average cost of capital may be used as the acceptance criterion. For example, if a firm produced only one product and all proposals considered were in conjunction with the marketing and production of that product, the use of the firm's overall cost of capital as the acceptance criterion probably would be appropriate. (Even here, however, there may be significant enough differences in risk among investment proposals to warrant separate consideration.) For a multiproduct firm with investment proposals of varying risk, the use of an overall required rate of return is inappropriate. Here the required rate of return for the specific proposal should be used, as determined with the methods proposed in the next section. The key, then, is the homogeneity of existing investment projects and investment proposals under consideration with respect to risk.

ACCEPTANCE CRITERION FOR INDIVIDUAL PROJECTS

When the existing investment projects of the firm and investment proposals under consideration are not homogeneous with respect to risk, the use of the firm's cost of capital as an acceptance criterion will not do. In these cases, we must formulate a specific acceptance criterion for the particular project involved. One means for doing so is with the capital-asset pricing model, and this approach is described in this section. We will see that certain underlying assumptions in the model as well as measurement problems make the approach applicable only under specific circumstances. As a result, management may wish to turn to other means for deciding on the merits of a risky investment. In such cases, it is able to evaluate information on the expected return and risk of a project. This assessment can be either in relation to the total risk of the firm or simply in relation to the risk of the proposal or proposals currently being evaluated. In subsequent sections, we explore these approaches. As we shall see, the critical factor, given the objective of maximizing shareholder wealth, is how accurately management is able to link risk-return information for an investment proposal with share price.

Capital-asset pricing model approach to projects

Essentially, the capital-asset pricing model approach is the same as that for determining the cost of equity capital of the firm. However, instead of the expected relation between excess returns for the stock (returns in excess of the risk-free rate) and those for the market portfolio, one is concerned with the expected relation of excess returns for the project and those for the market portfolio. The required return for the project would be

$$R_k = i + (\bar{R}_m - i)\beta_k \qquad (16\text{-}5)$$

where β_k is the slope of the characteristic line that describes the relationship between excess returns for project k and those for the market portfolio. As can be seen, this equation is identical to Eq. (16-4) except for the project return and its beta being substituted for those of the stock.

Assume that the firm intends to finance the project entirely with equity. The acceptance criterion then would be to invest in the project if its expected return exceeds the required return, R_k, as determined with Eq. (16-5). Recall from Chapter 15 that the market-determined relationship between systematic risk, as described by beta, and the required rate of return is depicted by the security market line. To illustrate the acceptance criterion for projects using this

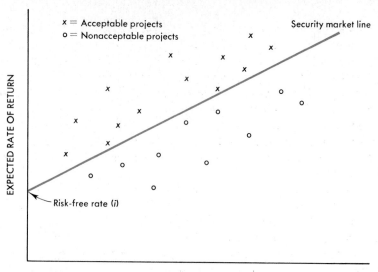

FIG. 16 · 1

The security market line
as applied to
risky investments

concept, we turn to Figure 16-1. All projects with internal rates of
return lying on or above the line should be accepted, for they provide
expected excess returns. These projects are depicted by the x's. All
projects lying below the line, shown by the o's, would be rejected. Note
that the greater the systematic risk of a project, the greater the return
that is required. If the project had no risk, only the risk-free rate
would be required. For projects with more risk, however, a risk premium is demanded, and it increases with the degree of systematic risk
of the project. The goal of the firm in this context is to search for investment opportunities lying above the line.

Because the capital-asset pricing model assumes that all risk other
than systematic risk is diversified away by investors in their portfolios
of stocks, implied is that diversification by the firm in the portfolio of
capital assets it holds is not worthwhile. In other words, the model implies that investors are able to achieve the same diversification as the
firm is able to do for them. Therefore, efforts by the firm to reduce
its total risk via diversification will not enhance its value, according to
this approach. More will be said about this shortly.

Application of the model. The difficulty in applying this approach is in estimating the beta for a project. Recall from Chapter 15
that derivation of the characteristic line is based on changes in market value for a stock and those for the market portfolio. It is therefore
necessary to estimate changes in the market value of the project over
time in relation to changes in value for the market portfolio. Estimation of the former represents unfamiliar ground for most people accustomed to thinking in terms of net-present values and internal rates of
return.

In many cases, however, the project is sufficiently similar to a company whose stock is publicly held so that one is able to use that com-

pany's beta in deriving the required rate of return for the project. In the case of large projects, such as new products, one frequently can identify publicly traded companies that are engaged entirely, or almost entirely, in this type of operation. The important thing is to identify a company or companies with systematic risk characteristics similar to those of the project in question.

Suppose, for example, that a steel company was considering the formation of a real estate subsidiary. As there are a number of real estate companies with publicly traded stocks, one simply could determine the beta for one of those companies or a group of them and use it in Eq. (16-5) to derive the required rate of return for the project. Note that the relevant required rate of return is not that for the steel company, but that for other real estate firms. Stated differently, the real estate venture of the steel company is viewed by the market in the same way as are other firms engaged solely in real estate. By concentrating on companies in the same line of business as that which the firm desires to enter, surrogates of this sort often can be found which approximate the systematic risk of the project. While an exact duplication of the project's risk is unlikely, reasonable approximations frequently are possible.

To illustrate the calculations, suppose that the average beta for a sample of real estate companies whose stocks were publicly traded and whose basic businesses were similar to the venture contemplated by the steel company was 1.6. We then could use this beta as a surrogate for the beta of the project. If we expected the average return on the market portfolio of stocks to be 10 percent and the risk-free rate to be 5 percent, the required rate of return for the project would be

$$R_k = .05 + (.10 - .05)1.6 = 13 \text{ percent}$$

Therefore, 13 percent would be used as the required rate of return for the project. If the real estate venture were expected to provide an internal rate of return in excess of or equal to this rate, the project would be accepted. If not, it would be rejected.

When there are no companies whose stocks are publicly traded that can be used as surrogates in determining the beta for the project, the task becomes much more difficult.[9] Even here, however, there sometimes exists information on the market value of the project in question. For machine tools, for example, a secondary market of sorts exists where prices are established for used machines of various ages. Other assets have similar markets where prices can be determined. Given these prices, one can measure the market return for a particular period and then use such information to derive an estimate of beta

[9] For a discussion of this problem, see Donald R. Lessard and Richard S. Bower, "An Operational Approach to Risk Screening," *Journal of Finance*, 27 (May 1973), 321–38.

for the project.[10] However, the approach is hampered by a number of measurement problems.

Unless one is able to use a company or companies whose stock is publicly traded as a proxy for the project, the derivation of a beta for a specific project is a difficult matter indeed. While the capital-asset model approach is rich in conceptual insight, its applicability is largely limited to situations where such company surrogates exist.

In addition to the practical problems, there is an underlying assumption in the capital-asset pricing model approach which must be questioned. As we know, this assumption is that only the systematic risk of the firm is important. However, the probability of a firm's becoming insolvent depends on its total risk, not just its systematic risk. When insolvency or bankruptcy costs are significant, investors may be served by the firm's paying attention to the impact of a project on the total risk of the firm. The latter is comprised of both systematic and residual risk. While the most important risk of a company to investors is its systematic risk, residual risk can be a factor of at least some importance.[11] The greater its importance, the less relevant is the capital-asset pricing model approach to risky investments.

Evaluation of projects on the basis of expected return and risk

When for either theoretical or practical reasons it is not appropriate to compute a required rate of return for a project using the capital-asset pricing model, we must turn to more subjective means for evaluating risky investments. In reality, most firms approach the problem in this manner. Many of course deal with risky investments in informal ways. The decision maker simply tries to incorporate risk into his judgment on the basis of his "feel" for the projects being evaluated. This "feel" can be improved upon by discussions with others familiar with the proposals and the risks inherent in them. Frequently, such discussions center around "what if" types of questions to each other. In a general way, then, an allowance can be made for risk in capital expenditure decisions. The problem with informal approaches to risk, of course, is that the information developed usually is sketchy and the treatment of it not consistent from project to project or over time.

We know from our discussion in Chapter 14 that expected return

[10]For such an example, see Van Horne, *Financial Management and Policy,* 4th ed., Chapter 7.

[11]When there are significant bankruptcy costs, these work to the detriment of stockholders as residual owners of the company. It therefore may be important for the firm to keep the probability of becoming bankrupt within reasonable bounds. To do so, it must consider the impact of the project on the firm's total risk (systematic and residual). This approach is taken up in the last section of the chapter.

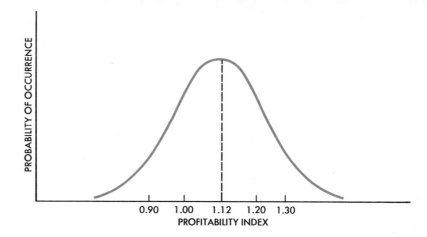

tribution to a probability distribution of possible profitability indexes. The converted probability distribution for the example problem is seen in Figure 16-2.

If management has specified maximum risk profiles for various expected values of profitability indexes, one would simply compare proposal X with the maximum risk profile for an expected value of profitability index of 1.12. If the dispersion of the proposal is less than that for the risk profile, the proposal would be accepted. If not, it would be rejected. The maximum level of dispersion permitted, as depicted by the risk profile, will increase with the expected value of profitability index. For a profitability index of 1.02, the dispersion of the maximum risk profile will be narrower than that for a profitability index of 1.10. An illustration of some hypothetical risk profiles is shown in Figure 16-3. We note that the greater the expected value of profitability index, the greater the dispersion that is tolerable to management.

The real problem, of course, is that the link to share price is not direct. Management is presented with information about the expected return and risk of a project and on the basis of this information reaches a decision. However, there is no direct link to the likely reaction of well-diversified investors. This link depends entirely upon the perceptiveness of management in judging investors' tradeoff between profitability and risk. Moreover, there is no analysis of the impact of the project on the total risk of the firm; as we know, this factor becomes important if capital markets are less than perfect. In essence, the project is evaluated in isolation of investors and of existing investment projects. For these reasons, the approach leaves much to be desired. Still, we must recognize that in practice most investment decisions are made by management in this way. By providing management with information about the dispersion of possible outcomes, more informed decisions are possible than in the conventional capital-budgeting analysis where only the expected values of cash flows are considered.

and risk can be quantified in a consistent manner. Given this information, the question becomes whether a project should be accepted or rejected. We will begin by examining how management might evaluate a single investment proposal and then move on to combinations of risky investments. All of these methods are firm-risk oriented in the sense that management does not consider explicitly the effect of the project on investors' portfolios. It does, however, assess the likely effect of the project(s) on the variability of cash flows and earnings of the firm. From this assessment, management then can estimate the likely effect on share price. The critical factor from the standpoint of valuation is how accurately management is able to link risk-profitability information for an investment proposal with share price. As we shall see, the linkage tends to be subjective, which detracts from the accuracy of the approaches.

Evaluation of a proposal. For purposes of illustration, we will work only with the expected value and standard deviation of the probability distribution of possible net-present values. Because the concepts presented are applicable for the internal-rate-of-return method, it is not necessary to illustrate them twice. Recall from Chapter 14 that the information generated for an investment proposal was the probability distribution of possible net-present values using the risk-free rate as the discount factor. From the distribution, one is able to derive the probability that the net-present value of the project will be zero or less. This probability corresponds to the probability that the project's internal rate of return will be less than the risk-free rate.

In the evaluation of a single proposal, it is unlikely that management would accept an investment proposal having an expected value of net-present value of zero unless the probability distribution had no dispersion. In this special case, the proposal, by definition, would be riskless. For risky investments, the net-present value would have to exceed zero. How much it would have to exceed zero before acceptance were warranted depends upon the amount of dispersion of the probability distribution and the utility preferences of management with respect to risk.

In order to facilitate project selection as well as to make it consistent over time, management may wish to formulate maximum risk profiles. To express the probability distributions in relative instead of absolute terms, we can convert the net-present value probability distribution into a distribution of possible profitability indexes. (Recall that the profitability index is simply the present value of future net cash flows over the initial cash outlay.) For proposal X, our example problem in Chapter 14, the initial cash outflow was $10,000 and the expected value of the probability distribution of net-present values was $1,173. Thus, the profitability index is ($1,173 + $10,000)/$10,000 = 1.12. The profitability index for zero net-present value is (0 + $10,000)/$10,000 = 1.00. Similarly, we can convert the entire probability dis-

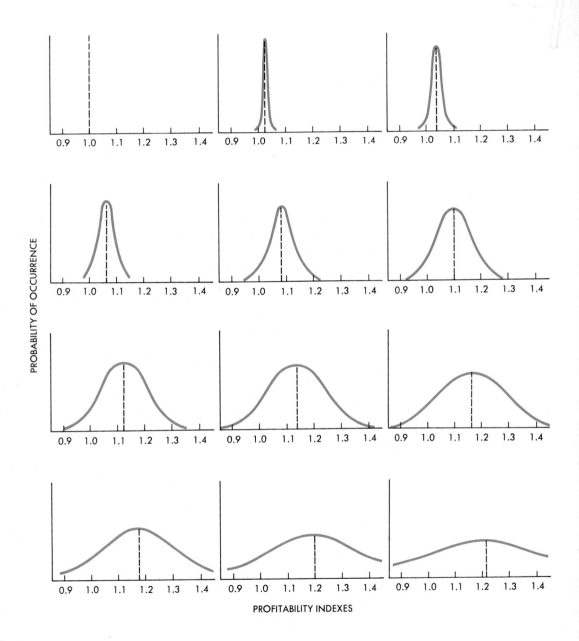

PROBABILITY OF OCCURRENCE

PROFITABILITY INDEXES

FIG. 16 · 3

Risk profiles

347

From Chapter 14, we know that the marginal risk of an individual proposal to the firm as a whole depends upon its correlation with existing projects as well as its correlation with proposals under consideration that might be accepted. We suggested that the appropriate information was the standard deviation and expected value of the probability distribution of possible net-present values for all feasible combinations of existing projects and investment proposals under consideration. We assume that management is interested only in the marginal impact of an investment proposal on the risk complexion of the firm as a whole.

The selection of the most desirable combination of investments will depend upon its utility preferences with respect to net-present value and variance, or standard deviation. To illustrate, Figure 16-4 shows various combinations of risky investments available to the firm. This figure is the same as Figure 14-6 in Chapter 14. Each dot represents a combination of proposals under consideration and existing investment projects for the firm. We see that certain dots dominate others in the sense that they represent a higher expected value of net-present value and the same standard deviation, a lower standard deviation and the same expected value of net-present value, or both a higher expected value and a lower standard deviation. The dots that dominate others are those that are farthest to the right. With information of this sort before it, management can eliminate most combinations of risky investments simply because they are dominated by other combinations.

In this case, management would probably consider only four combinations of risky investments—*B*, *H*, *L*, and *P*. From these it would choose the one that it felt offered the best combination of expected

FIG. 16 · 4

Opportunity set
of combinations
of projects

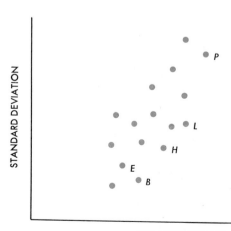

NET-PRESENT VALUE

348

return and risk. If it were moderately averse to risk, it might choose combination L. While combination P provides a somewhat higher expected value of net-present value, it also has a much higher standard deviation. Combinations B and H have lower risk, but also lower expected values of net-present values. If management were fairly averse to risk, however, one of these two combinations might be chosen.

As discussed in Chapter 14, the final selection determines the new investment proposal or proposals that will be accepted. An exception would occur only when the combination selected was comprised of existing projects. In this situation, no investment proposals under consideration would be accepted. If the portfolio of existing projects were represented by combination E in the figure, the selection of any of the four outlying combinations would imply the acceptance of one or more new investment proposals. Those investment proposals under consideration that were not in the combination finally selected would of course be rejected.

Conceptual implications

On the basis of the information presented, management is able to determine which investment proposals under consideration offer the best marginal contribution of expected value of net-present value and standard deviation to the firm as a whole. In determining the standard deviation for a combination, consideration is given to the correlation of an investment proposal with existing investment projects, as well as with other new investment proposals. Implied in this evaluation is that the total risk of the firm is what is important; investment decisions are made in light of their marginal impact on total risk.

This approach implies that from the standpoint of stockholders, management should be concerned with the firm's solvency. As discussed, such solvency depends on the total risk of the firm, not necessarily the risk of individual projects. Due to less than perfect correlation with each other, certain projects have diversification properties. As a result, the total risk of the firm will be less than the sum of the parts. Management will endeavor to accept investment proposals in such a way as to keep the probability of insolvency within reasonable bounds while maximizing net-present value.

As indicated before, the problem with this approach is that it ignores the fact that investors can diversify in the portfolios of common stocks that they hold. Therefore, diversification by the firm may not be a thing of value in the sense of doing something for investors that they cannot do for themselves. To the extent that investors are concerned only with the unavoidable or systematic risk of a project, the capital-asset pricing model approach illustrated earlier should be used.

In theory, the required rate of return for an investment project should be the rate that leaves unchanged the market price of the stock. If existing investment projects and investment proposals under consideration are homogeneous with respect to risk, it is appropriate to use the overall cost of capital of a company as the acceptance criterion. This can be a weighted-average cost of the various instruments with which the company intends to finance. By far the most difficult cost to measure is the cost of equity capital. Using a dividend-capitalization model, this cost is the rate of discount that equates the present value of the stream of expected future dividends with the market price of the stock. The key ingredient in the formula is the accuracy of one's estimates of expected future dividends. Approaching the problem directly, one can estimate the cost of equity capital with the capital-asset pricing model. The model itself was presented in the preceding chapter, and its application to determining equity costs was illustrated in this chapter. If this approach is used, it is important that the assumptions of the model be recognized and that they be reasonably applicable.

Given the measurement of marginal costs of debt, preferred stock, and equity, a weighted-average cost of capital can be computed. The weights employed should correspond to the proportions with which the firm intends to finance. Once computed, the weighted-average cost is used as a basis for accepting or rejecting investment proposals. The rationale for its use was discussed, as were certain qualifications. When investment projects, both existing and new, are widely variant with respect to risk, use of the company's overall cost of capital as an acceptance criterion is not appropriate.

In such cases, one should determine an acceptance criterion for each investment proposal or group of proposals under consideration. One means for computing a risk-adjusted required rate of return for a proposal is with the capital-asset pricing model. Instead of relating excess returns (in excess of the risk-free rate) for a stock to excess returns for the market portfolio, one relates excess returns for the project to excess returns for the market portfolio. Once a beta is determined, the required rate of return can easily be determined. The key to this approach is to find a company whose stock is publicly traded and whose business closely corresponds to the investment proposal being contemplated. This company's stock is then used as a surrogate for the proposal in computing beta. In the absence of a reasonable surrogate, this approach is very difficult. On a theoretical level, the capital-asset pricing model assumes that the only risk that is relevant is the systematic risk of the firm, an assumption that may not be appropriate in some situations.

A practical means for evaluating risky investments is to analyze the expected value and standard deviation of the probability distribution of possible returns for an investment proposal and, on the basis of this information, reach a decision. As taken up in Chapter 14, it is important that the discount rate employed be the risk-free rate. The greater the dispersion of the distribution, the greater the expected value that presumably would be required by management. The problem with this approach is that the link between the investment decision and share price is not direct. It depends on the perceptions of management with respect to likely investor reaction.

Finally, we examined the marginal impact of an investment project on the total risk of the firm. This becomes important if one is concerned with the possibility of insolvency. By analyzing the various possible combinations of existing projects and investment proposals under consideration as to their expected return and risk, management is able to select the best one, usually on the basis of dominance. The selection itself determines which proposals will be accepted and which will be rejected. With this approach, the diversification properties of a project are recognized in the computation of the standard deviation for a combination. Again this is important if one is concerned with the impact of investment proposals accepted on the total risk of the firm as opposed to only its systematic risk.

1. During 1974, interest rates on corporate bonds rose to historical highs. At the same time, stock prices dropped dramatically from the levels that prevailed in the early part of the year. Using Eq. (16-3), develop an explanation of the inverse relationship between interest rates and stock prices that occurred at that time.

2. Why is it important to use marginal weights in calculating a weighted-average cost of capital?

3. Under what circumstances is it appropriate to use the weighted-average cost of capital as an acceptance criterion?

4. Do the funds provided by sources such as accounts payable and accruals have a cost of capital? Explain.

5. What is the critical assumption inherent in the capital-asset pricing model as it relates to the acceptance criterion for risky investments?

6. What is the distinction between evaluating the expected value and standard deviation for an individual investment project and for a group or combination of projects?

7. If management of a company has significant holdings of stock in the company, with little in the way of "outside" wealth, how is this likely to affect its behavior with respect to risky investment decisions? Is this in the shareholders' best interests?

8. Trace the effects of the following on the cost of capital:
   (a) The Federal Reserve increases the money supply by buying bonds from the public.
   (b) The public decides to save a larger proportion of its income.
   (c) The capital-gains tax rate is lowered.
   (d) Major economic depressions are eliminated.
   (e) The corporation income tax rate is lowered.

1. Zapata Enterprises is financed by two sources of funds, bonds and stocks. The cost of capital for funds provided by bonds is K_i while K_e is the cost of capital for equity funds. The capital structure consists of amount B of bonds and S of stock. Compute the weighted-average cost of capital, K_o.

2. Assume B (Problem 1) is $3 million and S is $7 million. The bonds have a 6 percent cost of capital and the stock pays $500,000 in dividends. The growth rate of dividends has been 8 percent and is expected to continue at the same rate. Find the cost of capital if the tax rate on income is 40 percent.

3. Assuming a firm has a tax rate of 40 percent, compute the after-tax cost of the following:
   (a) A bond, sold at par, with a 9¼ percent coupon.

(b) A twenty-year 8½ percent, $1,000 par bond sold at $900 less a 5 percent underwriting commission. (Use an approximation method, footnote 3.)

(c) A preferred stock sold at $100 paying 7 percent with a call price of $110 if the company plans to call the issue in five years. (Use an approximation method.)

(d) A common stock selling at $20 and paying a $2 dividend which is expected to be continued indefinitely.

(e) The same common stock if dividends are expected to grow at the rate of 5 percent per year.

(f) A common stock, selling at $30 per share, of a company that engages in no external financing. The stock earns $5 per share, of which one-half is paid in dividends. The shareholders expect the company to earn a constant after-tax rate of 10 percent on investments.

4. On March 10, International Copy Machines (ICOM), one of the "favorites" of the stock market, was priced at $300 per share. This price was based on an expected annual growth rate of at least 20 percent for quite some time in the future. In July, economic indicators turned down, and investors revised downward to 15 percent their estimate for future growth of ICOM. What should happen to the price of the stock? Assume the following:

(a) A perpetual-growth valuation model is a reasonable representation of the way the market values ICOM.

(b) The measured cost of equity capital to the firm is the true cost.

(c) The firm does not change its dividend, the risk complexion of its assets, or its degree of financial leverage.

(d) The firm pays a current dividend of $3 per share.

5. K-Far Stores has launched an expansion program which should result in the saturation of the Bay Area marketing region of California in six years. As a result, the company is predicting a growth in earnings of 12 percent for three years, 6 percent for years four through six, after which it expects constant earnings forever. The company expects to increase its dividend per share, now $1, in keeping with this growth pattern. Currently, the market price of the stock is $25 per share. Estimate the company's cost of equity capital.

6. The Manx Company was recently formed to manufacture a new product. It has the following capital structure:

9% Debentures of 1990	$ 6,000,000
7% Preferred stock	2,000,000
Common stock (320,000 shares)	8,000,000
	$16,000,000

The common stock sells for $25 and is expected to pay a $2 dividend this year, which will grow at 10 percent for the foreseeable future. The company has a marginal tax rate of 50 percent. Compute a weighted-average cost of capital.

7. Cohn and Sitwell, Inc., is considering an investment proposal involving the manufacture of special drill bits and other equipment for oil rigs. This is currently regarded as a "hot" area, and the company has certain expertise by virtue of its having a large mechanical-engineering staff. Because of the large outlays required to get into the business, however, management is concerned that Cohn and Sitwell earn a proper return. Since the new venture is believed to be sufficiently different from the company's existing operations, management feels that a required rate of return other than the company's present one should be employed.

The financial manager's staff has identified several companies engaged solely in the manufacture and sale of oil-drilling equipment whose stocks are publicly traded. Over the last five years, the average beta for these companies has been 1.28. Cohn and Sitwell has an all-equity capital structure. The staff believes that 12 percent is a reasonable estimate of the average return on stocks in general for the foreseeable future and that the risk-free rate will be around 6 percent.

(a) On the basis of this information, determine a required rate of return for the project, using the capital-asset pricing model approach.

(b) Is the figure obtained likely to be a realistic estimate of the required rate of return on the project?

8. Benzo Tube Company wishes to evaluate three new investment proposals. It is concerned with the impact of the proposals on its total risk. Consequently, it has determined expected values and standard deviations of the probability distributions of possible net-present values for the possible combinations of existing projects, *E*, and investment proposals under consideration:

Combination	Expected Value of Net-Present Value (in thousands)	Standard Deviation (in thousands)
E	$6,500	$5,250
E, 1	6,800	5,000
E, 2	7,600	8,000
E, 3	7,200	6,500
E, 1, 2	7,900	7,500
E, 1, 3	7,500	5,600
E, 2, 3	8,300	8,500
E, 1, 2, 3	8,600	9,000

Which combination do you feel is most desirable? Which proposals should be accepted? Which should be rejected?

ALBERTS, W. W., and S. H. ARCHER, "Some Evidence on the Effect of Company Size on the Cost of Equity Capital," *Journal of Financial and Quantitative Analysis,* 8 (March 1973), 229–42.

ARCHER, STEPHEN H., and LEROY G. FAERBER, "Firm Size and the Cost of Equity Capital," *Journal of Finance,* 21 (March 1966), 69–84.

BERANEK, WILLIAM, "The Cost of Capital, Capital Budgeting, and the Maximization of Shareholder Wealth," *Journal of Financial and Quantitative Analysis,* 10 (March 1975), 1–21.

————, "A Little More on the Weighted Average Cost of Capital," *Journal of Financial and Quantitative Analysis,* 10 (December 1975), 892–96.

BIERMAN, HAROLD, JR., and JEROME E. HASS, "Capital Budgeting under Uncertainty: A Reformulation," *Journal of Finance,* 28 (March 1973), 119–30.

BRENNAN, MICHAEL J., "A New Look at the Weighted Average Cost of Capital," *Journal of Business Finance,* 5, No. 1 (1973), 24–30.

BRIGHAM, EUGENE F., and KEITH V. SMITH, "The Cost of Capital to the Small Firm," *Engineering Economist,* 13 (Fall 1967), 1–26.

ELTON, EDWIN J., and MARTIN J. GRUBER, "The Cost of Retained Earnings—Implications of Share Repurchase," *Industrial Management Review,* 9 (Spring 1968), 87–104.

GORDON, MYRON J., *The Investment, Financing and Valuation of the Corporation.* Homewood, Ill.: Richard D. Irwin, 1962.

GORDON, MYRON J., and PAUL J. HALPERN, "Cost of Capital for a Division of a Firm," *Journal of Finance,* 29 (September 1974), 1153–63.

HIGGINS, ROBERT C., and LAWRENCE D. SCHALL, "Corporate Bankruptcy and Conglomerate Merger," *Journal of Finance,* 30 (March 1975), 93–114.

LERNER, EUGENE M., and ALFRED RAPPAPORT, "Limit DCF in Capital Budgeting," *Harvard Business Review,* 46 (July–August 1968), 133–39.

LEWELLEN, WILBUR G., *The Cost of Capital.* Belmont, Calif.: Wadsworth, 1969.

LoCASCIO, VINCENT R., "The Cost of Capital in an Uncertain Universe," *Financial Executive,* 38 (October 1970), 70–78.

MYERS, STEWART C., "The Application of Finance Theory to Public Utility Rate Cases," *Bell Journal of Economics and Management Science,* 3 (Spring 1972), 58–97.

NANTELL, TIMOTHY J. and C. ROBERT CARLSON, "The Cost of Capital as a Weighted Average," *Journal of Finance,* 30 (December 1975), 1343–55.

OFER, AHARON R., "Investors' Expectations of Earnings Growth, Their Accuracy and Effects on the Structure of Realized Rates of Return," *Journal of Finance,* 30 (May 1975), 509–23.

PORTERFIELD, JAMES T. S., *Investment Decisions and Capital Costs.* Englewood Cliffs, N.J.: Prentice-Hall, 1965.

REILLY, RAYMOND R. and WILLIAM E. WECKER, "On the Weighted Average Cost of Capital," *Journal of Financial and Quantitative Analysis,* 8 (January 1973), 123–26.

ROBICHEK, ALEXANDER A., and STEWART C. MYERS, *Optimal Financing Decisions.* Englewood Cliffs, N.J.: Prentice-Hall, 1965.

ROBICHEK, ALEXANDER A., DONALD G. OGILVIE, and JOHN D. C. ROACH, "Capital Budgeting: A Pragmatic Approach," *Financial Executive,* 37 (April 1969), 26–38.

SOLOMON, EZRA, "Measuring a Company's Cost of Capital," *Journal of Business,* 28 (October 1955), 240–52.

VAN HORNE, JAMES C., *The Function and Analysis of Capital Market Rates.* Englewood Cliffs, N.J.: Prentice-Hall, 1970.

V Capital Structure and Dividend Policy

I'M going home at 2:50.

The Concept of Leverage

17

Leverage may be defined as the employment of an asset or funds for which the firm pays a fixed cost or fixed return. The fixed cost or return may be thought of as the fulcrum of a lever. When revenues less variable costs or earnings before interest and taxes exceed the fixed cost or fixed return, positive or favorable leverage results. When they do not, the result is unfavorable leverage. In this chapter, we explore the principles of operating and financial leverage, both individually and jointly. It is important to point out that our discussion of financial leverage is only in terms of the contractual, or explicit, costs associated with leverage. In the next chapter we take up the implicit, or opportunity, costs associated with financial leverage.

Have to spend money to make money

OPERATING LEVERAGE

Operating leverage occurs anytime a firm has fixed costs that must be met regardless of volume. In the very long run, of course, all costs are variable. Consequently, our analysis necessarily involves the short run. We employ assets with a fixed cost in the hope that volume will produce revenues more than sufficient to cover all fixed and variable costs. One of the more dramatic examples of operating leverage is in the airline industry, where a large portion of total costs are fixed. Beyond a certain break-even load factor, each additional passenger represents essentially straight profit to the airline. With fixed costs, the percentage change in profits accompanying a change in volume is greater than the percentage change in volume. This occurrence is known as operating leverage. Operating leverage may be studied by means of a break-even, or cost-volume-profit, analysis.

Break-even analysis

To illustrate break-even analysis, consider a firm that produces a quality testing machine that sells for $50 a unit. The company has annual fixed costs of $100,000, and variable costs are $25 a unit regardless of the volume sold. We wish to study the relationship between total costs and total revenues. One means for doing so is shown in the break-even chart in Figure 17-1, which depicts the relationship between profits, fixed costs, variable costs, and volume. By *profits,* we mean operating profits before taxes, excluding interest and other income and expenses.

The intersection of the total costs line with the total revenue line represents the break-even point. The fixed costs that must be recovered from the sales dollar after the deduction of variable costs deter-

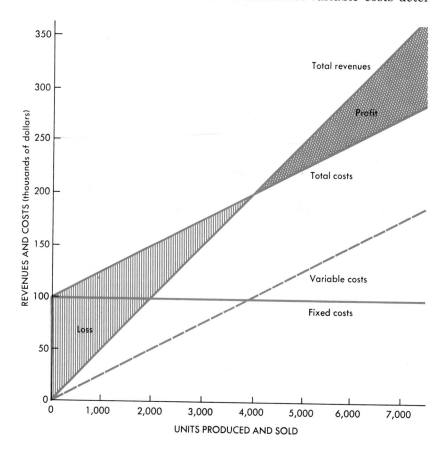

FIG. 17 · 1

Break-even analysis:
original conditions

mine the volume necessary to break even. In Figure 17-1, this break-even point is 4,000 units of output. At the break-even point, variable costs plus fixed costs equal total revenue:

$$F + V(X) = P(X) \qquad (17\text{-}1)$$

where F = fixed costs
  V = variable costs per unit
  X = volume of output (in units)
  P = price per unit

Rearranging Eq. (17-1), the break-even point is

$$X = F/(P - V)$$
$$= 100{,}000/(50 - 25) = 4{,}000$$

For each additional increment of volume above the break-even point, there is increasing profit represented by the cross-hatched area in the figure. Likewise, as volume falls below the break-even point, there are increasing losses, represented by the lined area. Table 17-1 shows the profit for various levels of volume. We see that the closer the volume to the break-even point, the greater the percentage change in profit in relation to a percentage change in volume.

TABLE 17·1

Relation between Profit and Volume

Volume (in thousand units)	0	1	2	3	4	5	6	7
Operating profit (in thousand dollars)	−$100	−$75	−$50	−$25	0	$25	$50	$75

The degree of operating leverage of a firm at a particular level of output is simply the percentage change in profits over the percentage change in output that causes the change in profits. Thus,

$$\text{Degree of operating leverage at } X \text{ units} = \frac{\text{Percentage change in profits}}{\text{Percentage change in output}} \qquad (17\text{-}2)$$

Rather than calculate the percentages involved directly, a simple formula is available for expressing the relationship:

$$\text{DOL at } X \text{ units} = \frac{X(P - V)}{X(P - V) - F} \qquad (17\text{-}3)$$

Suppose we wished to determine the degree of operating leverage for 5,000 units of output for our hypothetical example firm:

$$\text{DOL at 5,000 units} = \frac{5,000(50 - 25)}{5,000(50 - 25) - 100,000} = 5$$

For 6,000 units of output, we have

$$\text{DOL at 6,000 units} = \frac{6,000(50 - 25)}{6,000(50 - 25) - 100,000} = 3$$

We see then that the further the level of output is from the break-even point, the lower the degree of operating leverage.

A break-even chart, like that in Figure 17-1, tells us the relationship between operating profits and volume. The greater the ratio of price to variable costs per unit, the greater the absolute sensitivity of profits to volume and the greater the degree of operating leverage for all levels of

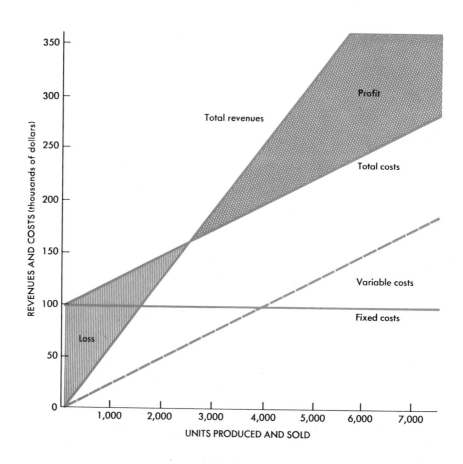

FIG. 17 · 2

Break-even analysis: price increase

[handwritten margin note: Highest degree of leverage at breakeven / larger # smaller leverage]

output. However, a change in volume is not the only factor that affects profits. Indeed, a change in selling price, in variable cost per unit, or in fixed costs will affect profits. In the light of Figure 17-1, we examine a favorable change in each of these factors, all other factors held constant.

Increase in price. Figure 17-2 shows the change for an increase in price from $50 to $65 per unit. We see that the break-even point is reduced from 4,000 units to 2,500 units as a result of this price increase; and, of course, profits are $15 per unit greater for each level of volume.

Decrease in fixed costs. For a decrease in fixed costs from $100,000 to $50,000, with the original $50 per unit price, the break-even point is reduced even further. Figure 17-3 illustrates this case. The break-even point now is 2,000 units, and total profits are increased by $50,000 for all levels of volume.

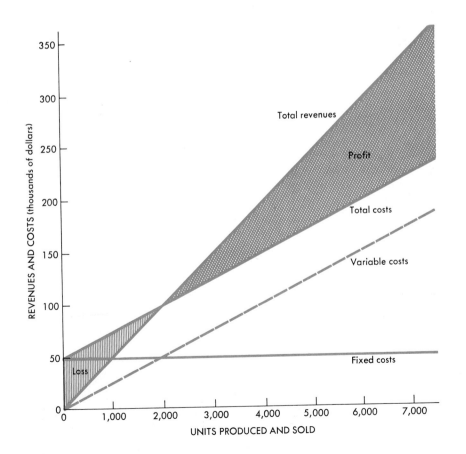

FIG. 17 · 3

Break-even analysis: decrease in fixed costs

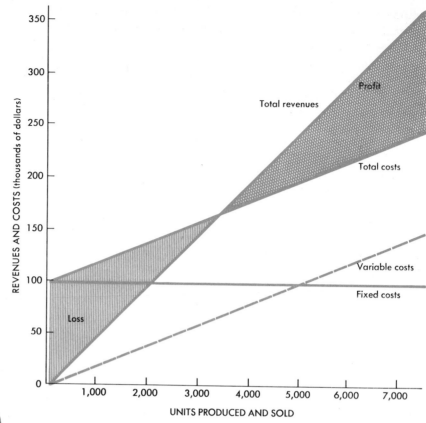

FIG. 17 · 4
Break-even analysis:
decrease in variable costs

Decrease in variable costs. Finally, Figure 17-4 shows the change when variable costs per unit are lowered from $25 to $20. The break-even point is lowered to 3,333 units, and profit is $5 greater per unit of output. Table 17-2 summarizes the profits for various levels of

TABLE 17 · 2

Relation between Profits and Volume

Volume (in units)	Original case	Price ($65)	Fixed Costs ($50,000)	Variable Costs ($20)	All Three
0	−$100	−$100	−$ 50	−$100	−$ 50
2,000	− 50	− 20	0	− 40	40
4,000	0	60	50	20	130
6,000	50	140	100	80	220
8,000	100	220	150	140	310

Profits (in thousands)

volume under the alternatives cited. The last column of the table shows the relationship between profits and volume if all three of the changes occur simultaneously.

Despite a number of limitations that we shall take up shortly, break-even analysis gives management a good deal of information about the operating and business risks of the company. Given an approximate break-even point, management can compare fluctuations in expected future volume with this point to ascertain the stability of profits. Knowledge of this stability is important to the financial manager in determining the ability of the firm to service debt. Such an analysis is important also when he plans the acquisition of assets that will require additional fixed costs. The expected future trend and stability of volume, together with the ratio of expected price to expected variable costs per unit, will bear heavily upon the decision to increase fixed costs. As we saw in the previous discussion, break-even analysis is useful in determining the change in profits that accompanies a change in pricing and costs. Depending upon the elasticity of demand and the ratio of price to variable costs, price cutting to boost volume may or may not be worthwhile. Break-even analysis provides us with a means for deciding.

Limitations

Although break-even analysis seems simple enough in concept—and this simplicity is one of its virtues—its effectiveness is limited in several ways. These limitations must be recognized and the method modified if it is to provide meaningful results. One assumption of the method is that there is a constant price and variable cost per unit, irrespective of volume. In many cases, the firm's sales volume may influence the market price of a product. For example, increased output may lead to a decline in market price. Moreover, variable costs are likely to increase as the firm approaches full capacity; for example, less efficient labor or costly overtime help may have to be used. These shortcomings of break-even analysis can be remedied by making the relationships between total sales and volume, and total costs and volume, nonlinear, to correspond with economic reality. Figure 17-5 (p. 364) shows an example of these curvilinear relationships.

Another difficulty with break-even analysis is the classification of costs as fixed or variable. In practice, many costs defy clear categorization because they are partly fixed and partly variable. These costs are known as semivariable costs. Moreover, we assume that costs classified as fixed remain unchanged over the entire volume range, but this range is limited by the immediate physical capacity of the firm. A steel company may have an idle marginal plant that it can put into operation if it needs additional output, but putting the plant into operation

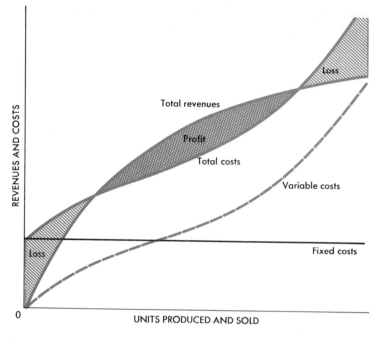

FIG. 17 · 5

Break-even analysis:
curvilinear relationship

may increase fixed costs. If the range of volume considered includes this plant, fixed costs would not be constant but would increase in a step function manner at the point in volume at which the plant was to be reopened. For most situations, however, new physical capacity must be constructed if volume is to be increased beyond some critical point. Consequently, a break-even analysis is relevant only for volume up to that point.

Another problem relates to multiple products. Break-even analysis probably is best suited for a one-product analysis. When there are multiple products, a single break-even analysis cannot be used unless the product mix remains unchanged. When the product mix does change, it may be necessary to prepare a separate break-even analysis for each product. Here, allocating expenses that are common to all product lines may present a problem.

The information inputs for break-even analysis usually are based upon historical relationships. However, these relationships may not be particularly stable over time. For extreme volume changes, there may be no historical precedent.

Finally, we must note that the short-term time horizon in break-even analysis is a limitation for longer-range planning. The benefits realized from certain expenditures, such as capital expenditures and research and development outlays, are not likely to be realized during the period of time encompassed by most break-even analyses. A break-even analysis would not justify these expenditures, but they may well be necessary to the continued life of the firm. Despite the

many limitations of break-even analysis, however, it can be an important tool to the financial manager if it is employed properly and if it is
reasonably appropriate to the situation.

365
Chapter 17
The Concept of Leverage

Financial leverage, as defined before, involves the use of funds obtained at a fixed cost in the hope of increasing the return to common
stockholders. Favorable or positive leverage is said to occur when the
firm earns more on the assets purchased with the funds than the fixed
cost of their use. Unfavorable or negative leverage occurs when the
firm does not earn as much as the funds cost. Again, it is important to
point out that we do not consider the opportunity costs associated with
debt in this chapter but do in the next. For our purposes in this chapter, financial leverage, or "trading on the equity" as it is called, is
judged in terms of its effect upon earnings per share to common stockholders. We are interested in determining the relationship between
earnings per share and earnings before interest and taxes (EBIT)
under various financing alternatives and the indifference points between these alternatives.

Calculation of earnings per share

To illustrate a break-even analysis of leverage, suppose Cherokee
Tire Company with long-term capitalization of $10 million, consisting
entirely of common stock, wishes to raise another $5 million for ex-
pansion through one of three possible financing plans. The company
may finance with (1) all common stock; (2) all debt, at 9 percent interest; or (3) all preferred stock with a 7 percent dividend. Present
annual earnings before interest and taxes are $1,400,000, the federal
income tax rate is 50 percent, and 200,000 shares of stock are presently outstanding. Common stock can be sold at $50 per share under
financing option 1, or 100,000 additional shares of stock.

In order to determine the EBIT break-even, or indifference, points
between the various financing alternatives, we begin by calculating
earnings per share for some hypothetical level of EBIT. Suppose we
wished to know what earnings per share would be under the three financing plans if EBIT were $2 million. The calculations are shown in
Table 17-3. We note that interest on debt is deducted before taxes,
while preferred-stock dividends are deducted after taxes. As a result,
earnings available to common stockholders are higher under the debt
alternative than they are under the preferred-stock alternative, despite the fact that the interest rate on debt is higher than the preferred-stock dividend rate.

TABLE 17·3

	All Common	All Debt	All Preferred
Earnings before interest and taxes (hypothetical)	$2,000,000	$2,000,000	$2,000,000
Interest	—	450,000	—
Earnings before taxes	$2,000,000	$1,550,000	$2,000,000
Income taxes	1,000,000	775,000	1,000,000
Earnings after taxes	$1,000,000	$ 775,000	$1,000,000
Preferred stock dividend	—	—	350,000
Earnings available to common stockholders	$1,000,000	$ 775,000	$ 650,000
Number of shares	300,000	200,000	200,000
Earnings per share	$3.33	$3.88	$3.25

Break-even, or indifference, analysis

Given the information in Table 17-3, we are able to construct a break-even or indifference chart similar to what we did for operating leverage. On the horizontal axis we plot earnings before interest and taxes (EBIT), and on the vertical axis, earnings per share (EPS). For each financing alternative, we must draw a straight line to reflect EPS for all possible levels of EBIT. To do so, we need two datum points for each alternative. The first is the EPS calculated for some hypothetical level of EBIT. For $2 million in EBIT, we see in Table 17-3 that earnings per share are $3.33, $3.88, and $3.25 for the common, debt, and preferred-stock financing alternatives. We simply plot these earnings per share at the $2 million mark in EBIT. It is important to recognize that it does not matter which hypothetical level of EBIT we choose for calculating EPS. Assuming good graph paper, one level is as good as the next.

The second datum point is simply the EBIT necessary to cover all fixed financial costs for a particular financing plan, and it is plotted on the horizontal axis. For the common-stock alternative, there are no fixed costs, so the intercept on the horizontal axis is zero. For the debt alternative, we must have EBIT of $450,000 to cover interest charges; so $450,000 becomes the horizontal axis intercept. For the preferred-stock alternative, we must divide total annual dividends by one minus the tax rate in order to obtain the EBIT necessary to cover these dividends. Thus, we need $700,000 in EBIT to cover $350,000 in preferred-stock dividends, assuming a 50 percent tax rate. Again, preferred dividends are deducted after taxes, so it takes more in before-tax earnings to cover them than it does to cover interest. Given the horizontal axis intercepts and earnings per share for some hypothetical level of EBIT, we draw a straight line through the two sets of points. The break-even, or indifference, chart for Cherokee Tire Company is shown in Figure 17-6.

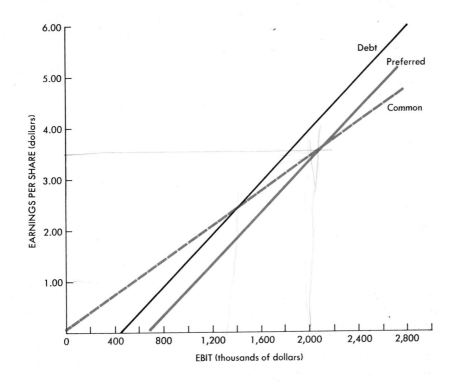

FIG. 17 · 6

Indifference chart
for three
financing alternatives

We see from the figure that the earnings-per-share indifference point between the debt and common-stock financing alternatives is $1,350,-000 in EBIT. If EBIT is below that point, the common-stock alternative will provide higher earnings per share; above that point the debt alternative is best. The indifference point between the preferred-stock and the common-stock alternatives is $2,100,000 in EBIT. Above it, the preferred-stock alternative is favored with respect to earnings per share; below it, the common-stock alternative is best. We note that there is no indifference point between the debt and preferred-stock alternatives. The debt alternative dominates for all levels of EBIT and by a constant amount of earnings per share, namely $0.63.

The degree of financial leverage at a particular level of EBIT is simply the percentage change in earnings per share in relation to a percentage change in EBIT. To illustrate, suppose EBIT were $2 million in our example. A $1 million increase would raise earnings per share from $3.88 to $6.38, or by approximately 64.4 percent. When this percentage increase is taken over the percentage increase in EBIT, 50 percent, the degree of financial leverage is found to be 1.29. An easier method for determining the degree of financial leverage is

$$\text{Degree of financial leverage at EBIT of } y = \frac{EBIT}{EBIT - C} \qquad (17\text{-}4)$$

where C as before is the annual interest expense or preferred-stock dividend on a before-tax basis. For our example, using the debt financing alternative at $2 million in EBIT, we have

$$\text{DFL at \$2 million} = \frac{2,000,000}{2,000,000 - 450,000} = 1.29$$

For the preferred-stock financing alternative, the degree of financial leverage is

$$\text{DFL at \$2 million} = \frac{2,000,000}{2,000,000 - 700,000} = 1.54$$

Here, a 100 percent increase in EBIT would result in a 154 percent increase in earnings per share. The higher degree of financial leverage for preferred stock is attributable, of course, to the higher financial costs on a before-tax basis.

Through an EBIT–EPS analysis, we can evaluate various financing plans or degrees of financial leverage with respect to their effect upon earnings per share. The presentation in this chapter has been devoted primarily to the construction of indifference charts as well as to providing other tools for analyzing financial leverage. In Chapter 18, the use of this information is considered in the overall context of determining an appropriate capital structure. At that time, implicit as well as explicit costs will be considered.

COMBINED EFFECT OF TWO TYPES OF LEVERAGE

When financial leverage is combined with operating leverage, the effect of a change in revenues on earnings per share is magnified. The combination of the two increases the dispersion and risk of possible earnings per share. To determine the effect of a change in units of output on earnings per share, we combine the equation for the degree of operating leverage, Eq. (17-3), with that for the degree of financial leverage, Eq. (17-4). Because EBIT is simply $X(P - V) - F$, where X is the units of output, P is price per unit, V is variable cost per unit, and

F is fixed costs, Eq. (17-4) can be expressed as

$$\frac{\text{EBIT}}{\text{EBIT} - C} = \frac{X(P - V) - F}{X(P - V) - F - C} \tag{17-5}$$

Combining this equation with that for the degree of operating leverage, Eq. (17-3), we obtain

$$\text{Degree of operating and financial leverage at } X \text{ units} = \frac{X(P - V)}{X(P - V) - F} \cdot \frac{X(P - V) - F}{X(P - V) - F - C}$$

$$= \frac{X(P - V)}{X(P - V) - F - C} \tag{17-6}$$

We see that the amount of fixed financial costs, C, increases the degree of combined leverage over what it would be with operating leverage alone.

Suppose that our hypothetical example firm used to illustrate operating leverage had $200,000 in debt at 8 percent interest. Recall that the selling price was $50 a unit, variable cost $25 a unit, and annual fixed costs were $100,000. Assume that the tax rate is 50 percent, that the number of shares of common stock outstanding is 10,000 shares, and that we wish to determine the combined degree of leverage at 8,000 units of output. Therefore,

$$\text{DO \& FL at 8,000 units} = \frac{8,000(50 - 25)}{8,000(50 - 25) - 100,000 - 16,000} = 2.38$$

Thus, a 10 percent increase in the number of units produced and sold would result in a 23.8 percent increase in earnings per share. Earnings per share at the two levels of output are:

	8,000 units	8,800 units
Sales less total variable costs	$200,000	$220,000
Fixed costs	100,000	100,000
EBIT	$100,000	$120,000
Interest	16,000	16,000
Profit before taxes	$ 84,000	$104,000
Taxes	42,000	52,000
Profit after taxes	$42,000	$52,000
Shares outstanding	10,000	10,000
Earnings per share	$4.20	$5.20

This degree of combined leverage compares with 2.00 for operating leverage alone. We see then the relative effect of adding financial leverage on top of operating leverage.

Operating and financial leverage can be combined in a number of different ways to obtain a desirable degree of overall leverage and risk of the firm. High operating risk can be offset with low financial risk and vice versa. The proper overall level of risk involves a tradeoff between total risk (the product of operating and financial risk) and expected return. This tradeoff must be made in keeping with the objective of the firm. The discussion here is meant to show how certain tools can be employed to provide information on the two types of leverage and their combined effect.

SUMMARY

Operating leverage may be defined as the employment of an asset with a fixed cost in the hope that sufficient revenue will be generated to cover all fixed and variable costs. We can study the operating leverage of a firm by using a break-even graph. This graph enables us to analyze the relationship between profits, volume, fixed costs, variable costs, and prices. By varying these factors, management may determine the sensitivity of profits and, in so doing, obtain a better understanding of the operating risk of the firm. Whereas break-even analysis is a very useful tool, certain limitations to its effectiveness must be recognized.

Financial leverage is defined as the use of funds with a fixed cost in order to increase earnings per share. By using an indifference chart, we can study the relationship between earnings before interest and taxes (EBIT) and earnings per share under various alternative methods of financing. The degree of sensitivity of earnings per share to EBIT is dependent upon the explicit cost of the method of financing, the number of shares of common stock to be issued, and the nearness to the indifference point. Although an EBIT–EPS chart is useful in analyzing the explicit costs of various methods of financing, it does not take into account any implicit costs inherent in the use of a specific method of financing.

For both operating and financial leverage, we can determine the degree of leverage. In the first case, we relate the change in profits that accompanies a change in output; in the second, the change in earnings per share that accompanies a change in earnings before interest and taxes. By combining the two formulas, we can determine the effect of a change in output upon earnings per share. In this way, we can better depict the relative influence of the two types of leverage.

1. Define the concept of *operating leverage*.

2. Can the concept of operating leverage be analyzed quantitatively? Is it a qualitative concept? Explain.

3. Define the concept of *financial leverage*.

4. Discuss the similarites and differences of financial and operating leverage.

5. Can the concept of financial leverage be analyzed quantitatively? Explain.

6. The EBIT-EPS chart suggests that the higher the debt ratio, the higher the earnings per share for any level of EBIT above the indifference point. Why do firms choose financing alternatives that do not maximize EPS?

7. Classify the following short-run manufacturing costs as either typically fixed or typically variable. Which costs are variable at management's discretion? Are any of these costs "fixed" in the long run?

    (a) Insurance *Fixed*
    (b) Direct labor ✔
    (c) Property taxes *F*
    (d) Interest expense *F*
    (e) R & D *F*
    (f) Advertising ✔

    (g) Raw materials ✔
    (h) Bad-debt loss ✔
    (i) Depletion ✔
    (j) Depreciation *F*
    (k) Maintenance ✔

8. Define the *break-even point*. Use this definition to explain the probable effect of an increase in each of the costs of Question 7. What would be the effect on the break-even point of the following:
    (a) Increased selling price ✔
    (b) Increase in the minimum wage ✔
    (c) Change from straight-line to accelerated depreciation
    (d) Increased sales *Stay Same*
    (e) A 5 percent surtax on corporate profits
    (f) A liberalized credit policy ✔

9. For what type of industry might break-even analysis be most suited? Why? Give an example.

1. The Madison Company earns, after taxes, $2,400 on sales of $88,000. The average tax rate of the company is 40 percent. The company's only product sells for $20, of which $15 is variable cost.
    (a) What is the monthly fixed cost of the Madison Company?
    (b) What is its break-even point in units? In dollars?

2. What would be the effect of the following on the break-even point of the Madison Company (Problem 1)?
   (a) An increase in price of $5 per unit (assume that volume is constant).
   (b) A decrease in fixed costs of $2,000.
   (c) A decrease in variable costs of $1 per unit and an increase in fixed costs of $6,000.

3. The D. T. Crary Horse Hotel has a capacity to stable fifty horses. The fee for stabling a horse is $100 per month. Maintenance, depreciation, property taxes, and other fixed costs total $1,200 per month. Variable costs per horse are $10 per month for hay and bedding and $9 per month for grain. Income is taxed at a 40 percent rate.
   (a) Determine the break-even point.
   (b) Compute the annual profits if an average of forty horses are stabled.

4. The D. T. Crary Horse Hotel (Problem 3) can be acquired for $100,000. Generate a range of earnings (EBIT–EPS) chart for the following financing alternatives:

	Debt	Preferred stock	Common stock
Alt. I	0	0	5,000 shares @ $20
Alt. II	25,000 @ 6%	0	3,750 shares @ $20
Alt. III	50,000 @ 7%	0	2,500 shares @ $20
Alt. IV	0	500 shares of $100 par, 7% dividend	2,500 shares @ $20

5. Assuming the occupancy rate for the D. T. Crary Horse Hotel (Problems 3 and 4) is expected to fluctuate between 60 percent and 100 percent, recommend the financing alternative in Problem 4 that you would use. Justify your choice.

6. The Botts Corporation is a new firm that wishes to determine an appropriate capital structure. It can issue 8 percent debt and 6 percent preferred and has a 50 percent tax rate. The initial capitalization of the firm will be $5 million, and common will be sold at $20 per share. The possible capital structures are:

Plan	Debt	Preferred	Equity
1	0	0	100%
2	30%	0	70%
3	30%	20%	50%
4	50%	0	50%
5	50%	20%	30%

(a) Construct an EBIT–EPS chart for the five plans.

(b) Determine the indifference points.

(c) Is the maximization of EPS at a given EBIT the sole function of a firm's capital structure? If not, are the points determined in (b) truly "indifference" points?

7. The Last Gasp Water Company sells distilled water by the gallon. The price per gallon is 75¢ and variable costs are 40¢ per gallon. Fixed costs involved in production are $1 million. The company has $5 million of 8 percent bonds outstanding.

(a) Compute the degree of operating leverage at 3 million gallons of water produced and sold, at 4 million gallons, at 5 million gallons, at 6 million gallons, and at 7 million gallons.

(b) Compute the degree of financial leverage at the above gallons of water produced and sold. Assume that EBIT is price minus variable cost per gallon times the number of gallons, less the amount of fixed costs.

(c) Compute the degree of combined operating and financial leverage at the above gallons of water produced and sold.

(d) What generalizations can you make?

SELECTED REFERENCES

CROWNINGSHIELD, GERALD R., and GEORGE L. BATTISTA, "Cost-Volume-Profit Analysis in Planning and Control," *N.A.A. Bulletin*, 45 (July 1963), 3–15.

HASLEM, JOHN A., "Leverage Effects on Corporate Earnings," *Arizona Review*, 19 (March 1970), 7–11.

HELFERT, ERICH A., *Techniques of Financial Analysis*, 3rd ed., Chapter 2. Homewood, Ill.: Richard D. Irwin, 1972.

HOBBS, J. B., "Volume-Mix-Price Cost Budget Variance Analysis: A Proper Approach," *Accounting Review*, 39 (October 1964), 905–13.

HUNT, PEARSON, "A Proposal for Precise Definitions of 'Trading on the Equity' and 'Leverage,'" *Journal of Finance*, 16 (September 1961), 377–86.

JAEDICKE, ROBERT K., and ALEXANDER A. ROBICHEK, "Cost-Volume-Profit Analysis under Conditions of Uncertainty," *Accounting Review*, 39 (October 1964), 917–26.

LEV, BARUCH, "On the Association between Operating Leverage and Risk," *Journal of Financial and Quantitative Analysis*, 9 (September 1974), 627–42.

PERCIVAL, JOHN R., Operating Leverage and Risk," *Journal of Business Research*, 2 (April 1974), 223–27.

REILLY, Frank K., and ROGER BENT, "A Specification, Measurement, and Analysis of Operating Leverage," Working Paper, University of Wyoming, 1974.

SHALIT, SOL S., "On the Mathematics of Financial Leverage," *Financial Management*, 4 (Spring 1975), 57–66.

18 Capital Structure of the Firm

In the preceding chapter, we considered financial leverage as it pertains to explicit costs. If one were to look only at these costs, there would be a tendency to take on very large amounts of debt in relation to the equity base of the firm. As long as the return on assets exceeded the interest cost on the debt used to finance such investments, leverage supposedly would be "favorable." But would it be favorable? To answer this question, we must explore the opportunity costs of debt. The critical question is whether financial leverage jeopardizes the return that investors in a firm's common stock expect. Put another way, do increasing amounts of debt make their investment more risky and, if so, what is the effect upon valuation?

To explore the question of debt opportunity costs, we first take up the theory of capital structure. Although necessarily this discussion is somewhat abstract, it provides rich insights into valuation. As we shall see, considerable controversy surrounds the question of optimal capital structure. Despite the unsettled nature of the matter, we hope that this presentation will provide the conceptual backdrop necessary to properly evaluate capital structure decisions. After consideration of the theory of capital structure, we move on to consider how a firm in practice can determine a capital structure suitable for its particular situation. Very much a part of this consideration is an analysis of a firm's cash-flow ability to service fixed charges. The reader will note that this discussion is far more practically oriented than our discussion of the theory. The change in focus is intentional as we move from a conceptual framework to applying the principles of such a framework to company decisions.

Financial risk defined

Whereas the investment decision determines the basic business risk of a firm, the financing decision determines its financial risk. Broadly defined, *financial risk* encompasses both the risk of possible insolvency and the variability in the earnings available to common stockholders. As a firm increases the proportion of debt, lease commitments, and preferred stock in its capital structure, fixed charges increase. All other things being the same, the probability that the firm will be unable to meet these fixed charges increases also. As the firm continues to lever itself, the probability of cash insolvency, which may lead to legal bankruptcy, increases. To illustrate this notion of financial risk, suppose that two firms have different degrees of leverage but are identical in every other respect. Each has expected annual cash earnings of $80,000 before interest and taxes. However, Firm A has no debt, while Firm B has $500,000 worth of 6% perpetual bonds outstanding. Thus, the total annual financial charges for Firm B are $30,000, whereas Firm A has no financial charges. If cash earnings for both firms happen to be 75 percent lower than expected—namely, $20,000—Firm B will be unable to cover its financial charges with cash earnings. We see, then, that the probability of cash insolvency increases with the financial charges incurred by the firm.

The second aspect of financial risk involves the relative dispersion of income available to common stockholders. To illustrate, suppose that the expected future annual operating incomes over the next five years for Firms A and B were subjective random variables where the expected values of the probability distributions were each $80,000 and the standard deviations, $40,000. As before, assume that Firm A has no debt, while Firm B has $500,000 in 6% bonds. If, for simplicity, we abstract from federal income taxes, the expected value of earnings available to common stockholders would be $80,000 for Firm A and $50,000 for Firm B. Because the standard deviation about the expected values is the same for both firms, the relative dispersion of expected earnings available to common stockholders is greater for Firm B than for Firm A. For Firm A,

$$\text{Coefficient of variation} = \frac{\$40,000}{\$80,000} = 0.50$$

while for Firm B,

$$\text{Coefficient of variation} = \frac{\$40,000}{\$50,000} = 0.80$$

Graphically, the relationship is shown in Figure 18-1. We see that the degree of dispersion from the expected value of earnings available to common stockholders is the same for both firms but that the expected value of these earnings is greater for Firm A than for Firm B. As a result, the relative dispersion, as measured by the coefficient of variation, is less for Firm A.

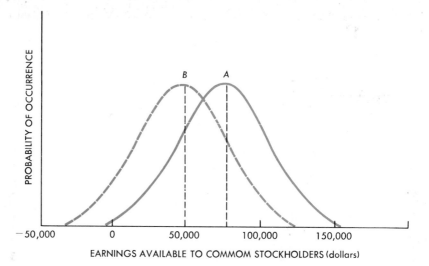

FIG. 18 · 1

Probability distribution
of earnings available
to common stockholders

The disperion in earnings available to common stockholders is to be distinguished from the dispersion of operating income, known as business risk. In our example above, both firms had the same degree of business risk, as defined, because the coefficient of variation of expected future operating income was the same:

$$\text{Coefficient of variation} = \frac{\$40,000}{\$80,000} = 0.50$$

Only in the degree of financial risk did the two firms differ. In summary, we regard financial risk as encompassing the volatility of earnings available to common stockholders as well as the probability of insolvency. Both aspects are related directly to the dispersion of expected operating income, or the business risk, of the firm.

The question we wish to explore first is whether or not a firm can affect its total valuation (debt plus equity) as well as its cost of capital by changing its financing mix. Our attention is directed to the total valuation of the firm and its cost of capital when the ratio of debt to equity, or degree of leverage, is varied.

Assumptions and definitions

So that the analysis that follows can be presented as simply as possible, we make the following facilitating assumptions:

1. We assume that there are no income taxes. This assumption is removed later.
2. The ratio of debt to equity for a firm is changed by issuing debt to repurchase stock or issuing stock to pay off debt. In other words, a change in capital structure is effected immediately. In this regard, we assume no transaction costs.
3. The firm has a policy of paying 100 percent of its earnings in dividends. Thus, we abstract from the dividend decision.
4. The expected future operating earnings for each company are the same for all investors in the market.
5. The operating earnings of the firm are not expected to grow. The expected operating earnings for all future periods are the same as present operating earnings.
6. The acceptance of an investment proposal or combination of investment proposals does not change the total business-risk complexion of the firm—in other words, business risk is held constant.

Using Solomon's symbols and some of his examples, we are concerned with the following three rates:[1]

$$k_i = \frac{F}{B} = \frac{\text{Annual interest charges}}{\text{Market value of debt outstanding}} \qquad (18\text{-}1)$$

In this equation, k_i is the yield on the company's debt, assuming this debt to be perpetual.

$$k_e = \frac{E}{S} = \frac{\text{Earnings available to common stockholders}}{\text{Market value of stock outstanding}} \qquad (18\text{-}2)$$

Given our restrictive assumptions of a firm whose earnings are not expected to grow and that has a 100 percent dividend-payout ratio, the earnings/price ratio represents the market rate of discount that equates the present value of the stream of expected future dividends with the current market price of the stock. This is not to say that it should be used as a general rule to depict the cost of equity capital. (See Chapter 16). We use it only because of its simplicity in illustrating the theory of capital structure. The final rate we consider is

$$k_o = \frac{O}{V} = \frac{\text{Net operating earnings}}{\text{Total market value of the firm}} \qquad (18\text{-}3)$$

[1] Ezra Solomon, *The Theory of Financial Management* (New York: Columbia University Press, 1963), Chapters 7–9.

where $V = B + S$. Here, k_o is an overall capitalization rate for the firm. It is defined as the weighted-average cost of capital, and may also be expressed as

$$k_o = k_i\left(\frac{B}{B + S}\right) + k_e\left(\frac{S}{B + S}\right) \qquad (18\text{-}4)$$

Our concern will be with what happens to k_i, k_e, and k_o when the degree of leverage, as denoted by the ratio B/S, increases.

Net income approach

Durand has proposed two approaches to the valuation of the earnings of a company: the net income approach (NI) and the net operating income approach (NOI).[2] These approaches represent the extremes in valuing the firm with respect to the degree of leverage. As they give us a basis for additional discussion, we consider them in turn. To illustrate the net income approach, assume that a firm has $3,000 in debt at 5 percent interest, that the expected value of annual net operating earnings is $1,000, and that the equity-capitalization rate, k_e, is 10 percent. Given this information, the value of the firm may be calculated as

O	Net operating earnings	$ 1,000
F	Interest	150
E	Earnings available to common stockholders	$ 850
k_e	Equity-capitalization rate (divide by)	0.10
S	Market value of stock	$ 8,500
B	Market value of debt	3,000
V	Total value of firm	$11,500

With the net income approach, earnings available to common stockholders are capitalized at a constant rate, k_e. The implied overall capitalization rate in the above example is

$$k_o = \frac{O}{V} = \frac{\$1,000}{\$11,500} = 8.7 \text{ percent}$$

[2]David Durand, "The Cost of Debt and Equity Funds for Business," in *The Management of Corporate Capital,* Ezra Solomon, ed. (New York: Free Press, 1959), pp. 91–116.

Assume now that the firm increases its debt from \$3,000 to \$6,000 and uses the proceeds of the debt issue to repurchase stock. Also, suppose that the interest rate on debt remains unchanged at 5 percent. The value of the firm then is

O	Net operating earnings	\$ 1,000
F	Interest	300
E	Earnings available to common stockholders	\$ 700
k_e	Equity-capitalization rate (divide by)	0.10
S	Market value of stock	\$ 7,000
B	Market value of debt	6,000
V	Total value of firm	\$13,000

The implied overall capitalization rate now is

$$k_o = \frac{O}{V} = \frac{\$1,000}{\$13,000} = 7.7 \text{ percent}$$

According to the net income approach, the firm is able to increase its total valuation, V, and lower its cost of capital, k_o, as it increases the degree of leverage. As a result, the market price per share increases. To illustrate, assume in our example that the firm with \$3,000 in debt has 850 shares of common stock outstanding. Thus, the market price per share is \$10 a share (\$8,500/850). The firm issues \$3,000 in additional debt and, at the same time, repurchases \$3,000 of stock at \$10 a share, or 300 shares in total. It then has 550 shares outstanding. We saw in the example that the total market value of the firm's stock after the change in capital structure is \$7,000. Therefore, the market price per share is \$7,000/550 = \$12.73, where before it was \$10.

Graphically, the approach is illustrated in Figure 18-2. The degree of leverage, B/S, is plotted along the horizontal axis, while the percentage rate for k_i, k_e, and k_o is on the vertical axis. This graph can be

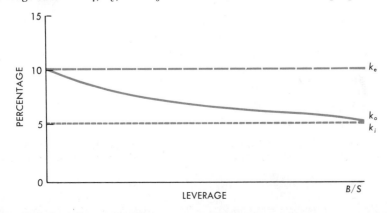

FIG. 18 · 2

Capital costs:
net income approach

constructed based upon the hypothetical examples we have shown. As can be seen, the critical assumptions of the net income approach are that k_i and, more particularly, k_e remain unchanged as the degree of leverage increases. As the proportion of cheaper debt funds in the capital structure is increased, the weighted-average cost of capital, k_o, decreases and approaches the cost of debt, k_i. The optimal capital structure would be the one at which the total value of the firm is greatest and the cost of capital the lowest. At that structure, the market price per share of stock is maximized. Using the net income approach, the optimal capital structure is the one farthest to the right in Figure 18-2. The significance of this approach is that a firm can lower its cost of capital continually and increase its total valuation by the use of debt funds. Again, the critical assumption is that the firm does not become increasingly more risky in the minds of investors and creditors as the degree of leverage is increased.

Net operating income approach

We turn now to the net operating income approach. The assumption here is that the overall capitalization rate of the firm, k_o, is constant for all degrees of leverage. Assume the same example as before but with k_o equal to 10 percent. For $3,000 in debt, we have

O	Net operating income	$ 1,000
k_o	Overall capitalization rate (divide by)	0.10
V	Total value of firm	$10,000
B	Market value of debt	3,000
S	Market value of stock	$ 7,000

The implied equity-capitalization rate in this case is

$$k_e = \frac{E}{S} = \frac{\$850}{\$7,000} = 12.1 \text{ percent}$$

With this approach, net operating income is capitalized at an overall capitalization rate to obtain the total market value of the firm. The market value of the debt then is deducted from the total market value to obtain the market value of the stock.

Suppose, as before, that the firm increases the amount of debt from $3,000 to $6,000 and uses the proceeds of the debt issue to repurchase stock. The valuation of the firm then is

O	Net operating income	$ 1,000
k_o	Overall capitalization rate (divide by)	0.10
V	Total value of firm	$10,000
B	Market value of debt	6,000
S	Market value of stock	$ 4,000

The implied equity-capitalization rate is

$$k_e = \frac{E}{S} = \frac{\$700}{\$4,000} = 17.5 \text{ percent}$$

We see that the equity-capitalization rate, k_e, rises with the degree of leverage. This approach implies that the total valuation of the firm is unaffected by its capital structure. Graphically, the approach is shown in Figure 18-3.

The critical assumption with this approach is that k_o is constant regardless of the degree of leverage. The market capitalizes the value of the firm as a whole; as a result, the breakdown between debt and equity is unimportant. An increase in the use of supposedly "cheaper" debt funds is offset exactly by the increase in the equity-capitalization

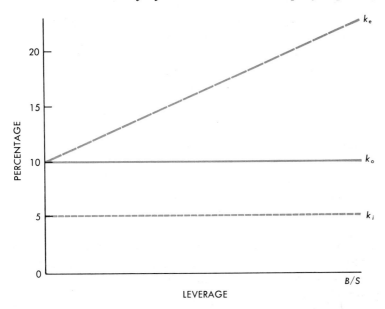

FIG. 18 · 3

Capital costs:
net operating income
approach

rate, k_e. Thus, the weighted average of k_e and k_i remains unchanged for all degrees of leverage. As the firm increases its degree of leverage, it becomes increasingly more risky; and investors penalize the stock by raising the equity-capitalization rate (lowering the P/E ratio) directly in keeping with the increase in the debt-to-equity ratio. As long as k_i remains constant, k_e is a constant linear function of the debt-to-equity ratio.

According to the net operating income approach, the real cost of debt and the real cost of equity are the same—namely, k_o. The cost of debt has two parts: the explicit cost represented by the rate of interest, and the implicit cost, or "hidden" cost, which is represented by the increase in the equity-capitalization rate that accompanies an increase in the proportion of debt to equity. As the cost of capital of the firm cannot be altered through leverage, this approach implies that there is no one optimal capital structure. All capital structures are optimal, for market price per share does not change with leverage. To illustrate, assume again that our example firm with $3,000 in debt has 850 shares of common stock outstanding. The market price per share in this case is $7,000/850 = $8.23. With the $3,000 in additional debt, the firm repurchases $3,000 of stock at $8.23 a share, or 364 shares in total. Therefore, the market price per share after the change in capital structure is $4,000/(850 − 364) = $8.23, the same as before. Thus, capital structure would be a matter of indifference to the investor.

So far, our discussion of the net operating income approach has been purely definitional; it lacks behavioral significance. However, Modigliani and Miller, in their famous 1958 article, offered behavioral support for the independence of the total valuation and the cost of capital of the firm from its capital structure.[3] Before taking up the implications of their position, however, we examine the traditional approach to valuation.

Traditional approach

The traditional approach to valuation and leverage assumes that there is an optimal capital structure and that the firm can increase the total value of the firm through the judicious use of leverage. Actually, this approach encompasses all the ground between the net income approach and the net operating income approach. To illustrate one variation of the approach, assume that our hypothetical firm has $3,000 in debt at 5 percent interest. Assume, however, that the equity-capitalization rate is 11 percent, rather than the 10 percent or 12.1 percent assumed with the net income or net operating income approaches illustrated previously. The valuation of the firm then is

[3]Franco Modigliani and Merton H. Miller, "The Cost of Capital, Corporation Finance and the Theory of Investment," *American Economic Review*, 48 (June 1958), 261–97.

O	Net operating income	$ 1,000
F	Interest on debt	150
E	Earnings available to common stockholders	$ 850
k_e	Equity-capitalization rate (divide by)	0.11
S	Market value of stock	$ 7,727
B	Market value of debt	3,000
V	Total value of firm	$10,727

The implied overall capitalization rate is

$$k_o = \frac{O}{V} = \frac{\$1,000}{\$10,727} = 9.3 \text{ percent}$$

This example suggests that the firm can lower its cost of capital and increase the total value of the firm and share price by leverage. With no leverage, $B/S = 0$; and the overall capitalization rate, k_o, is 10 percent. Although investors raise the equity-capitalization rate, k_e, as the firm becomes more financially risky with leverage, the increase in k_e does not offset entirely the benefit of using cheaper debt funds. As a result, total valuation and share price increase, and the cost of capital decreases. With $3,000 in debt and 850 shares outstanding, the market price per share is $7,727/850 = $9.09. This contrasts with $8.23 under the assumption of a net operating income approach to valuation.

The traditional approach implies that beyond some point, k_e rises at an increasing rate with leverage. Moreover, k_i also may rise beyond some point. To illustrate, suppose now that the firm increases its debt from $3,000 to $6,000 and uses the proceeds of the debt issue to repurchase stock. Assume also that the average rate of interest on all debt rises to 6 percent and that the equity-capitalization rate, k_e, at that degree of leverage is 14 percent. The valuation of the firm then is

O	Net operating income	$ 1,000
F	Interest on debt	360
E	Earnings available to common stockholders	$ 640
k_e	Equity-capitalization rate (divide by)	0.14
S	Market value of stock	$ 4,571
B	Market value of debt	6,000
V	Total value of firm	$10,571

The implied overall capitalization rate is

$$k_o = \frac{O}{V} = \frac{\$1,000}{\$10,571} = 9.5 \text{ percent}$$

Thus, the total valuation of the firm is lower and its cost of capital slightly higher than when the amount of debt was $3,000. This result is due to the increase in k_e and, to a lesser extent, the increase in k_i. From these two observations, we know that the optimal capital structure in this example occurs before a debt-to-equity ratio of 6,000/4,571, or 1.31.

Graphically, one variation of the traditional approach is shown in Figure 18-4. As can be seen in the figure, k_e is assumed to rise at an increasing rate with leverage, whereas k_i is assumed to rise only after significant leverage has occurred. At first, the weighted-average cost of capital declines with leverage because the rise in k_e does not offset entirely the use of cheaper debt funds. As a result, the weighted-average cost of capital, k_o, declines with moderate use of leverage. After a point, however, the increase in k_e more than offsets the use of cheaper debt funds in the capital structure, and k_o begins to rise. The rise in k_o is supported further once k_i begins to rise. The optimal capital structure is the point at which k_o bottoms out; in the figure, this optimal capital structure is point X.

Thus, the traditional position implies that the cost of capital is not independent of the capital structure of the firm and that there is an optimal capital structure. At that optimal structure, the marginal real cost of debt is the same as the marginal real cost of equity. For degrees of leverage before that point, the marginal real cost of debt is less than that of equity; beyond that point, the marginal real cost of debt exceeds that of equity. There are wide variations in the traditional approach. As we mentioned earlier, the approach falls somewhere between the extremes, the net income and the net operating income approaches.

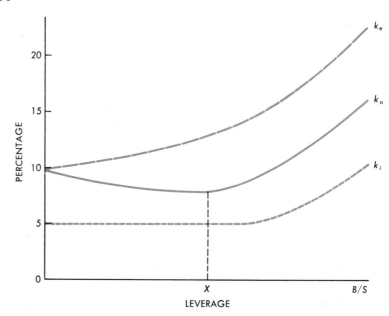

FIG. 18 · 4

Traditional approach

As discussed previously, Modigliani and Miller (MM) advocate that the relationship between leverage and the cost of capital is explained by the net operating income approach. They make a formidable attack on the traditional position by offering behavioral justification for having the cost of capital, k_o, remain constant throughout all degrees of leverage.

MM argue that the total risk for all security holders of a firm is not altered by changes in its capital structure. Therefore, the total value of the firm must be the same regardless of its financing mix. The crucial support for this hypothesis is the presence of arbitrage in the capital markets. Arbitrage precludes perfect substitutes from selling at different prices in the same market. In their case, the perfect substitutes are two or more firms in the same homogeneous risk class that differ only with respect to capital structure. MM contend that the total value of these firms has to be the same; otherwise, arbitragers will enter and drive the values of the two firms together. The essence of their argument is that arbitragers are able to substitute personal leverage for corporate leverage.[4]

Consider two firms that comprise a single risk class. These firms are identical in every respect except that Company A is not levered and Company B has $30,000 of 5% bonds outstanding. According to the traditional position, Company B may have a higher total value and lower average cost of capital than Company A. The valuation of the two firms is assumed to be the following:

		Company A	Company B
O	Net operating income	$ 10,000	$ 10,000
F	Interest on debt		1,500
E	Earnings available to common stockholders	$ 10,000	$ 8,500
k_e	Equity-capitalization rate (divide by)	0.10	0.11
S	Market value of stock	$100,000	$ 77,272
B	Market value of debt		30,000
V	Total value of firm	$100,000	$107,272
k_o	Implied overall capitalization rate	10%	9.3%
B/S	Debt-to-equity ratio	0	38.8%

MM maintain that this situation cannot continue, for arbitrage will drive the total values of the two firms together. Company B cannot command a higher total value simply because it has a different financing mix than Company A. MM argue that investors in Company B are able to obtain the same dollar return with no increase in financial risk by investing in Company A. Moreover, they are able to do so with a

[4]Ibid., pp. 268–70.

smaller investment outlay.[5] Because investors would be better off with the investment requiring the lesser outlay, they would sell their shares in Company B and buy shares in Company A. These arbitrage transactions would continue until Company B's shares declined in price and Company A's shares increased in price enough so that the total value of the two firms was identical.

To illustrate, suppose that a rational investor owned 1 percent of Company B, the levered firm, worth \$772.72 (market value). Given this situation, he should

1. Sell his stock in Company B for \$772.72.

2. Borrow \$300 at 5 percent interest. This personal debt is equal to 1 percent of the debt of Company B—his previous proportional ownership of the company.

3. Buy 1 percent of the shares of Company A, the unlevered firm, for \$1,000.

Prior to this series of transactions, the investor's expected return on investment in Company B was 11 percent on a \$772.72 investment, or \$85. His expected return on investment in Company A is 10 percent, or \$100 on an investment of \$1,000. From this return, he must deduct the interest charges on his personal borrowings. Thus, his net dollar return is

Return on investment in Company A	\$100
Less interest (300 × 0.05)	15
Net return	\$ 85

We see then that his net dollar return, \$85, is the same as it was for his investment in Company B. However, his cash outlay of \$700 (\$1,000 less personal borrowings of \$300) is less than the \$772.72 investment in Company B, the levered firm. Because of the lower investment, the investor would prefer to invest in Company A under the conditions described. In essence, the investor is able to "lever" the stock of the unlevered firm by taking on personal debt.

The action of a number of rational investors undertaking similar arbitrage transactions will tend to drive up the price of Company A shares, and lower its k_e, and drive down the price of Company B, increasing its k_e. This arbitrage process will continue until there is no further opportunity for reducing one's investment outlay and achieving the same dollar return. At this equilibrium, the total value of the two firms must be the same. As a result, their average costs of capital, k_o, also must be the same.

The important thing is the presence of rational investors in the market who are willing to substitute personal, or "homemade," leverage for corporate leverage. The analysis can be extended further to

[5]This arbitrage proof appears in Franco Modigliani and Merton H. Miller, "Reply to Heins and Sprenkle," *American Economic Review,* 59 (September 1969), 592–95.

cross risk classes and include general equilibrium in the capital markets. Here, however, we must take account of differences in business-risk premiums. On the basis of the arbitrage process illustrated, MM conclude that a firm cannot change its total value or its weighted-average cost of capital by leverage. Consequently, the financing decision does not matter from the standpoint of our objective of maximizing market price per share. One capital structure is as suitable as the next.

Arguments against the MM position. Given perfect capital markets, the arbitrage argument assures the validity of MM's thesis that the cost of capital and total valuation of a firm are independent of its capital structure. To dispute the MM position, one needs to look for reasons why the arbitrage process may not work perfectly. If perfect capital markets do not exist in practice, opponents of the MM position are able to contest its behavioral support and argue that the cost of capital can decline with the appropriate use of leverage. The following are the major arguments against the MM arbitrage process.

1. If there is a possibility of bankruptcy, and if administrative and other costs associated with bankruptcy are significant, the levered firm may be less attractive to investors than the unlevered one. With perfect capital markets, zero bankruptcy costs are assumed. If the firm goes bankrupt, assets presumably can be sold at their economic values with no liquidating or legal costs involved. Proceeds from the sale are distributed according to the claim on assets described in Chapter 27. If capital markets are less than perfect, however, there may be bankruptcy costs, and assets may have to be liquidated at less than their economic values. These costs and the "shortfall" in liquidating value from economic value represent a drain in the system from the standpoint of debt and equity holders. In the event of bankruptcy, security holders as a whole receive less than they would in the absence of bankruptcy costs. To the extent the levered firm has a greater possibility of bankruptcy than the unlevered one,[6] it would be a less attractive investment, all other things the same.[7] The possibility of bankruptcy is not a linear function of the debt/equity ratio but increases at an increasing rate beyond some threshold. As a result, the expected cost of bankruptcy increases in this manner and would be expected to have a corresponding negative effect upon the value of the firm and upon its cost of capital.

2. The perceived risks of personal leverage and corporate leverage may differ. Implied in the MM analysis is that personal and corporate leverage are perfect substitutes. In the case of corporate borrowings,

---

[6] It is possible, of course, that neither firm has a possibility of bankruptcy.

[7] For further discussion of this point, see Nevins D. Baxter, "Leverage, Risk of Ruin and the Cost of Capital," *Journal of Finance*, 22 (September 1967), 395–403.

the individual has only limited liability. In our first example, his loss is restricted to $772.72 if he remains invested in Company B, the levered firm. However, if he engages in the arbitrage transactions and invests in Company A, there is the possibility that he will lose his capital investment of $700 and be liable as well for borrowings of $300. Therefore his total risk exposure is greater with personal leverage and investment in the unlevered company than it is with a straight investment in the levered company.

In addition to greater risk, there are other reasons why investors may have a greater aversion to personal leverage than they do to corporate leverage. If the investor borrows personally and pledges his stock as collateral, he is subject to possible margin calls. Many investors view this possibility with considerable alarm. Moreover, personal leverage involves a certain amount of inconvenience on the part of the investor, which he does not experience with corporate leverage. For these reasons, personal leverage may not be a perfect substitute for corporate leverage in the minds of many investors.

3. Owing to market imperfections, the risk-adjusted cost of borrowing may be higher for the individual than for the corporation. If so, the levered company could have a somewhat greater total value than the unlevered firm for this reason alone.

4. Restrictions on investment behavior may retard the arbitrage process. Many institutional investors, such as pension funds and life insurance companies, are not allowed to engage in the "homemade" leverage that was described. In addition, stock and bond investments often are restricted by regulatory bodies to a list of companies meeting certain quality standards. One of these standards is that the company involved have only a "safe" amount of leverage. If a company breaches that amount, it may be removed from the acceptable list, thereby precluding certain institutions from investing in it. This reduction in investor demand can have an adverse effect on the market value of the company's financial instruments. Other restrictions also may have an effect. For example, the Federal Reserve regulates the percentage of advance under a margin loan. This requirement restricts the ability of arbitragers to substitute "homemade" leverage for corporate leverage.

5. Transaction costs tend to restrict the arbitrage process. Arbitrage will take place only up to the limits imposed by transaction costs, after which it is no longer profitable. As a result, the levered firm could have a slightly higher or slightly lower total value. The net effect of this imperfection is not predictable as to direction.

All of the factors listed above impede the effectiveness of the MM arbitrage process. If the arbitrage process is less than perfectly effective, a firm may be able to increase its total valuation and lower its cost of capital with an appropriate amount of leverage. As a result, the financing decision would matter, for it could affect the market value of the stock. The arbitrage argument is the behavioral foundation for the MM position.[8] Consequently, MM naturally deny the importance of these criticisms by arguing that they are too general. They suggest that as long as there are enough market participants at the margin that behave in a manner consistent with "homemade" leverage, the total value of the firm cannot be altered through leverage. According to them, the notion of "homemade" leverage as a substitute for corporate leverage cannot necessarily be rejected, even under real-world conditions.[9]

In the absence of corporate income taxes, the traditional position implies that capital structure does matter and that the firm can lower its cost of capital through a judicious amount of leverage. MM, on the other hand, contend that the cost of capital cannot be altered with leverage. If we assume perfect capital markets, we must accept the MM thesis on theoretical grounds. In practice, however, the majority of academicians and financial managers favor the traditional approach because of imperfections in the capital markets that hamper the perfect functioning of the arbitrage process.

The introduction of corporate income taxes

When we allow for corporate income taxes, we must reexamine the arguments presented so far. Because the payment of interest is deductible for tax purposes, leverage lowers the weighted-average after-tax cost of capital found with the MM position. To illustrate, suppose that the expected value of annual net operating income for two firms is $2,000 before taxes, the corporate income tax rate is 50 percent, the after-tax capitalization rate is 8 percent for both companies, and that Company A has no debt, whereas Company B has $8,000 in 5% bonds. According to the MM position, the total values of the two companies would be:

	Company A	Company B
1. Net operating income	$ 2,000	$ 2,000
2. Taxes	1,000	1,000
3. Profit before interest, but after taxes	$ 1,000	$ 1,000
4. After-tax capitalization rate for debt-free company (divide by)	.08	.08
5. Capitalized values of (3)	$12,500	$12,500
6. Interest on debt	0	400
7. (1 − Tax rate) (6)	0	200
8. Tax savings on interest	0	$ 200
9. Interest rate		.05
10. Capitalized value of (8)	0	$ 4,000
11. Total value of firm (5) + (10)	$12,500	$16,500

[8]See Modigliani and Miller, "The Cost of Capital, Corporation Finance, and the Theory of Investment: Reply," *American Economic Review*, 49 (September 1959), 655–69.

[9]Modigliani and Miller, "Cost of Capital, Corporation Finance, and the Theory of Investment," 274–76.

The higher total value of Company B is due to the deductibility of interest payments. Because of the tax benefit described, the firm can increase its total value with leverage under the MM position.

With taxes, the value of the firm, according to MM, is[10]

$$V = \frac{O(1 - t)}{\rho_k} + tB \tag{18-5}$$

where t = the corporate tax rate, ρ_k is the after-tax capitalization rate for a company with no debt in a given risk class, and O and B, as before, are expected net operating income and the market value of debt, respectively. As before, a 100 percent dividend-payout ratio is assumed. Equation (18-5) suggests that the valuation of the firm increases as more debt capital, denoted by B, is employed. In a sense, the government subsidizes the corporation so that the greater the debt used, the greater the firm's value. By the same token, the greater the leverage, the lower the cost of capital of the firm. The cost of capital on a tax-adjusted basis is expressed as[11]

$$k_o = \rho_k \left[1 - t \left(\frac{B}{B + S} \right) \right] \tag{18-6}$$

We see here that the greater the B, the lower the adjustment factor in the [ ] brackets and the lower the cost of capital of the firm.

Thus, MM recognize that with the introduction of corporate income taxes the cost of capital can be lowered with leverage.[12] We note, however, that their position implies that a firm can lower its cost of capital continually with increased leverage. The greater the leverage, the higher the total value of the firm and the lower its cost of capital. In order to achieve an optimal capital structure, the firm should strive for the maximum amount of leverage. The MM position in a world of taxes implies a capital structure consisting almost entirely of debt. Proponents of the traditional position argue that the cost of capital rises with extreme leverage owing to increased financial risk. As a result, the optimal capital structure would not call for a capital structure consisting almost entirely of debt. According to the traditional view, the cost of capital does not fall in the linear manner implied by Eq. (18-6), but rather rises beyond some point.

[10]Merton H. Miller and Franco Modigliani, "Some Estimates of the Cost of Capital to the Electric Utility Industry," *American Economic Review*, 56 (June 1966), 339–40.

[11]Ibid., p. 342.

[12]See Modigliani and Miller, "Corporate Income Taxes and the Cost of Capital: A Correction," *American Economic Review*, 53 (June 1963), 433–42.

A summing up

Where does this leave us with respect to the proportion of debt to employ? It should be apparent from the controversy presented that no universally accepted answer exists. It depends upon one's views of the strengths of the various arguments presented. If one believes that capital markets are perfect, that investors are rational, and that there are a sufficient number of arbitragers with funds to drive out any advantage between stocks differing only in the degree of leverage, then one must basically accept the MM position. In a world of taxes, this implies that an optimal capital structure will have in it a very high proportion of debt.

If one allows for bankruptcy costs, and if the probability of bankruptcy increases at an increasing rate with the degree of leverage, extreme leverage is likely to be penalized by investors. (As discussed earlier, bankruptcy costs represent a drain on the system to security holders.) In a world of both taxes and bankruptcy costs, there would likely be an optimal capital structure even if all of the other behavioral tenets of the MM position held. The cost of capital of a firm would decline as leverage was first employed because of the tax advantage of debt. Gradually, however, the prospect of bankruptcy would become increasingly important, causing the cost of capital to decrease at a decreasing rate as leverage increased. As leverage became extreme, the bankruptcy effect might more than offset the tax effect, causing the cost of capital of the firm to rise. By definition, this would be the point at which the capital structure of the firm was optimal. The joint effect of taxes and bankruptcy is illustrated in Figure 18-5 for a hypothetical firm.

If one feels that other imperfections and/or behavioral factors dilute the MM position further, the point at which the cost of capital line turns up would be earlier than that depicted in the figure. Consider now the cost of borrowing. After some point of leverage, the interest rate charged by creditors usually rises. The greater the leverage, of

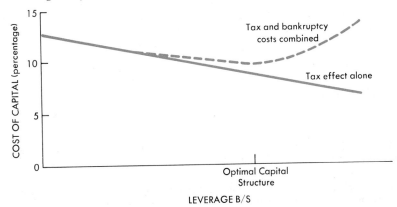

FIG. 18 · 5

Cost of capital with taxes
and bankruptcy costs

course, the lower the coverage of fixed charges, the more risky the loan, and generally the higher the interest rate charged. The MM position implies that any increase in interest costs is offset by the cost of equity capital increasing *at a decreasing rate*. Put another way, the P/E ratio would begin to decrease *at a decreasing rate* once interest costs began to rise. Implied is that investors become relatively *less* risk-averse with extreme leverage. Most find this contention to be quite objectionable and feel that the forces of arbitrage will not work to offset rising interest costs. Therefore, the cost of capital would likely turn up earlier than depicted in Figure 18-5, all other things the same.

Other capital-market imperfections work to hamper the arbitrage process so that "homemade" leverage is not a perfect substitute for corporate leverage. Recall that these imperfections include transaction costs, higher costs of borrowing for individuals than for corporations as a rule, institutional restrictions, and imperfections in information. The greater the importance one attaches to these factors, the less effective the arbitrage process becomes, and the greater the case that can be made for an optimal capital structure. In conclusion, there are a number of reasons for believing that an optimal capital structure exists in theory. Depending upon one's view as to the strengths of the various capital market and behavioral imperfections, the expected optimal capital structure may occur earlier or later along the scale of possible leverage.

THE APPROPRIATE CAPITAL STRUCTURE IN PRACTICE

If an optimal capital structure exists in concept, how can it be approximated in practice? In this section, we examine various ways to approach the problem. Our focus is on determining when the cost of capital line turns up as leverage is increased. In this regard, we are concerned with the implicit costs of leverage as they pertain to investors and creditors. Our purpose is to obtain insight into the perceived financial risk of the firm. By examining the effect of leverage from several different angles, we hope to be able to approximate when and in what manner the costs of debt and equity capital increase as increases in leverage occur.

EBIT–EPS analysis

One widely used method for examining the effect of leverage is to analyze the relationship between earnings before interest and taxes (EBIT) and earnings per share (EPS). The reader should be familiar with this method of analysis from the preceding chapter. In this chapter, we extend the method to take into account the likely future level and variability of EBIT. To illustrate with a different example, suppose a firm wished to compare the impact on earnings per share of financing a $10 million expansion program either with common stock at $50 a share or with 8 percent bonds. The tax rate is 50 percent, and the firm currently has an all-equity capital structure consisting of 800,000 shares of common stock. At $50 a share, the firm will need to sell 200,000 additional shares in order to raise $10 million. If we choose a hypothetical EBIT level of $8 million, earnings per share for the two alternatives would be:

	Common-Stock Financing	Debt Financing
EBIT	$8,000,000	$8,000,000
Interest	0	800,000
Earnings before taxes	$8,000,000	$7,200,000
Taxes	4,000,000	3,600,000
Earnings after taxes	$4,000,000	$3,600,000
Shares outstanding	1,000,000	800,000
Earnings per share	$4.00	$4.50

In order for the firm to show zero earnings per share under the debt alternative, it is clear that it will need to have EBIT of $800,000.

With this information, we are able to construct an EBIT–EPS chart, shown in Figure 18-6 (p. 394). The intercepts on the horizontal axis represent the amount of before-tax charges. For equity, the intercept is zero; for debt, it is $800,000. We then plot earnings per share for both alternatives under the assumption of an EBIT of $8 million. When we connect the intercepts with the appropriate EPS points at an EBIT level of $8 million, we obtain the straight lines shown. They tell us the earnings per share for the two financing alternatives that will occur under varying levels of EBIT.

Analysis of intersection. Because the debt line has a steeper slope, it intersects the common-stock line at an EBIT level of $4 million. At all levels of EBIT above $4 million, there is an earnings-per-share advantage to the use of debt. At levels of EBIT below $4 million, the advantage is in favor of common-stock financing.

Constructing an EBIT–EPS chart gives the financial manager information about the differential impact on earnings per share of alternative methods of financing. We note that as long as the firm is able to earn more than 8 percent before taxes on its investment, debt financing will show an EPS advantage. But the method does not con-

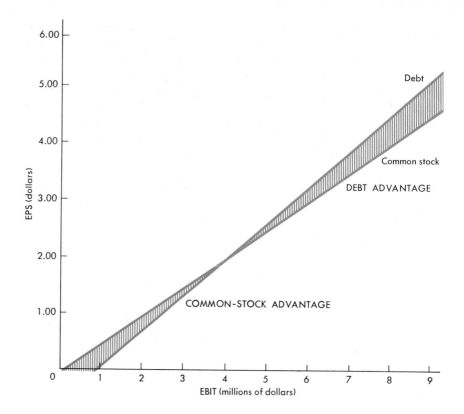

FIG. 18 · 6
EBIT–EPS chart

sider directly the implicit costs associated with debt. In an analysis of financial risk, however, an EBIT–EPS chart can be useful to the financial manager. He can compare the point of intersection with the most likely level of EBIT; he can also determine the probability that EBIT will fall below that point.

For example, suppose that the EBIT in the example presently is $7 million and that the company is considering the debt alternative. Given the business risk of the company and the possible fluctuations in EBIT, the financial manager should assess the probability of EBIT's falling below $4 million. If the probability is negligible, the use of the debt alternative would be supported. On the other hand, if EBIT presently is only slightly above the indifference point and the probability of EBIT's falling below this point is high, the financial manager may conclude that the debt alternative is too risky. In summary, the greater the level of EBIT and the lower the probability of downside fluctuation, the stronger the case that can be made for the use of debt.

To illustrate this concept further, suppose the firm were considering financing the $10 million expansion program not only with all common stock or all debt, but also with half common stock at $50 a share and half debt at 8 percent. Suppose further that if the economy is normal,

EBIT is expected to be $6 million. If a recession occurs, however, EBIT is expected to be $2 million, whereas if boom conditions occur, it is expected to be $10 million. The effect of these conditions on earnings per share under the various financing alternatives is shown in Table 18-1. We see that in the case of a recession, all common-stock financing has the most favorable impact on earnings per share, while under normal and boom economic conditions, all debt financing is the most favorable alternative. The table gives further insight into how leverage accelerates the impact of changes in EBIT on earnings per share.

Although an EBIT–EPS chart does not focus on the implicit costs of senior securities, the financial manager is able to obtain insight into these implicit costs through proper analysis. Although crude, the method is a useful supplement to other methods of analysis.

TABLE 18 · 1

Effect of Economic Conditions on Earnings per Share under the Various Financing Alternatives (in Millions of Dollars)

	Common-Stock Financing			Common-Stock and Debt Financing			Debt Financing		
	Recession	*Normal*	*Boom*	*Recession*	*Normal*	*Boom*	*Recession*	*Normal*	*Boom*
EBIT	$2.0	$6.0	$10.0	$2.0	$6.0	$10.0	$2.0	$6.0	$10.0
Interest	0	0	0	0.4	0.4	0.4	0.8	0.8	0.8
Earnings before taxes	$2.0	$6.0	$10.0	$1.6	$5.6	$ 9.6	$1.2	$5.2	$ 9.2
Taxes	1.0	3.0	5.0	0.8	2.8	4.8	0.6	2.6	4.6
Earnings after taxes	$1.0	$3.0	$ 5.0	$0.8	$2.8	$ 4.8	$0.6	$2.6	$ 4.6
Shares outstanding	1.0	1.0	1.0	0.9	0.9	0.9	0.8	0.8	0.8
Earnings per share	$1.00	$3.00	$5.00	$0.89	$3.11	$5.33	$0.75	$3.25	$5.75

Cash-flow analysis

When considering the appropriate capital structure, it is extremely important to analyze the cash-flow ability of the firm to service fixed charges. The greater the dollar amount of senior securities the firm issues and the shorter their maturity, the greater the fixed charges of the firm. These charges include principal and interest payments on debt, lease payments, and preferred-stock dividends. Before assuming additional fixed charges, the firm should analyze its expected future cash flows, for fixed charges must be met with cash. The inability to meet these charges, with the exception of preferred-stock dividends, may result in financial insolvency. The greater and more stable the expected future cash flows of the firm, the greater the debt capacity of the company. *Debt capacity* is used in a broad sense to mean all senior securities. From an internal standpoint, the financial risk associated with leverage should be analyzed on the basis of the firm's ability to service fixed charges. This analysis should include the preparation of cash budgets to determine whether the expected cash flows are sufficient to cover the fixed obligations.[13]

Necessarily, however, the analysis must consider the distribution of cash flows, for we are concerned with possible deviations in actual cash flows from those that are expected. As discussed in Chapter 4, cash budgets can be prepared for a range of possible outcomes, with a probability attached to each. This information is extremely valuable to the financial manager in evaluating the ability of the firm to meet fixed obligations. Given the probabilities of particular cash-flow sequences, he is able to determine the amount of fixed charges and debt the company can undertake while still remaining within insolvency limits tolerable to management.

Suppose management feels that a 5 percent probability of being out of cash is the maximum that can be tolerated, and that this probability corresponds to a cash budget prepared under pessimistic assumptions. In this case, debt might be undertaken up to the point where the cash balance under the pessimistic cash budget is just sufficient to cover the fixed charges associated with the debt. In other words, debt would be increased to the point at which the additional cash drain would cause the probability of cash insolvency to equal the risk tolerance specified by management. Note that the method of analysis simply provides a means for assessing the effect of increases in debt on the risk of cash insolvency. On the basis of this information, management would arrive at the most appropriate level of debt.

Donaldson has proposed a similar type of analysis.[14] He suggests that the ultimate concern of a company is whether cash balances during some future period will be involuntarily reduced below zero. Therefore, he advocates examining the cash flows of the company under the most adverse circumstances—that is, in his definition, under recession conditions. These conditions may or may not be the most adverse; however, in keeping with the spirit of his proposal, the firm should evaluate its cash flows under adverse circumstances. Donaldson defines the net cash balance during a recession as

---

[13]The preparation of cash budgets is discussed in Chapter 4.

[14]Gordon Donaldson, *Corporate Debt Capacity* (Boston: Division of Research, Harvard Business School, 1961). See also Donaldson, "Strategy for Financial Emergencies," *Harvard Business Review*, 47 (November–December 1969), 67–79.

$$CB_r = CB_o + NCF_r \qquad (18\text{-}7)$$

where CB_o = cash balance at start of recession
           NCF_r = net cash flows during recession

Donaldson then analyzes the cash-flow behavior of a firm during a recession by calculating a probability distribution of expected net cash flows.[15] By combining the beginning cash balances, CB_o, with the probability distribution of recession cash flows, NCF_r, he prepares a probability distribution of cash balances during the recession—CB_r.

To ascertain its debt capacity, a firm first would calculate the fixed charges associated with additional increments of debt. For each addition, the firm then would determine the probability of being out of cash. As before, management could set tolerance limits on the probability of being out of cash. For example, suppose the firm were considering issuing $20 million in additional debt and that the annual fixed charges were $3 million. By subtracting $3 million from the expected cash balances shown for the probability distribution of CB_r, we obtain the probability distribution of CB_r with the addition of $20 million in debt. If the probability of being out of cash with this increment of debt is negligible, Donaldson would contend that the company has unused debt capacity. Therefore, it would be possible to increase the amount of debt until the probability of being out of cash equaled the risk tolerance of management.

Donaldson extends his analysis to calculate the probability of cash inadequacy. Our discussion before was in terms of cash insolvency, which is defined as lack of cash after all nonessential expenditures have been cut. Cash inadequacy is said to occur if the firm is out of cash after making certain desired expenditures such as dividends, R & D expenditures, and capital expenditures. Thus, cash insolvency is the extreme form of cash inadequacy.

The analysis of the cash-flow ability of the firm to service fixed charges is perhaps the best way to analyze financial risk, but there is some question as to whether the external market analyzes a company in this manner. Sophisticated lenders and institutional investors certainly analyze the amount of fixed charges and evaluate financial risk in keeping with the ability of the firm to service these charges. However, individual investors may look more to the book value proportions of debt to equity in judging financial risk. There may or may not be a reasonable correspondence between the ratio of debt to equity and the amount of fixed charges relative to the firm's cash-flow ability to service these charges. Some firms may have relatively high ratios of

---

[15]The determinants of net cash flows with which he works are sales collections, other cash receipts, payroll expenditures, raw-material expenditures, and nondiscretionary cash expenditures. By analyzing each of these determinants, he determines the range and probability of recession net cash flows.

debt to equity but substantial cash-flow ability to service debt. Consequently, the analysis of debt-to-equity ratios alone can be deceiving, and an analysis of the magnitude and stability of cash flows relative to fixed charges is extremely important in determining the appropriate capital structure for the firm.

Comparison of capital structure ratios

Another method of analyzing the appropriate capital structure for a company is to evaluate the capital structure of other companies having similar business risk. Companies used in this comparison may be those in the same industry. If the firm is comtemplating a capital structure significantly out of line with that of similar companies, it is conspicuous to the marketplace. This is not to say, however, that the firm is wrong; other companies in the industry may be too conservative with respect to the use of debt. The optimal capital structure for all companies in the industry might call for a higher proportion of debt to equity than the industry average. As a result, the firm may well be able to justify more debt than the industry average. However, if the firm is noticeably out of line in either direction, it should be able to justify its position, because investment analysts and creditors tend to evaluate companies by industry.

Other methods

The firm may profit also by talking with investment analysts, institutional investors, and investment houses to obtain their views on the appropriate amount of leverage. These analysts examine many companies and are in the business of recommending stocks. Therefore, they have an influence upon the market, and their judgments with respect to how the market evaluates leverage may be very worthwhile. Similarly, a firm may wish to interview lenders to see how much debt it can undertake before the cost of borrowing is likely to rise. Finally, the management of a company may develop a "feel" for what has happened in the past to the market price of the stock when they have issued debt.

The methods described above for analyzing the appropriate amount of leverage do not give an exact answer. Nevertheless, by undertaking a variety of analyses, the financial manager should be able to determine, within some range, the appropriate capital structure for his firm. By necessity, the final decision has to be somewhat subjective. However, it can be based upon the best information available. In this way, the firm is able to obtain the capital structure most appropriate for its situation—the one that, hopefully, will tend to maximize the market price of the stock, all other factors held constant.

SUMMARY

A great deal of controversy has developed over whether the capital structure of a firm, as determined by its financing decision, affects its cost of capital. Traditionalists argue that the firm can lower its cost of capital and increase market value per share by the judicious use of leverage. However, as the company levers itself and becomes increasingly risky financially, lenders begin to charge higher interest rates on loans. Moreover, investors penalize the price/earnings ratio increasingly, all other things being the same. Beyond a point, the cost of capital begins to rise. According to the traditional position, that point denotes the optimal capital structure. Modigliani and Miller, on the other hand, argue that in the absence of corporate income taxes, the cost of capital is independent of the capital structure of the firm. They contend that the cost of capital and the total market value of the firm are the same for all degrees of leverage.

We saw that the behavioral support for their position was based upon perfect capital markets and the arbitrage process. Attacks on the MM hypothesis are centered on the validity of their assumptions. To the extent that the arbitrage process does not work perfectly, a case can be made for the view that the capital structure of the firm affects its cost of capital. With the introduction of corporate income taxes, debt has a tax advantage and serves to lower the cost of capital, even in the MM case. The traditional position implies, however, that the cost of capital will eventually rise with additional leverage, whereas the MM position implies a continually decreasing cost of capital with leverage. The combination of capital market imperfections, particularly bankruptcy costs, and the tax advantage of debt has led most to believe that an optimal capital structure does exist in theory.

In deciding upon an appropriate capital structure, the financial manager should consider a number of factors. He can obtain considerable insight from: an analysis of the cash-flow ability of the firm to service the fixed charges associated with senior securities and leasing; an analysis of the relationship between earnings before interest and taxes and earnings per share for alternative methods of financing; comparison of capital structure ratios for similar companies; and discussions with investment analysts, investment bankers, and lenders. Once an appropriate capital structure has been determined, the firm should finance investment projects in roughly those proportions.

1. Contrast the David Durand net operating income approach with the Modigliani-Miller approach to the theory of the capital structure.

2. As a financial manager who believes the cost of capital to the firm can be minimized by using moderate amounts of debt, you have been asked to defend your proposal to change the debt/equity proportions of the firm to the board of directors. The majority stockholder argues that the cost of capital to the firm is his return. Because you work for him, the majority stockholder wants your resignation unless you can defend wanting to minimize his return. Discuss your rebuttal.

3. Integrate the financial leverage approach in Chapter 17 with the following approaches to the capital structure:
   (a) Net income
   (b) Net operating income
   (c) Traditional
   (d) Modigliani-Miller

4. Why might you suspect that the optimal capital structure would differ significantly from one industry to another? Would the same factors produce differing optimal capital structures within all industry groupings?

5. What factors determine the interest rate a firm must pay for debt funds? Is it reasonable to expect this rate to rise with an increasing debt/equity ratio? Why?

6. Explain why the following three firms with similar asset structures and growth rates sell at different market prices. Are any of the firms overlevered? Explain carefully.

	Firm A	Firm B	Firm C
Dividend/share	$ 4	$ 3	$ 2
Market price	18	20	15

7. How can a company determine in practice if it has too much debt? Too little debt?

8. If there were not imperfections in financial markets, what capital structure should the firm seek? Why are market imperfections important in finance? Which imperfections are most important?

1. The E. W. Lambert Company has net operating earnings of $10 million and $20 million of debt with a 7 percent interest charge. In all cases, assume no taxes.

   (a) Using Durand's net income method and an equity-capitalization rate of 12 ½ percent, compute the total value of the firm and the implied overall capitalization rate.

   (b) Next, assume that the firm issues an additional $10 million in debt and uses the proceeds to retire stock; the interest rate and equity-capitalization rate remain the same. Compute the new total value of the firm and overall capitalization rate.

   (c) Using Durand's net operating income concept and an overall capitalization rate of 11 percent, compute the total market value, the stock market value, and the implied equity-capitalization rate for the E. W. Lambert Company prior to the sale of additional debt.

   (d) Determine the answers to (c) if the company were to sell the additional $10 million in debt.

2. Reconsider the E. W. Lambert Company, with its $10 million in net operating income, $20 million of 7 percent debt, and 12 ½ percent equity-capitalization rate.

   (a) Compute 1 (a) above if you have not already done so.

   (b) Assume that the E. W. Lambert Company now issues an additional $10 million of debt at an interest rate of 8 percent without altering the equity-capitalization rate. Compute the new total value of the firm and the implied overall capitalization rate.

   (c) Recompute (b) under the assumption that the sale of additional debt would have caused the equity capitalization to rise to 15 percent.

   (d) Recompute all of the above under the assumption that the company pays taxes at a 50 percent rate. Use an NI approach with a 12 ½ percent after-tax equity-capitalization rate. In (c) above, however, continue to use the 15 percent equity-capitalization rate.

3. The C. T. Carlisle Corporation has a $1 million capital structure and will always maintain this book value amount. Carlisle currently earns $250,000 per year before taxes of 50 percent, has an all-equity capital structure of 100,000 shares, and pays all earnings in dividends. The company is considering issuing some debt in order to retire some stock. The cost of the debt and the price of the stock at various levels of debt are given in the following table. It is assumed that the new capital structure would be reached all at once by purchasing stock at the current price. In other words, the table is a schedule at a point in time.

Amount of Debt	Average Cost of Debt	Price of Stock
$ —	—	$10.00
100,000	6.0%	10.00
200,000	6.0	10.50
300,000	6.5	10.75
400,000	7.0	11.00
500,000	8.0	10.50
600,000	10.0	9.50

(a) By observation, what do you think is the optimal capital structure?

(b) Construct a graph in terms of k_e, k_i, and k_o based upon the above data.

(c) Are your calculations in (a) confirmed?

4. The Crary Company and the Howard Company comprise a single risk class. These firms are identical in every respect except that the Crary Company is not levered, while the Howard Company has $1 million in 6 percent bonds outstanding. The valuation of the two firms is assumed to be the following:

		Crary	Howard
O	Net operating income	$ 300,000	$ 300,000
F	Interest on debt	—	60,000
E	Earnings to common	$ 300,000	$ 240,000
k_e	Equity-capitalization rate (divide by)	.125	.140
S	Market value of stock	$2,400,000	$1,714,000
B	Market value of debt	—	1,000,000
V	Total value of firm	$2,400,000	$2,714,000
k_o	Implied overall capitalization rate	12.5%	11.0%
B/S	Debt/equity ratio	0	58.4%

(a) An investor owns $10,000 worth of Howard stock. Show the process and the amount by which he could reduce his outlay through the use of arbitrage.

(b) How much of Crary would the investor own if he levered himself to the same debt/equity as in Howard?

(c) According to Modigliani-Miller, when will this arbitrage process cease?

(d) What arguments can be raised against the MM hypothesis?

5. Bakor Baking Company has an all-equity capital structure, net operating income before taxes of $400,000, and an after-tax capitalization rate of 10 percent. The corporate tax rate is 50 percent.

(a)   Assuming perfect capital markets, graph the cost of capital of the firm for various levels of debt. (Assume that the firm issues debt to repurchase stock, thereby effecting an immediate change in its capital structure.) What happens to the cost of capital with leverage?

(b)   Assume now that bankruptcy costs exist. What happens to the cost of capital in the above example as leverage increases?

6.   Hi Grade Regulator Company currently has 100,000 shares of common stock outstanding with a market price of $60 per share. It also has $2 million in 6 percent bonds. The company is considering a $3 million expansion program that it can finance with either (1) all common stock at $60 a share; (2) straight bonds at 8 percent interest; (3) preferred stock at 7 percent; (4) half common stock at $60 per share and half 8 percent bonds.

(a)   For a hypothetical EBIT level of $1 million, calculate the earnings per share for each of the alternative methods of financing. Assume a corporate tax rate of 50 percent.

(b)   Construct an EBIT–EPS chart. What are the indifference points between alternatives? What is your interpretation of them?

7.   Hi Grade Regulator Company (see Problem 6) expects the EBIT level after the expansion program to be $1 million, with a two-thirds probability that it will be between $600,000 and $1,400,000.

(a)   Which financing alternative do you prefer? Why?

(b)   Suppose that the expected EBIT level were $1.5 million and that there were a two-thirds probability that it would be between $1.3 million and $1.7 million. Which financing alternative do you prefer now? Why?

8.   Gamma Tube Company plans to undertake a $12 million capital improvement program and is considering how much debt to use. It feels that it could obtain debt financing at the following interest rates (assume that this debt is perpetual):

Amounts (in millions)	First $4	Next $3	Next $3	Next $2
Interest cost	7%	8%	9%	10%

The company has made projections of its net cash flows (exclusive of new financing) during a period of adversity such as a recession. In a recession, it expects a net cash flow of $3 million with a standard deviation of $2 million (assume a normal distribution). Its beginning cash balance is $500,000. If the company is willing to tolerate only a 5 percent probability of running out of cash during a recession, what is the maximum proportion of the $12 million capital improvement program that can be financed with debt? (Use the probability concepts discussed in Chapter 14 and the table in Appendix B to that chapter.)

ARDITTI, FRED D., "The Weighted Average Cost of Capital: Some Questions on Its Definition, Interpretation and Use," *Journal of Finance,* 28 (September 1973), 1001–9.

BARON, DAVID P., "Default Risk, Homemade Leverage, and the Modigliani-Miller Theorem," *American Economic Review,* 64 (March 1974), 176–82.

BAXTER, NEVINS D., "Leverage, Risk of Ruin, and the Cost of Capital," *Journal of Finance,* 22 (September 1967), 395–404.

BOOT, JOHN C. G., and **GEORGE M. FRANKFURTER,** "The Dynamics of Corporate Debt Management, Decision Rules, and Some Empirical Estimates," *Journal of Financial and Quantitative Analysis,* 7 (September 1972), 1956–66.

BRIGHAM, EUGENE F., and **MYRON J. GORDON,** "Leverage, Dividend Policy, and the Cost of Capital," *Journal of Finance,* 23 (March 1968), 85–104.

DONALDSON, GORDON, *Corporate Debt Capacity.* Boston: Division of Research, Harvard Business School, 1961.

————, "Strategy for Financial Emergencies," *Harvard Business Review,* 47 (November–December 1969), 67–79.

DURAND, DAVID, "Costs of Debt and Equity Funds for Business: Trends and Problems of Measurement," reprinted in *The Management of Corporate Capital,* ed. Ezra Solomon, pp. 91–116. New York: Free Press, 1959.

ELLIS, CHARLES D., "New Framework for Analyzing Capital Structure," *Financial Executive,* 37 (April 1969), 75–86.

FAMA, EUGENE F., and **MERTON H. MILLER,** *The Theory of Finance,* Chapter 4. New York: Holt, Rinehart & Winston, 1972.

GLENN, DAVID W., "Super Premium Security Prices and Optimal Corporate Financing Decisions," *Journal of Finance,* 31 (May 1976).

HALEY, CHARLES W., and **LAWRENCE D. SCHALL,** *The Theory of Financial Decisions,* Chapters 10 and 11. New York: McGraw-Hill, 1973.

HAMADA, ROBERT S., "The Effect of the Firm's Capital Structure on the Systematic Risk of Common Stocks," *Journal of Finance,* 27 (May 1972), 435–52.

HANDORF, WILLIAM C., "Flexible Debt Financing," *Financial Management,* 3 (Summer 1974), 17–23.

HEINS, A. JAMES, and **CASE M. SPRENKLE,** "A Comment on the Modigliani-Miller Cost of Capital Thesis," *American Economic Review,* 59 (September 1969), 590–92.

KEANE, SIMON M., "Some Aspects of the Cost of Debt," *Accounting and Business Research* (Autumn 1975), 298–304.

KUMAR, PREM, "Growth Stocks and Corporate Capital Structure Theory," *Journal of Finance,* 30 (May 1975), 533–47.

LEWELLEN, WILBUR G., *The Cost of Capital,* Chapters 3–4. Belmont, Calif.: Wadsworth, 1969.

MALKIEL, BURTON G., *The Debt-Equity Combination of the Firm and the Cost of Capital: An Introductory Analysis.* New York: General Learning Press, 1971.

MELNYK, Z. LEW, "Cost of Capital as a Function of Financial Leverage," *Decision Sciences,* 1 (July–October 1970), 327–56.

MERTON, ROBERT C., "On the Pricing of Corporate Debt: The Risk Structure of Interest Rates," *Journal of Finance,* 29 (May 1974), 449–70.

MILLER, M. H., and **FRANCO MODIGLIANI,** "Cost of Capital to Electric Utility Industry," *American Economic Review,* 56 (June 1966), 333–91.

MODIGLIANI, FRANCO, and **M. H. MILLER,** "The Cost of Capital, Corporation Finance, and the Theory of Investment," *American Economic Review,* 48 (June 1958), 261–97.

_____, "The Cost of Capital, Corporation Finance, and the Theory of Investment: Reply," *American Economic Review,* 51 (September 1959), 655–69; "Taxes and the Cost of Capital: A Correction," ibid., 53 (June 1963), 433–43; "Reply," ibid., 55 (June 1965), 524–27; "Reply to Heins and Sprenkle," ibid., 59 (September 1969), 592–95.

NANTELL, TIMOTHY J. and **C. ROBERT CARLSON,** "The Cost of Capital as a Weighted Average," *Journal of Finance,* 30 (December 1975), 1343–55.

PFAHL, JOHN K., DAVID T. CRARY, and **R. HAYDEN HOWARD,** "The Limits of Leverage," *Financial Executive,* 38 (May 1970), 48–56.

SCHALL, LAWRENCE D., "Firm Financial Structure and Investment," *Journal of Financial and Quantitative Analysis,* 6 (June 1971), 925–42.

SCHWARTZ, ELI, and **J. RICHARD ARONSON,** "Some Surrogate Evidence in Support of the Concept of Optimal Capital Structure," *Journal of Finance,* 22 (March 1967), 10–18.

SCOTT, DAVID F., JR. and **JOHN D. MARTIN,** "Industry Influence on Financial Structure," *Financial Management,* 4 (Spring 1975), 67–73.

SOLOMON, EZRA, "Leverage and the Cost of Capital," *Journal of Finance,* 18 (May 1963), 273–79.

_____, *The Theory of Financial Management.* New York: Columbia University Press, 1963.

TINSLEY, P. A., "Capital Structure, Precautionary Balances, and Valuation of the Firm: The Problem of Financial Risk," *Journal of Financial and Quantitative Analysis,* 5 (March 1970), 33–62.

19 Dividend Policy and Retained Earnings

In this chapter, we examine various aspects of dividend policy in relation to their effect on the value of the firm to its shareholders. The dividend-payout ratio, or the percentage of earnings paid to stockholders in cash, determines the amount of earnings retained in the firm. Over the years, retained earnings have been a very important source of financing for business corporations. Consequently, a dividend decision necessarily involves a financing decision. Although the dividend-payout ratio is a major aspect of the dividend policy of the firm, there are other aspects that affect valuation. In this chapter, we also consider the stability of dividends, certain factors that influence the payout ratio from the standpoint of the firm, stock dividends and stock splits, the repurchase of stock, and the procedural and legal elements of dividend policy.

DIVIDEND-PAYOUT RATIO

We investigate in this section the question of whether the payment of cash dividends can affect shareholder wealth and, if it can, the optimal dividend-payout ratio that will maximize shareholder wealth. Again, we assume that business risk is held constant. In order to evaluate the question of whether the dividend-payout ratio affects shareholder wealth, it is necessary to examine first the firm's policy solely as a financing decision involving the retention of earnings.

Consider the situation where the use of funds from earnings, and the dividend policy that results, is strictly a financing decision. As long as the firm has investment projects whose returns exceed its cost of capital, it will use retained earnings, and the amount of senior securities the increase in equity base will support, to finance these projects. If the firm has retained earnings left over after financing all acceptable investment opportunities, these earnings then would be distributed to stockholders in the form of cash dividends. If not, there would be no dividends. If the number of acceptable investment opportunities involves a total dollar amount that exceeds the amount of retained earnings plus the senior securities these retained earnings will support, the firm would finance the excess with a combination of a new equity issue and senior securities.

When we treat dividend policy strictly as a financing decision, the payment of cash dividends is a passive residual.[1] The amount of dividend payout will fluctuate from period to period in keeping with fluctuations in the amount of acceptable investment opportunities available to the firm. If these opportunities abound, the percentage of dividend payout is likely to be zero. On the other hand, if the firm is unable to find profitable investment opportunities, dividend payout will be 100 percent. For situations between these two extremes, the payout will be a fraction between 0 and 1.

Walter's formula

To illustrate dividend policy as a financing decision determined solely by the profitability of investment opportunities available, let us examine Walter's formula.[2] His model was one of the earlier theoretical dividend models, and certain later models correspond to this one. His formula is

$$P = \frac{D + \dfrac{r}{\rho}(E - D)}{\rho} \qquad (19\text{-}1)$$

where P = market price per share of common stock
D = dividends per share
E = earnings per share
r = return on investment
ρ = market capitalization rate

[1] Ezra Solomon, *The Theory of Financial Management* (New York: Columbia University Press, 1963), pp. 139–40.

[2] James E. Walter, "Dividend Policies and Common Stock Prices," *Journal of Finance,* 11 (March 1956), 29–41.

Suppose that r = 12 percent, ρ = 10 percent, E = \$4, and D = \$2. The market price per share would be

$$P = \frac{2 + (0.12/0.10)(4 - 2)}{0.10} = \$44$$

The optimal dividend-payout ratio is determined by varying D until you obtain the maximum market price per share. Under a strict interpretation of the Walter formula, the optimal dividend-payout ratio should be 0 if r is greater than ρ. Thus, in our example,

$$P = \frac{0 + (0.12/0.10)(4 - 0)}{0.10} = \$48$$

With a payout ratio of 0, market price per share is maximized. Similarly, if r is less than ρ, the optimal payout ratio should be 100 percent. Suppose that r = 8 percent, ρ = 10 percent, E = \$4, and D = \$2. The market price per share then would be

$$P = \frac{2 + (0.08/0.10)(4 - 2)}{0.10} = \$36$$

However, with a dividend-payout ratio of 100 percent,

$$P = \frac{4 + (0.08/0.10)(4 - 4)}{0.10} = \$40$$

Thus, market price per share can be maximized with a complete distribution of earnings. If r = ρ, market price per share is insensitive to the payout ratio.

The Walter formula implies that the optimal dividend payout should be determined solely by the profitability of investments. If the firm has an abundance of profitable investment opportunities, there should be no cash dividends, for the earnings are needed to finance these opportunities. On the other hand, if the firm has no profitable investment opportunities, all earnings should be distributed to stockholders in the form of dividends. In this case, the funds are not needed for financing.

Dividends as a passive residual

The treatment of dividend policy as a passive residual determined strictly by the availability of acceptable investment proposals implies that dividends are irrelevant; the investor is indifferent between dividends and capital gains. If investment opportunities promise a return greater than their required return, the investor would prefer to have the company retain earnings. If the return is equal to the required return, he would be indifferent between retention and dividends. Contrarily, if the return were less than the required return, he would prefer dividends. Supposedly, if the firm can earn more on projects than the required return, investors are perfectly happy to let the firm retain as much in earnings as it needs to finance the investments. With irrelevance, the required return is invariant with respect to changes in dividend payout. A question to raise is whether dividends are more than just a means of distributing unused funds. Should dividend policy in any way be an active decision variable? To answer these questions, we must examine more thoroughly the argument that dividends are irrelevant so that changes in the payout ratio (holding investment opportunities constant) do not affect shareholder wealth.

Irrelevance of dividends

The most comprehensive argument for the irrelevance of dividends is found in Modigliani and Miller's 1961 article.[3] They assert that, given the investment decision of the firm, the dividend-payout ratio is a mere detail. It does not affect the wealth of shareholders. MM argue that the value of the firm is determined solely by the earning power on the firm's assets, or its investment policy, and that the manner in which the earnings stream is split between dividends and retained earnings does not affect this value. The critical assumptions of MM are:

1. Perfect capital markets in which all investors are rational. Information is available to all at no cost; securities are infinitely divisible; transactions are instantaneous and without cost; and no investor is large enough to affect the market price of a security.

2. An absence of flotation costs on securities issued by the firm.

3. A world of no taxes.

4. A given investment policy for the firm, not subject to change.

5. Perfect certainty by every investor as to future investments and profits of the firm. (MM drop this assumption later.)

   Dividends versus terminal value. The crux of MM's position is that the effect of dividend payments on shareholder wealth is offset exactly by other means of financing. Consider first selling additional stock in lieu of retaining earnings. When the firm has made its invest-

[3] Merton H. Miller and Franco Modigliani, "Dividend Policy, Growth, and the Valuation of Shares," *Journal of Business,* 34 (October 1961), 411–33.

ment decision, it must decide whether to retain earnings, or to pay dividends and sell new stock in the amount of these dividends in order to finance the investments. MM suggest that the sum of the discounted value per share after financing and dividends paid is equal to the market value per share before the payment of dividends. In other words, the stock's decline in market price because of the dilution caused by external financing offsets exactly the payment of the dividend. Thus, the stockholder is said to be indifferent between dividends and the retention of earnings.

Given MM's assumptions of perfect certainty as well as their other assumptions, the irrelevance of dividends follows. As with our example for corporate leverage in the previous chapter, arbitrage assures that the sum of market value plus current dividends of two firms identical in all respects other than dividend-payout ratios will be the same. The individual investor can retain and invest his own earnings as well as the corporation can do it for him.[4] However, even under uncertainty MM maintain that dividend policy is irrelevant. It is this situation that we wish to analyze.

One point needs clarification, however. We have assumed that external financing involves the sale of new stock and that the effect of this sale on the market price of the stock offsets exactly the payment of dividends. What if the external financing involved debt? MM's position then rests upon their previous indifference thesis with respect to leverage: the real cost of debt is the same as the real cost of equity financing (see Chapter 18). Therefore, according to MM, the means of external financing used to offset the payment of dividends does not affect their hypothesis that dividends are irrelevant. Thus, we see the interdependency of MM's two positions. Dividend policy does not affect their thesis regarding leverage; in their position on dividends, the means of external financing is not a factor.

Arguments for relevance

A number of arguments have been advanced in support of the contrary position—namely, that dividends are relevant under conditions of uncertainty. In other words, the investor is not indifferent as to how the earnings stream is split between dividends and retained earnings. We shall examine these arguments under conditions of uncertainty but will keep intact MM's other assumptions—no transaction or flotation costs, the absence of taxes, and a given fixed investment policy of the

---

[4]For illustrations of the arbitrage process for the dividend decision, see Wilbur G. Lewellen, *The Cost of Capital* (Belmont, Calif.: Wadsworth, 1969), pp. 54–57; and James E. Walter, *Dividend Policy and Enterprise Valuation* (Belmont, Calif.: Wadsworth, 1967), pp. 106–10.

firm. Later, the first two of these assumptions will be removed when we investigate dividend policy under real-world conditions.

Resolution of uncertainty. It has been argued that the payment of current dividends resolves uncertainty in the minds of investors, and therefore, an investor is not indifferent between dividends and capital gains. He prefers dividends. Gordon, for example, contends that uncertainty on the part of investors increases at an increasing rate with the distance in the future of prospective cash payments.[5] According to Gordon, investors are not indifferent between current dividends and the retention of earnings with the prospect of future dividends, capital gains, or both. They prefer the early resolution of uncertainty and are willing to pay a higher price for the stock that offers the greater current dividend, all other things held constant. Thus, the rate of return required by investors would rise with the percentage of earnings retained.[6] This is not to say that the basic business risk of a firm's investments is affected by its dividend payout. Rather, it is contended that investors' *perception* of such riskiness, or their uncertainty, may be affected.[7]

Informational content of dividends. The argument above is allied closely to the "informational content of dividends" argument. The latter argument implies that dividends have an impact on share price because they communicate information to investors about the firm's profitability. When a firm has a target payout ratio that is stable over time, and it changes this ratio, investors may believe that management is announcing a change in the expected future profitability of the firm. Accordingly, the price of the stock may react to this change in dividends. Solomon contends that dividends may offer tangible evidence of the firm's ability to generate cash, and, as a result, the divi-

[5] Myron J. Gordon, "Optimal Investment and Financing Policy," *Journal of Finance,* 18 (May 1963), 264–72, and "The Savings Investment and Valuation of a Corporation," *Review of Economics and Statistics,* 44 (February 1962), 264–72.

[6] A number of authors have taken issue with Gordon. See Michael Brennan, "A Note on Dividend Irrelevance and the Gordon Valuation Model," *Journal of Finance,* 26 (December 1971), 1115–21; Robert C. Higgins, "Dividend Policy and Increasing Discount Rates: A Clarification," *Journal of Financial and Quantitative Analysis,* 7 (June 1972), 1757–62; and Robert E. Krainer, "A Pedagogic Note on Dividend Policy," *Journal of Financial and Quantitative Analysis,* 6 (September 1971), 1147–54. Even if current dividends are perceived as less risky than future ones, it is argued that stockholders are able to sell a portion of their shares to obtain the desired cash distribution. In essence, investors are able to manufacture "homemade dividends" in the same way as they are "homemade leverage" in the case of the capital structure decision. Because "homemade" dividends supposedly are perfect substitutes for corporate dividends, the Gordon argument is said not to hold. The company is not able to do anything for investors that they cannot do for themselves; therefore, dividend policy is not a thing of value.

[7] For amplification of this point, see Simon M. Keane, "Dividends and the Resolution of Uncertainty," *Journal of Business Finance & Accounting,* 1 (Autumn 1974), 389–93.

dend policy of the firm affects share price. "...in an uncertain world in which verbal statements can be ignored or misinterpreted, dividend action does provide a clear-cut means of 'making a statement' that 'speaks louder than a thousand words.'"[8] MM do not deny the possibility of this effect but continue to maintain that present and expected future earnings are what determine value. They assert that dividends are merely a reflection of these factors and do not in themselves determine value; therefore, the irrelevance proposition holds.[9] Thus, dividends are said to be used by investors as predictors of the firm's future performance; they convey management's expectation of the future.

Preference for current income. Another aspect of the uncertainty question involves investors who have a preference for current income. Under the irrelevance proposition, MM would argue that these investors can sell stock on a periodic basis to obtain income. With perfect markets, the investor always could sell part of his holdings or reinvest the dividends to satisfy his desire for consumption. Over the long run, the investor should be able to obtain the same income as he would with regular dividends. However, with uncertainty, stock prices fluctuate. Certain investors may regard as unsatisfactory the alternative of selling a portion of their stock for income at fluctuating prices. As a result, they may have a definite preference for current dividends. In addition to the uncertainty of the selling price, the inconvenience of selling a small portion of stock periodically for income may be a factor. For this reason alone, certain investors may prefer current dividends to capital gains.

Sale of stock at a lower price. The irrelevance doctrine also rests upon the assumption that the sale of stock by the firm to replace the dividend will be at the current price. In order to sell the stock, however, the firm must appeal to new investors or to existing stockholders to increase their holdings. With divergent investor expectations, Lintner contends that the equilibrium price of a share of stock will decline as the firm sells additional stock to replace dividends.[10] In other words, there is a downward sloping demand curve for the stock. With underpricing, the firm will need to sell more shares to replace the dividend. This dilution will cause a lower discounted value per share after financing than was true in the cases of the irrelevance example. Thus, a downward sloping demand curve for new issues of stock implies a preference toward retention, as opposed to paying higher dividends.

---

[8]Solomon, *Theory of Financial Management,* p. 142.

[9]Miller and Modigliani, "Dividend Policy," pp. 429–30.

[10]John Lintner, "Dividends, Earnings, Leverage, Stock Prices and the Supply of Capital to Corporations," *Review of Economics and Statistics,* 44 (August 1962), 243–69.

Removal of other assumptions

We now consider other factors that were assumed away by MM. Any attack on MM, however, must be based upon factors other than the ones we take up now. Nevertheless, the market imperfections we discuss are important in evaluating the effect of dividends upon valuation in the real world.

Tax effect. When we allow for taxes, there are a variety of effects. The most important is due to capital gains being taxed at a lower rate than dividends. Thus, there is a strong bias in favor of capital gains as opposed to dividends, and this bias favors the retention of earnings. Suppose a corporation pays a substantial dividend and expands by selling stock on a privileged-subscription basis to existing stockholders. These stockholders receive dividends, which are taxed at the ordinary income tax rate, and then purchase more stock. If the corporation had retained the earnings, the tax would have been avoided. The stockholder could realize value on his investment by selling some of his shares and paying only a capital-gains tax. The effect of the tax differential must be qualified to take account of the growing number of tax-free institutional investors. For these investors, the tax effect would not influence their preference for dividends or capital gains.

Other tax laws favor current dividends over capital gains. Individuals are able to exclude the first $100 of dividend income; such income is not taxed. Presumably, this tax provision creates a preference for current dividends on the part of small investors. For corporate investors, intercompany dividends are taxed at a rate below that applicable to capital gains. Accordingly, there would be a preference for current dividends on the part of these investors. However, the two effects described are overshadowed by the differential tax on dividends and capital gains, which, as stated earlier, creates a preference for capital gains.

Flotation costs. The irrelevance proposition is based upon the idea that, given the investment policy of the firm, funds paid out of the firm must be replaced by funds acquired through external financing. The introduction of flotation costs favors the retention of earnings in the firm. For each dollar paid out in dividends, the firm nets less than a dollar after flotation costs per dollar of external financing.

Transaction costs and divisibility of securities. Transaction costs involved in the sale of securities tend to restrict the arbitrage process in the same manner as that described for debt. The stockholder who desires current income must pay a brokerage fee on the sale of a portion of his stock if the dividend paid is not sufficient to satisfy his current desire for income. This fee varies inversely, per dollar of stock sold, with the size of the sale. For a small sale, the brokerage fee can be rather significant. As a result of this fee, stockholders with consumption desires in excess of current dividends will prefer the company to pay additional dividends. Perfect capital markets also assume that securities are infinitely divisible. The fact that the smallest integer is one share may result in "lumpiness" with respect to selling shares for current income. This too acts as a deterrent to the sale of stock in lieu of dividends. On the other hand, the stockholder not desiring dividends for current consumption purposes will need to reinvest his dividends. Here again transaction costs and divisibility problems work to the disadvantage of the stockholder, although in the opposite direction.

Thus, transaction costs and divisibility problems cut both ways. However, there is reason to believe that in recent years the net impact of these factors has created a slight bias on the side of a preference for current dividends. Many companies now have automatic dividend reinvestment plans. These plans allow the stockholder to specify a reduction in the amount of dividends he is to receive. This reduction is then used to purchase additional shares of stock in the company.[11] The reinvestment is administered by a bank in behalf of the company and is automatic. Transaction costs are lower than what a stockholder could do on his own, and there is virtually no inconvenience involved. Because of the increasing use of automatic dividend reinvestment programs, the scales may be tipped slightly in favor of the stockholder who desires to reinvest dividends as opposed to the one who desires greater current income. Transaction costs overall may therefore result in a net preference in the market for current dividends, all other things the same.

Other legal impediments. Certain institutional investors are restricted by law as to the types of common stock in which they can invest. The prescribed list of eligible securities is determined in part by the duration over which dividends have been paid. If a company does not pay dividends or has not paid them over a sufficiently long period of time, certain institutional investors are not able to invest in the stock. Universities, on the other hand, sometimes have restrictions on the expenditure of capital gains from their endowment. Although these two influences are small in aggregate, they work in the direction of a preference for current income as opposed to capital gains.

Of the market imperfections discussed in this section, the differential tax effect on dividends and capital gains is by far the strongest. As mentioned previously, this imperfection creates a preference for the retention of earnings in the firm.

[11] For a survey of the use of these plans, see Richard H. Pettway and R. Phil Malone, "Automatic Dividend Reinvestment Plans for Nonfinancial Corporations," *Financial Management*, 2 (Winter 1973), 11–18.

Investment opportunities and dividend policy

In theory, the optimal dividend policy of the firm should be determined in the light of the firm's investment opportunities and any preference that investors have for dividends as opposed to capital gains. The firm with abundant profitable investment opportunities will prefer a high retention rate because, owing to flotation costs, underpricing, and the differential tax treatment on dividends and capital gains, a sale of stock is a more expensive form of financing. The dividend decision, however, must take investors' preferences into consideration. If investors have a systematic preference for current dividends over capital gains, the profitability of the investment opportunities must be sufficiently attractive to offset this preference if the firm is to retain a high proportion of earnings and still maximize shareholder wealth. The key arguments supporting the idea that investors have a systematic preference for dividends are the resolution of uncertainty and the desire for current income.

For the firm that does not have enough attractive investment projects to utilize its entire earnings, a portion of these earnings should be paid out to stockholders in the form of dividends. If dividends do matter and are valued in the marketplace, the firm might pay an even higher dividend than is dictated by the amount of funds left over after investment. This policy eventually would necessitate issuing common stock. The difference in cost between the sale of stock and the retention of earnings then must be balanced against the opportunity cost of dividends foregone. Equilibrium would occur, of course, when the two were the same.

In conclusion, if dividend policy is not relevant, a firm should choose its dividend policy solely in keeping with its long-run investment opportunities. At the point at which the return on investment is less than the cost of capital, the firm should stop investing and should pay the unused funds out as dividends. The growth company that expands faster than its growth in earnings would pay no dividends, whereas the firm in a shrinking industry might have a 100 percent dividend payout or even a liquidating dividend. The firm need not pay out the exact unused portion of earnings every period. Some years, the payout may be more; other years, it may be less. Indeed, the firm may want to stabilize the absolute amount of dividends paid from period to period but in such a manner that over the long run the total earnings retained, plus the senior securities the increasing equity base will support, correspond to the amount of profitable investment opportunities available. Dividend policy would still be a passive decision variable determined by the amount of investment opportunities.

For the firm to be justified in paying a dividend larger than that dictated by the amount of profitable investment opportunities, the dividend must be relevant. The tax differential between current dividends and capital gains favors retention of earnings. Therefore, the investors' preference for current dividends must more than offset the tax differential. Although empirical evidence concerning the effect of dividends on the market price of a stock in this regard is lacking, many companies appear to behave as if dividends are relevant. For example, a number of growth companies which expand at a rate faster than their growth in earnings pay small dividends. If these companies believed dividends were irrelevant, they would retain all their earnings. A number of other companies that pay significant dividends go to the capital markets for additional equity capital rather than retain a greater portion of earnings. Examples include public utilities and airlines. Whereas these actions do not support the idea that dividends are relevant, they do indicate that many companies behave as though they were. The dividend-payout ratio that these firms believe is optimal is greater than that dictated by investment opportunities alone.

DIVIDEND STABILITY

In addition to the percentage of dividend payout of a company over the long run, investors may value stable dividends over this period. All other things being the same, the market price of the stock of a company may be higher if it pays a stable dividend over time than if it pays out a fixed percentage of earnings. To illustrate, suppose Company A has a long-run dividend-payout ratio of 50 percent of earnings. Suppose further that it has the policy of paying out this percentage every year, despite the fact that its earnings are cyclical. The dividends of Company A are shown in Figure 19-1. Company B, on the other hand, has exactly the same earnings and a long-run dividend-payout ratio of 50 percent, but it maintains a relatively stable dividend over time. It changes the absolute amount of dividend only in keeping with the underlying trend of earnings. The dividends of Company B are shown in Figure 19-2.

Over the long run, the total amount of dividends paid by these two firms is the same. However, the market price per share of Company B may be higher than that of Company A, all other things being the same. Investors may well place a positive utility on dividend stability and pay a premium for the company that offers such stability. To the extent that investors value dividend stability, the overall dividend policy of Company B would be better than that of Company A. This policy includes not only the percentage of dividend payout in relation to earnings but also the manner in which the actual dividends are paid. Rather than vary dividends directly with changes in earnings per share, Company B raises the dividend only when reasonably confident a higher dividend can be maintained.

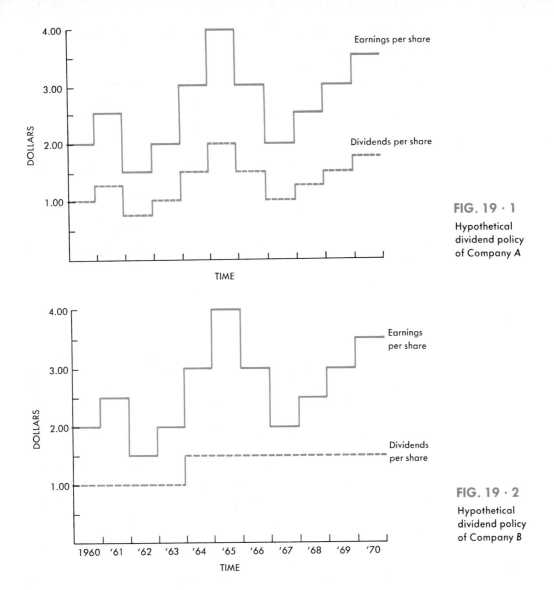

FIG. 19 · 1

Hypothetical dividend policy of Company A

FIG. 19 · 2

Hypothetical dividend policy of Company B

Valuation of stability

There are several reasons why investors may value stable dividends and pay a premium for the stock of the company providing such stability. These include the informational content of dividends, the desire of investors for current income, and certain legal considerations.

Informational content. When earnings drop and a company does not cut its dividend, the market's confidence in the stock may be bolstered over what it would be if the dividend were cut. The stable dividend may convey to investors management's view that the future of the company is better than the drop in earnings suggests. Thus, management may be able to affect the expectations of investors through the informational content of dividends. Management, however, cannot "fool" the market permanently. If there is a downward trend in earnings, a stable dividend will not convey forever an impression of a rosy future. Moreover, if a firm is in an unstable business with wide swings in earnings, a stable dividend cannot give the illusion of underlying stability.

Current income desires.   A second factor favoring stable dividends is that investors who desire a specific periodic income will prefer a company with stable dividends to one with unstable dividends, even though both companies may have the same pattern of earnings and long-run dividend payout. Although the investor can always sell a portion of his stock for income when the dividend is not sufficient to meet his current needs, many investors have an aversion to "dipping into principal." Moreover, when a company reduces its dividend, earnings usually are down and the market price of the stock depressed. As a result, the investor would have to sell his stock on unfavorable terms. Overall, it would seem that income-conscious investors place a positive utility on stable dividends.

Legal considerations.   Finally, a stable dividend may be advantageous from the legal standpoint of permitting certain institutional investors to invest in the stock. Various governmental bodies prepare legal lists of securities in which pension funds, savings banks, trustees, insurance companies, and others may invest. In order to qualify, a company must have an uninterrupted pattern of dividends. A cut in the dividend may result in the removal of a company from these legal lists.

The arguments presented in support of the notion that stable dividends have a positive effect upon the market price of the stock are only suggestive. There is little in the way of empirical evidence to shed light on the question. While studies of individual stocks often suggest that stable dividends buffer the market price of the stock when earnings turn down, there have been no comprehensive studies of a large sample of stocks dealing with the relationship between dividend stability and valuation. Nevertheless, most companies strive for stability in their dividend payments. This occurrence is illustrated in Figure 19-3, where total corporate dividends and net earnings after taxes are shown for the post-World War II period. Overall, corporations behave in a manner that is consistent with a belief that stable dividends have a positive effect on value.

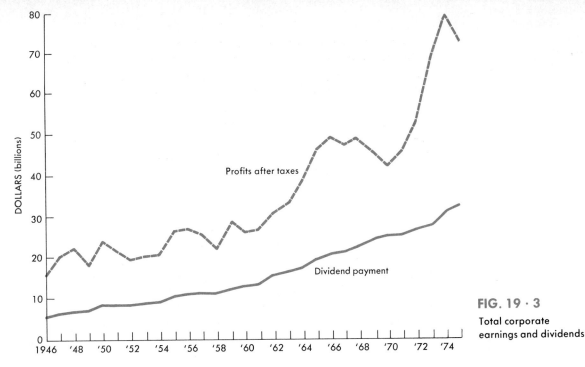

FIG. 19 · 3
Total corporate
earnings and dividends

Target payout ratios

It would appear that a number of companies follow the policy of a target dividend-payout ratio over the long run. Lintner contends that dividends are adjusted to changes in earnings, but only with a lag.[12] When earnings increase to a new level, dividends are increased only when it is felt that the increase in earnings can be maintained. In addition, there appears to be a definite reluctance on the part of companies to cut the absolute amount of their cash dividend. Both of these factors explain the lag in dividend changes behind changes in earnings. Given a lag relationship, retained earnings will increase relative to dividends in an economic upturn. In a contraction, however, retained earnings will decrease relative to dividends.

To illustrate the use of a target payout ratio and stable dividends, consider the case of Coleman Company. This company makes outdoor recreation equipment and central heating and air-conditioning units. These lines of business are somewhat cyclical, with resulting swings in earnings. However, the company maintained stable and increasing dividends in the sixties and early seventies; it seems to raise dividends once management and the board of directors are confident that the earnings can be sustained. The dividends per share and earnings per share for the company are shown in Figure 19-4. (Note the effect of the switch to Lifo for inventory purposes reduced earnings per share by sixty cents in 1974.)

[12] See John Lintner, "Distribution of Income of Corporations," *American Economic Review,* 46 (May 1956), 97–113.

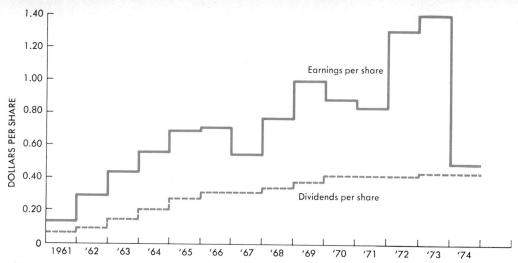

FIG. 19 · 4   Coleman Company, dividends and earnings per share, 1961–1974

Regular and extra dividends

One way for a company to increase its cash distribution in periods of prosperity is to declare an *extra* dividend in addition to the *regular* quarterly or semiannual dividend. By declaring an extra dividend, the company attempts to prevent investors from expecting that the dividend represents an increase in the established dividend rate. The declaration of an extra dividend is suitable particularly for companies with fluctuating earnings. General Motors, for example, has declared extra dividends in good car years. The use of the extra dividend enables the company to maintain a stable record of regular dividends but also to distribute to stockholders some of the rewards of prosperity. By paying extra dividends only when earnings are higher than usual, the company will not lead investors to count on the increased dividends in future periods. However, a company cannot pay extra dividends continuously without conveying to the market some impression of permanency. As soon as a certain level of dividends is recurrent, investors begin to expect that level regardless of the distinction between regular and extra dividends.

ADDITIONAL FACTORS

So far, we have related the dividend policy of a firm to the investment opportunities of that firm, to the magnitude and stability of earnings, to the possible preference of investors for dividends relative to capital gains, and to the fact that common stock is a more expensive form of financing than is the retention of earnings. However, there are a num-

ber of other considerations that influence a company in the dividend it
undertakes. These considerations tend to be of a more practical nature
than those discussed so far.

421
Chapter 19
Dividend Policy and
Retained Earnings

Liquidity

The liquidity of a company is an important consideration in many
dividend decisions. Because dividends represent a cash outflow, the
greater the cash position and overall liquidity of a company, the
greater its ability to pay a dividend. A company that is growing and
profitable may not be liquid, for its funds may go into fixed assets and
permanent working capital. Because the management of such a company usually desires to maintain some liquidity cushion to give it
flexibility and a protection against uncertainty, it may be reluctant to
jeopardize this position in order to pay a large dividend. The liquidity
of the company, of course, is determined by the firm's investment and
financing decisions. The investment decision determines the rate of
asset expansion and the firm's need for funds; and the financing decision determines the way in which this need will be financed.

Ability to borrow

A liquid position is not the only way to provide for flexibility and
thereby protect against uncertainty. If a firm has the ability to borrow on comparatively short notice, it may be relatively flexible. This
ability to borrow can be in the form of a line of credit or a revolving
credit from a bank, or simply the informal willingness on the part of a
financial institution to extend credit. In addition, flexibility can come
from the ability of a firm to go to the capital markets with a bond
issue. The larger and more established a company, the better its access
to the capital markets. The greater the ability of the firm to borrow,
the greater its flexibility, and the greater its ability to pay a cash dividend. With ready access to debt funds, management should be less
concerned with the effect that a cash dividend has upon its liquidity.

Control

If a company pays substantial dividends, it may need to raise capital at a later time through the sale of stock in order to finance profitable investment opportunities. Under such circumstances, the controlling interest of the company may be diluted if controlling stockholders
do not or cannot subscribe for additional shares. These stockholders
may prefer a low dividend payout and the financing of investment

needs with retained earnings. Such a dividend policy may not maximize overall shareholder wealth, but it still may be in the best interests of those in control.

Control can work two ways, however. In the case of a company being sought by another company or by individuals, a low dividend payout may work to the advantage of the "outsiders" seeking control. The outsiders may be able to convince stockholders that the company is not maximizing shareholder wealth and that they (the outsiders) can do a better job. Consequently, companies in danger of being acquired may establish a high dividend payout in order to please stockholders.

Nature of stockholders

When a firm is closely held, management usually knows the dividend desires of its stockholders and may act accordingly. If most stockholders are in high tax brackets and prefer capital gains to current income, the firm can establish a low dividend payout. The low payout, of course, would be predicated upon having profitable investment opportunities in which to employ the retained earnings. The corporation with a large number of stockholders does not know the dividend desires of its stockholders. It can judge these desires only in terms of the market price of its stock.

Timing of investment opportunities

A company may have profitable investment opportunities, but these opportunities may occur too sporadically for the company to be justified in retaining earnings. For example, a firm may know that it will need to build a major extension on its existing plant in about six years. If it retains earnings to finance this plant expansion, the funds will not be used for some period of time. During this period, the company will invest the funds in short-term securities yielding less than the required rate of return on retained earnings. However, shareholder wealth might be better maximized by paying out the intermediate earnings as dividends and raising the capital six years later with a stock issue. The sale of stock is a more desirable means than retained earnings by which to raise a large block of capital at one time.

Restrictions in bond indenture or loan agreement

The protective covenants in a bond indenture or loan agreement often include a restriction on the payment of dividends. This restriction is employed by the lender(s) to preserve the company's ability to service debt. Usually, it is expressed as a maximum percentage of cumulative earnings. When such a restriction is in force, it naturally influences the dividend policy of the firm. There are times when the management of a company welcomes a dividend restriction imposed by lenders because then it does not have to justify to stockholders the retention of earnings. It needs only to point to the restriction.[13]

Procedural aspect

When the board of directors of a corporation declares a cash dividend, it specifies a *date of record.* Holders of record on that date are entitled to the dividend declared. After the date of record, the stock is said to trade *ex-dividend,* for investors that purchase it are not entitled to receive the declared dividend. Theoretically, the market price of the stock should decline by the amount of the dividend when the stock goes ex-dividend. Because other factors influence the market price of the stock, this effect is sometimes difficult to measure. Once a dividend is declared, stockholders become creditors of the company until the dividend is actually paid; the declared but unpaid dividend is a current liability of the company.

Legal restrictions

Capital restriction.   Although state laws vary considerably, most states prohibit the payment of dividends if these dividends impair capital. *Capital* is defined in some states as the par value of the common stock. For example, if a firm had one million shares outstanding with a $2 par value, total capital would be $2 million. If the net worth of a company were $2.1 million, the company could not pay a cash dividend totaling $200,000 without impairing capital.

Other states define *capital* to include not only the par value of the common stock but also the capital surplus. Under such statutes, dividends can be paid only out of retained earnings. The purpose of the capital impairment laws is to protect creditors of a corporation. For a relatively new corporation, these laws may afford creditors a degree of protection. However, for established companies that have been profitable in the past and have built up retained earnings, substantial losses will usually have been incurred before the restriction has an effect. By

---

[13] For a more detailed examination of these restrictions, see Chapter 11.

this time, the situation may be sufficiently hopeless that the restriction gives creditors little protection.

Insolvency. Some states prohibit the payment of cash dividends if the company is insolvent. *Insolvency* is defined either in a legal sense, as liabilities exceeding assets, or in a technical sense, as the firm's being unable to pay its creditors as obligations come due. As the ability of the firm to pay its obligations is dependent upon its liquidity rather than upon its capital, the technical insolvency restriction gives creditors a good deal of protection. When cash is limited, a company is restricted from favoring stockholders to the detriment of creditors.

Excess accumulation of cash. The Internal Revenue Code prohibits the undue retention of earnings. Although *undue retention* is defined vaguely, it usually is thought to be retention significantly in excess of the present and future investment needs of the company. The purpose of the law is to prevent companies from retaining earnings for the sake of avoiding taxes. For example, a company might retain all its earnings and build up a substantial cash and marketable-securities position. The entire company then could be sold, and stockholders would be subject only to a capital-gains tax. If the excess earnings were distributed as dividends, the dividends would be taxed as ordinary income. If the IRS can prove unjustified retention, it can impose penalty tax rates on the accumulation. Whenever a company does build up a substantial liquid position, it has to be sure that it can justify the retention of these funds to the IRS. Otherwise, it may be in order to pay the excess funds out to stockholders as dividends.

STOCK DIVIDENDS AND STOCK SPLITS

In this section, we take up stock dividends and stock splits. In an economic sense, the two are very similar, although typically they are used for different purposes. Only from an accounting standpoint is there a significant difference.

Stock dividends

A stock dividend is simply the payment of additional stock to stockholders. It represents nothing more than a recapitalization of the company; a stockholder's proportional ownership remains unchanged. To illustrate, suppose a company had the following capital structure before issuing a stock dividend:

Common stock ($5 par, 400,000 shares)	$ 2,000,000
Capital surplus	1,000,000
Retained earnings	7,000,000
Net worth	$10,000,000

Now, suppose the company pays a 5 percent stock dividend, amounting to 20,000 additional shares of stock, and that the fair market value of the stock is $40 a share. For each twenty shares of stock owned, the stockholder receives an additional share. The balance sheet of the company after the stock dividend would be

Common stock ($5 par, 420,000 shares)	$ 2,100,000
Capital surplus	1,700,000
Retained earnings	6,200,000
Net worth	$10,000,000

With a stock dividend, $800,000 ($40 × 20,000 shares) is transferred from retained earnings to the common stock and capital surplus accounts. Because the par value stays the same, the increase in number of shares is reflected in a $100,000 increase in the common stock account ($5 × 20,000 shares). The residual of $700,000 goes into the capital surplus account. The net worth of the company remains the same.

Because the number of shares of stock outstanding is increased by 5 percent, earnings per share of the company are reduced proportionately. Suppose that total net profit after taxes were $1 million. Before the stock dividend, earnings per share would be $2.50, ($1 million/400,000). After the stock dividend, earnings per share are $2.38, ($1 million/420,000). Thus, the stockholder has more shares of stock but lower earnings per share. His proportion of total earnings available to common stockholders remains unchanged.

Value to investor. If the company pays no cash dividend, what does the stockholder receive with a stock dividend? In theory, he receives nothing but an additional stock certificate. His proportionate ownership of the company is unchanged. Presumably, the market price of the stock will drop, all other things being equal, so that the total market value of his holdings stays the same. For example, if he held 100 shares of stock previously, and market price per share were $40, the total value of his holdings would be $4,000. After the stock dividend, the price of the stock should drop by $40(1 − 1.00/1.05), or by $1.90. The total value of his holdings then would be $38.10 ×

105, or $4,000. Under these conditions, the stock dividend does not represent a thing of value to the stockholder. He simply has an additional stock certificate evidencing ownership.

To the extent that the investor wishes to sell a few shares of stock for income, the stock dividend may make it easier for him to do so. Without the stock dividend, of course, he also could sell a few shares of his original holdings for income. In either case, the sale of stock represents the sale of principal and is subject to the capital-gains tax. However, it is probable that certain investors do not look at the sale of a stock dividend as a sale of principal. To them, the stock dividend represents a windfall gain; they can sell it and still retain their original holdings. The stock dividend may have a favorable psychological effect on these stockholders.

The stock dividend can also be a thing of value to the investor if the company maintains the same cash dividend per share after the stock dividend as before. Suppose an investor owns 100 shares of a company paying a $1 dividend and that the company declares a 10 percent stock dividend and, at the same time, announces that the cash dividend per share will remain unchanged. The investor then will have 110 shares; and total cash dividends will be $110 rather than $100, as before. In this case, a stock dividend increases his total cash dividends. Whether this increase in cash dividend has a positive effect upon shareholder wealth will depend upon the tradeoff between current dividends and retained earnings, which we discussed earlier. Clearly, the stock dividend in this case represents a decision by the firm to increase modestly the amount of cash dividends.

Use of the stock dividend may convey some information. Stock dividends typically are associated with growth companies. Under these circumstances, the dividend may connote to investors that management expects earnings to continue to grow and to more than offset the dilution in earnings per share arising from the increase in the total number of shares. The underlying effect on value is growth, however, and not the stock dividend itself.

Advantages to company.   Frequently, a stock dividend is employed to "conserve cash." Instead of increasing the cash dividend as earnings rise, a company may desire to retain a greater portion of its earnings and declare a stock dividend. The decision then is to lower the dividend-payout ratio, for as earnings rise and the dividend remains the same, the payout ratio will decline. Whether shareholder wealth is increased by this action will depend upon considerations discussed previously. The decision to retain a higher proportion of earnings, of course, could be accomplished without a stock dividend. However, the stock dividend may tend to please certain investors by virtue of its informational content as well as its psychological impact. In addition, if the cash dividend per share is kept the same, total cash dividends will increase slowly in keeping with the increase in the number of shares.

In the discussion of advantages so far, the decision to issue a stock dividend has been based upon the availability of profitable investment opportunities. The percentage of cash dividend payout was reduced in order to finance a portion of these opportunities with retained earnings. Certain companies, however, have employed the stock dividend as a means of replacing the cash dividend because of financial difficulty. In these situations, the stock dividend should not connote the prospect of favorable earnings, but financial deterioration, and it should be so evaluated. It is doubtful whether many investors are fooled by the substitution.

The use of a stock dividend by a firm may also serve to keep the market price of the stock within a desired trading range. Certain companies do not like to see the market price of their stocks above a certain amount—say $60 a share—because a high price will not appeal to small investors. Consequently, they will endeavor to keep the price below a desired ceiling either by using stock dividends or, more commonly, by means of stock splits. Increasing the total number of shares outstanding may increase the total number of stockholders, resulting in greater overall popularity for the stock.

The principal disadvantage of stock dividends to the firm is that they are much more costly to administer than cash dividends. Another disadvantage is that small periodic stock dividends, perhaps 2 or 3 percent, may tend to distort downward the company's perceived growth in earnings. Whereas investment analysts adjust earnings per share for stock splits and significant stock dividends, many do not do so for small stock dividends. If earnings per share are not adjusted, the measured growth in earnings per share will be less than the true increase in earnings for the investor who held his stock over the period measured. Consequently, it is conceivable that the price/earnings ratio might be somewhat lower than it would be if earnings per share were adjusted.

Stock splits

With a stock split, the number of shares are increased through a proportional reduction in the par value of the stock. Suppose that the capital structure of a company before a two-for-one stock split were

Common stock ($5 par, 400,000 shares)	$ 2,000,000
Capital surplus	1,000,000
Retained earnings	7,000,000
Net worth	$10,000,000

After the split, the capital structure is

Common stock ($2.50 par, 800,000 shares)	$ 2,000,000
Capital surplus	1,000,000
Retained earnings	7,000,000
Net worth	$10,000,000

With a stock dividend, the par value is not reduced, whereas with a split, it is. As a result, the common stock, capital surplus, and retained earnings accounts remain unchanged. The net worth, of course, also stays the same; the only change is in the par value of the stock. Except in accounting treatment, the stock dividend and stock split are very similar. A stock split, however, is usually reserved for occasions when a company wishes to achieve a substantial reduction in the market price per share. The principal purpose of a split is to place the stock in a more popular trading range. The stock of a supergrowth company can rather quickly sell in excess of several hundred dollars a share unless it is split periodically and the total number of shares increased accordingly.

As was true of the stock dividend, the stock split does not represent a thing of value to the investor. He has more shares than before, but his proportional ownership of the company remains unchanged. The market price of the stock should decline proportionately, so that the total value of his holdings stays the same. Again, however, the split may have a favorable informational content. The announcement of the split may indicate to investors that management believes that earnings will continue to grow. As a result, the market price per share may increase upon the announcement of the split, or the rumor of an announcement, and remain higher.[14] However, the underlying cause for the increase in market price, again, is growth and not the split itself. It may be possible that the total market value of the firm is slightly higher if its shares are priced in a popular trading range rather than traded at a very high price.

---

[14]This occurrence is supported by the empirical work of Keith B. Johnson, "Stock Splits and Price Change," *Journal of Finance,* 21 (December 1966), 675–86. In testing the same data, however, W. H. Hausman, R. R. West, and J. A. Largay, "Stock Splits, Price Changes, and Trading Profits: A Synthesis," *Journal of Business,* 45 (January 1971), 69–77, concluded that the superior price performance of stocks that split occurred prior to the announcement of the split. Their results indicated that buying a stock on the announcement of the split does not lead to price appreciation greater than the appreciation expected by underlying valuation effects. This finding is similar to that of Eugene F. Fama, Lawrence Fisher, Michael Jensen, and Richard Roll, "The Adjustment of Stock Prices to New Information," *International Economic Review,* 10 (February 1969), 1–22, who tested the 1927–59 period.

Very seldom will a company maintain the same cash dividends per share after a split as it did before. However, it might increase the effective dividends to stockholders. For example, suppose a company splits its stock two-for-one and establishes a dividend rate of $1.20 a share, whereas before the rate was $2.00 a share. A stockholder owning 100 shares before the split would receive $200 in cash dividends per annum. After the split, he would own 200 shares and would receive $240 in dividends. The market price of the stock (on an after-split basis) may react favorably to the increase in cash dividends.

Reverse split.   Rather than increasing the number of shares of stock outstanding, a company may want to reduce the number. This reduction can be accomplished with a *reverse split*. In our example above, suppose that there were a one-to-four reverse split, instead of the two-for-one straight stock split. For each four shares held, the stockholder would receive one share in exchange. The par value per share would become $20, and there would be 100,000 shares outstanding rather than 400,000. Reverse stock splits are employed to increase the market price per share when the stock is considered to be selling at too low a price. Many companies have an aversion to seeing the price of their stock fall significantly below $10 per share. If, due to financial difficulty or other reasons, the price should fall into this range, the market price per share can be increased with a reverse split. The reverse split is regarded by many as an admission by the company that it is in financial difficulty. However, financial difficulty is not always the reason for the split, and the stock market's reaction to it depends primarily upon the company's past and expected future earnings.[15]

REPURCHASE OF STOCK

In recent years, the repurchase of stock has become increasingly popular, and a number of large companies have turned to it. There are several reasons for its popularity. Some companies repurchase stock in order to have it available for stock options. In this way, the total number of shares is not increased with the exercise of the options. Another reason for repurchase is to have shares available for the acquisition of other companies. In other situations, however, stock is repurchased with the full intention of retiring it. Under these circumstances, repurchase of stock may be treated as a part of the dividend decision of the firm.

[15] See Richard R. West and Alan B. Brouilette, "Reverse Stock Splits," *Financial Executive*, 38 (January 1970), 12–17.

Repurchasing as part of a dividend decision

If a firm has excess cash and insufficient profitable investment opportunities to justify the use of these funds, it may be in the shareholders' best interests to distribute the funds. The distribution can be
accomplished either by the repurchase of stock or by paying the funds
out in increased dividends. In the absence of personal income taxes
and transaction costs, it should make no difference to stockholders,
theoretically, which of the two alternatives is chosen. With repurchase,
fewer shares remain outstanding, and earnings per share rise. As a result, the market price per share should rise as well. In theory, the capital gain arising from repurchase should equal exactly the dividend
that otherwise would have been paid.

To illustrate, suppose a company has the following earnings and
market price per share:

Net profit after taxes	$2,000,000
Number of shares outstanding	500,000
Earnings per share	$4
Market price per share, ex-dividend	$60
Price/earnings ratio	15

Suppose further that the company is considering the distribution of
$1.5 million, either in cash dividends or in the repurchase of its own
stock. If investors are expecting the cash dividend, the value of a share
of stock before the dividend is paid will be $63—that is, $3 a share in
expected dividends ($1.5 million/500,000) plus the $60 market price.
Suppose, however, that the firm chooses to repurchase its stock and
makes a tender offer to stockholders at $63 a share. It then will be
able to repurchase $1.5 million/$63, or 23,810 shares. Earnings per
share will be

$$EPS = \$2,000,000/476,190 = \$4.20$$

If the price/earnings ratio stays at 15, the total market price per share
will be $63, (4.20 × 15), the same total value as under the dividend al-
ternative. Thus, the amount of distribution to stockholders is $3 per
share, whether dividends or repurchase of stock (and subsequent
capital gain) is used.

With a differential tax rate on dividends and capital gains, repurchase of stock offers a considerable tax advantage over payment of
dividends. The market-price increase resulting from a repurchase of
stock is subject to the capital-gains tax, whereas dividends are taxed

at the higher ordinary income tax rate.[16] The repurchase of stock is particularly advantageous when the firm has a large amount of unused funds to distribute. To pay the funds out through an extra dividend would result in a substantial tax to stockholders. The tax effect could be alleviated somewhat by paying the funds out as extra dividends over a period of time, but this action might result in investors' counting on the extra dividend. The firm must be careful not to undertake a steady program of repurchase in lieu of paying dividends. The Internal Revenue Service is likely to regard such a program as an attempt to allow stockholders to avoid the payment of taxes on dividends. Accordingly, it may impose a penalty.[17] Hence, it is important that the repurchase of stock be somewhat of a "one-shot" nature and not be used as a substitute for regular dividends or even for recurring extra dividends.

Investment or financing decision?

Some regard the repurchase of stock as an investment decision instead of a dividend decision. Indeed, in a strict sense, it is. However, stock held in the treasury does not provide an expected return as other investments do. No company can exist by investing only in its own stock. The decision to repurchase should involve distribution of unused funds when the firm's investment opportunities are not sufficiently attractive to employ those funds, either now or in the foreseeable future. Therefore, the repurchase of stock cannot be treated as an investment decision as we define the term.

Repurchase may be regarded as a financing decision, however, provided its purpose is to alter the capital-structure proportions of the firm. By issuing debt and repurchasing stock, a firm can immediately change its debt-to-equity ratio toward a greater proportion of debt. In this case, the repurchase of stock is a financing decision, because the alternative is to not pay out dividends.[18] Only when there is excess cash can the repurchase of stock be treated as a dividend decision.

---

[16] See Edwin J. Elton and Martin J. Gruber, "The Effect of Share Repurchases on the Value of the Firm," *Journal of Finance,* 23 (March 1968), 135–50.

[17] See Harold Bierman, Jr., and Richard West, "The Acquisition of Common Stock by the Corporate Issuer," *Journal of Finance,* 21 (December 1966), 687–96.

[18] Results of an empirical study by Allan Young, "Financial, Operating and Security Market Parameters of Repurchasing," *Financial Analysts Journal,* 25 (July–August 1969), 124, suggest that a number of companies use stock repurchase to effect major capitalization changes. Overall, however, Young's results are consistent with the fact that repurchasing companies have less favorable operating performances than non-repurchasing companies, which in turn is consistent with a lack of investment opportunities. Thus, the evidence is consistent with stock repurchase for most companies being a dividend decision.

Method of repurchase

The two most common methods of repurchase are through a tender offer and through the purchase of stock in the marketplace. With a tender offer, the company makes a formal offer to stockholders to purchase so many shares, typically at a set price. This bid price is above the current market price; stockholders can elect either to sell their stock at the specified price or to continue to hold it. In open-market purchases, a company buys its stock through a brokerage house in the same manner as does any other investor. If the repurchase program is gradual, its effect is to put steady upward pressure on the market price per share. This upward pressure, of course, is of benefit to stockholders. In general, the transaction costs to the firm in making a tender offer are much higher than those incurred in the purchase of stock in the open market.

Before the company repurchases stock, it is important that stockholders be informed of the company's intentions. In a tender offer, these intentions are announced by the offer itself. Even here, however, it is important that the company not withhold other information. For example, it would be unethical for a mining company to withhold information of a substantial ore discovery while making a tender offer to repurchase shares.

In open-market purchases, it is especially important to disclose the company's repurchase intentions. Otherwise, stockholders may sell their stock not knowing that a repurchase program is under way that will increase earnings per share. Given full information about the amount of repurchase and the objective of the company, the stockholder can sell his stock if he so chooses. Without proper disclosure, the selling stockholder may well be penalized.[19] When the amount of stock repurchased is substantial, a tender offer is particularly suitable, for it gives all stockholders equal treatment.

SUMMARY

The critical question in dividend policy is whether dividends have an influence upon the value of the firm, given its investment decision. If dividends are irrelevant, as Modigliani and Miller believe, the firm should retain earnings only in keeping with its investment opportunities. If there are not sufficient investment opportunities to provide expected returns in

[19] For a discussion of the ethics surrounding repurchase, see Richard Stevenson, "Corporate Stock Reacquisitions," *Accounting Review,* 41 (April 1966), 312–17.

excess of the cost of capital, the unused funds should be paid out as dividends. The key issue is whether dividends are more than just a means of distributing unused funds. If they do affect the value of the common stock, dividend policy becomes more than a passive variable determined solely by the investment opportunities. The firm could affect shareholder wealth by varying its dividend-payout ratio; as a result, there would be an optimal dividend policy. In this chapter, we have examined the various arguments for and against the relevance of dividends. If dividends are relevant, the net preference of investors for current dividends as opposed to capital gains must be balanced against the difference in cost between the sale of stock and the retention of earnings in determining the optimal dividend-payout ratio.

The stability of dividends is felt by many to have a positive effect upon the market price of the stock. Stable dividends may tend to resolve uncertainty in the minds of investors, particularly when earnings per share drop. They also may have a positive utility to investors interested in current periodic income. Many companies appear to follow the policy of a target dividend-payout ratio, increasing dividends only when it is felt that an increase in earnings can be sustained. The use of an extra dividend permits a cyclical company to maintain a stable record of regular dividends while paying additional dividends whenever earnings are unusually high.

Other considerations that affect the cash-dividend policy of the firm include the liquidity of the company, its ability to borrow, the desire to maintain control, the nature of the company's stockholders, the timing of investment opportunities, dividend restrictions in a bond indenture or loan agreement, procedural aspects, and legal restrictions.

A stock dividend represents the payment of additional stock to stockholders. It is used frequently as a means to conserve cash and to reduce the cash dividend-payout ratio of the firm. Theoretically, the stock dividend does not represent a thing of value to the stockholder unless cash dividends per share remain unchanged or are increased. A much more effective device for reducing market price per share is a stock split. With a split, the number of shares is increased by the terms of the split—for example, a three-for-one split means that the number of shares is tripled.

A company's repurchase of its own stock should be treated as a dividend decision when the firm has funds in excess of present and foreseeable future investment needs. It may distribute these funds either as dividends or by the repurchase of stock. In the absence of a tax differential between dividends and capital gains, the monetary value of the two alternatives should be about the same. With the tax differential, there is a considerable tax advantage to the repurchase of stock. Because of objections by the Internal Revenue Service, however, repurchase of stock cannot be used in lieu of regular dividends.

1. Justify borrowing money in order to have the liquidity with which to pay dividends on common stock.

2. What is the impact of a stock dividend on the wealth of stockholders? Is the answer different for a stock split?

3. The performance of some institutional investors (some pension funds, for example) is measured on the basis of income yield, recognizing capital gains or losses only if the securities are sold. Does this method of measuring performance have an impact on corporate dividend policy? Discuss the wisdom of this method of measuring performance.

4. Discuss the factors that would tend to bias dividend policy toward a high payout.

5. Discuss the factors that would tend to bias dividend policy toward a zero payout.

6. What effect would you expect on the firm's optimal dividend policy if the federal government began taxing all capital gains at the ordinary income tax rate?

7. What weakness do you see in the Walter formula as the indicator of an optimal policy? Consider carefully the firm's investment opportunities and optimal capital structure before you answer.

8. As the firm's financial manager, would you recommend to the board of directors that the firm adopt as policy a stable dividend payment per share or a stable payout ratio? What are the disadvantages of each? Would the firm's industry influence your decision? Why?

9. As an investor, would you prefer the firm to repurchase its stock by means of a tender offer or through open market operations? Why?

10. Why do companies with high growth rates tend to have low dividend-payout ratios, and companies with low growth rates high payout ratios?

1. The Peters Company's equity account (book value) is as follows:

    THE PETERS COMPANY EQUITY ACCOUNTS
    DECEMBER 31, 19—8

Common stock ($5 par, 1,000,000 shares)	$ 5,000,000
Contributed capital	5,000,000
Retained earnings	15,000,000
	$25,000,000

    Currently, Peters is under pressure from stockholders to pay some dividends. Peters's cash balance is $500,000, all of which is needed for transactions purposes. The stock is trading for $7/share.

    (a) What is the legal limit that can be paid in cash dividends?
    (b) What is the practical limit that can be paid in cash dividends?
    (c) Compute the equity accounts if the company pays a 20 percent stock dividend.
    (d) Compute the equity account if the company declares a 6-for-5 stock split.
    (e) Discuss the stock price movements that should occur after (c) and (d) above.

2. The L. B. Jones Corporation has the following optimal capital structure:

Bonds	30%
Preferred stock	20%
Common stock	50%

    New bonds have an after-tax cost of capital of 4 percent while preferred stock has a cost of capital of 8 percent. Stockholders expect a return of 15 percent on their capital. The current period earnings are $15 million, all of which are available for reinvestment or dividends.
    The capital budget reveals the following projects are available:

Project	Funds Required	After-tax Return on Investment
A	$10 million	20%
B	8 million	18
C	6 million	15
D	6 million	12

    (a) Determine the amount of dividends to be paid out in the current period, assuming funds will not be invested at below the cost of capital.

(b) Determine the incremental earnings available to common stockholders. Compute the return on incremental equity investment (r in Walter's formula).

(c) Using r in (b) above and the dividend in (a) above, compute the price of stock for the L. B. Jones Company using Walter's formula.

3. The T. N. Cox Company is owned by several wealthy Texas businessmen. The firm earned $3,500,000 after taxes this year. With one million shares outstanding, earnings per share were thus $3.50. The stock has recently traded at $72 per share, among the current stockholders. Two dollars of this value is accounted for by investor anticipation of a cash dividend. As financial manager of T. N. Cox, you have contemplated the alternative of repurchasing the company stock by means of a tender offer at $72 per share.

(a) How much stock could the firm repurchase if this alternative were selected?

(b) Ignoring taxes, which alternative should be selected?

(c) Considering taxes, which alternative should be selected?

(d) What might preclude the firm from choosing the preferred alternative?

4. The Axalt Corporation and the Baxalt Corporation have had remarkably similar earnings patterns over the last five years. In fact, both firms have had identical earnings per share. Further, both firms are in the same industry, produce the same product, and face the same business and financial risks. In short, these firms are carbon copies of each other in every respect but one: Axalt pays out a constant percentage of its earnings (50 percent) in dividends, while Baxalt has paid a constant cash dividend. The financial manager of the Axalt Corporation has been puzzled, however, by the fact that the price of his firm's stock has been generally lower than the price of Baxalt's stock, even though in some years Axalt's dividend was substantially larger than Baxalt's.

(a) What might account for the condition that has been puzzling the financial manager of Axalt?

(b) What might be done by both companies to increase the market prices of their stock?

	Axalt			Baxalt		
Years	EPS	Div.	Mkt. Price	EPS	Div.	Mkt. Price
19—1	$1.00	.50	$6	$1.00	.23	$4 7/8
19—2	.50	.25	4	.50	.23	4 3/8
19—3	−.25	nil	2	−.25	.23	4
19—4	.30	.15	3	.30	.23	4 1/4
19—5	.50	.25	3 1/2	.50	.23	4 1/2

5. The Xavier Cement Company has hired you as a financial consultant to advise the company with respect to its dividend policy. The cement industry has been very stable for some time, and the firm's stock has not appreciated significantly in market value for several years. However, the rapidly growing

southwestern market provides an excellent opportunity for this old, traditionally midwestern cement manufacturer to undertake a vigorous expansion program into a new market area. To do so, the company has decided to sell common stock for equity capital in the near future. The company expects its entrance into the southwestern market to be extremely profitable—returning approximately 25 percent on investment each year. In the following table, you will find data on earnings, dividends, and common stock prices.

	19—1	19—2	19—3	19—4	Anticipated 19—5
Earn./share	$ 4.32	$ 4.17	$ 4.61	$ 4.80	$ 4.75
Cash avail./share	$ 6.00	$ 5.90	$ 6.25	$ 6.35	$ 6.25
Dividend/share	$ 2.90	$ 2.80	$ 3.00	$ 3.20	?
Payout ratio	67%	67%	65%	67%	?
Avg. market price	$60.00	$58.00	$60.00	$67.00	$66.00
P/E ratio	14/1	14/1	13/1	14/1	14/1

What dividend policy recommendations would you make to the company? Specifically, what payout would you recommend for 19—5? Justify your position.

6. Malkor Instruments Company treats dividends as a residual decision. It expects to generate $2 million in net earnings after taxes in the coming year. The company has an all-equity capital structure and its cost of equity capital is 10 percent. The company treats this cost as the opportunity cost of retained earnings. Because of flotation costs and underpricing, the cost of common-stock financing is higher; it is 11 percent.

   (a) How much in dividends (out of the $2 million in earnings) should be paid if the company has $1.5 million in projects whose expected return exceeds 10 percent?

   (b) How much in dividends should be paid if it has $2 million in projects whose expected return exceeds 10 percent?

   (c) How much in dividends should be paid if it has $3 million in projects whose expected return exceeds 11 percent? What else should be done?

7. The Mann Company belongs to a risk class for which the appropriate capitalization rate is 10 percent. It currently has outstanding 100,000 shares selling at $100 each. The firm is contemplating the declaration of a $5 dividend at the end of the current fiscal year, which just began. Answer the following questions based on the Modigliani and Miller model and the assumption of no taxes.

   (a) What will be the price of the stock at the end of the year if a dividend is not declared? What will it be if one is?

   (b) Assuming that the firm pays the dividend, has net income of $1 million, and makes new investments of $2 million during the period, how many new shares must be issued?

   (c) Is the MM model realistic with respect to valuation? What factors might mar its validity?

8.

THE SHERILL CORPORATION CAPITAL STRUCTURE
DECEMBER 30, 19X3

Common stock ($1 par, 1,000,000 shares)	$1,000,000
Excess over par*	300,000
Retained earnings	1,700,000
Net worth	$3,000,000

*Also called capital surplus.

The firm earned $300,000 after taxes in 19X3 and paid out 50 percent of this in cash dividends. The price of the firm's stock on December 30 was $5.

(a) If the firm declared a stock dividend of 3 percent on December 31, what would the reformulated capital structure be?

(b) If the firm declared a 50 percent stock dividend rather than the 3 percent dividend, what would the reformulated capital structure be? *Hint:* In the case of a large stock dividend (over 25%), the reformulated capital structure should be calculated on a book value, and not a market value, basis.

(c) Assuming the firm paid no stock dividend, how much would earnings per share for 19X3 be? How much would dividends per share be?

(d) Assuming a 3 percent stock dividend, what would the EPS and DPS be for 19X3? Assuming a 50 percent dividend?

(e) What would the price of the stock be after the 3 percent dividend? After the 50 percent dividend?

SELECTED REFERENCES

BIERMAN, HAROLD, JR., and RICHARD WEST, "The Acquisition of Common Stock by the Corporate Issuer," *Journal of Finance*, 21 (December 1966), 687–96.

BLACK, FISCHER, and MYRON SCHOLES, "The Effects of Dividend Yield and Dividend Policy on Common Stock Prices and Returns," *Journal of Financial Economics*, 1 (May 1974), 1–22.

BRIGHAM, EUGENE F., and MYRON J. GORDON, "Leverage, Dividend Policy, and the Cost of Capital," *Journal of Finance*, 23 (March 1968), 85–104.

BRITTAIN, JOHN A., *Corporate Dividend Policy*. Washington, D.C.: Brookings Institution, 1966.

ELTON, EDWIN J., and MARTIN J. GRUBER, "The Cost of Retained Earnings—Implications of Share Repurchase," *Industrial Management Review*, 9 (Spring 1968), 87–104.

———, "The Effect of Share Repurchases on the Value of the Firm," *Journal of Finance*, 23 (March 1968), 135–50.

FAMA, EUGENE F., "The Empirical Relationships between the Dividend and Investment Decisions of Firms," *American Economic Review*, 64 (June 1974), 304–18.

FRIEND, IRWIN, and MARSHALL PUCKETT, "Dividends and Stock Prices," *American Economic Review*, 54 (September 1964), 656–82.

GRABOWSKI, HENRY G. and DENNIS C. MUELLER, "Life-Cycle Effects on Corporate Returns on Retentions," *Review of Economics and Statistics*, 58 (November 1975), 400–409.

HAUSMAN, W. H., R. R. WEST, and **J. A. LARGAY**, "Stock Splits, Price Changes, and Trading Profits: A Synthesis," *Journal of Business*, 45 (January 1971), 69–77.

HIGGINS, ROBERT C., "The Corporate Dividend-Saving Decision," *Journal of Financial and Quantitative Analysis*, 7 (March 1972), 1527–41.

––––––, "Dividend Policy and Increasing Discount Rate: A Clarification," *Journal of Financial and Quantitative Analysis*, 7 (June 1972), 1757–62.

JOHNSON, KEITH B., "Stock Splits and Price Changes," *Journal of Finance*, 21 (December 1966), 675–86.

KEANE, SIMON M., "Dividends and the Resolution of Uncertainty," *Journal of Finance & Accounting*, 1 (Autumn 1974), 389–93.

KRAINER, ROBERT E., "A Pedagogic Note on Dividend Policy," *Journal of Financial and Quantitative Analysis*, 6 (September 1971), 1147–54.

LAUB, P. MICHAEL and **ROSS WATTS**, "On the Informational Content of Dividends," *Journal of Business*, 49 (January 1976).

LINTNER, JOHN, "Distribution of Income of Corporations among Dividends, Retained Earnings, and Taxes," *American Economic Review* 46 (May 1956), 97–113.

––––––, "Dividends, Earnings, Leverage, Stock Prices and the Supply of Capital to Corporations," *Review of Economics and Statistics*, 44 (August 1962), 243–69.

MILLAR, JAMES A., and **BRUCE D. FIELITZ**, "Stock Splits, Stock Dividends and Share Price: Some Empirical Evidence," Paper presented at the Finance Management Association Meetings, San Antonio, October 1972.

MILLER, MERTON H., and **FRANCO MODIGLIANI**, "Dividend Policy, Growth, and the Valuation of Shares," *Journal of Business*, 34 (October 1961), 411–33.

PETTIT, R. RICHARDSON, "Dividend Announcements, Security Performance, and Capital Market Efficiency," *Journal of Finance*, 27 (December 1972), 993–1007.

––––––, "On the Impact of Dividend and Earnings Announcements," *Journal of Business*, 49 (January 1976).

PETTWAY, RICHARD H., and **R. PHIL MALONE**, "Automatic Dividend Reinvestment Plans of Nonfinancial Corporations," *Financial Management*, 2 (Winter 1973), 11–18.

PORTERFIELD, JAMES T. S., "Dividends, Dilution, and Delusion," *Harvard Business Review*, 37 (November–December 1959), 156–61.

––––––, *Investment Decisions and Capital Costs*, Chapter 6. Englewood Cliffs, N.J.: Prentice-Hall, 1965.

STEVENSON, RICHARD, "Corporate Stock Reacquisitions," *Accounting Review*, 41 (April 1966), 312–17.

VAN HORNE, JAMES C., and **JOHN G. McDONALD**, "Dividend Policy and New Equity Financing," *Journal of Finance*, 26 (May 1971), 507–19.

WALTER, JAMES E., "Dividend Policies and Common Stock Prices," *Journal of Finance*, 11 (March 1956), 29–41.

––––––, *Dividend Policy and Enterprise Valuation*. Belmont, Calif.: Wadsworth, 1967.

WEST, RICHARD R., and **ALAN B. BROUILETTE**, "Reverse Stock Splits," *Financial Executive*, 38 (January 1970), 12–17.

YOUNG, ALLAN, "Financial, Operating and Security Market Parameters of Repurchasing," *Financial Analysts Journal*, 25 (July–August 1969), 123–28.

VI Long-Term Financing

Money and Capital Markets *20*

The purpose of this chapter is to explore the money and capital markets from which a firm obtains external financing. In this regard, we study the flow of savings through financial markets as well as the role of interest rates in allocating funds among prospective users. Our initial focus is on the overall function of financial markets, but later we concentrate on how these markets affect the raising of funds by business firms. Hopefully, this chapter will provide the macrofinance setting preparatory to our discussion of long-term financing. In particular, an understanding here should make possible a better understanding of how business firms compete for funds in financial markets.

Different financial markets are classified according to the final maturity of the instrument involved. *Money* markets usually are regarded as including financial assets that are short-term, that are highly marketable, and that have a low degree of risk. Examples include Treasury bills, commercial paper, bankers' acceptances, and negotiable certificates of deposit. These instruments are traded in highly impersonal markets, where funds move on the basis of price and risk alone. Thus, a short-term loan negotiated between a company and a bank is not considered a money-market instrument. *Capital* markets include instruments with longer terms to maturity. Examples include the markets for government, corporate, and municipal bonds, corporate stocks, and mortgages. The maturity boundary that divides the money and capital markets is rather arbitrary, being one to five years, depending upon who is doing the classifying. In the section that follows, we consider the basics of why financial markets exist and their function.

Financial assets exist in an economy because the savings of various individuals, corporations, and governments during a period of time differ from their investment in real assets. If savings equaled investment for all economic units in an economy over all periods of time, there would be no external financing, no financial assets, and no money and capital markets. Each economic unit would be self-sufficient; current expenditures and investment in real assets would be paid for out of current income. A financial asset is created only when the investment of an economic unit in real assets exceeds its savings, and it finances this excess by borrowing or issuing equity securities. For an economic unit to finance, of course, another economic unit must be willing to lend. This interaction of borrowers with lenders determines interest rates. In the economy as a whole, funds are provided by savings-surplus economic units whose savings exceed their investment in real assets to savings-deficit units whose investment in real assets exceeds their savings. This exchange of funds is evidenced by pieces of paper representing a financial asset to the holder and a financial liability to the issuer.

Efficiency of financial markets

The purpose of financial markets is to allocate savings efficiently in an economy to ultimate users. If those economic units that saved were the same as those that engaged in capital formation, an economy could prosper without financial markets. In modern economies, however, the economic units most responsible for capital formation—nonfinancial corporations—invest in real assets in an amount in excess of their total savings. Households, on the other hand, have total savings in excess of total investment. The more diverse the patterns of desired savings and investment among economic units, the greater the need for efficient financial markets to channel savings to ultimate users. The ultimate investor in real assets and the ultimate saver should be brought together at the least possible cost and/or inconvenience to both.

Efficient financial markets are absolutely essential to assure adequate capital formation and economic growth in an economy. If there were no financial assets other than paper money, each economic unit could invest only to the extent that it saved. Without financial assets, then, an economic unit would be greatly constrained in its investment behavior. If the amounts required for investment in a real asset were large in relation to current savings, an economic unit simply would have to postpone investment until it had accumulated sufficient savings in the form of paper money. Because of the absence of financing, many worthwhile investment opportunities would have to be postponed or abandoned by economic units lacking sufficient savings.[1]

In such a system, savings in the economy would not be channeled to the most promising investment opportunities; and capital would be less than optimally allocated. Those economic units that lacked promising investment opportunities would have no alternative but to accumulate money. Likewise, economic units with very promising opportunities might not be able to accumulate sufficient savings rapidly enough to undertake the projects. Consequently, inferior investments might be undertaken by some economic units while very promising opportunities would be postponed or abandoned by others. It is not difficult to see the importance of being able to issue financial assets. However, even with this ability, there are still degrees of efficiency with which savings are channeled to investment opportunities.

A number of institutions have evolved to improve this efficiency. The more developed the financial markets of a country are, the greater the efficiency. One institution is the loan broker, whose purpose is to find savers and to bring them together with economic units needing funds. Because a broker is a specialist who is continually in the business of matching the need for funds with the supply, usually he is able to do it more efficiently and at a lower cost than are individual economic units themselves. Another institution that enhances the efficiency of the flow of savings is the secondary market, where existing securities can be bought or sold. With a viable secondary market, a purchaser of a financial instrument achieves marketability. If it needs to sell the security in the future, it will be able to do so. Thus, the existence of a strong secondary market enhances the primary market in which funds flow from ultimate savers to ultimate users. Investment bankers also enhance funds flows; and we study their role in depth in the next chapter.

Financial intermediaries

Up to now, we have considered only the direct flow of savings from savers to users of funds. However, the flow can be indirect if there are financial intermediaries in an economy. Financial intermediaries include such institutions as commercial banks, savings banks, savings and loan associations, life insurance companies, and pension and profit-sharing funds. These intermediaries come between ultimate borrowers and lenders by transforming direct claims into indirect ones. They purchase primary securities and, in turn, issue their own

---

[1] See John G. Gurley and Edward S. Shaw, *Money in a Theory of Finance* (Washington, D.C.: Brookings Institution, 1960); and John G. Gurley, "The Savings-Investment Process and the Market for Loanable Funds," reprinted in Lawrence S. Ritter, ed., *Money and Economic Activity* (Boston: Houghton Mifflin, 1967), pp. 50–55.

securities. For example, the primary security that a savings and loan association purchases is a mortgage; the indirect claim issued is a savings account or a certificate of deposit. A life insurance company, on the other hand, purchases corporate bonds, among other things, and issues life insurance policies.

Financial intermediaries transform funds in such a way as to make them more attractive.[2] A variety of services and economies are provided. For one, economies of scale are possible and may be passed on to the borrower and lender in the form of lower cost of operations. A financial intermediary also is able to pool savings to purchase primary securities of varying sizes. Most individual savers would have difficulty investing in a $20,000 mortgage. By putting funds in a savings and loan association, however, they are able to indirectly invest in a mortgage. Another service provided is diversification of risk—something not necessarily possible for the individual saver. Also, financial intermediaries are able to transform the maturity of a primary security into indirect securities of different maturities. As a result, the maturities may be more attractive to the ultimate lender than they would be if the loan were direct. Finally, the financial intermediary provides expertise in investing in primary securities which many savers do not have.

Thus, financial intermediaries tailor the denomination and type of indirect securities they issue to the desires of savers. Their purpose, of course, is to make a profit by purchasing primary securities yielding more than the return they must pay on the indirect securities issued and their expenses. In so doing, they channel funds from the ultimate lender to the ultimate borrower at a lower cost or with less inconvenience or both than is possible through a direct purchase of primary securities by the ultimate lender. Otherwise, they have no reason to exist.

Principal sectors in the economy

With the introduction of financial intermediaries, we have four main sectors in the economy: households, nonfinancial business firms, governments, and financial institutions. These four sectors form a matrix of claims against one another. This matrix is illustrated in Figure 20-1, which shows a hypothetical balance sheet for each sector. Households are the ultimate owners of all business enterprises, whether they be nonfinancial corporations or private financial institutions. The figure illustrates the distinct role of financial intermediaries. Their assets are primarily financial assets; they hold a relatively small amount of

---

[2] See Raymond W. Goldsmith, *Financial Institutions* (New York: Random House, 1968), pp. 22–23.

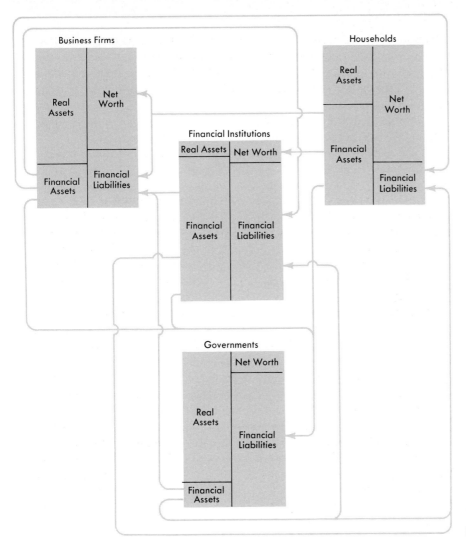

FIG. 20 · 1

Relationship of claims

real assets. On the right-hand side of their balance sheet, financial liabilities predominate. Financial institutions, then, are engaged in transforming direct claims into indirect ones that have a wider appeal.

Flow of funds matrix. We can study the flow of savings between sectors through the use of flow of funds data published in the *Federal Reserve Bulletin.* This system of social accounting provides an interlocking picture of funds flows in the economy.[3] Essentially, a source and use statement is prepared for each sector similar to the preparation in Chapter 4 of a source and use statement for an individual firm.

[3] See Lawrence S. Ritter, *The Flow of Funds Accounts: A Framework for Financial Analysis* (New York: Institute of Finance, New York University, 1968); and James C. Van Horne, *The Function and Analysis of Capital Market Rates* (Englewood Cliffs, N.J.: Prentice-Hall, 1970), Chapter 2, for further analysis of this system.

The flows are simply the changes in balance sheet figures between two moments in time. When source and use statements are combined, we obtain a matrix for the entire economy. A hypothetical matrix for a closed economy consisting of four sectors is shown in Table 20-1. In the table, we see that total uses of funds equals total sources for each sector; that is, the investment in real assets plus changes in financial assets must equal savings plus changes in financial liabilities.

We see also that business firms in aggregate invested in real assets to a greater extent than they saved. The difference was financed by issuing financial liabilities in excess of the increase in financial assets held. The existence of this large savings deficit sector implies the existence of one or more savings-surplus sectors. When we analyze the matrix, we see that households were a savings-surplus sector and primarily responsible for financing the business firms sector on a net basis. In addition, financial institutions were a savings-surplus sector, although the excess of savings over investment for this sector was small. This sector acts almost entirely as an intermediary, increasing its holdings of financial assets by issuing financial liabilities. Finally, governments, the fourth category, was a savings-deficit sector. Although governments make substantial expenditures for real assets, unfortunately they are not officially recorded. The budget deficit for governments is financed by an increase in financial liabilities in excess of the increase in financial assets. Because the financial institutions sector contains commercial banks and the monetary authorities, it "provides" money to other sectors in the economy. The $5 source of money for this sector represents an increase in demand deposits and currency held by the public and governments as claims against commercial banks and the monetary authorities.

TABLE 20 · 1

Matrix of Flow of Funds of Entire Economy, 19—

	Households		Business Firms		Financial Institutions		Governments		All Sectors	
	U	S	U	S	U	S	U	S	U	S
Net worth (savings)		101		77		4		−3		179
Real assets (investment)	82		96		1				179	
Money	2		2			5	1		5	5
Other financial assets	37		18		60		17		132	
Financial liabilities		20		39		52		21		132
	121	121	116	116	61	61	18	18	316	316

In the "All Sectors" column, we see that total uses equal total sources. More important, total savings for all sectors in the economy equal the total increase in real assets. Likewise, the total change in financial assets equals the total change in financial liabilities. Thus, financial assets and financial liabilities cancel out in the economy as a whole. In other words, there is no such thing as saving through financial assets for the economy as a whole. The financial asset held by one economic unit is the financial liability of another. However, individual economic units can save through financial assets, and this is the process we wish to study. The fact that financial assets wash out when they are totaled for all economic units in the economy is a recognized identity. It is the interaction between the issuers of financial claims and the potential holders of those claims that is important. In this regard, we consider business firms in detail. Unfortunately, space does not permit a like consideration of the other sectors.

CHANNELS OF FUNDS FLOWS TO AND FROM BUSINESS FIRMS

We know from our previous discussion that business firms are a savings-deficit sector. The major sources of funds to finance the excess of their investment in real assets over savings are households and financial institutions. The former represent a direct flow, while the latter represent an indirect one. Of course, business firms finance each other through accounts receivable and other arrangements, but these funds flows wash out when we consider business firms in aggregate. A precise breakdown of the sources and uses of funds for the 1969–74 period is shown in Table 20-2. We see that the principal use of funds by business firms is for plant and equipment. Of the total sources of funds, internal sources—comprised of retained earnings and depreciation allowances—account for nearly three-fifths, with external sources accounting for the remainder. Of the external sources, net new bond issues and stock issues were the most important categories, followed by mortgage debt and bank loans, both short-term and term.

The principal net investors in bond and stock issues (common and preferred) over the 1969–74 period, as well as the amounts held by them at 1974 year-end, are shown in Table 20-3. For corporate bonds, we note the importance of such institutional investors as life insurance companies, pension funds, and state and local government retirement funds as well as the importance of individual investors. With respect to corporate stocks, the most important investors on a net basis are pension funds, state and local government retirement funds, and life insurance companies. Note that during the period studied, individuals steadily reduced their holdings of stocks on a net basis. These reductions, together with net new issues, were largely picked up

TABLE 20 · 2

Sources and Uses of Corporate Funds (in $billions)

	Annual Net Increases in Amounts Outstanding					
	1969	1970	1971	1972	1973	1974E
Uses of funds:						
Plant and equipment	74.0	75.1	77.1	87.1	103.3	115.3
Land	7.7	7.8	8.2	9.3	10.9	11.9
Direct foreign investment	2.2	3.6	3.8	1.5	3.6	5.0
Residential construction	2.9	3.3	5.0	5.7	5.3	4.0
Inventories, adjusted for valuation	6.7	5.7	5.1	9.7	12.9	11.8
Total Physical Investment	93.5	95.5	99.2	113.3	136.0	148.0
Net Trade and Consumer Credit	2.1	1.6	6.4	8.9	4.0	9.0
Demand deposits and currency	2.6	0.9	0.5	−0.1	−0.3	−1.5
Time deposits	−2.4	1.7	3.6	3.1	1.4	7.0
U.S. governments	−2.8	0.4	2.1	−3.2	−3.0	1.5
Federal agencies	0.5	0.1	0.1	0.7	1.2	0.0
Open market paper	7.3	−0.1	−0.3	1.5	3.7	4.2
State and local securities	1.5	−0.8	2.1	−0.4	0.2	0.8
Repurchase agreements	1.4	−3.4	0.8	1.6	2.6	1.6
Foreign currencies	−0.4	−0.4	1.4	1.8	2.6	−0.4
Other financial assets (net)	−6.7	0.6	1.5	7.9	7.4	−6.7
Total Uses	96.6	96.1	117.4	135.1	155.8	163.5
Sources of funds:						
Internal cash generation	58.0	56.5	69.9	78.3	87.1	88.3
Mortgage debt	4.6	5.2	11.4	15.6	16.1	11.3
Bank term-loans	4.7	−0.5	−0.5	2.8	12.0	12.7
Bank short-term loans	7.1	6.1	4.9	10.7	18.6	18.1
Finance company loans	4.3	0.4	1.9	2.8	2.0	2.7
U.S. government loans	0.1	0.3	0.2	0.2	0.3	0.1
Net sales of open-market paper	2.3	2.2	−0.6	0.7	1.3	4.8
Net new stock issues	3.4	5.7	11.4	10.9	7.4	3.1
Net new tax-exempt bond issues	0.0	0.0	0.1	0.5	1.8	2.0
Net new taxable bond issues	12.1	20.2	18.7	12.6	9.2	20.4
Total external sources	38.6	39.6	47.5	56.8	68.7	75.2
Total sources	96.6	96.1	117.4	135.1	155.8	163.5

Source: *Supply and Demand for Credit in 1975* (New York: Salomon Brothers, 1975), p. 14.

TABLE 20 · 3

Changes in Ownership of Corporate Bonds and Stocks (in $billions)

	1969	1970	1971	1972	1973	1974	Amount Outstanding 12/31/74E
Corporate Bonds:							
Mutual savings banks	0.3	1.2	2.9	2.1	−1.4	0.8	13.9
Life insurance companies	1.6	1.2	5.4	6.4	5.1	4.9	88.4
Fire and casualty companies	0.8	2.2	0.3	−0.7	−0.1	0.2	7.8
Private non-insured pension funds	0.5	1.9	−0.7	−0.7	1.4	4.3	31.8
State and local retirement funds	3.2	3.7	3.9	4.3	3.5	5.5	48.8
Open-end mutual funds	0.2	0.7	0.6	0.2	−0.9	−0.5	3.7
Total non-bank investing institutions	6.6	10.9	12.4	11.6	7.6	15.2	194.4
Commercial Banks	−0.1	0.8	1.3	1.4	0.4	0.6	6.4
Foreigners	0.5	0.7	0.3	0.1	0.1	1.4	3.8
Residual: individuals and misc.	6.8	10.4	9.7	6.0	4.6	7.5	68.8
Total ownership	13.8	22.8	23.7	19.1	12.7	24.7	273.4
Corporate Stock (Common and Preferred):							
Mutual savings banks	0.3	0.3	0.5	0.6	0.4	0.2	3.6
Life insurance companies	1.7	2.0	3.7	3.7	3.5	2.0	24.0
Fire and casualty companies	0.8	1.2	2.6	3.2	2.2	1.2	16.0
Private non-insured pension funds	5.4	4.6	8.9	7.3	5.3	2.2	69.9
State and local retirement funds	1.8	2.1	3.2	3.5	3.9	3.6	17.3
Open-end mutual funds	1.7	1.2	0.4	−1.8	−2.3	0.0	28.1
Total non-bank investing institutions	11.7	11.4	19.3	16.5	13.0	9.2	158.9
Foreigners	1.6	0.7	0.8	2.3	2.8	0.6	18.7
Residual: individuals and misc.	−9.0	−5.3	−6.6	−5.8	−6.8	−6.6	458.4
Total ownership	4.3	6.8	13.5	13.0	9.0	3.2	636.0

Source: *Supply and Demand for Credit in 1975* (New York: Salomon Brothers, 1975), pp. 12, 15.

by institutional investors. This pattern has been going on since the early 1960s. Even with a significant reduction in holdings, however, individuals are by far the largest holders of corporate stocks. The last column of Table 20-3 shows that they accounted for 70 percent of the value of corporate stocks at 1974 year-end. However, individuals increasingly are becoming indirect rather than direct owners of corporate stocks by virtue of their indirect claims on financial institutions.

From the end of World War II through 1968, there was a negligible amount of net corporate stock financing. As a result, institutional investors could increase their holdings only by purchasing stock on a net basis from individuals. Since 1969, however, corporations have made moderate use of equity offerings as a means of financing. Table 20-3 points to the importance of financial intermediaries in channeling funds to business firms. In addition to their importance in investing in corporate bonds and stocks, they also are important in mortgage debt financing and bank loans, which are shown in Table 20-2. Mortgage debt comes primarily from such financial institutions as life insurance companies and commercial banks. Bank loans, of course, come from one of the largest intermediaries, commercial banks. The indirect claims that financial intermediaries issue ultimately are held by individuals. Thus, individuals are the ultimate source of net financing for business firms.

In summary, internal financing is the principal means for supporting asset growth by business firms, accounting for somewhat less than 60 percent of their total funds requirements. Corporate bonds and stocks followed by mortgage debt and bank loans are the principal means of external financing. A large portion of the funds received from a security issue do not come directly from ultimate savings-deficit economic units in society but rather through financial intermediaries. These intermediaries, in turn, issue indirect claims to ultimate savers.

ALLOCATION OF FUNDS THROUGH YIELDS

The allocation of savings in an economy occurs primarily on the basis of price, expressed in terms of expected yield. Economic units in need of funds must outbid others for their use. Although the allocation process is affected by capital rationing, government restrictions, and institutional constraints, yields are the primary mechanism whereby supply and demand are brought into balance for a particular financial instrument across financial markets. Holding risk constant, those economic units willing to pay the highest yield are the ones entitled to the use of funds. If rationality prevails, the economic units bidding the highest prices will be the ones with the most promising investment opportunities. As a result, savings will tend to be allocated to the most efficient uses.

It is important to recognize that the equilibration process by which savings are allocated in an economy occurs not only on the basis of expected return but on the basis of risk as well. Different financial instruments have different degrees of risk. In order for them to compete for funds, these instruments must provide different expected returns, or yields. If all financial instruments had exactly the same risk characteristics, they would provide the same yield in market equilibrium. Because of differences in default risk, marketability, maturity, and taxability, however, different instruments pose different degrees of risk and provide different effective returns to the investor. (A fifth factor, callability, is considered in detail in Chapter 22.)

Default risk

When we speak of default risk, we mean the risk of default on the part of the borrower in the payment of principal or interest. Investors demand a risk premium to invest in other than default-free securities. The greater the possibility that the borrower will default in his obligation, the greater the default risk and the premium demanded by the marketplace. Treasury securities usually are regarded as default-free, and other securities are judged in relation to them. The greater the default risk of a security issuer, then, the greater the expected return or yield of the security should be, all other things the same.[4]

For the typical investor, default risk is not judged directly but rather in terms of quality ratings assigned by Moody's Investor Service or Standard & Poor's. These investment agencies assign letter grades, which are published for the use of investors. In their ratings, the agencies attempt to rank issues according to the probability of default. A number of factors go into the analysis of an issue by an agency, including the cash-flow ability of the issuer to service debt, the amount and composition of existing debt, and the stability of cash flows. The highest-grade securities, whose default risk is felt to be negligible, are rated triple-A. The ratings used by the two agencies are shown in Table 20-4.[5]

---

[4]For empirical investigations of default risk premiums, see Lawrence Fisher, "Determinants of Risk Premiums on Corporate Bonds," *Journal of Political Economy*, 47 (June 1959), 217–37; Ramon E. Johnson, "Term Structure of Corporate Bond Yields," *Journal of Finance*, 22 (May 1967), 313–45; and Ray C. Fair and Burton G. Malkiel, "The Determination of Yield Differentials between Debt Instruments of the Same Maturity," *Journal of Money, Credit, and Banking*, pp. 733–49. For a much more extended discussion of default risk, see Van Horne, *Function and Analysis of Capital Market Rates*, Chapter 5.

[5]For an analysis of bond-rating methods, see James S. Ang and Kiritkumar A. Patel, "Bond Rating Methods: Comparison and Validation," *Journal of Finance*, 30 (May 1975), 631–40.

TABLE 20 · 4

Ratings by Investment Agencies

Moody's

Aaa	Best quality
Aa	High quality
A	Higher medium grade
Baa	Lower medium grade
Ba	Possess speculative elements
B	Generally lack characteristics of desirable investment
Caa	Poor standing; may be in default
Ca	Speculative in a high degree; often in default
C	Lowest grade

Standard & Poor's

AAA	Highest grade
AA	High grade
A	Upper medium grade
BBB	Medium grade
BB	Lower medium grade
B	Speculative
CCC–CC	Outright speculation
C	Reserved for income bonds
DDD–D	In default, with rating indicating relative salvage value

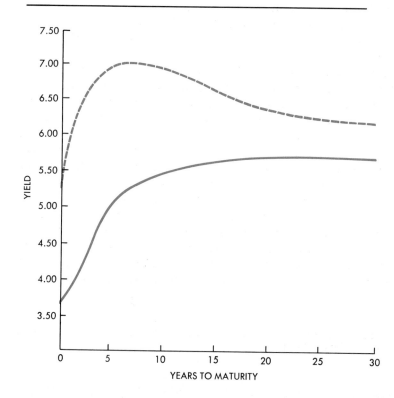

FIG. 20 · 2

Government yield curves

Marketability

Marketability of a security relates to the ability of the owner to convert it into cash. There are two dimensions: the price realized and the amount of time required to sell the asset. The two are interrelated in that it is often possible to sell an asset in a short period of time if enough price concession is given. For financial instruments, marketability is judged in relation to the ability to sell a significant volume of securities in a short period of time without significant price concession. The more marketable the security, the greater the ability to execute a large transaction near the quoted price. In general, the lower the marketability of a security, the greater the yield necessary to attract investors. Thus, the yield differential between different securities of the same maturity is caused not only by differences in default risk but also by differences in marketability.

Maturity

The relationship between yield and maturity can be studied graphically by plotting yield and maturity for securities differing only in the length of time to maturity. In practice, this means holding constant the degree of default risk. For example, we could study the yield-maturity relationship for default-free Treasury securities. An example of the yield-maturity relationship for Treasury securities on two separate dates is shown in Figure 20-2. Maturity is plotted on the horizontal axis and yield on the vertical; their relationship is described by a yield curve fitted to the observations.

Generally, when interest rates are expected to rise, the yield curve is upward-sloping, whereas it is humped and downward-sloping when they are expected to fall significantly. However, the yield differential between short- and long-term securities is greater for the steepest upward-sloping yield curve than the negative difference is for the steepest downward-sloping yield curve. In other words, there is a tendency for positive-sloped yield curves. Most economists attribute this tendency to the presence of risk for those who invest in long-term securities vis-à-vis short-term securities. In general, the longer the maturity, the greater the risk of fluctuation in the market value of the security. Consequently, investors need to be offered a risk premium to induce them to invest in long-term securities. Only when interest rates are expected to fall significantly are they willing to invest in long-term securities yielding less than short- and intermediate-term securities.[6]

---

[6]For a much deeper discussion of this concept, see Van Horne, *Function and Analysis of Capital Market Rates,* Chapter 4.

Taxability

Another factor affecting observed differences in market yields is the differential impact of taxes. The most important tax, and the only one we shall consider, is the income tax. The interest income on all but one category of securities is taxable to taxable investors. Interest income from state and local government securities is tax-exempt; as a result, they sell in the market at lower yields to maturity than Treasury and corporate securities of the same maturity. A differential impact on yields arises also because interest income is taxed at the ordinary tax rate, while capital gains on securities held more than six months are taxed at the more favorable capital-gains tax rate. As a result, fixed-income securities that sell at a discount because of a low coupon rate in relation to prevailing yields are attractive to taxable investors. The reason is that part of the yield to maturity is a capital gain. Because of the desirability of discount bonds, their yield to maturity tends to be lower than the yield on comparable bonds with higher coupon rates. The greater the discount, the greater the capital-gains attraction and the lower its yield relative to what it would be if the coupon rate were such that the security sold at par.

Behavior of yields on corporate securities

As a result of differences in default risk, marketability, maturity, and taxability, the costs of funds to business firms vary. In Figure 20-3, the yields on Aaa corporate bonds, Baa corporate bonds, and prime grade commercial paper are shown for the 1962–75 period. Because of the difference in default risk, Baa bonds provide a higher yield than do Aaa bonds. Moreover, this differential tends to widen during recessionary periods as investors become more risk-averse. This phenomenon is particularly evident in 1974–75. The difference in yield between Aaa bonds and prime commercial paper issued by corporations is due primarily to differences in maturity. As reflected in the figure, short-term interest rates, as typified by the commercial paper rate, fluctuate more than do long-term rates. This phenomenon is attributable to expectations of the future course of interest rates affecting short- and long-term rates in different ways. The maturity of a short-term instrument, by definition, is near. At maturity, the investor receives the face value of the instrument, assuming there is no default. Accordingly, there is far less investor uncertainty with respect to fluctuations in the market value of the instrument than there is with a long-term security.

The relevant expectations for commercial paper involve only the near future. The relevant expectations for bonds involve a much longer period of time. To illustrate the difference, suppose the economy were in a period of excessive inflation and that the monetary authorities had begun to tighten money. The accompanying reduction in the growth of the money supply would put upward pressure on short-term rates. However, by virtue of the monetary authorities tightening money, investors might believe that inflation would ultimately come under control and that interest rates would decline after a year or so. As a result, long-term bond yields might not rise and could actually decline some-

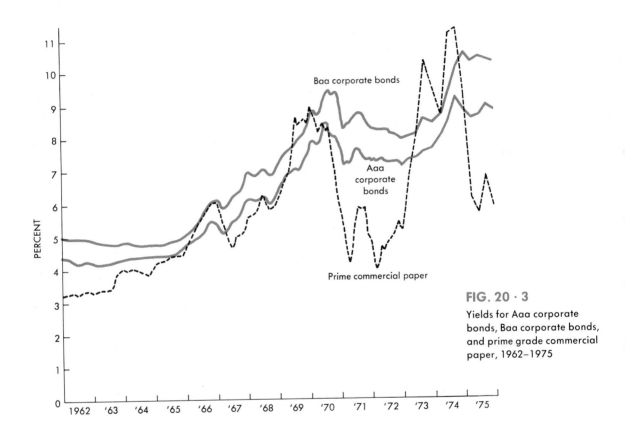

FIG. 20 · 3

Yields for Aaa corporate bonds, Baa corporate bonds, and prime grade commercial paper, 1962–1975

what in anticipation of interest rates eventually moving down. Thus, the two rates might temporarily move in opposite directions as they did in early 1970, in late 1972, and in late 1973-early 1974. Over the long run, however, short and long rates tend to move in the same direction as shown in the figure. The important point to all of this discussion, however, is that short-term rates reflect immediate supply and demand pressures in financial markets, while long-term rates are much more influenced by long-run expectations.

Factors affecting expectations

The most important factors affecting interest-rate expectations are general economic conditions, monetary policy, and fiscal policy. Economic conditions are the underlying determinant of the real rate of interest as well as of inflation. When the economy is booming, there typically is a high demand for funds to finance investment in real assets relative to savings. Moreover, inflation typically increases in the latter part of a boom. As a result, interest rates tend to rise. In a recession, on the other hand, demand for funds tends to be lower in relation to the supply, and inflation tends to decline in the face of excess capacity in productive resources and labor. As a result, interest rates tend to decline.[7] Thus, expectations of the future state of the economy have an extremely important effect upon interest rates in general and upon long-term rates in particular.

Monetary policy attempts to influence the rate of growth in economic activity and the rate of inflation by control over the supply of money. Consequently, it affects interest-rate expectations. Fiscal policy also influences economic activity and inflation because of the significant role the government plays in the economy. Policies with respect to expenditures, taxation, and borrowing have a substantial impact on economic activity and inflationary expectations. As a result, they affect interest-rate expectations. Moreover, the federal government is the largest single borrower in the money and capital markets. Therefore, it has a direct effect on the supply of securities in these markets and upon interest rates. In summary, all of these factors—economic activity, monetary policy, and fiscal policy—have an important influence on interest-rate expectations.

Bond versus stock yields

The expected return for common stocks is not as easily measured as is that for bonds. This return is comprised of dividends received plus the capital gain or loss that arises from the sale of the stock at the end of a holding period. Unfortunately, only the current dividend is directly observable. The capital-gains component must be estimated. As long as future dividends are expected to rise, the current dividend yield on a stock—that is, dividend per share divided by market price per share—will be less than the expected return from holding the stock. The current dividend yield simply omits the prospect for capital gains. Therefore, it is not appropriate to compare dividend yields on common stocks with the yields on bonds.

[7]There are exceptions, as evidenced in particular by 1974 when inflation and interest rates rose despite a recession. The topic of inflation is complicated by somewhat unpredictable lags and the interaction of many forces. A detailed discussion of inflation is beyond the scope of this book.

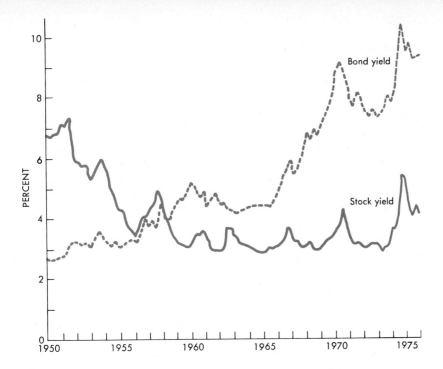

FIG. 20 · 4

Bond yields and
stock yields, 1950–1975

To illustrate this point, consider Figure 20-4, where the dividend yields for Standard & Poor's 500-market-stock index are compared with yields on Aa public utility bonds over the 1950–75 period.[8] Until the mid-1950s, stock yields were in excess of bond yields and had been for approximately fifty years. The popular reasoning for this spread was that stocks had to yield more than bonds because of the greater risk. In a rough sense, the yield spread between the two was thought to represent the risk premium necessary to attract investors into common stocks. When the bond yield line crossed the stock yield line in the mid-1950s, this type of reasoning was shattered. It became clear that the analysis of risk premiums was based upon an inappropriate measure of the return on common stocks. During the 1950s, growth expectations increased and prospective capital gains became an increasingly more important component of the expected return. This component was not reflected in the dividend yield. As a result, the direct comparison of corporate bond and stock yields was not a relevant guide to differences in expected return and risk.

The measurement of the expected return on common stocks must be based upon considerations similar to those discussed in Chapter 16, where we discussed the cost of equity capital. Recall that we attempted to estimate the expected future stream of dividends. The expected return from investment was then defined as the rate of discount which equated the present value of this stream with the market price of the stock.

[8]The Standard & Poor's 500-stock index is a broad-gauged market index that best typifies the market as a whole.

Financial assets exist in an economy because the investment in real assets by various economic units frequently differs from that unit's savings. An excess of investment over savings is financed by issuing a financial liability, while a surplus of savings over investment in real assets is held in the form of financial assets. The purpose of financial markets is to efficiently allocate savings in an economy to ultimate users of funds. A number of factors make financial markets efficient. Among the most important is the presence of financial intermediaries. A financial intermediary transforms the direct claim of an ultimate borrower into an indirect claim, which is sold to ultimate lenders. Intermediaries channel savings from ultimate savers to ultimate borrowers at a lower cost and with less inconvenience than is possible on a direct basis.

We can study the flow of savings from ultimate savers to ultimate borrowers through flow-of-funds data. We saw that for the economy as a whole, investment in real assets must equal savings. However, this is not true for individual economic units; they can have considerable divergence between savings and investment for a particular period. For business firms, the principal means for supporting investment in real assets is internal financing, or savings. However, business firms are a savings-deficit sector and make extensive use of external financing. The predominant sources of external financing are bond issues, stock issues, mortgage debt, and bank loans. The greatest portion of funds received do not come directly from individuals but indirectly through financial intermediaries.

The allocation of savings in an economy occurs primarily on the basis of expected return and risk. In turn, the overall risk of a security depends upon the likelihood of default, its marketability, its maturity, and certain tax considerations. Different financial instruments provide different yields because of differences in these factors. The differences in yields on Aaa corporate bonds, Baa corporate bonds, and prime commercial paper were studied in light of these factors. With respect to maturity, interest-rate expectations play an important role in distinguishing short-term instruments from long-term ones. The primary factors affecting such expectations are economic conditions, monetary policy, and fiscal policy. The expected return on investment in a common stock must include expected capital appreciation as well as the current dividend. The expected return on a stock is greater than its dividend yield, if future growth in earnings and dividends is expected. For this reason, it is inappropriate to compare the dividend yield on common stocks with the yield on bonds.

1. What is the purpose of financial markets? How can this purpose be accomplished efficiently?

2. Discuss the functions of financial intermediaries.

3. Business firms finance about two-thirds of their needs internally. As a result, many argue that professional management teams are isolated from investors; thus management teams run an enterprise for management, not for stockholders.
   (a) What forces in the economy might break down management's isolation from investors?
   (b) If management teams do in fact become isolated, what will be the impact on the efficiency of the economy?

4. The W. T. Grant Company bankruptcy, the Equity Funding scandal, Penn Central's bankruptcy, and other incidents that have made headlines cause investors to revise their expectation of risk and return associated with financial instruments. What is the impact of such incidents on capital formation and on the economic development of our society?

5. What is the purpose of stock market exchanges such as the New York Stock Exchange?

6. What would be the effect of the following occurrences on the money and capital markets?
   (a) The savings rate of individuals in the country declines.
   (b) Individuals increase their savings at savings and loan associations and decrease their savings at banks.
   (c) The government taxes capital gains at the ordinary income tax rate.
   (d) Unanticipated inflation of substantial magnitude occurs and price levels are rising rapidly.
   (e) Savings institutions and lenders increase the transaction charge for savings and for making loans.

7. Suppose nonfinancial corporations had relatively great liquidity. Nonetheless, there developed a great demand for funds by municipalities and the federal government. What would be the effect on interest rates for corporate bonds? What would be the effect if corporations developed a large need for funds but first financed themselves by reducing their liquidity?

8. Can you name an innovation in financial instrument, institution, or practice? What is the characteristic of a financial innovation? Whom do they benefit?

SELECTED REFERENCES

DOUGALL, HERBERT E., and **JACK E. GAUMNITZ**, *Capital Markets and Institutions*, 3rd ed. Englewood Cliffs, N.J.: Prentice-Hall, 1975.

GOLDSMITH, RAYMOND W., *Capital Market Analysis and the Financial Accounts of the Nation*. Morristown, N.J.: General Learning Press, 1972.

————, *Financial Institutions*. New York: Random House, 1968.

————, *The Flow of Capital Funds in the Postwar Economy*. New York: National Bureau of Economic Research, 1965.

GURLEY, JOHN G., "The Savings-Investment Process and the Market for Loanable Funds," reprinted in Lawrence S. Ritter, ed., *Money and Economic Activity*, pp. 50–55. Boston: Houghton Mifflin, 1967.

GURLEY, JOHN G., and **EDWARD S. SHAW**, *Money in a Theory of Finance*. Washington, D.C.: Brookings Institution, 1960.

HENNING, CHARLES N., **WILLIAM PIGOTT**, and **ROBERT H. SCOTT**, *Financial Markets and the Economy*. Englewood Cliffs, N.J.: Prentice-Hall, 1975.

HOMER, SIDNEY, and **MARTIN L. LEIBOWITZ**, *Inside the Yield Book*. Englewood Cliffs, N.J.: Prentice-Hall, 1972.

JACOBS, DONALD P., **LORING C. FARWELL**, and **EDWIN H. NEAVE**, *Financial Institutions*. Homewood, Ill.: Richard D. Irwin, 1972.

KAUFMAN, GEORGE G., *Money, the Financial System, and the Economy*. Chicago: Rand McNally, 1973.

MOORE, BASIL J., *An Introduction to the Theory of Finance*. New York: Free Press, 1968.

POLAKOFF, MURRAY E., et al., *Financial Institutions and Markets*. Boston: Houghton Mifflin, 1970.

RITTER, LAWRENCE S., *The Flow of Funds Accounts: A Framework for Financial Analysis*. New York: Institute of Finance, New York University, 1968.

RITTER, LAWRENCE S., and **WILLIAM L. SILBER**, *Principles of Money, Banking, and Financial Markets*. New York: Basic Books, 1974.

ROBINSON, ROLAND I., and **DWAYNE WRIGHTSMAN**, *Financial Markets: The Accumulation and Allocation of Wealth*. New York: McGraw-Hill, 1974.

SMITH, PAUL F., *Economics of Financial Institutions and Markets*. Homewood, Ill.: Richard D. Irwin, 1971.

VAN HORNE, JAMES C., *The Function and Analysis of Capital Market Rates*. Englewood Cliffs, N.J.: Prentice-Hall, 1970.

External Financing of Long-Term Needs 21

In the last chapter, we studied how business firms obtain funds in the money and capital markets. Although we investigated the sources of funds for corporate bond and stock offerings, we did not go into the details of how such funds are raised. The purpose of this chapter is to explore the ways in which bond and stock issues are sold. In this regard, we consider issues to the public placed through investment bankers, privileged subscriptions to the company's own stockholders, and direct placements by the firm to institutional investors.

OFFERINGS THROUGH INVESTMENT BANKERS

When a company issues securities to the public, it frequently avails itself of the services of an investment banker. The principal function of the investment banker is to buy the securities from the company and then resell them to investors. For this service, the investment banker receives the difference, or spread, between the price he pays for the security and the price at which the securities are resold to the public. Because most companies make only occasional trips to the capital market, they are not specialists in the distribution of securities. To sell securities on their own would be both costly and risky. On the other hand, investment banking firms have the know-how, the contacts, and the sales organization necessary to do an efficient job of marketing securities to investors. Because they are continually in the business of buying securities from companies and selling them to investors, investment bankers can perform this service at a lower cost than can the individual firm.

Competitive bidding versus negotiated offering

A security offering through an investment banker to investors other than the firm's own stockholders (known as a public offering) can be either on a competitive bid basis or on a negotiated basis. When new securities are sold by competitive bidding, the company issuing the securities invites bids from investment bankers. Frequently, two or more investment banking firms join together for the purpose of bidding on a security issue; the combination is known as a syndicate. The purpose underlying the formation of a syndicate is to spread the risk and to obtain a larger overall selling organization. The issuing company specifies the date that sealed bids will be received, and competing syndicates submit bids at the specified time and place. The syndicate with the highest bid wins the security issue. At that time, it pays the company the difference between its good-faith deposit and the bid price and then attempts to resell the issue at a higher price to investors.

With a negotiated offering, the company issuing the securities selects an investment banking firm and works directly with that firm in determining the essential features of the issue. Together they discuss and negotiate a price for the security and the timing of the issue. Depending upon the size of the issue, the investment banker may invite other firms to join it in sharing the risk and selling the issue. If a company has satisfactory experience with an investment banking firm, it usually will use the same firm for subsequent security issues.

From the standpoint of the issuing company, the key consideration in deciding between a competitive and a negotiated offering is the likely net price paid to it. Advocates of a competitive offering argue that the competition between bidding syndicates results in a higher price to the company and a lower profit spread to the investment banker than does a negotiated offering. For this reason, certain types of companies are required to issue securities on a competitive bid basis. For example, Rule 50 of the Public Utility Holding Company Act of 1935 mandates that utility holding companies receive at least two bids. Similarly, many state public utility commissions require that public utilities in their states issue securities by competitive bidding, unless an exemption is sought by the utility and approved by the commission. In addition, railroads are required by the Interstate Commerce Commission to use competitive bidding in the sale of their securities.

Advocates of negotiated offerings argue that such underwritings allow the investment banker more time to locate investors and to place the issue, which in turn results in a more favorable price than is possible under a competitive-bidding situation. In particular, this is said to be important in times of "demoralized" markets where security prices are falling, as well as in the case of a very large issue. In a "demoralized" market, certain investment bankers may refuse to enter into a competitive bid syndicate. Their absence, together with the reluctance of others to bid aggressively, could result in a lower net price to the company than would be the case with a negotiated offering.

Unfortunately, there has not been a great deal of empirical testing of competitive versus negotiated offerings with respect to corporate securities. Various studies of municipal bonds suggest that the issuer receives a higher net price with competitive bids than with a negotiated offering.[1] Two studies of corporate bonds suggest that the underwriter profit spread is lower for competitive bid offerings than it is for negotiated offerings.[2] In another study of public utility bond issues during the 1961–70 period, it was found that the underwriter spread was lower for the negotiated-offering method during periods of unstable market conditions, whereas it was lower for the competitive bid method in stable periods.[3] Overall, then, what limited evidence is available on corporate bonds is mixed and it pertains only to underwriter compensation, not to the net price paid to the company. Intuitively, many would contend that competition should result in a higher price to the company on average. However, we must allow for the difficulty of placing securities in a "demoralized" market.

Underwriting function

One of the key functions the investment banker performs is that of bearing risk. When an investment banker or group of investment bankers buys a security issue, he *underwrites* the sale of the issue by giving the company a check for the purchase price. At that time, the company is relieved of the risk of not being able to sell the issue to in-

[1] Reuben A. Kessel, "A Study of the Effects of Competition in the Tax-Exempt Bond Market," *Journal of Political Economy,* 79 (August 1971), 706–38; Richard R. West, "New Issue Concessions on Municipal Bonds: A Case of Monopsony Pricing," *Journal of Business,* 38 (April 1965), 135–48; and West, "Determinants of Underwriters' Spreads on Tax-Exempt Bond Issues," *Journal of Financial and Quantitative Analysis,* 2 (September 1967), 241–63.

[2] Avery B. Cohan, *Cost of Flotation and Long-Term Corporate Debt Since 1935* (Chapel Hill, N.C.: University of North Carolina Press, 1961); and Louis H. Ederington, "Uncertainty, Competition, and Costs of Corporate Bond Underwriting," *Journal of Financial Economics,* 2 (March 1975), 71–94.

[3] Gary D. Tallman, David F. Rush, and Ronald W. Melicher, "Competitive versus Negotiated Underwriting Costs of Regulated Industries," *Financial Management,* 3 (Summer 1974), 49–55.

vestors at the established price. If the issue does not sell well, either because of an adverse turn in the market or because it is overpriced, the underwriter, and not the company, takes the loss. Thus, the investment banker insures, or underwrites, the risk of adverse market-price fluctuations during the period of distribution.

Typically, the investment banker with whom a company discusses the offering does not handle the underwriting alone. In order to spread risk and obtain better distribution, he invites other investment bankers to participate in the offering. The originating house usually is the manager and has the largest participation. Other investment bankers are invited into the syndicate, and their participations are determined primarily on the basis of their ability to sell securities.[4] For the risk-bearing function of the offering, these investment bankers are compensated by an underwriting profit.

Underwriting commission. To illustrate the compensation of investment bankers, we turn to an example. Figure 21-1 shows the cover of the prospectus for a $150 million issue of $8\frac{7}{8}$ percent mortgage bonds of Southern California Edison Company. The issue was on a competitive bid basis, and the winning syndicate was comprised of 51 investment banking firms. The comanagers, Blyth Eastman Dillon & Co.; Halsey, Stuart & Co.; Kidder, Peabody & Co.; Merrill Lynch, Pierce, Fenner & Smith; and Salomon Brothers had the largest participations—$21.3 million, $10 million, $12 million, $28 million, and $28 million respectively. Other participations ranged from $8 million down to $150,000. We see in the figure that the syndicate bought the bonds from the company for $147,772,500, or $985.15 per bond. In turn, it priced the bonds to the public at $992.50 per bond, or $148,875,000 in total. The spread of $7.35 per bond represents the gross commission to the syndicate for underwriting the issue, for selling it, and for covering the various expenses incurred.

Of the total spread of $7.35 per bond, $3.35, or 46 percent, represents the gross underwriting profit. The remaining 54 percent represents the selling concession, which we will discuss shortly. This breakdown between underwriting and selling profits is typical for corporate bonds. A portion of the gross underwriting profit goes to the originating houses as managers of the offering. Though this figure is not given for the Southern California Edison issue, the typical fee is 15 to 20 percent of the total spread. After the bonds are sold, total underwriting profits less expenses and managers' fee are distributed to members of the syndicate on the basis of their percentage participation. It should be noted that the amount of underwriting profit to a member of a syndicate after expenses and the managers' fee is not particularly large. In

---

[4] For an insightful discussion of the traditions by which syndicates are formed, see Samuel L. Hayes III, "Investment Banking: Power Structure in Flux," *Harvard Business Review,* 49 (March–April 1971), 136–52.

$150,000,000

SOUTHERN CALIFORNIA EDISON COMPANY

8⅞%

FIRST AND REFUNDING MORTGAGE BONDS, SERIES FF, DUE 2000

The New Bonds will be redeemable at the option of the Company on 30 days' notice at prices set forth herein, but are not redeemable prior to March 1, 1980 through funds borrowed by the Company at an effective annual interest cost of less than 9.026%.

Interest Payable September 1 and March 1   Due March 1, 2000

Application will be made to list the New Bonds on the American Stock Exchange. Listing is subject to meeting the requirements of the Exchange including those relating to distribution of the New Bonds.

THESE SECURITIES HAVE NOT BEEN APPROVED OR DISAPPROVED BY THE SECURITIES AND EXCHANGE COMMISSION NOR HAS THE COMMISSION PASSED UPON THE ACCURACY OR ADEQUACY OF THIS PROSPECTUS. ANY REPRESENTATION TO THE CONTRARY IS A CRIMINAL OFFENSE.

	Price to Public(1)	Underwriting Discounts and Commissions(2)	Proceeds to Company(1)(3)
Per Unit	99.250%	0.735%	98.515%
Total	$148,875,000	$1,102,500	$147,772,500

(1) Plus accrued interest from March 1, 1975 to date of delivery and payment.

(2) The Company has agreed to indemnify the several Purchasers against certain civil liabilities, including liabilities under the Securities Act of 1933.

(3) Before deducting expenses payable by the Company estimated at $250,000.

The New Bonds are offered by the several Purchasers named herein subject to prior sale, when, as and if issued and accepted by the Purchasers and subject to their right to reject any orders for the purchase of the New Bonds, in whole or in part. It is expected that the New Bonds will be ready for delivery on or about March 13, 1975, in New York City.

BLYTH EASTMAN DILLON & CO.
INCORPORATED

HALSEY, STUART & CO. INC.
AFFILIATE of BACHE & CO. INCORPORATED

KIDDER, PEABODY & CO.
INCORPORATED

MERRILL LYNCH, PIERCE, FENNER & SMITH
INCORPORATED

SALOMON BROTHERS

The date of this Prospectus is March 6, 1975.

FIG. 21 · 1   Prospectus of the Southern California Edison Company

our example, it probably is somewhat over $2 a bond. The principal reward from participation comes from selling the securities.

Divided and undivided accounts.   Underwriting syndicates can be of two types: divided and undivided. A *divided account* is one in which the liability of members is limited to their percentage participation. If the member sells all the securities allotted to him under his participation, he has no liability, regardless of whether or not other members are able to sell their allotments. With an *undivided account*, each member is liable for his percentage participation in the unsold securities of the syndicate, regardless of the number of securities the individual member sells. If a member of a syndicate has a 20 percent participation in an offering involving 40,000 bonds, and 10,000 remain unsold at the termination of the syndicate, the member would be responsible for 2,000 bonds. His liability would be the same whether he had sold 20,000 bonds or none. It is important to recognize that virtually all syndicates involved in corporate securities are undivided. The principal use of divided accounts is in municipal securities.

Best-efforts offering.   Instead of underwriting a security issue, an investment banker may sell the issue on a *best-efforts* basis. Under this arrangement, the investment banker agrees to sell only as many securities as he can at an established price. The investment banker has no responsibility for securities that are unsold. In other words, he bears no risk. Investment bankers frequently are unwilling to underwrite a security issue of a small company. For these companies, the only feasible means by which to place securities may be through a best-efforts offering.

Making a market.   On occasion, the underwriter will make a market for a security after it is issued. In the case of a public offering of common stock for the first time, making a market is extremely important to investors. In making a market, the underwriter maintains a position in the stock and stands ready to buy and sell it at bid and ask prices he quotes. These quotations are based upon underlying supply and demand conditions. With a secondary market, the stock has greater liquidity to investors; this appeal enhances the success of the original offering.

Selling the securities

The second major function of the investment banker is that of selling the securities to investors. As we discussed earlier, investment bankers are invited into syndicates and their participations are determined primarily on the basis of their ability to distribute securities. For this function, an investment banker is rewarded by a selling concession of so many dollars a bond. In the case of the Southern California Edison offering, the selling concession was $4 per bond, or 54 percent of the total spread of $7.35. The ultimate seller can be either a member of the underwriting syndicate or a qualified outside security dealer. In order to earn the full concession, however, he must be a member of the syndicate. An outside security dealer must purchase the bond(s) from a member, obtaining only a dealer concession, which is less than the full selling concession. In our example, the outside dealer concession was $2.50 per bond out of a total selling concession of $4.00.

In a negotiated offering, the underwriters begin to line up prospective buyers before the actual offering date. A preliminary prospectus stating certain facts about the issue and the company is printed and given to interested investors. At this time, a price has not been established for the securities; the prospectus is known as a "red herring" because it contains, printed in red, a statement to the effect that a registration statement has been filed with the Securities and Exchange Commission but that it has not as yet been approved. Upon approval of the registration, the offering price to the public is established, and a final prospectus is printed. At that time, security salesmen seek orders from investors. If the issue is priced fairly, it will be sold within a day or two or, perhaps, even within a few hours. Sometimes "hot" issues are sold out in advance to preorder subscribers. Upon the sale of all the securities, the underwriting syndicate is dissolved.

Advising

In a negotiated offering, such as our example, the originating house is able to advise the company on a wide variety of matters pertinent to the success of the offering. For a company that makes infrequent trips to the capital markets, this advice can be very valuable, for the matters considered include the timing of the issue, its pricing, and features that are desirable to assure a successful sale. Because of his expertise and experience in the market, the investment banker is able to recommend the best package of terms for the particular issue under consideration. When the sale of securities is by competitive bid, the issuer does not receive the benefit of this advice because the underwriter enters the picture only after the bid is accepted and the price determined. Advice from investment bankers may be of a continuing nature, with the company consulting a certain investment banker or a group of bankers regularly.

Pricing the issue

In a negotiated offering, the issuing company and the investment banker determine the price. The investment banker would like to see a price low enough to assure a successful sale, but he is aware that if the price is too low, the issuing company will be dissatisfied. An investment banker can ill afford dissatisfied customers, for news of such dissatisfaction spreads quickly in the financial community. Moreover, the issuing company must agree to the price recommended by the underwriter. Otherwise, of course, there can be no offering.

In the case of bonds, the issue will be priced in relation to the price of other new issues of the same grade. For example, if the bond being issued were rated Baa, comparisons would be made with other Baa new issues. The underwriter and the issuing company must assess the tone of the market with respect to expectations as to future interest rates. In addition to recent interest rate movements in the money and capital markets, they consider the forthcoming supply of new issues, the expected future of the economy, and expectations as to monetary and fiscal policy. Typically, a new issue will have to be sold at a lower price and higher yield to maturity than a seasoned issue of the same maturity and grade. In a competitive-bidding situation, the syndicate will consider these same factors in determining the bid it will submit. The syndicate wants to submit a bid high enough to win the issue but low enough to be able to sell the issue readily to investors. For the negotiated issue, the underwriter wants a price that is high enough to satisfy the issuer but still low enough to increase the probability of a successful sale to investors.

For a common-stock issue, the problem of pricing is perhaps more difficult because of the greater volatility of the stock market. When a company already has stock outstanding that is held by the public, the principal factor that governs the price of any new issue is the market price of the existing stock. The new issue will need to be underpriced in order to sell, however. The degree of underpricing will depend upon the volatility of the stock and the tone of the market. When it becomes known in the marketplace that a company is going to offer new stock, downward pressure usually is exerted on the market price of the outstanding stock. This pressure reflects investors' concern over dilution in earnings per share. Pressure usually develops on the day the new issue is announced, or before, if rumors of the new issue are out. This pressure contributes to the problem of underpricing the issue properly. With a negotiated offering where stock already is held by the public, the price usually is not established until the night before the offering.

If a company is issuing stock to the public for the first time, the pricing problem is much more difficult because there is no current market price to serve as a benchmark. For privately held companies that are going public, a comparison with similar companies usually is made to determine the appropriate price/earnings ratio. For this comparison, regression studies and other types of statistical analyses may be helpful. However, some companies may be so specialized that comparison with other companies is very difficult. The pricing of these issues usually is resolved by consideration of such essentials as present earnings, the growth rate, and the volatility of earnings. For a company going public for the first time, the underwriter and company may agree on a price well before the offering. Because there is no secondary market for existing shares, it is not necessary to delay pricing to the last minute.

It is important to recognize that there exists a tradeoff between the price per share to the public and the underwriting spread. The higher the price, the greater the risk that the investment banker will be unable to sell the entire issue or that the distribution period will be prolonged. As a result of this greater risk, greater compensation is needed in the form of the spread between the price paid to the company and the reoffering price to the public.[5] The important thing to the company, of course, is the net price it is paid by the underwriter. In addition to this factor, it has been found that the underwriter spread varies inversely with the number of bidders and with the size of the issue. The first relationship is attributable to increased competition, while the second is due to economies of scale in underwriting.[6]

Stabilization of the market

During the period when the investment banker or syndicate is attempting to sell a new issue, it is important that the market price of the bond or stock be reasonably stable, to bolster investors' confidence in the issue. If the price should drop, the investment banker or syndicate stands to lose a great deal. To reduce this risk, the investment banker or managing underwriter for the syndicate often will attempt to stabilize the price during the distribution period, by placing orders to buy the security at a pegged price. For example, if the price of a bond to the public is $990, the managing underwriter may stand ready to buy any bonds offered at that price for the syndicate account. Thus, the market price cannot fall below $990 during the distribution period. In a sharply falling market, the managing underwriter may not

---

[5] See Ernest Bloch, "Pricing a Corporate Bond Issue: A Look Behind the Scenes," *Essays in Money and Credit,* Federal Reserve Bank of New York (December 1964), pp. 72–76.

[6] For an empirical investigation of this tradeoff with respect to unseasoned issues of common stock, see Dennis E. Logue and John R. Lindvall, "The Behavior of Investmant Bankers: An Econometric Investigation," *Journal of Finance,* 29 (March 1974), 203–15. For a theoretical investigation of the relationship between underwriter uncertainty in bidding for an issue, the offer price, and the underwriter spread, as well as an empirical test of the interrelationship, see Louis H. Ederington, "Uncertainty, Competition, and Costs in Corporate Bond Underwriting," *Journal of Financial Economics,* 2 (March 1975), 71–94.

be able to peg the price without having to buy the better part of the issue—a self-defeating process, to say the least. However, for an issue that is realistically priced in a reasonably stable market, the pegging operation does tend to reduce the risk of the underwriter. Without such stabilization, the risk to the underwriter would be greater; and he would compensate for it by bidding a lower price to the company and/or increasing the underwriter's spread.

Flotation costs

The flotation costs of a new issue of securities tend to vary with the size and the type of the issue. These costs include the underwriting spread, registration expenses, and other out-of-pocket expenses. Unfortunately, we have little in the way of recent empirical evidence on flotation costs. The results of a survey for the 1963–65 period showed that the larger the issue, the lower the cost of flotation as a percentage of gross proceeds.[7] As certain company expenses—printing and legal fees in particular—essentially are fixed, the larger the issue, the lower their percentage cost. The underwriter also has certain "fixed" expenses. Thus, the larger the issue, the smaller the underwriting expense. Additionally and more importantly, there usually is an inverse relationship between the size of an issue and the quality of the issuing company. The study also showed that the relative cost of flotation is highest for a common-stock issue and lowest for a debt issue—a fact not surprising in view of the differences in underwriting risk.

In a more recent study, Keith B. Johnson, T. Gregory Morton, and M. Chapman Findlay, III. used a large sample of corporate bond and common stock issues during the years 1971 and 1972 to test certain explanatory variables.[8] With flotation costs as the dependent variable, they found that the size of the issuer was the most significant variable in both cases (the larger the issuer, the lower the flotation costs). For bond issues, other significant variables were a surrogate for seasoning, a risk surrogate, whether or not warrants were attached, and variables for the type of offering (direct placement, underwriting, or best efforts). For stock issues, other significant variables were the type of offering (Underwriting or rights offering), and variables reflecting seasoning.

[7] *Cost of Flotation of Registered Equity Issues, 1963–65*, Securities and Exchange Commission (Washington, D.C.: Government Printing Office, March 1970); and Irwin Friend, James R. Longstreet, Morris Mendelson, Ervin Miller, and Arleigh P. Hess, Jr., *Investment Banking and the New Issues Market* (Cleveland: World Publishing, 1967), pp. 408–9. For an earlier study, see Avery Cohan, *Cost of Flotation of Long-Term Corporate Debt Since 1935* (Chapel Hill, N.C.: University of North Carolina Press, 1961).

[8] "An Empirical Analysis of the Flotation Cost of Corporate Securities," *Journal of Finance*, 30 (September 1975), 1129–33.

Instead of selling a security issue to the general public, many firms offer the securities first to existing shareholders on a privileged-subscription basis. This type of offering is known as a rights offering. Frequently, the corporate charter requires that a new issue of common stock or an issue of securities convertible into common be offered first to existing shareholders because of their preemptive right.

Preemptive right

Under a preemptive right, an existing common stockholder has the right to preserve his proportionate ownership in the corporation. If the corporation issues additional common stock, he must be given the right to subscribe to the new stock so that he maintains his pro rata interest in the company. Suppose an individual owns 100 shares of a corporation and the company decides to increase by 10 percent the number of shares outstanding through a new common-stock offering. If the stockholder has a preemptive right, then he must be given the option to buy ten additional shares so that he can preserve his proportionate ownership in the company. Various states differ with respect to laws regarding preemptive rights. However, the majority of the states provide that a stockholder does have a preemptive right unless the corporate charter otherwise denies it.

Terms of offering

When a company sells securities by privileged subscription, each stockholder is mailed one right for each share of stock he holds. With a common-stock offering, the rights give him the option to purchase additional shares according to the terms of the offering. The terms specify the number of rights required to subscribe for an additional share of stock, the subscription price per share, and the expiration date of the offering. The holder of rights has three choices: he can exercise them and subscribe for additional shares; he can sell them, as they are transferable; or he can simply do nothing and let them expire. The last usually occurs only if the value of a right is negligible and/or if the stockholder owns but a few shares of stock. Generally, the subscription period is thirty days or less. If a stockholder wishes to buy a share of additional stock but does not have the necessary number of rights, he may purchase additional rights. For example, suppose a person presently owns eighty-five shares of stock in a company, and the number of rights required to purchase one additional share is ten. Given his eighty-five rights, he can purchase only eight full shares of stock. He can, however, buy the ninth share by purchasing an additional five rights.

In a rights offering, the board of directors establishes a date of record. Investors who buy the stock prior to that date receive the right to subscribe to the new issue. The stock is said to sell with *rights on* prior to the date of record. After the date of record, the stock is said to sell *ex-rights;* that is, the stock is traded without the rights attached. An investor who buys the stock after this date does not receive the right to subscribe to additional stock.

Value of rights

The market value of a right is a function of the present market price of the stock, the subscription price, and the number of rights required to purchase an additional share of stock. The theoretical market value of one right after the offering is announced but while the stock is still selling rights-on is

$$R_o = \frac{P_o - S}{N + 1} \qquad (21\text{-}1)$$

where R_o = market value of one right when stock is selling rights-on
P_o = market value of a share of stock selling rights-on
S = subscription price per share
N = number of rights required to purchase one share of stock

For example, if the market price of a stock is $100 a share and the subscription price $90 a share, and it takes four rights to buy an additional share of stock, the theoretical value of a right when the stock is selling rights-on would be

$$R_o = \frac{100 - 90}{4 + 1} = \$2 \qquad (21\text{-}2)$$

We note that the market value of the stock with rights on contains the value of one right.

When the stock goes ex-rights, the market price theoretically declines, for investors no longer receive the right to subscribe to additional shares. The theoretical value of one share of stock when it goes ex-rights is

$$P_x = \frac{(P_o \times N) + S}{N + 1} \qquad (21\text{-}3)$$

where P_x = market price of stock when it goes ex-rights. For our example,

$$P_x = \frac{(100 \times 4) + 90}{4 + 1} = \$98 \qquad (21\text{-}4)$$

From this example, we see that, theoretically, the right does not represent a thing of value to the stockholder. His stock is worth $100 before the date of record; after the date of record, it is worth $98 a share. The decline in market price is offset exactly by the value of the right. Thus, theoretically, the stockholder does not benefit from a rights offering; the right represents merely a return of capital.

The theoretical value of a right when the stock sells ex-rights is

$$R_x = \frac{P_x - S}{N} \qquad (21\text{-}5)$$

where R_x = the market value of one right when the stock is selling ex-rights. If, in our example, the market price of the stock is $98 when it goes ex-rights,

$$R_x = \frac{98 - 90}{4} = \$2 \qquad (21\text{-}6)$$

or the same value as before.

It is important to recognize that the actual value of a right may differ somewhat from its theoretical value on account of transaction costs, speculation, and the irregular exercise and sale of rights over the subscription period. There is an old adage on Wall Street that says a stockholder should sell his rights early in the subscription period because at that time they have the maximum value. The high value, as the reasoning goes, is due to hesitation on the part of many stockholders either to exercise or to sell their rights in the early days of the subscription period. This hesitation is said to reflect a "wait and see" attitude. As a result, there is a shortage of rights early in the subscription period; and the market price of the right rises relative to its theoretical value. The opposite occurs near the end of the subscription period; stockholders are said to unload rights.

Although this behavior may seem logical enough, empirical studies have not revealed any distinct price pattern of rights over the subscription period.[9] One reason is that arbitrage limits the deviation of actual value from theoretical value. If the price of a right is significantly higher than its theoretical value, stockholders will sell their

---

[9] See Robert M. Soldofsky and Craig R. Johnson, "Rights Timing," *Financial Analysts Journal*, 23 (July–August 1967), 101–4.

rights and purchase the stock in the market. Such action will exert downward pressure on the market price of the right and upward pressure on its theoretical value. The latter occurs because of the upward pressure on the market price of the stock. If the price of the right is significantly lower than its theoretical value, arbitragers will buy the rights, exercise their option to buy stock, and then sell the stock in the market. This occurrence will exert upward pressure on the market price of the right and downward pressure on its theoretical value. These arbitrage actions will continue as long as they are profitable.

In the rights formulas presented, it is assumed implicitly that the relative earning power and risk complexion of the firm do not change as a result of the investment of funds raised in the offering. Implied also is that the firm's capital structure does not change—i.e., it employs the same financing mix as before. If these conditions do not hold, the market price of the common stock may well behave in a manner out of keeping with its previously computed theoretical value.

Success of the offering

One of the most important aspects of a successful rights offering is the subscription price. If the market price of the stock should fall below the subscription price, stockholders obviously will not subscribe to the stock, for they can buy it in the market at a lower price. Consequently, a company will set the subscription price at a value lower than the current market price to reduce the risk of the market price's falling below it. We know that the stock should fall in price when it goes ex-rights. Its new theoretical value is determined by Eq. (21-3); and we see that it depends importantly upon N, the number of rights required to purchase one share of stock. The greater the N, the less the theoretical price decline when the stock goes ex-rights. Thus, the risk that the market price will fall below the subscription price is inversely related to N.[10] To illustrate, suppose the following were true:

	Company A	Company B
Market value per share rights-on, P_o	$60.00	$60.00
Subscription price, S	$46.00	$46.00
Number of rights needed to purchase one share, N	1	10
Theoretical value of one share ex-rights, P_x	$53.00	$58.73

[10] See Haim Levy and Marshall Sarnat, "Risk, Dividend Policy, and the Optimal Pricing of a Rights Offering," *Journal of Money, Credit, and Banking*, 3 (November 1971), 840–49.

We see that Company *A* will have a greater decline in value per share when its stock goes ex-rights than will Company *B*. All other things the same, there is a greater probability, or risk, that Company *A*'s stock will fall below the subscription price of $46 than there is that Company *B*'s stock will fall below it.

   Amount of discount.   Apart from the number of rights required to purchase one share, the risk that the market price of a stock will fall below the subscription price is a function of the volatility of the company's stock, the tone of the market, expectations of earnings, and other factors. To avoid all risk, a company can set the subscription price so far below the market price that there is virtually no possibility that the market price will fall below it. The greater the discount from the current market price, the greater the value of the right, and the greater the probability of a successful sale of stock.[11] As long as the stockholder does not allow his rights to expire, theoretically he neither gains nor loses by the offering. Therefore, it might seem feasible to set the subscription price at a substantial discount in order to assure a successful sale.

   However, the greater the discount, the more shares that will have to be issued to raise a given amount of money, and the greater the dilution in earnings per share. This dilution may be a relevant consideration, for the investment community analyzes closely the growth trend in earnings per share. Significant underpricing of the new issue may excessively dampen the growth trend in earnings per share and result in a lower price/earnings ratio in the market. Although theoretically the stockholder should be equally well off regardless of the subscription price set, in practice the market value of his stock holdings may suffer if there is unnecessary dilution.

   Moreover, if the firm wishes to maintain the same dividend per share, underpricing, which will result in more shares issued, will increase the total amount of dividends the company will need to pay and lower its coverage ratio. The disadvantages of underpricing must be balanced against the risk of the market price's falling below the subscription price. The primary consideration in setting the subscription price is to reduce the probability of this occurrence to a tolerable level. If, then, the subscription price results in excessive dilution, the company should consider a public issue, wherein the amount of underpricing usually is less.

---

[11] Peter W. Bacon, "The Subscription Price in Rights Offerings," *Financial Management,* 1 (Summer 1972), 59–64, in a test of rights offerings for the 1965–68 period found at least some support for the notion that the relative size of the subscription discount influenced positively the success of the offering, as measured by the ratio of the number of shares subscribed for to the number of shares offered.

Other factors.   There are other factors that influence the success of a rights offering. The size of the capital outlay in relation to a stockholder's existing ownership of the stock is important.[12] Stockholders are likely to be more willing to subscribe to an issue amounting to a 10 percent addition to the stock they presently hold than to an issue amounting to a 50 percent addition. The mix of existing stockholders also may be a factor. If a substantial number of stockholders hold only a few shares, the success of the offering may be less than if most stockholders held units of 100 shares. The breakdown between institutional and individual investors also may bear upon the success of the rights offering. The current trend and tone of the stock market are extremely important. If the trend is upward and the market is relatively stable in this upward movement, the probability of a successful sale is quite high. The more uncertain the stock market, the greater the underpricing that will be necessary in order to sell the issue. In fact, there are times when the market is so unstable that an offering will have to be postponed.

Standby arrangement

A company can insure the complete success of a rights offering by having an investment banker or group of investment bankers "stand by" to underwrite the unsold portion of the issue. For this standby commitment, the underwriter charges a fee that varies with the risk involved in the offering. Often the fee consists of two parts: a flat fee and an additional fee for each unsold share of stock that the underwriter has to buy. From the standpoint of the company issuing the stock, the greater the risk of an unsuccessful sale, the more desirable a standby arrangement, although it also is more costly.

Privileged subscription versus public issue

By offering stock first to existing stockholders, the company taps investors who are familiar with the operations of the company. As a result, a successful sale is more probable. The principal sales tool is the discount from the current market price, whereas with a public issue, the major selling tool is the investment banking organization. Because the issue is not underwritten, the flotation costs of a rights offering are lower than the costs of an offering to the general public. Moreover, many stockholders feel that they should be given the first opportunity

---

[12] See Harry G. Guthmann and Herbert E. Dougall, *Corporate Financial Policy,* 4th ed. (Englewood Cliffs, N.J.: Prentice-Hall, 1962), p. 414.

to buy new common shares. Offsetting these advantages is the fact that a rights offering generally will have to be sold at a lower price than will an issue to the general public, with more dilution in earnings per share. As we have said, this greater dilution may work to the disadvantage of the company and its stockholders. If the company wishes to minimize dilution per share over the long run, it is better off with public issues than with rights offerings. Also, a public offering will result in a wider distribution of shares. Management can request stockholders with preemptive rights to waive them so that the company can sell stock to the general public. If the argument is persuasive enough or if management controls enough stock, the preemptive right may be waived.

GOVERNMENT REGULATION OF SECURITY OFFERINGS

Both the federal and state governments regulate the sale of new securities to the public. A company issuing securities must comply with these regulations. Of the two regulatory bodies, the federal authority is far more encompassing in its influence.

Federal regulation

With the collapse of the stock market in 1929 and the subsequent depression, there came a cry for the protection of investors from misinformation and fraud. Congress undertook extensive investigations and, in the end, proposed federal regulation of the securities industry. The *Securities Act of 1933* dealt with the sale of new securities and required the full disclosure of information to investors. The *Securities Exchange Act of 1934* dealt with the regulation of securities already outstanding. Moreover, it created the Securities and Exchange Commission to enforce the two acts.

Almost all corporations selling securities to the public must register the issue with the SEC. Certain types of corporations, such as railroads, are exempt because they are regulated by other authorities. In addition, a corporation selling $300,000 or less in new securities is required to file only a limited amount of information with the SEC. Other corporations, however, must file a detailed registration statement, which contains such information as the nature and history of the company, the use of the proceeds of the security issue, financial statements, the management and directors and their security holdings, competitive conditions and risks, legal opinions, and a description of the security being issued. Along with the registration statement, the corporation must file a copy of the *prospectus,* which is a summary of the essential information in the registration statement. As mentioned previously, this prospectus is known as a "red herring" because it has not yet been approved by the SEC. The prospectus must be available to prospective investors and others who request it.

The SEC reviews the registration statement and the prospectus to see that all the required information is presented and that it is not misleading. If the SEC is satisfied with the information, it approves the registration, and the company is then able to sell the securities. If not, it issues a *stop order,* which prevents the sale of the securities. Most deficiencies can be corrected by the company, and approval will usually be given eventually, except in cases of fraud or misrepresentation. For serious violations of the 1933 Securities Act, the SEC is empowered to go to court and seek an injunction. It should be pointed out that the SEC is not concerned with the investment value of the securities being issued, only with the presentation of complete and accurate information. The investor must make his own decision based upon that information. The security being issued may well be a highly speculative one subject to considerable risk. As long as the information is correct, the SEC will not prevent its sale.

The minimum period required between the time a registration statement is filed and the time it becomes effective is twenty days, sometimes known as a "cooling-off" period. During this time, investors can evaluate the information in the prospectus and reach a decision. The usual time lapse, however, is longer, around forty days.

The SEC regulates the sale of securities in the secondary markets in addition to the sale of new issues. In this regard, it regulates the activities of the security exchanges, the over-the-counter market, investment bankers and brokers, the National Association of Security Dealers, and investment companies. In its regulatory capacity, the SEC seeks to prevent fraudulent practices, excessive commissions, and other abuses affecting the investment public.

State regulation

Individual states have security commissions that regulate the issuance of new securities in their states. Like the SEC, these commissions seek to prevent the fraudulent sale of securities. The laws providing for state regulation of securities are known as "blue-sky" laws, because they attempt to prevent the false promotion and sale of securities representing nothing more than "blue sky." State regulations are particularly important when the amount of the issue is $300,000 or less and not subject to the rigorous scrutiny of the SEC. Unfortunately, the laws of the individual states vary greatly in their effectiveness. Some states are strict, but others are fairly permissive, with the result that misrepresentative promotion can thrive.

Rather than sell securities to the public or to existing stockholders through a privileged subscription, a corporation can sell the entire issue to a single institutional investor or a small group of such investors. This type of sale is known as a private or direct placement, for the company negotiates directly with the investor over the terms of the offering, eliminating the function of the underwriter. Some issues of common stock are placed privately, but the vast majority of private placements involve debt issues. Consequently, in the discussion that follows, we shall be concerned only with the direct placement of debt issues.

Private placements increased rapidly during the early sixties and accounted for about one-half of the total funds raised externally by corporations and for over three-fifths of the total debt issues by 1964. However, with the large increase in volume of corporate bond financing since 1965, the composition of financing has shifted toward public offerings. In recent years, private placements have accounted for approximately one-fourth of the total funds raised externally by corporations. However, the percentage fluctuates from year to year. This variation in private placements relative to public offerings reflects in part the limited capacity of the private placement market to handle volume. When the total volume of corporate bond financing increases sharply, the capacity of institutional investors does not increase proportionately. As a result, corporate borrowers must turn to public offerings for a larger portion of their requirements. This phenomenon was evident in 1970–71 and in 1974–75.

Advantages and disadvantages

What are the reasons for private placements? We may gain some insight by studying their advantages and disadvantages.

Flexibility.   One of the more frequently mentioned advantages of a private placement is the speed of the commitment. A public issue must be registered with the SEC, documents prepared and printed, and extensive negotiations undertaken; all this requires a certain lead time. In addition, the public issue always involves risks with respect to timing. With a private placement, the terms can be tailored to the needs of the borrower, and the financing can be consummated much more quickly. Because the issue is negotiated, the exact timing in the market is not a critical problem. The fact that there is but a single investor or small group of investors is attractive if it becomes necessary to change any of the terms of the issue. It is much easier to deal with a single investor than with a large group of public security holders.

Another advantage of a privately placed debt issue is that the actual borrowing does not necessarily have to take place all at once. The company can enter into an arrangement whereby it can borrow up to a fixed amount over a period of time. For this nonrevolving credit arrangement, the borrower usually will pay a commitment fee. This type of arrangement gives the company flexibility, allowing it to borrow only when it needs the funds. With a public issue, it is necessary to sell the entire issue at one time. Because the private placement does not have to be registered with the SEC, the company avoids making available to the public the detailed information required by the SEC.

Size of issue. Private placements allow medium-sized and sometimes small companies to sell a bond issue, whereas with a public offering the flotation costs would be prohibitive. Institutional investors are willing to invest in bonds of these smaller companies, provided the company is credit-worthy. It is doubtful that institutional investors would seek an issue of less than $100,000 (and many insist upon a higher minimum), but we must remember that a $5 million bond issue is considered small as a public offering.

Cost of issue. There are two costs to consider in comparing a private placement of debt with a public offering: the initial costs and the interest cost. As the negotiations usually are direct, private placement involves no underwriting or selling expenses. Frequently, however, a company seeks the services of an investment banker for advice in planning and negotiating the issue. Investment bankers have become increasingly involved as agents in private placements, thus offsetting to a certain degree the loss of underwriting and selling business. However, overall, the initial total cost of a private placement is significantly less than that of a public offering.[13]

The second aspect of the cost of a private placement of debt is the interest cost. Fragmentary evidence here indicates that the yield on private placements is significantly above that on public offerings. In addition to interest costs, institutional investors sometimes will request an equity "sweetener," such as warrants, to entice them to invest in the debt issue of a company. While the exact cost of this "sweetener" is difficult to measure, it certainly adds to the total cost of a private placement.[14]

[13] Avery B. Cohan, *Private Placements and Public Offerings: Market Shares Since 1935* (Chapel Hill, N.C.: School of Business Administration, University of North Carolina, 1961), Chapter 11.

[14] For a discussion of the implications of equity "sweeteners" for institutional investors and borrowers, see Samuel L. Hayes III, "New Interest in Incentive Financing," *Harvard Business Review*, 44 (July–August 1966), 99–112.

In summary, it would seem that the initial cost of a private placement of debt is less than that of a public offering. However, the interest cost and any additional compensation appear to be higher. For a long-term debt issue, the total cost is likely to be somewhat higher for a private placement than for a public offering. However, the difference in cost must be compared with the advantages of the private placement.

SUMMARY

When companies finance their long-term needs externally, they may obtain funds from the capital markets or directly from a single institutional investor or a small group of them. If the financing involves a public offering, the company will usually use the services of an investment banking firm. The investment banker's principal functions are risk-bearing, or underwriting, and selling the securities. For these functions, the investment banking firm is compensated by the spread between the price it pays for the securities and the price at which it resells the securities to investors. With a negotiated offering, the investment banker provides an additional service in advising the company as to the pricing and timing of the issue and as to procedures and features involved in the issue. With an offering on a competitive bid basis, the issue is sold to the investment banker or syndicate of investment bankers that submits the highest bid.

A company may give its existing stockholders the first opportunity to purchase a new security issue on a privileged-subscription basis. This type of issue is known as a rights offering, because existing stockholders receive one right for each share of stock they hold. A right represents an option to buy the new security at the subscription price; and it takes a specified number of rights to purchase the security. Depending upon the relationship between the current market price of the stock and the subscription price, a right will usually have a market value. Both security offerings to the general public and offerings on a privileged-subscription basis must comply with federal and state regulations. The enforcement agency for the federal government is the Securities and Exchange Commission, whose authority encompasses both the sale of new securities and the trading of existing securities in the secondary market.

Rather than offering securities to existing stockholders or the general public, a company may place them privately with an institutional investor. With a private placement, the company negotiates directly with the investor; there is no underwriting and no registration of the issue with the SEC. The private placement has the virtue of flexibility and affords the medium-sized and even the small company the opportunity to sell its securities.

1. Explain the rationale underlying the SEC rule that a firm's principal officers and directors may not sell the company stock short.

2. The financial manager handling a stock issue must choose between going directly or going through the intermediary, the investment banker, to the ultimate investor. Discuss the advantages and disadvantages of each alternative.

3. In issuing a new bond issue, the firm may decide to sell the bonds through a private placement or through a public issue. Evaluate these two alternatives.

4. There exists an inverse relationship between flotation costs and the size of the issue being sold. Explain the economic forces that cause this relationship.

5. For all sizes of issues, flotation costs for common stock are higher than those for preferred stock and flotation costs for common stock are higher than those for bonds. Explain this cost structure.

6. Does the full disclosure requirement of the SEC raise or lower the average cost of capital of a corporation? Explain the circumstances under which the cost would be (a) raised, (b) unchanged, and (c) lowered.

7. What factors enable the investment banker to continue to earn a profit on the underwriting and sale of securities? Are the banker's profits in the best interests of society as a whole? Why?

8. Rights offerings have been used extensively in the last ten years by many major U.S. corporations, notably Standard Oil of New Jersey and American Telephone and Telegraph. Why do you feel these corporations have chosen to raise funds with a rights offering rather than a new equity issue, especially when a fair percentage of the rights (2%–5%) are never exercised?

9. In direct placement of securities, small firms tend to pay much higher interest costs than do larger firms. Would you favor a proposal to limit by law the amount of interest the institutional investor could charge the small corporation?

1. The Ville Platte Artists School is considering the issuance of 200,000 shares of common stock at $40 per share through a subscribed issue. The 800,000 shares of stock currently outstanding have a market price of $50.
   (a) Compute the number of rights required to buy a share of stock at $40.
   (b) Compute the value of a right.
   (c) Compute the value of the stock ex-rights.
   (d) Prior to the rights being exercised but after the stock goes ex-rights, the price of the stock goes to $49.50. Determine the price of the right.
   (e) Compute the value of the rights in (d) if the price of stock ex-rights goes to $46.

2. The stock of the American Corporation is selling for $50 per share. The company then issues rights to subscribe to one new share at $40 for each five shares held.
    (a) What is the theoretical value of a right when the stock is selling rights-on?
    (b) What is the theoretical value of one share of stock when it goes ex-rights?
    (c) What is the theoretical value of a right when the stock sells ex-rights at $50?
    (d) Joe Speculator has $1,000 at the time American stock goes ex-rights at $50 per share. He feels that the price of the stock will rise to $60 by the time the rights expire. Compute his return on his $1,000 if he (1) buys American stock at $50 or (2) buys the rights at the price computed in (c) above if his price expectations are valid.

3. Instead of a rights offering, American Corporation (see Problem 2) could undertake a public offering at $45 per share with a 6 percent gross spread. American currently has 1.25 million shares outstanding and earns $45 million per year. All earnings are paid in dividends. In either case, American would sell enough shares to raise $1 million, which would be invested at an after-tax return of 10 percent.
    (a) Compute the earnings per share, dividends per share, and market price of the stock (assuming a 12.5 P/E ratio) for (1) the rights offering and (2) the public offering alternatives.
    (b) Mr. Brown owns one share of American stock. On a rights offering, he will sell the right (assume for $2) and use the proceeds to reduce his investment to $48. On a public offering, he would not buy any more shares. Compute Mr. Brown's earnings and dividend return on his investment and the price gain or loss on his investment under each of the two financing alternatives.

4. The Kramer Corporation wishes to raise $10 million of debt for twenty years. It can sell bonds publicly with an 8 percent coupon and a 1.50 percent gross spread, or it can place an 8½ percent note privately, with no other costs. Assuming that the Kramer Corporation would not repay the principal of either loan until maturity, would make annual interest payments, and is able to earn 12 percent before taxes on funds it employs, which plan would have the higher present value to the firm?

5. The stock of the Dunbar Company is selling for $150 per share. If the company were to issue rights to subscribe for one additional share of stock, at $125 a share, for each nine held, compute the following:
    (a) The theoretical value of a right when the stock is selling rights-on
    (b) The theoretical value of one share of stock when it goes ex-rights
    (c) The theoretical value of a right when the stock sells ex-rights, and the actual market price goes to $143 per share

6. Obtain a prospectus on a recent security issue of a corporation. Analyze it according to
    (a) The type of security being offered. Are there any special features? If a bond, is it secured? How is it secured?
    (b) The size of the issue and the type of company involved. How sound is

the company financially? How stable are its earnings? What is the growth potential? Is the size of the issue appropriate?

(c)   The flotation cost. What is the underwriter spread? Is it too high a percentage of gross proceeds? What portion of the spread was in support of underwriting? In support of selling? What was the dealer concession? Under what conditions may it be earned?

(d)   The underwriting syndicate. How many underwriters were there? What is the maximum participation? The minimum participation? Who was the manager? Were there provisions made for support of the price during the distribution period?

(e)   The pricing. Was the issue priced properly? From the standpoint of the company? Of the investor? Of the underwriter? How successful was the issue?

SELECTED REFERENCES

BACON, PETER W., "The Subscription Price in Rights Offerings," *Financial Management*, 1 (Summer 1972), 59–64.

BAUMOL, WILLIAM J., *The Stock Market and Economic Efficiency*. New York: Fordham University Press, 1965.

BEAR, ROBERT M., and ANTHONY J. CURLEY, "Unseasoned Equity Financing," *Journal of Financial and Quantitative Analysis*, 10 (June 1975), 311–26.

BLOCH, ERNEST, "Pricing a Corporate Bond Issue: A Look behind the Scenes," *Essays in Money and Credit*, pp. 72–76. New York: Federal Reserve Bank of New York, 1964.

COHAN, AVERY B., *Private Placements and Public Offerings: Market Shares since 1935*. Chapel Hill, N.C.: School of Business Administration, University of North Carolina, 1961.

——— , "Yields on New Underwritten Corporate Bonds," *Journal of Finance*, 17 (December 1962), 585–605.

DOUGALL, HERBERT E., and JACK E. GAUMNITZ, *Capital Markets and Institutions*. Englewood Cliffs, N.J.: Prentice-Hall, 1975.

EDERINGTON, LOUIS H., "Uncertainty, Competition, and Costs in Corporate Bond Underwriting," *Journal of Financial Economics*, 2 (March 1975), 71–94.

EIBOTT, PETER, "Trends in the Value of Individual Stockholdings," *Journal of Business*, 47 (July 1974), 339–48.

EVANS, G. H., JR., "The Theoretical Value of a Stock Right," *Journal of Finance*, 10 (March 1955), 55–61.

FRIEND, IRWIN, JAMES R. LONGSTREET, MORRIS MENDELSON, ERVIN MILLER, and ARLEIGH R. HESS, JR., *Investment Banking and the New Issue Market*. Cleveland: World Publishing, 1967.

HAYES, SAMUEL L., III, "Investment Banking: Power Structure in Flux," *Harvard Business Review*, 49 (March–April 1971), 136–52.

JOHNSON, KEITH B., T. GREGORY MORTON, and M. CHAPMAN FINDLAY, III, "An Empirical Analysis of the Flotation Cost of Corporate Securities, 1971–1972," *Journal of Finance*, 30 (September 1975), 1129–33.

KEANE, SIMON M., "The Significance of the Issue Price in Rights Issues," *Journal of Business Finance*, 4, No. 3 (1972), 40–45.

LEVY, HAIM, and MARSHALL SARNAT, "Risk, Dividend Policy, and the Optimal Pricing of a Rights Offering," *Journal of Money, Credit and Banking*, 3 (November 1971), 840–49.

LOGUE, DENNIS E., and **JOHN R. LINDVALL**, "The Behavior of Investment Bankers: An Econometric Investigation," *Journal of Finance*, 29 (March 1974), 203–16.

McDONALD, J. G., and **A. K. FISHER**, "New Issue Stock Price Behavior," *Journal of Finance*, 27 (March 1972), 97–102.

NAIR, RICHARD S., "Investment Banking: Judge Medina in Retrospect," *Financial Analysts Journal*, 16 (July–August 1960), 35–40.

NELSON, J. RUSSELL, "Price Effects in Rights Offerings," *Journal of Finance*, 20 (December 1965), 647–50.

SOLDOFSKY, ROBERT M., and **CRAIG R. JOHNSON**, "Rights Timing," *Financial Analysts Journal*, 23 (July–August 1967), 101–4.

TALLMAN, GARY D., DAVID F. RUSH and **RONALD W. MELICHER**, "Competitive versus Negotiated Underwriting Costs for Regulated Industries," *Financial Management*, 3 (Summer 1974), 49–55.

VAN HORNE, JAMES C., *The Function and Analysis of Capital Market Rates.* Englewood Cliffs, N.J.: Prentice-Hall, 1970

_____, "Implied Fixed Costs in Long-Term Debt Issues," *Journal of Financial and Quantitative Analysis*, 8 (December 1973).

WESTON, C. R., "Adjustment to Future Dividend Rates in the Prediction of Ex-Rights Prices," *Journal of Business Finance & Accounting*, 1 (Autumn 1974), 335–41.

WIESEN, JEREMY L., *Regulating Transactions in Securities.* St. Paul, Minn.: West Publishing, 1975.

22 Long-Term Debt

Our concern in this chapter is with long-term debt issues having an original maturity of more than ten years. We first take up the features of long-term debt, move on to consider various types of instruments, and then explore the nature of the call provision. Finally, the profitability of refunding an existing bond issue will be analyzed.

FEATURES OF DEBT

The fixed return of a long-term debt instrument is denoted by the *coupon rate*. For example, an 8½ percent debenture indicates that the issuer will pay the bondholder $85 per annum for every $1,000 face value bond he holds. The yield to maturity on a bond is determined by solving for the rate of discount that equates the present value of principal and interest payments with the current market price of the bond. (See Chapter 15 for the mathematics of bond interest.) The yield on a bond is the same as the internal rate of return for an investment project.

With a bond issue to the public, a qualified *trustee* is designated by the company to represent the interests of the bondholders. The obligations of a trustee are specified in the Trust Indenture Act of 1939, administered by the Securities and Exchange Commission. His responsibilities are to authenticate the bond issue as to its legality at the time of issuance; to watch over the financial condition and behavior of the borrower to make sure all contractual obligations are carried out; and to initiate appropriate actions if the borrower does not meet any of these obligations. The trustee is compensated directly by the corporation; this compensation adds to the cost of borrowing.

The legal agreement between the corporation issuing the bonds and the trustee, who represents the bondholders, is defined in the *indenture*. The indenture contains the terms of the bond issue as well as the restrictions placed upon the company. These restrictions, known as *protective covenants*, are very similar to those contained in a term-loan agreement. Because we analyzed protective covenants in Chapter 11, it is not necessary to describe these restrictions here. The terms contained in the indenture are established jointly by the borrower and trustee. If the issue is a negotiated underwriting, the underwriter also will be involved. Naturally, the borrower does not want the terms to be unduly restrictive. Nevertheless, he is mindful of the need to appeal to investors and to conform to certain legal requirements. If the corporation defaults under any of the provisions of the indenture, the trustee, on behalf of the bondholders, can take action to correct the situation. If not satisfied he then can call for the immediate payment of all outstanding bonds.

Retirement

The retirement of bonds may be accomplished in a number of ways. For example, bonds may be retired by payment at final maturity, by conversion if the bonds are convertible, by calling the bonds if there is a call feature, or by periodic repayment. Periodic repayment of the debt is possible if the bond issue is either a sinking-fund issue or a serial bond issue. Conversion is discussed in Chapter 24, and the calling of bonds is examined later in this chapter. We turn now to a discussion of sinking-fund and serial bonds.

Sinking funds. If a bond issue has a sinking fund, the corporation makes periodic sinking-fund payments to the trustee. In turn, the trustee uses these funds to purchase or redeem bonds and retire them. This operation generally is favorable to bondholders because it tends to support the market price of the bonds and assures the steady repayment of the issue. The trustee can retire bonds in two ways. He can purchase them in the open market. To prevent the purchase of bonds at too high a price, however, most sinking-fund bond issues provide for a *call price,* which enables the trustee to call the bonds for redemption. Usually, bonds are called on a lottery basis by their serial numbers, which are published in the *Wall Street Journal* and other papers. The trustee will purchase the bonds in the open market as long as the market price is less than the call price; when the market price exceeds the call price, he will call the bonds. For example, if the market price of a bond is $99.75 and the call price is $101.25, the trustee will purchase the necessary bonds in the market.

The amount of required sinking-fund payment may be either fixed or variable, depending upon the terms in the indenture. Under the former arrangement, the corporation makes fixed, equal periodic payments to the trustee. As the bonds are retired, the interest on the outstanding bonds becomes less and less. These fixed sinking-fund payments do not necessarily have to retire all the bonds by final maturity. For example, a $20 million, twenty-year bond issue might call for annual sinking-fund payments of only $500,000. Thus, a $10 million "balloon" payment at final maturity would be required to retire the remaining bonds.

Variable periodic sinking-fund payments are those that are not equal in amount. These payments may be tied to the earnings of the corporation, so that the greater the earnings, the greater the sinking-fund payment. This type of arrangement obviously is appealing to a company and its stockholders. In periods of poor earnings, the company is not constrained by the need to make a fixed sinking-fund payment. Bondholders, of course, would prefer fixed payments, because these payments assure a steady reduction of the debt over time. If the borrower cannot meet these payments, he would be in clear default under the terms of the indenture. This default enables the trustee to take corrective actions. In the case of variable sinking-fund payments, the borrower would not be in default, and the trustee would be powerless to take corrective measures. The amount of sinking-fund payment may vary also with the number of years to final maturity. For some bond issues, the amount of sinking-fund payment may increase over the years; for others, it may decrease. Overall, variable sinking-fund payments are employed far less often than are fixed payments.

Serial bonds. All sinking-fund bonds in an issue mature on the same date, although specific bonds are retired before that date. Serial bonds, however, mature periodically until final maturity. For example, a $20 million issue of serial bonds might have $1 million of the bonds maturing each year for twenty years. With a serial bond issue, the investor is able to choose the maturity that best suits his needs. Thus, a bond issue of this type appeals to a wider group of investors than an issue in which all the bonds have the same maturity. However, serial bonds are seldom used by corporations. Their principal use is found in the municipal bond market.

Debentures

The word *debenture* usually applies to the unsecured bonds of a corporation; the investor looks to the earning power of the corporation as his security. Because these general credit bonds are not secured by specific property, in the event of liquidation the holder becomes a general creditor. Although the bonds are unsecured, debenture holders are protected by the restrictions imposed in the indenture. One of the more important of these restrictions is a negative pledge clause, which precludes the corporation from pledging its assets to other creditors. This provision safeguards the investor in that the borrower's assets will not be impaired in the future. Because debenture holders must look to the general credit of the borrower to meet principal and interest payments, only well-established and credit-worthy companies are able to issue debentures.

Subordinated debentures

Subordinated debentures represent debt that ranks behind senior debt with respect to the claim on assets. In the event of liquidation, subordinated debenture holders would receive settlement only if all senior creditors were paid the full amount owed them. However, these holders still would rank ahead of preferred and common stockholders. In the event of liquidation, the existence of subordinated debentures works to the advantage of senior bondholders, because these holders are able to assume the claims of the subordinated debenture holders. To illustrate, suppose a corporation is liquidated for $600,000 and that it had $400,000 in straight debentures outstanding, $400,000 in subordinated debentures outstanding, and $400,000 in obligations owed to general creditors. One might suppose that the straight debenture holders and the general creditors would have an equal and prior claim in liquidation—that is, each would receive $300,000. However, the straight debenture holders are entitled to the subordinated debenture holders' claims, giving them $800,000 in total claims. As a result, they are entitled to two-thirds of the liquidating value, or $400,000; whereas general creditors are entitled to only one-third, or $200,000.

Because subordinated debentures are subordinate to all existing and future debt, senior creditors regard them as equity when evaluating the financial condition of the company. In fact, subordinated debt usually is employed to increase the equity base and support further borrowing. The popularity of the instrument stems in part from the fact that interest payments are deductible for tax purposes, whereas dividends on preferred stock, the closest substitute method of financing, are not. Because of the nature of the claim, a straight subordinated debenture issue has to provide a yield significantly higher than a regular debenture issue in order to be attractive to investors. Frequently, however, subordinated debentures are convertible into common stock and therefore may sell at a yield that actually is less than what the company would have to pay on an ordinary debenture. From the standpoint of a creditor, the equity base of the firm is the same whether the issue remains as subordinated debentures or is converted into common stock.

Mortgage bonds

A mortgage bond issue is secured by a lien on specific assets of the corporation—usually fixed assets. The specific property securing the bonds is described in detail in the mortgage, which is the legal document giving the bondholder a lien on the property. As with other secured lending arrangements, the market value of the collateral should exceed the amount of the bond issue by a reasonable margin of safety. If the corporation defaults in any of the provisions of the bond indenture, the trustee, on behalf of the bondholders, has the power to foreclose. In a foreclosure, the trustee takes over the property and sells it, using the proceeds to pay the bonds. If the proceeds are less than the amount of the issue outstanding, the bondholders become general creditors for the residual amount.

A company may have more than one bond issue secured by the same property. For example, a bond issue may be secured by a *second mortgage* on property already used to secure another bond issue under a *first mortgage.* In the event of foreclosure, the first-mortgage bondholders must be paid the full amount owed them before there can be any distribution to the second-mortgage bondholders. For the obvious reason of lack of appeal to investors, second-mortgage bonds seldom are used. When they are, the connotation usually is that financing has reached a rather desperate state.

A mortgage may be either *closed-end* or *open-end.* When a mortgage is closed, additional bonds cannot be issued under that lien. In order to raise additional funds through mortgage bonds, the company must mortgage additional properties. The result is frequently a hodgepodge of mortgage bond issues outstanding. Under an open-end mortgage, however, the company can issue additional bonds under an existing lien. This arrangement allows the company to issue various series of bonds at different times under the same lien. In this respect, it gives the company considerable flexibility in its financing. In order to protect the position of the bondholders of earlier series, certain restrictions usually are imposed that limit the amount of additional debt.

These restrictions include a maximum percentage on the amount of bonds in relation to the value of the property securing these bonds and a minimum earning power of the company in relation to the bonds outstanding. Public utilities and railroads have used open-end mortgages rather extensively and with notable success.

Many mortgage bond issues have an *after-acquired clause.* Under this clause, the lien covers acquisitions of property after the initial bond issue. The after-acquired clause affords investors additional protection, because any property acquired in the future is added to the lien. If the mortgage is open-end, which is almost always the case in this situation, the after-acquired clause does not restrict the company from additional mortgage financing. It merely assures existing bondholders that future bondholders will have exactly the same claim on assets as they do. It is important to recognize that *even with a mortgage bond issue, investors look to the earning power of the corporation as the primary test of credit-worthiness.*

Collateral trust bonds

A collateral trust bond is secured by stocks or bonds pledged by the corporation to the trustee. In the case of default, the trustee can sell the securities and pay the bondholders. Usually the securities held in collateral trust are securities of some other corporation. To a large extent, the quality of these securities determines the attractiveness of the collateral trust bonds to investors. This type of bond issue, sometimes employed in the past, now is used very infrequently.

Income bonds

With an income bond, a company is obligated to pay interest only when it is earned. There may be a cumulative feature in the issue where unpaid interest in a particular year accumulates. If the company does generate earnings, it will have to pay the cumulative interest to the extent that earnings permit. However, the cumulative obligation usually is limited to no more than three years. As should be evident, this type of security offers the investor a rather weak promise of a fixed return. Nevertheless, the income bond is still senior to preferred and common stock as well as to any subordinated debt. Moreover, the interest payment is deductible for tax purposes, unlike preferred-stock dividends. Because income bonds are not popular with investors, they have been used principally in reorganizations.[1]

---

[1] For a discussion of income bonds, see Bowman Brown, "Why Corporations Should Consider Income Bonds," *Financial Executive,* 35 (October 1967), 74–78; and Frank A. Halford, "Income Bonds," *Financial Analysts Journal,* 20 (January–February 1964), 73–79.

Equipment trust certificates

Although equipment trust financing is a form of lease financing, the certificates themselves represent an intermediate- to long-term fixed-income investment. This method of financing is used by railroads to finance the acquisition of "rolling stock." Under this method, the railroad arranges with a trustee to purchase equipment from a railway equipment manufacturer. The railroad signs a contract with the manufacturer for the construction of specific equipment. When the equipment is delivered, equipment trust certificates are sold to investors. The proceeds of this sale, together with the down payment by the railroad, are used to pay the manufacturer for the equipment. Title to the equipment is held by the trustee, who in turn leases the equipment to the railroad. Lease payments are used by the trustee to pay a fixed return on the certificates outstanding—actually a dividend —and to retire a specified portion of the certificates at regular intervals. Upon the final lease payment by the railroad, the last of the certificates is retired, and title to the equipment passes to the railroad.

The duration of the lease varies according to the equipment involved, but fifteen years is rather common. Because rolling stock is essential to the operation of a railroad and has a ready market value, equipment trust certificates enjoy a very high standing as fixed-income investments. As a result, railroads are able to acquire cars and locomotives on extremely favorable financing terms. In addition to railroads, airlines use a form of equipment trust certificate to finance jet aircraft. Though these certificates are usually sold to institutional investors, some issues are sold to the public.

Convertible bonds

A convertible bond is one that may be converted at the option of the holder into a certain number of shares of common stock of the corporation. The number of shares into which the bond is convertible is specified in the bond; and these shares remain unissued until actual conversion. Because we consider convertible securities in depth in Chapter 24, they are not discussed at this time.

Project financing

The term *project financing* is now being used to describe various financing arrangements for large individual investment projects. Often a separate legal entity is formed which owns the project. Suppliers of capital then look to the earnings stream of the project for repayment of their loan or for the return on their equity investment. With the energy problems of recent years, there has come the need to finance not only large explorations of gas, oil, and coal but also tankers, port facilities, refineries, and pipelines. Other projects include alumina plants, fertilizer plants, and nuclear plants. These projects require huge amounts of capital, which a single company cannot usually supply. Sometimes a consortium of companies is formed to finance the project. Part of the funds come from equity participations by the companies, and the rest come from lenders and/or lessors.

If the loan or lease is on a nonrecourse basis, the lender or lessor pays exclusive attention to the size of the equity participation and to the economic feasibility of the project. In other words, the lender or lessor can only look to the project for payout, so the larger the equity cushion and the more confidence that can be placed in the projections, the better the project. Sometimes the project's sponsors guarantee its completion, which simply assures the lender or lessor that the project will be completely built. After completion, however, the supplier of capital is on his own. Repayment must come from the project's earnings, so the economic feasibility of the project continues to be of major concern.[2] In still another type of arrangement, each sponsor may guarantee his share of the project's obligations. Under these circumstances, the lender or lessor places emphasis on the credit-worthiness of the sponsors as well as upon the economic feasibility of the project.

For the sponsors of the project, there are several types of sharing rules. In a "take-or-pay" type of arrangement, each sponsor agrees to purchase a specific percentage of the output of the project and to pay that percentage of the operating costs of the project plus debt-servicing charges. In a "through put" arrangement, which frequently involves pipelines, each sponsor is required to ship through the facility a certain amount, or percentage, of product. If the total shipped is insufficient to cover the expenses of running the facility, sponsors are assessed additional amounts to cover the shortfall. The amount of assessment is proportional to their participation. The maturity of the loan or lease corresponds to the likely ability of the project to generate cash over time. While the financing need not be long-term, in most cases it extends over eight or more years.

It is important to recognize that the term *project financing* conveys nothing more than the financing of a large project. The methods of financing are no different from those we have studied. They include debt and lease financing. What is different is the size and complexity of the financing. It is tailored to the needs of the sponsors as well as to the needs of potential suppliers of capital. Tax considerations become

[2] For further discussion of these two kinds of arrangements, see Grover R. Castle, "Project Financing—Guidelines for the Commercial Banker," *Journal of Commercial Bank Lending*, 57 (April 1975), 14–30.

very important in tailoring the financing to the best advantage of all parties. In addition, certain environmental restrictions must be observed, and these influence the type of financing undertaken. When the project is located on foreign soil, political risks arise. These may be reduced by guarantees from the Export-Import Bank, or from some other government agency. Nonetheless, foreign projects are complicated by different laws and political risks than those that prevail for domestic projects.

As indicated earlier, project financing has become important in recent years with the need to finance large energy-related investments. Their size necessitates financing apart from the sponsoring company's main line of business. This is particularly true when several sponsors enter into a consortium in order to spread risk. The key, then, is that the project stands alone in the sense that the sponsoring companies are liable for no more than their equity participations. With the continuing energy needs and the large amounts of capital financing such needs require, project financing is likely to become increasingly important in the future.

CALL PROVISION

Nearly all corporate bond issues provide for a call feature, which gives the corporation the option to buy back the bonds at a stated price before their maturity. The call price usually is above the par value of the bond and decreases over time. For example, a thirty-year bond issue might be callable at $106 ($1,060 per $1,000 face value bond) the first five years, $105 the second five years, and so on until the final five years, when it is callable at $101. Frequently, the call price in the first year is established at one year's interest above the face value of the bond. If the coupon rate is 8 percent, the initial call price may be $108 ($1,080 per $1,000 face value).

There are two types of call provision, according to when they can be exercised. Some issues state that the call privilege can be exercised immediately after issuance; with other issues, the call privilege is deferred for a period. The most widely used deferred call periods are five years for public utility bonds and ten years for industrial bonds. During this deferment period, the investor is protected from a call by the issuer.

The call provision gives the company flexibility in its financing. If interest rates should decline significantly, it can call the bonds and refinance the issue at a lower interest cost. Thus, the company does not have to wait until the final maturity to refinance. In addition, the provision may be advantageous to the company if it finds any of the protective covenants in the bond indenture to be unduly restrictive.

By calling the bonds before maturity, the company can eliminate these restrictions. Of course, if the issue is refinanced with bonds, similar restrictions may be imposed.

Value of call privilege

Although the call privilege is beneficial to the issuing corporation, it works to the detriment of investors. If interest rates fall and the bond issue is called, they can invest in other bonds only at a sacrifice in yield to maturity. Consequently, the call privilege usually does not come free to the borrower. Its cost, or value, is measured at the time of issuance by the difference in yield on the callable bond and the yield that would be necessary if the security were noncallable. This value is determined by supply and demand forces in the market for callable securities.

When interest rates are high and expected to fall, the call feature is likely to have significant value. Investors are unwilling to invest in callable bonds unless such bonds yield more than bonds that are non-callable, all other things the same. In other words, they must be compensated for assuming the risk that the bonds might be called. On the other hand, borrowers are willing to pay a premium in yield for the call privilege in the belief that yields will fall and that it will be advantageous to refund the bonds.

When interest rates are low and expected to rise, the call privilege may have a negligible value in that the company might pay the same yield if there were no call privilege. For the privilege to have value, interest rate expectations must be such that there is a possibility that the issue will be called. If interest rates are very low and not expected to fall further, there is little probability that the bonds will be called. The key factor is that the borrower has to be able to refund the issue at a profit. In order for him to do so, interest rates have to drop significantly; for the issuer must pay the call price, which is usually at a premium above par value, as well as the flotation costs involved in refinancing. If there is no probability that the borrower can refund the issue at a profit, the call privilege is unlikely to have a value.

Empirical evidence with respect to the yield differential between immediate callable and deferred callable bonds suggests that the call privilege has the most value and the most cost to the corporation when interest rates are high and are expected to fall.[3] By the same token, the call privilege has the greatest potential benefit to the corporation at these times. However, for this privilege, the corporation must pay a cost at the time the bonds are sold. We turn now to the question of refinancing an existing bond issue, given a call feature in the bond.

[3] See various references on call features at the end of this chapter.

In this section, we analyze the profitability of refunding a bond issue before its maturity.[4] We assume that the decision to refund is based upon profitability alone; other considerations, such as removing restrictive protective covenants, are ignored. The refunding decision can be regarded as a form of capital budgeting; there is an initial cash outlay followed by future interest savings. These savings are represented by the difference between the annual net cash outflow required under the old bonds and the net cash outflow required on the new, or refunding, bonds. Calculating the initial cash outlay is more complex. Consequently, it is best to use an example to illustrate the method of evaluation.

A hypothetical example

Suppose that a company has currently a $20 million, 8 percent debenture issue outstanding and that the issue still has twenty years to final maturity. In addition, assume that interest rates are significantly lower now than at the time of the original offering. As a result, the company can now sell a $20 million issue of twenty-year bonds at a coupon rate of 7 percent that will net it $19,600,000 after the underwriting spread.

For federal income tax purposes, the unamortized issuing expense of the old bonds, the call premium, and the unamortized discount of the old bonds, if they were sold at a discount, are deductible as expenses in the year of the refunding. Assume that the old bonds were sold originally at a slight discount from par value and that the unamortized portion now is $200,000. Moreover, the legal fees and other issuing expenses involved with the old bonds have an unamortized balance of $100,000. Finally, let us assume a call price on the old bonds of $105, issuing expenses on the new bonds of $150,000, a federal income tax rate of 50 percent, and a thirty-day period of overlap. The period of overlap is the lag between the time the new bonds are sold and the time the old bonds are called. This lag occurs because most companies wish to have the proceeds from the new issue on hand before they call the old issue. Otherwise, there is a certain amount of risk associated with calling the old issue and being at the "mercy" of the bond market in raising new funds. During the period of overlap, the company pays interest on both bond issues.

Framework for analysis. With this rather involved background information in mind, we can calculate the initial cash outflow

---

[4]This section draws heavily upon Oswald D. Bowlin, "The Refunding Decision: Another Special Case in Capital Budgeting," *Journal of Finance,* 21 (March 1966), 55–68. Its development assumes the reader has covered Chapter 13.

and the future cash benefits. The net cash outflow at the time of the refunding is as follows:

Cost of calling old bonds (call price $105)		$21,000,000
Net proceeds of new bond issue		19,600,000
Difference		$ 1,400,000
Expenses:		
Issuing expense of new bonds	$ 150,000	
Interest expense on ~~old~~ *New* bonds during overlap period	133,333 *116,667*	283,333
Gross cash outlay		$ ~~1,683,333~~ *1,666,667*
Less tax savings:		
Interest expense on ~~old~~ *New* bonds during overlap period	*116,667* ~~133,333~~	
Call premium	1,000,000	
Unamortized discount on old bonds	200,000	
Unamortized issuing expenses on old bonds	100,000	
Total	$1,433,333	
Tax savings (50% of amount above)		716,667
Net cash outflow		$ 966,666

The annual net cash benefits may be determined by calculating the difference between the net cash outflow required on the old bonds and the net cash outflow required on the new or refunding bonds. The annual net cash outflow on the old bonds is

Interest expense 8%		$1,600,000
Less tax savings:		
Interest expense	$1,600,000	
Amortization of bond discount ($200,000/20)	10,000	
Amortization of issuing costs ($100,000/20)	5,000	
Total	$1,615,000	
Tax savings (50% of amount above)		807,500
Annual net cash outflow—old bonds		$792,500

The annual net cash outflow on the new bonds is

10.5%

Interest expense 7%		$1,400,000
Less tax savings:		
Interest expense	$1,400,000	
Amortization of bond discount ($400,000/20)	20,000	
Amortization of issuing costs ($150,000/20)	7,500	
Total	$1,427,500	
Tax savings (50% of amount above)		713,750
Annual net cash outflow—new bonds		$686,250
Difference between annual net cash outflows ($792,500 − $686,250)		$ 106,250

Discounting. Thus, for an initial net cash outflow of $966,666, the company can achieve annual net cash benefits of $106,250 over the next twenty years. Because the net cash benefits occur in the future, they must be discounted back to present value. But what discount rate should be used? Certain authors advocate the use of the cost of capital. However, a refunding operation differs from other investment proposals. Once the new bonds are sold, the net cash benefits are known with certainty. From the standpoint of the corporation, the refunding operation is essentially a riskless investment project. The only risk associated with the cash flows is that of the firm defaulting in the payment of principal or interest. Because a premium for default risk is embodied in the market rate of interest the firm pays, the appropriate discount rate might be the after-tax cost of borrowing on the refunding bonds. Using this cost, 3.5 percent, as our discount factor, the refunding operation would be worthwhile if the net-present value were positive.[5] For our example, the net-present value is $543,400, indicating that the refunding operation is worthwhile. The internal rate of return is 9.2 percent, indicating again that the refunding is worthwhile, because the internal rate of return exceeds the required rate of 3.5 percent.

Other considerations

We must recognize, however, that just because a refunding operation is found to be worthwhile, it should not necessarily be undertaken right away. If interest rates are declining, and this decline is expected to continue, management may prefer to delay the refunding. At a later date, the refunding bonds can be sold at an even lower rate of interest, making the refunding operation even more worthwhile. The decision concerning timing must be based upon expectations of future interest rates.

Finally, two points should be raised with respect to the calculations in our example. First, most firms refund an existing issue with a new bond issue of a longer maturity. In our example, we assumed that the new bond issue has the same maturity as that of the old bond issue. Our analysis needs to be modified slightly when the maturity dates are different. The usual procedure is to consider only the net cash benefits up to the maturity of the old bonds. A second assumption in our example was that neither issue involved sinking-fund bonds or serial bonds. If either issue calls for periodic reduction of the debt, we must adjust our procedure for determining future net cash benefits.

---

[5] We recall from Chapter 13 that the net-present value is the present value of net cash benefits less the initial cash outflow.

Our concern in this chapter has been with the various features and types of long-term debt. The decision to use long-term debt in the capital structure and the amount of debt to be employed were considered in Chapter 18. The principal features of debt include the fixed return, the priority of claim on assets, the call privilege, and the method of retirement of the debt. We saw that periodic reduction of the debt can be accomplished by issuing either sinking-fund bonds or serial bonds. Types of debt financing examined included debentures, subordinated debentures, mortgage bonds, collateral trust bonds, income bonds, equipment trust certificates, and project financing.

In financing with long-term debt, the company must bargain with investors over the terms of the debt instrument. If the company wishes to include terms that are not beneficial to investors, it must be prepared to pay a higher yield in order to sell the instrument. For example, if debentures are subordinated, investors will demand a higher yield than if the issue involves straight debentures. Another interesting aspect of the bargaining process between the borrower and the investors relates to the call privilege. If interest rate expectations in the market are such that investors think that the issue may be called, the company will have to pay a higher yield for the privilege of being able to call it.

In the last section of the chapter, a method was proposed for analyzing the refunding of an existing bond issue before maturity. This method treats the refunding operation as a riskless capital-budgeting project.

1. Contrast serial bonds and bonds requiring a sinking fund.

2. Government requires certain financial intermediaries to invest mainly in corporate debt instruments. Discuss the rationale underlying this requirement.

3. In the refunding decision, differential cash flows are discounted at the after-tax cost of debt. Explain why these cash flows are not discounted at the average cost of capital.

4. Explain why a commercial bank loan officer would be particularly concerned with subordinating debt owed to the principal stockholders or officers of a company.

5. Which of the principal features of bond issues would you seek as a borrower and avoid as a lender under the following circumstances?
   (a) A continuing period of inflation.
   (b) A period of declining interest rates.

(c) Considerable short-term borrowing is projected in the near future.

(d) Cash inflows will exceed cash outflows for the foreseeable future.

6. Why would a corporation ever issue bonds that were immediately callable if the interest rate were higher than that for a deferred callable bond?

7. In issuing long-term debt, which types of instruments would be most used by railroads? By public utilities? By industrial firms?

8. Why would you expect very long-term bonds (30–50 years) to be *unsecured*? If the earning power of a secured bond's collateral is in doubt, would the collateral have any value to a bondholder?

PROBLEMS

1. The Hirsch Corporation is in bankruptcy. Mortgaged assets have been sold for $5 million and other assets have yielded $10 million. Hirsch has $10 million in mortgage bonds, $5 million in subordinated (to the mortgage bonds) debentures, $15 million owed to general creditors, and $10 million par value of common stock. How would distribution in bankruptcy be made?

2. In January 19X0, Lesikar, Inc., floated a 25-year $10 million bond issue with a $10\frac{1}{2}$ percent coupon. This issue, callable at 110, netted the firm $9.5 million. Investment bankers suggest refunding the issue with a $10 million, 9 percent bond to be issued in January 19X4 with a 21-year maturity. The new issue would net the firm $9.79 million. There would be a 30-day overlap between the issue of the new bonds and the calling of the old bonds. The tax rate is 50 percent.

(a) Compute the unamortized portion of the discount of the old bond.

(b) Compute the cash outlay required by the firm to refund the bond issue.

(c) Should the issue be refunded?

3. The Lemand Corporation has $10 million of 8 percent mortgage bonds outstanding under an open-end indenture. The indenture allows additional bonds to be issued as long as all of the following conditions are met:

(a) Pretax interest coverage [(income before taxes + bond interest)/bond interest] remains greater than 4.

(b) Net depreciated value of mortgaged assets remains twice the amount of mortgage debt.

(c) Debt/equity ratio remains below 0.5.

The Lemand Corporation has net income of $2 million and a 50 percent tax rate, $40 million in equity, and $30 million in depreciated assets, covered by the mortgage, which are depreciated at $2 million per year. Assuming that 50 percent of the proceeds of a new issue would be added to the base of mortgaged assets and that the company has no sinking-fund payments until next year, how much more 8 percent debt could be sold?

4. Research Project: Obtain copies of several bond indentures. Pay particular attention to the restrictive covenants concerning such things as dividends, working capital, additional debt, and nature of the business. Try to relate the cost of debt to the firm to the relative restrictiveness of these provisions.

Does management pay extra for discretion? If it does, can these covenants truly be said to be nonquantifiable? How would you go about finding a measure of the degree of restriction so that tradeoffs with interest could be made?

SELECTED REFERENCES

ANG, JAMES S., "The Two Faces of Bond Refunding," *Journal of Finance,* 30 (June 1975), 869–74.

BIERMAN, HAROLD, JR., and AMIR BARNEA, "Expected Short-Term Interest Rates in Bond Refunding," *Financial Management,* 3 (Spring 1974), 75–79.

BOWLIN, OSWALD D., "The Refunding Decision: Another Special Case in Capital Budgeting," *Journal of Finance,* 21 (March 1966), 55–68.

BROWN, BOWMAN, "Why Corporations Should Consider Income Bonds," *Financial Executive,* 35 (October 1967), 74–78.

EVERETT, EDWARD, "Subordinated Debt—Nature and Enforcement," *Business Lawyer,* 20 (July 1965), 953–87.

HALFORD, FRANK A., "Income Bonds," *Financial Analysts Journal,* 20 (January–February 1964), 73–79.

HICKMAN, W. B., *Corporate Bonds: Quality and Investment Performance,* Occasional Paper 59. New York: National Bureau of Economic Research, 1957.

JEN, FRANK C., and JAMES E. WERT, "The Deferred Call Provision and Corporate Bond Yields," *Journal of Financial and Quantitative Analysis,* 3 (June 1968), 157–69.

————, "The Effect of Call Risk on Corporate Bond Yields," *Journal of Finance,* 22 (December 1967), 637–51.

————, "The Value of the Deferred Call Privilege," *National Banking Review,* 3 (March 1966), 369–78.

JOHNSON, RODNEY, and RICHARD KLEIN, "Corporate Motives in Repurchases of Discounted Bonds," *Financial Management,* 3 (Autumn 1974), 44–49.

KOLODNY, RICHARD, "The Refunding Decision in Near Perfect Markets," *Journal of Finance,* 29 (December 1974), 1467–78.

MAYOR, THOMAS H., and KENNETH G. McCOIN, "The Rate of Discount in Bond Refunding," *Financial Management,* 3 (Autumn 1974), 54–58.

PINCHES, GEORGE E., and KENT A. MINGO, "The Role of Subordination and Industrial Bond Ratings," *Journal of Finance,* 30 (March 1975), 201–6.

SIBLEY, A. M., "Some Evidence on the Cash Flow Effects of Bond Refunding," *Financial Management,* 3 (Autumn 1974), 50–53.

VAN HORNE, JAMES C., *The Function and Analysis of Capital Market Rates,* Chapters 4–6. Englewood Cliffs, N.J.: Prentice-Hall, 1970.

————, "Implied Fixed Costs in Long-Term Debt Issues," *Journal of Financial and Quantitative Analysis,* 8 (December 1973).

WINN, WILLIS J., and ARLEIGH HESS, JR., "The Value of the Call Privilege," *Journal of Finance,* 14 (May 1959), 182–95.

23 Preferred Stock and Common Stock

In this chapter, we take up two forms of equity financing—preferred stock and common stock. Although they both fall under the same general heading, the differences between the two are far more pronounced than their similarities. From the standpoint of the ultimate owners of the corporation—namely, the common stockholders—preferred stock is a form of leverage to be evaluated in a manner similar to that of debt. Because the theory behind the use of these securities was discussed in Chapter 18, this chapter is devoted primarily to examining their features.

PREFERRED STOCK AND ITS FEATURES

Preferred stock is a hybrid form of financing, combining features of debt and common stock. In the event of liquidation, a preferred stockholder's claim on assets comes after that of creditors but before that of common stockholders. Usually, this claim is restricted to the par value of the stock. For example, if the par value of a share of preferred stock is $100, the investor will be entitled to a maximum of $100 in settlement of the principal amount. Although preferred stock carries a stipulated dividend, the actual payment of a dividend is a discretionary, rather than a fixed, obligation of the company. The omission of a dividend will not result in a default of the obligation or insolvency of the company. The board of directors has full power to omit a preferred-stock dividend if it so chooses.

The maximum return to preferred stockholders usually is limited to the specified dividend, and these stockholders ordinarily do not share in the residual earnings of the company. Thus, if an investor owns 100 shares of 6 percent preferred stock, $100 par value, the maximum return he can expect in any one year is $600; and this return is at the discretion of the board of directors. The corporation cannot deduct this dividend on its tax return; this fact is the principal shortcoming of preferred stock as a means of financing. In view of the fact that interest payments on debt are deductible for tax purposes, the company that treats a preferred-stock dividend as a fixed obligation finds the explicit cost to be rather high.

Cumulative feature

Almost all preferred stocks have a cumulative feature, providing for unpaid dividends in any one year to be carried forward. Before the company can pay a dividend on its common stock, it must pay the dividends *in arrears* on its preferred stock. For example, suppose that the board of directors of a company omitted the preferred-stock dividend on its 6 percent cumulative preferred stock for three consecutive years. If the stock has a $100 par value, the company would be $18 per share in arrears on its preferred stock. Before it can pay a dividend to its common stockholders, it must pay preferred stockholders $18 for each share of preferred stock held. It should be emphasized that just because preferred-stock dividends are in arrears, there is no guarantee that they ever will be paid. If the corporation has no intention of paying a common-stock dividend, there is no need to clear up the arrearage on the preferred. The preferred-stock dividend typically is omitted for lack of earnings, but the corporation does not have to pay a dividend if earnings are restored.

If the preferred-stock dividends are in arrears, and the company wishes to pay a common-stock dividend, it may choose not to clear up the arrearage but to make an exchange offering to preferred stockholders. For example, suppose that the dividend arrearages on an issue of $100 par value preferred stock are $56 and that the market price of the stock is $74 a share. The company might offer preferred stockholders common stock in the company, valued at $110, for each share of preferred stock held. Although theoretically the preferred stockholder is asked to give up $156 ($100 par value plus $56 dividend arrearages), the exchange offering promises him $110 relative to a current preferred-stock market value of only $74 per share. In order to eliminate the preferred stock, the company must obtain the approval of a required percentage of the stock outstanding, often two-thirds. Consequently, it probably will make its exchange offering contingent upon obtaining the required acceptance. If the incentive is attractive enough, preferred stockholders probably will accept the offer despite the fact that they are not satisfied to the full extent of the arrearages.[1]

If a preferred stock is noncumulative, dividends not paid in one year do not carry forward. As a result, a company can pay a common-stock dividend without regard to any dividends it did not pay in the past on its preferred stock. From the standpoint of an investor, a noncumulative preferred stock is little more than an income bond. In fact, there is somewhat less uncertainty with income bonds, for the conditions under which interest will be paid are specified clearly, and bondholders have a prior claim on assets. Because of the obvious disadvantage to investors, noncumulative preferred-stock issues are rare, although they may be used in reorganizations.

Participating feature

A participating feature allows preferred stockholders to participate in the residual earnings of the corporation according to some specified formula. For example, the preferred stockholder might be entitled to share equally with common shareholders in any common-stock dividend beyond a certain amount. Suppose that a 6 percent preferred stock ($100 par value) were participating, so that the holders were entitled to share equally in any common-stock dividends in excess of $6 a share. If the common-stock dividend is $7, the preferred stockholder will receive $1 in extra dividends for each share of stock owned. The formula for participation can vary greatly. The essential feature is that preferred stockholders have a prior claim on income and an opportunity for additional return if the dividends to common stockholders exceed a certain amount. Unfortunately for the investor, practically all preferred-stock issues are nonparticipating, with the maximum return limited to the specified dividend rate.

Voting power

Because of their prior claim on assets and income, preferred stockholders normally are not given a voice in management unless the company is unable to pay preferred-stock dividends during a specified period of time. For example, arrearages on four quarterly dividend payments might constitute such a default. Under such circumstances, preferred stockholders as a class will be entitled to elect a specific

---

[1] In 1962, the Virginia Carolina Chemical Company offered preferred stockholders a package of prior-preferred stock, convertible preferred stock, and common stock worth about $150 for each share of $100 par value preferred stock they owned. The dividend arrearages on the preferred stock were $96 a share, giving a preferred stockholder a theoretical claim of $196 a share.

number of directors. Usually, the number is rather small in relation to the total. Moreover, by the time the preferred stockholders are able to obtain a voice in management, the company probably is in considerable financial difficulty. Consequently, the voting power that preferred stockholders are granted may be virtually meaningless.

Depending upon the agreement between the preferred stockholders and the company, they may obtain voting power under other conditions as well. The company may default under certain restrictions in the agreement similar to those found in a loan agreement or a bond indenture. One of the more frequently imposed restrictions is that dividends on common stock are prohibited if the company does not satisfy certain financial ratios. We note, however, that default under any of the provisions of the agreement between the corporation and its preferred stockholders does not result in the obligation's becoming immediately payable, as does default under a loan agreement or bond indenture. The preferred stockholders merely are given a voice in management and assurance that common-stock dividends will not be paid during the period of default. Thus, preferred stockholders do not have nearly the same legal power in default as do debtholders.

Retirement of preferred stock

Preferred stock, like common stock, has no maturity. However, most preferred-stock issues are not regarded as a means of perpetual financing, because provision for retirement of the stock invariably is made.

Call feature. Practically all preferred-stock issues have a stated call price, which is above the original issuance price and may decrease over time. Like the call feature on bonds, the call feature on preferred stock affords the company flexibility. Because the market price of a straight preferred stock tends to fluctuate in keeping with interest-rate cycles, the value of the preferred-stock call feature is determined by the same considerations as is the call feature for bonds, which we discussed in Chapter 22. However, with long-term debt, unlike with preferred stock, there is a final maturity that assures the eventual retirement of the issue. Without a call feature on preferred stock, the corporation would be able to retire the issue only by the more expensive and less efficient methods of purchasing the stock in the open market, inviting *tenders* of the stock from preferred stockholders at a price above the market price, or offering the preferred stockholders another security in its place.

Sinking fund. Many preferred-stock issues provide for a sinking fund, which partially assures an orderly retirement of the stock. The trustee of the preferred-stock issue may use the sinking-fund payments to either buy stock in the open market or call a portion of it. In either case, the stock is retired. A sinking fund is advantageous to investors because the retirement process exerts upward pressure on the market price of the remaining shares. Also, the coverage ratio on the preferred-stock dividend is improved as the number of shares outstanding is reduced. The sinking fund works to the disadvantage of common stockholders because it represents another prior charge and, therefore, contributes to the financial risk of the company from their standpoint. A preferable arrangement for them would be a sinking-fund requirement wherein payments were variable in relation to earnings. Because the sinking fund is beneficial to preferred stockholders, the company should be able to sell the issue at a lower dividend yield than if it provided for no sinking fund. Overall, sinking funds are used much less with preferred stock than with bonds.

Convertibility. Certain preferred-stock issues are convertible into common stock at the option of the holder. Upon conversion, of course, the preferred stock is retired. Because practically all convertible securities have a call feature, the company can force conversion by calling the preferred stock if the market price of the preferred is significantly above the call price. Convertible preferred stock is used frequently in the acquisition of other companies.[2] In part, its use stems from the fact that the transaction is not taxable for the company that is acquired or its stockholders at the time of the acquisition. It becomes a taxable transaction only when the preferred stock is sold.[3] We shall examine convertible securities in much more detail in Chapter 24.

USE IN FINANCING

Nonconvertible preferred stock is not used extensively in financing; only public utilities employ it with any degree of regularity.[4] One of

---

[2] See Robert M. Soldofsky, "Convertible Preferred Stock: Renewed Life in an Old Form," *Business Lawyer* (July 1969), 1385–92.

[3] See Chapter 25 for a more detailed discussion of the tax effect.

[4] For a review of preferred-stock financing, see Donald E. Fisher and Glenn A. Wilt, Jr., "Nonconvertible Preferred Stock as a Financing Instrument," *Journal of Finance*, 23 (September 1968), 611–24. One reason for the use of preferred stock by utilities is that the Securities and Exchange Commission stated in 1952 that the capital structure of an electric utility should not exceed 60 percent debt, and that common stock should not be less than 30 percent. Thus, the 10 percent residual could be filled by preferred stock. Another reason is that a public utility is able to pass off the higher explicit cost of preferred stock, as compared with that of debt, in the rates it charges. Public utility commissions allow utilities to base their rates on their overall measured cost of capital.

the principal drawbacks to its use is the fact that the preferred dividend is not tax-deductible. With a 50 percent tax rate, the explicit cost of preferred stock is about twice that of bonds. As an investment, however, preferred stock may be more attractive to corporate investors than bonds because 85 percent of the dividends received are not subject to taxation. As a result, many preferred stocks sell at a lower yield than do the bonds of the same company, despite their lower priority of claim. In fact, the average yield differential between high-grade industrial bonds and high-grade preferred stocks has narrowed over the post-World War II period to where now preferred stocks yield less on the average. Thus, the after-tax cost disadvantage of preferred-stock financing has diminished somewhat during the last thirty years.

The advantage of preferred-stock financing is that it is a flexible financing arrangement. The dividend is not a legal obligation on the part of the corporation issuing the securities; if earnings turn bad and the financial condition of the company deteriorates, the dividend can be omitted. With debt financing, interest must be paid regardless of whether earnings are good or bad. To be sure, companies that are accustomed to paying dividends on their common stock certainly regard the preferred dividend as a fixed obligation. Nevertheless, under dire circumstances, a company that omits its common-stock dividend also can omit its preferred dividend.

Another advantage of a straight preferred-stock issue is that it has no final maturity; in essence, it is a perpetual loan. Also, the majority of preferred-stock issues do not require sinking-fund payments. Thus, a preferred-stock issue gives a corporation flexibility by allowing it not to make principal payments or plan for refinancing. Moreover, from the standpoint of creditors, preferred stock adds to the equity base of the company and thereby strengthens its financial condition. The additional equity base enhances the ability of the company to borrow in the future. Although the explicit cost of preferred stock is considerably higher than that of bonds, the implied benefits discussed above may offset this cost. In addition, the implicit cost of preferred-stock financing, from the standpoint of investors penalizing the price/earnings ratio of the common stock, may be somewhat less than that of debt financing.[5] To the extent that investors are apprehensive over legal bankruptcy, they would regard debt as a riskier form of leverage. Unlike creditors, preferred stockholders cannot force a company into legal bankruptcy.

[5]Gordon Donaldson, in "In Defense of Preferred Stock," *Harvard Business Review,* 40 (July–August 1962), 123–36, defends rigorously the use of preferred stock as a means of financing under certain circumstances. He argues that when a company has utilized its debt capacity, it may be able to finance further with preferred stock because the preferred-stock capacity of a company is distinct from its debt capacity.

The common stockholders of a corporation are its residual owners; collectively, they own the company and assume the ultimate risk associated with ownership. Their liability, however, is restricted to the amount of their investment. In the event of liquidation, these stockholders have a residual claim on the assets of the company after the claims of all creditors and preferred stockholders are settled in full. Common stock, like preferred stock, has no maturity date; and a holder can liquidate his investment by selling his stock in the secondary market.

Authorized, issued, and outstanding shares

The corporate charter of a company specifies the number of *authorized* shares of common stock, the maximum that the company can issue without amending its charter. Although amending the charter is not a difficult procedure, it does require the approval of existing stockholders, which takes time. For this reason, a company usually likes to have a certain number of shares that are authorized but unissued. These unissued shares allow flexibility in granting stock options, pursuing mergers, and splitting the stock. When authorized shares of common stock are sold, they become *issued* stock. *Outstanding* stock is the number of shares issued that actually are held by the public; the corporation can buy back part of its issued stock and hold it as *treasury* stock.

Par value

A share of common stock can be authorized either with or without par value. The par value of a stock is merely a stated figure in the corporate charter and is of little economic significance. However, a company should not issue stock at a price less than par value, because stockholders are liable to creditors for the difference between the price they paid and the par value. Consequently, the par values of most stocks are set at fairly low figures relative to their market values. Suppose a company sold 10,000 shares of new common stock at $45 a share and that the par value of the stock was $5 per share. The equity portion of the balance sheet would be

Common stock ($5 par value)	$ 50,000
Capital surplus	400,000
Net worth	$450,000

Stock can be authorized without par value, in which case the stock is carried on the books at the market price at which it is sold or at some stated value. The difference between the issuing price and the stated value is reflected as capital surplus.

Book value and liquidating value

The book value of a share of stock is the net worth of a corporation less the par value of preferred stock outstanding, divided by the number of shares outstanding. Suppose the equity portion of the balance sheet of a company is as follows:

Preferred stock ($100 par value)	$10,000,000
Common stock ($5 par value)	5,000,000
Capital surplus	10,000,000
Retained earnings	16,000,000
Net worth	$41,000,000

The book value of a share of common stock is $31 million/1 million shares = $31 per share. Theoretically, the book value of a share of stock should correspond to the liquidating value of the company, but this situation seldom occurs. Only if the assets of a corporation can be liquidated for the book values shown on the financial statement will book value per share correspond to the liquidating value per share. Even then, if liquidating costs are high, the liquidating value per share will be less than book value per share. For most companies, the liquidating value per share is less than book value per share because many of the assets can be liquidated only at distress prices. However, some companies carry certain assets—notably, land and mineral rights—at modest values on their books relative to the market value of the asset. For these companies, the liquidating value per share may be significantly higher than the book value. Sometimes investors calculate the net working capital per share in order to obtain a more conservative estimate of the possible liquidating value of a company.

To the extent that the liquidating value per share of a company exceeds its market value, the company may be subject to "raids." A "raider" buys a company's stock either in the open market or by a tender offer to existing stockholders until he obtains a controlling interest. Upon gaining control of the company, he liquidates it for a value in excess of the price paid for the stock. The managements of companies in which liquidating value per share exceeds market value per share watch all transactions in the company's stock very closely for signs of accumulation.

Market value

Market value per share is the current price at which the stock is traded. For listed companies and actively traded over-the-counter stocks, market-price quotations are readily available. However, the market for the stocks of many companies is thin and inactive, so that market-price information is difficult to obtain. Even when obtainable, the information may reflect only the sale of a few shares of stock and not typify the market value of the firm as a whole. For companies of this sort, care must be taken in interpreting market-price information.

The market value of a share of common stock usually will differ considerably from its book value and its liquidating value. It is a function of the current and expected future dividends of the company and the perceived risk of the stock on the part of investors. Because these factors bear only a partial relationship to the book value and liquidating value of the company, the market value per share is not tied closely to these values.

Sometimes the ability to transfer stock is restricted. An unregistered stock can be sold only under certain circumstances. For example, the holder might be able to sell it only to the corporation or he might be precluded from selling it at all for a certain length of time. Unregistered stock often is used as promotional stock being given to the founders of a company apart from any cash investment they might make. In addition to start-up situations, unregistered stock is also sold to institutional investors by going concerns as a means of raising equity capital. Because of the illiquid nature of the stock, it must be sold at significant discounts from the market price of registered shares outstanding.

Listing

Typically, the shares of a new company are traded in the over-the-counter market. In this market, one or more security dealers maintain an inventory in the stock and buy and sell it at bid and ask prices they quote. As a company grows in financial stature, number of stockholders, and volume of transactions, it may qualify for listing on a stock exchange. In contrast to the over-the-counter market, an exchange represents an auction market where buy and sell orders are matched. The listing requirements of the New York Stock Exchange are more stringent than those of the American Stock Exchange or of the regional stock exchanges, such as the Pacific Stock Exchange and the Midwest Stock Exchange.

Once a company satisfies the listing requirements of an exchange, it must decide whether or not to list. It may well want to continue in the over-the-counter market. In fact, stocks of many large companies with heavy volume are traded in the over-the-counter market. One reason

511
Chapter 23
*Preferred Stock
and Common Stock*

often cited for listing is the increased marketability of the stock. If
marketability is enhanced, stockholders will gain from the greater
liquidity associated with a stock listed on an exchange. Stockholders
also may gain from the greater collateral value attractiveness of a
listed stock as compared with an over-the-counter one. For the company, there may be a certain amount of prestige associated with being
listed on a major stock exchange. For these reasons, many feel that
listing on a major exchange improves the market price of the stock.
However, one empirical study suggests that listing of a stock from the
over-the-counter market to either the New York Stock Exchange or
the American Stock Exchange does not in itself create value.[6]

RIGHTS OF STOCKHOLDERS

Right to income

Common stockholders are entitled to share in the earnings of the
company only if cash dividends are paid. Stockholders prosper from
the market value appreciation of their stock, but they are entirely dependent upon the board of directors for the declaration of dividends
that give them income from the company. Thus, we see that the position of a common stockholder differs markedly from that of a creditor.
If the company fails to pay contractual interest and principal payments to creditors, the creditors are able to take legal action to assure
that payment is made or the company is liquidated. Stockholders, on
the other hand, have no legal recourse to a company for not distributing profits. Only if management, the board of directors, or both, are
engaged in fraud may they take their case to court and, possibly, force
the company to pay dividends. With stock options, however, the goals
of management are likely to approximate those of stockholders.

Voting power

Inasmuch as the common stockholders of a company are its owners,
they are entitled to elect a board of directors. In a large corporation,
stockholders usually exercise only indirect control through the board
of directors they elect. The board, in turn, selects the management;
and management actually controls the operations of the company.
With a proprietorship, partnership, or small corporation, the owners
usually control the operations of the business directly. With a large
corporation, however, there may be times when the goals of manage-

[6]James C. Van Horne, "New Listings and Their Price Behavior," *Journal of Finance*,
25 (September 1970), 783–94.

ment differ from those of the common stockholders. The only recourse of a stockholder to management is through the board of directors. Because common stockholders often are widely dispersed geographically and, therefore, disorganized, management can often exercise effective control of a large corporation if it controls only a small percentage of the stock outstanding. By proposing a slate of directors that is favorable to its own interests, management is able to maintain control. An outside stockholder, however, does have the right to expect that the directors will administer the affairs of the corporation properly in his behalf. If the directors act in a manner that results in personal gain, a stockholder can sue to recover. These suits are known as *derivative suits*. However, derivative suits are infrequent, partly because many states require that the stockholder bear the legal expenses of the corporation if he loses the suit. These laws were instigated to prevent stockholders from undertaking derivative suits at the least provocation.

Proxies

Each common stockholder is entitled to one vote for each share of stock he owns. Because most stockholders do not attend the annual meeting, they may vote by proxy. A proxy is simply a form by which the stockholder assigns his right to vote to another person. The SEC regulates the solicitation of proxies and also requires companies to disseminate information to its stockholders through proxy mailings. Prior to the annual meeting, management solicits proxies from stockholders to vote for the recommended slate of directors and for any other proposals requiring stockholder approval. If stockholders are satisfied with the company, they generally sign the proxy in favor of management, giving written authorization to management to vote their shares. If a stockholder does not vote his shares, the number of shares voted at the meeting and the number needed to constitute a majority are lower. Because of the proxy system and the fact that management is able to mail information to stockholders at the company's expense, management has a distinct advantage in the voting process. As a result, it usually is able to perpetuate existing practices if it so chooses.

Proxy contests

However, outsiders can seize control of a company through a proxy contest. Obviously, outsiders would not attempt a takeover if management controlled a large percentage of shares outstanding. When an outside group undertakes a proxy raid, it is required to register its proxy statement with the Securities and Exchange Commission to prevent the presentation of misleading or false information. The outside group attempts to persuade stockholders to sign a proxy giving them the authority to vote the stockholders' shares.

In a proxy contest, the odds favor existing management to win the contest. They have both the organization and the use of the company's resources to carry on the proxy fight. Insurgents are likely to be successful only when the earnings performance of the company has been bad and management obviously ineffective. The lower the rate of return, profit margins, dividend payout, and percentage of stock owned by management, the greater the probability of success for the insurgents.[7] In recent years, proxy contests have been relatively infrequent. To a large extent, they have been replaced by tender offer takeover bids, a topic considered in Chapter 25.

Voting procedures

Depending upon the corporate charter, the board of directors is elected either under a *majority voting system* or under a *cumulative voting system*. Under the former system, each stockholder has one vote for each share of stock he owns, and he must vote for each director position that is open. For example, if a stockholder owns 100 shares, he will be able to cast 100 votes for each director's position open. Because each person seeking a position on the board must win a majority of the total votes cast for that position, the system precludes minority interests from electing directors. If management can obtain proxies for over 50 percent of the shares voted, it can select the entire board.

Under a cumulative voting system, a stockholder is able to accumulate his votes and cast them for less than the total number of directors being elected. His total number of votes is the number of shares he owns times the number of directors being elected. For example, if a stockholder owns 100 shares, and twelve directors are to be elected, he will be entitled to cast 1,200 votes. He can cast these votes for whatever number of directors he chooses, the maximum being 1,200 votes for one director.

A cumulative voting system, in contrast to the majority system, permits minority interests to elect a certain number of directors. The minimum number of shares necessary to elect a specific number of directors is determined by

$$\frac{\text{Total shares outstanding times specific number of directors sought}}{\text{Total number of directors to be elected plus one}} + 1 \quad (23\text{-}1)$$

[7] See Richard M. Duvall and Douglas V. Austin, "Predicting the Results of Proxy Contests," *Journal of Finance*, 20 (September 1965), 464–71.

For example, if there are 3 million shares outstanding, the total number of directors to be elected is fourteen, and if a minority group wishes to elect two directors, it will need at least the following number of shares:

$$\frac{3,000,000 \times 2}{14 + 1} + 1 = 400,001$$

As is evident, cumulative voting gives minority interests a better opportunity to be represented on the board of directors of a corporation. Because the system is more democratic, a number of states require that companies in the state elect directors in this way. Even with cumulative voting, however, management sometimes can preclude minority interests from obtaining a seat on the board of directors by reducing the number of directors. For example, suppose the minority group above actually owns 400,001 shares. With fourteen directors to be elected, the group can elect two directors. However, if the board is reduced to six members, the minority group can elect no directors because the minimum number of shares needed to elect a single director is

$$\frac{3,000,000 \times 1}{6 + 1} + 1 = 428,572$$

Another method used to thwart a minority interest from obtaining representation is to stagger the terms of the directors so that only a portion is elected each year. For example, if a firm had twelve directors and the term was four years, only three would be elected each year. As a result, a minority group would need considerably more shares voted in its favor to elect a director than it would if all twelve directors came up for election each year.

Preemptive right

A preemptive right (see Chapter 21) entitles the common stockholder to maintain his proportional ownership in the corporation. He is given the first opportunity to purchase, on a pro rata basis, any new stock being offered or any new securities that are convertible into common.

Right to examine books

A stockholder legally is entitled to inspect the books and records of a corporation. However, this access is limited, for most corporations feel that the audited financial statement is sufficient to satisfy the requirement. To obtain more specific information, the stockholder may have to take his case to court in order to prove the necessity of obtaining this information. Stockholders are also entitled to a list of the stockholders of the corporation and their addresses. This list is vital to an insurgent group in a proxy contest. However, management may engage in delaying tactics by contending that the stockholder list will be misused. In these situations, the stockholder may have to go to court and demonstrate sufficient cause for obtaining the information. Upon a court order, management is required to provide the list.

CLASSIFIED COMMON STOCK

A company may have more than one class of common stock. Its common stock can be classified with respect to the claim on income and as to voting power. For example, the Class A common of a company may have no voting privilege but may be entitled to a prior claim to dividends, while the Class B common has voting rights but a lower claim to dividends. Usually, the promoters of a corporation and its management will hold the Class B common stock, whereas the Class A common is sold to the public. Actually, the Class A shares in this example are no more than a form of preferred stock. However, the Class A stock usually is given some voting power, but not as much as the Class B stock per dollar of investment. One incentive is that the New York Stock Exchange will not list a nonvoting stock, and other exchanges will do so only with reluctance.

Suppose, for example, that the Class A and Class B common stockholders of a company are entitled to one vote per share, but that the Class A stock is issued at an initial price of $20 a share. If $2 million is raised in the original offering through the issuance of 80,000 shares of Class A common for $1.6 million and 200,000 shares of Class B common for $400,000, the Class B stockholders will have over twice the number of votes as the Class A holders, despite the fact that their original investment is only one-quarter as large. Thus, the Class B holders have effective control of the company. Indeed, this is the purpose of classified stock.

For this control, the Class B holders must be willing to give something up in order to make Class A stock attractive to investors. Usually, they take a lower claim to dividends and a lower claim on assets. An appropriate balance must be struck between voting power and the claim to dividends and assets if the company is to bargain effectively for Class A equity funds. Sometimes, the Class B common simply is given to the promoters of a corporation without any cash investment on their part.

Ford Motor Company example

An example of a company with classified common stock is the Ford Motor Company. At December 31, 1974, the issued shares of capital stock for the company were:

	Shares Issued
Class B	12,089,395
Common stock	81,500,338
	93,589,733

The Class B common is owned by members of the Ford family and constitutes 40 percent of the total voting power of the company. The common is held by the general public and has 60 percent of the voting power of the company. The common stock was owned originally by the Ford Foundation, but was later sold by the foundation to the general public. A holder of common stock of Ford is entitled to one vote for each share he owns. A holder of Class B common is entitled to that number of votes per share that will make the voting power of the Class B common 40 percent of the total voting power of the corporation. At December 31, 1974, this number was

$$\frac{81,500,338}{12,089,395} \times \frac{0.40}{0.60} = 4.49 \text{ votes}$$

Each shareholder of Class B stock was entitled to 4.49 votes per share at the end of 1974. Thus, members of the Ford family retain substantial voting power in the company despite the fact that they hold far fewer shares than does the general public. All shares of common and Class B stock share equally in dividends and equally in their claim on assets in the event of liquidation.[8] The use of classified capital stock in this case affects only the voting power.

SUMMARY

Preferred stock is a hybrid form of security having characteristics of both debt and common stock. The payment of dividends is not a legal but a discretionary obligation, although many companies regard the obligation as fixed. Preferred stockholders' claims on assets and income come after

[8]*Annual Report,* Ford Motor Company, 1974; and *Prospectus* to Ford Motor Company Stock, November 20, 1963.

those of creditors but before those of common stockholders. The return on their investment is almost always limited to the specified dividend; very seldom do preferred stockholders participate in the residual earnings of the company. Although they may have some voting power, this power generally is restricted to situations where the company has evolved itself into financial difficulty.

Because preferred stock has no final maturity, almost all recent issues have had call features that give the corporation financial flexibility. Retirement of the preferred stock can also be accomplished by a sinking fund, by convertibility, or by an exchange offering. The principal disadvantage of preferred stock is that the dividend is not tax-deductible. Offsetting in some measure the difference in explicit costs between debt and preferred-stock financing are implicit benefits associated with debt capacity and financial flexibility. Despite these implicit benefits, however, preferred stock is little used as a method of financing.

The common stockholders of a corporation are its owners. As such, they are entitled to share in the residual earnings of the company if cash dividends are paid. As owners, however, they have only a residual claim on assets in the event of liquidation. Common stockholders are also entitled to a voice in management through the board of directors they elect. These directors can be elected under a majority voting system or a cumulative voting system; the latter system allows minority interests to obtain representation on the board of directors. The use of different classes of common stock allows the promoters and management of a corporation to retain voting control without having to make a large capital contribution.

QUESTIONS

1. Because the dividend payments on preferred stock are not a tax-deductible expense, the explicit cost of this form of financing is high. What are some of the offsetting advantages to the firm and to the investor that enable this type of security to be sold? Can you explain why the utilities are the principal preferred-stock issuers?

2. How can the issuance of preferred stock lower the firm's cost of capital?

3. Why would a preferred stockholder suffer a loss on those dividend payments in arrears even if the arrearage is ultimately paid up?

4. Why do you suppose Congress allows 85 percent of intercorporate preferred dividends to remain untaxed? Would a decrease in the percentage exemption raise or lower the amount of preferred stock issued? Why?

5. Preferred stock is said to combine the worst features of both common stock and debt. Do you agree with the contention? From whose point of view does it make sense?

6. What advantages to the firm are there from broad share distribution? Is the preemptive right in conflict with an objective of broad share distribution?

7. Why would a company ever wish to use classified common stock in its financing instead of straight common stock?

8. If not otherwise stated, what would you assume as usual with respect to the following features for a preferred stock: cumulative, participation, voting power, call feature, and claim on assets.

9. Why does most common stock have a low par value in relation to its market value?

10. Why does book value per share change over time?

PROBLEMS

1. Eleven years ago the Delano Corporation sold 10,000 shares of 6 percent, $100 par preferred callable at $105. After a year of paying dividends on this stock, Delano fell upon hard times, with the result that each share is now $60 in arrears. Conditions have improved, however, so that the net income after taxes has risen to a normal level of $250,000. The 50,000 common shares would ordinarily sell at a P/E multiple of 12, but the preferred arrearages have caused the common to sell at $30. The preferred has been quoted at $120, although any buying pressure would cause this price to rise significantly. Delano has a 50 percent tax rate and is faced with the following alternatives:
   (a) Exchange common for preferred on the basis of their market prices; or
   (b) Call the preferred, and finance the transaction with a 9 percent debenture.
   From the standpoint of current common shareholders, which alternative is preferable? What reservations do you have?

2. D. Sent, a disgruntled stockholder of the Zebec Corporation, desires representation on the board. The Zebec Corporation, which has ten directors, has 1 million shares outstanding.
   (a) How many shares would Sent have to control to be assured of one directorship under a majority voting system?
   (b) Recompute (a), assuming a cumulative voting system.
   (c) Recompute (a) and (b), assuming the number of directors was reduced to five.

3. The Southern Alabama Fire Insurance Company has an effective tax rate of 30 percent. It wishes to invest a portion of its portfolio in the securities of the Southern Alabama Manufacturing Company. The SAMC preferred stock currently sells at a price to yield 7 percent. SAFIC feels that the greater protection of a bond is worth 0.50 percent in after-tax yield to them. At what yield to maturity would a SAMC bond have to sell to be as attractive as the preferred stock to SAFIC?

4. The stock of the Moribund Corporation is currently selling in the market for $45 per share, yet it has a liquidation value of $70 per share. The Raid Corporation has decided to make a tender offer for the shares of Moribund. Raid feels that it must obtain at least 50 percent of the shares in order to effect the liquidation. Assuming Raid makes its tender offer on the expected relationship shown in the following table, at what price should the tender be made?

Price per Share	Expected Percentage of Shares Tendered
$55	50%
57	60
59	70
62	80
67	90
72	100

5. Lost Horizon Silver Mining Company has 200,000 shares of $7 cumulative preferred stock outstanding, $100 par value. The preferred stock has a participating feature. If dividends on the common stock exceed $1 per share, preferred stockholders receive additional dividends per share equal to one-half of the excess. In other words, if the common stock dividend were $2, preferred stockholders would receive an additional dividend of $0.50. The company has 1 million shares of common outstanding. What would dividends per share be on the preferred stock and on the common stock if earnings available for dividends in three successive years were (a) $1,000,000; $600,000; and $3,000,000; (b) $2,000,000; $2,400,000; and $4,600,000; and (c) $1,000,000; $2,500,000; and $5,700,000. (Assume all of the available earnings are paid in dividends, but nothing more is paid.)

SELECTED REFERENCES

BEAR, ROBERT M., and ANTHONY J. CURLEY, "Unseasoned Equity Financing," *Journal of Financial and Quantitative Analysis,* 10 (June 1975), 311–26.

BILDERSEE, JOHN S., "Some Aspects of the Performance of Non-Convertible Preferred Stocks," *Journal of Finance,* 28 (December 1973), 1187–1202.

DONALDSON, GORDON, "Financial Goals: Management vs. Stockholders," *Harvard Business Review,* 41 (May–June 1963), 116–29.

————, "In Defense of Preferred Stock," *Harvard Business Review,* 40 (July–August 1962), reprinted in *Foundations for Financial Management,* ed. James Van Horne, pp. 194–218. Homewood, Ill.: Richard D. Irwin, 1966.

DUVALL, RICHARD M., and DOUGLAS V. AUSTIN, "Predicting the Results of Proxy Contests," *Journal of Finance,* 20 (September 1965), 467–71.

EIBOTT, PETER, "Trends in the Value of Individual Stockholdings," *Journal of Business,* 47 (July 1974), 339–48.

ELSAID, HUSSEIN H., "The Function of Preferred Stock in the Corporate Financial Plan," *Financial Analysts Journal* (July–August 1969), 112–17.

FISHER, DONALD E., and GLENN A. WILT, JR., "Nonconvertible Preferred Stock as a Financing Instrument, 1950–1965," *Journal of Finance,* 23 (September 1968), 611–24.

FURST, RICHARD W., "Does Listing Increase the Market Price of Common Stocks?" *Journal of Business,* 43 (April 1970), 174–80.

McDONALD, J. G., and A. K. FISHER, "New-Issue Stock Price Behavior," *Journal of Finance,* 27 (March 1972), 97–102.

SOLDOFSKY, ROBERT M., "Classified Common Stock," *Business Lawyer,* April 1968, pp. 899–902.

STEVENSON, RICHARD A., "Retirement of Non-Callable Preferred Stock," *Journal of Finance,* 25 (December 1970), 1143–52.

VAN HORNE, JAMES C., "New Listings and Their Price Behavior," *Journal of Finance,* 25 (September 1970), 783–94.

YOUNG, ALAN, and WAYNE MARSHALL, "Controlling Shareholder Servicing Costs," *Harvard Business Review,* 49 (January–February 1971), 71–78.

Convertible Securities and Warrants 24

A convertible security is a bond or a share of preferred stock that can be converted at the option of the holder into the common stock of the same corporation. Once converted into common stock, the stock cannot be exchanged again for bonds or preferred stock. The ratio of exchange between the convertible security and the common stock can be stated in terms of either a *conversion price* or a *conversion ratio*. To illustrate, the Owens-Illinois, Inc., $4\frac{1}{2}$ percent convertible subordinated debentures ($1,000 face value), issued in November 1967, have a conversion price of $59, meaning that each debenture is convertible into 16.95 shares of common stock. We simply divide the face value of the security by the conversion price to obtain the conversion ratio, $1,000/$59 = 16.95. The conversion privilege can be stated in terms of either the conversion price or the conversion ratio.

The conversion terms are not necessarily constant over time. Many convertible issues provide for increases or "step-ups" in the conversion price at periodic intervals. For example, a $1,000 face value bond might have a conversion price of $100 a share for the first five years, $110 a share for the second five years, $120 for the third five, and so on. In this way, the bond converts into fewer shares of common stock as time goes by. Usually, the conversion price is adjusted for any stock splits or stock dividends that occur after the securities are sold. If the common stock were split two for one, for example, the conversion price would be halved. This provision protects the convertible bondholder and is known as an antidilution clause.

Conversion value and premium

The *conversion value* of a convertible security is the conversion ratio of the security times the market price per share of the common stock. If Owens-Illinois stock were selling for $60 per share, the conversion value of one convertible subordinated debenture would be 16.95 × $60, or $1,017.

The convertible security provides the investor with a fixed return, in the case of a bond, or with a specified dividend, in the case of preferred stock. In addition, he receives an option to convert the security into common stock; and he thereby participates in the possibility of capital gains associated with being a residual owner of the corporation. Because of this option, the company usually is able to sell the convertible security at a lower yield than it would have to pay on a straight bond or preferred-stock issue. At the time of issuance, the convertible security will be priced higher than its conversion value. The differential is known as the *conversion premium*. For example, the Owens-Illinois convertible subordinated debentures were sold to the public for $1,000 a bond. The market price of the common stock at the time of issuance (November 1967) was approximately $52. Therefore, the conversion value of each bond was 16.95 × $52, or $881; and the differential of $119 between this value and the issuing price represented the conversion premium. Frequently, this premium is expressed as a percentage; in our example, the conversion premium is $119/$881 = 13.5 percent.

Almost without exception, convertible securities provide for a *call price*. As was true with the straight bond or preferred stock, the call feature enables the corporation to call the security for redemption. Few convertible securities, however, are ever redeemed. Instead, the purpose of the call usually is to force conversion when the conversion value of the security is significantly above its call price.

How should a convertible be analyzed?

Because a convertible security is a bond or preferred stock at the time of issuance but is usually common stock later, it poses a certain amount of difficulty for the analyst examining the financial condition of the company. Convertible subordinated debt or convertible preferred stock can be treated as a part of the equity base by a creditor when he evaluates the financial condition of the issuer. In the event of liquidation, it makes no difference to the creditor if the issue is actually converted; for in either case he has a prior claim. The situation is different, however, in the case of a convertible bond that is not subordinated. As long as the bond is not converted, its holder would be a general creditor in the event of liquidation. Consequently, creditors tend to regard the convertible bond as debt until actual conversion takes place. For this reason, there is a strong incentive for the company to make the issue subordinated.

Investors in a company's common stock tend to recognize the potential dilution in their position before actual conversion takes place. To illustrate the dilution effect, suppose that a company issues $20 million in 6 percent convertible debentures and that the conversion price is $20 a share. The total number of additional shares upon conversion would be $20 million/$20 = 1 million shares. Assume further that the company has 3 million common shares outstanding and no other debt, that it expects earnings before interest and taxes two years from now to be $10 million, and that the federal income tax rate is 50 percent. Earnings per share under the two alternatives would be:

	Convertible Debentures Outstanding	Debentures Converted
Earnings before interest and taxes	$10,000,000	$10,000,000
Interest 6% debentures	1,200,000	—
Profit before taxes	$ 8,800,000	$10,000,000
Taxes	4,400,000	5,000,000
Profit after taxes	$ 4,400,000	$ 5,000,000
Shares outstanding	3,000,000	4,000,000
Earnings per share	$1.47	$1.25

We see that upon future conversion, there is dilution in earnings per share. It is important that the investor in common stock consider the impact of this dilution upon the market price of the stock. We note also that upon conversion, the company no longer has to pay interest on the debentures; this factor has a favorable influence upon earnings per share. If earnings were low enough, of course, the elimination of interest payments could result in an increase in earnings per share. However, this occurrence is the exception rather than the rule.

We should point out that it is necessary now for companies to report earnings per share on a fully diluted basis. In May 1969, the Accounting Principles Board of the American Institute of Certified Public Accountants required "fully diluted" earnings per share to be shown on the income statement with clarity equal to that of "primary," or undiluted, earnings per share. Full dilution means the maximum possible dilution if all convertible securities were converted into common stock and all warrants or options to purchase common stock were exercised. As a result of this opinion by the Accounting Principles Board, which is binding on public accountants in certifying financial statements, the common-stock investor is not likely to overlook the potential dilution inherent in a company's financing with convertible securities and warrants.

USE OF CONVERTIBLES

Convertible securities, in most cases, are employed as deferred common-stock financing.[1] Technically these securities represent debt or preferred stock, but in essence they are delayed common stock. Companies that issue convertibles expect them to be converted in the future. By selling a convertible security instead of common stock, they create less dilution in earnings per share, both now and in the future. The reason is that the conversion price on a convertible security is higher than the issuing price on a new issue of common stock.

To illustrate, suppose that the current market price of the common stock of ABC Corporation is $40 per share. If the company raises capital with an issue of common stock, it will have to underprice the issue in order to sell it in the market. Suppose that the company is able to sell the stock through underwriters and to realize net proceeds of $36 per share. If the company wishes to raise $18 million, the issue would involve 500,000 shares of additional stock. On the other hand, if ABC Corporation sells a convertible issue, it is able to set the conversion price above the current market price per share. If the conversion premium is 15 percent, the conversion price would be $46 per share. Assuming an $18 million issue of convertibles, the number of shares of additional stock after conversion would be

$$\frac{\$18 \text{ million}}{\$46} = 391,305$$

We see that potential dilution with a convertible issue is less than that with a common issue because fewer shares are being added.

As a financing strategy, management may wish to finance with convertible securities as opposed to common stock when its estimates of the firm's future are more favorable than those of the market. By so doing, it obtains lesser dilution for existing stockholders than it would if it financed with common stock. Once management's expectations are realized, the stock will presumably rise in price. Of course, the

[1] For presentation of a different concept of convertible financing, see Wilbur G. Lewellen and George A. Racette, "Convertible Debt Financing," *Journal of Financial and Quantitative Analysis*, 8 (December 1973), 777–92. The authors argue that the principal benefit of convertible financing is the tax deductibility of interest payments. As a result, they conclude that convertibles are an inefficient source of financing, inferior to that of straight debt.

merit of such a strategy depends upon management's estimates of the future being more accurate than those of the market. When the stock is depressed in price, however, it may be wise to avoid both common stock and convertible financing. This situation will be discussed later in the chapter when we consider the timing of a convertible issue.

Another advantage to the company in using convertible securities is that the interest rate or preferred-dividend rate typically is lower than the rate the company would have to pay on a straight bond or a straight preferred-stock issue. The conversion feature makes the issue more attractive to investors. The greater the value of the conversion feature to investors, the lower the yield the company will have to pay in order to sell the issue. For companies with relatively low credit ratings but good prospects for growth, it may be extremely difficult to sell a straight issue of bonds or preferred stock. However, the market may regard a convertible issue of these companies in a favorable light, not because of its quality as a bond or as preferred stock but because of its quality as common stock. Convertible securities can be sold during periods of tight money when it is very difficult for even a credit-worthy company to sell a straight bond or preferred stock. For these reasons, convertibles are attractive to many firms as a means of financing. Their use will be analyzed in the subsequent discussion.

Forcing and/or stimulating conversion

Companies usually issue convertible securities with the full expectation that these securities will be converted within a certain length of time. The investor can exercise his option voluntarily at any time and exchange the convertible security for common stock. However, he may simply prefer to hold the security, for its price will increase as the price of the common stock increases. In addition, he receives regular interest payments or preferred-stock dividends. For these reasons and others discussed later in this chapter, many investors do not want to convert their security even though its conversion value is more than what they paid for it.

In order to force conversion, companies issuing convertible securities usually must call the issue. To do so, the market price of the security must be significantly higher than the call price, so that investors will convert rather than accept the lower call price. Many companies regard a 20 percent premium of conversion value over call price as a sufficient cushion for possible declines in market price and for enticing investors to convert their securities. Suppose that the conversion price of a convertible debenture ($1,000 face value) were $50 and that the call price were $1,080. For the conversion value of the bond to equal the call price, the market price of the stock must be $1,080/20, or $54 a share. If the bonds are called when the market price is $54, many investors might choose to accept the call price rather than convert. The company then would have to redeem many of the bonds for cash, in part defeating the purpose of the original financing. In order to assure almost complete conversion, it might wait to call the debentures until the conversion value of the bond was 20 percent above the call price, a value that corresponds to a common-stock market price of approximately $65 a share. At this price, the investor would suffer a significant opportunity loss if he accepted the call price.[2]

Other means are available to a company for "stimulating," as opposed to "forcing," conversion. By establishing an acceleration or "step-up" in the conversion price at steady intervals in the future, there is persistent pressure on bondholders to convert, assuming the conversion value of the security is relatively high. For example, if the conversion price is scheduled to increase from $50 to $56 at the end of next month, convertible bondholders have an incentive to convert prior to that time, all other things the same. If the holder waits, he receives fewer shares of stock. Recognize that the "step-up" provision must be established at the time the convertible issue is sold. It cannot be used for purposes of stimulating conversion at a particular moment in time. Another means for stimulating conversion is to increase the dividend on the common stock, thereby making the common more attractive. In certain cases, the dividend income available on the common may exceed interest income on the convertible security. Although the two stimulants discussed above enhance conversion, invariably a portion of the convertible bondholders will not convert, owing to the downside protection of the bond, the superior legal claim on assets, and other reasons. Consequently, calling the issue may be the only means for assuring that the issue will be substantially converted.

Overhanging issue. If a company is unable to force or stimulate conversion because the market price of the stock has not risen sufficiently to entice the investor to convert, the convertible issue is said to be "overhanging." With an overhanging issue, the company is constrained in its ability to obtain new financing. It is difficult to sell another convertible security issue until the present one is converted. The overhanging issue creates apprehension in the market over the investment-worthiness of any new issue of convertibles and may even create apprehension over the worthiness of a nonconvertible security offering.

The risk of an overhanging issue and the loss of flexibility associated

---

[2]For a discussion of ways a company can notify bondholders of the call and to assure that a very high percentage exercise their option, see Alexander B. Miller, "How to Call Your Convertibles," *Harvard Business Review,* 49 (May–June 1971), 66–70.

with such an issue may offset, at least in part, the advantage in issuing price of the convertible security over a common-stock offering. With a common-stock offering, the firm obtains equity capital now. With a convertible security issue, it is uncertain when, if ever, the security will convert and the company will obtain equity capital.

Conversion premiums

For most issues of convertibles, the conversion premium ranges from 10 to 20 percent. Recall that this premium is the percentage by which the issuing price of the convertible exceeds its conversion value. If a convertible bond were sold for $1,000 with a conversion price of $50, and if the market price of common at the time of issuance were $43 a share, the conversion premium would be $7/$43, or 16.3 percent. For a growth company, the conversion premium can be in the upper part of the 10–20 percent range, or perhaps even higher in the case of a supergrowth stock. For companies with more moderate growth, however, the conversion premium may be closer to 10 percent. The range itself is established mainly by market tradition, in keeping, however, with the idea that the stock should be expected to rise in price so that it exceeds the conversion price within a reasonable period of time. The greater the growth in market price per share, the more quickly will the market price exceed the conversion price, all other things the same. Thus, the supergrowth company is able to command a higher conversion premium in the market than is a company with only moderate growth potential.

The higher the conversion premium, of course, the lower the dilution. If the company sets too high a conversion price, however, the issue will have to be sold as essentially a fixed-income security with a yield commensurate with what the company would pay on a straight debt or preferred-stock issue. Under such circumstances, the issue cannot be considered delayed equity financing. The ability of the firm to force conversion simply is too uncertain. For this reason, there are practical limits as to how high a conversion premium can be set. For most situations, it is 20 percent or less.

The appropriate timing of a convertible issue must be evaluated in relation to the market for the company's common stock. If it is a poor time to sell common stock because of a depressed market price, it usually is also a poor time to sell a convertible, even though the convertible issue can be sold at a conversion price higher than the price at which a common-stock issue can be sold. This is due both to the depressed market price of the stock and to variations in the conversion premium with market psychology. Because the dilution associated with a convertible issue depends directly upon its conversion price, which in turn is primarily a function of the market price of the stock, it is obvious that considerable dilution occurs when the stock is depressed in price. In addition to this influence, the conversion premium at which the issue can be sold is likely to be lower when the stock is depressed than when it is buoyant. Because the conversion premium is a function of expected growth, and because investors are less likely to expect growth when the stock is depressed than when it is strong, the conversion premium normally will be lower in a depressed market. These factors will result in greater dilution, the more depressed the market price of the stock. Thus, we see that the appropriate timing of a convertible issue follows very closely the market behavior of the company's stock.

VALUE OF CONVERTIBLE SECURITIES

The value of a convertible security to an investor is twofold: its value as a bond or preferred stock, and its potential value as common stock. (Because the principles of valuation of a convertible bond and a convertible preferred stock are nearly the same, our subsequent discussion will refer to convertible bonds.) The investor obtains a hedge when he purchases a convertible bond. If the market price of the stock rises, the value of the convertible is determined largely by its conversion value. However, if the market for the stock turns down, the investor still holds a bond whose value provides a floor below which the price of the convertible is unlikely to fall.

Bond value

The bond value of a convertible security is the price at which a straight bond of the same company would sell in the open market. It can be determined by solving the following equation for B:[3]

$$B = \sum_{t=1}^{n} \frac{I}{(1 + i)^t} + \frac{F}{(1 + i)^n} \qquad (24\text{-}1)$$

where B = straight bond value of the convertible
I = annual interest payments determined by the coupon rate
F = face value of the bond
n = years to final maturity
i = market yield to maturity on a straight bond of the same company

[3] In this equation, we assume that interest payments are annual and paid at the end of the year. If payments are semiannual, the equation should be modified according to the discussion in Chapter 15.

For example, suppose that ABC Company has outstanding a 6 percent convertible debenture issue with a final maturity twenty years hence. Suppose further that if the company is to sell a straight twenty-year debenture in the current market, the bond will have to yield 8 percent to maturity to be attractive to investors. For a twenty-year bond with a 6 percent coupon to yield 8 percent to maturity, the bond has to sell at a discount. More specifically, the market price has to be $804 for each $1,000 face value bond.[4] Thus, the bond-value floor of ABC's convertible bond would be $804. This floor suggests that if the price of the common stock were to fall sharply so that the conversion feature had negligible value, the price of the convertible would fall only to $804. At that price, the security would sell as a straight bond in keeping with prevailing bond yields for that grade of security.

The bond-value floor of a convertible is not constant over time. It varies with (1) interest rate movements in the capital market and (2) changes in the financial risk of the company involved. If interest rates in general rise, the bond value of a convertible will decline. For example, if the yield to maturity on a straight bond in our example increases from 8 to 9 percent, the bond value of the convertible will drop from $804 to $726. Moreover, the company's credit rating can either improve or deteriorate over time. If it improves, and the company is able to sell a straight bond at a lower yield to maturity, the bond value of the convertible security will increase, all other things held constant. However, if the company's credit standing deteriorates and the yield on a straight bond increases, the bond-value floor will decline. Unfortunately for the investor, when the market price of the stock falls because of poor earnings, the company may have financial difficulty, in which case its credit standing will suffer. As a result, the straight bond value of the convertible may decline along with the decline in its conversion value, giving the investor less downside protection than he might have expected originally.[5]

---

[4] Solving for Eq. (24-1),

$$B = \sum_{t=1}^{20} \frac{\$60}{(1.08)^t} + \frac{\$1,000}{(1.08)^{20}} = \$804$$

Fortunately, we need only consult a bond table to determine the market price. Given any three of the four variables above—namely, years to maturity, coupon rate, yield to maturity, and market price—we can quickly determine the fourth variable from the table.

[5] Mathematically, the straight bond value of a convertible security will rise over time, all other things held constant, if the face value of the convertible is above the straight bond value at the time of issuance. At final maturity, the straight bond value, of course, will equal the face value of the convertible.

Premiums

Convertible securities usually sell at premiums over both their bond value and their conversion value. Recall that the conversion value of a convertible is simply the current market price per share of the company's common stock times the number of shares into which the security is convertible. The fact that the convertible bond provides the investor with a degree of downside protection, given the qualifications mentioned above, usually results in its selling at a market price somewhat higher than its conversion value. How much higher will depend upon the probability that the conversion value of the security will fall below its bond value. Suppose, in our example, that the conversion price is $50 a share and the current market price of the common stock is $60 a share. The conversion value of the $1,000 face value bond will be $1,200. If the stock falls to $25 a share, the conversion value of the bond will plummet to $500. Assuming a straight bond value of $804, however, the market price of the convertible would not be expected to fall below $804. Consequently, the investor can reduce his risk by investing in a convertible security rather than in the common stock of a corporation. In general, the more volatile the price movements of the stock, the more valuable is the downside protection afforded by the bond-value floor. For this reason as well as for additional reasons discussed later, the market price of a convertible security often is above its conversion value. The difference is known as the *premium-over-conversion value.*

Moreover, a convertible bond usually will sell at a *premium-over-bond value,* primarily because of the conversion feature. Unless the market price of the stock is very low relative to the conversion price, the conversion feature usually will have value, in that investors may eventually find it profitable to convert the securities. To the extent that the conversion feature does have value, the convertible will sell at a premium over its straight bond value. The higher the market price of the common relative to the conversion price, the greater this premium.

Comparing the two premiums

By comparing the two premiums for a sample of convertible securities of similar companies, we gain insight into the tradeoff between conversion value and straight bond value. If we construct a scatter diagram with the percentage premium of market price of the convertible over its straight bond value on the vertical axis and the premium of market price over conversion value on the horizontal axis, we can examine the tradeoff empirically. Taking a cross-sectional sample of convertible securities, we can plot the premiums on the

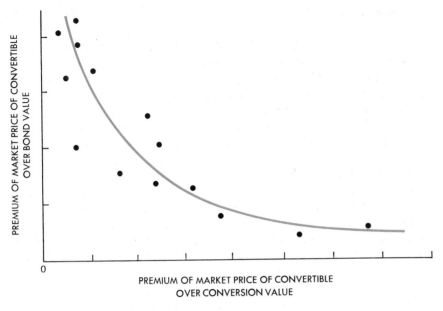

PREMIUM OF MARKET PRICE OF CONVERTIBLE
OVER BOND VALUE

PREMIUM OF MARKET PRICE OF CONVERTIBLE
OVER CONVERSION VALUE

FIG. 24 · 1

Convertible securities
tradeoff curve

scatter diagram and obtain a relationship that might be similar to that shown in Figure 24-1.

The figure suggests an inverse relationship between the two premiums.[6] At relatively high common-stock price levels, the value of the convertible as a bond is negligible. Consequently, its premium-over-bond value is high, whereas its premium-over-conversion value is slight. The security sells mainly for its stock equivalent. Investors are unwilling to pay a significant premium over conversion value for several reasons. First, the greater the premium of market price of the convertible over its bond value, the less valuable the bond-value protection to the investor. If the bond-value floor of a convertible bond is $900, for example, there is considerably more downside protection if the market price of the convertible is $1,000 than if it is $2,000. Second, when the conversion value is high, the convertible may be called; and if it is, the investor will want to convert rather than redeem the bond for the call price. Upon conversion, of course, the bond is worth only its conversion value. Finally, if the company increases the dividend on its common stock, the fixed return on the convertible declines relative to the return available on the stock equivalent. This occurrence contributes also to a narrowing of the premium as conversion value increases.

[6] Brigham undertakes a similar analysis using the ratio of the stock's initial market price over the conversion price on the horizontal axis and the ratio of the interest rate the company would pay on a straight bond over the rate it pays on a convertible bond on the vertical axis. Eugene F. Brigham, "An Analysis of Convertible Debentures: Theory and Some Empirical Evidence," *Journal of Finance*, 21 (March 1966), 41–48.

On the other hand, when the market value of the convertible is close to its straight bond value, the conversion feature has little value. At this level, the convertible security is valued primarily as a straight bond. Under these circumstances, the market price of the convertible is likely to exceed its conversion value by a substantial premium. Otherwise, the conversion feature would have a value, and the convertible security would sell at a premium over its bond value.

A tradeoff curve based upon a cross-sectional sample of convertible securities, such as that illustrated in Figure 24-1, is valuable to the financial manager in determining the appropriate yield and conversion premium on a new issue of convertible bonds. It gives him an idea of the additional yield that the firm would have to pay if it wanted a higher conversion premium, or, conversely, the decrease in conversion premium necessary to obtain a lower yield. In general, the higher the conversion premium, the higher must be the yield in order to entice market acceptance.

Other reasons for premiums

Although we have concentrated on the main reasons for premiums, other factors appear to have at least a modest influence on the premiums. For one thing, a convertible security is sometimes attractive to investors who operate on margin. In the past, the margin requirement on stock, which is set by the Federal Reserve, has been higher than that on convertible securities. This meant that market participants were able to borrow more for investment in convertible securities than they were for investment in stock. The greater collateral-value attractiveness of convertibles relative to that of stock resulted in a greater relative demand for convertibles; this demand, in turn, exerted upward pressure on the premiums. At the time of this writing, however, the margin requirement was the same for both types of securities, namely 50 percent. This means that the maximum loan a person could obtain from a bank or an investment house was 50 percent of the market value of the convertible securities or stock pledged. Therefore, the two types of securities had the same degree of collateral-value attractiveness.

Lower transaction costs on convertible bonds relative to those on common stocks also enhance the attractiveness of these bonds. An investor who wishes to acquire common stock of a company would incur lower transaction costs by purchasing a convertible bond and converting it into common stock than he would by purchasing the stock outright. This attraction should exert upward pressure on the premiums over conversion value and over bond value. The duration of the convertible option also should affect the premiums. In general, the longer the duration, the more valuable the option. Unlike other options, however, the duration until expiration is uncertain owing to the fact that the company can force conversion if the price of the common stock is high enough. The longest duration is the maturity of the security, but the actual duration typically is much shorter. Another factor is the dividend on the common. The greater the dividend, the greater the attraction of the common vis-à-vis the convertible security and the lower the premiums, all other things the same.[7]

WARRANTS AND THEIR VALUATION

A warrant is an option to purchase a specified number of shares of common stock at a stated price. When the holder exercises the option, he surrenders the warrant. Warrants are employed customarily as "sweeteners" to a public issue of bonds or debt that is privately placed.[8] The investor obtains not only the fixed return associated with debt but also an option to purchase common stock at a stated price. If the market price of the stock should rise, this option can be valuable. As a result, the corporation should be able to obtain a lower interest rate than it would otherwise. For companies that are marginal credit risks, the use of warrants may spell the difference between being able and not being able to raise funds through a debt issue. Additionally, during periods of tight money, some financially sound companies may have to provide warrants in order to make their debt issues attractive to investors. In addition to a "sweetener" to debt financing, warrants also are used in the origination of a company as compensation to underwriters and venture capitalists.

Features

The warrant itself contains the provisions of the option. It states the number of shares the holder can buy for each warrant he holds. For example, the Greyhound Corporation warrants provide an option to purchase one share of common stock for each warrant held; Braniff Airways warrants provide for the purchase of 3.18 shares for each warrant held. Another important provision is the price at which the warrant is exercisable. For example, Greyhound warrants are exercisable at $23.50 a share. The exercise price can be either fixed or "stepped up" over time. The Textron Inc. warrants, for example, are exercisable

---

[7] See Roman L. Weil, Jr., Joel E. Segall, and David Green, Jr., "Premiums on Convertible Bonds," *Journal of Finance*, 23 (June 1968), 445–47.

[8] For an analysis of the use of warrants in financing, see Samuel L. Hayes III and Henry B. Reiling, "Sophisticated Financing Tool: The Warrant," *Harvard Business Review*, 47 (January–February 1969), 137–50.

at $10.00 a share until May 1, 1979, and are exercisable at $11.25 after that time until their expiration in 1984.

Finally, the warrant must specify the date on which the option expires. Certain warrants, such as those of Alleghany Corporation, are perpetual, having no expiration date. Most warrants, however, have a stated expiration date. Warrants may be either detachable or nondetachable. Detachable warrants may be sold separately from the bond. Consequently, the bondholder does not have to exercise his option in order to obtain the value of the warrant. He simply can sell the warrant in the marketplace. Many detachable warrants are listed on the American Stock Exchange and the New York Stock Exchange. A nondetachable warrant cannot be sold separately from the bond; it can be detached only when the bondholder exercises his option and purchases stock.

Because a warrant is only an option to purchase stock, the warrant holder is not entitled to any cash dividends paid on the common stock, nor does he have voting power. If the common stock is split or a stock dividend is declared, the option price of the warrant usually is adjusted to take this change into account.

Exercise of warrants

Although warrants and convertible securities are similar in many respects, they differ with respect to the capitalization of the company after the option is taken. When convertible debentures are converted, new common stock is created, but the debentures are retired and there is no infusion of new capital into the company. However, when warrants are exercised, the common stock of the company is increased, and the bonds still remain outstanding.

To illustrate the difference, let us compare the results of financing with convertible bonds and financing with a straight bond issue with warrants attached. Suppose that ABC Corporation is raising $20 million in debt funds with either a convertible debenture issue or a straight debenture with warrants attached. Assume that the convertible debenture issue has a coupon rate of 6 percent and a conversion price of $50, whereas the straight debenture issue has a 7 percent coupon rate. With the straight debenture, the investor receives one warrant entitling him to purchase three shares of common stock at $60 a share for each bond ($1,000 face value) purchased. The capitalization of the company before financing, after financing, and after complete conversion or exercise of the option, is shown in Table 24-1. We assume that the retained earnings of the company remain unchanged and that the straight debenture issue has neither matured nor been called.

Table 24 · 1

	Before Financing	Convertible Debentures		Debentures With Warrants	
		Before Conversion	After Conversion	Before Exercise	After Exercise
Debentures		$20		$20	$20.0
Common stock					
($10 par value)	$10	10	$14	10	10.6
Capital surplus			16		3.0
Retained earnings	25	25	25	25	25.0
Net worth	$35	$35	$55	$35	$38.6
Total capitalization	$35	$55	$55	$55	$58.6

Upon conversion of all the debentures, the total number of shares of common stock increases by 400,000. However, total capitalization stays at $55 million, for the debentures are retired. In the case of the debentures with warrants attached, the debentures remain outstanding after all the warrants are exercised. Exercising their options, the warrant holders purchase 60,000 shares of common stock at $60 a share, or $3.6 million in total. Consequently, the total capitalization of the company is increased by $3.6 million. Dilution, of course, is greater upon conversion of the convertible debentures (400,000 new shares) than upon exercise of the warrants (60,000 new shares).

A company cannot force the exercise of the warrant option as it can force the exercise of the conversion option by calling a convertible security. Consequently, it is unable to control when the warrant will be exercised and when there will be an infusion of new equity capital into the corporation. Only the expiration date sets a limit on how long the warrants can remain outstanding and unexercised.

Valuation of warrants

The theoretical value of a warrant can be determined by

$$NP_s - O \qquad (24\text{-}2)$$

where N = the number of shares that can be purchased with one warrant
  P_s = the market price of one share of stock
  O = the option price associated with the purchase of N shares

On July 15, 1975, the common stock of Occidental Petroleum closed at $22\frac{1}{8}$ per share. The exercise price for Occidental warrants was $16\frac{1}{4}$, and it enabled the holder to purchase one share of common stock for each warrant held. Consequently, the theoretical value of an Occidental warrant on July 15, 1975, was

$$(1)(22\tfrac{1}{8}) - 16\tfrac{1}{4} = \$5\tfrac{7}{8}$$

The theoretical value of a warrant is the lowest level at which the warrant will generally sell. If, for some reason, the market price of a warrant were to go lower than its theoretical value, arbitragers would eliminate the differential by buying the warrants, exercising them, and selling the stock. A warrant is unlikely to sell below its theoretical value, and many warrants sell above that value. For example, the Occidental Petroleum warrants closed at $12\frac{1}{8}$ on July 15, 1975.

Premium over theoretical value. The primary reason that a warrant can sell at a price higher than its theoretical value is the opportunity for leverage. To illustrate the concept of leverage, consider the Textron warrants. For each warrant held, one share of common stock can be purchased, and the option price is $10. If the stock were selling at $12 a share, the theortical value of the warrant would be $2. Suppose, however, that the common stock increased by 25 percent in price to $15 a share. The theoretical value of the warrant would go from $2 to $5, a gain of 150 percent.

The opportunity for increased gain is attractive to investors when the common stock is selling near its option price. For a given investment, the investor can buy a greater number of warrants than he can shares of common stock. If the stock moves up in price, he will make more money on his investment in warrants than he would on an equal investment in common stock. Of course, leverage works both ways; the percentage change can be almost as pronounced on the downside. There is some downside protection, however, because it is unlikely that the price of the warrant will drop to zero. In order for the market price to drop to zero, there would have to be no probability that the market price of the stock would exceed the option price during the option period.

Because of the opportunity for favorable leverage as well as because of certain other factors, the market prices of most warrants are higher than their theoretical values. In particular, this event occurs when the market price of the associated common stock, NP_s in Eq. (24-2), is near the option price. When the market price of the stock increases, however, the degree of leverage decreases. For example, on July 15, 1975, Textron common stock closed at $24\frac{3}{4}$ per share. At that price, the theoretical value of a warrant was

$$(1)(24\tfrac{3}{4}) - 10 = \$14\tfrac{3}{4}$$

If an investor were to purchase Textron warrants at $14¾ and the market price of the stock increased 25 percent from $24¾ to $30⅞, the theoretical value of a warrant would increase 42 percent to $20⅞. Thus, there is less opportunity for leverage when the market price of the associated common stock is high relative to the option price than when it is close to the option price. As a result, warrants tend to sell around their theoretical values when the market price of the common is relatively high. For example, the Textron warrants closed at $15½ on July 15, 1975—slightly higher than their theoretical value.

The functional relationship between the market value of a warrant and the value of the associated common stock is shown in Figure 24-2. The theoretical value of the warrant is represented by the solid line in the figure, and the actual market value by the dashed line. When the market value of the associated stock is less than the option price, the theoretical value of the warrant is zero. When the value of the associated common stock is greater than the option price, the theoretical value of the warrant is positive, as depicted by the solid, diagonal line.

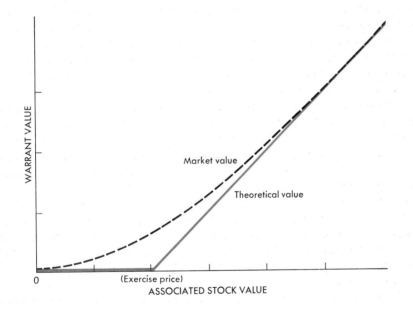

FIG. 24 · 2

Relation between theoretical and actual values of a warrant

When the market value of the associated common stock is low relative to the option price, the actual market value of a warrant usually exceeds its theoretical value. However, as the market value of the associated stock rises, the market value of the warrant usually approaches its theoretical value. The exact shape of the actual value line in Figure 24-2 will depend in part upon the remaining length of the option, the payment of dividends on the common stock, the volatility of the common stock, and the opportunity cost of funds to investors.[9] Although the behavior of warrant prices is a fascinating subject, further analysis is beyond the scope of this book.

SUMMARY

In this chapter, we have examined two types of options under which the holder can obtain common stock. The conversion feature enables the investor to convert a debt instrument or preferred stock into common stock, whereas a warrant attached to a bond enables the holder to purchase a specified number of shares of common stock at a specified price. With a warrant, the exercise of the option does not result in the elimination of the bonds. Convertibles are used more than warrants in financing.

The value of the convertible in the marketplace is determined by its value as a straight bond or preferred stock and its conversion value as common stock. For the corporation, convertibles represent delayed common-stock financing, and the timing of a convertible issue must be analyzed by the company in relation to the market for its common stock. There will be less dilution, for a given amount of financing, with a convertible issue than with a common-stock issue, assuming, of course, that the issue eventually converts. Offsetting in some measure this advantage is the risk of an "overhanging" issue, which occurs when the company is unable to force conversion because the market price of the stock has not risen sufficiently to raise the conversion value of the security significantly above the call price. An overhanging issue results in less financing flexibility for the issuer.

Normally, warrants are employed as a "sweetener" to a public or private issue of debt. The market value of a warrant usually is higher than its theoretical value when the market value of the stock is close to the option price, because this situation gives an opportunity for favorable leverage to the investor. When the market price of the stock is high relative to the option price, warrants tend to sell at about their theoretical values.

[9]See James C. Van Horne, "Warrant Valuation in Relation to Volatility and Opportunity Costs," *Industrial Management Review,* 10 (Spring 1969), 19–32.

1. Because the interest on convertible bonds is tax-deductible while the dividend on a convertible preferred is not, would a company be more inclined to force or stimulate conversion of a convertible preferred than it would a convertible bond?

2. Convertible securities are said to offer a hedge against both inflation and deflation. Can you explain why? Does your answer explain the widespread popularity of convertibles in the post-World War II period?

3. This chapter has argued that convertibles are a form of delayed equity financing allowing the sale of equity at a 10 to 20 percent premium over current market price. Yet most convertibles are finally called only if the current market price is well in excess of the conversion price. Wouldn't the firm have been better off to have waited and simply sold the common stock? Explain your position.

4. If convertible securities can be issued at a lower effective interest rate than long-term bonds, why would a company ever issue straight debt?

5. Why do warrants whose theoretical value is zero sell for positive prices?

6. Suppose you are the financial manager of a rather closely held small electronics firm. You have a favorable investment opportunity and are considering raising funds to finance it using subordinated convertible debentures or straight bonds with warrants attached. Equity funds are not a possibility, as you feel the current stock price has been unnecessarily penalized for recent start-up expenses and the firm's high debt ratio (relative to the industry). If you expect additional large future funds requirements, which financing alternative would you adopt? Why?

7. Why might a convertible bondholder elect to convert voluntarily?

8. What reasons can you offer for the use of warrants by small, rapidly growing companies?

1. The common stock of the Davidson Corporation earns $2.50 per share, has a 60 percent dividend payout, and sells at a P/E ratio of 10. Davidson wishes to offer $10 million of 6 percent, twenty-year convertible debentures with an initial conversion premium of 20 percent and a call price of $105. Davidson currently has 1 million common shares outstanding and has a 50 percent tax rate.
   (a) What is the conversion price?
   (b) What is the conversion ratio per $1,000 debenture?
   (c) What is the initial conversion value of each debenture?
   (d) How many new shares of common must be issued if all debentures are converted?

(e) If Davidson can increase operating earnings by $1 million per year with the proceeds of the debenture issue, compute the new earnings per share and earnings retained before and after conversion.

2. Assume that the Davidson Corporation (see Problem 1) raised the $10 million through an issue of stock (total gross spread and expenses = 10 percent of gross proceeds of issue). How many new shares would have to be issued? If operating earnings were increased by $1 million through the use of the proceeds, compute the new earnings per share and earnings retention. Compare your answers with those obtained in 1(e) above.

3. Assume that the Davidson Corporation (see Problem 1) could sell $10 million in straight debt at 9 percent as an alternative to the convertible issue.
    (a) Compute the earnings per share and earnings retained after issuance of the straight debt under the assumption of a $1 million increase in operating earnings and compare your answers with those obtained in 1(e) above.
    (b) Compute the bond value of the convertible debenture, assuming that interest is paid at the end of each year.
    (c) Compute the premium over bond value at issuance of the convertible debenture.

4. The Beruth Company is contemplating raising $10 million by means of a debt issue. It has the following alternatives:
    (a) A twenty-year, 6 percent convertible debenture issue with a $50 conversion price and $1,000 face value, or
    (b) A twenty-year, 8 percent straight debt issue with a detachable warrant to purchase four shares for $200 attached to each $1,000 bond.
    The company has a 50 percent tax rate, and its stock is currently selling at $40 per share. Its net income before interest and taxes is a constant 20 percent of its total capitalization, which currently appears as follows:

Common stock (par $5)	$ 5,000,000
Capital surplus	10,000,000
Retained earnings	15,000,000
Total	$30,000,000

    (a) Show the capitalizations resulting from each alternative, both before and after conversion or exercise (a total of four capitalizations).
    (b) Compute earnings per share currently and under each of the four capitalizations determined in (a).
    (c) If the price of Beruth stock went to $75, determine the theoretical value of each warrant issued under alternative (b) above.
    (d) Discuss the differences in the implicit costs of (1) straight debt, (2) convertible debt, (3) debt with warrants.

5. Eleven years ago Ardordyne issued 5 percent, 25-year convertible bonds at par. The bonds were convertible into common at $125 per share; the common was then selling at $100. The common was subsequently split two for one (the conversion price was adjusted) and currently sells at $47 with a

$1 dividend. Nonconvertible bonds of similar quality currently yield 9 percent. What price would you be willing to pay for one of these bonds? On what rational basis might investors in different circumstances be willing to pay a price different from yours?

6. Using Eq. (24-2), compute the theoretical value of each of the following warrants:

Warrant	N	P_s	O
(a)	5	$100	$400
(b)	10	10	60
(c)	2.3	4	10
(d)	3.54	27 ⅛	35.40

7. Stanley Zinc Company called its 7 percent convertible subordinated debentures for redemption on March 15, 1977. The call price was $106. A holder of a $1,000 bond was entitled to convert into 34.7 shares of stock. At the time of the call announcement, the common stock of Stanley Zinc was selling at $43 per share.
   (a) What is the approximate market price at which the debentures would be selling at the time of the announcement?
   (b) By what percentage would market price per share need to drop before bondholders would rationally accept the call price?

SELECTED REFERENCES

BACON, PETER W., and EDWARD L. WINN, Jr., "The Impact of Forced Conversion on Stock Prices," *Journal of Finance*, 24 (December 1969), 871–74.

BAUMOL, WILLIAM J., BURTON G. MALKIEL, and RICHARD E. QUANDT, "The Valuation of Convertible Securities," *Quarterly Journal of Economics*, 80 (February 1966), 48–59.

BLACK, FISCHER, and MYRON SCHOLES, "The Pricing of Options and Corporate Liabilities," *Journal of Political Economy*, 81 (May–June 1973), 637–54.

————, "The Valuation of Option Contracts and a Test of Market Efficiency," *Journal of Finance*, 27 (May 1972), 399–417.

BREALEY, RICHARD A., *Security Prices in a Competitive Market*, Chapters 16 and 17. Cambridge, Mass.: M.I.T. Press, 1971.

BRIGHAM, EUGENE F., "An Analysis of Convertible Debentures: Theory and Some Empirical Evidence," *Journal of Finance*, 21 (March 1966), 35–54.

FRANK, WERNER G., and CHARLES O. KRONCKE, "Classifying Conversions of Convertible Debentures over Four Years," *Financial Management*, 3 (Summer 1974), 33–42.

HAYES, SAMUEL L., III, and HENRY B. REILING, "Sophisticated Financing Tool: The Warrant," *Harvard Business Review*, 47 (January–February 1969), 137–50.

JENNINGS, EDWARD H., "An Estimate of Convertible Bond Premiums," *Journal of Financial and Quantitative Analysis*, 9 (January 1974), 33–56.

LEWELLEN, WILBUR G., and GEORGE A. RACETTE, "Convertible Debt Financing," *Journal of Financial and Quantitative Analysis*, 7 (December 1973), 777–92.

MERTON, ROBERT C., "On the Pricing of Corporate Debt," *Journal of Finance,* 29 (May 1974), 449–70.

———, "A Rational Theory of Option Pricing," *Bell Journal of Economics and Management Science,* 4 (Spring 1973).

MILLER, ALEXANDER B., "How to Call Your Convertible," *Harvard Business Review,* 49 (May–June 1971), 66–70.

PINCHES, GEORGE E., "Financing with Convertible Preferred Stocks, 1960–1967," *Journal of Finance,* 25 (March 1970), 53–64.

RUSH, DAVID F., and **RONALD W. MELICHER,** "An Empirical Examination of Factors Which Influence Warrant Prices," *Journal of Finance,* 29 (December 1974), 1449–66.

SAMUELSON, PAUL A., "Rational Theory of Warrant Pricing," *Industrial Management Review,* 6 (Spring 1965), 13–31.

SHELTON, JOHN P., "The Relation of the Price of a Warrant to the Price of Its Associated Stock," *Financial Analysts Journal,* 23 (May–June and July–August 1967), 143–51 and 88–99.

SKERRATT, L. C. L., "The Price Determination of Convertible Loan Stock: A UK Model," *Journal of Business Finance & Accounting,* 1 (Autumn 1974), 429–43.

SOLDOFSKY, ROBERT M., "Yield-Risk Performance of Convertible Securities," *Financial Analysts Journal,* 39 (March–April 1971), 61–65.

STEVENSON, RICHARD A., and **JOE LAVELY,** "Why a Bond Warrant Issue," *Financial Executive,* 38 (June 1970), 16–21.

VAN HORNE, JAMES C., *The Function and Analysis of Capital Market Rates,* pp. 166–71. Englewood Cliffs, N.J.: Prentice-Hall, 1970.

———, "Warrant Valuation in Relation to Volatility and Opportunity Costs," *Industrial Management Review,* 10 (Spring 1969), 19–32.

WEIL, ROMAN L., JR., JOEL E. SEGALL, and **DAVID GREEN, JR.,** "Premiums on Convertible Bonds," *Journal of Finance,* 23 (June 1968), 445–63.

VII
Expansion and Contraction

25 Mergers and Acquisitions

Growth is an essential ingredient to the success and vitality of many companies. Without it, a company has difficulty in generating a dedication of purpose and in attracting first-rate managers. Growth can be either internal or external. Up to now, we have considered only the former category, where a firm acquires specific assets and finances them by the retention of earnings and/or external financing. External growth, on the other hand, involves the acquisition of another company. In principle, growth by acquiring another company is little different from growth by acquiring a specific asset. Each requires an initial outlay, which is expected to be followed by future benefits. The objective of either type of acquisition is to maximize the value of the firm to existing shareholders.

By way of definition, a *statutory merger* is a combination of two corporations wherein one loses its corporate existence. The surviving company acquires both the assets and the liabilities of the merged company. A merger must be distinguished from a *statutory consolidation,* which is a combination of two companies whereby an entirely new corporation is formed. Both the old companies cease to exist, and shares of their common stock are exchanged for shares in the new company. When two companies of about the same size combine, they usually consolidate. When the two companies differ significantly in size, usually a merger is involved. Though it is important to understand the distinction, the words *merger* and *consolidation* tend to be used interchangeably to describe the combination of two companies.

The merger movement in the United States has gone through cycles which have roughly paralleled changes in the economic, social, and political environment. The greatest activity occurred in the 1890s and early 1900s when a number of giant corporations were formed. This was the period when U.S. Steel Corporation, Standard Oil Company, huge mining complexes, and a host of other corporate giants were launched. It was a day when antitrust and tax constraints as we know them today were virtually nonexistent. The next major period of merger activity occurred in the 1920s, following World War I. In the depression of the 1930s, merger activity virtually dried up. There was again a flurry in the late 1940s after World War II, followed by steady merger activity in the post-World War II period. In the mid-1960s, another peak was reached with the heightened interest in the conglomerate merger, in which unrelated businesses are combined.

REASONS FOR COMBINATION

The reasons for a combination are many and complex. Moreover, they are not mutually exclusive; more than one usually is involved in a combination. In this section, we consider various reasons for combinations, but recognize that they must be taken collectively.

Operating economies

Often, operating economies can be achieved through a combination of companies. Duplicate facilities can be eliminated, and marketing, purchasing, and other operations can be consolidated. For example, certain salesmen can be eliminated to avoid duplication of effort in a particular territory. The principal objective in a railroad merger is to realize economies of operation through elimination of duplicate facilities and runs. With an industrial company merger, a firm with a product that complements an existing product line can fill out that line and, hopefully, increase the total overall demand for the products of the acquiring company. The realization of operating economies is known as *synergism;* the fused company is of greater value than the sum of the parts— that is, $2 + 2 = 5$.

Operating economies can best be realized with a *horizontal merger,* in which two companies in the same line of business are combined. The economies achieved by this means result primarily from eliminating duplicate facilities and offering a broader product line in the hope of increasing total demand. A *vertical merger,* whereby a company either expands forward toward the ultimate consumer or backward toward the source of raw material, may also bring about economies.

This type of merger gives a company more control over its distribution and purchasing. In the formation of U.S. Steel Corporation in 1900, one of the purposes was a complete vertical integration of steel from extraction of ore to the final sale of the product. There are few operating economies in a *conglomerate merger*, where two companies in unrelated lines of business are combined.[1]

Management acquisition

Closely related to operating economies is the acquisition of management. If a firm finds that it is unable to hire top-quality management and that it has no one coming up through the ranks, it may seek a combination with another company having aggressive and competent management. The choice may be between gradual stagnation with an existing organization or combination with another company in order to obtain aggressive management and prospects for growth. To foster the long-run wealth of stockholders, the latter may be the only feasible alternative.

Growth

A company may not be able to grow at a fast or balanced enough rate by internal expansion and may find that its only way of achieving a desired growth rate is by acquiring other companies. The cost of growth by acquisition may well be cheaper than the real cost of internal growth; the numerous costs and risks involved in developing and embarking upon a new-product line may be avoided through acquisition of a going concern. In addition, it usually is quicker to acquire new products and facilities through mergers than through internal development. An important aspect of external growth may be the acquisition of the research capabilities of another firm. Because research tends to be individually oriented, the acquiring company may be unable to develop such capabilities on its own. Closely related to research is the possession of basic patents. A company having certain patent rights may be extremely valuable for this reason alone.

Although these factors may lead to higher future earnings and growth, the critical factor is the price paid for the acquisition. If the company to be acquired is priced rationally in the market (that is, it is not undervalued or overvalued), its acquisition is unlikely to increase share price *unless* there is synergism. Increased growth in *total* earnings is not the important thing—it is increased growth in earnings *per*

[1] See, for example, Dennis C. Mueller, "A Theory of Conglomerate Mergers," *Quarterly Journal of Economics*, 83 (November 1969), 652–53.

share, all other things the same. Unfortunately, in certain cases growth in sales, assets, and total earnings appears to have supplanted maximization of shareholder wealth as the primary goal of the firm. Robin Maris contends that because management's salaries, stock options, and prestige are more closely related to size than to profits, managers have considerable incentive to maximize growth.[2] If this is true, it is not difficult to understand the attractiveness of mergers in implementing such an objective, because in most cases growth can be achieved more easily through external acquisitions than through internal development.

Financing

Rapidly growing companies can run into difficulty in financing their growth. Rather than curtail their expansion, they may seek to combine with a company having the liquidity and stability necessary for financing the contemplated growth. The "cash-rich" company can benefit by being able to utilize its liquidity in a growth situation. The growing company benefits in that it does not have to give up exciting opportunities in order to provide for a period of "digestion."

Taxation

The avoidance of corporate income taxes is a factor in some mergers. A company with a tax loss carry-forward may want to acquire one or more profitable companies in order to be able to utilize its carry-forward. Otherwise, the carry-forward may expire at the end of five years for the lack of sufficient profits to utilize it completely. For this reason, a company may be willing to pay a fairly substantial price to acquire a profitable company.

Diversification

Diversification is the motive in some mergers. By acquiring a firm in a different line of business, a company may be able to reduce cyclical instability in earnings. Although it is virtually impossible to find two companies with negative correlation in earnings, it is possible to find

---

[2] *The Economic Theory of Managerial Capitalism* (New York: Free Press, 1964). See also Mueller, "Theory of Conglomerate Mergers," pp. 644–48. In contrast, Wilbur G. Lewellen and Blaine Huntsman, "Managerial Pay and Corporate Performance," *American Economic Review,* 60 (September 1970), 710–20, find in an empirical study that executive compensation is influenced more strongly by profit and stock performance than by sales.

situations in which there is only moderate correlation. Related to the argument for diversification is the notion of spreading risk. For a small company the risk exposure of undertaking a new-product line may be significant indeed. In fact, the potential loss may be so great in relation to the capital base of the company that management is unwilling to go ahead with the product development despite its considerable appeal. By combining with a larger company, however, the firm may be able to undertake the project, because the potential loss is not nearly as significant relative to the capital base of the surviving company.

To the extent that investors in a company's stock are averse to risk and are concerned only with the total risk of the firm, a reduction in earnings instability would have a favorable impact upon share price. This argument assumes that investors evaluate risk solely in relation to the *total* risk of the firm. We know from Chapters 15 and 16, however, that investors are able to diversify risk on their own. If they evaluate risk in an overall market context, they will diversify at least as effectively on their own as the firm is able to do for them. Particularly when the stock of the company being acquired is publicly traded, there is no reason to believe that investors are not able to diversify their portfolios efficiently. Because the firm is unable to do something for them that they cannot do for themselves, diversification as a reason for merging would not be a thing of value. Consequently, it would not lead to an increase in share price.

Personal reasons

In a tightly held company, the individuals who have controlling interest may want their company acquired by another company that has an established market for its stock. For estate tax purposes, it may be desirable for these individuals to hold shares of stock that are readily marketable and for which market-price quotations are available. The owners of a tightly held company may have too much of their wealth tied up in the company. By merging with a publicly held company, they obtain a marked improvement in their liquidity, enabling them to sell some of their stock and diversify their investments.

IMPACT OF TERMS OF MERGER

When two companies are combined, a ratio of exchange occurs that denotes the relative weighting of the firms. In this section, we consider the ratio of exchange with respect to the earnings, the market prices, and the book values of the stocks of the two companies involved. We assume that the combination is consummated in stock rather than in cash or debt. The objective in any merger should be to maximize the long-run wealth of existing stockholders. A successful merger, then, would be one that increases the market price of the firm's stock over what it would have been if the combination had not taken place.

Earnings impact

In evaluating the possibility of an acquisition, it is important to consider the effect the merger has on the earnings per share of the surviving corporation. Suppose Company A is considering the acquisition, by stock, of Company B. The financial data on the acquisition at the time it is being considered follows:

	Company A	Company B
Present earnings	$20,000,000	$5,000,000
Shares	5,000,000	2,000,000
Earnings per share	$ 4.00	$ 2.50
Price of stock	$64.00	$30.00
Price/earnings ratio	16	12

Assume that Company B has agreed to an offer of $35 a share to be paid in Company A's stock. The exchange ratio, then, is $35/$64, or about 0.547 shares of Company A's stock for each share of Company B's stock. In total 1,093,750 shares of Company A will need to be issued in order to acquire Company B. Assuming that the earnings of the component companies stay the same after the acquisition, earnings per share of the surviving company would be:

	Surviving Company A
Earnings	$25,000,000
Shares	6,093,750
Earnings per share	$4.10

Thus, there is an immediate improvement in earnings per share for Company A as a result of the merger. Company B's former stockholders experience a reduction in earnings per share, however. For each share of B's stock they had held, they now hold 0.547 shares of A. Thus, the earnings per share on each share of Company B's stock they held is (0.547)(4.10), or $2.24, compared with $2.50 before.

Assume, however, that the price agreed upon for Company B's stock is $45 a share. The ratio of exchange, then, would be $45/$64, or about

0.703 shares of A for each share of B. In total, 1,406,250 shares would have to be issued, and earnings per share after the merger would be:

	Surviving Company A
Earnings	$25,000,000
Shares	6,406,250
Earnings per share	$3.90

In this case, there is initial dilution in Company A's earnings per share on account of the acquisition of Company B.[3] Dilution in earnings per share will occur anytime the price/earnings ratio paid for a company exceeds the price/earnings ratio of the company doing the acquiring. In our example, the price/earnings ratio in the first case was $35.00/$2.50, or 14, and in the second case, it was $45.00/$2.50, or 18. Because the price/earnings ratio of Company A was 16, there was an increase in earnings per share in the first case and a decrease in the second.

Thus, both initial increases and decreases in earnings per share are possible. The *amount* of increase or decrease is a function of (1) the differential in price/earnings ratios, and (2) the relative size of the two firms as measured by total earnings.[4] The higher the price/earnings ratio of the acquiring company in relation to that of the company being acquired, and the larger the earnings of the acquired company in relation to those of the acquiring company, the greater the increase in earnings per share of the acquiring company. These relationships are illustrated in Figure 25-1 for three different earnings relationships. The a subscript for total earnings, T_a, and price/earnings ratio, P_a/E_a, denotes the acquiring company while the b subscript for T_b and P_b/E_b denotes the company being acquired.

Future earnings.   If the decision to acquire another company is based solely upon the initial impact on earnings per share, a company would never acquire another if there were an initial dilution in earnings per share. However, this type of analysis does not take into account the possibility of a future growth in earnings owing to the merger. If the earnings of Company B are expected to grow at a faster rate than those of Company A, a high ratio of exchange for the stock may be justified, despite the fact that there is initial dilution in earnings per share for stockholders of Company A. The superior growth in earnings of the acquired company may result eventually in higher earnings per share for these stockholders relative to earnings without the merger.

---

[3] Company B's former stockholders obtain an improvement in earnings per share. Earnings per share on each share of stock they had held is $2.74.

[4] See Walter J. Mead, "Instantaneous Merger Profit as a Conglomerate Merger Motive," *Western Economics Journal*, 7 (December 1969), 295–306.

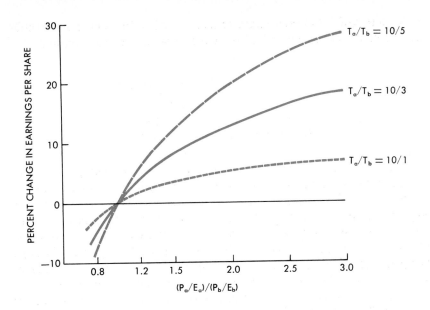

FIG. 25 · 1

Relationship between earnings per share change and the price/earnings ratio differential and relative earnings

It is useful to graph likely future earnings per share with and without the acquisition. Figure 25-2 shows this for a hypothetical merger. The graph tells us how long it will take for the dilution in earnings per share to be eliminated, and for an accretion to take place. In this example, it is three years; earnings per share drop $0.30 initially, but

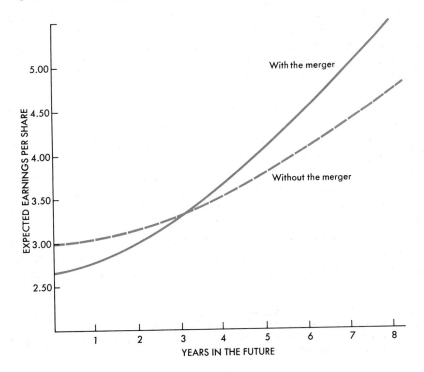

FIG. 25 · 2

Expected earnings per share with and without the merger

551

this relative dilution is eliminated by the start of the fourth year. The greater the duration of dilution, the less desirable the acquisition is from the standpoint of the acquiring company. Some companies set a ceiling on the number of years dilution will be tolerated, and this ceiling serves as a constraint in establishing the exchange ratio to be paid in the acquisition.

Another drawback to using the initial impact on earnings per share as the sole criterion for judging the value of a merger is that the earnings of the surviving company are not necessarily an additive affair, such that $2 + 2 = 4$. In many cases, there are *synergistic* effects, such that $2 + 2 = 5$. Because of operating economies, increases in demand, and so forth, earnings of the surviving company may be greater than the sum of the earnings of the two companies without the merger. In our example, suppose that total earnings three years after the merger are expected to be $36 million for the surviving company, whereas total earnings of Company A three years hence without the merger are expected to be $26 million. Assuming the price paid for Company B's stock is $45 a share, the expected earnings per share three years hence with and without the merger are

	With Merger	Without Merger
Expected earnings	$36,000,000	$26,000,000
Shares	6,406,250	5,000,000
Expected earnings per share	$5.62	$5.20

We see then that despite initial dilution, the acquisition of Company B produces a favorable effect upon future earnings per share over and above the expected growth in earnings per share for Company A without the merger.[5] We can graph expected earnings per share, as in Figure 25-2, with and without the acquisition under the assumption of synergism. In fact, when an acquisition is being considered, graphs should be prepared under differing assumptions as to the exchange ratio. They also should be made under differing earnings assumptions for the combination, for preparing such multiple graphs gives management greater information on which to base negotiations.

Dividends per share. The ratio of exchange of dividends per share sometimes is considered in the evaluation of a merger. However, the dividend decision really is separate from the merger decision. The important variable is prospective earnings, for dividends are a function of these earnings. The acquiring company can alter its dividend-

---

[5] See J. Fred Weston, "Determination of Share Exchange Ratios in Mergers," in William W. Alberts and Joel E. Segall, eds., *The Corporate Merger* (Chicago: University of Chicago Press, 1966), pp. 117–38.

payout ratio if the prospect of a higher total dividend is enticing to the stockholders of the company being acquired. Justification for this action, however, must be based upon an analysis of its effect upon shareholder wealth (see Chapter 19).

Market value impact

In addition to earnings, the major emphasis in the bargaining process is on the ratio of exchange of market prices per share. The market price of a publicly held stock is the focal judgment of investors as to the "intrinsic" value of that company. Accordingly, it reflects the earnings potential of the company, dividends, business risk, capital structure, asset values, and other factors that bear upon valuation. The ratio of exchange of market prices is simply

$$\frac{\text{Market price per share of acquiring company} \times \text{Number of shares offered}}{\text{Market price per share of acquired company}}$$

For example, if the market price of Company A is $60 per share and that of Company B is $30, and Company A offers a half share of its stock for each share of Company B, the ratio of exchange would be

$$\frac{\$60 \times 0.5}{\$30} = 1.00$$

In other words, the stocks of the two companies would be exchanged on a one-to-one market-price basis. If the market price of the surviving company is relatively stable at $60 a share, each set of stockholders is about as well off as before with respect to market value. However, there is little enticement to the company being acquired to accept a one-to-one market-value ratio of exchange. Consequently, the acquiring company usually must offer a price in excess of the current market price per share of the company it wishes to acquire. Instead of a half share of stock, Company A might have to offer 0.667 shares, or $40 a share in current market value.

Even when the acquiring company offers a price in excess of the current market price of the company being acquired, its own stockholders still may be better off with respect to market price per share. The reason is that there may be a difference in the price/earnings ratios of the two companies. Suppose that Company B is a moderate-sized company whose stock is traded in the over-the-counter market. Because, among other reasons, its stock is not particularly marketable, its price/earnings ratio is 10. Company A, on the other hand, has a price/earnings ratio of 18. Assume the following financial information:

	Company A	Company B
Present earnings	$20,000,000	$6,000,000
Shares	6,000,000	2,000,000
Earnings per share	$ 3.33	$ 3.00
Market price per share	$60.00	$30.00
Price/earnings ratio	18	10

With an offer of 0.667 shares of Company *A* for each share of Company *B*, or $40 a share in value, the market-price exchange ratio for Company *B* is

$$\frac{\$60 \times 0.667}{\$30} = 1.33$$

Stockholders of Company *B* are being offered a stock with a market value of $40 for each share of stock they own. Obviously, they benefit from the acquisition with respect to market price, because their stock was formerly worth $30 a share. However, the stockholders of Company *A* also stand to benefit, if the price/earnings ratio of the surviving company stays at 18. The market price per share of the surviving company after the acquisition, all other things held constant, would be:

	Surviving Company
Total earnings	$26,000,000
Number of shares	7,333,333
Earnings per share	$3.55
Price/earnings ratio	18
Market price per share	$63.90

The reason for this apparent bit of magic whereby the stockholders of both companies benefit is the difference in price/earnings ratios.

Thus, companies with high price/earnings ratios supposedly would be able to acquire companies with lower price/earnings ratios and obtain an immediate increase in earnings per share, despite the fact that they pay a premium with respect to the market value exchange ratio. The key factor, however, is what happens to the price/earnings ratio after the merger. If it stays the same, the market price of the stock will increase. As a result, an acquiring company would be able to show a steady growth in earnings per share if it acquired a sufficient number of companies over time in this manner.[6] Recognize that this increase

---

[6] For further illustration of this process, see Mead, "Instantaneous Merger Profit," pp. 298–99.

is not the result of operating economies or underlying growth but is due to the "bootstrap" increase in earnings per share through acquisitions. To the extent the marketplace values this illusory growth, a company presumably could increase shareholder wealth through acquisitions alone.

However, in reasonably efficient capital markets it seems unlikely that the market will hold constant the price/earnings ratio of a company that cannot demonstrate growth potential in ways other than acquiring companies with lower price/earnings ratios. The acquiring company must be able to manage the companies it acquires and show some degree of synergism if the benefit of acquisitions is to be lasting. If the market is relatively free from imperfections and if synergism is not anticipated, we would expect the price/earnings ratio of the surviving firm to approach a weighted average of the two previous price/earnings ratios. Under these circumstances, the acquisition of companies with lower price/earnings ratios would not enhance shareholder wealth. If synergism were expected, however, shareholder wealth could be increased through the acquisition.

Market values are unquestionably a major factor in most mergers; however, these values fluctuate greatly over time and in differing degrees for different companies. As a result, there may be considerable doubt as to just what is the appropriate market value of a company. Because of the fluctuation in market value, some companies vary their pursuit of acquisitions in keeping with the price of their stock. When the price is high, they may be aggressive in their pursuit of acquisitions; when it is relatively low, merger activity may dry up completely. Although certain mergers are based upon normalized market prices over a length of time, most are predicated upon the current market price. Consequently, fluctuations in this price are extremely important to the acquisition-minded company.

Book value impact

Book value per share is rather meaningless as a basis for valuation in most mergers. Whereas once it was the dominant factor, book value per share is important now only when it is significantly above market value. When the purpose of an acquisition is to obtain the liquidity of another company, book value per share and working capital per share become important in the terms of the exchange. For example, Textron acquired American Woolen primarily for the latter's liquidity. American Woolen's book value per share was approximately $60, its working capital per share was $24, and its market price per share was $16. Textron paid $25 a share in cash. The ratios of exchange of book value per share of two companies is calculated in the same manner as is the ratio for market values. The importance of this ratio in bargaining is restricted usually to situations in which a company is acquired for its liquidity and asset values rather than for its earning power.

NEGOTIATION OF A MERGER

The financial information developed earlier assists management only in negotiating more effectively; it does not establish the final terms. Management of the buying company must convince its counterpart in the selling company that a merger is in the latter's best interests. One must be mindful of the fact that if the prospective acquisition is attractive to the buying company, it is probably attractive to others as well.[7] Consequently, the selling company may have its pick of offers. Naturally, it will want to select the best.

But what constitutes the best offer? Obviously, the market-price exchange ratio is important, because it establishes the market price per share offered for the company. Apart from the exchange ratio, management of the potential acquisition often has to be convinced that a marriage of the two companies is in its best interest. Very much a part of the total picture is the role this management will play in the surviving company. To come to grips with this and related issues prior to negotiations, management of the acquiring company must thoroughly understand the operations of the potential acquisition. Then it must lay out a strategy with respect to the nonfinancial aspects of the prospective merger. These aspects include not only the role and compensation of management in the surviving company but also such things as the continuation and promotion of existing products, the opportunity to go into new markets, and the provision of financial resources to assure future growth.[8] Nonfinancial considerations can loom quite large in the minds of the selling company's management, often spelling the difference between going along with a merger or turning it down.

To the extent that synergism is possible, the buyer can be relatively generous in the exchange ratio offered, as well as in nonfinancial terms. Final terms depend upon the bargaining strengths of the two parties, the financial relationships described, and expectations regarding the future earnings performance of the surviving company. In the case of the buyer, negotiations should be framed in terms of what the seller will gain from the merger. Unless there is a reasonable gain, few companies will wish to sell. In contrast, the seller should think in terms of how much the merger is worth to the buyer. Simply because a merger will benefit the seller does not mean that the terms offered are the best that can be obtained by the seller.

[7] For an excellent exposition on negotiating strategy, see Gary E. MacDougal and Fred V. Malek, "Master Plan for Merger Negotiations," *Harvard Business Review,* 48 (January–February 1970), 77–82.

[8] See MacDougal and Malek, "Master Plan for Merger Negotiations," pp. 78–80.

Contingent payments

In order to provide a performance incentive to the management of the acquired company, the buyer sometimes uses a contingent payment plan based upon subsequent performance.[9] A down payment is made at the time of the merger and the contingent payment is based upon the seller's meeting or exceeding certain standards. Several conditions are necessary before a contingent payment plan is feasible. For one thing, the selling company needs to be operated after the merger as a separate division or subsidiary, with major decisions affecting profitability left in the hands of the management of the acquired company. Otherwise, management's influence on profitability is diluted. Other conditions that increase the feasibility of a contingent payment plan are the selling company's being closely held, relatively new, and having relatively low earnings.[10]

The down payment and performance standards must be firmly established by both parties. A number of variations are possible. The most common is to specify some level of future earnings, either year by year or an average. Contingent payments then are made on the basis of how much actual earnings exceed the earnings standards. Sometimes this excess is adjusted downward for the use of the parent company's capital. Other types of standards include a moving standard and a cumulative one.[11] When the acquisition is for cash, the contingent payment is simply excess earnings over the standard times some agreed percentage. When the acquisition is in stock, the number of shares given in a contingent payment varies according to the price of the parent company's stock at the time of the payment.

As should be apparent, the use of contingent payouts is applicable only under certain circumstances. The ground rules must be firmly established. It is no good from the standpoint of the buyer if the selling company "jacks up" earnings during the contingency period by postponing capital expenditures and research and development or "adjusts" accounting earnings. These actions work to the detriment of earnings in later years. If ground rules are equitable and firm, however, the incentive payment plan may be quite effective. The buyer benefits in that only proven performance is rewarded. If things turn bad, he is out only the down payment. The seller also may benefit in that the total price paid if postmerger earnings are good may be higher than the price paid if the total payment occurred at the time of the merger. Because of these features, the contingent payment plan has grown in importance in recent years.

---

[9] See W. Robert Reum and Thomas A. Steele III, "Contingent Payouts Cut Acquisition Risks," *Harvard Business Review*, 48 (March–April 1970), 83–91, upon which this section is based.

[10] Ibid., p. 84.

[11] Ibid, p. 85.

Tender offers

In our hypothetical examples, it was assumed that negotiations were confined to the managements and boards of directors of the companies involved. However, the acquiring company can make its appeal directly to the stockholders of the company it wishes to acquire, through a tender offer. A tender offer is an offer to purchase shares of stock of another company at a fixed price per share from any stockholder who "tenders" his shares. The tender price usually is set significantly above the present market price in order to provide an incentive to stockholders to tender their shares. Use of the tender offer allows the acquiring company to bypass the management of the company it wishes to acquire and, therefore, serves as a threat in any negotiations with that management. If management holds out for too high a price or otherwise balks at the offer of the acquiring company, that company can always make a tender offer.

The tender offer also can be used when there are no negotiations but when one company simply wants to acquire another. In a "surprise" tender offer, the acquiring company is very careful not to reveal its intentions prior to the actual offer. The primary selling tool is the premium that is offered over the existing market price of the stock. As a rule of thumb, many suggest a premium of 20 percent, which is adjusted up or down depending upon the circumstances.[12] In addition, brokers are often given very attractive commissions for shares tendered through them. The tender offer itself is usually communicated through financial newspapers. Direct mailings are made to the stockholders of the company being bid for if the bidder is able to obtain a stockholders' list. Although a company is legally obligated to provide such a list, it usually is able to delay delivery long enough to frustrate the bidder.

From the standpoint of the company being bid for, a number of defensive tactics are available. First, management may try to persuade its stockholders that the offer is not in their best interests. Usually, the argument is that the bid is too low in relation to the true, long-run value of the firm. However, in the face of an attractive premium, the long run may be too distant. Some companies raise the cash dividend or declare a stock split in hopes of gaining stockholder support. Legal actions are often undertaken, more to delay and frustrate the bidder than with the expectation of winning. To the extent that the two firms are competitors, an antitrust suit may prove a powerful deterrent to the bidder. As a last resort, management of the company being bid for may seek a merger with a "friendly" company.[13] Some of the strategies involved in tender offers are depicted in Figure 25-3.

[12] See Samuel L. Hayes III and Russell A. Taussig, "Tactics of Cash Takeover Bids," *Harvard Business Review,* 45 (March–April 1967), 139–40.

[13] For a more extensive discussion of these points, see ibid., pp. 135–48.

A bidder takes pains to keep his intentions secret until the last minute.
"Claude; Courtesy of *Fortune Magazine*."

Management often seeks to foil a bidder by
quickly arranging a merger with another company.
"Claude; Courtesy of *Fortune Magazine*."

Determined management opposition
can usually fend off an unwanted take-over bid.
"Claude; Courtesy of *Fortune Magazine*."

FIG. 25 · 3

Tender offers

Although the use of tender offers increased dramatically in the sixties, it declined in importance in the seventies. In part, this decline was due to coinciding changes in security regulations and accounting rules that tended to restrict the prospective acquirer.[14] There are many who oppose such restrictions because they believe tender offers contribute to corporate "democracy" and, thereby, serve a socially useful function. If management does not behave so as to maximize the

[14] See Richard E. Cheney, "What's New on the Corporate Takeover Scene," *Financial Executive*, 40 (April 1972), 18–21.

value of the firm to its shareholders, there is always the danger of a tender offer from another company. Whereas stockholders may not have enough control to effect a change otherwise, a tender offer may bring about a change and increase shareholder wealth. In recent years, the tender offer has largely displaced the proxy contest as a means of obtaining control of a company.

HOLDING COMPANIES

Instead of actually acquiring another company, a firm may purchase a portion of its stock and act as a holding company. By definition, a *holding company* owns sufficient voting stock to have a controlling interest in one or more other corporations. A holding company does not necessarily have to own 51 percent of the stock of another company in order to have control. For a widely held corporation, ownership of 20 percent or as little as 10 percent of the stock outstanding may constitute effective working control. The holding company had its origin in the latter part of the nineteenth century when the state of New Jersey first permitted corporations to exist for the sole purpose of owning stocks of other corporations.

Advantages

One of the advantages of a holding company is that it allows a company to acquire control of another with a much smaller investment than would be necessary with a merger. Moreover, by acquiring only a portion of the stock, the holding company usually does not have to pay as high a price per share as it would if it sought to purchase all the stock. It may purchase the stock gradually without undue upward pressure on the market price of the stock. Another advantage is that formal approval from stockholders of the acquiring company is not required. It is an informal arrangement. A further advantage of a holding company is the possibility that operating economies can be achieved through centralized management. The magnitude of economies possible here, however, is limited.

Disadvantages

One of the principal disadvantages of the holding company is that 15 percent of the dividends paid to it by the subsidiary is subject to taxation.[15] Thus, the holding company must pay a partial tax on dividends,

---

[15] If the holding company owns 80 percent or more of the voting stock of the subsidiary, the dividend is not subject to taxation.

and stockholders of the holding company also must pay a tax on dividends they receive. The partial tax could be avoided, of course, if the stockholders owned the operating companies directly.

Through pyramiding a series of holding companies, it is possible to obtain considerable leverage with respect to assets controlled and earnings. For example, suppose Holding Company A owns 20 percent of Holding Companies B, C, and D, which, in turn, own 20 percent controlling interest in nine operating companies. Thus, for every dollar of capital in each of the operating companies—$9 in all—Company A is able to control them with an investment of $0.36, (0.20 × 0.20 × $9), or 4 percent of the total capital of the operating companies. As long as the operating companies are profitable and able to pay dividends to the holding companies, all may go well. However, in the 1920s, there tended to be excessive pyramiding of holding companies, particularly with respect to public utilities. In the 1930s, the leverage of these companies magnified the losses, and a number of the pyramids crumbled. Because of the many abuses of holding companies, the Public Utility Holding Company Act of 1935 was passed to restrict the operation of holding companies in the public utility field.

ACQUISITIONS AND CAPITAL BUDGETING

From the standpoint of the buying corporation, acquisitions can be treated as another aspect of capital budgeting. In principle, the prospective acquisition should be evaluated in much the same manner as any capital-budgeting project. There is an initial outlay and expected future benefits. Whether the outlay be cash or stock, the firm should attempt to allocate capital optimally in order to increase shareholder wealth over the long run. The only difference is that, with acquisitions, the initial cost may not be established; indeed, it usually is subject to bargaining. If it can be assumed that the acquiring company intends to maintain its existing capital structure over the long run, it is appropriate to evaluate the prospective acquisition without reference to the way it is financed.

In evaluating the prospective acquisition, the buying company should estimate the future cash income after taxes that the acquisition is expected to add, net of any new investment.[16] The estimates should include consideration of any synergistic effects, for we are interested in the marginal impact of the acquisition. Moreover, the cash-flow estimates should be before any financial charges. The idea is to divorce the prospective acquisition's financial structure from its overall worth as an investment. Our concern is with operating cash flows that arise from operating the acquired company and not with prospective net

[16] See Samuel Schwartz, "Merger Analysis as a Capital Budgeting Problem," in Alberts and Segall, eds., *Corporate Merger*, pp. 139-50, on which this section draws.

income after financial charges. On the basis of these considerations, suppose the following incremental cash flows are expected from a prospective acquisition:

	Average for Years (in thousands)				
	1–5	6–10	11–15	16–20	21–25
Annual cash income after taxes from acquisition	$2,000	$1,800	$1,400	$800	$200
New investment	600	300	—	—	—
Cash flow after taxes	$1,400	$1,500	$1,400	$800	$200

If the acquisition is not expected to increase or decrease the business-risk complexion of the firm as perceived by suppliers of capital, the appropriate discount rate would be the cost of capital. Assuming this rate to be 10 percent after taxes, the present value of the expected net cash flows shown above will be $11,723,000. If the prospective acquisition has no debt, this figure suggests that the company can pay a maximum price of $11,723,000 for the acquisition and still be acting in the best interests of the company's stockholders. The actual price paid will be subject to negotiation. However, the present value of the prospective acquisition should represent an upper boundary for the acquiring company. Any price up to this amount should result in a worthwhile investment for the company. As a result, the market price per share of the firm's stock should increase over the long run. If the price paid is in excess of the acquisition's present value, this suggests that capital is less than optimally allocated.

Estimating cash flows

In an acquisition, there are the usual problems with respect to estimating future cash flows. However, the process may be somewhat easier than for a capital-budgeting proposal because the company being acquired is a going concern. The acquiring company buys more than assets; it buys experience, an organization, and proven performance. The estimates of sales and costs are based upon past results; consequently, they are likely to be more accurate than the estimates for a new investment proposal. Less uncertainty involved in the estimates means less dispersion of expected outcomes and lower risk, all other things held constant.[17] An additional problem, however, is introduced when the acquisition is to be integrated into the acquiring company. Under these circumstances, the acquisition cannot be evalu-

---

[17] Seymour Friedland, *The Economics of Corporate Finance* (Englewood Cliffs, N.J.: Prentice-Hall, 1966), p. 235.

ated as a separate operation; the synergistic effects must be considered. Estimates of these effects are difficult, particularly if the organization that results from the acquisition is complex.

563
Chapter 25
Mergers and
Acquisitions

ated as a separate operation; the synergistic effects must be considered. Estimates of these effects are difficult, particularly if the organization that results from the acquisition is complex.

PROCEDURAL ASPECTS INVOLVED IN MERGERS

A merger or consolidation often begins with negotiations between the managements of the two companies. Usually, the boards of directors of the companies are kept up to date on the negotiations. When initial agreement is reached as to terms, the respective boards must ratify these terms. Upon ratification, the agreement is submitted to the common stockholders of both companies for approval. Depending upon the corporate charter, an established majority—usually two-thirds—of the total shares is required. After approval by the common stockholders, the merger or consolidation can take place once the necessary papers are filed with the states in which the companies are incorporated.

One hurdle remains, however—that neither the Antitrust Division of the Department of Justice nor the Federal Trade Commission brings suit to block the combination. In order to actually block a merger or consolidation, the government, under Section 7 of the Clayton Act, must prove that a "substantial lessening of competition" might occur on account of it. Because the costs in executive time, legal expenses, and other expenses of waging an antitrust battle are so great, most companies want to be reasonably sure that they will not be challenged before going ahead with a combination.

Accounting treatment

From an accounting standpoint, a combination of two companies is treated either as a *purchase* or as a *pooling of interests.* With a purchase, the acquired company is treated as an investment by the buyer. The excess of the price paid above the company's net worth must be reflected as goodwill. Moreover, this goodwill usually is written off against future income, the logic being that it will be reflected in such income. Like any asset, an estimate must be made of its life; and goodwill is amortized over this period.[18] Thus, earnings are reduced by the amount of the charge. It is important to recognize that goodwill charges are not deductible for tax purposes. Therefore, the reduction of reported future earnings associated with this accounting treatment is viewed as a disadvantage by the acquiring firm.

In a pooling of interests, the balance sheets of the two companies are combined, with assets and liabilities simply being added together. As

---

[18]The maximum period over which goodwill can be written off is forty years.

a result, goodwill is not reflected in the combination, and there is no charge against future income. Because reported earnings will be higher with the pooling-of-interests accounting treatment than they will be with the purchase treatment, most acquiring companies prefer it when the goodwill being acquired is substantial.

In August 1970, however, the Accounting Principles Board of the American Institute of Certified Public Accountants significantly restricted the conditions under which a pooling of interests could occur. The conditions that now must be met include: [19]

1. Each of the combined companies must be autonomous for at least two years prior to the pooling and independent of the others in the sense that no more than 10 percent of the stock is owned.

2. The combination must be consummated in a single transaction *or* in accordance with a specific plan within one year after the plan is initiated. In this regard, no contingent payments are permitted.

3. The acquiring corporation can issue only common stock, with rights identical to those of the majority of outstanding voting stock, in exchange for *substantially* all of the voting common stock of another company. Here, "substantially" means 90 percent or more.

4. The surviving corporation must not later retire or reacquire common stock issued in connection with the combination, must not enter into an arrangement for the benefit of former stockholders, and must not dispose of a significant portion of the assets of the combining companies for at least two years.

The most important condition is number 3, which states that common must be exchanged for common. Before, debt and other instruments could be used. The next most important condition is the prohibition of contingent payments. The result of these conditions is a significant reduction in the number of poolings of interest. Though there are certain inequities in the rules, [20] their overall effect is to reduce distortions in reported earnings per share caused by the pooling-of-interests accounting method.

Purchase of assets or purchase of stock

The acquisition of another company can take place either by the purchase of assets or by the purchase of the common stock of the company being acquired. Under the former arrangement, the buying company may purchase all or a portion of the assets of another company and pay for this purchase either with cash or with its own stock. Frequently, the buyer acquires only the assets of the other company

[19] *Opinions of the Accounting Principles Board,* No. 16 (New York: American Institute of Certified Public Accountants, August 1970).

[20] See Arthur R. Wyatt, "Inequities in Accounting for Business Combinations," *Financial Executive,* 40 (December 1972), 28–35.

and does not assume its liabilities. If all the assets are purchased, the selling company is but a corporate shell. After the sale, its assets are composed entirely of cash or the stock of the buying company. The selling company can either hold the cash or stock or it can distribute the cash or stock to its stockholders as a liquidating dividend, after which the company is dissolved.

Thus, when its assets are purchased, the selling company can continue to exist if it holds the cash or stock arising from the sale. If it has cash, it may invest in other assets, such as a division of another company. Obviously, if only a portion of its assets are sold, the selling company will continue as a corporate entity. If paid in cash, the transaction is taxable to the selling company or its stockholders; that is, they must recognize the capital gain or loss on the sale of the assets at the time of the sale.[21] If payment is made in preferred or common stock, however, the transaction is not taxable at the time of sale. The capital gain or loss is recognized only when the stock is sold. A purchase of assets is easier to effect than a purchase of stock, for all that is needed on the part of the buying company is approval by the board of directors. The selling company, however, needs the approval of its stockholders.

When an acquiring company purchases the stock of another company, the latter is merged into the acquiring company. The company that is acquired ceases to exist, and the surviving company assumes all its assets and liabilities. As with a purchase of assets, the means of payment to the stockholders of the company being acquired can be either cash or stock. If cash, the transaction is taxable to the stockholders of the acquired company at the time of the acquisition. If stock, the transaction is not taxable to the stockholders until the stock is sold.

Dissenting stockholders

Although a combination generally depends only upon the approval of a required majority of the total number of shares outstanding, minority stockholders can contest the price paid for their stock. If a dissenting stockholder and the company fail to agree as to a just settlement on a voluntary basis, the stockholder can take his case to court and demand an appraisal of his shares and a settlement in cash. After a "fair market price" has been established by the court, the dissenting stockholder receives payment in cash for his shares. If the number of dissenting stockholders is large, they can cause considerable trouble. If the transaction is in stock, the demands for cash payments on the part of these stockholders may put a severe financial strain on the

---

[21] Likewise, payment with a debt instrument of the acquiring company is also taxable at the time of sale.

combination. Thus, most combinations depend not only upon obtaining approval of a required majority of stockholders but also upon minimizing the number of dissenting stockholders by making the offer attractive to all. Dissenting stockholders may be able to block the combination if they suspect that fraud is involved, even though the required majority of stockholders has approved it.

SUMMARY

A company may grow internally, or it may grow externally through acquisitions. The objective of the firm in either case is to maximize existing shareholder wealth. Both types of expansion can be regarded as capital-budgeting decisions. The criteria for acceptance are essentially the same: capital should be allocated so as to increase shareholder wealth. When two companies combine and one loses its corporate existence, the combination is known as a merger. If two companies combine and form a new corporation, the combination is known as a consolidation. Rather than acquiring another company in its entirety, a company can acquire working control and act as a holding company.

There are a number of reasons for merging, all of which relate to expected return and risk. Among the more important are operating economies, acquisition of management, growth potential, financing, taxation, diversification, and personal reasons. The relative valuation of two companies may be based upon earnings, market values, book values, or a combination of the three. Because the market price reflects the judgment of investors as to everything that affects value, it is the foundation upon which most exchange ratios are based.

Once sufficient financial information is developed, management of the acquiring company usually negotiates directly with management of the prospective acquisition. The acquiring company can, however, make its appeal directly to the stockholders of the prospective acquisition through a tender offer to purchase their shares. Another company can be acquired through the purchase of either its assets or its stock. In turn, the means of payment can be cash, or it can be stock. From the standpoint of accounting, the combination of two companies can be treated either as a purchase or as a pooling of interests. The latter treatment may give rise to more favorably reported earnings per share, but the pooling method has been restricted in recent years.

QUESTIONS

1. Explain the concept of *synergism*.
2. Illustrate and explain how the ratio of P/E multiples for two stocks affects the growth rate of reported earnings.

3. Why is the book value of a firm important in determining the exchange ratio of stock in a merger?

4. Some argue that the method of payment in a merger (stock-for-stock transaction at one end of the spectrum and cash-for-stock at the other, with various combinations of bonds, convertibles, etc., for stock in between the two extremes) is the most important factor in determining the price of the acquired firm. Explain this position.

5. Explain why the accounting treatment (purchase versus pooling) of the acquisition of a going concern should be different from the treatment given the acquisition of any other asset.

6. Explain the concept of instantaneous merger profit. What assumptions are made about economies of scale in explaining the concept?

7. It has been noted that the number of mergers tends to vary directly with the level of relative business activity. Why would this be?

8. Can a merger with a large, stable company serve as an effective way to raise capital for a growth-oriented smaller company?

9. Company X and Company Y both have considerable variability in their earnings, but they are in unrelated industries. Could a merger of the two companies reduce the risk for stockholders of both companies? Could investors lower the risk on their own?

PROBLEMS

1. The following data are pertinent for Companies A and B:

	Company A	Company B
Present earnings (in millions)	$20	$ 4
Shares (in millions)	10	1
Price/earnings ratio	18	10

(a) If the two companies were to merge and the exchange ratio were one share of Company A for each share of Company B, what would be the initial impact on earnings per share of the two companies? What is the market value exchange ratio? Is a merger likely to take place?
(b) If the exchange ratio were two shares of Company A for each share of Company B, what happens with respect to the above?
(c) If the exchange ratio were 1.5 shares of Company A for each share of Company B, what happens?
(d) What exchange ratio would you suggest?

2.

	Expected Earnings	Number of Shares	Market Price per Share	Tax Rate
Hargrave Company	$5,000,000	1,000,000	$100	50%
Hooper Company	3,000,000	500,000	60	50%

The Hargrave Company wishes to acquire the Hooper Company. If the merger were effected through an exchange of stock, Hargrave would be willing to pay a 25 percent premium for the Hooper shares. If done for cash, the terms would have to be as favorable to the Hooper shareholders; to obtain the cash, Hargrave would have to sell its own stock in the market.

(a) Compute the exchange ratio and the combined expected earnings per share if an exchange of stock were accomplished.

(b) Compute the growth of earnings per share as a result of the merger.

(c) If we assume that all Hooper shareholders have held their stock for more than six months, have a 40 percent marginal tax rate, and paid an average of $14 for their shares, what cash price would have to be offered to be as attractive as the terms in (a) above?

(d) Why might the computation in (c) overstate the premium that would have to be paid to make the cash price comparable to the exchange of stock offer? Upon what factor would the size of premium depend?

(e) If the cash [see (c) above] were obtained by means of a stock issue at the current stock prices (with total expenses of 10 percent), what would the earnings per share of the new Hargrave be?

3. Suppose that the current balance sheets of Hargrave and Hooper (see Problem 2) are as follows:

	Hargrave	Hooper
Cash	$ 10,000,000	$12,000,000
Accounts receivable	17,000,000	14,000,000
Inventories	20,000,000	15,000,000
Prepaid expenses	3,000,000	4,000,000
Total current assets	$ 50,000,000	$45,000,000
Fixed assets, net	100,000,000	30,000,000
Total assets	$150,000,000	$75,000,000
Notes payable	$ 15,000,000	$ —
Accounts payable	25,000,000	16,000,000
Accrued wages and taxes	10,000,000	10,000,000
Total current liabilities	$ 50,000,000	$26,000,000
Long-term debt	50,000,000	24,000,000
Common stock	10,000,000	7,500,000
Capital surplus	20,000,000	7,500,000
Retained earnings	20,000,000	10,000,000
Total liabilities and net worth	$150,000,000	$75,000,000

(a) Derive the balance sheet of new Hargrave if the exchange of stock [see 2(a)] were effected. Compute the old and new book value per share.

(b) Recompute (a), assuming instead that the Hooper holders are paid in cash, as outlined in 2(c) and (e). Assume that the Hooper assets cannot be written up. Also compute an old and new net tangible assets per share.

4. Assume the exchange of Hargrave shares for Hooper shares as outlined in Problems 2 and 3 above.
   (a) What is the ratio of exchange?
   (b) Compare the earnings per Hooper share before and after the merger. Compare the earnings per Hargrave share. On this basis alone, which group fared better? Why?
   (c) What would you expect to happen to the share price of Hargrave after the merger? What would you expect to happen to the P/E ratio? Must they both move together?
   (d) Why do you imagine that old Hargrave commanded a higher P/E than Hooper? What should be the change in P/E ratio resulting from the merger? Does this conflict with your answer to (c)? Why?
   (e) If the Hargrave Company is in a high-technology growth industry and Hooper makes cement, would you revise your answers?
   (f) In determining the appropriate P/E ratio for Hargrave, should the increase in earnings resulting from this merger be added as a growth factor?

5. Three years and twenty mergers later, Hargrave (see Problems 2–4), under pressure to report earnings growth, is looking at a proposed merger.

	Expected Earnings	Number of Shares	Market Price
Hargrave	$35,000,000	3,500,000	$200
Fontenot	3,000,000	500,000	90

Assume the merger is consumated under the same terms as Problem 2.
   (a) Compute the exchange ratio and the combined expected earnings per share if an exchange of stock were accomplished.
   (b) Compute the growth rate of earnings per share as a result of the merger and compare this growth with 2(b).
   (c) Explain the difference in 2(b) and 5(b).
   (d) What do you think will happen to the P/E ratio?

6. Collect data on situations where one company made a tender offer for the shares of another, and management hurriedly conducted negotations with a third company. Compare the terms of the two offers, especially with regard to the price of the offer. Did the offer endorsed by management always bear the highest price? Should this not be the case under the theory? Examine the other terms of the offers, including employment contracts, options, bonuses, and retirement provisions. Correlate management's endorsement with
   (a) Those offers having the highest price, and then
   (b) Those having the most favorable employment terms.
   Which correlation is higher? Why? Finally, determine which offer was accepted by the stockholders. Correlate this with
   (a) Those having the highest price, and
   (b) Those endorsed by management.

7. The Resin Corporation, which has an 8 percent after-tax cost of capital, is considering the acquisition of the Smythe Company. If the merger were effected, the incremental cash flows would be as follows:

AVERAGE FOR YEARS (IN MILLIONS)

	1–5	6–10	11–15	16–20
Annual net income attributable to Smythe	$10	$15	$20	$15
Required new investment	2	5	10	10
Net after-tax cash flow	$ 8	$10	$10	$ 5

What is the maximum price that Resin should pay for Smythe?

8. Let it be assumed that a holding company can always be set up with 50 percent debt at 8 percent and 20 percent preferred stock at 6 percent. Further assume that all companies pay a tax rate of 50 percent, that the 85 percent intercorporate dividend exclusion applies in all cases, and that ownership of 40 percent of the stock of another company constitutes control. The shares of the Target Company can be obtained at their book value.

TARGET COMPANY

Total assets	$30,000,000	Debt (8%)	$15,000,000
		Preferred (6%)	5,000,000
		Common	10,000,000
			$30,000,000

(a) A group of investors has set up Holding Company A to acquire control of the Target Company. If the group holds all the equity of Holding Company A, how much money must they put up? If Target has operating earnings equal to 20 percent of total assets and pays all earnings in dividends, what return on investment will the group earn?

(b) Suppose the group sets up Holding Company B to acquire control of Holding Company A. If the group holds all the equity of B, how much money must they put up? If A pays all earnings in dividends, what return on investment will the group earn? How many dollars of operating assets does the group control per dollar of their own investment?

(c) How would your answers change if Target had operating earnings equal to 8 percent of total assets?

SELECTED REFERENCES

ALBERTS, WILLIAM W., and JOEL E. SEGALL, eds., *The Corporate Merger.* Chicago: University of Chicago Press, 1966.

APPLEYARD, A. R. and G. K. YARROW, "The Relationship Between Take-over Activity and Share Valuation," *Journal of Finance,* 30 (December 1975), 1239–50.

CROWTHER, JOHN F., "Peril Point Acquisition Prices," *Harvard Business Review,* 47 (September–October 1969), 58–62.

CUNITZ, JONATHAN A., "Valuing Potential Acquisitions," *Financial Executive,* 39 (April 1971), 16–28.

HAUGEN, ROBERT A., and TERENCE C. LANGETIEG, "An Empirical Test for Synergism in Merger," *Journal of Finance*, 30 (September 1975), 1003–14.

HAYES, SAMUEL L., III, and RUSSELL A. TAUSSIG, "Tactics in Cash Takeover Bids," *Harvard Business Review*, 45 (March–April 1967), 135–48.

HEATH, JOHN, JR., "Valuation Factors and Techniques in Mergers and Acquisitions," *Financial Executive*, 40 (April 1972), 34–44.

HEXTER, RICHARD M., "How to Sell Your Company," *Harvard Business Review*, 46 (May–June 1968), 71–77.

HIGGINS, ROBERT C., and LAWRENCE D. SCHALL, "Corporate Bankruptcy and Conglomerate Merger," *Journal of Finance*, 30 (March 1975), 93–114.

HOGARTY, THOMAS F., "The Profitability of Corporate Mergers," *Journal of Business*, 43 (July 1970), 317–27.

HOWELL, ROBERT A., "Plan to Integrate Your Acquisitions," *Harvard Business Review*, 48 (November–December 1970), 66–76.

LARSON, KERMIT D., and NICHOLAS J. GONEDES, "Business Combinations: An Exchange-Ratio Determination Model," *Accounting Review*, 44 (October 1969), 720–28.

LEV, BARUCH, and GERSHON MANDELKER, "The Microeconomic Consequences of Corporate Mergers," *Journal of Business*, 45 (January 1972), 85–104.

LEWELLEN, WILBUR G., "A Pure Financial Rationale for the Conglomerate Merger," *Journal of Finance*, 26 (May 1971), 521–37.

LORIE, J. H., and P. HALPERN, "Conglomerates: The Rhetoric and the Evidence," *Journal of Law and Economics*, 13 (April 1970), 149–66.

MACDOUGAL, GARY E., and FRED V. MALEK, "Master Plan for Merger Negotiations," *Harvard Business Review*, 48 (January–February 1970), 71–82.

MEAD, WALTER J., "Instantaneous Merger Profit as a Conglomerate Merger Motive," *Western Economic Review*, 7 (December 1969), 295–306.

MELICHER, RONALD W., and THOMAS R. HARTER, "Stock Price Movements of Firms Engaging in Large Acquisitions," *Journal of Financial and Quantitative Analysis*, 7 (March 1972), 1469–75.

MELICHER, RONALD W., and DAVID F. RUSH, "Evidence on the Acquisition-Related Performance of Conglomerate Firms," *Journal of Finance*, 29 (March 1974), 141–50.

NIELSEN, JAMES F., and RONALD W. MELICHER, "A Financial Analysis of Acquisition and Merger Premiums," *Journal of Financial and Quantitative Analysis*, 8 (March 1973), 139–48.

REILLY, FRANK K., "What Determines the Ratio of Exchange in Corporate Mergers?" *Financial Analysts Journal*, 18 (November–December 1972), 47–50.

REUM, W. ROBERT, and THOMAS A. STEEL III, "Contingent Payouts Cut Acquisition Risks," *Harvard Business Review*, 48 (March–April 1970), 83–91.

ROCKWELL, WILLARD F., JR., "How to Acquire a Company." *Harvard Business Review*, 46 (May–June 1968), 121–32.

SHAD, JOHN S. R., "The Financial Realities of Mergers," *Harvard Business Review*, 47 (November–December 1969), 133–46.

SHICK, RICHARD A., "The Analysis of Mergers and Acquisitions," *Journal of Finance*, 27 (May 1972), 495–502.

SHICK, RICHARD A., and FRANK C. JEN, "Merger Benefits to Shareholders of Acquiring Firms," *Financial Management*, 3 (Winter 1974), 45–53.

SMALTER, DONALD J., and RODERIC C. LANCEY, "P/E Analysis in Acquisition Strategy," *Harvard Business Review*, 44 (November–December 1966), 85–95.

STEVENS, DONALD L., "Financial Characteristics of Merged Firms: A Multivariate Analysis," *Journal of Financial and Quantitative Analysis*, 8 (March 1973), 149–58.

WESTON, J. FRED, and SURENDRA K. MANSINGHKA, "Tests of the Efficiency of Conglomerate Firms," *Journal of Finance*, 26 (September 1971), 919–36.

WESTON, J. FRED, and SAM PELTZMAN, eds., *Public Policy toward Mergers*. Pacific Palisades, Calif.: Goodyear, 1969.

26 Growth through Multinational Operations

In recent years, international trade has grown in importance to where it now constitutes a major portion of the total activity of many business firms. In the wake of this surge has come the development of the multinational enterprise. By definition, a *multinational business* is one with investment and sales in two or more countries. For some companies, foreign sales represent only a small portion of total revenues and we would not regard these companies as multinational in any real sense. However, companies like IBM, Gillette, Pfizer, and American Smelting and Refining derive over half their profits from international operations and are truly multinational in scope. Although the United States depends less upon foreign trade than most nations, this trade has shown significant growth in recent years, as evidenced in Figure 26-1.

How does financial management in a multinational enterprise differ from that in a domestic business firm? In principle, the concepts of efficient allocation of funds among assets and the raising of funds on as favorable terms as possible are the same for both types of companies. However, the environment in which these decisions are made is different. The purpose of this chapter is to consider the institutional factors that make investing and financing for a multinational company somewhat different from that for a domestic company. In this regard, we examine such things as the tax environment, political risks, foreign exchange risk, investment constraints imposed by the government, financing instruments, and certain specialized documents used in

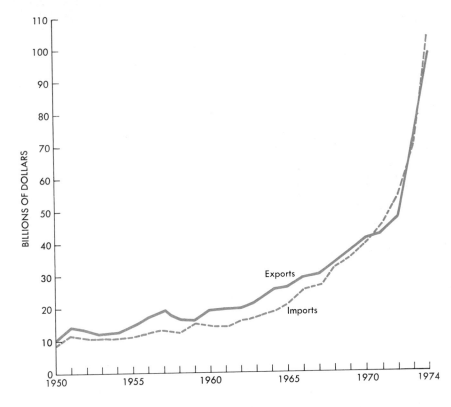

FIG. 26 · 1

U.S. imports and exports

foreign trade. Our purpose is not an in-depth understanding but rather an exposure to those factors that influence the basic decisions of the firm in an international setting.

FOREIGN INVESTMENT

The decision to invest capital in a project abroad should be based upon considerations of expected return and risk the same as any investment proposal. Quantifying these parameters is more complex, however, owing to disparities in currency exchange rates, differences in taxes, differences in accounting practices, and differences in factors affecting risk. However, once expected return and risk are quantified, the evaluation of the project itself is the same whether it be domestic or foreign in origin. Consequently, we shall concentrate on examining the various factors that make foreign investment unique rather than the evaluation process itself. That process was taken up earlier in the book and has not changed.

Reasons for foreign investment

Risk considerations. By diversifying a portfolio of assets internationally, a company often is able to reduce its risk in relation to expected return more effectively than it can through domestic diversification. Recall from our discussion of portfolio risk in Chapter 14 that the key element was the correlation among projects in the asset portfolio. By combining projects with low degrees of correlation with each other, a firm is able to reduce risk in relation to expected return. However, domestic investment projects tend to be correlated with each other because most are highly dependent on the state of the economy. One advantage of foreign investments is that the economic cycles of different countries do not tend to be completely synchronized. As a result, it is possible to reduce risk relative to expected return by investing across countries.

To illustrate, suppose a company were in the machine tool business. If it invested in another plant domestically, the return is likely to be highly correlated with the return from existing assets. Consequently, there would be little reduction in relative risk. However, if it invested in a plant to market machine tools in a country whose economy was not highly correlated with the domestic economy, the project's return is not likely to be highly correlated with the return from existing assets. Consequently, it may be possible to reduce risk relative to expected return by investing in the same industry internationally where such investment domestically would not result in a relative risk reduction. The idea is simply that returns on investment projects tend to be less correlated among countries than they are in any one particular country.

Whether foreign diversification by a company benefits its stockholders depends on whether or not capital markets between countries are segmented. If they are not, there is little reason to believe that foreign diversification by a company will increase its value. However, if currency restrictions, investment barriers, legal restrictions, lack of information, and other capital market imperfections of this sort exist, capital markets between countries may be segmented. Under these circumstances, foreign diversification may enhance shareholder wealth. In general, studies of common-stock investments across countries have supported the diversification potential of international investments, though there is disagreement on the degree of capital market segmentation.[1]

[1]See Haim Levy and Marshall Sarnat, "International Diversification of Investment Portfolios," *American Economic Review,* 60 (September 1970), 668–75; Donald Lessard, "International Portfolio Diversification: A Multivariate Analysis for a Group of Latin American Countries," *Journal of Finance,* 28 (June 1973), 619–34; H. G. Grubel, "Internationally Diversified Portfolios," *American Economic Review,* 63 (December 1968), 1299–1314; Bruno H. Solnik, *European Capital Markets* (Boston: Lexington Books, 1973); Tamir Agmon, "The Relations among Equity Markets: A Study of Share Price Co-Movements in the United States, United Kingdom, Germany, and Japan," *Journal*

The concept of diversification is applicable also to the acquisition of foreign companies. To the extent again that market imperfections exist which result in segmentation among international capital markets, the diversification properties associated with a foreign acquisition may be of value. Recall from Chapters 16 and 25, which dealt with domestic acquisitions, that acquisitions were a thing of value only if the acquiring company could do something for its investors that they could not do for themselves. In the case of a company with a publicly traded stock, there was little reason to believe that stockholders could not achieve the same diversification on their own by investing directly in the company involved. In the case of foreign acquisitions, however, the acquiring company may be able to do something for investors that they cannot do for themselves if international capital markets in fact are segmented. As a result, the risk-reduction properties associated with the foreign acquisition may be a thing of value.[2]

Return considerations. The other reason for investing abroad is the expectation of a higher return for a given level of risk. Given a firm's particular expertise, there may be gaps in markets abroad where excess returns can be earned. Domestically, competitive pressures may be such that only a normal rate of return can be earned. Although expansion into foreign markets is the reason for most investment abroad, there are other reasons. Some firms invest in order to produce more efficiently. Where labor and/or other costs are less in another country, a company may seek foreign production facilities simply to produce a product at a lower cost. In the electronics industry, for example, there has been a movement toward foreign production facilities for this reason. Finally, some companies invest abroad to secure necessary raw materials. Oil companies and mining companies in particular invest abroad for this reason. All of these pursuits—markets, production facilities, and raw materials—are in keeping with an objective of securing a higher rate of return than is possible through domestic operations alone.

As brought out earlier, however, there are a number of factors that make investment abroad different from investment domestically. These include tax differences, political and foreign exchange risk, and government constraints on foreign investment. We consider each in turn. First, however, we should point out that there is more risk to a foreign investment than simply the political and foreign exchange

---

of Finance, 28 (September 1972), 839–55; Gerald A. Pogue and Bruno H. Solnik, "The Market Model Applied to European Common Stocks: Some Empirical Results," *Journal of Financial and Quantitative Analysis,* 9 (December 1974), 917–44; and Tamir Agmon and Donald Lessard, "International Diversification and the Multinational Corporation: An Investigation of Price Behavior of the Shares of U.S. Based Multinational Corporations on the NYSE," Working Paper (Sloan School, Massachusetts Institute of Technology, 1975).

[2] For further analysis of this issue, see Michael Adler and Bernard Dumas, "Optimal International Acquisitions," *Journal of Finance,* 30 (March 1975), 1–20.

risks. In many cases the most important risk is business risk. However, we discussed methods for analyzing this risk in Chapters 14 and 16, so it is unnecessary to repeat the discussion here.

Taxation

Owing to different tax laws and different treatments of foreign investment, the taxation of a multinational firm is extremely complex. Our purpose is to discuss some of the more important aspects of the problem. We begin by looking at the way the United States government taxes a company with foreign operations and then move on to consider taxation by foreign countries.

Taxation by U.S. government. If a U.S. corporation carries on business abroad through a branch or a division, the income from that operation is reported on the company's U.S. tax form and taxed in the same way as domestic income. If business is carried on through a foreign subsidiary, however, the income normally is not taxed in the U.S. until it is distributed to the parent in the form of dividends. The advantage here, of course, is that the tax is deferred until the parent receives a cash return. In the meantime, earnings are reinvested in the subsidiary to finance expansion. Unlike dividends from a domestic corporation (85 percent exempt), dividends received by a U.S. corporation from a foreign subsidiary are fully taxable.

In certain cases, income of a foreign subsidiary is subject to U.S. taxation prior to its actual remission in the form of dividends. In order to prevent tax havens, where U.S. taxes are deferred through transfer price and other arrangements between a U.S. company and its foreign subsidiary, Subpart F of the Revenue Act of 1962 was instigated. Under this provision, a U.S. stockholder owning more than 10 percent of a foreign company is taxed on certain types of income from that company. The provision is complicated, and presentation of the types of income subject to taxation is beyond the scope of this book. Its purpose is simply to prevent the excessive accumulation of earnings in tax havens and the resulting deferral of U.S. taxes.[3]

In order to encourage exports, the U.S. government provides favorable tax treatment for certain types of operation. One type is a Western Hemisphere Trade Corporation, which is a domestic company whose business is entirely in the Western Hemisphere and which receives at least 95 percent of its gross income from sources outside the U.S. The maximum marginal tax rate for such a company is 34 percent instead of the regular corporate rate of 48 percent.

---

[3]Also in the Revenue Act of 1962 is a provision dealing with the liquidation of a foreign subsidiary. The capital gain is largely treated as dividend income and not subject to the more favorable capital-gains tax.

A Domestic International Sales Corporation (DISC) also receives a tax incentive to encourage exports. A company must have exports of at least 95 percent of its gross receipts as well as satisfy certain other provisions in order to qualify as a DISC. The tax advantage of a DISC comes in its being able to defer taxes on one-half its income until such income is distributed to stockholders. The other half of the DISC's income is treated as if it were paid to stockholders as a dividend and is subject to ordinary income taxes. Thus, the DISC itself pays no income tax, but stockholders do on one-half the income. In recent years, DISC companies have come under fire in Congress. Pressures have grown to end the ability of such companies to defer income taxes. If DISC tax benefits are repealed, it will have a significant effect on such large exporters as machinery companies, grain companies, aircraft companies, and automobile companies, which have made extensive use of the DISC.

Taxation by foreign governments. Every country taxes income of foreign companies doing business in that country. The type of tax imposed varies. However, most of the larger industrial countries impose taxes on corporate income that correspond roughly to the corporate rate in the U.S. Some of these countries differentiate distributed income to stockholders from undistributed income, with a lower tax on distributed income. Less-developed countries frequently have lower taxes and provide certain other tax incentives in order to encourage foreign investment. One method of taxation that has become very important in Europe is the value-added tax. In essence, the value-added tax is a sales tax wherein each stage of production is taxed on the value added. Suppose an aluminum fabricator buys aluminum sheets for $1,000 and cuts, shapes, and otherwise works them into doors which are sold for $1,800. The value added is $800, and the fabricator would be taxed on this amount. If the fabricator sold its doors to a wholesaler who, in turn, sold them to retailers for $2,000, the value added would be $200 and taxed accordingly. In the future, the value-added tax is likely to become increasingly important.

In order to avoid double taxation, the U.S. gives a federal income tax credit for foreign taxes paid by a U.S. corporation. If a foreign country has a tax rate of less than 48 percent, the U.S. corporation would pay combined taxes at the 48 percent rate. Part of the taxes paid would be to the foreign government and the other part to the U.S. To illustrate, suppose a foreign branch of a U.S. corporation had earnings of $100,000 and the foreign income tax rate was 35 percent. The company would pay $35,000 in foreign income taxes. Suppose further that the $100,000 earnings were subject to the 48 percent rate domestically, or $48,000 in taxes. In this case, the company receives a tax credit of $35,000; thus, it pays only $13,000 in U.S. taxes on the earnings of its foreign branch. If the foreign tax rate were 55 percent, however, the company would pay $55,000 in foreign taxes and nothing in U.S. taxes. Here, total taxes paid would obviously be higher. The same tax credit arrangement applies to dividends received from a foreign subsidiary.

Political risk

The political risks facing a multinational company range from mild interference to complete confiscation of all assets. Interference includes such things as laws that specify a minimum percentage of nationals that must be employed in various positions, required investment in environmental and social projects, and restrictions on the convertibility of currencies. The ultimate political risk is expropriation and it occurred, for example, in Chile in 1971 when the country took over the copper companies. There are a number of degrees of risk between mild interference and outright expropriation. Such discriminatory practices as higher taxes, higher utility charges, and the requirement to pay higher wages than a national company are examples. In essence, they place the foreign operation of the U.S. company at a competitive disadvantage.

Because political risk has an important influence upon the overall risk of an investment project, it must be assessed realistically. Essentially, the job is one of forecasting political instability. How stable is the government involved? What are the prevailing political winds? What is likely to be a new government's view as to foreign investment? How efficient is the government in processing requests? How much inflation and economic stability is there? How strong and equitable are the courts? Answers to these questions should give considerable insight into the political risk involved in an investment. Some companies have categorized countries according to their political risk. If a country is classified in the undesirable category, probably no investment will be permitted no matter how high its expected return.

Once a company decides to invest, it should take steps to protect itself. By cooperating with the host country in hiring nationals, making the "right" types of investment, and in other ways being desirable, political risk can be reduced.[4] A joint venture with a company in the host country can improve the public image of the operation. Though effort should be made to protect an investment once it is made, when sharp political changes occur often there is nothing that can be done. The time to look hardest at political risk is before the investment is made.

---

[4]For a discussion of the appropriate organizational approach to this problem, see Louis T. Wells, Jr., "The Multinational Business Enterprise: What Kind of International Organization?" *International Organization*, 25 (September 1971), 447–64.

In the case of investments in certain less-developed countries, it is possible to insure projects through the Overseas Private Investment Corporation (OPIC). The OPIC is government owned and insures against inconvertibility into dollars as well as against loss due to expropriation. It also insures against normal buiness losses. Where uncertainty is great, this insurance makes a good deal of sense to the investing company.

Foreign exchange risk

Foreign exchange risk is the risk that the currency of a country in which a U.S. firm does business is devalued relative to the dollar, that the market price of the currency declines relative to the dollar in the absence of an official devaluation, and/or that its convertibility is restricted. (If the dollar declines in value relative to the currency in question, this works to the advantage of the company.) When a currency is devalued relative to the dollar, the U.S. company suffers a loss on the currency and on the assets payable in currency it holds. For example, suppose the British pound is worth $1.80. If XYZ Multinational Company held currency and receivables amounting to 500,000 pounds and the pound were devalued by 10 percent, XYZ would suffer a loss in dollar terms of $90,000. Thus a significant devaluation or drop in price of a currency can be very costly to the multinational company.

Actually, the exchange-risk exposure of a company is not confined to changes in the value of monetary assets. It encompasses all factors that give rise to the foreign operation's cash flows. When a devaluation occurs, for example, this may affect future sales, costs, and remittances. This effect is in addition to the immediate effect of the devaluation on the operation's monetary position. The former effect often influences total value to a greater extent than does the latter. However, the long-run effects of a devaluation on cash flows and value are difficult to quantify.[5] As the treatment of these effects, though cer-

[5] For a general discussion of some of these issues, see Rita M. Rodriguez, "Management of Foreign Exchange Risk in the U.S. Multinationals," *Journal of Financial and Quantitative Analysis,* 9 (November 1974), 849–57; and Ruediger Naumann-Etienne, "A Framework for Financial Decisions in Multinational Corporations—Summary of Recent Research," *Journal of Financial and Quantitative Analysis,* 9 (November 1974), 859–74. For an analysis of the implications of exchange-risk exposure on the present value of cash flows, see Donald Heckerman, "The Exchange Risk of Foreign Operations," *Journal of Business,* 45 (January 1972), 42–48. For a portfolio approach to the problem where the devaluation exposure of each asset and liability is quantified in terms of probabilities, see Bernard A. Lietaer, *Financial Management of Foreign Exchange: An Operational Technique to Reduce Risk* (Cambridge, Mass.: M.I.T. Press, 1971); and Lietaer, "Managing Risks in Foreign Exchange, *Harvard Business Review,* 48 (March–April 1970), 127–38. In the end, Lietaer provides a means for evaluating various hedging strategies as to their expected cost and risk. Depending on the risk preferences of management, an optimal strategy will be selected in the manner described in Chapter 16 for the portfolio selection of risky investments.

tainly important, is beyond the scope of this book, we will concentrate our examination on the effect of a devaluation on the monetary assets and liabilities of a company. In what follows in this section, we will discuss the various ways a company can protect itself against foreign exchange risk.

Balancing monetary assets and liabilities. If a company believed that a country were going to devalue its currency, it would make sense to reduce monetary assets in that currency to as low a figure as possible and to borrow extensively in that currency. A devaluation works to the advantage of a net debtor and to the disadvantage of a net creditor. In the absence of accurate forecasts of devaluation—which few of us have—a multinational company can hedge its monetary position in order to protect itself against devaluation. By *hedging,* we mean offsetting monetary assets, such as cash, marketable securities, and receivables, with monetary liabilities, such as payables and loans, of the same amount. If a devaluation occurs, monetary assets and liabilities will be equally affected and the company will suffer neither a gain nor a loss. Its net monetary position (assets less liabilities) is zero before and after the devaluation.

Use of forward market. In addition to hedging, a company can protect itself against devaluation by use of the forward exchange market. In this market, one buys a futures contract for the exchange of one currency for another at a specific future date and at a specific exchange ratio. By buying a futures contract, one assures himself of being able to obtain conversion into the currency he desires at a specific exchange ratio.

To illustrate, suppose Balog Manufacturing Company sold machinery to a British customer through its U.K. branch for 100,000 pounds sterling with terms of 90 days. Upon payment, Balog intends to convert the pounds to dollars. Suppose the spot rate and 90-day futures rate on British pounds were the following:

Spot rate	$1.80
Ninety-day future	1.76

The spot rate is simply the current market-determined exchange rate for pounds. If Balog wishes to avoid foreign exchange risk, it should sell 100,000 pounds forward 90 days. When it delivers the 100,000 pounds 90 days hence, it will receive $176,000. If the spot rate stays at $1.80, of course, Balog would have been better off not to have sold pounds forward. (It could sell the 100,000 pounds in the spot market for $180,000.) However, if the pound were devalued or otherwise declined by more than 2 percent during the 90 days, it would profit from the use of the forward market. Thus, the forward exchange market allows a company to insure against devaluation and market-determined declines in value. In the case illustrated above, there is a cost if the spot rate remains at $1.80. The cost is .04 per pound, and on an annual basis it can be expressed as

$$\left(\frac{.04}{1.80}\right)\left(\frac{360}{90}\right) = 8.89 \text{ percent}$$

Put another way, Balog paid $4,000 to insure its ability to convert pounds to dollars. In so doing, it protected itself against declines in value of the pound which might erode the $180,000 sale of machinery.

In summary, the forward exchange market permits a multinational company to protect itself against foreign exchange risk. This risk embodies both devaluation, where a sharp decline in value occurs, and downside fluctuations in the spot rate. For this protection, there is a cost which is determined by the relationship between the forward rate and the future spot rate. Whether or not one wishes to use the forward market depends upon one's view of the future and one's risk-aversion. The greater the possibility of devaluation and the greater the risk-aversion, the greater the case that can be made for use of the forward market. If others feel the same way, however, the cost of this insurance will rise.

Foreign currency swap. Yet another means for hedging against foreign exchange risk is a swap arrangement. This arrangement is simply an agreement between two parties to exchange one currency for another at a specific future date and at a specified exchange ratio. In effect, the swap is a simultaneous spot and forward transaction with the latter reversing the original swap transaction. For example, a U.S. parent company might wish to transfer funds temporarily abroad to a foreign subsidiary with the understanding that they would be returned in 120 days. In order to protect itself against exchange risk, it might enter into a swap arrangement with a private trader or commercial bank. This arrangement assures the company that it will be able to get dollars back 120 days hence. The cost of the arrangement is the difference in exchange ratios at the time of the initial swap and at reversion 120 days later. Because the latter exchange ratio is set in advance, the cost can be determined in the same way as the cost of a forward transaction.

Swap arrangements also are made available by foreign governments and central banks in an effort to encourage international trade and investment. When economic conditions are volatile and the currency markets unsettled because of the possibility of devaluation, the government often is the only party able to effectively underwrite exchange risk. In recent years, central banks have been active in currency swaps as a means for stabilizing their own currencies. For example, the Federal Reserve Bank has engaged in a number of swaps with central banks in Europe to stabilize the dollar. These swaps, of course, do not involve companies but are directly between central banks. As shown, however, the currency swap affords protection to the firm against devaluation and is particularly important in transactions with countries whose currency is soft and where viable forward exchange markets are lacking.

Adjustment of intracompany accounts. Finally, a company with multiple foreign operations can protect itself against foreign exchange risks by adjusting transfer of funds commitments between countries.[6] To illustrate, suppose one believed that the German mark would be revalued upward in the near future while the French franc would hold steady. Suppose further that a company had foreign subsidiaries in both countries and that the French subsidiary purchased approximately $100,000 of goods each month from the German subsidiary. Normal billing calls for payment three months after delivery of the goods. Instead of this arrangement, the French subsidiary might be instructed to pay for the goods on delivery, in view of the likely revaluation upward of the German mark.

Government restrictions

In addition to the influences on foreign investment discussed above, in the past there have been a number of direct constraints imposed by the U.S. government. The purpose of these controls was to reduce the outflow of capital abroad. With the chronic U.S. balance-of-payments problems in the sixties, it was felt that direct controls were needed to lessen the problem. In the middle and late sixties, then, the U.S. government established certain limits on foreign investment by U.S. multinational companies. At first, these restrictions were largely voluntary. As time passed and the balance-of-payments situation deteriorated further, they became involuntary and more severe.

In general, the controls restricted investment to a percentage of that which occurred in a base year. In addition, the restriction was much more lenient for investment in an underdeveloped country than it was for investment in a developed country. With the movement in the early seventies toward freer trade and the breaking down of trade barriers among countries, restrictions on foreign investments were removed altogether in 1974. As a result, this former constraint on the in-

---

[6]Discussion of this method is based on Newton H. Hoyt, Jr., "The Management of Currency Exchange Risk by the Singer Company," *Financial Management,* 1 (Spring 1972), 18–19. The article also shows how a company uses other approaches to protect itself.

vestment of funds abroad is no longer a factor. However, government restrictions may reappear in the future, and if they do, it is important to understand their influence on foreign investment decisions.[7]

The second major facet of financial management is raising funds on as favorable terms as possible. In the case of a multinational company, this involves raising funds to finance a foreign affiliate. These funds can come from either internal or external sources. The former are comprised of equity investment and loans from the U.S. parent, retained earnings, and depreciation and depletion allowances. Recently, internal sources of funds have accounted for somewhat over 70 percent of the total financing of U.S.-owned foreign affiliates. Of the internal sources, approximately three-quarters is comprised of retained earnings and depreciation and depletion allowances.

External Financing

Although the major sources of funds for a foreign affiliate are internal, external sources are important as well. In particular, external financing is important in cases involving less-permanent funds requirements. There are a wide variety of sources of external financing available to the foreign affiliate. These range from commercial bank loans within the host country to loans from international lending agencies. In this section, we consider the more important sources of external financing.

Commercial bank loans and trade bills.   One of the major sources of financing abroad is the commercial bank. These banks perform essentially the same financing function as domestic banks—a topic discussed in Chapters 10 and 11. One subtle difference is that banking practices in Europe allow longer-term loans than are available in the United States. Another is that loans tend to be on an overdraft basis. That is, a company writes a check that overdraws its account and is charged interest on the overdraft. Accompanying the growth in multinational companies has been a corresponding growth in international banking by U.S. banks. The number of branches of U.S. banks abroad has expanded rapidly, and now there is no important

---

[7]For a probabilistic analysis of the combined influence of exchange risk, risk of nationalization, and risk of government restrictions as they affect project cash flows, see Lawrence J. Gitman, "A Multinational Firm Investment Model," *Journal of Economics and Business*, 26 (Fall 1973), 41–48.

city in the free world that does not have a branch or office of a U.S. bank. Under the Edge Act, American banks may act as holding companies and own stock in foreign banks. These banks may be either wholly owned subsidiaries or owned in part by nationals. Thus, U.S. banks are able to provide, directly or indirectly, banking arrangements for foreign affiliates in almost any country. For reasons of contact and familiarization with local practices and customs, however, the affiliate may wish to do business with a local bank as opposed to a U.S. bank.

In addition to commercial bank loans, the discounting of trade bills is a common method of short-term financing. Although this method of financing is not used extensively in the United States, it is used extensively in Europe to finance both domestic and international trade. More will be said about the instruments involved later in the chapter.

Eurodollar and Eurobond financing. A *Eurodollar* is defined as a dollar deposit held in a bank outside the United States. Since the late fifties, an active market has developed for these deposits. Foreign banks and foreign branches of U.S. banks, mostly in Europe, bid actively for Eurodollar deposits, paying interest rates that fluctuate in keeping with supply and demand conditions. These deposits are in large denominations, frequently $100,000 or more. The banks use the Eurodollar deposits they receive to make dollar loans to prime borrowers. These loans are made at a rate in excess of the deposit rate; the differential varies according to the relative risk of the borrower. All loans are unsecured. Essentially, the borrowing and lending of Eurodollars represent a wholesale operation, with far fewer costs than are usually associated with banking. The market itself is free from government restrictions and is truly international in scope.

The Eurodollar market serves as an important source of short-term financing for the working-capital requirements of the multinational company. Many American firms arrange for lines of credit and revolving credits from Eurodollar banks. For the latter arrangement, the firm pays a commitment fee the same as it does for a domestic revolving credit. The interest rate on loans is based upon the Eurodollar deposit rate and bears only an indirect relationship to the prime rate. Typically, the rate on a Eurodollar loan exceeds the prime rate and is much more volatile. Consequently, it is more difficult to project the cost of a Eurodollar loan than that of a domestic loan. Nevertheless, no compensating balances are required, thus enhancing the attractiveness of this kind of financing.

The Eurobond market developed in the late 1960s into an important source of long-term funds for the multinational company. A *Eurobond* is simply a bond issued abroad which is denominated in dollars. In concept, it is the same as a Eurodollar loan except that it is long-term in nature. With the capital restraints on foreign investment imposed in the sixties, U.S. corporations turned to raising funds abroad for their foreign affiliates. A sizable portion of the funds raised was through Eurobonds. Not only did foreign affiliates of U.S. companies borrow in this market but foreign companies did as well. Both straight bond issues and convertible issues were sold. With the removal of capital restrictions in 1974, however, Eurobonds declined in importance as a means of financing foreign operations.

Development banks. Many countries have development banks that make intermediate- and long-term loans. The purpose of these loans is to support economic development within the country. If the investment project or international transaction qualifies, financing through a development bank may be a viable financing alternative. The bank itself can be either a governmental agency or run privately. In order to obtain a better understanding of their operation, we will discuss briefly several of the larger development banks.

The *Export-Import Bank* is an independent agency of the U.S. government. This bank, known as the Exim Bank, was established in 1934; and its purpose is to facilitate the financing of exports from the United States. It accomplishes this purpose in several ways. Its major program is making long-term loans to foreigners which enable them to purchase U.S. goods and services. In this regard, the Exim Bank tries to supplement rather than compete with private capital. It will participate with private lenders in extending credit, and this arrangement has been used with success. The bank also guarantees payment of medium-term financing incurred in the export of U.S. goods and services.

The *Agency for International Development* (AID) was established in 1961 to carry out U.S. foreign assistance programs. One aspect of its program is development loans to friendly governments and private enterprises. The effort here is to stimulate investment in underdeveloped countries. The *Inter-American Development Bank* was formed in 1959 by a number of Latin American countries together with the United States. It is an example of a regional development bank which makes both public and private loans for purposes of enhancing economic development in the member countries. The development banks of individual countries are too numerous to list. To mention only a few of the larger, there is the *Industrial Reorganization Corporation* in Britain, *National Financiera, S.A.,* in Mexico, *Credit National* in France, *Kreditanstalt für Wiederaufbau* in West Germany, and *Instituto Mobiliare Italiano* in Italy. An example of a privately owned development bank is *Adela,* which was formed in 1964. It makes private investments in Latin American firms, usually in participation with other investors.

World Bank group. The World Bank group is comprised of three financial institutions. The *International Bank for Reconstruction and Development* was established in 1944 and is commonly known as the

World Bank. It is owned by over one hundred member countries and its purpose is to make loans to finance economic development. Examples of loans include the financing of irrigation projects, schools, roads, electric power plants, dams, agricultural projects, and basic industries. The major emphasis is upon loans to less-developed countries. Loans are made either to member governments or to private firms where the loan is guaranteed by the government.

The *International Finance Corporation* (IFC) was established in 1956 as an affiliate of the World Bank. It, in association with private investors, makes loans to private enterprises in developing countries. These loans are not guaranteed by the government and, in general, are of higher risk than those made by the World Bank. The participation of the IFC in a financing is always less than 50 percent of the total financing. The IFC also invests in development banks which, in turn, lend to private enterprises. The final member of the World Bank group is the *International Development Association* (IDA). It was created in 1960 to make loans on "soft" terms to countries with limited capacity to service debt. Maturities typically are long, and grace periods are given before the first payment is expected. Projects financed are usually of a social overhead type, such as schools, roads, and housing in very underdeveloped countries.

FINANCING INTERNATIONAL TRADE

Foreign trade differs from domestic trade with respect to the instruments and documents employed. Most domestic sales are an open-account credit where the customer is billed and has so many days to pay. In international trade, the seller is seldom able to obtain as accurate or as thorough credit information on the potential buyer as he is with a domestic sale. Communication is more cumbersome and transportation of the goods slower and less certain. Moreover, the channels for legal settlement in cases of default are complicated and more costly to pursue than is true when a domestic customer defaults. For these reasons, a set of procedures has evolved for international trade which differ from those for domestic trade. There are three key documents: an order to pay, or draft; a bill of lading, which involves the physical movement of the goods; and a letter of credit, which guarantees the credit-worthiness of the buyer. We examine each in turn.

The trade draft

The international draft, sometimes called a bill of exchange, is simply a written statement by the exporter ordering the importer to pay a specific amount of money at a specific time. Though the word "order"

$10,000.00 January 26, 1977

------ Ninety ----------- Days after sight

Pay to the order of OURSELVES

Ten thousand and no/100 --------------------------------- Dollars

To

Dorts Imports

Hamburg, West Germany

J. Kelly Company, Exporters

Palto Alto, California, U.S.A.

By Joseph Kelly

FIG. 26 · 2
A trade draft

may seem harsh, it is the customary way of doing business internationally. The draft may be either a *sight* draft or a *time* draft. A sight draft is payable on presentation to the party to whom the draft is addressed. This party is known as the *drawee*. If the drawee, or importer, does not pay the amount specified upon presentation of the draft, he defaults and redressment is achieved through the letter of credit arrangement to be discussed later. A time draft is payable so many days after presentation to the drawee.[8] For example, a 90-day time draft indicates that the draft is payable 90 days after sight. An example of a time draft is shown in Figure 26-2.

Several features should be noted about the draft. First, it is an unconditional order in writing signed by the drawer, the exporter. It specifies an exact amount of money that the drawee, the importer, must pay. Finally, it specifies an exact interval after sight at which time this amount must be paid. Upon presentation of the time draft to the drawee, it is accepted. The *acceptance* can be by either the drawee or a bank. If the drawee accepts the draft, he acknowledges on the back of the draft in writing his obligation to pay the amount specified 90 days hence. The draft then is known as a trade acceptance. If a bank accepts the draft, it is known as a bank acceptance. The bank accepts responsibility for payment and thereby substitutes its creditworthiness for that of the drawee.

If the bank is large and well known, and most banks accepting drafts are, the instrument becomes highly marketable upon acceptance. As a result, the drawer, or exporter, does not have to hold the draft until the due date; he can sell it in the market. In fact, an active

[8]The draft itself can be either "clean" or "documentary." A clean draft is one where documents of title are not attached, while with a documentary draft they are attached and delivered to the importer at the time the draft is presented. Clean drafts are usually used for situations in which there is no trade as such and the drawer is simply collecting a bill. Most drafts are documentary.

market exists for bankers' acceptances of well-known banks. To illustrate the arrangement, assume that we have a 90-day draft for $10,000, that it is accepted by a well-known bank, and that 90-day interest rates in the bankers' acceptance market are 6 percent. The drawer then could sell the draft to an investor for $9,850, $10,000 − [$10,000 × .06(90/360)]. At the end of 90 days, the investor would present the acceptance to the accepting bank for payment and would receive $10,000. Thus, the existence of a strong secondary market for bankers' acceptances has facilitated international trade by providing liquidity to the exporter.

Bills of lading

A bill of lading is a shipping document used in the transportation of goods from the exporter to the importer. It has several functions. First, it serves as a receipt from the transportation company to the exporter that specified goods have been received. Second, it serves as a contract between the transportation company and the exporter to ship the goods and deliver them to a specific party at a specific point of destination. Finally, the bill of lading can serve as a document of title. It gives the holder title to the goods. The importer, for example, cannot take title until he receives the bill of lading from the transportation company or its agent. This bill will not be released until the importer satisfies all the conditions of the draft.[9]

The bill of lading accompanies the draft, and the procedures by which the two are handled are well established. Banks and other institutions able to handle these documents efficiently exist in virtually every country. Moreover, the procedures by which goods are transferred internationally are well grounded in international law. These procedures allow an exporter in one country to sell goods to an unknown importer in another and not release possession of the goods until paid, in the case of a sight draft, or until the obligation is acknowledged, in the case of a time draft.

Letters of credit

A commercial letter of credit is issued by a bank on behalf of the importer. In the document, the bank agrees to honor a draft drawn on the importer provided the bill of lading and other details are in order. In essence, the bank substitutes its credit for that of the importer. Obviously, the local bank will not issue a letter of credit unless it feels the importer is credit-worthy and will pay the draft. The letter of

---

[9]The bill of lading can be negotiable, if specified at the time it is made out; and it also can be used as collateral for a loan.

IRREVOCABLE COMMERCIAL LETTER OF CREDIT

Since 1852

WELLS FARGO BANK, N.A.

FORMERLY WELLS FARGO BANK AMERICAN TRUST COMPANY
HEAD OFFICE: 464 CALIFORNIA STREET, SAN FRANCISCO, CALIFORNIA 94120

INTERNATIONAL DIVISION — COMMERCIAL L/C DEPARTMENT — CABLE ADDRESS WELLS

OUR LETTER OF CREDIT NO.
THIS NUMBER MUST BE MENTIONED ON ALL DRAFTS AND CORRESPONDENCE

AMOUNT SPECIMEN

DATE

SPECIMEN

AIR MAIL TO:

PLEASE FORWARD THE ENCLOSED ORIGINAL CREDIT TO THE BENEFICIARY

GENTLEMEN:

BY ORDER OF

AND FOR ACCOUNT OF

WE HEREBY AUTHORIZE YOU TO DRAW ON

UP TO AN AGGREGATE AMOUNT OF SPECIMEN

AVAILABLE BY YOUR DRAFTS AT
ACCOMPANIED BY

C
O
P
Y

S P E C I M E N

DRAFTS MUST BE DRAWN AND NEGOTIATED NOT LATER THAN SPECIMEN
ALL DRAFTS DRAWN UNDER THIS CREDIT MUST BEAR ITS DATE AND NUMBER AND THE AMOUNTS MUST BE ENDORSED ON THE REVERSE SIDE OF THIS LETTER OF CREDIT BY THE NEGOTIATING BANK.
WE HEREBY AGREE WITH THE DRAWERS, ENDORSERS, AND BONA FIDE HOLDERS OF ALL DRAFTS DRAWN UNDER AND IN COMPLIANCE WITH THE TERMS OF THIS CREDIT, THAT SUCH DRAFTS WILL BE DULY HONORED UPON PRESENTATION TO THE DRAWEE.
THIS CREDIT IS SUBJECT TO THE UNIFORM CUSTOMS AND PRACTICE FOR DOCUMENTARY CREDITS (1962 REVISION), INTERNATIONAL CHAMBER OF COMMERCE BROCHURE NO. 222.

SPECIMEN
AUTHORIZED SIGNATURE

FIG. 26 · 3
Letter of credit form

credit arrangement reduces almost entirely the risk to the exporter of selling goods to an unknown importer in another country. An example of a letter of credit form is shown in Figure 26-3.

Illustration of a confirmed letter. The arrangement is strengthened further if a bank in the exporter's country *confirms* the letter of credit. To illustrate, suppose a New York exporter wishes to ship goods to a Brazilian importer located in Rio de Janeiro. The importer's bank in Rio regards the importer as a sound credit risk and is willing to issue a letter of credit guaranteeing payment for the goods when they are received. Thus, the Rio bank substitutes its credit for that of the importer. The contract is now between the Rio bank and the beneficiary of the letter of credit, the New York exporter. However, the exporter may wish to work through its bank, because he has little knowledge of the Rio bank. He asks his New York bank to confirm the Rio bank's letter of credit. If the New York bank is satisfied with the credit-worthiness of the Rio bank, it will agree to do so. When it does, it obligates itself to honor drafts drawn in keeping with the letter of credit arrangement.

Thus, when the exporter ships the goods, he draws a draft in accordance with the terms of the letter of credit arrangement. He presents the draft to his New York bank and the bank pays him the amount designated, assuming all the conditions of shipment are met. As a result of this arrangement, the exporter has his money with no worries as to payment. The New York bank then forwards the draft and other documents to the Rio bank. Upon affirming that the goods have been shipped in a proper manner, the Rio bank honors the draft and pays the New York bank. In turn, it goes to the Brazilian importer and collects from him once the goods have arrived in Rio and are delivered.

Facilitation of trade. From the description, it is easy to see why the letter of credit facilitates international trade. Rather than an exporter extending credit directly to an importer, he relies on one or more banks; and their credit-worthiness is substituted for that of the importer. The letter itself can be either *irrevocable* or *revocable*. Drafts drawn under an irrevocable letter must be honored by the issuing bank. This obligation can be neither canceled nor modified without the consent of all parties. On the other hand, a revocable letter of credit can be canceled or amended by the issuing bank. This type of letter specifies an arrangement for payment but is no guarantee that the draft will be paid. Most letters of credit are irrevocable, and the process described above assumes an irrevocable letter.

The three documents described—the draft, the bill of lading, and the letter of credit—are required in most international transactions. Established procedures exist for doing business on this basis. Together, they afford the exporter protection in selling goods to unknown importers in other countries. They also give the importer assurance that the goods will be shipped and delivered in a proper manner. The financial manager should be acquainted with the mechanics of these transactions if the firm is engaged in exporting or importing.

SUMMARY

A multinational business is one that does business in two or more countries, and it has grown in importance in recent years. As with domestic operations, the financial manager is concerned with the allocation of capital to investment projects and the raising of funds. Foreign investments should be judged on the basis of expected returns and risk, the same as a domestic project. Foreign projects often afford risk-reduction properties that are not available in domestic projects. Expansion abroad is for reasons of going into new markets, acquiring less costly production facilities, and securing raw materials.

A number of factors make foreign investment different from domestic investment. For one thing, taxation is different and this dimension was explored. Political and foreign exchange risk exist. With respect to the former, forecasting of potential instability and the effect of this instability on expected returns is essential at the time an investment is being considered. Foreign exchange risk is the risk that a foreign currency will be devalued relative to the dollar and/or that convertibility will be restricted. A company can protect itself against this risk by balancing foreign monetary assets and liabilities, by use of the forward exchange market, by engaging in a foreign currency swap arrangement, or by adjusting intracompany account arrangements. Both political and foreign exchange risk must be integrated with business risk in judging the overall risk of a foreign investment. A final factor sometimes influencing foreign investment decisions is that of government restrictions on investment abroad.

Raising funds abroad is the second major function of the financial manager. Although internal financing—comprised of equity investments and loans from the parent, retained earnings, and depreciation and depletion allowances—is the most important source of funds, external financing is important as well. The major sources of external funds are commercial banks, Eurodollar loans, Eurobonds, development banks, and the World Bank group. Financing international trade differs from domestic trade in the procedures employed. The differences in procedures are attributable to the lower quality of credit information, poorer communications, slower transportation, and different legal processes. There are three principal documents involved in international trade. The draft is an order by the exporter to the importer to pay a specified amount of money either upon presentation of the draft or a certain number of days after presentation. A bill of lading is a shipping document that can serve as a receipt, as a shipping contract, and as title to the goods involved. The final document, a letter of credit, is an agreement by a bank to honor a draft drawn on the importer. It greatly reduces the risk to the exporter and may be confirmed by another bank. These three documents greatly facilitate international trade.

QUESTIONS

1. As a result of the trade deficits in the early seventies, the United States devalued the dollar twice while other countries revalued their currency. Explain

what this currency realignment meant in terms of profitability from prior investments abroad by U.S. businessmen.

2. Explain the function performed by the Eurodollar market.

3. What are the functions of the bill of lading?

4. Explain the concept of a "floating" exchange rate in contrast to a fixed exchange rate.

5. Many countries require that nationals control more than 50 percent of the voting stock in any venture. Is this wise? Explain.

6. In the early seventies, the Chilean government took over most of the American-owned businesses in Chile. Explain the impact of such action on the short-run and long-run productivity of the assets that were taken over. Project the impact of these actions on future development of the underdeveloped countries.

7. In 1971, Congress passed the Domestic International Sales Corporation Act (DISC), whose purpose was to provide tax incentives for U.S. corporations selling abroad in order to stimulate exports. Is there any moral or theoretical justification for U.S. taxpayers to subsidize the foreign consumption of U.S. goods? Explain.

8. The U.S. trade deficits of the late sixties and early seventies were to be corrected by a devaluation of the dollar and a revaluation of the yen and the mark. Explain how these changes were to correct the trade deficit.

9. Identify factors that will prevent the correction of a trade deficit by currency realignment (devaluation or revaluation).

PROBLEMS

1. The U.S. Imports Company purchased 100,000 marks worth of machines from a firm in Dortmund, West Germany. The value of the dollar in terms of the mark has been decreasing. The firm in Dortmund offers 2/10, net 90 terms. The spot rate for the mark is $0.3856, while the ninety-day future rate is $0.3906.
   (a) Compute the dollar cost of paying the account within the 10 days.
   (b) Compute the dollar cost of buying a future to liquidate the account in 90 days.
   (c) The differential between (a) and (b) is the result of the time value of money (the discount for prepayment) and devaluation. Determine the magnitude of each of these components.
   (d) Determine the annual percentage cost of capital and the annual percentage cost of protection against devaluation.

2. Financiera de Nuevo León in Mexico offers to pay 12 percent on one-year certificates of deposit. The Mexican government taxes interest income at the source through a withholding system much like the U.S. system of withholding on personal income. The Mexican tax rate is 21 percent. An American businessman who is in the 40 percent tax rate in the U.S. invests $50,000 in the Financiera (Savings and Loan).
   (a) Determine the taxes paid to the Mexican government.

(b) Determine the taxes paid to the U.S. government on the income from Mexico.

(c) Qualitatively, assess the riches being borne by the American investor.

3. An American manufacturer is going to increase its inventories in Europe financed by either a Eurodollar loan with 18-months maturity at an annual rate of 8 percent payable at maturity or with British pounds at an annual rate of 12 percent. If the latter alternative is chosen, the position will be hedged with a future contract at $1.913 per pound. The current exchange rate is $2.05 per pound. Choose the better financing alternative.

SELECTED REFERENCES

ADLER, MICHAEL, and BERNARD DUMAS, "Optimal International Acquisitions," *Journal of Finance,* 30 (March 1975), 1–20.

EITEMAN, DAVID K., and ARTHUR I. STONEHILL, *Multinational Business Finance.* Reading, Mass.: Addison-Wesley, 1973.

GITMAN, LAWRENCE J., "A Multinational Firm Investment Model," *Journal of Economics and Business,* 26 (Fall 1973), 41–48.

HOYT, NEWTON H., JR., "The Management of Currency Exchange Risk by the Singer Company," *Financial Management,* 1 (Spring 1972), 13–20.

HUGHES, JOHN S., DENNIS E. LOGUE, and JAMES SWEENEY, "Corporate International Diversification and Market Assigned Measures of Risk and Diversification," *Journal of Financial and Quantitative Analysis,* 10 (November 1975), 627–37.

LESSARD, DONALD, "International Portfolio Diversification: A Multivariate Analysis for a Group of Latin American Countries," *Journal of Finance,* 28 (June 1973), 619–34.

LEVY, HAIM, and MARSHALL SARNAT, "International Diversification of Investment Portfolios," *American Economic Review,* 60 (September 1970), 668–75.

LIETAER, BERNARD A., *Financial Management of Foreign Exchange: An Operational Technique to Reduce Risk.* Cambridge, Mass.: M.I.T. Press, 1971.

NAUMANN-ETIENNE, RUEDIGER, "A Framework for Financial Decisions in Multinational Corporations—Summary of Recent Research," *Journal of Financial and Quantitative Analysis,* 9 (November 1974), 859–74.

NEHRT, LEE C., *International Finance for Multinational Business,* 2nd ed. Scranton, Pa.: Intext, 1972.

PETTY, J. WILLIAM, II, and ERNEST W. WALKER, "Optimal Transfer Pricing for the Multinational Firm," *Financial Management,* 1 (Winter 1972), 74–87.

ROBBINS, SIDNEY M., and ROBERT B. STOBAUGH, *Money in the Multinational Enterprise: A Study of Financial Policy.* New York: Basic Books, 1973.

RODRIGUEZ, RITA M., "Management of Foreign Exchange Risk in the U.S. Multinationals," *Journal of Financial and Quantitative Analysis,* 9 (November 1974), 849–57.

ROLL, RICHARD W., and BRUNO H. SOLNIK, "Interest Rates and Exchange Risk," *Journal of Finance,* 31 (May 1976).

RUTENBERG, DAVID P., "Maneuvering Liquid Assets in a Multinational Company: Formulation and Deterministic Solution Procedures," *Management Science,* 16 (June 1970), 671–84.

SAFARIAN, A. E., "Perspectives on Foreign Direct Investment from the Viewpoint of a Capital Receiving Country," *Journal of Finance,* 28 (May 1973), 419–38.

SHAPIRO, ALAN C., "Exchange Rate Changes, Inflation, and the Valuation of the Multinational Corporation," *Journal of Finance,* 30 (May 1975), 485–502.

_____, "Optimal Inventory and Credit-Granting Strategies under Inflation and Devaluation," *Journal of Financial and Quantitative Analysis,* 8 (January 1973), 37–46.

SMITH, DAN THROOP, "Financial Variables in International Business," *Harvard Business Review,* 44 (January–February 1966), 93–104.

SOLNIK, BRUNO H., *European Capital Markets.* Boston: Lexington Books, 1973.

VERNON, RAYMOND, *Manager in the International Economy,* 2nd ed. Englewood Cliffs, N.J.: Prentice-Hall, 1972.

WEINROBE, MAURICE D., "Corporate Taxes and the U.S. Balance of Trade," *National Tax Journal,* 24 (March 1971), 79–86.

WELLS, LOUIS T., JR., "The Multinational Business Enterprise: What Kind of International Organization?" *International Organization,* 25 (September 1971), 447–64.

WESTON, J. FRED, and **BART W. SORGE**, *International Business Finance.* Homewood, Ill.: Richard D. Irwin, 1972.

ZENOFF, DAVID B., and **JACK ZWICK**, *International Financial Management.* Englewood Cliffs, N.J.: Prentice-Hall, 1969.

Failure and Reorganization 27

Our analysis throughout most of this book has assumed that the firm is a going concern; nevertheless, we must not lose sight of the fact that some firms fail. Recognition of failure is important both from the standpoint of internal management and from the standpoint of a creditor with amounts owing from a company in distress. This point was brought into sharp perspective in the 1970s with the bankruptcy of large companies such as Penn Central and W. T. Grant. Previously, bankruptcy was regarded as a phenomenon restricted to small firms—the depression of the thirties being the last time major corporations had failed.

The word "failure" is vague, partly because there are varying degrees of failure. For example, a company is regarded as technically insolvent if it is unable to meet its current obligations. However, such insolvency may be only temporary and subject to remedy.[1] Technical insolvency, then, denotes only a lack of liquidity. Insolvency in bankruptcy, on the other hand, means that the liabilities of a company exceed its assets; in other words, the net worth of the company is negative. Financial failure includes the entire range of possibilities between these extremes.

[1] See James E. Walter, "Determination of Technical Insolvency," *Journal of Business*, 30 (January 1957), 30–43.

The remedies available to save a failing company vary in harshness according to the degree of financial difficulty. If the outlook is sufficiently hopeless, liquidation may be the only feasible alternative. However, many failing firms can be rehabilitated to the gain of creditors, stockholders, and society. Although the major purpose of a liquidation or rehabilitation is to protect creditors, the interests of the owners also are considered. (In the thirties, they were all but neglected.) Still, legal procedures favor creditors. Otherwise, they would hesitate to extend credit, and the allocation of funds in the economy would be less than efficient.

Signs of failure

Although the causes of financial difficulty are numerous, many failures are attributable either directly or indirectly to management. Usually, nonfinancial problems lead to losses which, in turn, lead to financial strain and eventual failure. Very seldom is one bad decision the cause of the difficulty; usually the cause is a series of errors, and the difficulty evolves gradually. Because with most companies the signs of potential distress are evident prior to actual failure, a creditor may be able to take corrective action before failure finally occurs. If the cause of the difficulty is financial mismanagement and the company is profitable, the situation almost invariably can be salvaged. However, when the underlying cause is principally external, and there is no way for management to curtail losses, the inevitable result is liquidation.

Despite difficulties caused by past mistakes, many companies can be preserved as going concerns and can make an economic contribution to society. Sometimes the rehabilitation is severe, in keeping with the degree of financial difficulty. Nevertheless, these measures may be necessary if the firm is to obtain a new lease on life.

In the remainder of this chapter, we take up the full spectrum of remedies available to a firm in financial distress. It is important to recognize that at the time this chapter was being written, Congress was considering a major reform of the Bankruptcy Act. In 1976, however, it was unclear which direction the proposed legislation would take and, if legislated, the date of transition to the new Bankruptcy Act. In what follows, then, we describe the remedies available to a failing firm under the existing Bankruptcy Act, beginning with remedies that are voluntary on the part of creditors and the company and then examining legal actions that can be taken in connection with a failing company. In the last section of the chapter, we examine the major features of the proposed legislation and the ways in which it will change existing procedures.

Extensions

An extension involves nothing more than creditors extending the maturity of their obligations. In cases of temporary insolvency of a basically sound company, creditors may prefer to work the problem out with the company. By not forcing the issue with legal proceedings, creditors avoid considerable legal expense and the possible shrinkage of value in liquidation. Moreover, they maintain their full claim against the company involved; they do not agree to a partial settlement. The ability of a creditor to realize the full value of his claim depends, of course, upon the company improving its operations and its liquidity. In an extension situation, existing creditors often are unwilling to grant further credit on new sales and insist upon current purchases being paid for in cash. Obviously, no one creditor is going to extend his obligation unless others do likewise. Consequently, a creditors' committee is usually formed by the major creditors to negotiate with the company and to formulate a plan mutually satisfactory to all concerned.

We must point out, however, that no one creditor is obligated to go along with the plan. If there are dissenting creditors and they have small amounts owing, they may be paid off in order to avoid legal proceedings. The number of dissenters cannot be too large, for the remaining creditors must, in essence, assume their obligations. Obviously, the remaining creditors do not want to be left "holding the bag." If an extension is worked out, the creditors can institute controls over the company to assure proper management and to increase the probability of speedy recovery. In addition, they may elect to take security if marketable assets are available. The ultimate threat on the part of creditors is to initiate bankruptcy proceedings against the company and to force it into liquidation. By making an extension, however, they show an inclination to cooperate with the company.

Composition

A composition involves a pro rata settlement of creditors' claims in cash or in cash and promissory notes. The creditors must agree to accept a partial settlement in discharge of their entire claim. For example, a debtor may propose a settlement of sixty cents on the dollar. If creditors feel that the settlement is more than they could obtain in liquidation after legal expenses, they will probably accept. Even if it is somewhat less, they may still accept, because no company likes to be responsible for forcing another into bankruptcy. The settlement is a "friendly" one in the sense that legal proceedings are avoided.

As in an extension, however, the settlement must be agreed to by all creditors. Dissenting creditors must be paid in full, or they can force the company into bankruptcy. These creditors can be a considerable nuisance and may all but preclude a voluntary settlement. Overall, voluntary settlements can be advantageous to creditors as well as to the debtors, for they avoid legal expenses and complications. The settlements are informal and, as a result, tend to be more efficiently administered than legal settlements. Too often the latter are both cumbersome and lengthy.

Creditors having operating control

Creditors may agree to a voluntary settlement only if the present management is relieved of its reponsibility. A creditors' committee may be appointed by creditors to control the operations of the company until the claims can be settled. The company enters into an agreement with creditors, giving them control of the company. One problem with this arrangement is the possibility of stockholder suits against the creditors for mismanagement of the company. Consequently, creditors are reluctant to become too active in the management of a failing company.

Liquidation

In certain circumstances, creditors may feel that the company should not be preserved, because further financial deterioration seems inevitable. When liquidation is the only realistic solution, it can be accomplished either through a private settlement or through bankruptcy proceedings. An orderly private liquidation is likely to be more efficient and result in a significantly higher settlement. With a liquidation in bankruptcy, much time is expended in court scheduling and other legal formalities, not to mention the legal and other expenses involved. The opportunity costs of delays as well as the direct expenses usually are much less with a private liquidation.

A private liquidation can be effected through an assignment in which the debtor assigns its assets to a trustee. In turn, the trustee liquidates the assets and distributes the proceeds to creditors on a pro rata basis. The liquidation itself can be on a piecemeal basis, asset by asset over time, or through a public auction where assets are sold all at once. The assignment of assets by the debtor does not release him from his obligations. For all practical purposes, however, creditors have little prospect for obtaining further settlement from a company once all of its assets are liquidated. The assignment can be either informal or formal. In an informal, or common-law assignment, creditors agree upon a trustee and proceed informally. In a formal, or statutory, assignment the court appoints the trustee and oversees the settlement. The liquidation is still voluntary, however, in the sense that it is agreed to by all creditors. Because voluntary settlements must have such agreement, they usually are restricted to companies with a limited number of creditors and to situations where the securities outstanding are not publicly held.

LEGAL PROCEDURES

Most legal procedures undertaken in connection with failing companies fall under the Bankruptcy Act of 1898, as amended by the Chandler Act of 1938. This act provides for both the liquidation of a company and its reorganization.[2] In most cases, the courts take over the operation of the company and preserve the *status quo* until a decision is reached whether to liquidate the company or keep it alive through reorganization.

Liquidation

If there is no hope for the successful operation of a company, liquidation is the only feasible alternative. The federal district court, then, declares the firm bankrupt and proceeds with a plan for orderly liquidation. Bankruptcy proceedings may be either voluntary or involuntary. With a voluntary bankruptcy, the company files a petition of bankruptcy with a federal district court. In an involuntary bankruptcy, three or more creditors with claims in excess of $500 initiate the action by filing a petition with the court. If the total number of creditors of a firm is less than twelve, any one creditor can file a petition. The federal court will declare the company an involuntary bankrupt if it violates one of the six acts of bankruptcy.

These acts can be summarized as follows:

1. The debtor conceals some or all of its assets or it transfers its property, both with the intent of defrauding creditors.

2. Cash or other assets are transferred to one creditor in preference to others. This preferential treatment gives the creditor involved a more favorable settlement than other creditors will receive.

3. The insolvent debtor gives specific creditors a lien on its property.

[2] Before the thirties, companies were reorganized under equity receiverships. This process is no longer in use.

4. The debtor makes a general assignment for the benefit of creditors.

5. The debtor, while insolvent, appoints a receiver or trustee to take charge of his property.

6. The debtor admits in writing that he is unable to pay his debt and that he is willing to be judged a bankrupt.

Upon the declaration of bankruptcy, the court usually appoints a *referee* to take over the operation of the company temporarily and call a meeting of the creditors. At the meeting, claims of the creditors are proven, and the creditors are given the opportunity to elect a *trustee in bankruptcy*. The trustee has the responsibility of liquidating the assets of the company and distributing liquidating dividends to the creditors. The conduct of the trustee in carrying out these responsibilities is under the supervision of the court.

Priority of claims. In the distribution of the proceeds of a liquidation, the priority of claims must be observed. The administrative costs involved in the bankruptcy, taxes, and certain other claims must be paid before creditors are entitled to receive settlement. Secured creditors are entitled to the proceeds realized from the liquidation of specific assets on which they have a lien. If any balance of the claim is not realized from the sale of the collateral, these creditors become general creditors. General creditors are paid liquidating dividends on a pro rata basis from the total liquidation of unencumbered assets. If all of these claims are paid in full, liquidating dividends then can be paid to subordinated debtholders, to preferred stockholders, and, finally, to common stockholders. It is unlikely, however, that common stockholders will receive much in the way of distribution from a liquidation.

To illustrate the priority of claims, suppose Bar K Products Company had the balance sheet shown in Table 27-1 at the time of bank-

TABLE 27 · 1

Balance Sheet of Bar K Products at Time of Bankruptcy

Current assets	$2,600,000	Accounts payable	$ 900,000
		Accrued wages	600,000
		Bank loan	1,100,000
		Current liabilities	$2,600,000
		First mortgage bonds	1,000,000
		Long-term debentures	600,000
Net fixed assets	5,200,000	Preferred stock	1,000,000
		Common stock	4,000,000
		Retained earnings	(1,400,000)
	$7,800,000		$7,800,000

ruptcy. The claims of creditors are shown on the right-hand side. Suppose in liquidating the assets of the company the trustee in bankruptcy realizes $1,500,000 on the current assets and $2,500,000 on the sale of fixed assets, or $4,000,000 in total. The first claims on these proceeds are the administrative expenses involved in liquidation. Suppose these expenses amount to $500,000, which leaves $3,500,000 for creditors. Next in priority come the wages due employees, which total $600,000. The mortgage bonds are paid from the sale of the specific property securing them. Suppose the proceeds from this sale are $800,000. The claims discussed thus far constitute priority items. After they are settled, the residual is available to general creditors and it is:

Proceeds from sale of all assets	$4,000,000
Less: Liquidation expenses	500,000
Wages due employees	600,000
Mortgage bonds, paid from sale of property	800,000
Amount available to general creditors	$2,100,000

General creditor claims include accounts payable of $900,000, a bank loan of $1,100,000, the $200,000 in unsatisfied claim of the first mortgage bondholders ($1,000,000 claim less $800,000 proceeds from the sale of the property securing the bonds), and long-term debentures of $600,000. These claims total $2,800,000. Thus, the claims of general creditors of Bar K Products Company exceed the amount available to them. As a result, general creditor claims are settled on a pro rata basis of $2,100,000/$2,800,000 = 75 percent. The specific settlements are as follows:

	General Creditor Claims	Amount of Settlement
Accounts payable	$ 900,000	$ 675,000
Bank loan	1,100,000	825,000
First mortgage	200,000	150,000
Long-term debentures	600,000	450,000
	$2,800,000	$2,100,000

Obviously, nothing remains for preferred stockholders or common stockholders in this particular case. If the amount available for general creditors exceeds total claims, the residual is applied first to preferred stockholders and, if anything remains, to common stockholders.

Appointment of a receiver and final discharge. When a trustee cannot be appointed quickly, the court appoints a *receiver* to manage the operation of the company and conserve its assets until a trustee can be selected. After that, the procedure is the same as before. Upon the payment of all liquidating dividends, the bankrupt is discharged, thereby being relieved of any further claim. The principal objective of bankruptcy proceedings is an orderly liquidation of assets and an equitable distribution to creditors on a formal basis. The disadvantage of these proceedings is that they are slower and usually more expensive than a private liquidation. Some court-appointed officials are inefficient, being more concerned with their remuneration than with the proceeds available to creditors. As a result, a liquidation in bankruptcy may be less efficient than a private liquidation, providing creditors with a lower settlement. However, when creditors cannot come together in a voluntary manner, bankruptcy proceedings are the only recourse.

REORGANIZATION

It may be in the best interests of all concerned to reorganize a company rather than liquidate it. A reorganization is an effort to keep a company alive by changing its capital structure. The rehabilitation involves the reduction of fixed charges by substituting equity and limited-income securities for fixed-income securities. In essence, a reorganization is similar to a composition in that claims are scaled down. The decision to go with a reorganization as opposed to liquidation must be based upon the likely future profitability of the company. If there is little prospect for profitable operations in the foreseeable future, creditors will want to liquidate the company and take whatever losses they must at the time. Only if the present value of the company as a going concern exceeds its liquidating value will a reorganization be worthwhile from the standpoint of creditors.

Procedure

Most reorganizations of industrial and public utility companies occur under Chapter X of the Bankruptcy Act. Reorganization procedures are initiated in the same general manner as a liquidation in bankruptcy. The federal district court appoints a *trustee* to operate the debtor's business until a reorganization plan is put into effect.[3] If the debts of the company are in excess of $250,000, the court must

---

[3]The company is declared a "debtor" in a reorganization as opposed to a "bankrupt" in a liquidation.

appoint a "disinterested" trustee—that is, a party independent of the debtor. In addition to managing the operations of the debtor temporarily, the trustee must compile all the essential information required by the court, creditors, and—if the securities are publicly held—the Securities and Exchange Commission. Included is information pertaining to the value of assets, the nature of the liabilities, and the operating potential of the debtor from the standpoint of profitability.

Most important, the trustee is charged with the responsibility of drawing up a plan of reorganization. This plan is proposed after a thorough review of the situation and discussions with creditors and stockholders. Committees may be formed by the various classes of creditors and stockholders to represent and protect the interests of each class. The plan then is submitted to the court for hearings and approval. If liabilities exceed $3 million, and the securities are publicly held, the plan must also be submitted to the SEC. The SEC acts only in an advisory capacity to the court; it prepares a report on the proposed plan and submits it to the court. The final decision is that of the court. The SEC has no right to appeal this decision, although it may participate in appeals undertaken by other parties.

Fair, equitable, and feasible standards. If the court feels the plan is fair, equitable, and feasible, it will approve the plan. The fair and equitable standard means that all parties are treated according to their priority of claim. Junior security holders cannot receive a new security of the same value as senior security holders. The superior rights of senior security holders must be recognized in the reorganization. Feasibility has to do with the plan being workable with respect to earning power relative to the financial structure of the reorganized company. A company cannot have too great an amount of fixed financial charges in relation to its expected earning power. If the reorganized company does not have adequate coverage of fixed charges, the court will conclude the plan is not feasible and the trustee will need to submit another plan.

Once a plan is approved by the court, it is submitted to the creditor and stockholder groups for approval. In order to become effective, it must be accepted by a two-thirds majority of each class of debtholders and by a simple majority of each class of stockholders. Upon approval by the majority of a particular class of security holders, the plan is binding on dissenters in that class.

Railroad reorganizations. The reorganization procedure for railroads is similar to other reorganizations, except that the Interstate Commerce Commision plays an active role in the reorganization. Railroad reorganizations occur under Section 77 of the Bankruptcy Act and the Mahaffe Act of 1948. The reorganization plan must be submitted to the ICC, which approves the trustee. The ICC holds hearings and then either approves the proposed reorganization plan or submits its own plan to the court. The concern of the ICC is that the reorganization plan be compatible with the public's interest. The court, however, must approve the plan on the basis of whether it is fair, equitable, and feasible.

Reorganization plan

The difficult aspect of a reorganization is the recasting of the company's capital structure to reduce the amount of fixed charges. In formulating a reorganization plan, the trustee must carry out three steps. These steps are: (1) determination of the total valuation of the reorganized company, (2) formulation of a new capital structure, and (3) assignment of valuation to the old securities in exchange for the new securities.

Determining a total valuation. The first step, determining the total valuation of the reorganized company, is perhaps the most difficult but the most important. The technique favored by trustees is a capitalization of prospective earnings. For example, if future annual earnings of the reorganized company are expected to be $2 million, and the overall capitalization rate of similar companies averages 10 percent, a total valuation of $20 million would be set for the company. The valuation figure is subject to considerable variation owing to the difficulty of estimating prospective earnings and determining an appropriate capitalization rate. Thus, the valuation figure represents nothing more than a best estimate of potential value. Although the capitalization of prospective earnings is the generally accepted approach to valuing a company in reorganization, the valuation may be adjusted upward if the assets have substantial liquidating value. The common stockholders of the company, of course, would like to see as high a valuation figure as possible. If the valuation figure the trustee proposes is below the liquidating value of the company, common stockholders will argue for liquidation rather than reorganization.

Formulating a capital structure. Once a valuation figure has been determined, the next step is to formulate a new capital structure for the company to reduce fixed charges to that there will be an adequate coverage margin. To reduce these charges, the total debt of the firm is scaled down by being partly shifted to income bonds, preferred stock, and common stock. In addition to being scaled down, the terms of the debt may be changed. The maturity of the debt can be extended to reduce the amount of annual sinking-fund obligation. The trustee is very mindful of the need to achieve a proper balance of debt or equity in relation to the prospective earnings of the company. If it appears that the reorganized company will need new financing in the future, the trustee may feel that a more conservative ratio of debt to equity is in order to provide for future financial flexibility.

Valuation of old securities. Once a new capital structure is established, the last step involves the valuation of the old securities and their exchange for new securities. Under an *absolute priority rule,* which is required in reorganization under Chapter X of the Bankruptcy Act, all senior claims on assets must be settled in full before a junior claim can be settled. For example, in the exchange process, a bondholder must receive the par value of his bond in another security before there can be any distribution to preferred stockholders. The total valuation figure arrived at in step one sets an upper limit on the amount of securities that can be issued. Suppose the existing capital structure of a company undergoing reorganization is as follows:

Debentures	$ 9 million
Subordinated debentures	3 million
Preferred stock	6 million
Common stock equity (at book value)	10 million
	$28 million

If the total valuation of the reorganized company is to be $20 million, the trustee might establish the following capital structure in step two:

Debentures	$ 3 million
Income bonds	6 million
Preferred stock	3 million
Common stock	8 million
	$20 million

Having established the "appropriate" capital structure for the reorganized company, the trustee then must allocate the new securities. In this regard, he may propose that the debenture holders exchange their $9 million in debentures for $3 million in new debentures and $6 million in income bonds; that the subordinated debenture holders exchange their $3 million in securities for preferred stock; and that preferred stockholders exchange their securities for $6 million of common stock in the reorganized company. The common stockholders then would be entitled to $2 million in stock in the reorganized company, or 25 percent of the total common stock of the reorganized company. Before, these stockholders held 100 percent of the stock. It is easy to see why common stockholders would like to see as high a valuation figure as possible. To encourage high valuation, they may attempt to discount the troubles of the company as temporary and argue that the earning potential of the company is favorable.

Thus, each claim is settled in full before a junior claim is settled. The example above represents a relatively "mild" reorganization. In a "harsh" reorganization, debt instruments may be exchanged entirely for common stock in the reorganized company and the old common stock eliminated completely. Had the total valuation figure in the example been $12 million, the trustee might have proposed a new capital structure consisting of $3 million in preferred stock and $9 million in common stock. Only the straight and subordinated debenture holders would receive a settlement in this case. The preferred and the common stockholders of the old company would receive nothing.

Absolute versus relative priority. These examples serve to show that the common stockholders of a company undergoing reorganization suffer under an absolute priority rule, whereby claims must be settled in the order of their legal priority. From their standpoint, they would much prefer to see claims settled on a *relative priority basis*. Under this rule, new securities are allocated on the basis of the relative market prices of the securities. The common stockholders could never obtain senior securities in a reorganization, but they would be entitled to some common stock if their present stock had value. Because the company is not actually being liquidated, common stockholders argue that a rule of relative priority is really the fairest. However, the absolute priority rule has been upheld by the Supreme Court (*Case* v. *Los Angeles Lumber Products Company,* 1939). Their only recourse is to question whether the reorganization plan is fair and equitable to all security holders and not whether the absolute priority of claims is valid.

The absolute priority rule does not imply that fixed-income security holders must receive securities of the same grade. They can and usually do receive in part a security of a grade inferior to the one they held. However, their superior rights, relative to stockholders, must be recognized. Moreover, the securities they receive must be reasonably sound in the sense that their actual values in the market approximate the face values assigned in the reorganization. It would be unfair, for example, to assign a new bond with a face value of $1,000 if, because of a low interest rate and considerable default risk, it sells for only $500 in the capital markets. In this case, a greater amount of the new securities would need to be assigned in the reorganization.

Chapter XI procedures

Chapter XI of the Bankruptcy Act permits a failing company to seek an *arrangement*. In essence, an arrangement is a "legal" extension or composition. Only the company itself can initiate an arrangement, by filing a voluntary petition with a federal district court attesting to the fact that it is unable to pay unsecured creditors and proposing a plan of action. Once the petition is filed, creditors cannot push for collection while an arrangement is being worked out. The court appoints a referee to call a meeting of creditors and discuss the plan proposed by the debtor. In addition, the court may appoint a receiver or trustee if the situation so warrants. The plan proposed by the debtor is subject to amendments by the creditors. Once a plan is approved by the majority of creditors and is judged by the court to be fair, equitable, and feasible, however, it becomes binding on all. In this respect, the arrangement has an advantage over a voluntary extension or composition, wherein creditors do not necessarily have to accept the plan. A large creditor can easily prevent a voluntary settlement from working.

The arrangement applies only to unsecured creditors, however. The claims of secured creditors are left intact; the debtor must pay secured creditors according to the terms of the obligations. An arrangement usually is a cheaper and quicker form of settlement than other types of legal settlements. The method is well suited for the company whose creditors are mostly trade creditors and that has no publicly held fixed-income securities. If a company has publicly held securities and substantial changes in its capital structure are required, these changes usually will be effected under Chapter X, rather than under Chapter XI, of the Bankruptcy Act.

REFORM OF THE BANKRUPTCY ACT

At the time of this writing, Congress was considering a major reform of the bankruptcy laws of the United States. Two bills were being considered, one drafted by the Commission of the Bankruptcy Laws (H.R. 31), and the other by the National Conference of Bankruptcy Judges (H.R. 32). It is not clear which of these two bills, if either, will emerge. However, it does seem clear that there will be a major overhaul of the bankruptcy system. Of the two bills, the first calls for the more sweeping changes. Therefore, we will focus our attention on the important changes contained in it. However, major differences between the two bills will be pointed out as we go along. Hopefully, the reader will gain insight into what is likely to come in the way of changes of the Bankruptcy Act.

Bankruptcy courts

Under each bill, U.S. bankruptcy courts are established with judges appointed for fifteen-year terms. In the Commission bill, the judges are appointed by the president, whereas in the National Conference of Bankruptcy Judges bill, they are appointed by the judicial council for the particular circuit involved. The number and location of bankruptcy courts will be determined by the Judicial Conference of the United States on the basis of a comprehensive survey of case loads. Unlike the present system, the individual courts need not be self-supporting, as expenses will be paid out of appropriations by the federal government. This is the same general revenue support as occurs for other courts.

Bankruptcy administration

In the Commission bill, a separate administrative body is established in the executive branch of the government. Called the U.S. Bankruptcy Administration, its function is to administer the litigated estate. Under the old law, such administration is under the auspices of the court. Frequently, there have been conflicts of interest and inefficiencies under this system. The Commission has therefore recommended the severance of administrative from judicial functions within the bankruptcy system.

The U.S. Bankruptcy Administration would be staffed by permanent employees, and their duties would include many of those now performed by referees, trustees, auctioneers, appraisers, accountants, and attorneys. This would largely replace the appointment of outside administrators by the court, where often there is absence of effective control and where there is little uniformity across the United States. Hopefully, there would also be economies arising from increased efficiency. Headquartered in Washington, the Bankruptcy Administration would have some regional and many local offices.

Under the second bill, H.R. 32, the present system of administration is largely retained and various outside parties are appointed by the court to administer the estate. The most important of these is the trustee. In all cases, the court oversees the administration of the estate. This difference in administration is perhaps the key difference between the two bills.

Involuntary petitions and other changes

Under the existing Bankruptcy Act, one of the six acts of bankruptcy must be proven. This frequently results in delays, during which time the debtor's assets are further depleted. Under the first bill, the concept of an act of bankruptcy is abolished and involuntary proceedings can be initiated by a creditor if the business ceases to pay its obligations. To protect the debtor against ill-founded petitions by creditors, however, the court is required to hold immediate hearings after the filing of an involuntary petition. After the filing of the petition and pending determination of the issues involved, the court may order the Bankruptcy Administration to take possession of the property in order to prevent depletion.

In the hearing, the court must determine whether the relief sought in the petition is in the best interests of the debtor and creditors. After due consideration of the issues of the case, the court either decides that the case is valid and direct relief is in order, or it dismisses the case.

The bill also provides for a number of changes designed to streamline the administration of a bankrupt estate. Certain red tape involved in the sale of property is eliminated so as to reduce administrative expenses and delays. Changes also are made in the treatment of the recovery of assets transferred before bankruptcy, so as to make it more equitable.

With respect to the distribution of assets, the bill proposes a major simplification of the provisions to make them more equitable among unsecured creditors. Wages to employees and claims for contributions to employee benefit plans are given substantial priority—in preference to all other creditors with the exception of administrative expenses, which come first. Third in priority come taxes accruing within one year prior to bankruptcy. This reduces the government's priority of claim, as the limit now is three years. All other outside claims are lumped together under the heading of general creditors, and the burden of proof of a legally enforceable and allowable claim is made less onerous. However, claims by officers, directors, affiliates, and stockholders are subordinated to those of the general creditors. When the estate is sufficient to pay some but not all of the claimants in a particular priority class, the distribution is made on a pro rata basis.

Business rehabilitation

To eliminate the overlap and confusion involved in Chapters X, XI, and XII in the present Bankruptcy Act, the three chapters are consolidated into one chapter under the first bill, H.R. 31. Under the second bill, H.R. 32, consolidation occurs, but there is a separate chapter for arrangements.

Under the first bill, the court determines whether a trustee is needed on the basis of the circumstances of the case. Where debts exceed $1 million or where there are more than three hundred security holders, however, the presumption is that a trustee will be appointed. The selection itself is by the Bankruptcy Administration, subject to the approval of the court. In reorganizations, the use of a receiver is eliminated.

Rather than have the creditors themselves determine the election of a creditors' committee, the selection is made by the Bankruptcy Administration and the committee usually will be composed of the seven largest creditors. This change is expected to eliminate certain infighting among different creditors and lawyers. Also, the direct involvement of the Securities and Exchange Commission is reduced and its function assumed by the Bankruptcy Administration.

The basic concept of fair and equitable as applied to publicly held securities in a reorganization is retained. However, recognition is given to the fact that the valuation placed on the company is at best an educated guess about the future. An effort is made to expedite the formulation and consummation of a reorganization plan so as to eliminate the unreasonable delays that now occur. The rule of absolute priority is modified to allow equityholders to participate in the plan if they make future contributions that are important to the operation of the reorganized company. The degree of participation in the plan is determined on a basis that will approximate the value of such contributions. This represents a marked departure from the absolute priority rule established in *Case* v. *Los Angeles Lumber Products Company*, 1939.

After all plans for the reorganization of a company are submitted to the Bankruptcy Administration within the allotted time, they are turned over to the court and a date for approval hearings is set. At the hearings, the court evaluates each plan according to its feasibility, the reasonableness of the valuation placed on the company, and the fair and equitable criteria. On the basis of these considerations, the court then approves or disapproves each plan. Approved plans are transmitted to those creditors and equityholders that are entitled to accept or reject a plan. These security holders then accept or reject each of the plans.

The court then sets hearings for the confirmation of any plans that have the requisite majority of acceptances. The court will confirm a plan if it has majority acceptance by each creditor class and majority acceptance by equityholders. If more than one plan has majority acceptance, the court considers the preferences indicated by creditors and equityholders in determining which plan to confirm. Upon confirmation of a plan, it becomes binding on all parties. All rights and interests of equityholders and all claims of creditors other than those contained in the confirmed plan are then terminated.

SUMMARY

Business failure encompasses a wide range of financial difficulty; it occurs whenever a company is unable to meet its current obligations. The remedies applied to a failing company vary in severity with the degree of financial difficulty. Voluntary settlements are informal and must be agreed to by all creditors and the company itself. The difficulty with a voluntary settlement is in obtaining agreement of all parties concerned. Included in voluntary settlements are extensions, compositions, a creditors' committee controlling the operations of the company, and a private liquidation.

Legal settlements are effected, for the most part, under Chapters X and XI of the Bankruptcy Act, as amended by the Chandler Act of 1938. Railroads are reorganized under Section 77 of the Bankruptcy Act. The least "harsh" of the legal procedures is an arrangement under Chapter XI. An arrangement is simply a formal extension or composition. Reorganizations and liquidations occur mostly under Chapter X. In a reorganization, the capital structure of the company is changed so as to reduce the total amount of fixed charges. The reorganized plan has to be fair, equitable, and feasible, as determined by the court and approved by a two-thirds majority of each class of debtholders and a majority of each class of stockholders. If the company cannot be rehabilitated, it will be declared bankrupt by the court and liquidated by a trustee in bankruptcy. Creditors receive liquidating dividends according to the priority of their claims.

In the last section, we described the two bills that at the time of this writing were being considered by Congress to reform the Bankruptcy Act. Depending upon the outcome, the act could be changed in a significant way.

1. Contrast a technically insolvent situation with an insolvency-in-bankruptcy situation.

2. Why are taxes and administrative costs involved in the bankruptcy paid prior to any creditor's claim?

3. It is argued that a small number of bankruptcies is a healthy sign of economic development. Explain.

4. As a creditor to a financially troubled concern, would you prefer liquidation or financial reorganization? Why? Would you always prefer liquidation if the market value of the firm was less than the liquidation value?

5. Can you explain why utilities, railroads, and banks are seldom liquidated? Are the risks in these industries less than those in other industrial corporations?

6. Before a firm can be reorganized, there must be a valuation placed on it. How should this valuation be arrived at? What conceptual problems would you encounter in the process?

7. Contrast an extension and composition with a reorganization of a firm in distress.

8. When a firm goes through reorganization, what implicit assumption is being

made about the profitability of assets? Was this assumption valid in the Penn Central reorganization?

9. Contrast absolute and relative priority bases for settling claims.

1. The Greenwood Corporation is in bankruptcy. The trustee has estimated that the company can earn $1.5 million before interest and taxes (50 percent) in the future. In the new capitalization, he feels that debentures should bear a coupon of 6 percent and have coverage of five times, income bonds (6 percent) should have overall coverage of two times, preferred stock (6.25 percent) should have after-tax coverage of three times, and common stock should be issued on a P/E basis of twelve times. Determine the capital structure that conforms to the trustee's criteria.

2. Assume that the Greenwood Corporation (see Problem 1) originally had the following capital structure:

	Book Value	Market Value
Senior debentures	$10,000,000	$ 9,000,000
Subordinated debentures	15,000,000	12,000,000
Junior subordinated debentures	5,000,000	2,000,000
Preferred stock (par $100)	5,000,000	1,000,000
Common stock (1,000,000 shares, par value $10)	− 10,000,000	1,000,000
	$25,000,000	$25,000,000

Determine which of the new securities each class of old securities holders would get under:
(a) The absolute priority rule
(b) The relative priority rule

3. The Vent Corporation can be liquidated under bankruptcy proceedings. The book and liquidation values are as follows:

	Book	Liquidation
Cash	700,000	700,000
Accounts receivable	2,000,000	1,600,000
Inventory	3,500,000	2,000,000
Office building	5,000,000	3,000,000
Plant	8,000,000	5,000,000
Equipment	7,000,000	3,000,000
Total	$26,200,000	$15,300,000

The liability and equity accounts are as follows:

Accounts payable	$ 2,000,000
Accrued federal taxes	500,000
Accrued local taxes	200,000
Notes payable (7% annual interest)	1,000,000
Accrued wages	500,000
Total current liabilities	$ 4,200,000
Mortgage on office building (8% coupon)	$ 3,000,000
First mortgage on plant (8% coupon)	3,000,000
Second mortgage on plant (9% coupon)	2,000,000
Subordinated debentures (10% coupon)	5,000,000
Total long-term debt	$13,000,000
Preferred stock (8% dividend)	$ 5,000,000
Common stock	7,000,000
Retained earnings	(3,000,000)
Total	$ 9,000,000
Total	$26,200,000

Expenses of liquidation (lawyers' fees, court costs, etc.) are expected to be 20 percent of the proceeds. The debentures are subordinated only to the two first mortgage bonds. All of the accrued wages are less than three months old and less than $600 per employee. Determine the appropriate distribution of the proceeds of liquidation.

4. **FALL CORPORATION BALANCE SHEET**

Cash	$ 1,000,000	Note payable	$ 1,000,000
Accounts receivable	2,000,000	Accounts payable	4,000,000
Inventories	5,000,000	Accrued wages	3,000,000
Prepaid expenses	1,000,000	Accrued taxes	1,000,000
Total current		Total current	
assets	$ 9,000,000	liabilities	$ 9,000,000
Fixed assets, net	8,000,000	Long-term debt	12,000,000
Goodwill	5,000,000	Equity	1,000,000
Total assets	$22,000,000		$22,000,000

(a) Do you feel it likely that the Fall Corporation either is now or will soon be technically insolvent? Why? What steps could management take to correct this situation?

(b) Answer (a) with respect to the bankruptcy concept of insolvency.

(c) Compare and contrast these two concepts of insolvency.

(d) Is it possible that attempts to alleviate one form of insolvency could aggravate the other? How?

(e) Is the balance sheet the best tool for determining technical or fundamental insolvency? Can you suggest better ones?

ALTMAN, EDWARD I., *Corporate Bankruptcy in America.* Lexington, Mass.: Heath Lexington Books, 1971.

————, "Corporate Bankruptcy Potential, Stockholder Returns and Share Valuation," *Journal of Finance,* 24 (December 1969), 887–900.

————, "Equity Securities of Bankrupt Firms," *Financial Analysts Journal,* 25 (July–August 1969), 129–33.

BROWSTEIN, GERALD W., "Awarding Fair Fees in Bankruptcy: Recent Developments," *Commercial Law Journal,* 76 (March 1971), 64–68.

Collier on Bankruptcy, 14th ed., Vol. 2. New York: Mathew Bender and Company, 1971.

COOGAN, PETER F., RICHARD BROUDE, and HERMAN GLATT, "Comments on Some Reorganization Provisions of the Pending Bankruptcy Bills," *Business Lawyer,* 30 (July 1975).

CYR, CONRAD K., "Setting the Record Straight for a Comprehensive Revision of the Bankruptcy Act of 1898," *American Bankruptcy Law Journal,* 49 (Spring 1975).

GORDON, MYRON J., "Towards a Theory of Financial Distress," *Journal of Finance,* 26 (May 1971), 347–56.

KRAUSE, SIDNEY, "Chapters X and XI—A Study in Contrasts," *Business Lawyer,* 19 (January 1964), 511–26.

LEV, BARUCH, *Financial Statement Analysis: A New Approach.* Englewood Cliffs, N.J.: Prentice-Hall, 1974.

MURPHY, PATRICK A., "Restraint and Reimbursement: The Secured Creditor in Reorganization and Arrangement Proceedings," *Business Lawyer,* 30 (November 1974).

MURRAY, ROGER F., "The Penn Central Debacle: Lessons for Financial Analysis," *Journal of Finance,* 26 (May 1971), 327–32.

Report of the Commission on the Bankruptcy Laws of the United States. Committee on the Judiciary, 93rd Cong., 1st sess. Washington, D.C.: Government Printing Office, 1973.

RUTBERG, SIDNEY, *Ten Cents on the Dollar.* New York: Simon & Schuster, 1973.

STANLEY, DAVID T., and MARJORIE GIRTH, *Bankruptcy: Problem, Process, Reform.* Washington, D.C.: Brookings Institution, 1971.

WALTER, JAMES E., "Determination of Technical Insolvency," *Journal of Business,* 30 (January 1957), 30–43.

WESTON, J. FRED, "The Industrial Economics Background of the Penn Central Bankruptcy," *Journal of Finance,* 26 (May 1971), 311–26.

Appendix
Present-Value
Tables

TABLE A · 1

Present Value of One Dollar Due at the End of N Years

N	1%	2%	3%	4%	5%	6%	7%	8%	9%	10%	N
01	0.99010	0.98039	0.97007	0.96154	0.95238	0.94340	0.93458	0.92593	0.91743	0.90909	01
02	.98030	.96117	.94260	.92456	.90703	.89000	.87344	.85734	.84168	.82645	02
03	.97059	.94232	.91514	.88900	.86384	.83962	.81630	.79383	.77218	.75131	03
04	.96098	.92385	.88849	.85480	.82270	.79209	.76290	.73503	.70843	.68301	04
05	.95147	.90573	.86261	.82193	.78353	.74726	.71299	.68058	.64993	.62092	05
06	.94204	.88797	.83748	.79031	.74622	.70496	.66634	.60317	.59627	.56447	06
07	.93272	.87056	.81309	.75992	.71068	.66506	.62275	.58349	.54703	.51316	07
08	.92348	.85349	.78941	.73069	.67684	.62741	.58201	.54027	.50187	.46651	08
09	.91434	.83675	.76642	.70259	.64461	.59190	.54393	.50025	.46043	.42410	09
10	.90529	.82035	.74409	.67556	.61391	.55839	.50835	.46319	.42241	.38554	10
11	.89632	.80426	.72242	.64958	.58468	.52679	.47509	.42888	.38753	.35049	11
12	.88745	.78849	.70138	.62460	.55684	.49697	.44401	.39711	.35553	.31863	12
13	.87866	.77303	.68095	.60057	.53032	.46884	.41496	.36770	.32618	.28966	13
14	.86996	.75787	.66112	.57747	.50507	.44230	.38782	.34046	.29925	.26333	14
15	.86135	.74301	.64186	.55526	.48102	.41726	.36245	.31524	.27454	.23939	15
16	.85282	.72845	.62317	.53391	.45811	.39365	.33873	.29189	.25187	.21763	16
17	.84438	.71416	.60502	.51337	.43630	.37136	.31657	.27027	.23107	.19784	17
18	.83602	.70016	.58739	.49363	.41552	.35034	.29586	.25025	.21199	.17986	18
19	.82774	.68643	.57029	.47464	.39573	.33051	.27651	.23171	.19449	.16351	19
20	.81954	.67297	.55367	.45639	.37689	.31180	.25842	.21455	.17843	.14864	20
21	.81143	.65978	.53755	.43883	.35894	.29415	.24151	.19866	.16370	.13513	21
22	.80340	.64684	.52189	.42195	.34185	.27750	.22571	.18394	.15018	.12285	22
23	.79544	.63416	.50669	.40573	.32557	.26180	.21095	.17031	.13778	.11168	23
24	.78757	.62172	.49193	.39012	.31007	.24698	.19715	.15770	.12640	.10153	24
25	.77977	.60953	.47760	.37512	.29530	.23300	.18425	.14602	.11597	.09230	25

Source: Ezra Solomon, ed., *The Management of Corporate Capital* (New York: The Free Press of of Glencoe, Inc., 1959), pp 313–16.

TABLE A · 1

Present Value of One Dollar Due at the End of N Years

N	11%	12%	13%	14%	15%	16%	17%	18%	19%	20%	N
01	0.90090	0.89286	0.88496	0.87719	0.86957	0.86207	0.85470	0.84746	0.84034	0.83333	01
02	.81162	.79719	.78315	.76947	.75614	.74316	.73051	.71818	.70616	.69444	02
03	.73119	.71178	.69305	.67497	.65752	.64066	.62437	.60863	.59342	.57870	03
04	.65873	.63552	.61332	.59208	.57175	.55229	.53365	.51579	.49867	.48225	04
05	.59345	.56743	.54276	.51937	.49718	.47611	.45611	.43711	.41905	.40188	05
06	.53464	.50663	.48032	.45559	.43233	.41044	.38984	.37043	.35214	.33490	06
07	.48166	.45235	.42506	.39964	.37594	.35383	.33320	.31392	.29592	.27908	07
08	.43393	.40388	.37616	.35056	.32690	.30503	.28478	.26604	.24867	.23257	08
09	.39092	.36061	.33288	.30751	.28426	.26295	.24340	.22546	.20897	.19381	09
10	.35218	.32197	.29459	.26974	.24718	.22668	.20804	.19106	.17560	.16151	10
11	.31728	.28748	.26070	.23662	.21494	.19542	.17781	.16192	.14756	.13459	11
12	.28584	.25667	.23071	.20756	.18691	.16846	.15197	.13722	.12400	.11216	12
13	.25751	.22917	.20416	.18207	.16253	.14523	.12989	.11629	.10420	.09346	13
14	.23199	.20462	.18068	.15971	.14133	.12520	.11102	.09855	.08757	.07789	14
15	.20900	.18270	.15989	.14010	.12289	.10793	.09489	.08352	.07359	.06491	15
16	.18829	.16312	.14150	.12289	.10686	.09304	.08110	.07078	.06184	.05409	16
17	.16963	.14564	.12522	.10780	.09293	.08021	.06932	.05998	.05196	.04507	17
18	.15282	.13004	.11081	.09456	.08080	.06914	.05925	.05083	.04367	.03756	18
19	.13768	.11611	.09806	.08295	.07026	.05961	.05064	.04308	.03669	.03130	19
20	.12403	.10367	.08678	.07276	.06110	.05139	.04328	.03651	.03084	.02608	20
21	.11174	.09256	.07680	.06383	.05313	.04430	.03699	.03094	.02591	.02174	21
22	.10067	.08264	.06796	.05599	.04620	.03819	.03162	.02622	.02178	.01811	22
23	.09069	.07379	.06014	.04911	.04017	.03292	.02702	.02222	.01830	.01509	23
24	.08170	.06588	.05322	.04308	.03493	.02838	.02310	.01883	.01538	.01258	24
25	.07361	.05882	.04710	.03779	.03038	.02447	.01974	.01596	.01292	.01048	25

TABLE A · 1

Present Value of One Dollar Due at the End of N Years

N	21%	22%	23%	24%	25%	26%	27%	28%	29%	30%	N
01	0.82645	0.81967	0.81301	0.80645	0.80000	0.79365	0.78740	0.78125	0.77519	0.76923	01
02	.68301	.67186	.66098	.65036	.64000	.62988	.62000	.61035	.60093	.59172	02
03	.56447	.55071	.53738	.52449	.51200	.49991	.48819	.47684	.46583	.45517	03
04	.46651	.45140	.43690	.42297	.40906	.39675	.38440	.37253	.36111	.35013	04
05	.38554	.37000	.35520	.34111	.32768	.31488	.30268	.29104	.27993	.26933	05
06	.31863	.30328	.28878	.27509	.26214	.24991	.23833	.22737	.21700	.20718	06
07	.26333	.24859	.23478	.22184	.20972	.19834	.18766	.17764	.16822	.15937	07
08	.21763	.20376	.19088	.17891	.16777	.15741	.14776	.13878	.13040	.12259	08
09	.17986	.16702	.15519	.14428	.13422	.12493	.11635	.10842	.10109	.09430	09
10	.14864	.13690	.12617	.11635	.10737	.09915	.09161	.08470	.07836	.07254	10
11	.12285	.11221	.10258	.09383	.08590	.07869	.07214	.06617	.06075	.05580	11
12	.10153	.09198	.08339	.07567	.06872	.06245	.05680	.05170	.04709	.04292	12
13	.08391	.07539	.06780	.06103	.05498	.04957	.04472	.04039	.03650	.03302	13
14	.06934	.06180	.05512	.04921	.04398	.03934	.03522	.03155	.02830	.02540	14
15	.05731	.05065	.04481	.03969	.03518	.03122	.02773	.02465	.02194	.01954	15
16	.04736	.04152	.03643	.03201	.02815	.02478	.02183	.01926	.01700	.01503	16
17	.03914	.03403	.02962	.02581	.02252	.01967	.01719	.01505	.01318	.01156	17
18	.03235	.02789	.02408	.02082	.01801	.01561	.01354	.01175	.01022	.00889	18
19	.02673	.02286	.01958	.01679	.01441	.01239	.01066	.00918	.00792	.00684	19
20	.02209	.01874	.01592	.01354	.01153	.00983	.00839	.00717	.00614	.00526	20
21	.01826	.01536	.01294	.01092	.00922	.00780	.00661	.00561	.00476	.00405	21
22	.01509	.01259	.01052	.00880	.00738	.00619	.00520	.00438	.00369	.00311	22
23	.01247	.01032	.00855	.00710	.00590	.00491	.00410	.00342	.00286	.00239	23
24	.01031	.00846	.00695	.00573	.00472	.00390	.00323	.00267	.00222	.00184	24
25	.00852	.00693	.00565	.00462	.00378	.00310	.00254	.00209	.00172	.00142	25

TABLE A · 1

Present Value of One Dollar Due at the End of N Years

N	31%	32%	33%	34%	35%	36%	37%	38%	39%	40%	N
01	0.76336	0.75758	0.75188	0.74627	0.74074	0.73529	0.72993	0.72464	0.71942	0.71429	01
02	.58272	.57392	.56532	.55692	.54870	.54066	.53279	.52510	.51757	.51020	02
03	.44482	.43479	.42505	.41561	.40644	.39754	.38890	.38051	.37235	.36443	03
04	.33956	.32939	.31959	.31016	.30107	.29231	.28387	.27573	.26788	.26031	04
05	.25920	.24953	.24029	.23146	.22301	.21493	.20720	.19980	.19272	.18593	05
06	.19787	.18904	.18067	.17273	.16520	.15804	.15124	.14479	.13865	.13281	06
07	.15104	.14321	.13584	.12890	.12237	.11621	.11040	.10492	.09975	.09486	07
08	.11530	.10849	.10214	.09620	.09064	.08545	.08058	.07603	.07176	.06776	08
09	.08802	.08219	.07680	.07179	.06714	.06283	.05882	.05509	.05163	.04840	09
10	.06719	.06227	.05774	.05357	.04973	.04620	.04293	.03992	.03714	.03457	10
11	.05129	.04717	.04341	.03998	.03684	.03397	.03134	.02893	.02672	.02469	11
12	.03915	.03574	.03264	.02984	.02729	.02498	.02287	.02096	.01922	.01764	12
13	.02989	.02707	.02454	.02227	.02021	.01837	.01670	.01519	.01383	.01260	13
14	.02281	.02051	.01845	.01662	.01497	.01350	.01219	.01101	.00995	.00900	14
15	.01742	.01554	.01387	.01240	.01109	.00993	.00890	.00798	.00716	.00643	15
16	.01329	.01177	.01043	.00925	.00822	.00730	.00649	.00578	.00515	.00459	16
17	.01015	.00892	.00784	.00691	.00609	.00537	.00474	.00419	.00370	.00328	17
18	.00775	.00676	.00590	.00515	.00451	.00395	.00346	.00304	.00267	.00234	18
19	.00591	.00512	.00443	.00385	.00334	.00290	.00253	.00220	.00192	.00167	19
20	.00451	.00388	.00333	.00287	.00247	.00213	.00184	.00159	.00138	.00120	20
21	.00345	.00294	.00251	.00214	.00183	.00157	.00135	.00115	.00099	.00085	21
22	.00263	.00223	.00188	.00160	.00136	.00115	.00098	.00084	.00071	.00061	22
23	.00201	.00169	.00142	.00119	.00101	.00085	.00072	.00061	.00051	.00044	23
24	.00153	.00128	.00107	.00089	.00074	.00062	.00052	.00044	.00037	.00031	24
25	.00117	.00097	.00080	.00066	.00055	.00046	.00038	.00032	.00027	.00022	25

TABLE A · 2

Year	1%	2%	3%	4%	5%	6%	7%	8%	9%	10%	Year
1	0.9901	0.9804	0.9709	0.9615	0.9524	0.9434	0.9346	0.9259	0.9174	0.9091	1
2	1.9704	1.9416	1.9135	1.8861	1.8594	1.8334	1.8080	1.7833	1.7591	1.7355	2
3	2.9410	2.8839	2.8286	2.7751	2.7232	2.6730	2.6243	2.5771	2.5313	2.4868	3
4	3.9020	3.8077	3.7171	3.6299	3.5459	3.4651	3.3872	3.3121	3.2397	3.1699	4
5	4.8535	4.7134	4.5797	4.4518	4.3295	4.2123	4.1002	3.9927	3.8896	3.7908	5
6	5.7955	5.6014	5.4172	5.2421	5.0757	4.9173	4.7665	4.6229	4.4859	4.3553	6
7	6.7282	6.4720	6.2302	6.0020	5.7863	5.5824	5.3893	5.2064	5.0329	4.8684	7
8	7.6517	7.3254	7.0196	6.7327	6.4632	6.2098	5.9713	5.7466	5.5348	5.3349	8
9	8.5661	8.1622	7.7861	7.4353	7.1078	6.8017	6.5152	6.2469	5.9852	5.7590	9
10	9.4714	8.9825	8.5302	8.1109	7.7217	7.3601	7.0236	6.7101	6.4176	6.1446	10
11	10.3677	9.7868	9.2526	8.7604	8.3064	7.8868	7.4987	7.1389	6.8052	6.4951	11
12	11.2552	10.5753	9.9539	9.3850	8.8632	8.3838	7.9427	7.5361	7.1607	6.8137	12
13	12.1338	11.3483	10.6349	9.9856	9.3935	8.8527	8.3576	7.9038	7.4869	7.1034	13
14	13.0038	12.1062	11.2960	10.5631	9.8986	9.2950	8.7454	8.2442	7.7861	7.3667	14
15	13.8651	12.8492	11.9379	11.1183	10.3796	9.7122	9.1079	8.5595	8.0607	7.6061	15
16	14.7180	13.5777	12.5610	11.6522	10.8377	10.1059	9.4466	8.8514	8.3125	7.8237	16
17	15.5624	14.2918	13.1660	12.1656	11.2740	10.4772	9.7632	9.1216	8.5436	8.0215	17
18	16.3984	14.9920	13.7534	12.6592	11.6895	10.8276	10.0591	9.3719	8.7556	8.2014	18
19	17.2261	15.6784	14.3237	13.1339	12.0853	11.1581	10.3356	9.6036	8.9501	8.3649	19
20	18.0457	16.3514	14.8774	13.5903	12.4622	11.4699	10.5940	9.8181	9.1285	8.5136	20
21	18.8571	17.0111	15.4149	14.0291	12.8211	11.7640	10.8355	10.0168	9.2922	8.6487	21
22	19.6605	17.6580	15.9368	14.4511	13.1630	12.0416	11.0612	10.2007	9.4424	8.7715	22
23	20.4559	18.2921	16.4435	14.8568	13.4885	12.3033	11.2722	10.3710	9.5802	8.8832	23
24	21.2435	18.9139	16.9355	15.2469	13.7986	12.5503	11.4693	10.5287	9.7066	8.9847	24
25	22.0233	19.5234	17.4131	15.6220	14.0939	12.7833	11.6536	10.6748	9.8226	9.0770	25

Source: Solomon, op. cit., pp. 317–20.

TABLE A · 2

Present Value of One Dollar Per Year. *N* Years at *r*%

Year	11%	12%	13%	14%	15%	16%	17%	18%	19%	20%	Year
1	0.9009	0.8929	0.8850	0.8772	0.8696	0.8621	0.8547	0.8475	0.8403	0.8333	1
2	1.7125	1.6901	1.6681	1.6467	1.6257	1.6052	1.5852	1.5656	1.5465	1.5278	2
3	2.4437	2.4018	2.3612	2.3216	2.2832	2.2459	2.2096	2.1743	2.1399	2.1065	3
4	3.1024	3.0373	2.9745	2.9137	2.8550	2.7982	2.7432	2.6901	2.6386	2.5887	4
5	3.6959	3.6048	3.5172	3.4331	3.3522	3.2743	3.1993	3.1272	3.0576	2.9906	5
6	4.2305	4.1114	3.9976	3.8887	3.7845	3.6847	3.5892	3.4976	3.4098	3.3255	6
7	4.7122	4.5638	4.4226	4.2883	4.1604	4.0386	3.9224	3.8115	3.7057	3.6046	7
8	5.1461	4.9676	4.7988	4.6389	4.4873	4.3436	4.2072	4.0776	3.9544	3.8372	8
9	5.5370	5.3282	5.1317	4.9464	4.7716	4.6065	4.4506	4.3030	4.1633	4.0310	9
10	5.8892	5.6502	5.4262	5.2161	5.0188	4.8332	4.6586	4.4941	4.3389	4.1925	10
11	6.2065	5.9377	5.6869	5.4527	5.2337	5.0286	4.8364	4.6560	4.4865	4.3271	11
12	6.4924	6.1944	5.9176	5.6603	5.4206	5.1971	4.9884	4.7932	4.6105	4.4392	12
13	6.7499	6.4235	6.1218	5.8424	5.5831	5.3423	5.1183	4.9095	4.7147	4.5327	13
14	6.9819	6.6282	6.3025	6.0021	5.7245	5.4675	5.2293	5.0081	4.8023	4.6106	14
15	7.1909	6.8109	6.4624	6.1422	5.8474	5.5755	5.3242	5.0916	4.8759	4.6755	15
16	7.3792	6.9740	6.6039	6.2651	5.9542	5.6685	5.4053	5.1624	4.9377	4.7296	16
17	7.5488	7.1196	6.7291	6.3729	6.0472	5.7487	5.4746	5.2223	4.9897	4.7746	17
18	7.7016	7.2497	6.8399	6.4674	6.1280	5.8178	5.5339	5.2732	5.0333	4.8122	18
19	7.8393	7.3658	6.9380	6.5504	6.1982	5.8775	5.5845	5.3162	5.0700	4.8435	19
20	7.9633	7.4694	7.0248	6.6231	6.2593	5.9288	5.6278	5.3527	5.1009	4.8696	20
21	8.0751	7.5620	7.1016	6.6870	6.3125	5.9731	5.6648	5.3837	5.1268	4.8913	21
22	8.1757	7.6446	7.1695	6.7429	6.3587	6.0113	5.6964	5.4099	5.1486	4.9094	22
23	8.2664	7.7184	7.2297	6.7921	6.3988	6.0442	5.7234	5.4321	5.1668	4.9245	23
24	8.3481	7.7843	7.2829	6.8351	6.4338	6.0726	5.7465	5.4509	5.1822	4.9371	24
25	8.4217	7.8431	7.3300	6.8729	6.4641	6.0971	5.7662	5.4669	5.1951	4.9476	25

TABLE A · 2

Year	21%	22%	23%	24%	25%	26%	27%	28%	29%	30%	Year
1	0.8264	0.8197	0.8130	0.8065	0.8000	0.7937	0.7874	0.7813	0.7752	0.7692	1
2	1.5095	1.4915	1.4740	1.4568	1.4400	1.4235	1.4074	1.3916	1.3761	1.3609	2
3	2.0739	2.0422	2.0114	1.9813	1.9520	1.9234	1.8956	1.8684	1.8420	1.8161	3
4	2.5404	2.4936	2.4483	2.4043	2.3616	2.3202	2.2800	2.2410	2.2031	2.1662	4
5	2.9260	2.8636	2.8035	2.7454	2.6893	2.6351	2.5827	2.5320	2.4830	2.4356	5
6	3.2446	3.1669	3.0923	3.0205	2.9514	2.8850	2.8210	2.7594	2.7000	2.6427	6
7	3.5079	3.4155	3.3270	3.2423	3.1611	3.0833	3.0087	2.9370	2.8682	2.8021	7
8	3.7256	3.6193	3.5179	3.4212	3.3289	3.2407	3.1564	3.0758	2.9986	2.9247	8
9	3.9054	3.7863	3.6731	3.5655	3.4631	3.3657	3.2728	3.1842	3.0997	3.0190	9
10	4.0541	3.9232	3.7993	3.6819	3.5705	3.4648	3.3644	3.2689	3.1781	3.0915	10
11	4.1769	4.0354	3.9018	3.7757	3.6564	3.5435	3.4365	3.3351	3.2388	3.1473	11
12	4.2785	4.1274	3.9852	3.8514	3.7251	3.6060	3.4933	3.3868	3.2859	3.1903	12
13	4.3624	4.2028	4.0530	3.9124	3.7801	3.6555	3.6381	3.4272	3.3224	3.2233	13
14	4.4317	4.2646	4.1082	3.9616	3.8241	3.6949	3.5733	3.4587	3.3507	3.2487	14
15	4.4890	4.3152	4.1530	4.0013	3.8593	3.7261	3.6010	3.4834	3.3726	3.2682	15
16	4.5364	4.3567	4.1894	4.0333	3.8874	3.7509	3.6228	3.5026	3.3896	3.2832	16
17	4.5755	4.3908	4.2190	4.0591	3.9099	3.7705	3.6400	3.5177	3.4028	3.2948	17
18	4.6079	4.4187	4.2431	4.0799	3.9279	3.7861	3.6536	3.5294	3.4130	3.3037	18
19	4.6346	4.4415	4.2627	4.0967	3.9424	3.7985	3.6642	3.5386	3.4210	3.3105	19
20	4.6567	4.4603	4.2786	4.1103	3.9539	3.8083	3.6726	3.5458	3.4271	3.3158	20
21	4.6750	4.4756	4.2916	4.1212	3.9631	3.8161	3.6792	3.5514	3.4319	3.3198	21
22	4.6900	4.4882	4.3021	4.1300	3.9705	3.8223	3.6844	3.5558	3.4356	3.3230	22
23	4.7025	4.4985	4.3106	4.1371	3.9764	3.8273	3.6885	3.5592	3.4384	3.3254	23
24	4.7128	4.5070	4.3176	4.1428	3.9811	3.8312	3.6918	3.5619	3.4406	3.3272	24
25	4.7213	4.5139	4.3232	4.1474	3.9849	3.8342	3.6943	3.5640	3.4423	3.3286	25

TABLE A · 2

Present Value of One Dollar Per Year. N Years at r%

Year	31%	32%	33%	34%	35%	36%	37%	38%	39%	40%	Year
1	0.7634	0.7576	0.7519	0.7463	0.7407	0.7353	0.7299	0.7246	0.7194	0.7143	1
2	1.3461	1.3315	1.3172	1.3032	1.2894	1.2760	1.2627	1.2497	1.2370	1.2245	2
3	1.7909	1.7663	1.7423	1.7188	1.6959	1.6735	1.6516	1.6302	1.6093	1.5889	3
4	2.1305	2.0957	2.0618	2.0290	1.9969	1.9658	1.9355	1.9060	1.8772	1.8492	4
5	2.3897	2.3452	2.3021	2.2604	2.2200	2.1807	2.1427	2.1058	2.0699	2.0352	5
6	2.5875	2.5342	2.4828	2.4331	2.3852	2.3388	2.2939	2.2506	2.2086	2.1680	6
7	2.7386	2.6775	2.6187	2.5620	2.5075	2.4550	2.4043	2.3555	2.3083	2.2628	7
8	2.8539	2.7860	2.7208	2.6582	2.5982	2.5404	2.4849	2.4315	2.3801	2.3306	8
9	2.9419	2.8681	2.7976	2.7300	2.6653	2.6033	2.5437	2.4866	2.4317	2.3790	9
10	3.0091	2.9304	2.8553	2.7836	2.7150	2.6495	2.5867	2.5265	2.4689	2.4136	10
11	3.0604	2.9776	2.8987	2.8236	2.7519	2.6834	2.6180	2.5555	2.4956	2.4383	11
12	3.0995	3.0133	2.9314	2.8534	2.7792	2.7084	2.6409	2.5764	2.5148	2.4559	12
13	3.1294	3.0404	2.9559	2.8757	2.7994	2.7268	2.6576	2.5916	2.5286	2.4685	13
14	3.1522	3.0609	2.9744	2.8923	2.8144	2.7403	2.6698	2.6026	2.5386	2.4775	14
15	3.1696	3.0764	2.9883	2.9047	2.8255	2.7502	2.6787	2.6106	2.5457	2.4839	15
16	3.1829	3.0882	2.9987	2.9140	2.8337	2.7575	2.6852	2.6164	2.5509	2.4885	16
17	3.1931	3.0971	3.0065	2.9209	2.8398	2.7629	2.6899	2.6206	2.5546	2.4918	17
18	3.2008	3.1039	3.0124	2.9260	2.8443	2.7668	2.6934	2.6236	2.5573	2.4941	18
19	3.2067	3.1090	3.0169	2.9299	2.8476	2.7697	2.6959	2.6258	2.5592	2.4958	19
20	3.2112	3.1129	3.0202	2.9327	2.8501	2.7718	2.6977	2.6274	2.5606	2.4970	20
21	3.2147	3.1158	3.0227	2.9349	2.8519	2.7734	2.6991	2.6285	2.5616	2.4979	21
22	3.2173	3.1180	3.0246	2.9365	2.8533	2.7746	2.7000	2.6294	2.5623	2.4985	22
23	3.2193	3.1197	3.0260	2.9377	2.8543	2.7754	2.7008	2.6300	2.5628	2.4989	23
24	3.2209	3.1210	3.0271	2.9386	2.8550	2.7760	2.7013	2.6304	2.5632	2.4992	24
25	3.2220	3.1220	3.0279	2.9392	2.8556	2.7765	2.7017	2.6307	2.5634	2.4994	25

Index